If You Ever Need Me, *I Won't Be Far Away*

If You Ever Need Me, *I Won't Be Far Away*

Bruce Farrell Rosen

Alma Rose Publishing
San Francisco ~ CA

For information contact:
Alma Rose Publishing
2443 Fillmore Street No. 338
San Francisco, CA 94115
www.almarosepublishing.com

Front and back cover photos by Susan Rosen

Design, layout and typesetting by
Liquid Pictures
www.liquidpictures.com

ISBN Number: 978-0-615-49943-7
Library of Congress Number: 2011937959

Printed in the United States of America

For Mom

Michael's Quote

~

I see her best when I close my eyes. She was Alma to a few, Lorraine to many, and grandmother to me. I sit, eyes closed, and concentrate, as one minute becomes ten and ten become one. She was Alma the girl, Alma the woman, Alma the lover, Alma the mother. And she was Lorraine the seer, Lorraine the healer, Lorraine the mystic, Lorraine the intangible. It is no surprise she resides in this place, where the empirical flirts with the spiritual.

Sometimes I'll see her when I am in an elevator, or while I am walking, or when I am preoccupied. She is disguised as rose buds and smoke, a scent she inhabited in life and clung to in death. This smell, perhaps ordinary to many, awakens my potential and purpose. It is my mantra, my catalyst, perpetuating cycles of thought leading back to that one brief moment.

Birth is a Beginning

Birth is a beginning
And death is a destination
And life is a journey;
From childhood to maturity
And youth to age;
From innocence to knowing;
From foolishness to discretion
And then, perhaps, to wisdom;
From weakness to strength
Or strength to weakness—
And, often, back again;
From health to sickness
And back, we pray, to health again;
From offense to forgiveness
From loneliness to love!
From joy to gratitude
From pain to compassion
And grief to understanding
From fear to faith;
From defeat to defeat to defeat—
Until looking backward or ahead,
We see that victory lies, not at some high place along the way
But having made the journey,
Stage by stage,
A sacred pilgrimage;
Birth is a beginning
And death a destination
And life is a journey;
A sacred pilgrimage—
To life's everlasting

Acknowledgements

~

There have been a few key people in my life that have been anchors during the writing of these pages. I thank Susan Rosen for her openness and acceptance of the deep feelings that I have expressed in these pages, many of them about her. And it means alot to me that she loves this book. Though our paths have diverged, I trust and respect her totally. And I have gratitude to her for many things, especially our wonderful sons. She is also the photographer of the front and back cover photos.

Gwen Jones has been a source of healing for me over the past several years. She has been there through many turbulent moments (and many joyful ones), often simply listening when I had much to say, providing a kind and compassionate smile, allowing me to enter the serenity of her personal space. Her practice of Network Chiropractic--her healing touch--has been calming and liberating.

I thank my two sons, Michael and Jonathan, just for being Michael and Jonathan. But, in particular, I thank them for always reminding me that I must finish this book, to not let too much time pass before going back to it.

I thank my sister, Heidi, for her insights, and she often reminds me of my mom. She is a profound woman, a sister and true friend.

I offer my thanks to Marlowe Rafelle for her attention to detail in the proofing of the manuscript, as well as the questions that she asked as a result of her careful reading. She is excellent.

I owe an enormous thank you to my editor, Simon Hayes, for his deeply intuitive reading of this book. It is almost as if he had written it himself.

A big thank you to Isabella Michon who has been key in the preparation of the materials that bring this book to the public. She has been a true partner in this project.

I have profound appreciation for the tireless work of Jeffrey Reynolds of Liquid Pictures. He was incredibly competent and professional in translating the changes of the final edit to print.

The requirements of my "day job" in the financial world are demanding, and I wouldn't have been able to write freely in the evening if it were not for the absolute "bedrock" support of my assistant, Mary DuSablon. And she was instrumental in providing research for the writing. Many thanks to Mary.

And, of course, the publication of this book owes so much to the insight, experience, intelligence, friendship of Donald S. Ellis. He is extraordinary. Don, I am grateful that our paths have connected.

Bruce Farrell Rosen

Author's Introduction

~

It is an interesting phenomena of memory that through recollection we are clearer about "who we were" than "who we are." As we think back over our lives—the music, the feelings and the places where we stood; the scent of perfume, a flower, bus exhaust, the sweet scent of hashish at a concert, the taste of a kiss that triggers the passion of love—we gain objectivity of who we were, our ambitions, fears, longings—our essential qualities. One of the reasons that I must visit London every chance I get is because of the "London scent" that I ingested when, at the age of eighteen, my mom (with little means) made a high school graduation trip to Europe possible for me. It was a surprise that she could make this trip happen, and I fell in Love with London above anywhere else, the scent a combination of bus and car exhaust, Indian aromas wafting through the air, strong unfiltered tobacco, warm beer, British accents dripping with an almost edible flavor, all set against a backdrop of the red buildings of Chelsea and Knightsbridge, the green of Hyde, St.James, Green Parks. I fell in love with this place; and there will always be the eighteen year old in me discovering London for the first time, every time I return, and return I must till the end of my time.

It has always been a fact of my life that I have endeavored to record the sights, sounds, fragrances and tonal qualities of my experience. The voice of my departed mom is as clear to me in memory as it was audible during her lifetime. I hear the voices of my children at younger ages, Michael telling me with pure sweetness at the age of eight that he would like a sip of water as we walked through Alta Plaza Park in San Francisco; Jonathan laughing and dancing, singing along with me to "Catch the Wind" by Donavan. I used to tease him that trying to capture him and hold onto him for a little extra time was like "trying to catch the wind." Music always touched me in deep ways; in these pages I strive to tell what it was like to hear some of the fabled rock bands when they arrived, the feeling of who I was when the lights went out, the pounding rhythms of Led Zeppellin's "Whole Lotta Love" starting the show. How well I know that 16 year old, perhaps much more so than this person in his mid-50's today. It is true that such is always the case, and that the person I am today will be more clearly revealed in a few years time.

In these pages I have sought to be true to the person that I have been, because in clearly knowing who we were, we gain a better understanding of who we are. I will be forever changed by the night a man broke into our home and tried to rape my mom, my father out of town. I must have screamed at the top of my lungs, because it chased the man away, but my recollection is that I wasn't creating any sound at all. I do know and understand that boy, and how that boy was affected in that moment. I'll never forget where I was—who I was—when my boyhood idol, Sandy Koufax, pitched a perfect game against the Chicago Cubs, that September night in 1965. I idolized the man—living in a neighborhood where there were, virtually, no Jews; he represented heroism, dignity, to me—and I think the experience of that "perfect game" as broadcast by Vin Scully—his echoing, resonating voice spiritual in a deeply baseball way—affected me forever. How does one not remember who they were, and how they changed, that night in 1964 when the Beatles burst on the scene on the stage of the Ed Sullivan show? So much of my life after that was affected by the perfect harmonies of John and Paul, the scents, the sounds, the kisses, the joy and sadness infused with the DNA of the music of the Beatles.

As the story unfolds, I sought to understand myself through memory, but to also understand memory through being true to the self that I am today. I strive for honesty in the present and the past. This is a book of philosophy, understanding our actions, their cause and effect against the notion of free will or determinism. We discover Eastern philosophy, spirituality, premonition, love of family, loyalty of friendship, loss, hope, belief, redemption, paying a price for choices, the joy of sport, music, and the desire to understand the events that unfold around us during these tumultuous times. It is a book that strives to understand responsibility, personal boundaries, the notion of regret and whether it is necessary to regret. Ultimately, it is a book about joy, the memory of joy, the joy that we carry with us, joy in the present. Ultimately, I believe this book is guided by simple love; my hope for readers is that they will rediscover themselves, perhaps understand themselves through memory, and heal their wounds as they read these pages.

Bruce Farrell Rosen

If You Ever Need Me,
I Won't Be Far Away

“M”

I really didn’t have to ask her out for a glass of wine after the play that night. We could have parted with a compassionate handshake, suggestive of some sort of recognition that there is a kinship here, a kind of knowing of one another that would seem improbable given that we had just met several hours ago when I walked through those Steinway doors in Midtown Manhattan. She was there to audition a few pianos for me, a concert pianist in her younger days, her delicate, symphony hall touch hardly diminished by aging hands and the grinding pressures of having to retain her prominent position as a leader in the annual tally of pianos sold, dollars delivered to the company.

I had come from San Francisco to buy a piano for my son; Michael was in New Hampshire at a summer music composition camp and would be attending the Oberlin Conservatory in the fall on a music scholarship. He had just performed a stirring Shostakovich a couple of weeks earlier, in his chamber orchestra, had received a standing ovation from the Marin Academy audience; and in a matter of just a few months would be able to pursue music virtually full time at the Conservatory.

He had worked so damn hard in school, and I so much wanted to reward him with a Steinway piano, something he would treasure for the rest of his life. The ability to buy that piano had not come easy to me. I had not been born with a silver or even silver plated spoon, but had become pretty successful at managing bond money, particularly tax-exempt bond money for all sorts of clients, the very affluent as well as those who needed to save a little on taxes. I had worked painfully hard to develop this clientele, starting at a small municipal bond firm on receiving a graduate degree in International Relations at San Francisco State. I had written a thesis on terrorism, a popular subject in the years to come. I had started out cold-calling about 10 hours a day, and after about a year had some pretty nice relationships with some families. Twenty-four years later, many of these families have become like family to me.

My approach was always to err on the conservative side, and it served me well over the years. Indeed, the money didn't come easy, but come it did. Nothing was ever taken for granted, and as I walked through those doors into that opulent Steinway showroom, there was a pride, a joy, a type of satisfaction that I had never quite known, the sense that I could give something so profound to this young man who demanded so little of me. I was filled with love for him as we auditioned pianos.

We sampled pianos, but there was a sort of hypnosis at work. I wanted to know her a bit better—her playing seduced me and her voice charmed me. I offered her the ticket to the play that night, the ticket having just fallen in my lap from a friend who at the last minute would not be able to go. I didn't have to offer her that ticket; I could have gone alone, and she didn't have to accept. But a few hours later she did accept, we did go together, and we did drink that wine.

It was a ruby-red Italian that we drank that night, July 23rd, 2005, at an Italian outdoor café, on a little side street just off the theater district. The night felt like velvet, the humidity not oppressive, almost a kind of trade wind lending a softness, a tranquility to the jagged edges of this intense place. We each finished our glasses of wine, ordering seconds with a salad. We drank the seconds, shared the salad, our forks sort of bumping into each other all over the plate, the city of New York becoming a masterpiece.

I had never had an affair nor had gone in search of one—but my passion for this woman was overwhelming, a charm that was so intoxicating. I felt intensely happy that night, and there was a cathartic release of emotion as I poured out to her everything that I was feeling; and I had no idea that this much had been bottled up inside. There was a feeling of awakening to something that had been dormant or sleeping within me for a long time, certainly since before my mom passed in 1999. I surrendered to this feeling in the moment, tried to prolong it as long as it might last, wanted to be courageous and allow myself to feel it. But in short time the edges of my soul began to hurt, because Susan, my wife, was at home, impervious to the effects of a woman on her husband.

In the years before my mom died, Susan and I had been busy raising two boys, and we were giving it everything that we had. Neither of us had been raised with much money, but the success that I was having in the bond business, along with her steady pharmacist's income permitted us to buy a home in the costly city of San Francisco, as well as put these two boys through the area's better schools, which meant private. We recognized a talent for music in my older son, Michael, and supplemented his education with music training at the S. F. Music Conservatory. Our younger son, Jonathan, had shown an uncanny ability to memorize sentences, moved like a dancer, and was passionate and dramatic in virtually everything he did. We enrolled him in the American Conservatory Theater's Young Conservatory for children.

Susan and I felt a deep kinship with one another, and we blanketed our boys in a protective cocoon filled with gratitude for the blessings of this family. We felt a kind of love that most parents know—selflessness, a desire to be present and enjoy the moments before us, a recognition that life doesn't get any sweeter than these cherished times when a family is together.

The presence of my mom in the life of our family added a depth, richness and guidance to our lives that I tried to embrace as much as I could while she was alive. So when she died of lung cancer on September 7,1999, the cavity in my heart and gut would be too much to comprehend. God, I do know, truly does give us just as much and no more than we can handle at any moment in time. The loss of my mom will take a lifetime to digest, so profound was her influence.

How might one take in and grasp in the moment and immediate aftermath of her death the gravity and meaning of her life and loss? I could only absorb it in doses; and however large these doses seemed, they are pieces of a much larger hole that will be amortized over a lifetime. As I write this today, eight years later, sadly estranged from my lovely wife, Susan, looking over the city and the San Francisco Bay, I continue to make meaning of my mom's life and passing. I endeavor to consider the life that she would want (and does want) me to live, and try to keep my heart as open as I possibly can so that I can feel her presence.

There is an ebullience, a joy, an overflowing fountain of compassion that my mom brought to this world, and it touched so many souls. The more that I am able to remain open and not be weighed down by the gravity of work, or guilt, or regret, or responsibility (though highly responsible I cannot help but be), the deeper I am able to connect with the gifts that come from my mom, an appreciation for everything that life puts in our pathway, the smooth rides and the struggles. And to the extent that I am able to remain open to life, to not hide from truth, to be present in the company of others and to really listen, I am able to live a kind of joy, which is the inheritance from my mom. Of course, the expansion that does come from being awake allows one to hear the voices of those deeply cherished, so I continue to experience in unit doses the grief of her loss.

Absorbing the loss of my mom took a toll on our marriage, as I retreated to places within myself to which only I could go. I could go to this inner place of comfort, but I had to go alone; Sue couldn't find me in this foreign territory. I believe that I would have enjoyed the comfort of company in this foreign soil; perhaps it would not have seemed so solitary. But she couldn't find me. I cannot blame her for this; deeply did she grieve as well. We continued to pour ourselves into our boys all the more, and as we did perhaps a bit of intimacy was sacrificed

Indeed, the wine had gone a bit to my head. The sultry breeze enveloping this section of Manhattan began to feel even more tropical. We had been laughing with gusto, and "M" had a kind of effervescence that seemed to bring me out of myself. Suddenly, everything seemed to be infused with energy and truth. The play we had seen that night was called "Doubt," and on that warm, sultry night in New York, I discovered a bit of myself in her. There was a similarity in her smile to that of my mom, and the way she laughed from the soul, with abandon, also reminded me of my mom's joy in laughter. Yes, the play we saw that night was called "Doubt," but in this moment I did not afford myself the luxury of self-doubt; there was no way to doubt the moment.

Beatlemania

I was born in 1955, and experienced as a young teenager the tail end of the 1960s, but the full effect of the '70s. I'll never forget that night in 1964 when my father—vehemently overriding my bit of whining to his suggestion—demanded (practically threatening a strapping) that my brother and I come into the den and listen to this new group, The Beatles, being introduced on "The Ed Sullivan Show." I did like Ed Sullivan's shows, but I was doing something else at the moment and didn't want to be bothered. My dad really insisted and he really threatened. So we entered the room, just in time for the introduction. The Beatles had obviously been a phenomenon in England, and had caught on in the U.S. But it took that one Ed Sullivan appearance to really do the damage. Nothing was the same in this country after that performance. The insanely shrieking girls and entranced boys shown in the audience will be forever emblazoned in my consciousness.

Beatlemania catapulted the country into an excited state that involved the lives of virtually every teenager in the country. The country so desperately needed a bit of fun, the assassination of John F. Kennedy having occurred just a few months before. From the moment of that first Ed Sullivan appearance, I was hooked. I had already had a fascination with things British, and was always charmed when I met an English lad my age or happened to be introduced to a movie filmed in England. But, boy, this Beatles thing really put me over the top.

I started out loving McCartney, and though I never lost the affection, I moved into a lifelong appreciation for all things John Lennon. And, as I got older, the Lennon fascination and enjoyment continued to grow. Sure, I enjoyed "Penny Lane," but nothing could match "Strawberry Fields" for sheer inner revelation. "Hey Jude" was great, really great, but has there ever been a more profound moment in the history of music than those opening chords to "A Day in the Life," followed by the vibrating, intoning vocals of Lennon starting, "I read the news today, oh boy."

I could go on for pages about the Beatles, and no doubt there will be much to say about them as I ponder my life, so great was their influence on me. The meaning of John Lennon for me now, though, in this context, is that his music was essentially an aphrodisiac in the budding passion with this New York woman.

I had recently seen the Lennon musical in San Francisco with my family, it having played in the city before heading to Broadway. And I heard that some changes had been made to the New York show that made the performances even stronger, some superfluous stuff had apparently been removed. As we were drinking that second glass of wine I called the concierge at my hotel to see if she might obtain a couple of tickets to the show. She took my cell phone number and promised to call me back either way. It was late at night, so I assumed that all of her connections would be shut down for the night. However, she came through. And as we were finishing that second glass of wine, the concierge informed me that she had obtained third-row tickets for the next day's performance.

I met my New York friend there the following day and we were entranced by the music and memories. She is a few years older than myself, and it dredged up for her a lot of feelings and thoughts that she hadn't experienced in many years, so involved had she been in her adult life performing piano concerts and selling. Tears welled in her eyes during the performance, memories of her precious sister whom she had lost at a very young age, forcing themselves on her consciousness. And memories of happy things as well—the sheer innocence, naiveté and joy of the music overtaking both of us.

I appreciated being with her that afternoon, experiencing the music and feelings again, and I felt something else as well, a sort of respect that she had been a few years older than me when this music was happening; that she was even more a product of that era. There was something that very much turned me on about that fact. Indeed, the whole experience of being with her was taking on the quality of a dream, where time seems to exist in a different dimension than it usually does in an ordinary day. And as much as I was enjoying these moments, this sort of letting go, how on earth could I not acknowledge or forget that I was married, and that Susan and I did very much love one another?

The two worlds coexisted for a moment, but I had a foreboding that these two worlds could not and must not coexist for very long. Yet, there was this passion over which I did not seem to have much control. I had always been (while not a control freak) a person certainly in control of my behavior. What had happened here? I simply could not understand it myself. I seemed to be losing boundaries. But how not to? I started feeling things so intensely that I did not know what to do with the feelings. Was it she? Was it I? Was this just the time and place, the weather a perfect conduit, to let myself out, to just allow something deep within to be released?

We took a ride on New York harbor that night, the Statue of Liberty a beacon of freedom in the offing. Perhaps there had been a kind of liberation for me that night, a brave willingness to just let myself out, damn the consequences. This realization, though, did not come lightly; there was no doubting my love for Susan, my love and responsibility for family, the pain that I was feeling on the other side of this liberation.

Alma Lorraine Rush Rosen

My mother, Alma Lorraine Rush Rosen, was born January 2, 1934, to Abraham and Mary Rush, delivered by a midwife in a cramped upstairs flat in the Chinatown district of Toronto, Canada. She was the youngest of six children, three older brothers and two sisters having come before her. She was the youngest by several years, and it had been a foregone conclusion that there would not be any more children after number five. These were the depression years, and Alma was an unexpected addition to a family of three very tough brothers, each one a paper boy who, at one time or another, successfully fought off the intrusions of neighborhood bullies intent on stealing their money, newspapers and corners.

The brothers were tough, but they had to be. Anti-Semitism was not confined to Europe, and if Jews were being blamed in Germany for the downfall of their society, there was, no doubt, a stench of this mentality in pockets all across North America. The Rush sisters grew to be extremely attractive: Yettie a buxom redhead, Sarah, a green-eyed blonde who had the local royalty chasing after her; but Alma took the prize for beauty. She could pass for many nationalities. Italians claimed her as their own; Spaniards would swear that she was from that culture's Sephardim; and she had an Egyptian or Middle-Eastern look as well. Her complexion was of smooth olive, a figure that was just unbelievable, and large brown eyes, almost biblical in appearance, the eyes of a seer.

At the age of 17, Alma entered the Miss Toronto beauty pageant and was one of the top two or three runners-up. Many thought that there had to have been a bribe for her not to have come in first, so absolutely stunning was she. Her brothers were friends with some pretty well-known prizefighters, and one in particular—a guy who went on to become a world champion—would have given just about anything to date her. But Alma's parents were protective and they would have none of it. It was, however, a tough life for her growing up. Abe, her father, was a tyrant of a man, but he had to be to keep Isaac, Dave and Meyer in line.

Abe was of Russian stock, his grandfather having been a bootmaker to the Czar, and his wife, Mary, of a more delicate, Austrian lineage. Theirs had been, as so many in those days, a matchmaker marriage. The union worked for many years—six children had to be raised—but over time the oppressive nature of this Russian tailor left Mary pleading for some time alone. She just couldn't take the terror anymore. It is because of this that there is some question about Alma's parentage. Abraham had left Mary some time around a year before Alma was born, and didn't return until she was about a month or two old. He went off to Vancouver to sow some oats, Mary remaining behind to support the family—with the help of her sons and their paperboy money—as a seamstress. Abe would send some funds back from time to time, just enough to keep everything afloat. In any event, many in the know suggest strongly that while Abe was gone, Mary fell in love with an Egyptian psychic, the girl with the Mediterranean features so different from her siblings belonging to him. Indeed, the timing of Abe's travels would suggest that this could very well be the case.

When Alma was quite young, perhaps six or seven years old, she befriended a couple of elder English sisters. These sisters claimed to be psychic, and saw in the young Alma a very profound spiritualism, an old soul. They discovered in Alma a kind of clairvoyance that they had not seen in anyone before. They readily admitted to the young girl that she had an astounding gift—one far deeper than their own—and wanted to help her develop it. They did this by showing Alma the art of tea-leaf reading, helping her to decipher the meanings of the images that she would discover in the cup. She began to tell these ladies facts of their own lives that were astounding to them. In short time she began to do this for others. She read for her brothers and sisters; she was so good that word got out and people were willing to pay her money—tough to come by in those years—for a reading.

She read for her mother one day and that would be it for a while, as far as the readings would go. Her information was so precise and accurate that Mary became frightened for her daughter. She saw the downside in this—that her daughter might become exploited or worse for this gift—and she told Alma in no uncertain terms that she had to keep this gift to herself for a while. No more readings. So she stopped the readings, but that didn't mean that her psychic gift lay dormant.

One day her father asked if she would like to go along to help him collect rents, the family now owning an apartment house. She thought that would be fun. As Abraham came to the part of a dark alley where he would turn toward the apartment house, Alma said, "Pa, don't go out there, please don't; there is a man hiding and he is going to try and kill you with something." Her father scoffed and began to open the door. And as he did, a man with a crowbar came from behind with just that weapon Alma had seen in her mind. She screamed, and as she did Abraham looked up to discover the man with the weapon. He was able to slam the door and take off, perhaps just in time to save his life.

When Larry first laid eyes on Alma, he had to have her, so he pursued her—eventually winning The Prize. I am the result of his success. Approximately 1959, California.

Alma Rush around age 20.

By the age of 18, Alma couldn't take it anymore, she had to get away from this family, Her brothers were very, very tough and there always seemed to be some sort of trouble following at least one of them at almost any time. And her father, whose protectiveness bordered on cruelty. Not to mention the protectiveness of her brothers. The break came on a weekend trip, when Mary asked if Alma would accompany her on a trip to Montreal to visit a noteworthy reader of cards, Gertie Rosen. Gertie, A French Jew with roots dating to the origins of Montreal, was well known in Montreal as a very good fortuneteller. Mary had thought that it would be a nice getaway for mother and daughter, so they went off to see Gertie at 100 Villeneuve Street in what was at the time a Jewish and Greek neighborhood of Montreal. She lived across the street from Saul's pharmacy on one side, his best seller a medicine called 222s, an over-the-counter painkiller composed mainly of codeine. Directly across the street on the other side was the neighborhood store—Rifka's—smelling of everything sweet and sour.

Gertie had a live-in person who helped her cook and clean, named Bella. Bella looked as the name sounds. She was a very large woman, with a kind of pimply birthmark from which one would always try to look away. The kitchen always smelled like a mixture of borsht, tongue, herring and oily, overcooked chicken soup. Gertie was married to Max, but they slept in separate bedrooms. When he was home, he would greet the guests for Gertie, and when he wasn't home, he ran one of the leading taxicab companies in Montreal. He was a redhead of Polish descent, and they had two sons and a daughter—Larry was the oldest, followed by Sollie and their daughter, Vivian. When he wasn't driving taxis for his father, Larry played jazz clarinet and saxophone in some local bands. He looked very much like his father, perhaps about five-feet, six-inches tall, thin, with wiry, red hair, kinky, curly. He had fallen asleep the previous night in soiled clothes. And when he awoke late the next morning, he got up to discover one of the most beautiful girls he had ever seen.

He came upon Alma, waiting in the parlor to see his mother. He spoke to her and had to have her. She wasn't interested at first, he was not a very attractive sight in soiled clothes with a pale complexion. But Larry made sure he obtained her phone number, and within a few days was off to Toronto to woo this beauty. Alma wasn't that attracted, but she needed to get away. Within a few months, they eloped, Alma's father and brothers searching every motel from Toronto to Montreal for them. They vowed to "kill the bastard" if they could find him. Find him they couldn't, and a few years later, on March 6, 1955, I was born in Toronto's Mt. Sinai Hospital.

❒

The story of my birth, as told to me many times by my mother when I was growing up, made it into the significant medical record books of the time. The pregnancy had been physically very difficult for her, and as sensitive as she was as an intuitive, she was equally vulnerable to major episodes of illness. She had been diagnosed with a heart murmur in her teens, and was also quite susceptible to serious colds, the flu and pneumonia. She had to be hospitalized a few times during the term. When labor started, it was accompanied by some serious hemorrhaging.

As the bleeding continued, the labor became ever more painful; it started to become apparent that the mother or the child and possibly both might not make it through this alive. The doctors told Larry that they might not be able to save the mother and the baby, and that one might have to be sacrificed. "Obviously, save the mother, save the mother," he pleaded. "We'll do all that we can," was the response.

Alma had slipped into a kind of coma, an unconsciousness, and in this state she was visited by a middle-aged doctor, speaking in a calm, but serious and measured voice. "Alma," he said, "There is a button next to you and I want you to push it. You are bleeding quite seriously, and that button will bring the nurses. Push the button and everything will be okay. You are about to have a boy, and he will be a very special boy. So press the button now."

Alma pressed the button, and almost immediately on doing so a frenzy of activity occurred around her, the lives of her and her baby very much in jeopardy. "Thank you doctor, thank you so much for your help," she started. But there was only a team of nurses in the room, and there, apparently, had not been a doctor in the room speaking to her at all. "Alma, you are delirious," one of the nurses said to her. "Where did the doctor go?" Alma replied.

"There hasn't been a doctor in this room; you were in here alone for a while. And you are a very, very lucky woman that you pushed that button. You have been bleeding very seriously, but it looks as though we have been able to control it. You might have died."

"I know that there was a doctor there—he is the one who told me to push the button." "You are imagining it, Alma, but you are very fortunate tonight, very fortunate tonight," came the answer. I almost didn't make it that night, and the same is true of my mom.

Apparently, a whole team of doctors was called into that Mt. Sinai delivery room that night. They were there to watch the top doctors attempt to save the lives of mother and baby. My birth was a case of placenta previa, where the placenta precedes the baby—there being no fluid for delivery. Infant death due to suffocation or other causes is a real possibility in this state of affairs, and given the weakened condition of mother, the loss of both might have happened.

San Francisco

March 19th, 2007

My mom lived to tell me this story many times as I was growing up, and as I sit here tonight, reflecting on my life, and looking on the darkened San Francisco Bay, the lights of the city sparkling like diamonds in the foreground, and the elemental, illuminated Golden Gate Bridge—draped in pearls of light—I feel an intense anxiety in my neck and stomach. Sue and I are separated from one another, and I can't quite diagnose the reasons for it. There is some sort of force at work that seems to have demagnetized our magnetic attraction. I love her deeply, but it had become unbearably intense since the revelations of New York City. At least in this apartment to which I have moved I do not have to explain what I am feeling and whether or not I am feeling. I am alone, but there is quiet. And over the past several months I have so desperately needed some quiet.

❐

Michael is in college, and Jonathan will be a college freshman in the fall. Sue and I have been in emotional agony since the New York City revelations, so perhaps it was just better to leave while Jonathan was still home, rather than when the house was totally empty. The loneliness aches, my having been so much a part of the family for the last 20 years. Though the quiet is sometimes deafening, there are other moments when I drink in the space and quiet. I often miss Susan, but if I walk to the house to see her, I experience our separation acutely. I look into her eyes and witness a biblical depth; I often told her that I thought that she might have been Ruth from the Old Testament in a past life. She is one of the top and most-respected pharmacists in the city. She read all the right books, and raised the boys with the kind of love and tenderness—bringing out the best in them and providing structure and kindness in large doses—that affords them the opportunity to love deeply in their lives, to live full lives filled with compassion.

Yet, we are not together, and might not ever be together in the same way again. This causes me great pain. But as I sit here at this moment, I just don't feel that I can put the eggshells back together. Something happened, and I can't say what it is. Perhaps I know, and I tell myself that I really don't know. Maybe I love her deeply, but I am not in love. Perhaps we make way too much out of being in love, as a society. We dwell on the romance, but forget the need for friendship. Sue and I will be friends till death do us part, but I hadn't felt the romantic spark for quite a long time. Maybe it is possible that romance and friendship can also exist till death do us part. Maybe that will yet happen with Sue again. Perhaps it won't. Maybe there is another love in store for me in this life; I just don't know. The uncertainty can be liberating, but the lack of stability and predictability can be quite painful. Romance can be a drug, and I am not interested in filling my void with any kind of ephemeral drug of passion or any other kind. I guess I'll have to just wait and see. That is all I really know at this moment—except that I feel quite sad and I miss my mom.

There are many messages—some might call them psychic realizations—that my mom presented to me over my life about my own life. For me, though, these were truths. When she saw something clearly, I just took it as fact. And I always took her advice when she told me of a particular direction that I should take. Many of her clients would listen to her advice, feel that she was probably correct, then willfully follow their own desires. Many of these people—several have become clients of mine in my own business—have relayed to me over the years since her death that they often realized the errors of their ways when they deviated from her advice, and were even more inclined to strictly adhere to her words when she saw something clearly.

❐

A tea-leaf reading might last five minutes if there was not much to see, or if there was perhaps one significant point that needed to be revealed. She would never labor over a teacup just to give people their money's worth. Other readings might last 45 minutes or longer. And, of course, she always left room for questions at the end. There were a few times—one in particular that she told me about—when she would look into a cup, see something quite unsavory about the person and then just put the cup back down, saying, "You'll have to go to some one else; I just can't read you." In the particular instance of which she made me aware, she had seen a serious crime the person was about to commit. In telling the person that they would have to go to someone else, she added, "My advice to you is not to do it. That is all I will say." The person, the way my mom told it, became as "white as a ghost." She never told me what she saw in that particular person's teacup, but I know from her tone of voice that it was very, very serious. I didn't probe her.

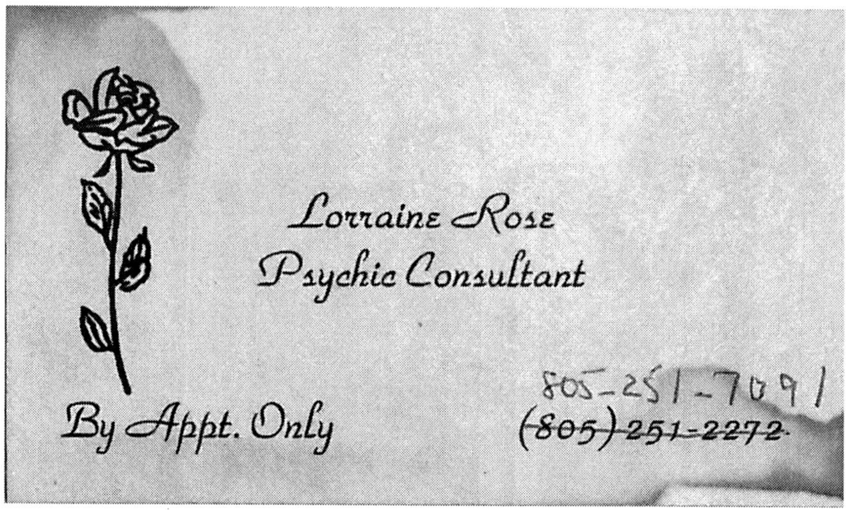

Mom's Psychic Consultant business card.

Lorraine Rose was her professional name. She would often read for the poor and "down and out" people for free, but would receive with tips some handsome payments from the glamorous and wealthy who could afford it. On one particular occasion when I came to her home in Canyon Country, a high-desert community about 30 minutes north of the San Fernando Valley, to visit her on break from attending college at the University of California, Santa Barbara, she had just finished talking to someone who must have been quite interesting, either that or the conversation had been provocative or funny, given the expression on her face. I had been out having a couple of beers with friends and walked in the door around midnight. "What are you thinking about, Mom?" I asked her. "Who were you just talking to? Anything happen? What were you talking about?" "Oh, nothing special," she said with a bit of a wry smile. "Oh something happened; just tell me," I pushed. "Come on, Mom, who were you talking to?" "Well Marlon Brando just asked me out on a date," she replied. (My mom and dad had been separated for a number of years.)

My father had left the house in Los Angeles to go back to Canada when I was 16, the year 1971. I am the eldest of four kids, and at that point, my youngest sibling, Heidi, was nine; Elliot, the next youngest, was 11; and Jeff, 15 months junior to myself, was 15. Lorraine Rush raised us without any additional support, solely from her readings. She had always read as sort of a hobby for friends, but when my father left, it became—like it or not—her livelihood. Her reputation spread quickly without the help of advertising. She was very humble, and didn't want any notoriety. Although, and within a few years she was reading for the rich and famous (though quite confidentially).

Marlon Brando had apparently been coming to her for help with his love life, and there was a Japanese woman for whom he had some deep feelings. Lorraine Rose had been advising Mr. Brando with respect to this woman, but in the process he was developing an affection for her. These conversations had been going on for some time, and (having been at school) I really had no clue that this was happening. My sister, Heidi, living at home had known the whole story for some time, and later brought me up to speed on the nature of their conversations. I really don't know if they ever went out on a date; she never told me, though I did ask. I do know, though, that he had come to the house for a reading, and that she had gone to his home to read for him as well. Most of the sessions took place on the phone, and they took place for quite some time after I went back to college.

A few years earlier than the Brando conversation, I was also home visiting from college. I had been sitting on the back patio, looking at the mountains in the distance, when I walked back into the house to see a very elegantly dressed, highly attractive woman getting up to leave after a reading. Just after she left I asked, "Mom, who was that? Wow, what a knockout!" She nonchalantly answered that it was the actress Yvette Mimieux. "What did you see in her cup?" I asked, the randy college student getting the best of me. "You know I can't tell you that," she answered, and very quietly went on about her business, washing the day's build-up of teacups.

The most profound message that my mother ever gave to me in a tea-leaf reading concerned something no less than my destiny. As a philosophy major in college, I spent many hours discussing and grappling with the questions of free will versus determinism, fate versus chance, the role of choice versus inaction. At this stage of my life, I have come to the belief that, as human beings, we do have choice; we can choose to act or not act. We have volition, will power and can choose to exercise it or not. The existentialists believed that our destinies are the product of our free will, and that we create our futures through our own actions for better or worse. I do believe this to a point, but I have no doubt that there is something else at work, something over which we have little control.

Life presents itself to us, and we can either succumb to its clear path or not. And we often avoid the path that seems the clearest only to find it again at a later time. But sometimes it doesn't come again, and we miss the opportunity. There is, thus, a fate before us, but it is up to us to follow it or not. As discussed, there were many people who heard what Lorraine Rush had to say, but chose to not follow. Very often they wished that they had, and in due time they were back on course. But there are those who will fight vigorously for their free will and choose not to follow the signs or road map in front of them, and often miss the proper turn-off on the freeway. However, grace often does prevail, and even in those instances where we think we have free choice, and the exercise of that choice seems to be leading us in a direction we know not where, destiny or fate does prevail, free choice or not.

I could have ignored the reading that Lorraine gave me on that gorgeous early summer day, when I came home to visit during my break from graduate school in San Francisco, as we sat in the backyard overlooking the foothills north of Los Angeles. But it really would not have mattered, so clear was her vision for my life. Free will or not, what she saw that day had the weight of destiny. She put my cup down and told me the standard, "Twirl it around three times and make a wish." I complied and made the wish, which was to finally meet a person with whom I would fall in love and eventually raise a family. I was 25 and very much wanted to meet this person. I had been dating and was tiring of the shallow nature of these encounters. My mom looked into my cup and said, "Your wish is going to come true, and it will be relatively soon. Your wish is very clearly to be in love—there are hearts and cupids all over your cup." She stopped to point these out to me. "You will not be able to find this person yourself," she continued. "She'll find you. Remember what I am saying, don't try so hard to find her; you'll have to wait for her to find you."

She went on to tell me that this person would be of light complexion, light hair and, probably, blue eyes. She averred that the woman would be quite smart, "just as smart as you, but

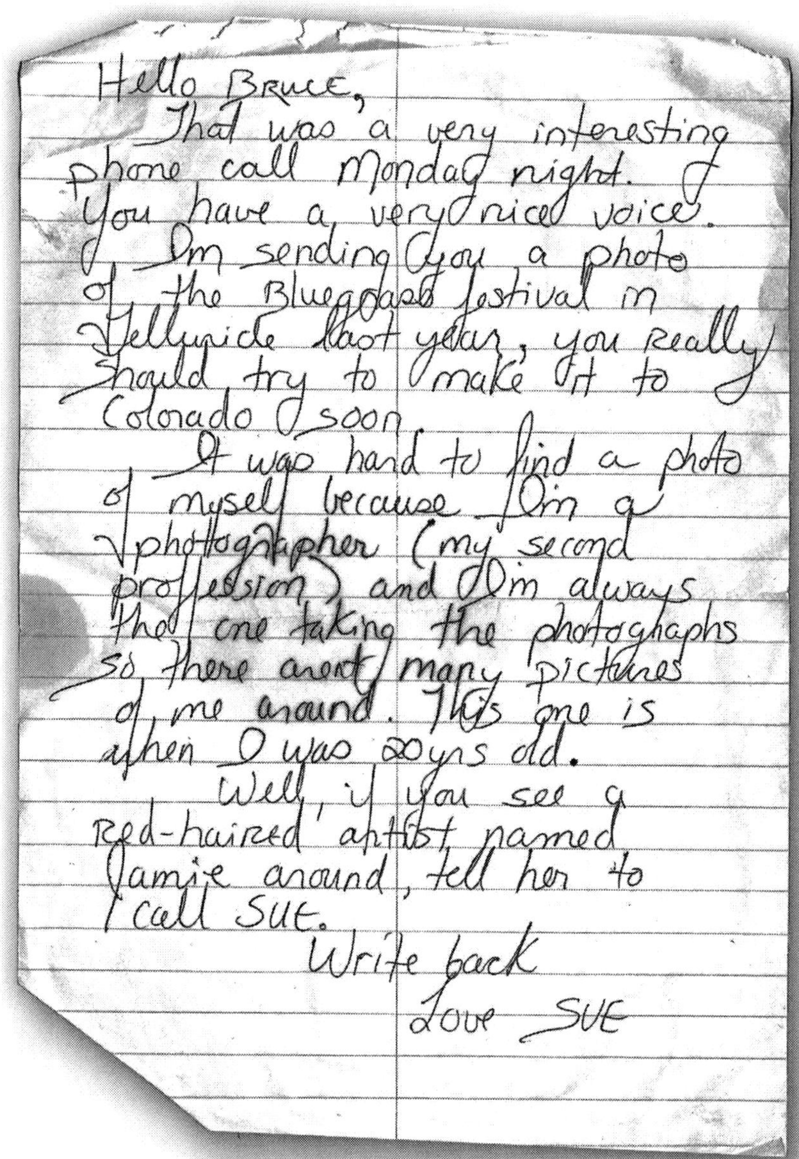

Hello Bruce,
That was a very interesting phone call Monday night. You have a very nice voice.
I'm sending you a photo of the Bluegrass festival in Telluride last year, you really should try to make it to Colorado soon.
It was hard to find a photo of myself because I'm a photographer (my second profession) and I'm always the one taking the photographs so there aren't many pictures of me around. This one is when I was 20 yrs old.
Well, if you see a Red-haired artist named Jamie around, tell her to call SUE.
Write back
Love SUE

Sue finds Bruce as predicted by Alma in the tea-leaf reading.

Dear Sue,

It was a wonderful surprise to receive your letter, all of a sudden I find myself thinking about the fascinating occurrence of Monday night when I was so attracted to you on the telephone.

I must say that you certainly do take beautiful Photographs, as you capture it, the Town of Telluride seems very intriguing. I have never been to Colorado, but, perhaps you might be a very good reason to do so.

Aside from the attractiveness of Colorado, Sue, you certainly are very pretty. Your hair is about the color that I had visualized, and it is a very beautiful setting in which the picture is taken.

I am enclosing a picture that I had taken in a photo-booth a few weeks ago. I think it captures me at one of my unrelaxed moments.

In any case I look forward to keeping in touch with you—and very possiby meeting you in the near future. I really would like to visit Colorado, And I'm sure that you have a soft spot for San Francisco.

Talk To You Soon,

Love

Bruce

The wrong number that turns into the right number—Bruce writes Sue.

in a different way." This from a mother who thought that I was absolutely brilliant, so this was high praise for the other person. She added that the father would be quiet, but would like me very much. "But remember, don't go looking for her; she'll find you." "Any questions?" she asked, as she customarily did at the end of a reading. "Well, what is her name?" I asked, "Just give me a name." She picked up the cup, reflected for a moment then uttered the word, "Sue." "Her name is Sue," she said, her thoughts drifting for a moment. "Well," I answered, "I know a Suzanne, but she has dark hair, and I really don't think that I could fall in love with her." "It's not she," she answered. "You haven't met her yet, but it is coming soon," and then she put the cup down.

While I was down in southern California, the friend with whom I moved to San Francisco to attend graduate school—and with whom I shared a room—arranged to install separate telephones for the two of us. We had previously shared a telephone, but since he was a guitarist and was starting a business of playing around town, a separate phone number would be best. A couple of days after my mom's reading, I returned to San Francisco and entered my room, replete with this new phone. I put the bags down, lingering in the living room with my roommate, Jeff, asking how the business was doing (had he acquired any new gigs?), while he asked me about L.A., being from the same general area. We had been talking for about an hour when my telephone rang. It was a sweet-sounding voice, and the connection seemed to be long distance. "Is Jamie there?" she asked. "Jamie? There is no Jamie here," I answered. "I think that you have the wrong number." But she didn't hang up right away, nor did I. When I could tell that she had lingered for a moment, I continued. "This sounds like long distance," I said, "and you have a really sweet voice." She sort of giggled, telling me that she also liked the sound of my voice. "Is this long distance? Where are you calling from?" "I am in Denver. My friend, Jamie, moved to San Francisco about a year ago, and I haven't spoken to her in a while. She must have moved," she answered. "Well, you really do have a very nice, soft voice," I reiterated. "What is your name?" "Sue," she answered. "So you are Sue from Denver. I'm sorry that you can't find your friend, Jamie—by the way is that a girl?—but I wouldn't mind talking to you further."

Indeed, Jamie had been a girlfriend from childhood, and she was quite a talented artist who had moved to the Haight-Ashbury district of San Francisco, the same neighborhood where I was living at the time. She had recently moved and the changeover in phone numbers had me with her old one.

Sue and I continued to talk on that initial "wrong number" for a while, concluding by deciding that we would send each other our pictures. "I have one that I have recently taken in one of those picture booths, but I look quite uptight in it," I said. "It is the only one that I have."

"Send it," she said, "and I'll send you one that I took a couple of years ago in Florence."

The conversation ended and the pictures were sent. Now, did I really know during that conversation that this "Sue" was the woman that I would marry one day? No way. Did the thought cross my mind that this was quite a coincidence? Yes; absolutely yes. However, a very strange, sort of "all-knowing" revelation took place for me a few days later. When her picture arrived, I looked at it and saw an almost unbelievable familiarity in this person. When I saw it, I realized instantly that this was the woman that I would one day marry. One year later, after graduating pharmacy school, Sue moved in with me. A year after that, we were married in San Francisco.

We were married at city hall in San Francisco by a judge, just like Marilyn Monroe and Joe DiMaggio. The ceremony was attended by my friend, Jeff, with whom I had shared the phone; by my mother; my aunt Yettie, Alma's sister; by Sue's mother; and by Jamie, the girl whose number I had acquired. We have had two amazing kids, Michael and Jonathan. And indeed, Sue has all the physical characteristics that my mother had seen in the cup, the fair complexion, light hair and blue eyes. Her father liked me very much, and I shared the same feelings for him. We became very good friends, though he passed away from complications due to Alzheimer's several years ago.

As I write this, looking over the darkened bay, the lights strewn across the Golden Gate Bridge, the dome of the Palace of Fine Arts lit up like a thick wedding band, I have an anxiety and sadness, assuaged only by this requirement that I write.

❒

The reservation was to fly to New York on Jet Blue late in the day on the 22nd of July, the day before the arranged appointment to view pianos. I had initially called Steinway a few weeks before the appointment, happened on a Russian saleswoman who seemed cold and detached, not that informative. So, I looked around locally, thinking it would be easier to just purchase the instrument at one of the outlets nearby.

Sue and I gathered knowledge about sizes, models and prices; we investigated some previously owned instruments, almost buying one at quite a good price. However, we became concerned that perhaps the sales lady was giving us a con job—she seemed a little too aggressive and in a hurry to make the sale. So, we settled on the thought that it would have to be a new Steinway, the Model M being the most practical in terms of price and size.

The plan was to stop in New York City for a day or two and buy the piano before my planned trip to visit my cousins, Jerry and Madeleine, in London. Jerry and Matty are the son and daughter of David Rush, my mom's brother who was a legend in Toronto.

The Rush Family

Rising from defending a street corner with his brother Meyer during the depression years, Davey went on to own, through his affiliation with stock-market promoters, a series of mining companies; his knowledge and information with regard to when to sell these companies put him on the financial front pages of Toronto newspapers. Considerable wealth was created through his involvement in owning companies, and this eventually led to his ownership of a chain of department stores, and some of the prime real estate in Toronto. Meyer was an antihero of considerable notoriety in Toronto during the late 1950s and 1960s, and as tough as Dave was—truly, there were very few people who would want to take him on with their fists, a man just filled with power in his upper body—Meyer was, probably, double that. In 1967, Meyer had been accused by the Canadian Government of having committed a $100-million stock fraud—stories of his dealings and alleged exploits had been commonplace reading in Toronto newspapers. Mike, as he was also known, had vehemently denied the charges, firmly believing that some were trying to enrich themselves politically by concocting such a vast crime—making him the fall guy for all of the cover-ups that were taking place within organized crime and proper government circles—and finding a stooge of whom they could make a serious example to the public.

Mike was convinced that there was a conspiracy at work here. He confided in me that he had been approached by leading figures in organized crime and government circles to let them in on the take, and that he would have none of it. Later in that year, 1967, a bomb blew up under his bed in Toronto's Sutton Place Hotel, knocking out windows across the street, with people being treated for shock. He had been prepared to testify and name names. And, of course, this would be a surefire way to kill him. Who tried to kill him? He wasn't sure—but he did know the reasons behind it. Some high-ranking people had a lot to lose, so he said. He died three times on the way to the hospital, but was brought back to life each time by a young, determined doctor. In an amazing coincidence of fate, a key reason that he was able to survive the bombing long enough for the doctor to keep him alive had to do with the mattress stuffing that filled his wounds, absorbing some of the flow of blood. The bed had been manufactured by his brother-in-law, Morris Kornblum, his sister Sarah's husband.

Meyer had been pronounced dead on Canadian national radio—I heard it myself. My father had taken our family from California to Canada for a couple of years when I was 12. During the second year, we moved from Montreal to an outpost way up in the province of New Brunswick, settling in a town called Campbellton. My father had been offered an engineering job, so instead of going back to California, which I so desperately wanted to do, we moved farther to the northeast, and settled into a bitter, bitter winter. I had come home from school early on one of these frigid cold days and my mom was the color of a sheet. She had just heard from a sister that her brother had been blown up while sleeping in his bed.

The radio was on, and not long after being home I heard the commentator say that, "Toronto stock promoter, Meyer Rush, standing trial in a $100-million stock fraud, has died after being blown up by a bomb while sleeping." A couple of hours later, the radio announced that, "Meyer Rush, originally pronounced dead from a bomb placed under his bed in Toronto's Sutton Place Hotel, is clinging to life." He did live. And a couple of months later, while recuperating in Panama—where he owned some land—he was spotted by a Toronto reporter who recognized him. He pursued Meyer relentlessly for a few days, until he gave the guy a story. Shortly thereafter, the picture of Meyer Rush, skin grafts readily apparent across his neck, looking muscular in short sleeves, his foot on a jeep, emblazoned the front page of a Canadian national magazine.

❒

Several months before the bombing, some men broke into his home in the middle of the night, wielding baseball bats. They proceeded to beat him about the arms, legs, and head. From his slumber, he managed to gain some recognition of one of the attackers. Emerging from the hospital, Meyer went to the lineup, the police believing that they might have found one of the perpetrators.

As the men were presented to Meyer, he slowly walked from one end of the line to the other, casually glancing at the face of each one. He walked a couple of times, eventually stopping in front of one of the men. "You dirty son of a bitch," Meyer uttered, then proceeded to drive his fist into the guys mouth and jaw, blood splattering all around. Upon knocking the guy out, a detective approached Meyer and asked if that meant that he had made a successful identification. "I don't tell no tales," Meyer Rush responded, walking away. I just loved that guy, Meyer Rush.

The notoriety of Meyer Rush became too much for his brother Dave to handle. So in short time, Dave left Toronto to retire in London. While in retirement, he started a very successful glass company, making double-glazing for windows and patio doors. Central heating had not been that common in England, and the country had a serious need for well-insulated windows. Dave became one of the pioneers of that business in England, and made a mint doing it.

When I graduated college in 1978, I moved from Santa Barbara to London to work with my uncle. It was at this time that I became more familiar with my cousins, Jerry and Matty. I went to visit them by myself a few months after my mom died in 1999, finding them a real comfort at that time. And, indeed, London brought back some fond memories for me, so it was a good visit, and it helped me with my grief. I had gotten into the habit of visiting them almost every year since then, sometimes with my family, other times not. When Jerry told me that it wouldn't be a good idea to come in July, 2005, I made the plans to stay a while longer in New York—I'd never really been there for more than a day.

London had just experienced those two serious terror attacks, hitting the buses and the underground. I still considered going to London after the first attack, but when the second one hit, I heeded his advice and looked forward to the museums, theater, skyline and streets of New York City.

The Russian woman had been uninviting and not very informative on the phone, but when I called back to enquire again about pianos and to arrange for the appointment—this time armed with a bit more information on the subject—it was a very different person with whom I spoke. The second woman was charming, playful, inquisitive, and a bit flirtatious. There was a musical timbre to her voice, a slight hoarseness and huskiness that played quite well on the telephone. She wasn't highly aggressive, but just enough to hold my attention and interest regarding what I might find in the Steinway showroom in New York City. "When are you coming to New York?" she wanted to know; and "You ought to come soon," she persuaded, quite invitingly, with a bit of a giggle. I told her that I was considering looking at another shop as well, one that specialized in vintage, previously owned and refurbished Steinway pianos. She knew of the shop and sought to convince me that one could never be sure that a refurbished piano could be made with the same custom workmanship and parts as the original—and that the trade-in value would never be as good. I let her know that I would consider what she was saying, but that I would very likely visit the aforementioned shop and then come to a decision. I let her know that the other shop had been referred to me by a very talented musician friend of mine. We agreed to talk again in a week or so about the date of my visit.

She was readily available when I did call back—but my proposed time for meeting was problematic for her. The Saturday that I would be visiting would be the eighth straight day of her working, and she would desperately need a day off. "Well, put me through to someone else, and I'll see to it that if I buy, you'll get a referral fee," I volunteered. "Don't get me wrong, I have nothing against Russians, but just don't give me that Russian lady, she sounded very cold and unhelpful when I called the first time. I didn't even give her my name when she asked." "You know what?" she offered, "I'll come in on my day off. I want to make sure that if you come this far, you'll receive the right kind of attention." "I really don't feel good about taking up your day off," I answered. "No, I'll do it; don't worry about it."

The date was set.

I am not the best traveler by airplane the world has ever seen, but nor am I the worst. Indeed, I do get quite nervous in airplanes and turbulence does get to me, but not always. There are times that I can fly peacefully, surrendering to the whole experience. I had worked feverishly the day of my flight to New York; I was trying to get in all of my bond trades before being gone for a week and a half to visit New York, and then on to New Hampshire, where my son, Michael, would be debuting a piece of music that he had written during a composition program at the Walden School. It had been several months since I had taken any kind of a break, so when I boarded that plane, I truly was in the mood to surrender. I felt relaxed and ready to get away.

Once we were up in the air, I settled in nicely, turning on my iPod and listening to some of my favorite music that I hadn't heard for awhile. I hadn't really drunk much water the whole day, nor had I had much on the flight. It was somewhere over Chicago that I began to feel quite warm. "Sweet Melissa," my favorite Allman Brothers song had just come on, and I really didn't feel like getting up. But as the song played on, I began to feel more uncomfortable; I was continuing to feel quite warm and noticed that I was sweating. So I decided to get up to have some water and use the restroom, and as I did, I became quite light-headed. And when this happened I became dizzy and started to panic. My heart was racing and I was sweating profusely. And I had the sensation—one that I had never, ever had quite like this—that I could not get any air. It truly felt like all the air had been sucked out of the cabin. I thought that it couldn't be only me who was feeling this, and started to look around the plane to see if oxygen masks were being released. But I didn't see any such thing. People seemed relaxed, reading, eating, sleeping, not a look of panic on anyone's face. That was reassuring at first, until I realized that something, then, must be happening to me. Breathing very heavily, almost gasping for air and sweating profusely, I walked over to the steward, saying that I thought that I needed some oxygen. The service and attention was phenomenal. Immediately he brought me to the back of the plane, sat me down and tied an oxygen mask to my face. I was feeling quite embarrassed about this, not wanting anyone to know that I was having any difficulty. He reassured me—and so did the stewardesses that made their way to the back of the plane—that I would be okay. But I wasn't quite so sure. I didn't know what was happening to me, and at that point, I just wanted to be off that airplane and in some cozy place. Giving me plenty of room and monitoring my breathing, they announced the need for a doctor to come to the back of the plane. Well, I was relieved to know that there would be some medical attention, but not so thrilled to be the object of so much attention.

The doctor noticed that my eyes were dilated and that I was showing signs of dehydration. My blood pressure was quite low, and the heartbeat rapid. He told me that orange juice, because it had electrolytes, would be better than just water, and proceeded to fill me with the juice. He stayed there, monitoring my pressure and breathing, until I started to become more stable. I stretched out, slowly starting to calm down. The doctor calmed me down by talking about comforting things; it turned out that his boys went to the same high school as my own. He took my blood pressure a few more times, and by the time we were ready to descend to JFK, I was, essentially, back to normal. Nonetheless, surmising that it had been dehydration mixed with panic, but not being totally sure, he recommended that on landing I allow a paramedic team to bring me to the local emergency room. "Let them check you out, so that when you go to sleep tonight, you can do so confidently," he suggested. Since I would be in New York for a few days, and certainly wanted to have a bit of a good time, it just made sense that I take care of this unexpected health business.

I walked out of the airplane on my own power, and was greeted on the runway by several paramedics intent on bringing me to the emergency room at Jamaica Queens. I wouldn't be able to retrieve my bags, but they assured me that they would be stored in a safe place, ready to be retrieved when I was free to leave the hospital; and if I had to be admitted, arrangements would be made to have them sent over. So, moments after arriving in New York City, I found myself not headed to the Four Seasons in Midtown but in an ambulance en route to an emergency room. It took hours to be admitted, and once admitted, it took a few more hours to be tested and to get the results. They performed an EKG, among other tests. In the process, a different kind of New York City was being revealed to me. As I sat with an IV in my arm to hydrate me as I waited for the results of my tests, the activity was frenetic and the action intense, people suffering from knife or gunshot wounds vying for attention with others suffering from drug or alcohol overdoses. In several cases, medical personnel were urgently struggling to save lives, a few of those who I had seen brought in on stretchers that night not surviving. Amidst all of this activity, at least one nurse on staff was, perhaps, excessively jaded. She just watched as I struggled to pull out my phone and carry the I.V stand to a location where I might inform family of my whereabouts. She continued to watch in a bemused fashion, until an orderly came by and put the stand on a cart with wheels. "Thanks a lot," I said, and then stared at the nurse, giving my best glare from the days when I was captain of my hockey team. It didn't faze her, though; she had no doubt seen far worse than my cold stare in her time spent in emergency rooms. And, as she was on the receiving end of my acknowledgement, another patient was giving her serious hell for ignoring her as she was writhing in pain.

The tests cam back fine, and I was discharged from the hospital at about three o'clock in the morning. I was not in any frame of mind to head back to the airport to retrieve my bags, so the hotel, for a small fee, arranged to do that for me. Actually, it was quite nice of them to be so accommodating in the wee hours of the morning. I exited the hospital, drained from the experience, but relieved that I was all right. I couldn't find any taxis upon leaving, just a few unmarked cars, resembling limousines. One motioned for me to come in, said that he would take me where I wanted to go. But I would have none of it. At 3:00 A.M., as I left Jamaica Queens emergency room, I was holding in abeyance my confidence and trust in anything. It actually felt as though a part of me had died on that plane, and that I had been reborn into a very strange world. I demanded that the driver show me his identification. And even when he did, I wanted to see a bit more. Finally I committed myself to travel with this driver into Midtown, but as I did, I made sure that the driver got a dose of my intense hockey glare, the one that didn't seem to faze Nurse Ratched. The glare must have worked this time, because at about 3:45 that morning I made it to my hotel room, the bags arriving just a few minutes later. I didn't fall asleep as easily as I would have wanted, when I hit that bed. But sleep eventually came to me, and when I awoke it was almost time to make that appointment. From that airplane ride forward, life has not been quite the same for me. And, again, as I sit here overlooking this darkened bay, I struggle to make sense of everything.

April 17th, 2007

I have just arrived home from attending a dinner at an Italian Restaurant in North Beach for my son Jonathan's 18th birthday. Sue and a few of his friends were gathering at a place on Columbus Avenue and Jonathan had called me at work with the address. I was at the place a few minutes before the appointed time of 7:30 and waited until almost 8:00 without seeing anybody. It was a quiet night in the restaurant and the owner/waiter—Sicilian with a thick Italian accent, quite a peacock the way he ordered the waitresses around as he surveyed his kingdom—was in a hurry for people to arrive. Our business (Jonathan had made a reservation for nine) would be the lion's share of his revenue that night, so it would seem. Whenever a taxi stopped near the restaurant, he would ask me if that was them. "No, I said, let's be patient, they'll be here in due time. My son tends to run a bit late." In the meantime, I ordered a glass of water, and just sort of dozed off at the table, following a long, tiring day of work, my tongue raw from saying so many words today.

❒

Since our separation in January, my days have been filled with an unsettled feeling, an uncomfortable anxiety that I feel in the center of my stomach, that then works its way into the back of my neck and shoulders. This tension seems to crystallize into an impetus to work and create, and my production at work has not faltered since the move, and in the quiet of my empty apartment, I write about my life. The unsettled feelings that accompany this transition leave my body tense, my jaws often tight at the end of the day. But in the quiet moments when the day is over (such as when sitting at the table, waiting for the birthday party to arrive), or late at night when I sit in my comfortable chair and listen to some soulful Coltrane or Bill Evans or a current favorite, Joshua Redman, the rough edges of the anxiety soften and I become tired and peaceful.

By 8:00, Jonathan and friends still hadn't arrived, and the Sicilian peacock was getting antsy. I had given him enough time to be late, so I decided to call him. "Jonathan, I've been sitting in this restaurant that you picked out, and I am almost the only one in here; where are you guys?" "We've been waiting in the restaurant for you, dad. Everybody is here except you." He started giggling as he said this; I think he had just had a glass of wine. "Jonathan, I've been waiting for you at the address that you gave me. I think that you guys must have gone to the wrong restaurant." Indeed, I was at the correct restaurant, if one goes by address. But they were clearly at the right restaurant from the standpoint of being in the better place for his birthday.

There was a lot of laughter in the background, some music, the toasting of glasses, waiters trying to talk over the patrons. In front of me were merely a couple of guests, eating dinner quietly and alone, and a waiter pacing back and forth. Next door to the restaurant where I sat was another restaurant, and I believed that this was where the birthday party ended up. "Jonathan, I think I am next door to you. Go outside for a moment, and I'll also go outside." "Okay Dad." Twenty seconds later, we were looking at each other from about 30 feet apart. "Oh God, I am so embarrassed," Jonathan said. "I really liked the way this restaurant looked, it looked fun and I thought that it was the right place," he laughed, slightly buzzed from a glass of wine. "Don't worry about it sweetie—I'll be over there in just a minute," I followed. He had been having such a good time, and he was certainly in the right place to celebrate his 18th birthday.

I went back to tell the brooding guy about the mistake. I apologized, then asked how much I owed him for the water. I would have felt worse for his losing the business if he hadn't seemed so arrogant. "It is $30 for the bottle of water; it took us some time to set up the tables," his thick accent not disguising anger and hostility. "Thirty dollars, I'm not paying you $30 for a bottle of water. And the cost of setting up—it took you five minutes to set up, and you only did it after I arrived. I'm not going to pay $30 for that water." If he hadn't been so greedy and aggressive, I would have gladly given him $30 or more for the error. But he was just rubbing me the wrong way tonight. "You know what, I'll give you 20 bucks for the water, but only because I feel badly that you are out the business." There was a momentary look on his face that suggested hatred and violence. Then he caught himself, probably realizing that you really cannot treat customers like this. I put $20 down on the table, and upon walking out, met his stare with my own hockey glare—the tough look that one gets after taking a slash to the back of the legs upon chasing a puck into the corner.

I was elected captain of my hockey team in high school, and being tough had something to do with it. I wasn't very big as a hockey player, but quite fast and strong. My shot was timed at about 90 miles an hour, and I scored my share of goals. I was good enough to go on to a top college program, but gave it up to do something mellow, in particular, surf. But that hockey glare comes back to me now and then—and when it does, I just let it out. I left the restaurant and made my way toward the festive atmosphere of my son's birthday party. Just as I got outside, my cell phone rang. There was a woman on the other end, and she had quite an appealing, soft voice, noticeable even on a cell phone. She asked for a guy named John. I told her that she had the wrong number and, upon hanging up, said, "What is your name? If I see a John, I'll tell him that you called." She chuckled, adding, "Susan, Susan Sweet." "That is a very nice name, I hope that you find John. I'm going to my son's birthday; gotta go and good-luck." What was the universe trying to tell me here? It sure felt like it was saying something to me tonight. Susan Sweet? I made my way into the festive place and sat down next to my wife Sue—she just couldn't stop laughing at the silly little mistake Jonathan had made about the restaurant—and I thought to myself that I have never doubted her sweetness for a minute.

Jonathan is such an amazing kid. As I sit here, a large freighter the only light on the bay at the moment, I miss him terribly. I just saw him, but I miss everything about him. I miss his childhood; and of course that of his brother, Michael. I grieve the fact that I do not see him every day, now—though he does spend some nights here at the apartment. And of course, looking ahead, he will be off to college in the fall. I am acutely feeling the passage of time. His birthday filled me up a couple of hours ago; but at the moment it is a void that I feel. My life is changing, as all of our lives change. I strive to hang onto the preciousness of the moments. He is a fantastic actor, Jonathan. He just completed a one-month run in a highly coveted role at the Magic Theatre in San Francisco. The play was called, "Bot," and Jonathan played a central role as Charlie, a brilliant, socially inept teenager who replicates himself on a computer. Bay Area newspapers reviewed him wonderfully, one calling him, "grounded and excellent," and another saying that he played his role "with nervous intelligence." Closing night, the playwright raved to me about Jonathan, thinking that his performance brought the character to life in just the way she had imagined it. He is also a filmmaker, and one of his films appeared in last year's youth festival of the San Francisco International Film Festival. His singing and songwriting—it just brings tears to my eyes. I'm a proud dad, I know, but his music sounds like a cross between Bob Dylan and Paul Simon. Perhaps I am getting carried away, but he is just a phenomenal kid, and not only for his talent. It is his soul and goodness. It was bittersweet watching him tonight. He is leaving for college soon, growing up, and we are not together as a family in the same way we once were—though the love for one another certainly hasn't diminished.

Prior to our separation, Sue and I had been having some really tough times, and it had been going on for months. Jonathan and Michael, aware of our struggles and pain, came to both of us with the advice that we separate. Everybody was in a state of limbo, and such decisive action would ultimately reveal a direction. Their consent, permission, was a gift—one that did not come easily to our boys. Our family is on a journey, and as I sit here in the waning hours of Jonathan's birthday, I pray for truth and guidance, a glimpse of the future. I try to listen, carefully listen, to the words of Alma Rush—I know that she has something to tell me.

We have been separated since early January of this year, 2007. The night before the movers were to come and bring my belongings, we went down to Harry's Bar on Fillmore Street for a Kobe burger and a drink. I had a glass of red wine and Sue, wine not often agreeing with her, had a Stella Artois. It was college football bowl season and the crowd was quite loud, games on the overhead screens competing in volume with the loudness of the crowd. Why were we in this situation? Why had we followed through on this idea? Why hadn't there been something to intervene? "I love you," I told Sue. "I love you very, very much and I will always love you," I continued. "Whatever happens, I will always be there for you; you can count on it," I continued. "I just love you so much and I love our family—I would lay down my life for this family." "I love you very much," she followed. "But I guess that we have to do this, otherwise you'll never know what you really want," she continued, and began to sob. "I know that you're right, I know," I followed, "but it just hurts like fucking hell, like fucking hell," tears pouring down my cheeks. Sue's turquoise eyes were quiet, still, reflective and filled with tears.

I shook my head a few times, not believing that we were at this place in our lives, and in this physical place in the restaurant looking at each other, knowing love, but being so unsure of anything that concerned our future together. "We might very well not come back together, Sue" I said, "and the thought of it just tears me up. It's almost as if there is some kind of force at work here, and we don't seem to have much control over it," I went on. "I know, Bruce," she added, "I just wonder what your mom would say about all of this." "I don't know what she would say, but I think that she might feel that what we are going through is inevitable, and that we just have to go through it and find out what lies on the other side. She never fought nature; she flowed with it until she could see where it was taking her. When she was able to get a grip on her life, she could change direction on a dime, and she had to do that several times. But she never fought the flow of things; she went along with it in the same way that water takes its own natural direction. She followed the Tao." Sue looked at me like maybe I was getting too "out there" for her. "All I know is that you're going to have to decide, and I can't see any other way." I nodded, the tears still uncontrollable. "I guess this will all make sense at some point, but it just hurts, it just hurts. I suppose my soul is aching, struggling for some kind of freedom," I went on. A slight tinge of anger appeared behind her tears. "If freedom is what you want, then that is what you'll have," she started. "You are just going to have to figure it out."

We went back to the house where I filled several boxes with important papers, not wanting the movers to see any of my private stuff. A couple of hours later, she drove me over to the apartment, where I dropped off the boxes in the empty apartment. It was a cold, clear winter night and the view out the apartment window was precise and sharp. The lights of the Golden Gate Bridge glistened clearly and intensely against the black sky and dark waters of the bay. I opened the window and a chill breeze pushed itself through the small opening. The breeze was different up here on top of the hill in this apartment; it was stronger than it was through the opening in our bedroom window at the house. Yes, indeed I would be free; indeed, I would feel some liberation, absolutely: I was listening to and feeding my soul. But at what price? "Time will tell," I whispered to myself. "Time will tell." I sat on top of one of the boxes for at least an hour and a half, maybe two. I left the window open slightly—the air blowing outward from my soul, merging with the cool wind blowing into the apartment. Memories of our family started flooding through me. The ski trips to Colorado or Utah or Canada, Jonathan jumping up and down imploring "I want to Ski, I want to Ski." I tease him about that to this day. Whenever we go skiing together, I mimic his jumping up and down from the days when he was four or five. To an outsider, it might have looked like a spoiled kid impatiently wanting to ski; but it wasn't that at all. It was just the beautiful innocence of this treasure of a boy not wanting to waste any time, just impatient to be up there and get on the snow like everybody else.

❒

My mind then moved to the time when Jonathan was, maybe, a couple of years old and his brother, Michael, perhaps four and a half. We went down to the restaurant (this was on the beach at Maui), Michael slowly following behind, taking it all in. When we got to the restaurant and ordered, Michael realized that he had gone out with just a long T-shirt, no underwear beneath. The look of embarrassment was just unforgettable. We looked at him and couldn't contain our laughter, which made him all the more shy. It was a family moment that none of us will ever forget. Or the time, before Jonathan was born, when Michael sat in a high chair at the very same restaurant where he forgot his underwear, devouring grapes. They offered him grapes, and he had never tasted them before. He loved them. And all he could ask for was "beeps"—his word for grapes. I tease him to this day about "beeps," whenever I see him eating them.

My mom, Michael called her "Tudy"—a name that stayed with her until her death—was there with us in Hawaii for the "beeps." She just couldn't get over the preciousness of it, and often remembered those moments with me when the boys started to get older. Hours before moving, and these thoughts are just pouring through me. I am alone in this apartment, preparing to move in. I want to talk to my mom so desperately at this moment; I want to have a deep conversation with her about my life. But I can only find her in my thoughts, but in my thoughts I hear her voice. "It really will all be okay," she says. "Everything is meant; it is very important that you understand that," she insists. I feel a warm breeze blowing from within and merging with the coolness coming from outside. I hear my mom's voice as I sit on these boxes, looking into the dark waters from this empty apartment. In several short hours, I will be moving in here. I try to be still as I realize that there is nothing else to do but surrender.

Breaking with "M"

The woman from New York—oh, she is more than that, I have to give her a name, I'll call her "M"—doesn't know that I have separated. It has been about four months since the move, but I cannot let her know. Breaking it off with her was so very difficult, and my feelings for her cannot be separated from the anguish between Sue and myself that I associate with them. So, I have decided not to let her know. I cannot say that I will never see her again, though that is a very strong possibility, perhaps likelihood. Jonathan will be going to Bard college, about an hour and a half out of New York City, and, no doubt, I will be going to the city often, but I truly believe that I will not see "M" on these visits.

The relationship continued from its inception in July 23rd, 2005, with daily and often many more than daily phone calls. Some days we would talk three or four times a day. Her voice was electrically charged for me, and as we spoke we became quite desperate to see one another. We spoke about many things. She had never overcome the loss of her beautiful, sister—"M" described her as an angel on earth and her best friend in the world—who had been healthy and then, suddenly, was overcome with an illness that took her life within a few weeks. Tears that she had buried over the loss of this sister poured through the telephone lines. It seemed that "M" had, perhaps, never experienced the kind of warm and compassionate response from a friend or lover that she desperately needed for this painful loss, and my words and understanding of her grief calmed her.

We talked about the loss of my mom, and she listened with tenderness as the tears poured out of me during some evening conversations from my office after a long day of trading bonds. But there was also a great deal of laughter. And I turned her on to some music—often putting the telephone up to the CD player—that she certainly knew, but had not heard much during her days of intense classical musical study. She knew of the Grateful Dead, but never realized how much of a "Dead Head" she could become until I played her "Sugar Magnolia," "Truckin'," "Uncle John's Band," "St. Stephen," "Friend of the Devil," "Broken Down Palace," and other masterpieces. She said that it was good she hadn't really listened to that music when she was studying, because she might have left altogether, perhaps on a motorcycle for California. She had heard some of Bob Dylan, but had never really listened. But at the end of one of those long days, when finding a few good bond trades seemed impossible but finally came through—clients pinching me much of the afternoon over penny debits and understanding the changes to their statements—we listened to "Highway 61." She was hooked from the opening chord of "Like a Rolling Stone," and as her musical intelligence took over, she really seemed to "get" that talking/singing style that Dylan hones to irreverent perfection. We listened to that whole album, right up to the final ironic phrases of "Desolation Row."

She had heard the Rolling Stones of course; but never the way that I had her listen to them. At the end of one of our conversations, I told her to "go out and buy the 'Sticky Fingers' album tomorrow; call me when you get home with it, but not before drinking a glass and a half of red wine. Then, when you call me, have 'Moonlight Mile' cued up and ready to go." She followed these instructions perfectly, and as she did she realized that she had never, ever heard a song quite like this. The seductive, sultry, orgasmic intensity of Richards' guitar, combined with Jagger's steamy moaning, the carefully placed "yeah," "ah," "oh," produced an "x-rated" moment, the wine only heightening the virtues of it all. From that instant, she just had to experience the Rolling Stones live. She realized how much she had been missing. Most of what we did over the telephone was play music for one another. There was so much music that we played together. She had never heard of Roxy Music, so when I played her "More Than This" and "Avalon" she was transported to another musical dimension. She had a very high degree of musical sensitivity, so when she listened to the sophisticated rhythms and romanticism of Bryan Ferry's sound, she went to a sublime place. And I was experiencing all of this again through her. It was profound. Our conversations took on an addictive aspect. And how not to when she would call me from within the Steinway practice room, playing her favorite Chopin ballads.

There developed a sort of chemical dependency to our phone calls, and it was that way for both of us. She would often call me during the day, saying she just had to get in her 50 milligrams. I would begin to feel a kind of withdrawal, a depletion of energy, when the end of the day came and we hadn't spoken. I had never had a dependency on anything, person, food, place, drug, but this had certainly become one. As it continued over several months, it started to feel toxic to me. I couldn't escape from the dependency, and I started to become scared. I couldn't continue this double life of being this partner to "M," and still husband to Sue. "M" wanted to see me and I, her. This tension to see one another had put a strain on the conversations. How could we sustain this friendship without contact? It just had to be that way, I reasoned, because I was not prepared to surrender my marriage.

Sue had long since known about the conversations, and we were in therapy over the situation. She had discovered the phone calls on my cell phone, and when confronted, I was honest about the friendship. I just could not be 100 percent up front about the intensity of the passion; I am not sure that I really understood its power. Perhaps I thought that it was a friendship, and that it could remain one. But over the months it became clear that this was an addiction and that for the wellbeing of all concerned, I had to break it off. So, last spring, about a year ago, I decided in one of our last therapy sessions that I would cut this off—giving our marriage a chance. It was excruciatingly painful to do this, because it felt like I was killing something living. I wrote "M" the following letter:

My dear "M,"

The soul resides in the heart, and the heart speaks a language that reason and intellect can only begin to comprehend. A little more than six months ago, the intoxicating power of Hurricane "M" turned my sense of reason upside down, quickened my heart rate, twirled me around like a top, clockwise then counterclockwise, the calm eye eventually coming to rest in the center of my soul. The strength of our feelings for each other, the desire to spend precious moments together, has produced sadness, anguish, loneliness, and hope and fear of the unknown. I fell in love with you.

It is, though, the unknown that we face. My feelings for you are sometimes so powerful that I just want to run away from everything to be with you, to walk in the park with you on a snowy day. It often hurts terribly to visualize my life without you. However the gravity of the situation takes over, and (as we have discussed) I realize that there is a family to feel the consequences of anything that I do. Thus, I caution myself, attempt to gain perspective, try to figure out whether these feelings that I have for you can continue to be acted on—whether I might have a future with you or if that future will produce too much heartache for those about whom I also care deeply. In the end I have to be true to my heart and soul, and it is this message that I so struggle to understand. There is within me a constant conflict: I do not want you to go away, and yet I am not sure that I can have you. I do not want to make a rash decision that will result in more harm and pain for all concerned. I do not want to act when I feel weakened by so much strife. I need to gain clarity with regard to the direction my life must go. I hope and pray that this clarity will come to me in the not distant future, and if it does, I will act with a sense of conviction that it must be that way. I have deep love and compassion for the people close to me in my life. I so desperately do not want to hurt those for whom I care so much. So much of the time, I just do not know what to do, confusion and strife so much a part of my insides.

"M," we've talked about talking much less so that I can gain clarity; perhaps arrive at the perspective that will provide answers. This, however, has been so painfully difficult to do, tears inescapable. It is, though, probably the answer in the short term. My humanity, values, sense of who I am require that I seriously look at my marriage so that I can understand its meaning for Susan and myself, comprehend what it means to me now and in the future. I cannot walk away from it without gaining this understanding. This, no doubt, will take some time. And in the time that it takes, I risk not having you—I risk losing you. It deeply saddens me to realize this, and yet I cannot do otherwise at this moment. I truly believe that if we are meant to be, we will come together again. This is *where I let God take over. I know in my depths that God has a plan for each of us, and when we reach our limitations as human beings, God does take over.*

My dear "M," I love you very much, Bruce

Shortly after cutting off this relationship, I wrote a prose poem that I read in a therapy session. I had talked about it the session before, and Sue wanted to hear it:

I ride horseback through the dusty, barren streets of my mind. I hear the silent echoes of music that once played, empty reverberations of a distant laughter, vacant glimpses of flirtatious, amorous glances. Just an empty quiet now as I sit atop this tired black horse, fatigued from the long uphill ride, the unsteady path falling downhill into the rough river that we had to navigate to pass. He is nervous, now, my black horse. Nervous and very tired. And I am fatigued and agitated as I sit astride, having thrown away miles back the saddle, this beaten-down, ripped-apart leather. No, there is no music anymore on the streets of this ghost town where sand fills the air. The wind picks up and dirt blows into my eyes, the black horse shaking his head to one side to avoid the stinging pellets to his eyes. Yes, these streets are filled with dust, but not a soul to be discovered as I nonchalantly dismiss the bullet-riddled walls of the saloon and jailhouse. The courthouse where marriages were once performed is a cemetery to warm embraces, passions, vows no longer remembered, except, maybe, to God, if he exists, and within my mind, if these visions are to be trusted. I am tall enough on this bareback to stare into the saloon, glasses still on the bar, scattered about, perhaps festively. A trace of lipstick near the top of a shot—glass, another on a wine glass, no doubt a kiss or two no longer remembered.

I am nervous atop this horse, very tired too. My hand rests on the holster pocket, and I am ready to shoot if I must. But what is there to fear, just the ghosts of unfulfilled passions, promised futures, unrequited longings, evicted memories. But it is all right, these phantoms have no power over me anymore; they were once filled with the blood of dreams, but they are now as empty and barren as these deserted streets within the ghost town of my mind. But I won't stop here, because hope brings another day and another day brings hope. I'll shoulder it, feed this tired black horse, nourish him with water, find a resting stop in the verdant green hills above this empty place. Yes, hope brings another day and another day brings hope.

Sue sobbed when I read this during the session. She, too, felt tired after riding through dusty lifeless streets where sweet songs had once been sung. She desperately needed nourishment and hoped to find it somewhere, hopefully in the green pasture perceptible above the town. We both needed to find some place of tranquility, and it seemed that neither of us could provide that for the other. It is painful when, after so many years, two people cannot seem to be the medicine, the tonic for the other. Actually, it is a quite desperate, helpless feeling—there is a person, a husband, a wife, that we want to help, for whom we strive to make it all better, and we just can't do it. But, indeed, we can always look forward to tomorrow—hope does bring another day, and another day does bring hope.

The relationship that I was having with "M" came to Sue in a dream. She approached me one morning in early October as I was getting out of the shower—it had been about two-and-a-half months since meeting "M"—by telling me that we should sit down and talk, that she had had a very profound dream about me during the night. The thought that crossed my mind as she mentioned the dream was that, "Yes, indeed, I expected this—I knew that she would have a dream about this relationship. She is very intuitive and, of course, it would come to her in this way." My mother had appeared to her in a dream, but it wasn't so much a deep dream, as it was a vision, or a visitation. Apparently it occurred somewhere between consciousness and unconsciousness—a place where the details were quite clear. My mom had told her that I had met a person with whom I felt very close, and that it was more of a spiritual relationship than a physical affair. This woman, she told Sue in the dream, had connected with me in a very deep way, and that it was going to be very difficult for me to break it off with her—but break it off I would eventually do. The situation would last for a while, but it would eventually end. I was basically stunned, as Sue told me the details of the dream. Truly, as mentioned, I expected some kind of awakening for her in a dream, but not anything like this.

I took a deep breath, realized that my mom had done us both a great service by doing this, because, really, how long could this level of emotion continue without my having to share it with Sue? I knew that I simply would not be able to experience these feelings of attraction without getting it out in the open. I know myself, and

I knew on meeting "M" that if these feelings did not go away, I would have to bring it all to the surface. I cannot live a dual life.

We are separated because, even though there is no "M" in my life, I am trying to discover what it is I really feel, what my soul is truly saying. It isn't saying that it strives for carnal knowledge; while physical pleasures are nice, they are empty without intimacy. It is an expansion that my soul seems to require, and it is something over which I do not have much control. I am not sure what the expansion entails, except to say that as painful as it sometimes is to be alone, no longer living in the house we had lived in together for so many years—feeling separated from many of the familiar comforts that I have known—my body and consciousness feel as though they are stretching. Perhaps I had to take leave to enter into deeper relationships with those that I love, God and myself.

The dream had stunned me, and when I regained some composure, I struggled to explain the relationship. I couldn't continue, though, without having to take a breather more than once to ask, "Is that really how it came to you, my mom brought it to your attention in a dream?" And each time I asked it, Sue swore to God that this is how it came to her.

It was amazing to me then, absolutely astounding, and every bit as much at the moment, as I sit here a couple days after the Golden State Warriors defeated the Dallas Mavericks in what is being described as the greatest upset in the history of the NBA, but the San Jose Sharks (my hockey team) have gone down three games to two in a series that was theirs for the taking. I shake my head, though, as I realize that those about whom we care so deeply and lose to the "other side," have it within their means to come back to us with their love and messages. And as clear and prescient as Alma Lorraine Rush was in life, she is no less in the afterlife.

The revelation that night changed our lives. Sue entered a phase where she was on a mission, intent on finding out all that she could about this person in New York. She looked her up on the internet, obtaining reviews of her piano concerts when she was younger. And, indeed, she discovered that I had been speaking to her more than quite a bit, basically every day. She had discovered in my diaries things I had written about my feelings for "M," and wanted me to explain them to her. I was honest and did my best. But none of this was easy, and the tension continued to build. It built because I did not deny that I was speaking to her, and couldn't promise that I would stop. We entered therapy over the relationship; and by the time we discontinued it about six months later, in the spring of 2006, I had decided to do my best to sever this tie. A few months later, when Michael arrived home from college at Oberlin, we took a family vacation in Maui. My mom had always told me that if you need to cut a relationship that seems difficult to break, take a piece of string or thread and cut it in half, while saying goodbye and wishing the person well. On a beautiful blue-sky day, sounds of kids laughing in the background, the laughter of my own boys playing football behind me on the beach, I brought scissors and a string to the waters edge and said goodbye to "M." I swam in that purifying ocean until my arms had virtually nothing left; the warm salty water had cleansed my spirit, but freeing the mind would be a bit more difficult.

Even though I had cut the cord with "M" in my mind, I was not able to tell her, definitively, that there was no chance for us; that our friendship had to be over. I think that I had felt that by not watering the relationship, by essentially communicating less and less, the same would be true on her end and, over time, the situation would become more a memory, less a fantasy. But, of course, that had not been communicated to "M." Again closure, even though I had cut the string and let the breeze blow it into the Maui ocean, has always been very difficult for me, and, in truth, there had not been many relationships in my life where I had to take the initiative to say goodbye. I never went out with a lot of women growing up, and when a relationship did come to an end, it was mutual, seemingly inevitable, and part of a path that brought mutual growth to both. This, though, was different; it was different because a volcano had erupted deep from within and it had enveloped my psyche. It seemed to affect every aspect of my being. The feelings could not be contained, but they had to be cut off—and it felt my duty to say farewell.

"M" continued to call me and periodically send e-mails. And during these communications I did my best to let her know that we really must stop talking, that really we were involved in something that would never be brought to a kind of consummation or fruition that we had seemed desperate to have. The more we discussed this, the more we both believed that perhaps we had succumb to a fantasy, an illusory world where time either stopped or moved so quickly that it existed in another dimension. The dimension in which it had existed was pure joy, but now it had been giving way to sorrow. During our waning conversations, tears would fill both of our eyes. I would try to console "M"; I tried to get her to see that our relationship opened both of us up, and now she would be ready to finally find true love in her life, a kind of love that would be available to her. I was convinced, and tried to get her to see that her presence had been a tonic for me; that there was an innocence to the whole thing that allowed me to relive feelings bottled up since being a kid, and many other feelings certainly shut down since my mom's death. We philosophized and rationalized, but in the end it hurt like hell. Even though we were speaking less and less, the voice messages and e-mails were intoxicating. And when I returned any of them, there was that voice—that voice that just seemed to paralyze me. I have no claim to be anything like Superman, but I have an understanding of what "kryptonite" did to him—in its presence, he momentarily lost his power. "M's" voice was like kryptonite to me—and when I heard it, I felt a loss of control, almost a paralysis, over which I struggled to gain control. It didn't help when she would notify me of some of the fun things that were happening at Steinway. Billy Joel had been trying out a piano in the Rotunda, essentially putting on a private concert for those lucky enough to be sitting nearby. God, how I wanted to be there next to her listening to that. I cut the conversation short, and returned to what I had been doing, getting bids on a list of bonds for a client. On another occasion, Judy Collins was in the room, elegant and graceful with her sterling gray hair and clear, pure blue eyes. The music of Judy Collins, my God, how stirring it is. She would call me from the balcony, overlooking central park, of this actor or that actress, all of them famous. I am not incredibly impressed by famous people, but the whole thing sounded like so much fun—and it was a kind of fun I had said no to and realized that I would never have with "M."

Our conversations became less and less frequent over time, until eventually there were almost none at all. Yet even now, there is the occasional e-mail or note dropped from "M." And I respond with an acknowledgement when they come. But as I sit here tonight, May 11, 2007—my San Jose Sharks hockey team eliminated from the playoffs by the Detroit Red Wings as I feared they might be (Jonathan and I were at the game when we were within 30 or so seconds from going up three games to one, only to see the game tied and lost in overtime)—I strive to gain perspective on that relationship that was Hurricane "M." I am alone now; lord knows my life has changed.

May 10th, 2007

Barry Bonds hit his 745th home run the other night; I was at the game, sitting in the first row behind home plate. I invited Sue to the game with me that night—though she left a little early because it started to get chilly for her. She was there for the home run, however. Barry hit it to the deepest part of the ballpark, straight away center field. He is among the league leaders in home runs at the moment, and he cannot be doing it with steroids now. The whole country is watching. He needs only 10 home runs to catch Henry Aaron, and I will definitely applaud when it happens. It bothers me that he has been demonized—the nation is rightly troubled by the steroids problems in sports, and Bonds has become the poster boy to take the blame. This is happening because Barry is threatening a hallowed record, he seems arrogant and dishonest in his denials about steroids. He most likely took the supplements, but so did so many other players. This doesn't make it right, but it also doesn't make him Darth Vader, an evil force contaminating all of baseball, indeed all of sports in America. Baseball, no doubt, knew this stuff was going on and chose to ignore it until it became a serious problem. Certainly the teams knew that something unnatural was happening when so many players were becoming like Hercules practically overnight. It is a horrible problem, and as some players did it, pressure was placed on others to keep up. So it became insidious. But Barry is hardly to blame for the steroid evils in America. Give the man his due, applaud the accomplishment when he does break the record, and let's make sure that steroids are removed from sports at all levels. But if Bonds' statistics are tainted (and certainly most of his home runs were hit before the steroids era), then how many other statistical accomplishments in the game over the past several years should be questioned? We cannot say for certain that many of our favorite players over the past few years—people that put up exceptional numbers or had incredible longevity—didn't take steroids. Give the guy his home run record when it happens, applaud the unbelievable accomplishment that it is, and let's move on.

It was nice going to the baseball game with Sue the other night; and when she left early and I went home alone there was an empty feeling that ran through me. And yet, when I ask myself if I can rejoin her in a life together at the moment, I just cannot say that I can. I do not feel good much of the time, there is a daily anxiety that does not seem to go away. It is there through much of every day and into every night. Yet there is a freedom that I have that is difficult to give up right now. It is not so much a freedom to go out with a bunch of women, though I go out from time to time, but one that allows me to fill a room with my own space. It is my internal space that fills this room; there is a kind of letting out of myself that I need to go through at this point in time. But very often that space that has expanded to fill a room feels empty—and what I have is an expanded consciousness of emptiness.

Tonight was particularly bittersweet. It is the night of Jonathan's senior prom, and as I sit here at the moment reflecting on the years that we have raised him, and that he will be off to college in a few short months, he is no doubt laughing and enjoying himself immensely with his sweet, beautiful girlfriend Ana. But it is that expanded consciousness of emptiness that I feel right now, and it really hurts. Sue, Jonathan and I went to his friend's house in Marin County to take pre-prom pictures, along with all the other parents. Other parents were together—Sue and I were together but apart. There was a joy on the kids' faces, and even though they are seniors, sitting at the zenith of the high school experience, there is a naiveté as they begin their journey into the unknown. The pictures that we took together tonight will be markers, reference points as Jonathan looks back 10, 15, 20 years from now. The memories from that senior prom can last forever, and it is certainly my deepest prayer that as Jonathan looks on these pictures frozen in time, it will be from a vantage point where they represent happy moments of youth en route to a very fulfilled life. The truth, though, is that time is passing quickly, and I never would have thought as I was raising my boys that moments as magical as these would occur with this kind of sadness. When we parted Sue went off to a friend's birthday party, and I came home to write. Putting down these thoughts brings comfort. There were people that wanted to go out with me tonight, but I just couldn't. I want to be here by the phone and speak to Jonathan as he is on his way to the party after the prom. I want to hear his voice tonight. I sometimes ask myself about fate and the direction my life must go. I realize that it is not until we push ourselves up against the unknown and feel the consequences do we get a sense of that of which we are capable. Time will tell the direction one will go; and much will be determined by whether we can find calm within the anxiety, even joy.

When we push ourselves into the unknown—and sometimes we do this because we realize that something in ourselves is changing, and externally there has to be a change—we discover what we are and are not capable of doing. We may desire to live a certain kind of life, but realize that we are not capable of doing it—sometimes there is just too much internal resistance. We may endeavor to overcome that resistance and perhaps we will be successful and move into a more fulfilling life. Or perhaps that resistance is the language of the soul informing us of what is possible and what is not. We push ourselves up against the unknown when we must, and in so doing we enter that junction—we encounter it first hand—where free will and determinism meet. It becomes clear that nothing is free of limitations, including free will—there are obstacles to its free exercise, and one might call this determinism or fate. The obstacles can be perceived to be internal or external, but it really doesn't matter—when free will meets its limitations the internal and external worlds are one and the same. We desire something, we want to change our lives, we seek fulfillment and the realization of our potential, there is success and then something slows us down. Sometimes our minds are slowing us down for a reason, call it determinism if you like. Perhaps our minds slow us down because of an external change, maybe a relationship that looked promising is now changing—the mind perceives this and reacts. Internal and external, they are one and the same when freedom meets its limitations.

My dear mom, Alma Lorraine Rush, would always tell me to look for the signs, follow the signs. I strive to do this; I just wish that I could sit down next to her, have her look into my teacup and reveal the signs to me. However, I am on my own—she isn't there to do that for me. No, I am wrong in this. She is there to do that for me—she just wants me to do the hard work first. She'll help me to see clearly when the options have narrowed. I slow down and listen as my soul speaks—at the moment it is speaking to and hearing from Alma.

❒

During that period in the late spring of '06, exactly one year ago, when I was struggling to let go of "M," I received significant information from my dreams. In one dream, I was playing baseball with my two brothers, Jeff and Elliot, and some old friends from high school. One of the friends was Phil, or Rusty as we called him—an Arkansas boy and the most loyal friend one could ever have—and I was catching some of his wicked fastballs. The field was in the high desert of southern California, where I attended high school. It was a bit breezy and there was some sand blowing. Back behind the first base line and set near a chain link fence were some benches, and that is where "M" sat watching. I motioned for her to come closer, but she didn't want to—she didn't feel like she fit in with this group. I realized, also, that she didn't fit in with this group, as much as I really wanted her to. I interpreted this dream to mean that there were differences between "M" and I that could not be bridged—that as much as I wanted to think that she could be with me, I had to acknowledge that she could not.

Shortly thereafter there was another dream. "M," who is a practicing Catholic, asked me to attend a mass with her. This dream occurred in rich detail and vivid color. I attended the mass, sitting next to "M." The worshipers stood to repeat prayers, and as we stood, I observed the vivid religious scenes portrayed on purple, blue, red, yellow and orange baroque-style stained glass windows. "M" and the worshipers were repeating the prayers being chanted by the priest in Latin, while I stood quietly, my back rigid. The mass was in Latin, the cathedral looked Gothic, with arches and spires, and the service seemed very heavy, an organ music that seemed to inculcate a sense of guilt and the notion that Jesus Christ is the only salvation for mankind. I experienced the truth of this worship for "M" and the other "true believers," and in the dream

I apprehended the stark beauty of the religion. But try as I might, I just couldn't force myself to see the world this way. I looked around during the service, observing the severity on everyone's face, including "M," and realized that this just isn't for me. "I'm Jewish," I said to myself. "This is just too stifling for me. My mind needs to be free. This God is real, but it is not how I perceive him. I have to be free to see God in my own way." These were the thoughts that occurred to me in the dream. And I again interpreted them to mean that "M" and I are just too different—that I had to let go. I realized that I needed to be free of this relationship.

A week or two later the third dream took place in a dentist's office. There was a tooth that needed to be pulled. I really resisted having the tooth pulled, asking the dentist if there could be some other remedy. Not only was there no other remedy, the tooth had to be pulled without any painkiller, and with a string attached to it. The dentist had tied a long string to the tooth, and from the other end of the office proceeded to pull it. He told me that this was going to be painful, but assured me that I would be able to tolerate the pain. The tooth was pulled and it did hurt a lot. Yet, I was surprised that it did not hurt more than it did. I expected it to be so painful that I might be rendered unconscious. That did not happen. The significance of the dream was obvious to me. I so much didn't want to lose that tooth, but it had to go. I delayed so long that it had become infected, and had to be pulled out the hard way. I had no choice in the matter; it had to go. As much as I was attracted to "M," and desperately wanted her, I had to let her go. Perhaps setting her free would enable her to find a man who was truly available.

The fourth dream occurred about a week after the third. In the dream, I had been put in the hospital because a kidney had to be removed. I was nervous, but the nurse—dressed in pure white medical clothes—assured me that the surgery would not be serious and that I would recover well. "There will be pain and discomfort for a few days, but I am sure that you will come through it very well," she assured me. I underwent the surgery, and when I awoke—it had seemed that no more than a second had elapsed, but it was now the next morning—the same nurse was right there to tell me that it had gone well. She asked me if I wanted more medicine for the pain, but I refused, telling her that I felt that I could handle the pain without any extra painkillers. I interpreted this dream in much the same way that I felt about the dentists office—there was an organ within me that needed to be removed, it just had to happen, and it was something over which I did not have any control.

The adrenalin of the relationship with "M" had poured through my veins for many months, but the dualism with which I was living was tearing me up. The desire to be truly present in my marriage, to be the person that I had always been, to be emotionally centered and grounded in the "I" and "Thou" of our relationship never ceased, but it encountered, indeed clashed with, this instinct to hang on to the connectedness with "M." The anxiety I lived with was intense, acute, and I was always on edge. My bond trading did not suffer at all, probably because the daily activities represented a release of anxiety into which I could perform and feel myself. The problem, though, is that the day could never become night for me. Sue, never demanding in our marriage, wanted much more of me now; she clearly felt insecure in our relationship and took it personally that I could not easily find my way back to her. She seemed to always be looking for emotional clues, facial expressions, a body language of love, and when these did not meet her satisfaction or expectations, she would fall into a kind of emotional despair. It took its toll in a gradual, but steady loss of weight. I started to become quite scared as her weight loss went to an unacceptable level. I had been letting go of "M," I knew that I had to, and the dreams clarified this for me, but it was excruciatingly difficult to stop communicating "cold turkey." The abrupt halt to an "organic" relationship with "M" produced some desperate moments for the two of us. The emotional connection of the relationship had a gravitational pull, and it felt like I needed a blood transfusion to remove the drug from my system. I thought about how desperately horrible it would be to try and kick an addiction to a drug—how a user innocently falls into something and in the end needs the help of angels to save their life. My life was not at risk, but my inner life felt tortured as I struggled, but I could not be the medicine for Sue or "M." We were all hurting, and I just could not find the boundaries to separate myself from it all.

I have always believed in God. From earliest memory, not prodded by anyone, I have gone to my knees at night and said prayers to the God that I envision in my mind. I am Jewish, and I feel the soul of Judaism in the very core of me. My perception of God is of a kind of limitlessness. To conceive of him would be like trying to place boundaries on an expanding universe; it is a loving, transcendent force that is bounded by nothing but itself externally, but is as infinitely deep within as it is without. God is where the depths of our soul meet the eternity of space and time—in him, internal and external merge. And if there is a form to God, the form can be represented by intermittent broken lines, between which are spaces that let the light of eternity into the universe and into our souls. Thus, it would not be my vision of God to perceive of him in the form of a person. But, indeed, I must admit that something very unusual happened to me one night when I prayed amidst all of the anguish.

I prayed for answers, I prayed for serenity, I prayed to hear my mom's voice. I started to become quite quiet, and it was a kind of quiet that I hadn't expected, and as I became quiet, there was a joy, a compassion, a love that I experienced. Love was all around, it surrounded me; I started to feel very light. Then came the image of Jesus Christ. I saw, felt, embraced, and was embraced by Jesus Christ. I did not become a Christian after this; my conception of God had not been altered. But I did know at that moment the spirit that had fostered the great religion of Christianity. I experienced the spirit of Christ, the beauty, the limitless love and compassion that is the soul of Christianity. I have always respected the truth of religious experience, and have never been skeptical of the testimonies of those whose lives have been transformed by profound religious experience. Violence does not belong in this conversation; that is the product of manipulation. I experienced a compassion and grace when I prayed that night, but within the experience there was a message. The message was that I should tell "M" of the experience; to remind her that, as a Catholic, this experience of Christ was available to her, and that all she needed to do was to surrender to her beliefs. "Tell her that there is help for her, and it is in the person of Jesus Christ," came the message. In one of our last phone calls, I delivered this message to "M."

❒

The inner turmoil stayed with me for weeks, and I began looking for some way to alleviate the tension. I have a Chinese friend who teaches and practices acupuncture and dispenses herbs; he gave me a very mild herb that calmed the spirit somewhat. I started looking into yoga, tai chi, forms of meditation. Taking my walks on Saturday or Sunday, or even in the middle of the afternoon during the week in the financial district, I would keep my eye open for some kind of holistic practice that might offer a kind of reprieve or retreat from this adrenalin or toxicity that seemed to be keeping me unbalanced, uneven, uncomfortable. On a June afternoon at about 4:00, I went for a walk, thinking that I would come back to the office in about half hour to finish the day's phone calls. Walking up Sansome Street, on my way to Telegraph Hill, I stopped just before the London Wine Bar to read a brochure describing the services of the Moksha Life Center.

"Moksha," now there is a name that I appreciated. I had studied eastern religions in college and recognized moksha to mean release or liberation. The pamphlet described a kind of chiropractic known as "Network," a noninvasive technique of light touching and gentle movements whose long-term benefits would be to open up the body in such a way that we can remember who we really are. It spoke of releasing the tensions that are the effects of suppressed memories that are stored within our bones and on a cellular level. It described how Dr. Gwendolyn Jones, the practitioner of the method, brought to this practice a knowledge of biology (she had studied cellular biology in Boston) and shamanism, based on experiences in the Brazilian Amazon with tribal leaders. It sounded interesting to me, but I decided to take a pass on it, continuing to walk up Sansome Street toward Telegraph Hill.

On my way back, I stopped to look at the brochure again. There was something very intriguing for me about the practice, so I decided to ring the bell. I really didn't expect anyone to answer the call, but a buzzer rang, so I proceeded up the stairs. The space was apparently being used by a theater troupe, rehearsing for an upcoming play. I asked a guy at the front desk if he knew anything about this "Network Chiropractic" being advertised down on the street. He said that he did not, that he was renting the space to rehearse, but that if I waited around, he would find the woman for me. The troupe disappeared into another room, and after a few minutes I made my way to the door to leave. But just as I was leaving, the same gentleman came back, advising me not to leave, that he was sure that he could locate the woman soon. I decided to stick around a few more minutes. A minute or two later, he returned with a very pretty woman, large blue eyes with an Asian aspect. The turquoise eyes were set against long dark hair and an infectious smile. She asked me what brought me in, "What is up with you?" I started to tell her about what I was going through, particularly the anxiety. She was such a good listener that I just kept going. She listened to me for more than an hour; there was, no doubt, an urgency and tension to my voice as I struggled to get the energy out of my system. After listening to me, she described how she believed that the work in which she was involved would be highly useful to me. What she was doing, she said, was work that allows people, over time, to connect with their spirit. She talked about a physical and emotional component to stored memories, and that the innovative approach of this methodology allowed one to release the physical and emotional blockages that impede us from reaching our potential. I decided to try this therapy on an introductory level, and continue to do it today; and, perhaps, there is a kind of inner calm that I have gained during this past year.

My life is clearly unsettled at the moment, and as I write this, the bay is very dark and the wind is blowing. I cannot remember a spring in which the wind has blown so constantly. I hurt deeply over the fact that the future of my marriage is unknown, and I just cannot find the answers or predict the outcome. It is an unsettled time for me, but I go forward, perhaps with more inner peace.

❐

Michael came home for the summer from Oberlin a few days ago, and, my God, was it nice to give him a huge hug. Well he isn't actually home for the summer; he'll be going to Paris for the month of July to study electronic music. He played a couple of pieces of electronic/ technological music that he wrote. I was struck, listening to it, that the whole concept of music must be changing, evolving to include sounds that appear as something other than notes, but are apparently connected conceptually to be classified as musical. Oberlin is, from what I am hearing, at the cutting edge of this new musical paradigm, and if this is true, Michael must be creating music that is very cutting edge, being so talented and creative. The music had the sound of a sort of "intergalactic noise," but there was an intelligence and direction to it. I felt that it was taking me somewhere, but I never arrived. Perhaps as he becomes more advanced the music will take me to new worlds, or maybe I will hear—as he channels it—the language of other civilizations sending us their messages. He has been performing this music in a group at school, and it is performed not on a piano, but on a laptop computer. "So you are playing a laptop computer in a musical group—this is where all that hard-earned money that I saved is going?" I joked. "Michael, you are an incredible pianist, don't forget that instrument, Okay?"

He went on to tell me how amazing it is to be playing music that is breaking new ground, and to be part of a group—performing his own compositions—where he sits as a musical engineer on a keyboard, weaving a sort of magic that blends with the other instruments. In any event, it was phenomenal to look into his serious, deep blue eyes, hugging him for dear life. It was a difficult year for him, processing the separation of his parents, while working intensely to create music and satisfy the Conservatory's demanding expectations. He'll be going to Paris, and I have decided to meet him in London first, then go over to Paris with him. I desperately need a break. I have been working at a break-neck pace trying to keep everything moving forward in business, satisfying the customers, studying the bond market and economy to be the best that I can be. But the anxiety has continued to build. My stomach churns every morning, my neck, shoulders, back tightening as the day wears on. It seems that the anxiousness has seemingly gone to another level. I suppose we are getting closer, as time moves on, to making some decision about our lives, our marriage, though Sue and I do not get together to talk about it very much. There is, though, no doubt that a dialogue is occurring below the surface between us—and it happens even when we are not talking or seeing each other. We seem to be moving closer, perhaps to a divorce—there is almost an inexorable aspect to it, and I can't seem to be able to get my arms around this conceptually, spiritually or in any other way. I do love her—there is no doubt about that. We were given the gift of one another—and the beauty of these boys brings selflessness, compassion, love and gratitude. Yet, our process continues.

I have been dating, and there is no reason to think that Sue isn't doing the same. Have we reached that point at which we will not come back together? Are the pangs of anxiety and uncertainty a kind of language of the soul, telling me something, if only I could decipher it? When Sue and I are together, I feel the gravity of our relationship, the pull of our memories, our creations, the boys, the dog, the house in which she lives and that we struggled to buy together. The gravity tugs at me, but I resist—I struggle to get beyond its reach, struggling hard against the tide. And I do this at my own expense. It hurts like hell to let go, but there is something in me that wants to float above the ground, survey the terrain, resist the temptation of certainty, just experience a feeling of freedom that I have never known. But will I ever really be free? This tension often feels like a prison. And I do, very much, want connection. I crave intimacy—and the more I am alone, the deeper the recognition of that fact. And so, therein, lies the paradox: I am alone because I have sought the freedom, but experiencing the freedom intensifies the desire for intimacy. And yet, our divorce is becoming an increasing possibility.

There have been books written about Sacred Contracts—and I am not sure that I subscribe to the idea. The notion is that we determine before birth who we will marry, the kind of life we will live, the work we will do, the children we will have. And in this context, perhaps our marriage is concluding because our contract with one another has reached fulfillment. There is a nice sort of cognitive dissonance to this type of thinking—it explains a lot for which we do not have answers. But is it cognitive dissonance, or is there something spiritually true about it? I have always been a concrete, rational person, and there is a large part of me that wants to relegate this idea to the world of "mumbo jumbo." But in this, as in many things, we really can't be sure. Maybe there is something at work here along those lines. I guess it really doesn't matter—what will be will be. And I do know one thing for sure: I am doing the very best that I can.

Indeed, it will be very nice to get away and go to Paris with Michael. But it isn't only Michael that I will spending time with when I go—Jonathan graduates from high school next Saturday, and a few days after that, he'll be off to Europe with some friends for six weeks. I have always been so protective of him—it is going to be quite difficult for me to not know where he is every day. He is a big boy, though, and I traveled to Europe when I was 18—though I went on a tour. There is nothing else that I can do but surrender to his freedom and let him grow up. This, of course, I'll do. But in the process of doing it, I'll catch up with him after I leave Michael.

A couple of nights ago, Michael and I went to a baseball game together—we sat in the first row behind home plate. The Giants were playing the Houston Astros, and had just brought up this kid named Tim Lincecum, a phenomenon in the minor leagues. The kid didn't disappoint, throwing 97 MPH fastballs, with a hard curve ball that just fell off the table. The kid pitched a gem, and I'm pretty sure we're going to be hearing his name quite a lot in the future. However, Barry Bonds did not hit a home run, still sitting at 745 home runs, 10 shy of tying Hank Aaron. It has been two and a half weeks since he hit one, after getting off to such a torrid start. There were moments of pure joy being at the game with Michael—that tension clearing and lifting for whole sections of time. There are those who can't enter into the world of baseball, finding it too boring and slow. I have loved the sport from early childhood, a true-blue Dodger fan at a young age, listening to the resonating, echoing, golden voice of Vin Scully and following every game that I could of Sandy Koufax. Baseball is slow in the same sense that a conversation is slow—when we enter a conversation with a friend, we really don't count the words. The conversation may be slow and thoughtful, but with a good friend we lose ourselves in the moment, hours often seeming like just minutes. Such is the case when one enters into the dialogue with baseball—that inner conversation with the game that transports one into a kind of timelessness. I had that sort of experience with Michael the other night—baseball has always brought me back to myself, and it did so again the other night. My father found it difficult to take me to many baseball games when I was kid, so I made sure that I was often included when my friends went. I have been just the opposite with my boys—I'm taking them to games even when they may want to do something else. I have always felt there is no better way for a father to spend time with a son. Just magic.

≈

May 29th, 2007

Jonathan is just a few days away from graduating high school—the ceremony will be this Saturday. This launching of Jonathan into the world feels bittersweet. He will be off to New York soon to begin his college and adult life, and his days at home are limited. I think back to when he was about eight or nine and was showing great promise as an actor. I enrolled him in a program called "Kids on Camera," where he learned to recite monologues as he was being filmed. It was here that I first realized his uncanny ability to memorize massive amounts of words. And the camera just loved him. He would dance, sing, perform, never at a loss for his words as his eyes twinkled in front of the camera. He loved these theatrical moments every Saturday, but by the time the next Saturday came around, I had to insist that he go back. This became the modus operandi for Jonathan—in these early childhood years, I had to push him to attend performance classes, and when he would go he didn't want to leave. Jonathan was one of a few kids in his "Kids on Camera" class who was given an offer to be represented by an agent. So he signed, and we had fun with that for a while. He would go to photographic shoots for clothing or toys, or would be asked to audition for a movie or two. He came pretty close, one of a couple of finalists, to landing a major role opposite Robin Williams; there's a very sweet picture of him, soft brown eyes, wavy hair blowing in the wind decorating the package of a successful toy. A couple of years ago, that toy was still being sold—I stumbled on the toy in a Toys R Us store, and it was quite amusing and nostalgic to see it, his eyes cast downward as he held some kind of a sweeper toy that he moved along the ground looking for hidden treasures in the grass. He eventually started to act quite seriously, and was picked for some roles in American Conservatory Theater's mainstage productions. He did "A Christmas Carol" a couple of times, but it was his role as "the boy" in a Beckett's "Waiting for Godot" that brought about a heightened maturity and stage presence. He had been working with some of ACT's best actors, and they became mentors for him. This release of his energies on the stage was a nice diversion for him and our family. My mom had passed away maybe a year before, and it served us all quite well to so see Jonathan performing his role on that stage in front of packed audiences. He loved my mom deeply, and it was a wonderful release for him. It was a joy to see it amidst the sadness. He has continued to act right up to the present, just finishing a role in which he played a boy who replicates himself on a computer in a Magic Theatre Production. Various reviews called him "riveting," and this recent appearance added a bit of distraction to these difficult times of separation. And it is, thus, during these difficult times of separation that we prepare to launch him into the world. I cannot think of any other term that more accurately describes the feeling than "bittersweet."

Jonathan has been living at home, occasionally sleeping here with me. Sue is about to experience those stinging pangs of the empty nest, a feeling that I, perhaps, had to deal with a bit earlier when I moved into this apartment alone. She remains in the house and Jonathan will not be around writing and singing his songs. It is going to hurt a lot. I feel so much for what Sue is experiencing—neither of us could have prepared to be sending off our boy from separate stations in life. It is a joyful moment for Jonathan, a time of liberation. It is my hope that Sue and I will experience the sweetness that we deserve to feel at this moment, that our minds will meet in a mutual love and appreciation for everything that we have worked through to bring us to this time and place. It is my prayer this will happen. Yet it will be bittersweet as we acknowledge that Jonathan's journey forward leaves us in a position to examine ever more acutely where we stand in relation to one another. It is this impending situation that has, no doubt, produced this increasing anxiety for me. I will miss Jonathan's availability intensely, but my heart pours out to Sue. I so much want her to prosper, thrive, succeed. I cannot take away her pain, just as I can't seem to alleviate my own inner tension. Jonathan's venture into the world was inevitable, and it would have touched us in a profound and deep way, changing our lives, even if we were together. But we face this apart. I wish for many blessings, health and safety for my dear son as he enters the world, and may we all share precious moments in the future, even if they are experienced in ways other than what we anticipated.

June 2, 2007, and Jonathan's graduation has now passed. At the moment he is attending the after-graduation party, and from what I hear, the Mill Valley Recreation Center has been turned into a fantasyland, resembling something like a scene from Arabian Nights. There is hypnotic Mid-Eastern music, tents filled with delectable foods, and belly dancers writhing to the music, moving in and out of the tents. And all of this under the watchful eyes of Marin Academy parents, who are the chaperones tonight. Sue is one of these guardians. I spoke with her about an hour ago from the fantasy world and her spirit seems to have improved compared to how she was when we finished the after-graduation dinner. Sue, myself, Jonathan, Michael and their friends all attended dinner tonight at a really great place in Mill Valley, the Buckeye Road House. The chicken, the lamb, the fish, the beef, the desserts, the wines are just first rate. It is the place we went to celebrate Michael's graduation and my 50th birthday, a little over two years ago. There was a sense of joy and celebration as we toasted Jonathan, his hair getting very long and curly now, expressing his freedom through not cutting it the past several months. He looks a lot like Bob Dylan as he appeared on the cover of Blond on Blond. And he is writing and singing a lot of songs these days that reflect Dylan's influence. Some of these songs move me to my core; a friend of mine produces music and on Jonathan's last day of school we recorded several of them. Much of this music reflects his grappling with transition from a life filled with the comfort of sweet, supportive, creative and nurturing friends to one in which he will move 3,000 miles to a new school and a new world. The songs deal with his desire, perhaps struggle, to understand intellectually and accept emotionally the separation of his parents—the shaking up of a world that had always been so secure as a child for him. He understood the necessity of the separation, encouraged me to go out and create space for everyone when he saw the tortured struggle taking place between his mom and dad—he had a very zen-like attitude, a mature acknowledgement that one simply cannot force change but must accept life as it is. These realizations and mature understandings occurred on one level, but underneath it all he is a young man whose hormones are erupting, body changing, emotions searching for a home and safe harbor in a world where the comfort of his family is not quite delivering the sense of security that it once had. Just before sitting down to write these thoughts tonight, I put on one of my favorite of his songs. In this particular one, "Bridges and Boats," Jonathan is admitting to his loneliness and my internal struggle to gain some peace of mind. With the sincerity of heaven he sings, "Blank walls, and I'm sleeping on the ground, it is empty in the day. Though I try to put this behind me now, it never went away. He stands by a window in the room, staring at the bay, and all the bridges and the boats, fade away." My God, how I love this boy, and with all of the poignancy that life contains, I celebrate his graduation tonight. So, indeed, we toasted Jonathan, and for moments Sue and I looked away from these difficult times. She drank a huge glass of an exotic wheat beer from Belgium, and I picked out a velvety Pinot Noir from Sonoma.

The alcohol worked its magic—Michael drank his share of the wine, and I sneaked a glass under the table to Jonathan—but, of course, the come down from the drinks occurred, hitting Sue particularly hard. The life went out of her as we waited in line to get the car. Tears were streaming beneath her dark glasses—and I so desperately wanted to make it all good. "I know it is hard Sue, the heaviness wipes me out everyday." "I'm doing well," she said, "I'm just not doing well right now." "This transition is hard, Sue, it is really hard, there is joy and sadness," I went on. But she didn't hear me or didn't want to hear me and started to walk away. As she walked, I thought of her on the field of the graduation. The day had been warm, as it is in San Rafael in June. But the cool breeze that has infiltrated and permeated San Francisco all spring started to set in, and I got up to find a sunny spot behind the rows of chairs. I had come in short sleeves and she made herself warm with a sweater that she had brought for just this eventuality.

As I watched the graduation from behind the rows of chairs, Sue's hair looked lovely, reddish-blond, long and thick, blowing in the wind. My words could not comfort her as she walked away toward the car. But there were no words that she even attempted to offer me. It seems that she really doesn't even try to understand my interior life—perhaps she just thinks that I am reveling in the joy of my solitude. She would want for us to go back to what we once were, but she doesn't seem to want to take a look at where I am in the moment. It is that intimacy that I crave, and it is the only hope for our marriage. I want to go forward with a kind of intimacy that we did not have in those days of raising children, but she doesn't seem to want to look into my eyes and see the despair or gain an understanding of my hope.

The boys were not aware of this moment as we waited for the car, and they remained in a special bond of brothers and friends. But as I write this and think of the day, Jonathan's words affect me deeply: "He stands by a window in the room, staring at the bay, and all the bridges and the boats, fade away."

In just a few days, Jonathan will be going to Europe with his best three friends; he rose to the occasion in so many ways this past year—learning to be philosophical amidst the pain of his parents' separation; taking on a significant role in a major play; academically succeeding—that a trip like this is sweet reward. But the trip, for me, is adding another layer of anxiety to what I am already feeling these days. I love this boy so much; I just want to keep him in a protective cocoon. This of course is not possible, and it shouldn't be. He will be visiting six countries during five weeks on this trip—and for him there will be an abundance of moments of pure joy. And I have every confidence that he'll be safe—so it is more for me that this tension exists, not as much for him. I am concerned about how I will deal with not knowing where he is much of the time—and the frustration that I am sure to feel when I haven't heard from him or try to reach him on his international cell phone but cannot. It doesn't get much better than exploring the possibilities of freedom with one's best friends at an age when one is finally acquiring the wings to fly above the ground and survey the landscape. But I do remind myself that he is 18, not 21 or 25. They are still somewhat kids at this age, and can be prone to some serious lapses of maturity. So when I reflect on that idea, I start punishing myself for letting him go—and I tell myself that Sue and I should have been more together on this subject—that our own difficulties prevented us from seeing this situation clearly. But then another part of me, a larger part, a surrendering side, takes over and says that he has so earned this trip, that he is smart and traveling with mature friends, that to have deprived him of this opportunity would have inhibited him from discovering this part of the world and conquering some of his own insecurity. In essence, he will grow and develop confidence from this trip; it will be a celebration for him that he has reached a mature enough point in his life that he is permitted to take leave. One is only this age once, he'll probably not again have this opportunity to experience the world in this way with his three best friends in life—and if there are epiphanies of joy to be experienced, I want him to have those moments. I just wish the summer were over already, and that he were safely on his new college campus hitting the books. We'll get there soon enough.

Europe 1973

I took a trip to Europe at the age of 18, but I would not have been permitted to go without supervision. My father had left my mom a couple of years before, to go back to his birthplace, Montreal. It had been a relief for him to go, because he would become vicious from time to time, sometimes becoming violent with me and my younger brothers, Jeff and Elliot. And as much as I forgive him today—I long ago released my anger over his often cold, distant and sometimes violent treatment of my youth; it is just too much work to hold on to anger, and it is unhealthy—I cannot deny that his fatherhood left me so desperately wanting for the companionship of a father.

So, my father was gone and my mother, without the help of any support or care packages, raised her four children through her gift. Throughout my high school years the house would be filled with eight, 10, 12, sometimes 15 people there to obtain one of her coveted tea-leaf readings. She earned enough to save some, but it was mostly enough to pay the bills and provide the food. We were wealthy though, because it is impossible to put a price on her love. Even though she was probably among the most psychic people to have ever lived, it was her love, her bountiful compassion that people treasured most of all—they came from all destinations to listen to the softness of her voice and rest in the fullness of her presence which suggested that everything was going to be all right, that all would work out according to the way it should. If everything is a commodity, including love, then the experience of being with my mom, Alma Lorraine Rush, was priceless.

It was after one of these house-filled, tea-leaf reading nights that I walked in with the news that my school would be taking a bunch of students to Europe during the upcoming summer. Europe had seemed a fantasy, I so much wanted to go, but I never thought that she would ever think to send me. I gave her the news that this would happen, but truly I did not mention it thinking that I would ever be going. We just didn't have the money; I knew that. "You'll go," she said to me. "You'll go." It was as simple as that. She didn't amplify her words, expound on them in any way. "You'll go." "Come on mom, how are we going to do that?" I asked. She became a tad annoyed with me at my question. "You'll go; tell them you'll go," she insisted. And indeed, I did go. She raised the money through the readings, taking on a few extra every week for the next several months. And, of course, she looked after all of the other needs of her family as well. Indeed, I did go. And the trip brought tears to my eyes.

I had always had a love affair with things British, and when we arrived in London, the first stop on the six-week tour, I was mesmerized. Every one spoke with that English accent that I could not get enough of. The girls were cute, most of them braless, and they all spoke with those accents—what a total turn-on. I walked lap after lap around Hyde Park, stopping at the Speakers Corner to hear some of the wittiest banter I had ever known. I had been on the school's debating team, performing quite well in winning a few contests. But my skill seemed small in comparison to some of these people who would make their way out of the crowd and argue with the highly articulate person standing on the podium. I have been told on a recent trip to London that this period of debate in Hyde Park, 1973, was a golden age for this activity; it was considered great sport in those days and it brought out the very best of the city's academics. The Vietnam War was still raging, Nixon was being investigated for Watergate, the English economy was in a fix, the discussions were dignified and lively. Indeed, in listening to the exchanges recently at the Corner, banter is not nearly as fun nor as challenging or stimulating. There seems to be a lot more anger than I had heard then. Or maybe it was just the thrill of being in London, in the shadows of Buckingham Palace, for the first time, 18 years young and enjoying every ounce of London, especially those magnificent accents—the sound, the lilt touched the pleasure center of my brain. There was so much to enjoy on the trip. And, for sure, some of it made me very sad.

Outside Munich, we walked through the gas chambers and barracks of Dachau, and I will always remember the stench of gas and decayed bodies that infiltrated the air. Other students noticed it too, and when I asked one of the guides what the smell was, they admitted that they thought that it was the lingering reminder of what had gone on there, that they had not been able to remove the odor. The pictures in the museum where brain surgery had been performed on healthy young men were very disturbing. There were pictures of young people virtually starving to death—skin and bones—and they looked 80 when they were probably 20. There was an exhibit of the shoes of an entire family that had been murdered. There was a vessel holding the gold fillings that had been extracted from those who had been incinerated. And the housing where, in something that looked like dark barns, dozens were made to sleep on a kind of bed that could not have been big enough to hold eight. Approaching Dachau one exits from train tracks, much like if not exactly the same as those that brought these Jews, my people, to this place. In Berlin, a city divided between Russia and the West, very much in the center of the cold war, we traveled from west to east through "Check Point Charlie," past the East German guards, some of whom no doubt had fired those guns at Easterners trying to escape. We had heard that just a few days earlier there had been a killing of a student who had tried to escape over the wall.

From Berlin on to Amsterdam, where I smoked hashish in the park, a group of kids from all over the world crowding around a friend of mine who was playing some great rock guitar. We went up and down the canals, eventually making our way into "the most famous red light district in the world." I didn't partake of the action, but I probably would have if I hadn't been concerned about spending too much money in one place. I couldn't get over how seductive these women appeared—most of them unbelievable busty knockouts who were too luscious to resist for an 18-year-old guy. In Amsterdam there was the serious moment of visiting the house of Anne Frank. It was astounding to me that I was climbing into those same hiding places where this young woman—gifted young writer with the eyes of a seer—refused to surrender to anything but optimism and belief in the goodness of human beings. I took a moment to try to listen to what it would have sounded like as Nazis walked up and down the very streets that I was gazing on from this hiding place in the attic.

In Rome, there was the Coliseum, where I had a vision of being one of those slaves from Judea forced to defend myself in the theater—I really did feel that I had had a past life in that place in just that way. We made our way to the Papal City, and after walking through a labyrinth of hallways—each one decorated with marble and sculptures of the renaissance—we entered the Sistine Chapel. I simply could not comprehend that masterpiece on first viewing. I stood for an hour just staring up at the frescoes on the ceiling, each one illuminating a scene from creation and the unfolding of the biblical world. The image of God breathing life into Adam just astounded, as did the painting of the Last Supper.

As a work of art this ceiling is a masterpiece of the ages, but as a feat of endurance it was Herculean. The ceiling of Sistine Chapel is a marriage of genius and bewildering endurance. Just try lying flat and holding your arms up for an hour, barely letting them down for more than a moment before extending them again. The muscles burn with exhaustion after awhile. To think that Michelangelo did this for hours a day over a period of years, at the same time portraying artistic brilliance is astounding.

Then on to Florence, where I saw the David at the Accademia. I had read about the sculpture—how David's blood flowed through that cold marble—but I was speechless when I actually saw it. How did Michelangelo place a beating heart, a vital life force flowing through those thick veins and muscles, within that stone? Greatness is too small a word for this man. Michelangelo's work was spellbinding to me—my mind expanded as I comprehended that this man had the ability to bring heavenly form to this earthly plane. Plato talked much of the ideal forms of beauty, truth, justice that existed on a celestial level that mankind interprets and reproduces on earth. Plato's ideas have always been intuitively accurate for me, but he had never encountered a Michelangelo. Michelangelo was able to ascend the mount of the Gods, perceive heavenly forms, and place them in front of the eyes of human beings. They are not interpretations or representations of heaven, but divinity frozen in time and placed before men. Prior to coming to Europe I read Irving Stone's story of Michelangelo, "The Agony and the Ecstasy." The book introduced me to much of the work of the artist, and it also exposed me to his thinking—the research into his letters was prodigious. After reading the book, I told my mom that I had found Michelangelo fascinating, and that from what I read I could very much relate to the way that he thought. "Mom," I said, "I am going to look up his astrological sign; I wouldn't be surprised if we were born under the same one. Well, I was flabbergasted. Not only were we born under the same sign, but we shared the identical birthday, March 6. Now, please do not get me wrong—I am not delusional about what I am capable of doing on this planet, but to this day I find it astonishing that I so related to his thinking that I decided to look up his birthday, only to find out that it is the very same as mine.

In Paris, we were able to see the Mona Lisa without a glass case surrounding it, and the crowds were nothing like they are today. Back in London, we took a trip down 10 Downing Street—totally blocked off these days—and could have walked right up to the door, just a few guards standing sentry. I marveled at being able to walk right up to the residential door of England's Prime Minister. And, of course, there was the trip Savile Row, London's high fashion street of tailors that housed the studio where the Beatles worked and eventually performed their concert on the roof, made famous in the movie "Let it Be," that break-up movie showing the disillusionment that was clearly visible on the faces of the four lads. But that concert on the roof—Wow!—McCartney, black, full beard, hair blowing back in the wind, Lennon in full flight as they rocked to "Get Back": "Jojo was a man who thought he was a woman." I imagined the concert as I stood on the street in front of the building. This was a conservative street, even in the '60s, and I was told that many people on the street were perturbed by the disruption to business. "How ridiculous, how totally ridiculous," I couldn't help but think. What I would have given to have been in London for that moment—it would be the highlight of a life. This was bliss, and it was Mom, hard working and asking for nothing in return, except that I get the most that I could out of this trip, who had made this possible. How I loved her then, loved her all my life, and miss her so deeply.

❐

That trip to Europe was liberation for me after a couple of very difficult years. There is some old, grainy footage from when I was about two years old taken on a summer day at Lake Ontario. In the film my father is holding me up above the water by my arms, nearly stretching them out of their sockets. It is clear that this stretching hurts—I am making all sorts of pained faces—but the most difficult thing is that he keeps dunking me in the water against my will. I am being held and stretched above the water, then let down as my head submerges. He does this not once or twice or three times, but maybe 10 times, each plunge beneath the water scaring me more and more, and the pain from the stretching obviously increasing. The look on my face becomes one of pure fright. Eventually my mom, just stunning in her one-piece swimsuit, not long removed from being runner-up in the Miss Toronto pageant, comes over and scolds my dad, removing me from his possession. His laughter as she took me from him revealed the extent to which he was totally unaware of the trauma he was inflicting. The joke went a bit too far, but that was my dad, he had a very undeveloped sensitivity gene that would prevent him from understanding the harsh effect he could have on his children and wife. That dunking in the waters of Lake Ontario is a metaphor for so much that I would experience under the sometimes-martial law of my father.

When he got mad during my childhood, he would hit, not talk. My mom often objected to these tactics, and more than once put herself in a difficult situation where she tried to separate him from one of his kids who he was intent on punishing. There is an instance that has never left my consciousness. It took place when I was 10 years old and playing baseball with some friends at the school field down the hill from my house in Simi Valley, southern California. The kid next door, Mike Carniglia, was known in the neighborhood as a real troublemaker. He would act all chummy and before you knew it he was picking a fight with someone, stealing the ball or throwing it over the fence. We had all learned our lesson with this kid, so we would spurn him anytime he came around and ask to join our game. On a beautiful mid-summer late afternoon in 1965—I had been listening to the album "Beatles 65" earlier in the day for the first time and had just fallen in love with the song, "No Reply" because, aside from the ecstatic pleasure of its harmonies, it told my story of trying to make it with the girl down the street whose parents kept saying wasn't home: "I tried to telephone, they said you were not home, that's a lie, 'cause I know where you've been and I saw you walk in your door."

We had been reaching the peak moment of our baseball game. I was at the plate with the bases loaded, down a run. My friends had been talking about how difficult it was to defend me when I was at the plate because I sprayed the ball to all fields. Just as my friend Timmy went into the wind-up to throw the pitch, Mike Carniglia came running onto the field asking to play. I drop the bat and walk over to tell him that this is an important moment in our game and not a good time for us to be interrupted. He made a huge fuss, so I told him that I would kick his ass if he didn't get out of here. Mike then yells up at his father, Dick Carniglia, to tell him that the punk down the street, Bruce Rosen, will not let him play. Dick, sitting in his lawn chair, informs my father who had just come over to visit—he had recently decided to chum up to Dick for some reason, though he had never paid any attention to him since we had moved in a few years earlier—that I had decided not to let his son play baseball with the other guys. My father yells "bloody murder" at me from the bluff above the field, immediately running down and chasing me with intent to punch. I run from him and the game comes to an unfinished end. To this day, I wish that I would have had the chance to drive the runners in. My father never caught me that afternoon, and I didn't come home for dinner, which alarmed my mom.

The whole event was observed by my genteel friend, a 60-year-old, gray-haired, English retired bank president, Jack Hussey, who lived a few doors further down the street from Mr. Carniglia. Mr. Hussey enjoyed an unobstructed vantage point of the field from the best patio in the neighborhood. He had a great swimming pool that I was allowed to use anytime I wanted, and an awesome barbecue. The smell of the ribs he was barbecuing was in the air that late afternoon when my father chased me around the field. The disruption to our game disturbed Mr. Hussey greatly. A few days later, I was walking down the sidewalk in front of his house when he called me over to say the words that ring clear to this day: "Bruce, I saw what your father did the other day when you boys were playing so nicely down on the field. I had just remarked to Muriel (his wife) how much I was enjoying the sound of your game when your father comes chasing you like a lunatic. I just want you to know, Bruce, that that was very wrong of him—and I am going to tell him so when I see him. I hope you boys go back and finish your game." He said all of this in a sort of dignified, English, bank president way. I really loved Jack Hussey—he took to me and I to him. He had been a soccer star when he was younger and regaled me with stories of his soccer exploits, as well as tales of his experiences as captain of a submarine during World War II. About a year later, we moved from there to return to my father's roots in Montreal. I greatly missed California, my friends, though not Mike Carniglia, but most of all Jack Hussey.

6-6-66

On June 6, 1966 my parents pulled myself and brother Jeff out of school a week early (the teachers wondered why they couldn't have waited a week for school to end) and set their course for Montreal, Quebec, Canada, my father's birthplace. My father had started a business, Simi Valley T.V., which became the dominant television repair service in the new communities of Simi and Santa Susana, indeed the entire Simi Valley. He had locked up contracts with many of the top department stores at the time, including May Company, Sears and others. The business was really expanding, new contracts coming in all the time, and my mom had much more than a full time job taking care of the business and her four children, myself, Jeff and the two small ones, Heidi and Elliot. Yet, despite the success and his talent for repair, the desire to return to his roots in Montreal—overriding the objections of my mom, as well as my fervent desire as an 11 year old to stay in California and be with my friends, to keep playing baseball in the backyard field—turned us away from the comfortable and into a world where success is difficult without knowing a large amount of the French language.

The trip was quite fun at first, and I have some vivid recollections of it. I clearly remember the long stretch of highway, hundreds of miles of open road, mirages of water appearing and disappearing, and sandstorms covering the windshield in dust from time to time, as we moved through the cactus-filled landscape of Arizona into New Mexico. The road signs kept reminding us that we were getting closer to Albuquerque, and the idea of that was appealing to me. I worshiped the L.A. Dodgers at this age, absolutely idolizing my Jewish hero, Sandy Koufax. Vin Scully, the Dodgers' announcer—the mesmerizing stories of the game that he would tell, his resonating, lingering, echoing voice capturing my baseball imagination—would often tell of players who were being called up or sent down to the farm team in Albuquerque. "Maybe we can catch an Albuquerque Dodger game," I remember saying to my Dad, only to be told that we would just be passing through, there would not be enough time.

From New Mexico we headed northward through Oklahoma—I remember seeing the sign for Broken Arrow, Oklahoma, which a few years later I identified as the birthplace of the smooth shortstop for the Dodgers, Bill Russell. I was surprised at how green Oklahoma seemed, and I loved the accents. There were many Native American sites along the way, and it was fascinating to me when we stopped and I could look at the pipes, beads, jewelry, and indigenous rocks that were used in tribal ritual. I felt that I was experiencing a deep bond or affinity with these people as we traveled through this territory. Stopping in Oklahoma one night, I dreamt of a kind of Native American celebration, seeing in rich color the turquoise, red, yellow, and white feathers of the chief's headdress. I remember thinking, even at this age of 11, that I had been a Native American in a past life.

We continued east, eventually making our way into New York City. My parents had remembered the Hotel Astor from earlier years growing up, and as we saw its sign in Times Square they decided that we would stay there. It was a dive. Obviously, the place had fallen on hard times, and we left very early the next morning for Montreal.

My father's anger started to really show itself the further east we went. And on the drive from New York to Montreal, he was ready to slug myself or Jeff if we complained about anything. I suppose that, although he was being pulled to Montreal to rediscover his roots, to be near his parents, get back in touch with childhood friends, he was stressed about bringing his family into a place where we would have to stay with his sister until he found a job and place to live. He had moved from a virtual expert in his field with an expanding and promising business—he had sold the name Simi Valley T.V. for enough of a sum to move us to Montreal—to a place, though familiar, where he had no career whatsoever. And all of this with four young kids. The closer we got to Montreal, the tighter his face became, his complexion becoming whiter as the tension became increasingly palpable.

We had been staying with his sister, Vivian, for a few weeks when a childhood friend of my father's, Lefty, a stocky Greek Jew with thick forearms and raven black hair, came over for a visit. He really liked me, and had an interest in virtually every sport. We had been speaking of Sandy Koufax, Don Drysdale and my Dodgers for a while when Lefty, my Dad sitting next to him, said that the three of us should go next week to a practice of the Montreal Alouettes, Montreal's Canadian Football League team. The season hadn't started yet, and the summer practices were open to the public. I was thrilled to have the chance to do that, and with Lefty present, my father agreed that on a certain day next week we would go.

There was not a lot for me to be excited about in Montreal; I really missed my friends and everything about my home, California. California was dry where this place was sticky, hot and humid. Everybody spoke French and I didn't know a word. I really wanted to be back home, but I knew that I would have to make the most of it. Perhaps, I would never be back in California, almost certainly not as a kid again. I was extremely excited about going to that football practice. I had never been to a professional practice of any kind. Lefty had assured me that he would be there, and my father assured Lefty that he would bring me. The day arrived and there were four hours to go before the practice, but my father was not around. Then there were three hours to go, and he could not be found. Then two, then one, then practice time, then the practice was most certainly over, but my father never showed up. He came in a few hours after the practice had surely ended, with no explanation for why he hadn't taken me. I was heartbroken, nearly destroyed over what he had done. "Dad, why didn't you show up? The practice is over now; you promised," I said with some anger and sadness. "Shut up; don't you dare talk to your father with that disrespect," he lashed at me. "I'm your father" "You promised me, you really promised me," I responded to him, probably not in the tone he wanted to hear. And as I said this, he slashed me across the mouth and nose with the back of his hand and knuckles, blood from my face splattering everywhere. He smashed my lip and bloodied my nose. I went away crying, sobbing, bleeding into a bedroom, my mother and aunt coming in to comfort me. I was inconsolable for a while; nothing could help. I'll never forget what I heard next: "You dirty Goddamn son of a bitch," my mother yelled. "I am finished with you, Larry. I am finished with you." Later that night and the next day, my father apologized. But what could I say. The damage had been done, and really, it was irreparable. My mother would later tell me, after they had divorced, that in her mind it was Larry's vicious blow to my face in that tight Montreal apartment that turned her away from him for good.

❒

A few years later we returned to California, my mom having promised me during our stay in Canada that we would do so. It is 1971, my hair is really long and curly, and all of my friends are surfing. So, naturally I want to surf. I was a really good athlete, captain of my ice hockey team, and I just knew that I could do that surfing thing. My mom had gone out and gotten a job at a country music publishing company, working for country singers Dusty Rhodes and Buck Owens. She was making some money and wasn't so dependent those days on my father's paycheck. So she promised me that I could have a surfboard, that she would buy it for me with her next paycheck. When my father heard about this he went white with rage. No son of his would take part in that surfing with those kids hanging around the house. He didn't like the look of those boys; certainly drugs would be involved, and either I would have to leave or he would leave if I were allowed to surf. My mom told him that she was going to buy me that surfboard, and if that meant his leaving then the door was open. She bought the board, I did surf, my hair grew longer and more curly, my body a deep bronze from the Malibu sun, and my father was filled with anger. He had been waking up early, driving me to hockey practice in the years since returning to California. He had a strong interest in the sport, became president of the local hockey club, and was generally pretty nice to me on hockey days. But now that I had this surfboard, he vowed that my hockey days were over. His first edict was to deny me the privilege of going up north to San Francisco with my brother, Jeff, who had qualified for the all-star team as a goalie, while I had been picked as a right-winger. We were to play against a San Francisco team, and had we won, the trip would have continued to Seattle. It was a huge honor to make that team, and to play with my brother would have been phenomenal. But this is where Larry had the power. He denied me that opportunity, and there was nothing that anyone could do about it. “Screw it,” my mom told me. “You don’t need hockey. I was going to ask you to quit anyway. I’ve seen you play lately, and you have too much anger. Either you are going to get hurt, or you’ll hurt somebody. I want you to quit. Just quit, okay? You can surf instead.” I followed her advice; my hockey days were over but I was starting to become a pretty good surfer. And, indeed, I do realize my mom was correct in making that request. As I think back, I know that my game was no longer about the enjoyment of playing, but had become a vehicle for my release of anger. Not a good reason to play the game.

≈

June 17th, 2007

Today is Fathers Day, and it is the first Father's day where I am alone. Michael has set off to a reunion at the Walden School in New Hampshire, where he will be performing his own composition. From there he goes to London, where I will meet him. We will then go to Paris together, where he will study music during the month of July. From there I will go to Florence, where I will meet Jonathan for lunch. Michael left yesterday, and Sue did not want to come back to an empty house. She drove him to the airport, and continued on to Monterey for a few days. It is Father's Day and I am alone with these thoughts. I am sad and lonely today, but at least I have the tranquility of my thoughts. This tranquility and solitude was interrupted for a brief and startling moment by an exclamation mark when my cell phone rang late this afternoon. The ringer on the phone sounded different, though the tone was the same as always. Yet there was an urgency to it; it almost demanded that I run to that phone and pay attention. I wanted to ignore the phone, I felt too reflective and deep within my thoughts to speak to anyone. But it might have been Jonathan calling from Europe, so I ran over to look at the incoming number. I wanted to speak to Jonathan, but it wasn't he who was calling.

It was a phone number that I hadn't seen light up on my phone for several months—it was "M's" cell phone number. I wasn't tempted to pick up the phone; I just didn't have it in me. After a minute or two, the phone made that sound showing that the caller had left a message. She sounded like she had had a glass of wine or two, and she was wishing me a happy Father's Day. The voice—attractive as always—did not pull me in. I no longer occupy that space of obsession, the place where I was being filled with the Dionysian joy of intoxicating surrender.

❐

The earth rotates on its axis and we move with it—we just don't realize it. But then one day the space we had been filling is empty, and with all our might we cannot re-enter it. We occupy another place, and though we sometimes do not clearly understand our location, we know something for sure—we know that as surely as the planet rotates on its axis and moves around the sun our perceptions change in subtle ways. And in relationships, we either change and adapt together or we move apart. Over time the accumulation of subtle changes results in different perspectives on our lives—and sadly we might continue to love and cherish people in our lives, but we no longer share the same experience or, rather, a similar understanding of our experience. So we can force ourselves to stay together through cherished memories—though not moving forward in ways that we once had—or we might push forward, breaking new ground as we enter the unknown. I am pulled in each of these two ways today—and it is a difficult time. After listening to "M's" message, I decided to call my father. I reached him at Radio Shack where he works. He sounded a bit fatigued, after all he is 76 years old now and working almost full time. He had surgery on his stomach recently and recovered quickly enough to go back to work in less than a month. He rushed it, but he obviously has endurance. I wished him love on this day, and he quietly did the same to me. He asked how I had been doing, and how the situation was with Sue. "It's the same," I said, "We're doing about the same." He didn't have much to say to that. "Well, happy Father's Day," he repeated, his voice sort of trailing off to nowhere. "Well, I'll keep in touch, talk to you soon," I replied, and the conversation was over.

It is a few days after Father's Day. Jonathan is well into his trip now, and he has been a good boy, checking in every few days. I was glad to see that he made it through Amsterdam and its temptations. He and his friends were moved to tears by the visit to the Anne Frank house. The boys, all of them highly sensitive and intelligent, felt that they could feel the energy of Anne—and Jonathan described to me how he could visualize the Nazis patrolling the street below. He described his inspiration as he struggled to take in as much as was possible of Van Gogh's visions in the museum dedicated to this man who hardly sold a painting in his lifetime. And the Vermeer paintings, he was just astounded by the way this genius mastered the various shadings of light and texture.

But it wasn't solely the cultural that they were experiencing in Amsterdam—they had been spending a fair amount of time sampling the offerings in the legal marijuana bars. Its okay, I did the same when I was his age on my tour. I'm glad he was able to tell me about it in vivid detail. They sat on the roof of their hostel, smoking and overlooking the city. Can't take that away from him—it will be an experience that he'll remember the rest of his life. He called me from Denmark today, someplace north of Copenhagen. The Danish mother of a school friend has a place there on a pristine lake; and they have been spending a few days swimming and walking through the forest, writing songs, singing, being alive. I am thrilled for him, and I will be okay as long as he continues to check in with me every few days.

Disappearing on a Freight Train

Checking in is not something that I did for my mom when I was 16 years old, a few months before my father left for Canada for good. I could no longer handle his daily threats to take something away from me if I didn't cut my hair, or change my friends and clothes, or stop surfing. My anger and resentment toward him was building and I was acquiring a strong wanderlust. I had heard one too many times his refrain to my mom that, "either he goes or I go." So, one afternoon, I filled a duffel bag full of clothes, threw in a couple of canned goods, sneaked a couple of $20 bills from my mom's purse, and set out on an adventure that became one of the most traumatic periods in my mom's life. I told my mom that I would be gone for a while, and that I was planning to hitchhike to New York to visit my cousin, Sephra. Sephra's life sounded like a lot of fun; she ran her father's business, and her father was the widely known and respected, Sam Herman, one of the top jazz arrangers in the world. Sephra had been telling me about the interesting, exciting people she had been working with—Aretha Franklin, Roberta Flack, George Benson, Sarah Vaughn and others—and I just had to get away from this father of mine. My mom looked at me like I was out of my mind when I told her this, and she clearly did not believe me. I was prepared go alone, but a good friend of mine, Steve Pencille, wanted to come along.

Steve was a very good-looking kid; the girls were crazy about him. He was almost one hundred percent Native American—Cherokee—with a dash of French for accent. He had thick black hair, green eyes, a complexion that was, perhaps, a shade lighter than olive, lean and fit, and could definitely take care of himself if it came to that. I knew that he would be the ideal traveling companion for this kind of trip. Steve loaded up his bag, said good-bye to no one and joined me down by the railroad tracks, where we stuck out our thumbs for a ride headed east toward the desert.

❒

It was May, 1971, and we had decided that we had finished school for the year. Not long before this, I had been introduced to the mind-altering substances of Panama Red and black Afghanistan hash. And in the process, I discovered that music could sound much different than it ever had. Under the effect of Panama Red marijuana—indeed it really was red, many strains of red leaf running through it—I listened to Jim Hendrix' "Electric Ladyland" for the first time using headphones. It was electrifying; no other word can describe it. The song "Crosstown Traffic" screeched through my brain. I journeyed to distant lands as Jimmy sang,

"Have you ever been (to Electric Ladyland?)" sung in a bluesy, ballad sort of way that felt like soft velvet. Then there was the, "No reason to get excited, the thief he kindly spoke, there are some here among us who think that life is but a joke," of "All Along the Watchtower"—scintillating, as he gave us this electrified vision of a Jimmy Hendrix world of jokers, demons and seers.

Under the influence of the black Afghanistan hash, I heard the "Led Zeppelin 1" album for the first time. Has there ever been a more fully realized debut album? I think not. The hard, sharp, electric exclamation marks, followed by John Bonham's pounding beat as we go into Robert Plants high, piercing crescendo in the song "Good Times Bad Times," and it introduced me to a musical ecstasy of which I had to have more. And, as I vibrated to the energy of it, I was put into a mood where I just had to run, had to travel, had to ramble. The song is followed by, "Babe I'm Gonna Leave You," and as I listened to the deep bluesy tones of it, I thought about how I would tell my girlfriend, Debbie, of the straight, waist-length hair and the awesome hips—I had the words, "Debbie Love," painted across my bedroom wall—that I would be off for a while. "Dazed and Confused," "Your Time is Gonna Come," "Communication Breakdown," has there ever been a more paradigm-shattering album?—Well maybe the Beatles' "Sgt. Pepper's Lonely Hearts Club Band," totally mind-bending at the time—let alone debut album? I was ready to move, I was ready to travel.

A few rides took us to the edge of the desert, to the town of Indio. We spent the first night in a little ravine near the road, tucked into our sleeping bags. Steve and myself broke some Coke bottles in half, so that we would have some jagged glass edges by our sides as weapons should it be needed. It was cold that night, a lot colder than I had anticipated; my army jacket, replete with an ironed-on marijuana leaf on the back, the words underneath it saying, "Cannabis Sativa," didn't keep me as warm as it should have.

The following morning we realized that we didn't have enough food to keep us going, so we filled our bags with oranges and apples from a fruit stall that we found in the center of town. We were quick and darted away before anyone could discover our theft. We tried to continue hitchhiking, but after a couple of hours there hadn't been any offering of a ride. We were close to the railroad tracks and not far from a stopping place for trains. In short order a train came to a crossing and stopped, remained there for quite a while. "Steve," I said, "let's grab this train; let's hop trains to New York." Without thinking, this raven-haired adventurer, Native American explorer said, "Yeah, great idea, let's do it!" We ran over to the train, jogging quickly up and down its length to find the most comfortable car for transport. We discovered a series of flat cars with an indentation down the middle, the bottom of which held a pulley for the brakes. The car offered some shelter in the form of a fruit truck that rested atop the flat car—giving us a ceiling as shelter from the elements. There remained some room on either side of the car, affording us the opportunity to dangle our legs along the side and stare into the wilderness. We decided on that car and jumped on it, just as the train was beginning to move.

In a couple of hours we were looking at the Salton Sea, a big lake in the middle of the desert that I had always heard of but had never seen. It was impressive; I hadn't realized that it would be so large. The ride continued into the night, our second night on the journey. The indentation in the middle of the flat car looked like it would be a comfortable sleeping place on first glance, but it didn't fulfill its promise. All night long, just as I was falling asleep, the pulley would move up and down, moving against various parts of my back and spine. I slept, but it certainly wasn't a good night's sleep. We awoke to the sunrise over the Arizona desert; and it was a sight to behold. The freedom and the wide-open landscape, cactus as far as the eye could see, reddish mountains in the distance, permitted my mind to wander, my mind to open, my soul to expand. But as the day went on there was a creeping anxiety that, probably, there were people back home worrying about me. And, of course, there was no way to let anyone know my whereabouts. However, I relegated these thoughts to the back of my mind, as I allowed myself the freedom to enjoy this journey. As we continued, we ate the canned chili that we heated with matches and sticks, enjoyed our bounty of fruit, and enjoyed each other's company. I'll never forget the look on Steve's face that afternoon as he sat off by himself, his Native American soul coming alive and being reborn in the desert of his ancestry, just gazing intensely into the distance. He was like an animal that had been released back into its natural habitat—thoughts from whence he came were nowhere in his mind.

Day became night, and as the night grew darker, we found ourselves in the Tucson train yard. We had run out of peanut butter and were getting low on water—reinforcements were definitely in order. There was a little grocery store across the road from the train station, and to get there meant jumping off the train, running across some tracks, jumping over another train and darting across the road. This had to be done quickly, and I volunteered to do the job, Steve staying behind to direct me back to the proper train with his voice. The excursion was further complicated by floodlights, which were trained on the trains in the yard to find stowaways, such as ourselves. And everywhere in the train yard were posted signs that described the penalties and fines that would be imposed on those guilty of illegal entry upon trains. The challenge was daunting, but I took it on. I darted out of the train, across some tracks, jumped on and then out of the other side of the flat car on another train, ran across the road, purchased a jar of peanut butter and jelly mixed together in one jar—how efficient—purchased some water, and ran back holding a large bag. I returned the way I came, the experience very treacherous as I tried to stay low beneath the floodlights. As I looked into the distance, my train started moving—and it was starting to pick up speed pretty quickly. I started to lose sight of our place on the train when Steve spotted me and yelled his location. I found him, jumped on the flat car just before him, and climbed onto our car. I barely made it onto the train; it had really started to move quickly. As I think about it now, it is no exaggeration or fantasy to say that this was a dangerous maneuver. I got back to our car, Steve giving me a huge hug. I sat there for a moment, contemplating the bravery of what I had done. In Steve's Native American eyes, I had shown my worth, and would forever be seen by him as a warrior. I had earned his respect, and it was revealed in his eyes.

I slept that night a little better than I had the previous night, but the pulley continued to move up and down our backs. When we awoke we were in the Red desert of Texas. There was very little vegetation, just red desert sand. About mid-day, the train stopped, and didn't start again for a few hours. We were truly in the middle of nowhere, not a road, nor a city or a telephone pole within miles and miles and miles. We sat in that red dirt desert, eating our spoils, peanut butter and jelly in the one jar on some bread. We still had plenty of oranges, and they were delicious. Eventually the train started moving, and by the next morning we found ourselves in the train yard of El Paso. This was a safer train yard, much more open and spread out than the one in Tucson. There were no floodlights, but of course it was daytime. I was starting to feel the pangs of anxiety a bit more acutely—I was now starting to have a strong sense that my mom was worrying about me. I knew that I had to call her and let her know that I was okay. Steve had no interest in finding a phone, but I made my way over to one and managed to call home. The phone rang and rang and rang, but no one answered—no answering machines in those days. About an hour later I called again; still no answer. The time had come to catch another train—and this one was bound for Chicago. We'd go to Chicago, and then continue on to New York. This train did not have a flat car, but a large open boxcar filled with hay. I slept so so that night, the floor rather hard, and there was not enough hay to do much softening of the ground. This was a pretty fast train and made very few stops, and when it did stop, it was only for a moment. Within a couple of days we were in Oklahoma, Kansas, Missouri. Somewhere in Missouri it started to rain, and it rained very hard. Dampness permeated the car, and I was starting to wheeze from the combination of dampness and straw. I had had serious asthma as a kid, but had not had an attack for a few years. Now I was having an asthma attack. I couldn't breathe. I was gasping for air—and I was becoming quite afraid. I took long, slow breaths, and after awhile—easily one of the longest hours of my life—the attack started to lift. A few hours later, I was in the clear. I hid the attack from Steve—I didn't want him to become alarmed, and I guess I did not want him to see any weakness in me. But the attack changed my perspective on this trip. I was becoming acutely aware that my mom was worrying about me greatly, and I was beginning to decide that I would turn around and come back when we hit Chicago. I did not tell Steve of my plans, but I kept hearing the words in my head saying, "Bruce, the only way to go back is to do it; it won't happen if you keep going in this direction." As I was hearing these words, I also kept hearing the words to that Bob Dylan song, "Like A Rolling Stone": "How does it feel to be on your own, no direction home, a complete unknown, like a rolling stone?" The words were playing in my mind over and over again. They were sending me a message that I had to return.

We made our way into Illinois, and stopped in the outskirts of East Moline, Illinois. There was a little canteen store outside the train tracks, and I went in to get some change.

I went to the phone booth and called my mom. This time she answered. "Brucie, is that you?" "Yeah, Mom, it's me; I'm in East Moline, Illinois, not far from Chicago." "Brucie, I have been worried sick over you; I didn't know if you were alive or dead. Are you all right? Did you have an asthma attack? I have a feeling that you did." "Yeah Mom, I'm okay, and yes I did have an asthma attack. But I got through it okay. I'm going to come home, Mom, but I'm going to do it the way I came. I'll hop freight trains back." "No you won't, Brucie, she yelled at me." "Are you near a store or any place that has a phone number?" "There are some stores around me," I answered. "Don't hang up the phone, leave it off the hook, run over and get a phone number for me, please!" she exclaimed nervously and urgently. "And give me the phone number to the phone booth where you are if we get disconnected." I gave her the number, and assured her that if we were to get disconnected, I would definitely call back. I brought back the phone number from the little grocery store, and within a minute she had arranged for a person to watch over me, bring me to a Western Union station where funds would be wired, and organize a plane ticket for my return to Southern California. I called her back to tell her that, really, I would prefer to come back the way I traveled—to make it back on my own. But, obviously, she'd have none of it. "All right Mom, I'll take your plane back. I'll be back soon; and I'm really looking forward to seeing you." "I can't wait to see you too, Brucie; I'm so thankful that you're all right," and she started crying loudly. I don't think that I had ever heard my mom cry before, and I was startled by this. I was tired, drained from the asthma attack, and her tears shocked me into a new reality. I had felt that she had worried about me—I just did not realize it was this severe.

The guy brought me to the Western Union station to pick up the money, then up to his apartment where I was fed before catching the plane ride later that evening. But before going off with him, I had a heart-to-heart with Steve, telling him that I was heading back. I described how my mom was going out of her mind, and suggested that he call his parents as well. But he would have none of it. He was going to continue. "I really want to go back the way I came," I told him, "but my mom is insisting. I am going to fly back tonight." We embraced, shook hands, hugged—looking into each other's eyes and recognizing the warrior in the other.

We made it back to the guy's apartment, which was upstairs from a post office. When I went to use his restroom, I saw my face in a mirror for the first time since leaving, although I had gained a hint of my appearance when I saw my reflection on the metal of the telephone. It was caked with grease. I must have been quite a sight: that grease-stained army jacket with the cannabis leaf on the back; long frizzed-out curly black hair, encircled by a Jimmy Hendrix-style headband. I grabbed a towel and washed my face. I walked back into the front room, and was greeted by a huge, heavyset woman with very short, boyish-length brown hair—she was so large she basically filled the entire bed. The guy introduced me to her as Bertha. "Bertha," he said to her as he introduced me—"I've got a real hippy for you here; he just hopped trains across the country. You want some of this?" Then he looked over at me, saying, "You want some of Bertha?" "It's okay," I answered a bit shyly. I'm ready to get moving on home." Bertha then looked over at me and smiled. "Maybe, I will have a bit of him," she said. He's pretty cute." "Thanks, Bertha, maybe I'll come back and see you some day," I answered. "You do that," she said, "you be sure and do that."

That evening, I was home; it had taken me about five days to make it that far, and I was back in about three-and-a-half hours. My father looked away when he saw me; apparently he had shut down his emotions, trying not to show any fear. But clearly, he had to have been worried. My mom, sister Heidi, and brothers were there to greet me at the airport—and boy did they show their love. I don't think that I had ever seen that much joy on my mom's face as when she first laid eyes on me that night. About a month later, Steve Pencille returned, arriving by train the way he started. He had landed in Chicago, making a living by parking cars, then sleeping in them. He came over to my place when he arrived back, and we smoked a bit of that black Afghan hash. We went into my room and left the headphones off: blasting out of my speakers were the driving opening lines to "Good Times, Bad Times," Robert Plant's searing singing, Bonham's drums pounding, Jimmy Page's guitar slicing the air.

The Hugging Saint

June 23rd, 2007

A couple of nights ago, I went to see the Hindu "hugging saint," Amma. I hadn't heard of her nor was aware of her and the thousands of people who make their pilgrimage to hear the inspiring words and enjoy being in the presence of radiant energy. My friend, Gwen Jones, the woman who has been working her Network Chiropractic magic on me, applying that light, penetrating, comforting touch to my back a couple of times a week, the woman of charm and substance that I had stumbled on that day when I was searching for a way to heal from "M," asked if I would accompany her to see Amma.

Over the previous couple of weeks, Gwen has shown me some of Amma's writings and led me to a website which includes her teachings, hopes, prayers and positive visions for our species and planet. It also included testimonials reflecting on the healing power of Amma's hug. It sounded interesting and I didn't have anything planned that night, so I accepted the invitation. The event took place at her Ashram in the East Bay. As we approached, the inviting and intoxicating aromas—sweet and spicy—of Indian curry wafted through the air. These aromas immediately stimulated for me an appetite that was quite intense—and in reflecting on it, it was an appetite for more than just the curry, it was a hunger for the spiritual peace that seemed to underlie everything in front of me. We worked our way through a thick throng of people, intent on finding the source of these delicious aromas, and as we got closer, our minds were tranquilized by rhythmic Hindu chanting. The meditative sounds eventually fell into a soft, still, quiet, from which emerged a hypnotic, captivating Indian music—the perfectly executed beat of tablas blending with an angelic sitar and harp. A flute then accompanied the sound, and then from the depths of quiet, the chanting began again. The night was warm, but not stifling, and a cooling, but not chilly, breeze from the bay began to settle in over the East Bay hills. It all suddenly felt like magic. We dined, chanted, walked paths bordered with all sorts of tapestries, Indian spices, teas, books, candles, meditation tapes, simple and colorful clothing, Vedic astrology and so much more. We found our way to a booth where numbers were being handed out to determine one's place in line to be hugged by Amma. Since there had been so many before us, our numbers were quite high, which meant that we would not be able to receive our hugs until the following morning. I simply wouldn't and couldn't wait that long for the hug.

I told the woman who was handing out the tickets that I was very much enjoying the atmosphere, but that I would have to leave in a while, perhaps without experiencing the hug. I told Gwen that she was welcome to stay around for the hug if she wanted, but that I couldn't possibly wait until sunrise.

Gwen kindly, calmly, patiently recommended that we simply enjoy the place, and that if I really wanted to leave in a while, she'd bring me back to the city in a few hours (we had gone in her car). The woman in the booth, seeing my consternation over such a long wait, told me that by all means I should find a way to stay for the hug—that it would be something memorable. And she went one step further by telling me that if I came back in an hour, she would offer the two of us any returned numbers that would get us to an earlier "hugging time."

That was a sweet, loving gesture by this woman, and after walking around a bit more, drinking some chai tea and eating a delicious curry-spiced chopped salad, we made our way back to receive the pleasant surprise that we now were in possession of numbers that would get us to the "hug" within an hour.

The time moved quickly, and as the procession moved its way toward Amma, we were getting closer by the minute. As we got closer I was struck by two things: the look of joyful beatitude on Amma's face, and her ability to hug hundreds, indeed thousands of people without having to get up and use the restroom. I was told that she could sit there for a full twenty-four hours hugging people, not having to get up and use the restroom, even once—totally amazing. And so was the hug. Gwen started shaking as we made our way to the dais, now just a few feet away from this soulful woman filled with love. Amma radiated a pure energy of love and compassion. She first hugged Gwen, then myself, then the two of us together. She was uttering words that sounded like, "Ma, Ma, Ma, Ma, Ma." She looked into my eyes and I saw a look that I had seen in my mother's eyes. It was a look of deep insight and love: It said to me, "I am here for you; I care very much for you; everything will be okay."

June 27th, 2007

I am, perhaps, excessively, obsessively concerned about the safety of my 21- and 18-year-old sons; I am often on "pins and needles" when I do not know where they are and cannot reach them. Fortunately in this great modern era, I am able to maintain contact with them through cell phones, including international ones. And as I contrast this accessibility to their whereabouts—perhaps the stress of not reaching them is only intensified by the ability to reach them most of the time—I gain a vivid glimpse of what it must have been like for my mom to not know my whereabouts as I disappeared for days, hopping those freight trains across the country. That would have been total hell for me, if I had been in her place—and I am sure it was no less for her. My God, the anguish she must have felt. Yet I did only what I had to do, which was to break away from the strains of my home. I love my mom to the depths of my soul as I sit here on this British Airways jet bound for Europe where I will meet my sons. I recognize how much she would have wanted to see these grandchildren at this stage of their lives, and I know that she was more successful at handling the uncertainties in life than I seem to be at controlling my worry over my sons' lives. I inhabit her propensity for worry, but she seemed to be able to surrender better than I can—knowing in her heart that all would be okay. Who knows, maybe it was the LSD that I took in my late teens that causes me to go to this place of fear—a lesson for all the young people out there: Don't take that stuff at all, even if you think that you are immune from anxiety. We tend to think that nothing can happen to us when we are young, and I saw too many people lose it and not quite regain themselves from LSD. And a number of those kids seemed quite strong and solid before taking the stuff.

I am very sensitive, miscommunicated feelings, pretentious assumptions about another's thoughts, people not in accord with one another, often trouble and unsettle me—and in this regard I am very much like my mother. She didn't like discord. And she worried constantly about her children, but as stated, she seemed to have a better mechanism for ultimate surrender than I do. I struggle with my need to gain a sense of control over events, particularly when it concerns my boys. So, it is consoling that Jonathan has been checking in so responsibly as he travels through Europe, (and I am trying not to abuse that, to let him have the full sense of freedom by avoiding calling him during those times when my anxiety rises). The plane is hitting a few bumps at the moment, and so I transfer that tension in this moment to Jonathan—where is he right now, damn it, this is tough stuff, letting go. And, again, my thoughts return to Alma Rush; I had told her that I would be traveling across the country, but that seemed too ludicrous to be true for her. She didn't know whether I was alive or dead. I want to embrace her with all I've got right now. I want to thank her for knowing me so well and filling me with vision, for understanding that I needed to see vistas beyond my back door, though my father would have prevented all of it if he could have. And though I would tell her how sorry I am for putting her through, perhaps the most traumatic week of her life, she would no doubt understand how necessary that trip was for my development. It gave me a grasp of the wilds of life, how it feels to be uprooted ("to be on your own, no direction home, a complete unknown, like a rolling stone," as Dylan repeated sang in my ear), and to have an appreciation for safety and security—it felt blissful to be back in my own bed after that trip, sheltered from the elements, a brake pulley no longer running up and down against my back. I continued to have dreams of those freight trains for years—dreams that celebrated and craved the adventure, but were also filled with the trauma of the moments. It was a trip that had to be taken, and it was the triggering mechanism that led to my fathers leaving for good.

❒

My father no doubt worried about me during the week that I disappeared. But to hear my mother and sister, Heidi, tell the story he showed no emotion at all. Alma could not go to him at all for any comfort—his attitude, apparently, was that, "What will come, will come," and it did not make a lot of sense to spend extra emotion on worry. Alma Rush could not take this mental desertion any longer—she was prepared and had become eager for him to go. And Larry Rosen wanted to leave. It became more clear than ever a few days after my return. I had been back at the house less than a week when Larry Rosen decided that he would stop me from doing what I loved at the time, surfing. He told me that I would have to give that surfboard away, because I would not be permitted to use it in his presence. So I said to him, "Well, I guess I won't use it in your presence—you'll just have to leave. You were able to stop me from playing hockey, but you won't stop me from surfing." He came at me with that "white anger," that tightness of face. "You talk like that to your father? You talk like that to your father?" he yelled, as he ran at me with intent to punch. This time though—and it was the only time in my life that it has ever happened, neither before or since—I stood my ground, raised my fists, saying in a controlled way, "Dad, you'd better stop, because if you come at me, I'm going to knock you down." He had never heard those words before—he was accustomed to seeing me run—and the look on my face was new to him. It was a look that said, "Please don't make me do it, because I will do it. He backed away, turned and walked into the living room. That night he offered my mom an ultimatum: "Either I go or he goes." She told him to leave, and within a couple of weeks, my father was on the road, once again heading back to his roots in Montreal, Quebec—only this time alone.

Parc Monceau

July 2nd, 2007

Sitting in Parc Monceau in Paris, the day a bit cooler than what I had dressed for, large billowing clouds and a splash of drizzle in the air. I entered the park off of Rue Rembrandt, taking about a dozen pictures of, maybe, the most architecturally evocative, atmospheric, textured corner of the world—it certainly felt that way to me. There is the curvature of the buildings, spellbinding elegance, graceful in its symmetry such that it evokes musical harmony and peace as one enters this oasis of green lawns, stone walkways meandering through the middle and eventually encircling the entire landscape, benches situated all along these walkways for people to actually sit down and reflect—they are set up just far enough apart to allow one personal space, but abundant enough to accommodate virtually anyone who would wish to find solace in this restful place. Some parks are designed for recreation and play, and though there are children with toys here, joggers

Park Monceau, Paris, as looked upon from the architecturally elegant homes and flats.

running along the pathways, it seems that this place—perhaps it is the alignment of the benches as virtually all of them catch a glimpse of the stone facades and intricately designed gold and wrought iron balconies of the flats that encircle it—is designed for excavating one's inner thoughts, then reflecting on how they fit in a world that begins in Paris, then extends to all places in one's personal geography. There is a sublime balance of energy within this park, a special chi—the Chinese term referring to flow of life force—that softens the edges and breaks down complexities into simple parts. I feel calm as I sit here, and there is an ease at the moment—one that I have not felt in quite a while. I look down at the stones on the ground, and everywhere I see a curved line running through them, showing me that within all appearances as in all thought, the world is composed of yin/yang. Every moment embraces the passive/aggressive, soft/hard, warm/cool, positive/negative, masculine/feminine, joyful and sad moments of life.

❐

In this moment, I feel sad for Sue back at home, helpless to ease her hurt. She is soft and highly sensitive inside, but her exterior attitude has been quite hard lately—she'll call to check in with me, then abruptly say that she has to go, saying, "Bye-bye," and hanging up. She does this a lot. I feel somewhat empty after that happens, and I am trying to separate myself from what she is feeling, so that I can enjoy or perhaps simply know independence of thought and emotion. This is very difficult to do after being married for 25 years.

I called her last night to tell her that I had brought Michael safely to his destination on the outskirts of Paris, a place where he will be studying modern music and technology for the rest of the month. I had left a message, which she later returned. I'd just had a glass of red wine, and was enjoying the streets when the phone rang. I couldn't get to it right away, but called back a few minutes later. I told her about the funky, sketchy area of Parisian suburbs where Michael would be staying, after which she asked how I was doing. I started to tell her, when she said that she had to go pay for something, then abruptly hung up.

I'm sure that it hurts that her two sons are over her in Europe, now that I am here taking part, while she remains by herself in San Francisco. She is working intensely in her new job as a pharmacist in charge of a retirement facility and wouldn't have been able to take this time, even if she had wanted to—though I did tell her when she took the job that, perhaps, she could inform the employers that she had a previous commitment to be in Paris with her sons. I had suggested that she take a week or more for herself and be here with Michael, getting a bit of time in Paris and with her cherished son.

Paris is her favorite city (Florence just a neck behind), and between moments with Michael, she could have taken the walks that she loves, enjoyed the coffee and reading in the cafes, being amidst the spellbinding magic of this place. But she wasn't interested—perhaps the thought of being here without romance was too painful a consideration. She wasn't interested at all, though I did try; I so much want her to be happy, to enjoy life in its richness. Sometimes I am so sad that she is sad. But I really do not think that it goes the other way very often. I do not believe that she thinks much of the grief that I feel over our marriage. She cannot be my medicine, but often, I would like to be hers. And when I try, I get pulled into a place of sadness from which it can take a few days to emerge. I strive to observe borders, to recognize limitations, but the lines are often amorphous—emotions, thoughts, feelings just spilling over like a faucet that continues to pour into an already-full glass.

❐

I know that it is often over-stated, a fantasy excessively indulged to the point of being a cliché, but I reflect on it as I sit here in this park of romance: Is there a more naturally stylish, evocative, seductive, appealing, inviting woman on this planet than the French woman? I think not. The romance of the language and its whispery inflections certainly enhance the effect, but there is something much more than that, a certain "je ne sais pas" in the smile, the glances, the toss of the hair, the simple skirt, blouse and heels that adds up to more than the sum of its parts. Some of the women, as with all nationalities, are striking—there is not a lot of subtlety to magnificently stunning women—but it is with the women that are not so obviously beautiful where the French shine. There is a difficult to grasp, almost unfathomable sexiness to so many of the French femmes that do not turn heads; it is an essence that is hard to define. I am enjoying trying to define it as I sit here in this park, luxuriating in the variety of French ladies walking past, sparks occurring in some of the exchanged glances.

I am looking at a woman sitting on a bench across the path from me to the right; I cannot take my eyes away from the way one ankle is resting on the other, white high heels, black pants that are tight at the calves, reddish brown hair catching a bit of a breeze, a sideways glance that catches my eye, then back to the book. Her sexiness is awesome. Or the woman, a while ago, short black hair, black high heels, legs straddling a motor scooter and unflinchingly staring at me as I entered the park. There was a look that I do not see anywhere else. The look was feminine and passive, but fully self-possessed. It was inviting, curious and slightly aggressive. It is a look that might keep me coming back to Paris forever.

I stop for a moment and reflect, again, on this sublime Parc Monceau. I observe the exquisite row of stone mansions and flats behind me, black wrought-iron balconies looking out on these landscaped lawns, trees and gardens. The buildings made of stone are different shades of beige and off pink. There are a few places on this planet where I have fantasized about living: the homes that overlook Hyde Park and Green Park in London from the vantage points of Knightsbridge, Mayfair, St. James; the brownstones along fifth avenue in New York City, looking down on Central Park. But as I sit here today, if there could be one wish that I might have come true—aside from the good health and happiness of those for whom I care so deeply—it would be to have at my disposal a flat overlooking this Parisian oasis. It is, I think, the most sublime of all locations.

❒

In the film, "Paris Je T'Aime," a postal worker from Denver reflects on her life and her falling in love with herself as she falls in love with Paris. It is the last and most poignantly moving of all of the short films that make up this movie's impressions of Paris life. The scene takes place in this Parc Monceau. And as I sit here today, reflecting on it all as a group of small children look at me curiously, glancing at what I am writing, I realize that aside from the tough stuff that it takes to survive—hard work, dealing with bosses and clients—life is simple. Yet, for it to remain simple, one must practice the simple things—taking enough time to sit in a quiet space and hear one's thoughts, perhaps allowing a long glance at that woman with the high heels whose style is, essentially, incomprehensible. And, of course, all that we have on this earth is ourselves and one another—and to be a gift to the other, we really must allow ourselves to love ourselves. We can find inspiration on any park bench in any patch of green in the world—today as I get up and walk into the streets of Paris, I was given the gift of Parc Monceau.

≈

July 4th, 2007

I am on a train from Paris to Milan, from which I will catch another train that will take me to Florence. Last night I had dinner at a restaurant just off of Boulevard St. Michelle, in the Latin Quarter, with Michael and a friend from Oberlin who is studying with him at a studio in the sketchy outskirts of Paris; there is some genius in the field of musical technology that has drawn them there, but the area definitely made me nervous when I left him. As borderline as this suburb appears, I remind myself that people simply do not resort to violent crime in France or in Europe as easily as occurs in any American city.

I have spoken to several people who have admonished me for letting my sons travel to Europe this summer. "You're letting them go to Europe," they say, "Don't you know how dangerous it is over there?" I'm not about to get into arguments over this; I usually calmly answer that, "They will be fine, just because it is foreign doesn't mean it's more dangerous than America." "To the contrary," I add, "Europeans have more to fear when they send their sons and daughters to American streets for the summer." In any event, the school is located in a "questionable area" of Paris's outskirts, but as questionable as it might seem in Paris, it would feel quite tame if it were America. He'll be fine, no doubt; I just have some work to do to control my anxiety.

The food that we enjoyed at the restaurant last night was excellent. I had vibes that it would be good—it was the only one in the Quarter where there was a line waiting outside. We shared a bottle of Bordeaux—the waiter said that it was their finest red—and it went down like pure elegance. I told Michael that if he plays piano or composes music to the excellence of this wine, then he is definitely going places. The friend—a really friendly girl buddy of his from Oberlin—delighted in the wine and meal; she was really appreciative to have the opportunity to dine at a place like this on a school budget, the newness and joy of the experience present in her eyes. It was special to be with two intelligent young people, so appreciative of the experience they were having. It was a thrill for me to be with them, and it was especially nice—given that I had been to Paris several times in my life—to watch them take it in for the first time. After a couple of glasses of wine, Michael blurted out that, "this city is amazing; I've never been to a place where an entire city is set up for people to have fun." Indeed, Paris does seem that way much of the time. It is a gift when the heaviness lifts, and everything feels light. The stiffness of the neck is gone, and one cannot feel the heavy pack that is ever-present on the shoulders—so much so that we take the weight for granted. But I felt that way during this dinner with Michael and friend; I was with my son in Paris, and we were enjoying one another very much. Life had given us this unexpected gift, and it was ours to enjoy.

Close Encounters

I met Michael at Heathrow Airport in London about a week ago. He flew in from New York after attending his Walden composition reunion in New Hampshire. I had flown directly from San Francisco. Even though Michael's plane had been delayed several hours due to lightning in New York, and he arrived several hours after I did, though he had been scheduled to arrive a few hours before me, he was raring to go when he got off that plane. He was eager to hear some music and have a pint or two. So after checking into our hotel, located just a few blocks from Piccadilly Circus, in the West End, I led him over to Soho, where we had a sub-par Chinese meal (he was certain that he would have selected a better restaurant). I led him to Soho for a reason—it is the neighborhood of Ronnie Scott's Club, one of the best, most intimate jazz clubs in the world. I didn't know if there would be any tickets available for anyone playing that night, but I was delighted to discover that we were just in time to see—and there were just a couple of tickets remaining—Tower of Power. I am not a big fan of funk, but I wasn't going to turn down an opportunity to see these "world class funksters" from my own back yard, the Bay Area. And they did not disappoint. They played what they play very well—"You're still a young man," "What is Hip," and so on—and Michael genuinely appreciated their talents. I was surprised that he had never heard of "Tower of Power" before; I thought everyone had at least heard of that name. I told him that I had actually dated one of the singers of this group when I first moved to San Francisco in 1979. He wanted to know if she was "hot," and I answered, "Yes, very, a little too hot to go out with more than a few times." I had a couple of glasses of wine at the show, the jet lag starting to kick in, while Michael seemed unfazed by a couple of pints of lager. Tired, dazed, but feeling quite happy we made our way out of Soho, up Piccadilly and to our hotel at Waterloo Place.

We slept soundly until I was awakened by a phone call from my sister, Heidi. She was nervous and wanted to know if I was aware of the news regarding London. She had just turned on the news, and CNN was showing a whole section of London that had been cordoned off due to police finding a car loaded with enough explosives to kill more than a thousand people. The section that she was describing sounded like our neighborhood—she mentioned the Trocadero, and I knew that we were just around the corner from that spot. I looked out the window to discover that the whole area around the hotel had been blocked off to traffic—there was an odd quiet for this busy a section of London. I called the front desk after watching CNN for a while, and they informed me that much of the area was being searched by bomb squad experts, and that if we were leaving the hotel, various detours would have to be taken. I woke up Michael to show him what was going on, a serious awakening after the previous night's careless enjoyment. We exited the hotel a little while later, seeing first hand the international reporters describing the scene and interviewing various onlookers. Literally about 100 yards from the hotel was the car, a Mercedes that was being hauled away, that had held the explosives. The car, apparently, had been parked there about 2:00 A.M., and we had walked down that very alley coming back from Ronnie Scotts about an hour and a half before that. The news reported that an emergency medical crew had been summonsed to the nightclub beside which this car had been parked. A woman had taken ill in the nightclub, and on arriving, they discovered smoke coming from the Mercedes. As we looked on this cordoned off street, the car being readied to be hauled away for inspection, fear was palpable in the air. I told Michael that the official report is that the emergency crew discovered the car "in the nick of time" due to the woman taking sick, but that I knew the real story. The real story, I told him, is that his grandmother, Alma Lorraine Rush, or "Tudy" as he had called her when he was a child, created the sickness in the girl, this summoned the emergency crew which discovered the smoke that she caused to be observed. And you know what? There is a part of me that believes this.

Later that day there were more road closings; Park Lane was closed due to the discovery of another bomb across the street at Hyde Park. Then there was news that a Trafalgar Square parking garage was closed due to suspicious packages. Everywhere we walked, Piccadilly, Regent Street, Oxford Street, there were shrieking alarms of police, fire and rescue vehicles. Later that night, the news stations were filled with the story of the terrorist who had tried to drive a car bomb into the entrance to the Glasgow,

Scotland, Airport. The media that were congregating just a few yards to the front of our hotel were now broadcasting details to the world of the new events in Glasgow.

Going out for a walk that evening, Michael back in the room enjoying room service, I stopped in front of the truck that was the transmitter for several international broadcasts. There was a very attractive NBC reporter, blond and elegant—the engineer told me that she was a Canadian broadcaster working for that station. The BBC was reporting, as was the CBC and the Aussie broadcasting station. However it was that sublime Canadian reporter who really got to me. I didn't see a ring on her finger—so I was tempted to linger for a while and see if we might talk. As she left she gave me a sort of sweet glance and smile, turning her head toward me, then walking straight toward an escorted Mercedes limousine. Her hair blew softly and sweetly across her face as she got into the car, a quick acceleration and she was off. I wandered away with thoughts of fantasy—what might have been, what could have been—and worked my way into the throng of people that is Piccadilly Circus.

It was a day of aborted terror in London, and no doubt the intention behind these attempts was to send a message to the new Prime Minister—Brown had just replaced Blair as Prime Minister—that he had better review his Iraq policy. The objective was to intimidate the new government, affect its policies. Intimidation of governments, political terror, has become oddly familiar to me recently.

❐

Last September, before our separation, when the struggle to stay together was becoming too difficult for the two of us to endure, I took a trip to Thailand to get away. I have a doctor friend in Bangkok, an American guy who practices medicine and runs a clinic that brings medical relief into the developing world. On one particular night he brought me to one of those delicious parts of town that men often think of when they think of Bangkok, a street known as Soi Cowboy. Beautiful Thai women were performing unusual and seductive treats onstage, some of which I had never even heard of before, like creating the sound of firecrackers from between their thighs, a trace of gunpowder lingering in the air. During the stage entertainment, women were making the rounds, erotically slithering into the laps of the gentlemen in the audience. The beers were going down well, when I looked up at the overhead television monitor to see a newsflash come over the screen, which was turned to CNN. "Crisis in Thailand," it read.

Given that I had a few beers in my system, and this very scantily clad, outrageously feminine woman was doing her best to make herself known to me, I didn't take the message all that seriously. I was conscious of it, but assigned it to a computer file that I did not need at the moment. But then another news flash occurred, a silky Thai girl encircling my lap, doing her best to distract me from the news. This time, I was more focused on world events. This was a picture of tanks moving through the streets of Bangkok, the very Bangkok where I now sat, the caption reading, "Military junta seizes control of Thailand; Bangkok in crisis." In

Prior to my separation from Sue, I went to Thailand for some meditation. There was a coup d'etat during my visit.

the scene, tanks were following one after the other, stern-faced soldiers atop them, the streets damp with a steady drizzle. I shook my doctor friend, Eric, snapping him out of the trance into which he had fallen due to the deliciously sexy women who were surrounding him. "Eric, look at the screen, there is a military junta taking place outside!" "Wow," he said, "that is just a few blocks away. Goodness! I can't believe it. I've been in countries before a coup, and in countries after a coup, but never during a coup." I was filled with equal parts apprehension and excitement. It seemed almost, not quite, but almost, astonishing to me that nobody in this place was aware of, or perhaps, cared about, what was going on outside. Nero was fiddling while Rome was burning, only it was happening in Bangkok.

Within about an hour we left the club. Eric lived nearby, while I had to find a taxi to take me across town to the Oriental Hotel by the river. The streets were wet and empty, except for a row of taxis and very pretty women, who Eric informed me were men. The whole scene was exotic and surreal—what the hell was I doing in Bangkok I wondered. The streets were deserted, except for a few people leaving the bars in the middle of a coup. As I looked for a cab, I was being checked out by a row of gorgeous women, absolutely too beautiful to be men. Eric assured me that I would be just fine getting back, that all of the taxis would be safe. But how did he know, and how could I know for sure. I'd never been in a military junta before. I didn't want to be taken to some military outpost. I reviewed the row of taxis, asking each driver if he spoke English. Suddenly, everything was looking a bit suspicious to me, seeing a bit of strangeness in the smile of every driver who didn't speak English. "God, isn't there any cab driver who speaks English?" I uttered under my breath, Eric probably comfortably at home by now. Finally I found a guy, a smiling face, goodness everyone smiles brightly in Thailand, I think I'd have liked a frown by about then. "The Oriental Hotel, please," I asked. He nodded his head in agreement

Thailand wasn't just the coup. Here I am experiencing some very peaceful moments.

As the driver brought me across town, I started to recognize some of the sites I had seen when I started out pre-coup, several hours earlier to see Eric. "Okay, I can relax," I thought. When I got back to the hotel, there were several messages from Sue wanting to know if I was safe. She was scared that westerners would be prime targets for the Muslim general who had seized control of the government, and that my being Jewish and western might make me a likely candidate for being rounded up and put away. I called back to say I was all right, and I also returned the calls of my two brothers, Jeff and Elliot, who only knew what they saw on CNN, specifically that Bangkok was under siege. I assured them that I was fine and that I had no intention of interrupting my trip and leaving Thailand. "I'll come back early only if it is really necessary, really, really necessary," I assured everyone. I stayed in Thailand nearly two weeks, eventually making my way up to Chiang Mai to the north, an area of lush tropical flora, a night market where the air is intoxicating, with the sweetest-smelling coconut I had ever encountered, fruits whose names I cannot remember but whose flavors I will never forget for their ability to stimulate sheer bliss, and gemstones said to be mined right there in the area of the hill people, gorgeous pieces of jade, from the deepest greens to the richest lavenders. The area is dotted with hillside Buddhist shrines and temples, and religious relics eventually make their way into your hands, the convincing stall keepers assuring that some are several hundred years old.

I stayed at the Four Seasons resort just outside of Chiang Mai, an idyllic Shangri-La of serene tropical grounds, with pathways that lead one to hidden benches where one cannot help but hear one's own thoughts and confront what lies within. There is nothing to intercept your thoughts here, no exotic dancers or religious temptations. Just pure quiet and being alone. And, indeed, it was quiet, probably even quieter than it should have been—apparently more than 70 percent of the expected tourists had cancelled due to the coup, and I felt very much alone. Thus, there was no need to make reservations at the spa here, and so I just walked into a place where the body was treated as a temple housing the soul. My feet were bathed in flowers, and I was given a ginger tea that tasted as though I was swimming in a pool of pure ginger sweetened with honey. The massage, not the traditional stretching Thai massage, was sensual to the point of transcendence, but it wasn't sexy. The hands caressed until I felt as though I had taken leave of my body, so immersed was I in my senses. It was just amazing.

❐

As it turned out, that massage was the last that I would truly enjoy of that trip to Thailand. That night when I went to bed, I was overcome with a fever of 103, and an ache in the body that I couldn't understand. My back hurt with a kind of pain and ache that was unfamiliar to me; it covered all of it, and I simply could not move from the bed. I could not get up to brush my teeth, wash my face, or lock the door to the room. I could not move at all. I knew the temperature was 103 because I sat up and dialed the phone, asking that they bring a thermometer. They did so, and were so kindly concerned for me. A few hours later they sent someone by to make sure I was all right, and the next day, they arranged, without my asking for it, for a doctor to visit. It was not a respiratory virus he said, but a total body flu, not uncommon for first time visitors to this area, but my temperature had been higher than most. Prior to the doctor visiting, I called my doctor friend, Eric, in Bangkok. "Welcome to the club," he slightly jokingly offered me. "This is what happens to westerners when they come over here for the first time—I see it all the time. You either have food poisoning or just a nasty case of the flu, I'd bet the latter, since you are not throwing up. Get the hotel to go out and get you a week's worth of Cipro and take it," he suggested. "I never go into the bush without it." "I've got some," I answered, "My doctor in San Francisco gave me a prescription before I left." "Smart doctor," he said. "Hey Bruce, you woke me up; I'm going back to bed. Call me when you get back to Bangkok." "If I get back to Bangkok, Eric." "Naw, don't worry about it Brucie boy, it won't kill you. You'll be okay. In a few days. Going back to bed," Eric said, clearly yawning. "See you if I can, when I get back to Bangkok," I replied.

That flu was severe and for the next few days the best that I could do was get some soup or an egg down, and by the time I got back to Bangkok I was in no mood for revelry. It was almost as though my body had said to me in Chiang Mai, especially after the serenity of the massage, "This is where you are going to slow down to a virtual stop. You went away for reflection and to be alone with your thoughts and this is where it is going to happen, right here in this Shangri-La where no harm can come to you." Indeed, it did work out that way.

The humidity and the fever slowed my body to a standstill, and as does happen during high fevers, the mind entered a dimension where the pace of thinking had become altogether different from its usual course.

Life was moving in slow motion, and as I lay in this condition it became clear to me—as thoughts sometimes become clear during periods of fasting for me during Yom Kippur, the Hebrew day of atonement—the reason that I lay in this far-away place in Thailand, entirely by myself: it had to do with surrender, truly surrendering to loneliness and fear. In so doing, I could feel the essence of myself pouring out through my pores. It was among the sickest and most lonely I had ever felt, those moments when I could not move in this beautiful Shangri-La, but I don't know when I'd ever felt more myself. At that moment I felt kindness and tenderness for myself, and I realized that I truly respect and love myself, that I do my best to be there for everyone as I strive to gain a bit of freedom to encounter this world and make sense of it.

As I lay there it occurred to me that an observer might find me a bit delirious as my mind drifted and my mouth mumbled thoughts and realizations in an abbreviated shorthand, not complete ideas. I was aware that I was mumbling, and with this self-consciousness I became a bit scared, "My God, I don't want to die alone in this hotel room in Thailand." But I recognized the need to surrender on a very deep level, and as I did this, I cut through the fear. In this state of mind, truly a kind of lightness of being, it all made sense: the relationship with "M," the strain of our marriage that was causing so much pain, the love that I felt to the core of my being for Sue and the boys, and yet the struggle to be free, all made sense as I drifted in and out of wakefulness.

❒

The train bound for Italy from Paris is moving quickly at the moment, passing through fields that are too green for the middle of summer, landscape dotted with farmhouses and granite cliffs off in the distance, as I contemplate that first night of the flu in Chiang Mai. I don't ever want to feel that sick again, but it is an experience that I would not want to trade. That fever burned into me with a sense of self, and I will never forget it.

It is important to note that Bangkok is much more than Soi Cowboy. The smiles that I encountered throughout this city, even by the soldiers sitting atop tanks, were gracious and dignified. The people are raised from a young age to smile, and it is disarming, putting one at ease. Eric, hard-core realist that he is, says that there are things going on beneath some of those smiles that you wouldn't want to know; be that as it may, I still contend that I have never seen a people more self-effacing and generous with kindness and courtesy than the Thai people during my short stay. It is called "the Land of a Thousand Smiles," and I can see why.

Bangkok is truly a wonder to behold. It comes at you and confronts the senses in every way. The Golden Buddhist Temples and Shrines are everywhere, and the food is amazing, even the mom-and-pop restaurants putting one into a Thai wonderland of flavors. An experience that is indelible for me, and this occurred when I arrived in Bangkok, before the trip to Chiang Mai, is a ride on a barge up the river. In a matter of just a few minutes outside of Bangkok we moved past tropical fruit plantations, golden-domed temples visible alongside cabins built on stilts, roofs made of sticks or corrugated tin, meditative incense wafting from either side of the river, as the water laps meditatively against the sides of the boat. Heading up the river, the barge deviates; the water is not always deep enough to make its way up some very narrow, shallow locks. Now the tropical fruit plantations are densely lush on either side, and the scent of mangos, passion fruit, bananas, and other types of sweetness that I do not recognize is everywhere.

The boat docks near the end of this lock, and we make our way into a Buddhist temple, small but ornately designed with golden images of the Buddha and a Golden Pagoda dome, which is slightly hidden by mango trees. Taking my shoes off, I walk to the back of the Temple, where I see a young man, maybe 15 years old, deep in thought, studying a text as he writes notes. He has the shaved head of a young monk. I gaze at him, then down at the text, trying to gain a glimpse of what he is reading, then others come around him as well. But he remains impassive, unaffected or distracted. He wears the look of a young Buddha, neither a smile nor a frown, and as I look at him, I want to bring some of that serenity to my own life. Will he be so serene at 51? I cannot say. But there is an inner calm within him that will last a lifetime, I'm sure.

The train speeds toward the granite cliffs that a few minutes ago seemed quite far away; we have moved out of the pastures and vineyards and into some rugged territory, though not extremely mountainous. We are somewhere in the south of France, but not quite to the coast. I'm thinking back now to what my sister, Heidi, said to me when I got back to her in London, after she woke me up that morning to tell me of the terror plot that had been aborted. "What is it with you," she said to me, "can't you go to a place where there is quiet and no danger?" "I don't know, Heidi," I answered, "I guess I'm just drawn to the action. By the way, I think Mom defused that bomb." "I think you are right," she answered, "I'm sure you're right."

The train moves swiftly as we find ourselves amidst serene, green pastureland, sheep, horses and cows grazing as it approaches these sheer faces of the cliffs. As we get closer, these cliffs are steeper and more rugged than what I would have thought from a distance. Then, all of a sudden, we are in a forest with waterfalls, and if I didn't know that I was in France, someone might have convinced me that we were in the geography leading to Yosemite. Just gorgeous scenery as we make our way past a village where all is stone. First we are greeted by the church, the bell in the hardened rock bell tower ringing at the moment; now we approach a school, then the center of the village. Thoughts are pouring through my consciousness like a quickly moving stream, held together by a centered source that is Bruce Farrell Rosen.

❒

The Herald Tribune reports that Barry Bonds is still stuck at 750 home runs, five shy of catching Henry Aaron. My prediction is that he'll do it sometime in the early part of August. I'm returning to San Francisco on the 11th of July, and I do not know at this moment if Bonds was selected to the all-star game to be played in San Francisco on the 10th. I would have attended that game if I were coming back a day earlier, but I shall not complain. The time is moving very rapidly, and these days of letting my mind wander will conclude much too quickly.

I am not in a hurry to return to my desk, where this subprime mortgage fiasco is proving to be a contagion that is undermining foreign as well as domestic banks. I just read of a German bank that invested heavily in the speculative securities secured by these mortgages that is on the verge of failing, if it does not receive a bailout by the country's banking industry.

The fallout from these subprime mortgages, where lenders basically gave away variable interest rate money—loans where the rates are escalating quickly due to the Fed raising rates several months ago—to unqualified buyers with virtually nothing down in deposit, is that high-quality mortgage bonds, corporate bonds, U.S.

Government agency bonds, are plummeting in value as the market flees to the safety of U.S. Treasury securities. People are defaulting on these subprime loans to the tune of something like 20 percent of all of this type of debt, and there is panic out there among corporations, banks and insurance companies.

These entities have basically no idea how much of this troubled debt is in their investment portfolios, and the chaos could get worse before it gets better. Banks made these loans to people, thinking that if they made a mistake in lending, the escalating real estate values would bail them out. But nothing, including real estate, goes up in value indefinitely, and once again we witness another round where greed got the best of good judgment and common sense. The problem is that as bankers of the baby boom generation age, they are being replaced by young bankers without an appreciation for risk. The Savings and Loan Crisis of the early 1990s, the stock market crash of 1987, where the market lost 20 percent of its value in a few days, are distant history to many of them.

They remember the dot com boom and bust, but real estate values soared after that as the Fed cut rates in the aftermath of September 11, 2001. Money became virtually free; and conservative thinking was just thrown out the window. I specialize in bonds, all types of conservative bonds, particularly tax-free issues. These high quality issues are getting hit as investors start selling in fear; many of these sellers are large institutions that need to raise money fast, in case the reserves tumble to unacceptable levels. When I get back I'll focus on that; so while I'd like to go to the all-star game, I will enjoy the delicious remaining moments of this train journey through Europe.

❒

My thoughts move quickly, in sync with the speed of this fast moving train. I'm thinking of baseball again, and the game I saw just before leaving for this trip. The New York Yankees were in town on the weekend, and I caught the Saturday game. It was the first time since 1962 that the Yankees had visited San Francisco, when the Yanks defeated the Giants in seven games, considered by some the greatest World Series ever played. I went to that Saturday game with a sports buddy, Phil Barbieri. We have sat next to each other at San Francisco 49er games since I acquired my seats in 1982, the beginning of the Bill Walsh, Joe Montana era. Phil and his father, Phil, Sr., had their seats long before I acquired mine, dating back to early 1960s when the 49ers played their games at the old, backbreaking, wooden-benched Kezar Stadium in the city. Together the two Phils, myself, Sue and my boys experienced, perhaps, the greatest quarterback and football dynasty of all time (Packer fans might disagree), Joe Montana, Bill Walsh and the San Francisco 49ers. Joe Montana walked on air; he had an uncanny ability, an unbelievable instinct, to sense when pressure was about to devour him, adroitly stepping up at the last microsecond to find a second, third, fourth target downfield. And, of course, he had some phenomenal targets: Dwight Clark, Freddie Solomon, Roger Craig, John Taylor, Jerry Rice. On the other side of the ball, the Niners had, probably, the greatest defensive back of all time, Ronnie Lott. Thus I witnessed with the Barbieris some of the greatest football of all time, replete with the all-time best quarterback, Mr. Montana, the absolute best wide-receiver ever, Jerry Rice, and Mr. Lott on defense.

My seats are close to the field and I saw Lott make some hits that were sheer grace in the way a guided missile might look beautiful. I do not know how some of those guys ever got up after being hit by him. The Montana era became the Steve Young era, and the coach shifted from the charismatic genius of Bill Walsh, to the cerebral, stoic, no-nonsense George Seifert. And we won another world championship. Steve Young had to wait behind Montana for several years to get his chance, and then he became a Hall of Fame quarterback. Two Hall of Fame quarterbacks in a row! What an amazing time to go to 49er football games.

Phil's dad treated me like a son when we would sit together at the games. He had been a butcher during his career at Safeway markets, and he always had with him a delicious Italian sandwich, which he would always offer to share with me. On a warm day, he would tell me that it was good that I was at the game, because I had to get rid of that "office pallor." He'd put his arm around me as we watched Montana warm up on the sidelines before the opening kickoff, asking me about the investment market, the economy, my opinions as to the political situation at the time. He loved Ronald Reagan, just like he adored Joe Montana, but he couldn't warm up to the first George Bush, just like he never quite accepted Steve Young after Joe Montana. We'd talk and then watch football, and we met at these games rain or shine.

There was one game when the 49ers were playing the Miami Dolphins when we, Phil, Phil and myself, sat through, probably, the wettest game in 49er history. There was a torrential downpour, the field and parking lots underwater. We stayed for the whole game, knowing we were being macho for doing so, but telling one another that we had to be totally crazy. The elder Phil died a couple of years back, just as the 49ers were beginning their descent to football oblivion, may he rest in peace.

Phil junior went with me to this Yankee game, his first baseball game of the season. His mother had died within the last year, and he hadn't been that motivated to attend public events. He tries not to show it, but the grief is all over his face. We sat in the first row behind home plate, gaining an unobstructed view of Yankee players that I never get a chance to see in person. There is a distinct contrast between Alex Rodriquez and Derek Jeter, two players who will be in the Hall of Fame five years after they retire, unless there are startling revelations that appear, which is the case so often these days. I don't have the sense that anything like that will happen to these guys. Jeter has that sweet, dimpled smile, and he gets cute with the crowd, enjoying the banter, a bit of give and take, the demeanor one of a classy elegance. Studying him in the on-deck circle, one is aware of a kind of baseball royalty. Rodriquez also exudes a quality of Baseball Royal Family, but his status is Baronial to the Princely nature of Jeter. It is an interesting study to watch Alex Rodriguez in the on-deck circle, staring directly ahead, always in full, handsome, chiseled profile, as he swings a series of bats to loosen up. He is clearly aware that eyes are on him as he gets loose, but he does his best to not glance at the onlookers. He is taller than I would have thought, and is pure fluidity in motion. His gait is as smooth as they come, and he is a phenomenal-looking athlete. The women, no doubt, are hypnotized by this guy. A-Rod hit a home run to the deepest part of the ballpark, straight away center field, in the eighth inning to tie the game, but the Giants finally won it in the 13th on a bloop single. Amazingly, the Giants took two out of three from the Yankees that weekend, one of the few series they have won all year. But these Yankees are not the same Yankees as in the recent past, sitting four games below 500. However, I have a suspicion that when all is said and done, Joe Torre will have these guys in the playoffs again. I think they just got a bit bored and need the pressure to get themselves going. Torre is probably in his final season, and I adore the man. Yankee fans are so lucky to have had this guy around for so long. I remember him as a kid growing up, addicted to baseball and my idol Sandy Koufax. Torre was always one of those solid durable guys, and the moment that you might take him for granted at the plate, he'd put his team ahead with a double up the alley, driving in two runs. I love listening to Torre talk baseball, and it was a thrill to see him right in front of me as I sat in that first row behind the plate. Torre is also a member of Baseball's Royal Family, a military commander and a member of the Baseball House of Lords.

❐

I am on way to Florence now, just out of Milan, and I am looking forward to eventually meeting up with Jonathan and the boys. I'll be in Florence for a few days, then on to Portofino where I will charter a boat and meet the guys in Cinque Terre for lunch and a few hours on the Mediterranean. I expect they'll enjoy the ride, after the last month of hostels and cafeteria fare. Jonathan, though, pulled a fast one on me a few days ago.

I spoke too soon when I said he was keeping me well informed. A few nights after Michael and I had arrived in London, I had this strange feeling that something had changed with Jonathan's trip; my antennae were picking up something, and I didn't know what it was. But I just couldn't relax, laying awake all night long focusing on something that seemed irregular about their trip. I knew that something was up. I initially felt that my apprehension was fueled by the nervousness in London at the time, but there was something else to this feeling, something distinct from what was happening in the background. They were supposed to have arrived in Florence, but after my night of lying awake all night, I called the hotel where they were supposed to be staying. The attendant said that three boys had checked in not four, and the names of the three boys were Jonathan's traveling mates, but he was not on the list. Fear started running through me; I tried to reach him once, twice, three times and more on his cell phone, but there was no answer. This had become a very unpleasant morning for me, and I was quite stressed after a night of no sleep. Finally, to my great relief, he did answer! "Where are you, Jonathan? I called your hotel in Florence, and your had friends checked in but not you!" Memories of my mom finally speaking to me, when I reached her from Moline, Illinois, the end of my railroad journey. "I'm playing my guitar, writing a song, and my feet are dangling over the pier here in Venice," he answered. "I came to see Ana, I had to see her. Otherwise I won't get a chance to see her until the end of the summer, and right after that I have to go away to college," he answered. His beautiful girlfriend Ana has introduced him to a lot of new music; it is so great when the woman you like can turn you on to interesting, exciting new music, it is very sexy, particularly some rare Bob Dylan, and had kept him anchored during the difficult emotional year of our separation.

"I didn't sleep last night," he went on to tell me, "because there was a family with a sick child that would have had to stand. So I gave them my seat, and I slept in the aisle."

"Jonathan, that makes two of us who didn't sleep last night," I responded, relieved that he was okay. "Your dad is really psychic," I continued, "I couldn't sleep at all last night; I knew something was up. I was very nervous. "You always get nervous, Dad," he answered. "This time more than usual, this was a different kind of feeling. I am really relieved that you are all right, Jonathan; I'm not going to give you a hard time. But this was a breach of our contract. You said that you'd keep me informed, and you didn't. I had to find out for myself, the hard way. It would have been fine with me, if you had told me that you were going to take a detour to Venice. I would have arranged for you to have a place to go to when you arrive, just in case Ana didn't arrive." "I have the name and address of a good hostel, and I have money, so you don't have to worry. But I am sorry that I didn't tell you. There is just no way that I wasn't going to come to see her."

"Jonathan, I wouldn't have tried to stop you. But we had an agreement, and in the future I expect you to be honest with me. I have to be able to trust you." "Can we talk about this later, dad? I'm really tired and I'm writing a song." "No problem, sweetie, no problem. Just keep your phone charged so that I can reach you from time to time. And please be sure to let me know when you catch the train to rejoin your friends. Are you meeting them back in Florence?" "Yeah, Dad, I'll be sure to call you and let you know." I love you sweetie," I answered. "I love you very, very much; have a great time with Ana, and please call me when she arrives. And call me if you need help with anything."

As I am saying this, I am aware of how my father would have treated me, if he had discovered this sort of breach. First of all, I'd never be here in the first place, if he had been home when I was 18, and secondly, I would have been threatened to no end if I had ever somehow made it here. Just as I thought the conversation was over and was ready to hit the disconnect button, I heard, "Dad, I do want to tell you something. I want you to know that I did try to call you when I arrived here in Venice. My phone ran out of battery, and you should have seen me, tired, a guitar on my back, my hair long and straggly, sneaking into little cafes to find an outlet for my charger. I would find one in a place and plug the cord into it, then the owner would give me a weird look. So after just a few minutes I would leave. I kept trying to sneak into place after place, trying not to be observed so that I could charge the phone to call you." This admission brought tears to my eyes, listening to his tired voice, sweet and soft, telling me this story. I could imagine what he looked like. It reminded me of when I looked into the mirror for the first time after hopping those freights. "Jonathan, I just love you; I totally love you. Have a good time; just call me." I was proud of how I spoke to my son, and given how protective I had been during his growing up years, I honored myself in that moment for being able to let go.

A couple of days later, Jonathan called me upon leaving Venice, and then again when he met up with his friends in Florence. He had had a magical time with Ana and her family, gondola rides through the tiny canals, as they meander alongside the greens and reds of the apartments, whose balconies have witnessed so many sighs of love and bewilderment in the past several hundred years. He needed to take a trip like this, and I am glad that it happened for him, despite myself.

❒

In about an hour or so we'll be arriving in Florence. The sun is starting to wane over this Tuscan countryside, bathing the rolling hills, vineyards and villages of beige and terra cotta in a pinkish hue; an interesting couple, a retired school teacher and the principal she married just offered me a glass of Tuscan white from a recently opened bottle. Nice people this couple; they are continuing on to Rome. Part of me wishes that I could keep going. Though I am looking forward to Florence, I really don't want to stop. It would be nice to keep sipping the wine with this couple.

They are African Americans from Oakland; and the conductor has just come by to tell them that they are talking too loud. I was talking with them; but he didn't look at me. Is that because I am white? I hope not. But I felt slightly embarrassed for them, though they didn't show any fluster. Perhaps they have just grown up with this sort of nonsense all their life. But this bothered me. "You guys aren't talking loudly at all," I offered, "What's up with this guy—he doesn't like the sound of people?" "Ah don't worry about it," the somewhat rotund elder gentleman, balding with full gray at the temples, said to me, his voice deep, hoarse and profound. "All right," I said, "I just don't like it when people can't let others be," I responded. "The world is filled with people like that, and you'll go crazy if you get mad at all of them or try to fix them all," he replied. "Yeah, you're right," I said.

"You've been writing here for quite a while, are you writing a book?" "Indeed I am," I answered. "What is it about?" his wife wanted to know. She was quite pretty, middle aged, full-breasted and quite charming. She was about 12 to 15 years younger than he, and I can see why he fell for her, and she for him. "It's about my life, a memoir of growing up," I answered. "Are you a published writer?" she continued. "I have never published a book, but I have published articles and essays," I answered. "Do you do that full time?" he wanted to know. "By day I manage money, and in my free time, I write. This is something that I have wanted to do for a long time; circumstances have presented themselves now that I am able to write this piece." "So tell me a bit about some of the things that you have written," he wanted to know. "Well I have written editorials and opinions for a number of Bay Area papers. When the Bill Clinton, Monica Lewinsky scandal broke, a piece that I wrote, "Mr. Clinton, a Time For Honesty," was published in the San Francisco Chronicle. They have run other opinion pieces of mine as well. I write an occasional column on business for a monthly. And a few years ago, I wrote and recorded a series of 'slice of life essays' for the BBC. They really enjoyed those stories." As they continued to drink their wine, they became more and more interested in me. "How did the BBC thing happen?" he wanted to know. "Well, I was very moved by the death of Princess Diana, I absolutely adored her, so I wrote a poetic piece about her that was published with her picture in the Chronicle. I sent it to the BBC, eventually hearing from someone that wanted to read it on the air; they were asking my permission. Of course I gave it. This conversation led to a brainstorming session a few weeks later, and the producer asked if I would write a sort of pilot essay, from which others might follow, if it was liked. Well, they kept asking me for more, so we did about 12. I recorded them on a special line they set up, and eventually I went over to the BBC studios and recorded several in the studio next to where the Beatles played before coming to America. Boy that was hallowed ground," I went on. "I lived through the Beatles as a kid growing up; to take a tour of the room where they recorded for the country, and to record essays that I wrote, which would be broadcast all over the country and the world was an incredible feeling." "Can't wait to read the book when it comes out," he said. "Well, hopefully that will happen someday," I answered. "Going through some tough stuff right now, and I am writing about it," said I as I took in about the fourth good sip of this tasty wine.

"Any other stuff you like to write about, what about sports?" he said. "I love sports, most sports," I answered. "And, perhaps the favorite thing that I have written is about Sandy Koufax. He was my boyhood idol. A Jewish athlete, probably the greatest pitcher of all time—I looked up to him, almost like a father figure. It was during the baseball strike several years ago, and to fill the space where baseball normally would appear, stations played classic games. I happened to turn on the T.V. and I stumbled upon a game from my childhood. Koufax was pitching, and the game was being announced in a serious, important way, there was a gravitas to the event; a second or two later, I could see the big number 32 on the back, as Koufax went into his wind-up. "Strike three," exclaimed the announcer. He had just retired the side, and I think it was Harmon Killebrew who had just gone down. At the commercial, we were being told that we were watching game seven of the 1965 World Series, Dodgers against Twins. But I had already figured that out. It was the most important game of my childhood. I knew instantly what game that was. The footage was in a grainy black and white, and after the break, the greatest baseball announcer of all time, at least to my mind, came on to call the action, it was Vin Scully. Apparently each team's announcer would alternate calling the game for the national audience; now it was Scully's turn. I live in San Francisco, so I don't often get a chance to hear Vin call a game, but I sure wish that I could hear him more often. His voice, that echoing, resonating intonation, just fills me with memories, and when I heard him calling this game, my childhood came pouring through me. I was the class president, so I was afforded the opportunity to listen to this game during class—as you know, they were day games then in the World Series—then dutifully go up to the board to draw the score into a box for each inning. I was the only kid in the class who knew what was happening in the game, but I wasn't allowed to tell until after the inning, and any kid that disturbed me would be sent out of the room. And, of course, the kids were interested; this was L.A., where we were living. Koufax had pitched that game on two-days' rest, and it wasn't known until just moments before game time if Koufax or Drysdale would be pitching. The skipper, Walter Alston, announced to the team that the 'Lefty' would be going today—Drysdale was told to be ready. The Dodgers won that game, and on the T.V., the champagne flowed at the end. What a game that was to watch again. I wrote a piece about it, and it was published by a weekly Marin county paper. I sent it to them, since I was living in Marin at the time. A friend of mine who read the article suggested that I send it to the Baseball Hall of Fame Museum, which I did. I really didn't expect anything to happen. But about a week after sending it in, I received a phone call from the director of the Hall of Fame, asking if it would be all right if they published it in a newsletter. He told me that it would go out to all the members of the Hall, including Sandy. Wow! This was something that I did not expect. Eventually,

Sandy Koufax came to San Francisco on an autograph show. I was out of town at the time, but a friend of mine took my piece to him to be signed. So, now, I have on my wall my article as published in the magazine, with Koufax's signature on it. I treasure that. So, there you have it." "Great story," they said in unison. "Don't write so much that you don't enjoy yourself while you're here, gotta have a good time," he advised. "I'll take that to heart," I answered. What a fun, thoughtful couple; he took my card and plans to call when they get back to Oakland. I do hope that he does.

❒

It is the fourth of July, and I am thinking a lot about Sue. Though we are separated, our bond is thicker than boundaries. I hope that she is okay today—a holiday. Her family is here in Europe, and she is, no doubt, in a weird place emotionally. I just want her to be all right, to enjoy the day. I'll call her when I arrive in Florence. On this train there are several couples sitting side by side, a shared comradery as they discuss their lives, reveling in the pleasure of the experience unfolding at this moment, the pinkish hues of the Italian countryside deepening into light shades of blue as well. Sue and I shared our lives for nearly 25 years—indeed blood is thicker than boundaries. We have a shared history, just like these affectionate couples on the train. We raised a family with Love. But we are not together now. And as this train speeds toward Florence, a sweeping pain envelops me. I had been listening to my iPod a couple of hours ago, and one of my favorite songs came on. It is "Everybody Hurts," by R.E.M. The singer for this group, Michael Stype, has such an unusual, ironic, beautiful and tearfully sad voice—it casts a spell. The texture of his voice, and the words to his songs go directly to my heart; they touch a nerve:

When the day is long and the night, the night is yours alone,
when you're sure you've had enough of this life, well hang on.
Don't let yourself go, everybody cries and everybody hurts sometimes...
If you're on your own in this life, the days and nights are long...
Well, everybody hurts sometimes,
everybody cries. And everybody hurts sometimes.

Another R.E.M. song comes on, and I'm thinking intensely about my mother. As I traveled back and forth to Los Angeles in the final weeks of her life, I kept hearing a particular song—and the words and mood went to the heart of what I was feeling. I was looking for answers from the "great beyond." As I returned from my mom's house to San Francisco for the final time that she was still alive, these words played on my headphones:

I've watched the stars fall silent from your eyes...
I'm breaking through
I'm bending spoons
I'm keeping flowers in full bloom
I'm looking for answers from the great beyond.

We are approaching Florence now, and I vow to drink a couple of glasses of wine after I check in. I'm ready to lose myself for a bit in Michelangelo's city—after all we were born on the same day.

Florence

It felt like not much more than a few minutes, but my watch (a Mickey Mouse watch that I have had for about 25 years, and it attracts a lot of attention) informed me that it was about an hour and a half of focused attention that I had just spent captivated by Michelangelo's awesome David in the Accademia. One first encounters "courage" in its purest form—a Platonic ideal of "courage" that the master apprehends in the divine realm of pure form, then makes it human as he places a soul within this chiseled masterpiece—on first glances at the David. But then something else becomes present, the face revealing a sense of inner struggle, courage and determination eventually subduing insecurity and fear as this young man prepares to wage this "long-shot battle" against the Giant. Logic may dictate that this battle has little promise of success, and that in all probability David will meet his demise—and as one studies David's face, one sees that recognition—but David summons an inner strength, and the emotion changes back to one of certain victory. David has conquered his fear, and that determination becomes very clear. This is not a mere statue of marble; Michelangelo has placed the Divinity of a soul within stone. And as I fell under David's spell, I recognized within myself the aspiration to be clear in my thinking, to live a life of virtue and to conquer fear. It was truly an amazing experience as I concentrated on the face, then walked around and around this piece of "flesh and blood."

It had already been a full day by the time I arrived at the Accademia to see the David. The day had started quite cool for July but became hot by midday when, after several hours of walking, I settled into a cozy little café on a very narrow cobblestone street, just off the Piazza Repubblica. The streets on this side of the Piazza are so narrow that there are just inches of room—one being forced to firmly press against the stone wall of a building behind—when a car appears. It is, actually, daunting, and if one has had a glass of wine, you'd better hold on for "dear life." The morning walk resulted in a full hunger that was satisfied by an incredibly delicious Pizza Margherita, the tomato sauce richer than anything I could remember. As I ate the pizza and downed a full liter of water, I entered into a conversation with a highly pretty, engaging, talkative Italian woman with clear blue eyes, smooth Mediterranean complexion and long black hair. Her companion had just left, he was balding attractively, a man of about 60, gray at the temples, a full black mustache, the head tanned by the Italian sun, and she was clearly in the mood to talk. At first she started to speak to me in Italian, then noticing my inability to understand, switched to English, asking me if I was enjoying my stay, and was I from Spain. I laughed, telling her that it was kind of funny that she was asking me in English if I was Spanish. "Well I don't speak Spanish," she said," but you look like you are from a Mediterranean country, and since you obviously don't speak Italian, I thought I'd ask you in the only other language that I know, my little bit of English." I explained to her that I was from San Francisco, just traveling on my own to see this area of the world. "You are on your own?" she asked. "You must have a woman back home, and she trusts you to travel alone?" "It is something of a story," I answered. "I'm just traveling to get some quiet in my life, to see this beautiful place and have time to myself." I really didn't want to talk about my internal dynamics at the moment, so I switched the subject to the cobblestone streets. "Are you Florentine?" I asked, "Are you from here?" "Yes, I live here," she answered. "These streets," I continued, "these cobblestone streets, they are so old and beautiful, but they are dangerous. They are always uneven; I keep tripping over them. I almost landed on my face a few times." This produced a giggle from her, which was followed by a slightly sardonic smile. She informed that, indeed, it was quite a problem in Florence. She rides bicycles virtually everywhere she goes in the city, and she had taken more than one tumble during her bike-riding career. "You always have to look down when you ride bikes, or even walk in Florence; if you don't you could land on your "face." She struggled for that last word, "face," it finally coming to her in time to finish the sentence. "Florence is a beautiful place for tourists," she went on, "the art, the food, the beautiful buildings. But it is not easy to live here. It is so crowded and noisy, and they do not spend enough money taking care of our streets. Ah, but there is nothing that I can do about it; I am a Florentine, I will not live anywhere else, so I just put up with it." I nodded in agreement; I was enjoying how those clear blue eyes were being so expressive of her feelings toward Florence. "Yes, it is always more difficult to live in a city than to visit it," I answered, as I paid my bill and started to get up. "It's really been fun talking with you" I said, "but I've got an appointment at the Accademia to see the David, so I better get going." "Oh, that statue is amazing," she said. "It is really amazing." "Can't wait to see it," I answered, and as I got up, I kid you not, I stumbled over a piece of cobblestone, nearly falling on my face. She laughed, covering her very attractive mouth so as not to appear to be making fun of me. "See what I mean?" she said. "Yes, I definitely see what you mean," I answered, making my way to the gelato stand next door for a large scoop of the banana.

The gelato store had too many amazing-looking flavors to settle for just one. So I ordered a scoop of strawberry to sit atop the banana and made my way outside, sitting at a little table against the narrow cobblestone street. Strong coffee was being poured next to me, and the aroma blended with the thick, sweet tobacco from the cigar of a passerby. The tobacco-coffee combination was further enriched by the delicious fragrance of an absolutely ravishing, stunning woman—long, bronzed, Mediterranean legs culminating in an absolutely impeccable ass and black high heels, no less. She was speaking Italian to a good looking, clearly Italian man in his 30s, with raven black hair combed straight back to the bottom of his neck. He was wearing black pants with a white, long-sleeved shirt, rolled up to the forearms. He looked like he might be a waiter on a lunch break. As they walked by she probably noticed my intense gaze, giving a quick turn of the head, her long, straight black hair wrapping around her neck. She offered a quick smile before turning her head back to her partner in conversation. She was clearly cognizant of what I was thinking, and I don't think my thoughts were much different from other men who took a break from what they were doing to take a notice. A couple of guys were drinking wine at the table next to me, but I can never drink during the day. I need mental clarity while the sun shines; it is the evening when I can surrender to the elixir, enjoying the sweet release of the feelings and sentiments of the heart. I finished the gelato—it felt like a whole movie had transpired while eating it—and made my way to the Accademia, where I had arranged in advance for a guaranteed time to see the David, thereby avoiding the long line to get in.

The David has a slingshot over his shoulder and a rock in his hand as he prepares to take on a force far more powerful than himself. There is a look of nobility on the face of the David; a courage despite the overwhelming odds against him. The nose is long, finely chiseled and dignified, and though there is a fearlessness in his eyes, one can also see a weariness and a tinge of doubt. David looks slightly tired, as though he has been thinking about this moment for quite a while. There is fear, but the fear is covered over by a look of total surrender as he accepts his fate, come what may. The statue transported me to another place for a while; it brought me to, perhaps, a place that Michelangelo wanted me to visit—a world where ideal forms meet human frailty. In this statue, I could hear music. The beauty of this form generated for me an inner sound; I would not be able to describe the instruments, except to say that the cascading melodies of the harp were audible.

After the fulfilling day, I made my way back to the hotel to rest. After a few hours I emerged, making my way to a restaurant where the enjoyment of food found full expression in the jovial patrons, the waiters exceptionally good-natured as they invited me into their special place on Earth. The concierge had told me about the place—Garga, I believe it is called—and it was a superb suggestion. The place was filled with color and ambience—scenes of Florence, wine bottles adorning the walls, wine flowing freely between tables so close to one another that strangers might soon become lifelong friends, if only for the moment. The waiter brought me to a table that seemed right in the center of all the action. It was a solo table, but I was clearly not alone. The wine was flowing freely and happiness filled the air. I started to look at the wine list, when a waiter came up to me and said in English," "You relax, I'll pick the wine for you. You want red?" "Yes," I offered, "that'll be great." "You want it by the glass or the bottle? Don't answer; I'm bringing a bottle of something that you'll love. Just trust me!" "I absolutely trust you," I answered. He brought the wine and it didn't disappoint. It was from Tuscany and was really good. I ordered a salad filled with virtually every vegetable under the sun, which was followed by a lasagna—the cheeses and tomato sauce otherworldly.

At the table next to me was a woman sitting alone, blond hair flipping up like a "page boy" atop her shoulders, very cute, with a low-cut blouse revealing a full and "silky" bust. She was keeping to herself, and so was I, but our eyes met warmly and she asked me where I was from. When I told her she said, "I thought so; you seem like a San Franciscan." "Well what does that mean?" I responded quizzically, and a bit buzzed from the wine. "Oh, you just give off that vibe; you seem to know what wines you like—a very northern California thing—and you seem to be really having fun in a light-hearted way." She was on her second glass of wine when I moved over to her table. We talked for quite awhile, drinking wine together, enjoying the company of one another. I told her what I was going through in my life; the anguish I often felt over the direction of my marriage; the relief it was to get away for a while; the book that I was writing. She listened exceptionally well, intently, and had a gorgeous smile. "Are you traveling alone?" I asked. "Yes," she answered. She was from Seattle, and she had carefully planned a three-week trip to Italy for her 10th wedding anniversary. Her husband at the last minute could not make the trip due to business, and she wasn't about to cancel it. She decided to go alone. We talked and laughed, talked and laughed. I would throw out the name of a song to her and she would tell me who recorded it, and other versions of it. She really liked James Taylor, Jackson Browne, and one Stones album in particular—Sticky Fingers—which is my favorite. There is a profound difference between good and bad wine, and the good wine that we were drinking had filled even the subtlest corners of my interior. I started singing—and frankly I surprised myself with how well I intoned it—that opening line to Wild Horses, "Idle living is easy to do, the things you wanted, I bought them for you," and this was followed by a re-creation of the opening chords of "Moonlight Mile," followed by those deep Jagger groans—simply the sultriest, most erotic song I have ever heard. She dug it and we just kept on laughing. I told her that the best album of all time, bar none, was "Abbey Road," and she didn't just agree, she firmly agreed. Feeling ecstasy in every nook and cranny, I serenaded her with, "Her majesty's a pretty nice girl, but she doesn't have a lot to say; her majesty's a pretty nice girl, but she changes from day to day; I want to tell her that I love her a lot, but I gotta get a belly full of wine; her majesty's a pretty nice girl, some day I'm gonna make her mine, oh yeah, some day I'm gonna make her mine." From the Beatles I moved to Led Zeppelin. She was envious as I described seeing Zep in Los Angeles, not once but in three successive years of the early '70s. And, as if to match each year with a glass of wine, I filled my glass a third time, breaking into the opening riffs of "Whole Lotta Love"—"You need cooling, baby I'm not fooling." She laughed at me amusedly but with affection. And beneath that affection was passion—a guy just knows these things. At that moment there was nothing in the world that I wanted more than to make love to this woman. I continued in the "Whole Lotta Love" vein, describing the power of Bonham's beat; Page's stance; Plant's flowing golden locks; John Paul Jones' steady, stoic bass line. This was the one group that she regretted not having been able to see live. She was in her early 40s and Zeppelin had disbanded by the time she had come of rock-concert age. We left the restaurant together, our hands softly but certainly coming together as we made our way through the little squares en route to the Duomo.

Time stood still as we walked past the multicolored frescoes of the Renaissance. I walked her back to her hotel, crossing the bridge to get to the other side of the Arno. She was staying in a converted palace; she had been telling me of the amazing view of Florence from the rooftop of her hotel. Arriving at the hotel, we made our way up several flights of stairs to this vantage point from which all of Florence opened up to us. We held hands as we looked at the view—blood was pouring through both of us as the river, the bridges, the intoxication that is Florence spread before us. "I would love to kiss you right now, but I can't," she said to me. "I just can't." "I understand, I understand," was my reply. A few moments later we said goodbye. "You know, we'll probably never see or speak to each other again," I said to her. But I will never forget this evening as long as I live." "Nor will I" she answered. Sometimes love lasts for years; sometimes days; sometimes months. And sometimes it exists eternally in the moment. Such was the case on this evening in Florence with this golden woman from Seattle. We hugged each other passionately as we made our way down the stairs. She stopped on the third floor to go to her room, while I continued down to the lobby, nodded to the doorman, and made my way into the streets of Florence.

❐

The next morning was quite difficult—memories of the previous evening were fresh, and I was having difficulty moving into a higher gear. I was a bit "hung over" and feeling quite down. I walked around Florence the whole day, a sense of loneliness and waywardness overcoming me from time to time. I walked past the same places we had visited the previous night—but they no longer embodied the same "life," and they had become infused with a sense of nostalgia. Later in the day my spirits did pick up a bit, as I walked across the river to Piazza Michelangelo, where the view of Florence is stunning. I walked miles this day; and when I got back to the hotel I was tired and a bit melancholy.

"Where is my life going?" I asked myself. "Where is it going, and what am I doing? Mom, do you have an answer for me?" And as I asked this question, I noticed that there was "Alma" embroidered on the leather pillow decorating the bed. The leather pillow had not been there the previous day, so it had to have been placed on the bed that afternoon. I was weary and had asked a question of my mom, and now as I look up I see her name on a pillow? Amazing. Alma is not a very common name. And the timing of it—it just seemed amazing. The answer to me was clear: "Bruce, I am here for you, and you are on a journey right now, a discovery. All is all right with you, and I will never leave your side." I took a bath and went out for a walk. When I returned, the pillow was gone—nor was it there at all the next day, as it had not been the previous one.

❐

Seeing "Alma" on the pillows, the word bringing a visage of my mom and her voice to me, dispelling a sense of confusion with the illumination of heaven brought me back to the moment when, a week after her passing, her name appeared directly in front of me immediately on my asking for some kind of sign of her presence. I needed some time off from work in the aftermath of my mom's passing—I had been strong during the weeks of her worsening cancer, taking care of my family and her household financially when she was incapable of reading tea leaves any longer—surrendering to my grief would be the only way to return functionally to the daily tortures of the financial world. I did not know how long it would take me to return, mentally I put aside a month, but I knew that to bury this grief and jump back in would eventually manifest in an uncontainable sadness that would be overwhelming. The grief had to be encountered in the moment, and for about a week and a half, I would retreat to the attic of our home—out of the reach of anybody—and sob, sometimes uncontrollably. I might be sitting quietly for a period of time, finding solace in my thoughts and an inner peace that is the gift of God when a person is feeling intense loss, when a wave of grief would overcome me, necessitating that I go to a place where I could cry. It came on in waves, as does nausea, and I knew that these waves and surges erupted from the soul, as does a volcanic fire from deep within the earth's crust, and spoke to me of my deep connection to my mother, the intense love of her, the desperate sense of loss, and of my humanity to feel so deeply. The pain was at times very difficult to bear—in the Jewish tradition we attach a black piece of cloth to our clothes to represent a kind of grief that can be so severe that we want to tear our clothes off of our bodies—and, indeed, I passed into a state of mind where I just wanted to rip my shirt from my body.

The intensity of the grief started to lighten after about a week, and it was at about this time that I took a long walk through the streets of San Francisco. My boys were attending Town School for Boys at the time, a school on Jackson Street that sits across from Alta Plaza Park in Pacific Heights, the views of the city are gorgeous from this park. After a few hours of walking I made way to Alta Plaza Park, looking south as the city stretched out before me. It was about the time when the boys would be getting out of school for the day, and after a long day of walking, I thought that it would be nice to go in the direction of the school, perhaps seeing Michael or Jonathan as they were heading home. Walking to the Jackson Street side of the park, I sat on the little wall that encircled the park, offering a good view of the school, boys starting to walk past me now as they headed home. In this moment a wave of sadness came on me, and I couldn't control the tears from streaming down my face. My mom's grandchildren would, no doubt, be passing by soon, and they would never see their beloved grandmother, Tudy, again, and my mom would not make it to Michael's Bar Mitzvah, the event she started to help Sue plan for a year earlier, and something she dreamed of attending since the boys were small. In this moment, I spoke out loud to my mom: "Mom, you always told me that you would watch over me from the other side, when you someday pass away. Mom, I need to know that you are there; I have to know that you are here right now, and that you can see and hear me. I need some proof, please show me, please." I stood up and started to walk to my right, thinking about heading home. I walked about 10 steps and to my astonishment a license plate appears in front of me—I had asked this question no more than 30 seconds earlier—with the words, "Alma loves ten." This is astounding, astonishing to me. Never in my life had I seen my mom's name on a license plate, and now as I am asking her to reveal her presence to me, it appears in a message of love. I thought for a moment about the people she loved most deeply—and as I counted her children, grandchildren and Sue, the number equaled ten. One can go through life trying to interpret the signs, looking for meaning or not. But sometimes a message is clear and unavoidable, it is spelled out right before our eyes—all it takes is the will to believe.

I am on an airplane headed home, looking down on the outlying areas of Edmonton, Alberta, Canada. And I am thinking about one of the best days of my life. From Florence, I went to Portofino, an absolute gem of a location, startling in its verdant green cascading—villas of orange, red, blue, white, green, each with windows offering glamorous, wine-filled day or night dreams of a world that can be perfect—into the deepest turquoise and aquamarine. Stunning is the right word to describe this place that is not diminished even with the fashionable boutiques that attract a jeweled crowd. Yet, there is still a local fishermen's village feel to the place, a sense that many that still live here or have moved nearby, started fishing locally as children and never left, or began their careers as struggling artists in small quarters that now go for millions of dollars.

I had arranged in advance with my hotel to charter a small boat and skipper for the full day, meeting up with Jonathan and his friends in one of the villages of Cinque Terre, about an hour's ride from Portofino. The bed that I had slept in the previous night was tiny and hard, but somehow I had slept well, feeling full of passion and life for my journey to meet my son on these beautiful waters. The day offered to be warm but not scorching, and the sky promised to be purely summer Mediterranean blue the whole day. I made my way down to the harbor, where Roberto greeted me at the launch that took us to the boat. He was all smiles and sunglasses as he took command of the boat, bringing us into the open sea, the sun brilliant as we graced the waters, gliding over the tops of swells, the dreamy Italian Riviera coastline dotted with villages in the offing. I hadn't felt this nice in I don't know how long, surrendering to the freedom and joy of being in this place. We approached the little village of Vernazza, little houses with windows on the village and sea, descending to the harbor, awnings and facades of orange, cream, green, red gold. Along the waterfront were numerous restaurants—each with its own fish specialty—that seemed to be filled almost wholly by local village people. Good-natured banter in Italian over the course of the dominos game reached the beach across the street where bronzed young women were organizing themselves around patches of sand, some jumping in the water before settling on towels. A big haul of fish was being brought in by a guy with rough-hewn, thick, meaty, bronzed and freckled hands, a negotiation taking place with a gentleman in an apron, the owner or manager of the little diner.

"Jonathan, I'm here," I enthusiastically yelled as he answered his phone, having just arrived at the waterfront to meet me. "God, this is beautiful, I just can't believe how beautiful this place is," I said to him. "Can we go to lunch? We're starving; we walked here from the next village, we walked an hour and a half, we haven't had any breakfast and we're starving." "Absolutely, we're going to lunch right now! I made a reservation at my hotel; the guy said the restaurant is great, and you guys can order anything that you like." "Where are you, Dad?" he asked. "I'm standing just beyond the water, where the launch let me out—look straight ahead; I see you." He came over to me—memories of my sleepless night in London, and the following morning when I found out that three boys and not he had checked into the hotel quickly giving way to the comfort of his being right in front of me—huge smile, long brown hair made golden by his travels in the sun falling underneath a leather cowboy hat, and we hugged tightly. It was a hug with the fullness of father and son. His friends were all smiles and very hungry. I rarely have pasta in the middle of the day; it slows me down to a crawl. But on this day, I had two plates, then a banana gelato, before meeting the launch that brought us to the boat. As the boys arrived at the boat, they offered practically every teenage adjective ever invented to describe pleasure. Roberto took us along the coast to the villages of Cinque Terre, eventually stopping in an aqua harbor where we swam to our hearts' content. Life just doesn't get any better than that; we were together—all of us together—in a sphere of heaven where nothing external could interrupt our joy. The sun lulled us, the water cleansed and refreshed, the stomachs were satisfied, and the rest was Italy. I had become a hero to the boys. They thanked me profusely, saying that this had gone to the top of the list of their highlights. As we lay on the boat after swimming, I told the boys that this is an experience that would stay with them their whole lives, it would never be forgotten. "At various times in your lives, you will come back to this moment," I said. "When life offers greater responsibilities, you'll write about this moment, dream of it, put it to song, reflect on it as one of the golden moments of youth. You'll remember being with your best friends, the freedom, the sensation of swimming in these waters and lying under the Italian sun. I love you guys; I'm so happy to be here with you today; I'm just thrilled to be a part of it." The boys responded by not responding; they lay in the sun, the energy of profound, intelligent, youthful self-reflection practically audible. And then Alex—affable, kind, thin and lean muscled, handsome with pretty green eyes, black hair that has a sort of "blown away from the face look," freckles about the nose and cheeks even more pronounced by his European summer in the sun—broke the reflective silence by asking me (in the very Alex manner of speaking quickly to get the idea out right away) if I could recall an experience in my youth that had deeply affected me.

Costa Rica

"Absolutely, Alex; Absolutely; Costa Rica when I was 20 years old and a sophomore in college." "I know this story," said Jonathan, "Tell it to us." "Well you know a lot of it, Jonathan," I said, "but you know the partially edited version. It isn't that it is X-Rated or anything, but there were a few sexual situations that I never mentioned." "Bruiser, tell us the story" started Wyatt, also a really good-looking young man. Wyatt—soon to be at Oberlin College, my son Michael's school, on a soccer scholarship—is a darkly handsome young man, with deeply set large brown eyes.

He is about Alex's height, a muscular frame but not bulky. He has a very offbeat sense of humor, a quite eccentric kid; a deep thinker who knows how to have a good time. He had the habit of collecting the funniest, craziest hat he could find in each city they visited on their trip. He lay on his towel with this pink, floppy hat, crazy-looking green flowers seemingly painted on it, covering his face. The boys liked to call me "Bruiser" from the tales of my hockey exploits. "Okay, Wyatt, I will:

"My second year of college had ended that very day—I had finished my last philosophy exam for the year. The 'Bruiser' wasn't just brawny you know; the girls liked him for his brain as well. Sitting down in my chair, I had this brainstorm. I wanted to go to sea; I wanted to be on some boat going to a tropical place; I didn't want to be around a lot of people; and even if I did, I didn't have enough money for some cruise ship. And I really didn't want to go on a cruise ship. I'd read in some travel magazine about booking passage on 'Merchant Marine' ships, how they were available to travelers who wanted to get away from the big social setting of cruise ships, and how they went to exotic ports. The article spoke of the cozy quarters and good food on these boats, and that often one didn't know where the ship was going until receiving orders at sea. But these 'Merchant Marine experiences' usually book up at least a year in advance, sometimes two years. There are only a few passengers per ship.

"I had read the article during the preceding winter, digested it, fantasized about the travel, then put it out of my thoughts. But the thought hit me hard as I sat down in my chair, literally moments after finishing that final exam. I was inspired; 'I bet I can find a room on one of those boats,' I thought to myself, 'I bet I can, I just feel it.' I looked in the yellow pages under 'Merchant Marine,' and stumbled on the 'United Fruit Company.' I called it, it was about three in the afternoon, and a middle aged–sounding woman answered. She had a bit of a chuckle in her voice, and sounded as if she had picked up the phone while still laughing from an office joke. 'Hello,' I said, trying to give her my softest, most appealing voice. My friends used to call me 'the voice' for my ability to get into long, sexy conversations with telephone operators, or women who would answer the phone at the other end of random dialing. 'This may sound a bit off the wall and unexpected, but I just finished my last final exam for the year at college, and I had this wave of inspiration that I would be able to find a Merchant Marine ship that has an opening for a passenger or two.' I said two, because if this were successful, there was a good friend of mine, Glen, who would no doubt want to go with me. 'Mmm,' she said; 'you are looking for an adventure, ha. Well, one of these ships is a great way to do it. You know that people have to book a few years in advance for these journeys, they are becoming very popular.' 'God, it would just be incredible if something like that opened up—any possibilities, anything opening up?' I offered, enthusiastically, unwilling to give in to the strong likelihood of, 'No, nothing here, you'll have to try another line.' But that was not the answer I received. 'You know what? I just might have something for you; no promises at the moment, but I might have something. I had heard earlier today of two elderly women who were going to have to cancel our next voyage through the canal to Ecuador—they want a full refund which we could not promise at this late notice—and I'll have to make some calls to see if they are still planning on canceling. Do you definitely want to go? And do you have valid passports, and you'll have to get current with shots, small pox is needed for sure, if these women want to cancel. If you can go and are qualified to go, we might be able to give them the full refund they are asking for.' 'This is unbelievable,' I shot back. 'This is incredible. Absolutely, I'll go; and if you have a room with two beds—you say there were two elderly women—then I have a friend who surely would go. You say the ship is headed for Ecuador, through the Panama Canal!' 'Yes, that is the expected destination, but things can change while at sea. The ship can make an unexpected stop; it can go to the expected destination, and on to another one. It is expected to be a 10-day trip to Ecuador, but it may be longer. You boys have the time?' 'Absolutely, I hope it is longer,' I answered. 'I'll take it for a month or more' 'Well, I don't think it will be gone that long, but let me get your phone number and I'll look into this for you. I doubt that I will be able to get back to you today, but I'm sure I can get an answer by tomorrow.' 'I really want to do this,' I responded. And I very much wanted her to know of my excitement. 'Don't forget me overnight,' I pleaded, 'Please don't forget this.' 'I promise I won't,' she replied. 'It will be fun for you and it will get these ladies off the hook, if it works out,' she replied. 'But remember, you'll need valid passports and shots, if you do go. Be prepared to tell me if you are able to go when I call tomorrow.' 'I will; I absolutely will. You know what, call me by 2:00 in the afternoon tomorrow if you can, and if I don't hear from you then I'll give you a call.' 'Deal,' she said, 'If you do not hear from me first, then go ahead and give me a call.'

"Man, I couldn't believe what had just happened. I was practically on my way to South America on a Merchant Marine ship; 30 minutes ago, I had been on my way home for the summer. I could barely contain my excitement. I ran outside and jumped into the swimming pool at my apartment. I swam about 10 quick laps, and when I came out, I ran back up the steps to the apartment, sat down on the couch—wet bathing suit and all—and called my friend, Glen. Glen was a philosophy major like myself; he had a light complexion, long, frizzy, reddish hair, just about down to his shoulders, and he was very bookish. He loved to argue, and we used to sharpen our wits against each other by constantly trying to find the flaws in the other's thinking. I'll never forget one conversation we had when, looking at a really gorgeous girl at school, I told him how I can appreciate the 'aesthetic' beauty of a woman, without feeling that I have to have her, possess her, have sex with her. 'I wouldn't throw her out of bed, obviously,' I would say, but I really do appreciate beauty; I am astounded by it sometimes. 'That's a bunch of nonsense,' he would answer, 'Of course you want to possess it, own it, experience it in a physical way—it is the consciousness that you are seeking.' 'Of course,' I would add, 'Of course I want to experience the consciousness of being physical with her, that goes without saying, but I can separate the beauty of the form, from my desire for the form.' 'Bullshit,' Glen would fire back, and so it went.

" 'You're fuckin' amazing,' Glen responded when I told him about the potential for this trip. 'If you pull this off, you're fuckin' amazing,' 'Glen, I don't know, I just had the feeling like it might be possible; in that moment when I called, I truly expected the answer would be 'yes.' 'Absolutely, I'll go if this happens,' Glen fired back."

"She called me before I had to call her. The call came in at about 1:30, and I was waiting for it. 'You're on,' she said. 'There will be two beds in the berth; you said you have a friend that wants to go. Otherwise, you'll have to pay for the cabin yourself. The cost is $1100 round trip, and that includes three great meals a day. You'll be dining with the captain. So, if you have someone to go with, it will be $550.00 per person. The ladies are very happy to get their money back—though they are disappointed that they cannot make it. You know, there is a waiting list, but I am putting you ahead of the others. Don't you say a word about that. I just loved your excitement—I couldn't turn you down. Do you have the passports? And you boys will definitely need shots.' 'We've got the passports, and we've already arranged for the shots. We'll be there. Thanks so much; thanks so much for making this happen!' I exclaimed. 'I got you on the ship, but you made it happen,' she answered. 'You called at just the right time.'

"Guys, this trip was unbelievable. We boarded the boat at San Pedro Harbor, just outside Long Beach in L.A. We were introduced to our room—two really comfortable twin beds at each end of the cabin. There was a nice big picture window—and off the room was a bathroom with a bathtub. And on the other side of the bathroom was a sitting room, with a liquor cabinet. We were told that as long as we didn't overdo it—get that guys, don't overdo it—we could have a few drinks at night from the liquor cabinet." "Wow," responded Woods—a boyish-looking lad with straight blond hair down to his shoulders, sweet blue eyes, and freckles all over his face; he had grown about a foot in the last year and was headed to Stanford as a freshman—"I'm loving this story." "Well, I'll go on:

"The captain came and introduced himself to us; he was Dutch and, he told us, would be steering the ship through the Panama Canal. We would be dining with him and a few officers for dinner, and it would be very informal. We could wear shorts. We'd be on our own for the other meals. We then went to the upper deck, the captain conducting his pre-voyage safety inspection, giving the crew of Honduran sailors instructions for conducting business during an emergency. The captain then introduced us to each of his sailors—and I had never been greeted with so many warm smiles, handshakes, jovial expressions and warm hugs within 30 minutes in my life before. We had just met, and they were really happy to see us. These were muscular sailors, experienced seamen, guys who had been at sea for much of their adult lives; I think they saw in us—no doubt they saw it in me—this sense of adventure in our eyes. Perhaps they saw their own lives at sea differently for a moment—that they were wise men, learned in the ways of the ocean-going life, and what a joy it would be to share some of it with a couple of young men, eager for adventure. Perhaps the people that book passage on these vessels are usually much older, more staid in their ways. Now they had a couple of college students—guys with really long hair, intent on having some fun. It would be an adventure for them as well."

Alex interrupts me for a moment, speaking in his typically quick way, as though getting the words out gets in the way of moving on to the next thought. "Bruiser, what year was this and what was going on in the world at the time?" "Alex, it was late June 1974, and the impeachment of Richard Nixon over Watergate—I'm sure you guys have heard about Watergate—" "aha," came from each boy, their heads nodding affirmatively—"was on the front burner. Nixon did some good things—he was a brilliant man with an understanding of economics and foreign affairs—such as recognizing the need to 'open the door to China,' but he had a serious blind spot. He stood by these small-time burglars, and loyally covered up for his staff. He lied about his role in this affair, and it was so unnecessary. He was going to trounce George McGovern in the election, anyway; why not fire a few guys and be honest with the investigation from the get-go? The problem was that he had this little clique of inside men—Gordon Liddy, H.R. Halderman, John Dean, they were totally loyal to him, Nixon totally loyal to them—that he would use for all sorts of dirty tricks that he kept from the public." "What kinds of dirty tricks?" asked Jonathan. "Oh, he spied on people who he thought were enemies, particularly blacks and Jews. He hated the 'free speech movement' taking place on campuses across the country, and tried to concoct stories that would get the leaders arrested. He tried to get John Lennon kicked out of the country; he eavesdropped on Martin Luther King; spied on a lot of his perceived enemies. He used this circle of advisors to do it, and these practices had been going for quite awhile, and so it isn't surprising that these guys would do something so stupid as break into his opponents' headquarters to get information. This is the type of stuff these guys did. And it isn't surprising that Nixon stood by these guys all the way to his resignation. See, he wasn't impeached; he resigned before that could happen. He handed the presidency over to Gerald Ford, who lost a couple of years later to Jimmy Carter. So that is what was going on as we set sail on the Merchant Marine ship. A couple of months later, Nixon would resign, and about a year after that, we finally got out of Vietnam—and we did it the hard way, in defeat. The Viet Cong had taken control of their whole country, our men leaving in helicopters on the roofs of buildings. I'll never forget the reports coming from Vietnam of soldiers dying every day." "Sort of like Iraq," offered Wyatt. "Yeah, a bit like Iraq, but there are some differences; in Iraq we really were after a 'mini Hitler,' Saddam Hussein—it is good that the guy is gone—but our country was lied to with regard to what we were after. Weapons of mass destruction? Yeah, maybe there was some legitimate concern that the guy might acquire such things—but it turns out that we knew that he wasn't anywhere close to having them. We put together all kinds of evidence that he was in possession of such things—put together a case that didn't allow for any contrary, contradictory evidence; this is what happens when a president surrounds himself with people who see the world only as he does—and entered the country thinking that the vast majority of Iraqis would welcome us with open arms. It was a huge mistake—now I've gotten started—the way it was handled. There was total anarchy; we never should have dismantled the entire police force—we needed these people for law and order. And I'm sure there were plenty of military and police people who hated Hussein even more than Bush, and would have been willing to work with us toward putting in place some authority.

"We didn't protect the ancient artifacts in their museums—there were all kinds of looting of the country's treasures. And that is not a small thing; maybe it doesn't seem important, but it really is. Truth be told, we wanted to be in the right place at the right time as far as controlling Iraq's oil. We didn't want this guy in charge of one of the world's greatest oil reserves, and I understand this, but the rest of the world was in favor of controlling this guy, without invading and starting a civil war. We could have worked with the rest of the world and monitored affairs there, perhaps putting a noose around him so tight that he was unable to do anything on the world stage, eventually to be deposed by his own people. Who knows? But what I do think is that our government lied to us, knowingly. This is my opinion. I want you guys to read up and come to your own conclusions. Anyway, enough about Iraq, for now. It is a horrible situation; if we leave there will be a civil war, so I'm not sure we will leave. And I don't want to see any of you boys going to fight a war so the oil companies can get rich. One more thing: What really gets me angry about Iraq is that our government was handing out contracts to rebuild Iraq even before we went to war. If I am a soldier sitting in that hot desert, preparing to go to war, I don't want to know that some corporate executive is planning his riches at my expense. Okay, back to Costa Rica.

"We set sail thinking that we were headed to South America through the Panama Canal. That first night Glen and I had a nice full glass of Costa Rican rum mixed with Coke, went to the front of the ship and lay on the bow looking up at the stars. Land was not visible, or if it was, there were no lights and nothing could be seen. We were making our way off the coast of Baja California. The stars were just insane; I had never seen so many in my life. A zillion, zillion stars—and you could see that band of dust that makes up the Milky Way galaxy. The sea was black that first night, but the blackness was constantly broken by the white foam splashed up from the small swells as they gently sprayed the front of the ship. The white foam looked fluorescent, made up of countless fragments of green and blue. I had never slept better in my life than I did that night on the ship. The slow rocking movement of the boat, sometimes gently forward, other times like a cradle moving from side to side, put me into the deepest sleep of my life. And I had this type of sleep every night I was on the ship. I dreamed the deepest of dreams, filled with all kinds of color. They were imaginative, fantasy types of dreams. I can't remember the content of any of them—all I remember is that they were dreams that took control of mind and body, bringing me to a deep womblike place where nothing existed except the most pleasant calm I had ever known and have ever known to this day. The further south we got over the next few days, the deeper the blue of the sea. By day we could see the outlines of Puerto Vallarta, Acapulco, then a few lights barely visible of tiny Mexican villages or settlements, giving way to the blackness of the land. Then the stars would come out—I was under the influence of my nightly Costa Rican rum and Coke, though I never drank very much, just enough to feel it—and I would go to the bow and lie on my back, drifting among the stars. Sometimes Glen would come with me to the front of the ship, but at other times he'd visit our friends up in the radio room, listening for signals from far-off lands or distant ships. After my nightly visit with the stars, I would join Glen up in the radio room—sometimes it was very late and he had already gone to bed—sitting in this dark place, the only illumination being the little streaks of orange, blue, green, red coming from the inside of electrical tubes on a panel. We made very good friends with the Honduran radio engineer; the wire-rimmed glasses and sterling gray hair afforded him a bookish, professorial sort of look, but the sandals, shorts, South American skin roasted to a rawhide brown revealed his roots as a sailor. He spoke fluent English, and he started to laugh when I asked him the question of UFOs. I wanted to know if he had ever seen any, or thought that he'd ever seen any during the many years of his sitting in these radio rooms in the dark nights at sea. And I also wondered if he ever heard radio signs that, perhaps, sounded like alien intelligence trying to communicate with us. He chuckled because he liked my curiosity, imagination and enthusiasm, but he gave me a slow, measured, serious answer. 'I have never seen anything resembling a UFO at sea—though I have seen comets and spectacular shooting stars—but I have wondered, myself, about some of the frequencies that I have picked up on the radio from time to time. Alien intelligence? Yes, it has crossed my mind, from time to time.' I nodded, asking if he would turn the dial to see if we could pick up anything. He kindly obliged. The night was black, the boat gently swaying, the stars visible everywhere through these windows, as he turned the dial from frequency to frequency, the fiery little orange within the knob on the panel of the radio moving from left to right, and back again. We picked up a bit of Spanish here—quite audible and loud, so it wasn't far away—and a bit of German there, coming in quickly then disappearing behind the hiss of white noise. 'Where is that coming from?' I asked. 'Probably somewhere in the North Sea,' he answered. 'Sounds like a German commercial vessel.' We picked up some dignified, official, British accent, saying something about Richard Nixon—it had to be the BBC—and that slowly faded to soft static. Continuing up and down the radio, we heard more and more of the hissing white static, as it blended with the darkened room and blackness of the star-filled sky. It was the softest, most peaceful static the world has ever known."

"The third day at sea the air became absolutely still. The water was the deepest blue that I had ever seen, and that includes the pristine turquoise off the islands of Hawaii. The water appeared almost entirely still, save for the tiny ripples that moved across the surface and flattened out, the way a mountain lake serenely becomes placid as it approaches the shore. The stillness of this massive bathtub—ripples soft enough to float a toy boat—on which we sailed reflected the rays of a summertime, Central American orb of bright yellow, situated in the middle of a blue, rivaled by the color of Sue's eyes and that of my son, Michael, as well." "Bruiser," interrupted Woods, "you're getting a bit syrupy with this blue-eyed stuff. Okay." "Woods, your eyes rivaled the beauty of the sea as well—feel better now?" "Much better," he answered, and everyone chuckled, even Roberto, who was quite transfixed by this story as well.

"I'll continue. The sea penetrated me, a slight saltiness that entered my lungs with the sweetness of the Costa Rican coffee we had been drinking on board. The air had the high notes of a pristine, fragrant Chardonnay wine, the kind that starts out dry then becomes a bouquet of fresh flowers as the tongue discerns a delicacy that comes directly from God. The kind of wine that leaves on one's breath an aftertaste of licorice root and fresh mint. The air was intoxicating; trying to enjoy as much of it as I could, I breathed deeply for a good few minutes. A Honduran sailor walked by, big smile full of beautiful, straight, white teeth, and dropped a net into the water for some reason. I was curious, but didn't ask him anything about it, just noticed quizzically as he pulled it up without catching anything, sea water spilling through it and dropping back into the 'bath water.' I thought that, maybe, he was playing a game of some sort. But I did say to him, that I couldn't believe how still the water was, that it seemed that we were barely moving. He answered me in English, a very deep voice like from the inside of a hollow coconut. 'Doldrums,' he said, 'we're in the Doldrums, and we'll be sailing through it for the next day or so. In the Doldrums there is no wind, and the water barely moves. One can be stuck in here for days if you have a sailboat and the engine breaks down.' 'Interesting, very interesting,' I commented. 'I never knew such a place existed.' Are there other places like this, where everything is so still at sea?' I asked. 'This is the only Doldrums I know about,' he answered. 'Mmm, I wonder if this place is responsible for the term 'Doldrums?' I wondered out loud. 'I think it is; I think it is,' he responded, looking serious and thinking about that for a moment."

"After about a day and night sailing through the Doldrums, the following morning brought a full breeze, the green, Panamanian flag unfurling and flapping, a snapping sound as it caught the air. The breeze was strong through most of the day and remained steady through the night. It was strange how it came on so suddenly. It wasn't accompanied by any kind of weather front, the sky remained almost cloudless—but the breeze seemed to come on us like magic, almost on cue for a movie set. It is something I remember so well, and it was a really sweet breeze. It was moist and tropical, just bathing your skin. I'll never forget that softness—the air felt like silk, the swells picking up and splashing that serious blue against the boat.

"We had been at sea about five days when the Dutch Norwegian captain—very proper in the way he addressed us, as though we were fellow officers—told us at dinner that we would be making a stop the following morning, early, at a little banana port in Costa Rica, called Golfito. We would be there all day, anchoring there for the evening, before heading through the canal to Ecuador and possibly other South American ports. We were, of course, free to wander the town, just as long as we made it back for the launch to bring us back to the boat at 10:00 P.M. 'If you miss that, you'll be spending the night in Golfito—or staying awake,' he said, 'because there is only one hotel in the port, and I don't think you'd enjoy it very much. A lot of shall we say—and out came his proper English (a bit of tongue in cheek) with the Dutch accent—'hookers use that hotel, and the sheets aren't changed, if you know what I mean. Only hearsay,' he added in that proper English Dutch, 'can't say that I know for sure.' He grinned, then chuckled a bit.

" 'Looking forward to it; it'll be fun to get my feet on land for a bit, see what a little Latin American port is like,' I answered. 'It isn't much of a port, just a tiny little place set up to handle the banana business. Quite lush, though, surrounded by jungle,' he offered. 'We'll be pulling into the port quite early, at sunrise,' he concluded, as he graciously excused himself to do his ship's business."

"The ship cradled me into another dreamy, all-encompassing sleep that night, as it had every previous night. Yet, I was aware that we had pulled into the port, because for the first time there was a sense that we were no longer moving. I was too tired to get up, but Glen, whose bed was underneath the porthole window, pushed himself up from the covers, saying, 'Wow, is this place green. It is a freaking jungle out there.' I worked hard at getting myself out of bed, finally did it and looked at the most amazing sight I had ever seen. We were the only boat in what looked to be a super tiny harbor, and to our left, to our right, was a jungle hillside so densely filled with palm trees and all kinds of tropical-looking plants that it had to be a movie set. 'My God, Glen, this is fantasyland,' I said. 'I can't wait to get out there.' The first sight of land, except for seeing it off in the distance as we sailed down the coast, and we enter this incredible verdant forest behind us, palm trees everywhere, the sky an incredible blue, little canoes just off the pier in the turquoise water, darkly bronzed shirtless men fishing, even this early in the morning. Guys, it was an incredible sight."

"In just a few minutes we were on the deck, the sea saltier now that we were on shore, a kind of burnt coconut scent wafting through the air—someone, somewhere must have been burning it for breakfast or some such reason—drinking that deep brown Costa Rican coffee we had been savoring each day at sea. It tasted different now that we were on shore; the flavor no longer originated from the depths of the sea but now was borne in the heart of that enticing jungle. The flavor of the coffee, its effect on me stimulated my desire for this port. Glen felt no less entranced, and I couldn't wait to explore. We were told by the captain that on the outskirts of this jungle port—about a mile from where we were; it couldn't be seen because of the curvature of the shoreline—was a man, Captain John, who built out the inside of an old pirate ship on returning from Vietnam, living on fruit, eating what he grew. I asked if the captain had ever seen or met the guy—indeed he had, he answered, 'long white hair down to his waist, an oddball character, but he has the right to live how he wants, I suppose. He went to Vietnam and he has the right to be left alone. The locals call him "Crazy Captain John," but they seem to like the man. He brings no harm.' 'Interesting,' I answered. 'Glen, let's go see this guy, if we can.' Glen gave me a questioning, quizzical look, then nodded his head affirmatively. 'Yeah, let's try to find the guy after we look around the port a bit,' he responded.

"The village port was, essentially, about a quarter mile strip of a few little cantinas for drinking and dancing at night; a couple of tiny, hole-in-the-wall grocery stores whose backyard was the base of the jungle as it sloped downward to the port; a restaurant without a roof—canvas acted as a roof at night, was pulled to the side during the day, and back again when it started to rain; a little hotel, this had to be the place the captain had told us about; and then a larger bar with a stairwell in the back going upstairs. A bit further along this port road were wooden shacks, some built on stilts, others looking like little outhouses that you'd find in Yosemite Valley, and also some tin cottages, little places where people lived, the exterior made of aluminum or tin. We looked into the window of one of the cottages—you couldn't miss it, the window was wide open and was at eye level as we walked by—and saw two voluptuous, dark women sitting in panties and thin white bras that could barely hold the full breasts that were pouring out of them. They each winked at both of us, and being me, of course, I had to stop and try to talk to them. They were a huge turn-on. And in the hot tropical sun—something about being 19 years old, you've been at sea for about a week, you are in this place surrounded by jungle, the sun getting hot, the air moist and humid—I felt the juices flowing. They didn't speak a word of English, but they motioned us to come in. And I would have, but Glen was the conservative one. 'You don't know if they have some kind of disease, and who knows, maybe they have a machete back there.' 'Glen, I'd like to go in.' 'Suit yourself, but I'm gonna keep on walking—think I'll go see if I can find Captain John.' 'All right, I'll shine it on,' I answered. 'Suit yourself; go in if you like; don't let me stop you,' he replied. 'No, I'll keep on going; maybe we'll see what happens on the way back.'

"We kept on walking several hundred yards, until the road came to an end. But just before it did, there was a footpath that led up the hill into the jungle. The trail led us right into the jungle—the shrieks of monkeys in the distance, thick fragrance of dried bamboo, the chirping and singing of rainforest birds—and about 15 minutes of walking later, we stumbled upon an enclosed area being used as a shower, a rubber hose filling it with the pristine water of a waterfall behind. Next to the shower was a little outhouse toilet, with some plumbing that flushed the sewage into what looked like a septic tank. Further along, we happened on a place that looked like someone's living room made from a hollowed-out motorboat. In it was a couch, some chairs, a large umbrella for shade, and strung to a couple of trees behind it was a large hammock made of pillows and cushions. Still no sign of anyone yet, but in no time, the path turned back out of the jungle and down to the shore. And as we approached the shore, I could hear the hearty laughter of a man with a deep voice, followed by that of a woman. Suddenly there appeared a big, burly guy, sort of looked like a heavyweight wrestler—skin tanned and reddened by the sun—with a bushy gray beard, gray hair down to his waist. He was with a woman—more European looking—with waist-length brown hair, streaked with gray. She was, probably, late 30s, with some full boobs hanging out of her tank top. The long-haired guy stopped chuckling for a moment, as did his woman. Noticing a touch of alarm, I yelled 'Hey, how are you? We just got off the ship, taking a walk. Are you the Captain John that I heard about?' A big smile returned to the guy's face, the woman grabbing him around the waist, and he yelled out, 'Sounds like you speak American; come on over have a look around.' 'Sounds great,' I yelled back. 'Cool,' yelled Glen. Now guys, you gotta remember, we both had long hair as well, especially mine. I had on a headband, and looked like a cross between Jimmy Page and Jimmy Hendrix. As we approached Captain John, he stuck out his hand to give the 'you're one of us' handshake of the hippie generation—the one where you wrap your thumbs around one another, clasping hands. Here, Jonathan, it's like this." Jonathan wrapped his hand around mine, knowing just what to do. That kid of mine would have loved coming of age in the 60s—he has the singing voice and musical talent to have made it big time, with a Kerouac, Dylan, wandering-minstrel kind of spirit. 'You guys rock stars, you look like rock stars?' Captain John offered approvingly, his woman—now I could see those Judy Collins-blue eyes—smiling, looking a bit flirtatious." "She probably wasn't flirtatious, you were just horny," derided Wyatt, getting up to down a glass of water before returning to his cozy spot on the cushioned chair, his funny hat once again covering his face from the sun. "Well, Wyatt, I was definitely horny—I think we've established that— but the look was one of approval, shall we say. Where was I? Oh, she didn't say much, but she was mature-looking and very beautiful, though she had a tired look, like she'd seen and experienced a lot. 'Come on you guys, let me show you around,' said Captain John. 'Just saw your shower,' I answered. 'What a brilliant contraption.' 'And I love that little living room made out of the motor boat, little hammock in the back,' offered Glen, clearly dazzled, but not uncomfortable in this exotic place.

"Captain John took us down the pathway toward the water, arriving at this pirate ship that had become his home. 'It's a real pirate ship,' he offered, 'not a gimmick. I bought it when I got back from Southeast Asia; you know that war going on over there? Bad scene, but Sammy doesn't want me to talk about it, do you Sammy? By way of proper introduction, this is Sammy, the lady of my life.' 'Nice to make your acquaintance,' offered Sammy in a mock dignified way. 'You look like a couple of very nice, refined, handsome young men. Where are you from, exactly?' As she spoke, it became clear that Sammy was British, though she spoke in an accent that had lost some of its strength. 'Met Sammy in Thailand on the way back from Vietnam—but that is another story, isn't it Sammy?' 'Indeed it is,' she answered. And the rest remained unspoken. Something had happened over there in Thailand when Captain John left Vietnam, something interesting and odd, I felt. But I never asked, and they didn't seem to want to tell it. But to this day, I wonder how they met. I wish I'd asked. So guys, take this as a lesson; never be afraid to ask questions. Oh, I take that back; use your discretion in asking questions. I guess it is important to know when not to be curious—don't want your curiosity getting you in trouble." "Dad, get on with the story, will you?" reprimanded my Jonathan. "Okay, will do. Not much more to tell about Captain John. He sat us down in this funky pirate ship, gave us a bowl of fruit with a cold beer. That beer went down so well. I asked him if he ever gets visits from Americans or Europeans, did he ever see other people in this secluded place. 'Oh yeah,' he answered, 'A few sailors out there know Captain John. But nobody ever just stumbles on the place like you guys did. A few of my buddies have come to visit after getting out of Nam, before moving on with their lives. The local people leave us alone—we never get any visits from anybody in the port. We're good neighbors up here,' he continued. After the beer and the fruit, we said our goodbyes and made our way back into the port, walking back the same way we had come, past that ingenious shower filled with water from the waterfall.

"We walked back through the jungle path, stayed correctly to the left—curious about going to the right though, it probably would have brought us deeper into the rain forest toward the monkeys—ending up again on that strip of road alongside the harbor. We walked once again past the tin or aluminum cottages, but this time the Latin women with those voluptuous boobs spilling out of their bras were not in the window. The window was closed, a curtain obscuring a full view. 'Lost my chance, Glen, and you might have had a good time as well,' I said, sort of half kidding. It was kind of tongue in cheek for me. Glen was right, we might have contracted some sort of disease. 'You had your chance; don't blame it on me. Anyway, we might not have met Captain John.' 'No, just kidding,' I answered. 'It worked out real well.' We continued along the road a few hundred yards, eventually stumbling on a hole-in-the-wall little restaurant offering Mexican tacos. There was an enticing, spicy scent filtering through the open door; we were getting real hungry, the fruit alleviating our appetites for just a short while. We sat down at a table at the front next to a window. Mosquitoes were making their high pitched sound, flies were on the wall, the table needed a washing, sweat was dripping down our necks—it was very humid, the air felt still, except for a fan that didn't help at all—but those chicken tacos were out of this world. They put some green sauce on them, with a spiciness I had never encountered before. I couldn't find anything like that flavor when I got back to Los Angeles, and I still have not tasted anything like it, despite going to a lot of Mexican restaurants in my lifetime. Maybe it was the exotic place we were in that brought out the extra flavor in those tacos—but it wasn't only that. Maybe they make it with tequila or something, but that sauce was unbelievable. We left that place hot, covered in sweat, but very satisfied. Walking a bit slowly in this thick, moist air, we came on the large bar with a room full of tables in the front, the stairs leading up to a second story in the back—the place we had passed on our way to Captain John's. Two Honduran sailors from the ship—I remember one guy had a front tooth that was totally silver, the other shorter, stockier, thick neck with a tattoo of a thin-waisted, large-breasted woman—caught sight of us, and motioned for us to come in. We hadn't had much conversation with them on the ship, but like all the sailors we met they were filled with good vibes, always 'filling us up' with big smiles and a sense of the camaraderie of fellow seamen. I think we saw them before they saw us—each had just downed a full whiskey glass of something. After motioning for us to come in, they decided to take matters into their own hands by running up to greet us at the old west saloon-style front door—the kind with the two low doors that swing back and forth. Throwing their arms around us, they immediately bought us shots to drink—we had offered to buy the round, but they would have none of that. 'Tequila,' said the silver-toothed, leaner sailor. 'Oh yes,' responded his mate. 'Tequila goes down well in this climate.' 'Tequila it is then,' said the adventurous Glen. 'Sure, why not?' I followed. 'The mescal plant never disappoints.' We downed that shot, chased it with a beer, then finished off a second shot of the same. But I always knew my limit—a lesson for you boys—even then, at the age of 19. That was enough, and Glen and I were feeling damn good. We offered to buy the sailors a round, but they wouldn't have any of it. And they weren't about to let us pay for our own—and we certainly weren't about to fight them over it.

" 'Thanks guys, you guys are great. Look, a Costa Rican dog, Glen—a Costa Rican dog! I bet he speaks Spanish,' I said, feeling so damn good, as I stood up to leave. 'Boys, we want to bring you upstairs for a minute, come with us,' said the silver-toothed one, his words slurred just a bit, but speaking understandable English. 'What's up there?' I asked. 'I think we'll just go on out and see this jungle place a little more,' I continued. 'Boys, come with us upstairs, really, just for a minute,' followed the stocky one, that sexy tattoo jumping off his arm. Glen and I looked at each other—we were feeling no pain at this moment—and nodded affirmatively to each other. These guys weren't going to do us any harm—that was obvious. 'What's up there?' I asked. 'Come with us, you'll see—you'll have no complaints,' offered the silver-toothed gentleman. We walked with them to the top of the stairs, reaching a little porch or landing, turned right a few steps, then left to the entrance of a long corridor. As we made our way down the corridor, bare-breasted Latina beauties—nothing on except little panties—opened doors to little rooms on either side of the corridor. Door after door opened as we walked down this hallway that was, maybe, 50-feet long. There must have been 10 women on each side—I swear—each one a knock-out, full breasts, dark-skinned, long black hair, red toenails, red lipstick, red fingernails, each putting on the most inviting expression to invite us in. 'Glad you followed us up, boys,' the stocky one said, the silver-toothed friend, drunk and full of laughter. 'My god,' I said; 'fuckin' shit,' submitted Glen. 'We'll leave you guys alone,' the stocky one said. 'It'll cost you guys about 10 bucks a piece in Costa Rican, a little more if you're happy and want to give a tip,' offered my silver-toothed friend. 'Can you handle it?' he said. 'No problem,' Glen answered. 'We'll see you boys back on the ship tonight, maybe,' they offered. And then they turned around and left, drunken sailors, laughing, arms around one another, a friendship as deep as the sea, borne of the hard work of the ship, nurtured by the lustiness of the hot, tropical sun. We walked up the corridor, then back. I submitted to the charms of Melba, her stall was about half way down the corridor. I selected her on the way back to the front of the corridor, after taking in the full length of the offerings. Glen ended up right next door to me with Patrice. Patrice was the taller of the two ladies. Her breasts were round and full, but not as large and voluptuous as the two women we had seen earlier in the day in the tin cottage, nor were they as lust-inspiring as some of the other women along the corridor." "It is a bit embarrassing to hear this stuff from my Dad," interjected Jonathan. "I love the story, but it is embarrassing. You left some of this stuff out when you told me your Costa Rican story before." "Well, I can stop, if it is embarrassing; I don't want you feeling uncomfortable," I went on. "No, I love the story, it is just that you're my dad, know what I mean?" "I do know; I think I would probably have felt the same way at your age, if my dad had told me some kinky story from his childhood. But my dad never shared anything with me in those days.

"I can't remember that he's ever told me a story about anything." "No, I really like it," Jonathan responded. "Great story," offered Alex. "Awesome," chirped Woods. "Man, it's ridiculous," chimed Wyatt. "Great story," our skipper, Roberto agreed. "I never had anything like that happen to me when I was 19," he continued. "Jonathan, should I continue?" "Yeah, go ahead. It's a fun story, and I like the way you tell it. You should put this in your book." "I will, Jonathan; I'll try to fit it in. I'll go on, but I'll spare you guys the graphic stuff.

"Patrice was taller than Melba, and she had native features that blended with the Spanish. Her skin looked incredibly soft, though I didn't have the opportunity to touch her. She was a bit lighter than the other women, with a few freckles around her nose. Glen said that she was the best lay he had ever had, and that she kissed as though she was trying to lure him into her web. As I got busy with Melba, I could hear the squeaking of the bed next to me. And she made a lot of noise, that Patrice. Melba was smashing. She had a deep bronze skin, and black hair, with a bit of a wave as it approached her waist. She was the most aggressive in pursuing me, but she didn't need to be. I had already decided on her on my first trip down the corridor. She was about five feet four, with a narrow waist, and full hips, and her breasts were large, full, luscious. Besides her body, her selling point was that in pretty good English she told me as I walked past the first time that she would do things to me that I would remember for the rest of my life. Some of the women simply said 'fucky, fucky,' as I walked past. 'I am study to be a doctor,' Melba said; 'I know what gives a man pleasure.' Those words stuck in my mind, still in full flight from the shots of tequila. I submitted to her on my return trip down the corridor. And, given that this might be embarrass you, Jonathan, I will only say that she told the truth. She did things to an inexperienced 19 year old that had not been done before and, dare I say it, have never been done in quite the same way since. Melba was amazing. She had a sexual power about her. Okay, that's where I'll stop with Melba."

"I emerged from Melba's stall before Glen did from Patrice's room. I made my way downstairs where the seats at the bar were filled with several more sailors from our boat, though the two gentlemen who had brought us upstairs were no longer there. A lot of shots were being put down, boisterous Spanish reveling in the joy of the moment loudly spoken. A couple of sailors—one of them stocky, black hair wet from the humidity, the part in his hair beginning about two inches from his left ear, two front teeth framed by silver; the other, younger and about a head taller, a bit of a 'ladies' man' with black hair combed straight back like Elvis Presley—recognized me instantly, each giving me the kind of wink that a man gives to another man when he is aware that some action has been had. 'You have some fun up there?' the Elvis look-alike said to me. 'My brothers take care of you boys? Where is your friend? Still getting some?' he continued with full laughter. 'I'm buying you a drink; I'm sure you're thirsty after your experience up there,' said the stockier one with the jet black, oddly parted hair. 'No guys, let me buy you one,' I demanded. 'No way; no way,' they said at practically the same time. And at just this moment Glen comes down, pushing his frizzy, reddish blond hair away from his face, picks up my smile and flashes a fatigued one in return. The Elvis sailor sees Glen and yells, 'looking a little tired, senor—you lasted longer than your friend here. A drink for the thirsty senor.' Glen comes to the bar, gives me a shake of his head, as I down the shot of tequila that had just been handed to me. 'A drink for the thirsty lover-boy,' shouts my stocky friend. And then

Glen downs in one gulp that shot of tequila. If we had been a bit tired after our sessions, we weren't feeling it any longer.

" 'That Patrice, man she can kiss—I was falling in love up there,' Glen offered, a look of satisfaction all over his face. 'I hope you used a "rubber," Glen,' I admonished. 'Used two of them,' he answered. 'How did it go with Melba?' 'Let's just say that Melba lived up to her name,' I replied. 'I've never known a Melba who didn't,' Glen said wryly, a large grin taking over his whole face, the tequila, no doubt, just hitting his pleasure center. Shortly thereafter, we said our goodbyes to the sailors—big bear hugs given to both of us—and we were out into the hot, moist, still air of this jungle port, Golfito, Costa Rica."

"A nice rest and a meal would be in order, so we made our way to the launch that brought us back to the ship. We took a nap, showered, then went to the dining quarters where the Dutch captain was having his meal. Dressed in cool white clothing, our captain—again speaking a gentleman's English with a Dutch accent—asked if we got a chance to see a bit of Golfito, and 'What did you think of it?' Glen and I looked at each other, smiled knowingly at each other like a couple of brothers sharing a special secret, but also like a couple of kids who had just been caught grabbing some sweets before dinner. The captain looking at myself, then Glen, then taking in the two of us at once said, 'So which jungle did you get a chance to see, the one upstairs from the bar, or the other one where Captain John lives?' 'Both,' I said; 'interesting guy that Captain John—had the most incredible shower, I could ever imagine. Fed by a waterfall.' 'I've seen it,' offered the captain. 'A man of great ingenuity, that Captain John,' he continued. 'And the other jungle; you made it to the other jungle, did you?' he smiled with all seriousness. 'Yeah, some of your boys showed us the other jungle,' but we're not giving up any names,' offered Glen. 'Don't worry, I won't ask, gentlemen; I won't ask. So you had a good day in Golfito, then.' 'Incredible day, just an amazing day,'

I answered. And at this point, the Dutch captain offered a large, compassionate smile.

" 'That's what it's all about,' he said, 'that's what it's all about. Enjoy your youth, have some fun. Oh to be young. Before you know it, you'll be older and filled with responsibilities. Enjoy your youth; enjoy the freedom; enjoy this time.' And so guys, I say the same to you. Enjoy this time; everything in moderation, though. Just know where to draw the line. But by all means enjoy this moment, this day, this place, each other, the music, the laughter. Not that there won't be other special times in your life—there will be many enjoyable times in your lives. But this time is very special. I'll tell you a bit more about Costa Rica; and then let's go for a swim."

"After dinner, Glen and I went back to the port. We walked up and down the roadway that borders the marina, eventually making our way back into the saloon below the corridor graced by Melba and Patrice. The place was now very full and lively, and in the background were English accents. Earlier in the day the place felt like an intimate party, the American English of Glen and myself the only native-English being spoken. Now the place was packed to the walls, a British Merchant Marine ship having arrived just a few hours before. Since I started with tequila earlier in the day, I was sticking with it tonight. Glen occupied himself with some sailors from our ship at the bar, while I ambled over to the table occupied by the English seamen. 'From England, ha,' I offered, feeling just so damn good. 'I really love it there; visited London last summer and really loved it. And, of course, I just love the music. Zeppelin, Cream, Jagger and the Stones; nobody on earth I'd like to talk to more than John Lennon.' 'You a rock star matey?' challenged a red-faced sailor, a big anchor tattooed on each thick forearm, golden-colored hair that was thinning and covering his head like straw. 'Second time someone has asked me that today,' I answered. 'Why else would a guy with such long hair, speaking American, be in a godforsaken place like this?' he said with a thick accent, borne of the docklands. 'Hey have a seat, matey,' he said, pulling a chair to his table from the one right next. 'We booked passage on a Merchant Marine ship that started out in Los Angeles; this is our first stop. My friend and myself—that's my buddy over there at the bar, the long-haired guy'—'Oh, another rock star,' he interrupted—'booked passage on this Honduran ship, captained by a Dutchman. Been a great ride, and we like this place so much, we're thinking of getting out here in Costa Rica, and joining the ship when it comes back through the canal on its return. We're kind of deciding that we want to see a lot more of this country.' 'Enjoy yourselves, matey,' he said. 'But I've seen enough bush in my life. Seen bush all over the world—the jungle kind and the kind you get upstairs—you know what's up those stairs, matey?' 'We've been introduced,' I answered. 'You have, have you, you American rock star. You know what it is with you Americans? You like to get to the action before everybody else. You guys just love action. Found more than you could handle in Vietnam, didn't you?' He had just downed another shot of something, and was starting to get a bit feisty. 'Save a little for the rest of the world, will you?' he continued. 'Well you know what it is with you British?' I said after a second shot of tequila. Now guys, I may have looked like a rock star, but I was a very athletic one. I certainly wasn't about to fight this sailor, but my juices were starting to flow. But for me, and I'm sure for him, it was all in good fun. 'You know, that's really a low blow about Vietnam. A lot of guys have died, and are dying over there, and we take it seriously. Look at all the wars the Brits have started—very few places on earth you haven't wanted to call your own. The problem with the Brits is that you guys are always looking for something, but never see what is right in front of your eyes.' I must have hit some sort of truth for him, because he stopped, looked me right in the eyes, then said: 'Matey, you're right about that. We are that way—we are always looking around but rarely see what is right in front of us. Didn't mean that comment about Vietnam. You guys have your hands full over there.'

" 'That's for sure,' I answered. 'That's for sure.' There was a lot of noise in the room, glasses clicking, ladies from upstairs making their way among the men. Gladly, we didn't see any sign of Melba or Patrice. The jukebox was playing some Latin dance music—not sure what it was, a local group I think—and then came one of my favorite songs in the world. It was the liquid, fiery guitar of Carlos Santana, the bluesy, sultry opening lines of 'Samba Pa Ti' building to a crescendo. Chasing the tequila with a beer, I closed my eyes and surrendered to the seduction of Costa Rica. It just doesn't get any better than that. The British sailor also started to nod to the intoxicating solo guitar of Carlos. 'Ah, Carlos,' he said. 'Yeah, Carlos.' When the song ended, I got up to make my way over to Glen at the bar—he had been there the whole time. But not before clasping the hand of my English friend, saying 'I love you British; always will.' 'Take care of yourself, rock star,' he answered. I made my way over to Glen, and together we went outside to catch some air.

"We still had a couple of hours before having to meet the last launch of the evening back to the ship. There wasn't a lot more to do in Golfito, but the exotic nature of this jungle port had penetrated our bloodstreams. And we were thinking really seriously about looking into the possibility of working out an arrangement with the shipping company to meet the ship on the way back to Los Angeles, thereby spending that time seeing other parts of this country. We walked back along the frontage road in the direction of the tin cottages where we had been titillated earlier that morning, the pathway heading into the jungle toward Captain John a few hundred yards beyond that. Once away from the saloon, all became dark. The scent of the density of life coming from the jungle blended with the thick salt of the sea, and in this thick air, under the influence of tequila and a black sky filled with a billion stars, these two scents merged into a third exotic aroma that felt as though it contained the origins of all life on the planet. In a place like this life seems to want to constantly recreate itself for its own pleasure.

" 'What are you trying to say here, Bruiser?' chuckled Woods, the soon-to-be Stanford freshman with the lanky frame, long blond surfer's hair and sweet face. "Well Woods, to put it bluntly, a place like this makes you want to fuck." "Dad," laughed Jonathan nervously. "Sorry, but that's the way it felt to a 19-year-old me." "Yes, I know what you mean, I know what you mean," offered Roberto in his strong Italian accent. "I have been a sailor my whole life; I love this story of the sea. I was in the Italian Navy; I know what that jungle feels like. It makes you feel—what is the word in English—wild." "Yeah, absolutely," I agreed.

" 'Glen,' I said, 'Let's not head back to the ship. Let's go see if we can find Melba and Patrice.' 'Good idea,' responded the thoughtful Glen. 'Hopefully, we won't have to wait in line,' he continued. 'What do we have to lose? We'll see if we can find them,' I responded. We made our way back into the saloon, and it was still packed to capacity. Santana's "Black Magic Woman"—I kid you not—was playing on the jukebox, loudly above the cacophony of the customers. 'A Black Magic Woman, she's trying to make a Devil out of me' poured the words as we made our way up the stairs, sailors and ladies twisting their bodies around each other in an area set aside for dancing. We walked down the hallway where earlier that day we had been beckoned by a couple of dozen women. There was no beckoning this time, just a lot of groans and moans coming from occupied stalls.

"To Glen's delight, Patrice was not booked, and was really excited to see him. They starting making out as though they were lovers. Melba's stall was not occupied; she wasn't in the room. Patrice said that she was out getting something to eat, and that she'd be back pretty soon. 'Just wait in her room; she won't mind,' Patrice said. And then Patrice and Glen went into her stall, closed the door and went at it. I could hear the uninhibited sounds of love making while I waited for Melba. She came back about 30 minutes later looking quite surprised to see me. 'I am happy to see you; I'm so happy to see you. You pay a little, and we spend the night together,' she offered. Melba was all business, Patrice and Glen—well that appeared to be something different. 'Sounds good Melba; we spend the night together.' 'You lie down here—make comfortable and I come back soon,' she answered. Well, an hour went by, then another hour—the lovemaking hot and furious, then quiet and sleepy in Patrice's stall next to me. I waited and waited, but no Melba. I had fallen asleep when, a few hours later, it was about 3:00 in the morning, Melba frantically rushes into the stall, shakes me saying, 'You must leave; you must leave now! Somebody is trying to kill me; somebody is trying to kill me. You must leave; you must leave!' I jump to my feet—I had been lying naked in her bed—put my clothes on quickly, trying to make sense of what was happening. 'Someone is trying to kill you; someone is trying to kill you? Why? What happened?' I ask. 'No time for questions; you must leave; someone is trying to kill me!' she repeats. The adrenalin kicks in, and I yell over at Glen: 'Glen get up; get up. We've got to leave. Someone is trying to kill Melba!' 'What the fuck,' exclaims my groggy friend. 'Glen, no fucking around. Someone is trying to kill her. We've got to leave now.' In a couple of seconds emerges Glen, Patrice not seeming all that flustered. Perhaps Melba had pulled this before—who knows? But in any event we were out of there in a flash. We made our way out of the dark, empty saloon downstairs and into the deserted street. Glen and I were alone—the sailors no doubt back where they belonged, on the ship. We walked over to the little pier by the launch. We could see the ship a couple of hundred yards at sea—but there was no way to get there. Within a couple of hours the sun climbed out of the jungle, life appeared in the waters, the launch-man arrived, and we were back on the ship for breakfast. After breakfast, we hit the beds and slept into the afternoon. We relaxed on the ship the rest of the day, but our desire to get off the ship and see this land had not diminished. The captain arranged for us to leave the ship; we were given clear instructions about when it would be returning and where we needed to be. The following morning we were off to see Costa Rica. The Captain had told us about a little resort on the sea, surrounded by rainforests. The village was called Puntarenas. A bus would be leaving in a few hours, and Glen and I made that bus.

"About an hour out of Golfito, the bus began to ascend into hilly and ravishingly beautiful countryside. The further along we went the more open became the scenery—no longer jungle terrain—as we drove amidst wide open fields of dense green, clusters of palms decorating the landscape where horses were roaming freely. The air coming in through the wide-open windows of the bus was cooler, lighter, still moist and warm, but filled with a lot more oxygen than Golfito. Glen and I were quiet, taking in the scenery, our long hair blowing wildly in the breeze. I think we were the only tourists on this bus, if you could call us that. There was a classroom full of young girls, maybe 11, 12 years old, white blouses and blue skirts their uniform, most with long, dark hair, smooth complexions, smiling faces. They were speaking amongst themselves, every once in a while one taking a curious, quizzical glance at Glen or me. We must have been quite a sight; I'm sure we weren't quite the sight the kids were used to seeing on their local bus ride. About an hour later, the bus emptied out almost entirely, Glen and I alone to the end of the line, Puntarenas. We climbed through this hilly, lush, grassy landscape for about two-and-a-half hours, and as we did, our consciousness became more and more euphoric. But then a weird thing happened. As the bus descended down toward the resort town, our moods started to become a bit low. It was probably that we were more tired than we had recognized from our Golfito experience, but Glen and myself talked about this once we arrived in the town. 'Glen,' I said, 'it's strange, but I was elated, absolutely euphoric as we were climbing through that hilly scenery, but as we started to descend, I started to get a bit low. I don't know why, this place is gorgeous, but there was something about climbing and then descending that changed my consciousness.' Glen and I were always interested in analyzing ideas, emotions, consciousness—our friendship was based on our affinity for exploring concepts, feelings, understanding our moods. As much as we were capable of being totally 'Dionysian,' surrendering to the moment, the event, the place, we could be almost, obsessively, Apollonian together. We could spend hours dissecting some nuance. Often Glen would disagree with me, but this time he had had the same experience. 'Wow, that is strange; I had the same experience on that bus. I was flying when we were climbing, but I started to have a real comedown when we started to descend. It's pretty weird—maybe it is the vibe or the energy of the place we were heading toward, perhaps our level of excitement couldn't be sustained and had no place to go but down—sort of like a cocaine comedown—maybe it is something we ate, but we were both tapped into that same feeling.' 'Yeah, I haven't experienced anything like that before,' I answered. 'Let's go find a hotel, take a nap, have some dinner, and then check out the sunset. We'll get our second wind,' I followed.

"We went to one, two, three hotels—the officer in control of the radio room had given us the names—but they were all booked. Nice places, along the beach—beautiful patio restaurants —but not a room to be had. We were directed to a hotel further down the beach 'that was sure to have rooms.' Now, guys, we weren't looking for anything even remotely extravagant, just like you guys on your trip. I'm sure you're staying in some pretty low-budget hostels. But this place was one for the ages. We were pretty enthused on approaching it—it looked on a gorgeous, smooth white-sand beach maybe 100 yards from the premises. 'Yes, we have a room with two single beds,' we were told, 'It is the last one available. You will be able to see the sea.' We grabbed the key, taking it sight unseen. We entered the room and, man, what a bummer. Low-flying bugs and mosquitoes had the airspace entirely to themselves. The walls had flies all over them, and the room was hot, humid, uninhabitable. 'Glen, now I know why we shared in a joint comedown—we were apprehending, intuiting that we would end up in a place like this.' 'Yep, you got it Bruce; our minds were getting the message before our bodies,' he followed. 'Let's go take a walk by the ocean and figure something out,' I suggested. 'Agreed,' he answered.

"It was about 4:30 in the afternoon; the sand was pristine white, but the beach not that crowded. We each waded, then swam into these perfect waters—I guess about as perfect as the waters we're on now, don't you think, Roberto?" "It doesn't get much more perfect than this," answered my Italian friend. " 'Glen, let's do something else—let's head to San Jose,' I said, 'I'm sure there are buses that'll get us there tonight. Can't be more than a four-or-five hour ride,' I went on. I was, indeed, correct. We would be able to make it to San Jose, but it would take some doing. There was a little provincial town on the other end of the rain forest from Puntarenas. We would be able to catch a bus from there in a few hours—it would take us directly to San Jose. But for whatever reason, there wasn't any transportation to this village—so to get there meant a walk through a rainforest. The town was about three miles away, so we'd have to start right away if we were going to make it. 'You should be fine walking through there,' someone had said, 'but be a little careful, there are wild boar that go on that road from time to time.' I was up for it, but Glen gave me a look like what the hell are you getting us into here. I think if someone were to look at our body language as we prepared to hike to the next town, mine would have been filled with vigor, ready for the athletic challenge. Glen had a 'what the fuck' expression, his shoulders turned in, suggesting that he wasn't really up for this schlep. Well, we made it through that rain forest, Glen telling me about half way through—Glen was two years older than me and liked to use it against me when it was advantageous—that he was too old to be doing this shit. 'Come on Glen; come on,' I responded like a drill sergeant or hockey coach. We made it to the next village, but not in time to catch the bus to San Jose. No worries, we found a cozy air-conditioned room for the night; our schedule for the next day was to get to the bus station just a few doors down, for our journey to San Jose."

"Guys, when I was in my teens and into my 20s there was a coffee commercial that used to play on TV for MJB coffee, I think it was. Or maybe it was Hill Brothers, I can't remember which. I'm not sure if either of these coffee companies is around today. Maybe one bought the other, or they were both bought by someone else, I don't know. But in any event, the TV commercial had this South American coffee grower named Juan Valdez. The commercials aired over many years and the television-watching audience got to know him in his various guises. His appearance was stereotypical South American. Big Sombrero; full, burly mustache; brown eyes and a full, wide face, the skin slightly dry looking, browned and freckled by the South American sun. Some commercials would have him on a horse surveying his coffee fields; others might show him mingling amongst his workers with a big smile on his face. But it seems to me that every commercial had the same two ingredients: a scene of Juan holding the "rich" coffee beans in his large, rough, coffee-growing hands; the other of him drinking a sip of this coffee, the look on his face one of pure ecstasy. So boys, as we approached San Jose on this bus of local working-class Costa Ricans—along the way someone would put on the seat next to him a cage with a few chickens or a rooster in it; at another stop a family with about 20 members took over all the remaining seats as well as the standing room, selling bunches of bananas to anyone interested—we entered gorgeous, hilly coffee country. And as Glen and I shared a bunch of bananas that we had purchased—these bananas were different from what you find in California; they were very small, about a dozen in a bunch, absolutely delicious—we expected to find Juan Valdez. This was just great. We were rested, brimming with enthusiasm at being in this exotic coffee land, enjoying this foreign land of Latin America. And then there appeared Juan Valdez, and then another Juan Valdez, and then another. This was real life, and it was a kick, so much fun. The scent of dried coffee wafted through the air as the bus made its way into San Jose through the rolling hills.

"And then we were in the big city. What a contrast this was to Golfito. It seemed quite compact and densely populated. It appeared to be fairly affluent, lots of professional, well-dressed business people going to and from destinations. And though we must have looked like quite a sight with our hair, men and women were quite friendly, a lot of smiling. As we walked toward a travel center to find a hotel, we came on several little public squares, filled with atmosphere. 'Glen, this place has every bit the texture that you find in Europe,' I said. 'It does remind me of Spain,' he answered, 'but it has its own special charm,' he continued. I agreed. This place felt really nice, really friendly. We sat down and had a sublime cup of Juan Valdez, the coffee dark as mud, which we filled with cream. It was delicious, and in the background there was an announcer—it sounded as though it were a public radio station—providing information of some sort in a deep, Spanish accent. The language in the background, the little square, the coffee, the friendly faces walking past, this place was second to nothing.

"We found a nice hotel, a place with super-comfortable beds. That night we went out, found a little club with a nice jukebox and drank some Costa Rican rum. I went to the jukebox and selected about 10 Santana songs—choosing "Samba Pa Ti" about three times. And each time the song came on, I fell deeper in love with Costa Rica. By the end of the evening, I was dancing slowly with a beautiful senorita, about my age. We had started talking; she was a school teacher; she told me that Costa Rica had the highest percentage of school teachers of any country in Latin America, maybe even the world—and eventually we ended up dancing in a slow, rhythmic sultry way with one another. I'll never forget—and I really mean never—that moment when that fiery, ecstatic guitar of Carlos came on, our faces together, everything Latin, everything just incredible. We stayed in San Jose about four nights, and on that last night, I left Glen all alone to fend for himself in the wilds of San Jose. By prior arrangement, this lovely, educated, soft, cheerful, romantic Costa Rican young woman met me for dinner at a restaurant in an area near to her apartment, not far from the commercial district. It was an area of relatively low-rise apartment buildings, each about 10-to-12 floors high. We had pasta that night, and a few beers. After dinner we walked to a little club that was playing live music, and what I remember distinctly about the music that night is that the group—all with long hair, making me feel quite at home—opened with a really sexy version of that early Santana song, "Oye Como Va," which was followed by "Evil Ways." We swayed, our bodies touching then pulling apart, the lyrics intoned in a deeply Latin way, 'You've got to change your evil ways, baby, before I start loving you. This can't go on, baby.' The music was intoxicating, the woman, Maria, was very pretty, with large, round brown eyes, shoulder-length brown hair, and full lips that were always smiling. She was really pretty, and when we went to her apartment at the end of the night, I tried to capture the moment in time with a mental picture of her, essentially knowing that we probably wouldn't see each other again. Her place was on one of the higher floors of one of these bland, modern apartment buildings. There was a view of the streets below; don't get embarrassed, Jonathan, but we made love that night. She called a taxi for me about three in the morning, which brought me back to the hotel room where Glen was sound asleep. As I walked in, Glen stirred, sat up for a moment, looked at me with squinted eyes, saying, 'Had fun tonight, did you?' 'No question, Glen boy; no question. Tell you about it in the morning.'

"While in San Jose, we had been told that we should not miss Puerto Limon, on the Caribbean coast. The train ride there from San Jose had to be experienced to be believed, it was said. And guys, it was amazing. Apparently, hundreds had died building this route from the hilly country outside San Jose, through the dense rain forests as they descended to the seaport of Puerto Limon. The tracks started in the rolling hills, and in no time one entered this jungle paradise, waterfalls cascading down cliffs into a steep ravine with a rushing river. About halfway toward Limon, the train stopped for about an hour. During this time, local villagers approached the train with bunches of bananas, which we purchased. These were fairly young girls and boys, barefoot, the boys shirtless, quite poor. But there wasn't any sense of desperation about them; they were not poorly fed, and were smiling. But, I was surprised by how many people came with bananas, other fruit, little trinkets. It seemed that a whole village had paid a visit to the train. Eventually, the train started moving, descending ever more deeply into this densely tropical land. The further we traveled, the closer to the Caribbean side, the greater the differences in the housing and people. Whereas the villagers in the forests closer to San Jose appeared to be of Spanish or native descent, living in homes that seemed to be made of clay, now the population was black, clearly more African. Because of the immense amount of rain the area must receive, houses were built on stilts. Everywhere were little cottages built high above the ground on stilts, African-looking Costa Ricans waving at the train as we traveled past. Eventually we were in Puerto Limon, where we stayed three nights. Even though it was Costa Rica, this was an island in the Caribbean. It was a different country from San Jose, certainly, and everything on the Pacific coast. Limon was hot and extremely humid—every bit as much as Golfito. There was no avoiding the mosquitoes, and our room was no exception. But it wasn't anything like the hotel room we escaped from in Puntarenas.

"While in Limon we had a funny experience. We found a lotion to safeguard us against being bitten, covering ourselves in it. And it worked. It chased away the bugs. And it proved to be a lady magnet. Dancing in a couple of steamy cantinas, the girls loved our scent. More than one time, we were told that the cologne we were wearing was really nice. It would be our secret. But finally we broke down and told a couple of girls with whom we had been dancing that it was a mosquito repellant. The looks on their faces were funny—smiling, giggling, covering their mouths with their hands. It was quite funny to them. Limon was fun, and the people were so nice. It was exotic to us, the blend of the African and

Spanish in this deeply tropical port. Before leaving, we stumbled upon a plaque saying in Spanish and English that this was the place where Columbus had landed on his "discovery" of this land. It was an interesting moment; standing on these grounds, looking out at the sea, getting a sense of how it might have seemed. There was not a lot of civilization on this coastline; much of it probably looked similar to what Columbus saw. Puerto Limon; it had been quite an experience, but we were ready to escape the mosquitoes and make our way back to the cooler climate of San Jose.

"We were told that there was a little airstrip on the outskirts of Limon, and that we could take a plane back to San Jose. We had about three days before we were due to catch the return ship from Golfito, and since the train ride was a whole day, we took the plane to give ourselves more time in San Jose. We thought that it would be cool to experience more of Juan Valdez country, getting out into the coffee plantations. It was a real small plane—apparently purchased by the Costa Rican domestic airlines from some small American airlines. You'd never get me on one of those planes today, but back then it didn't bother me much. It was a smooth ride—the pilot pointing out the dense rain forest that we had traversed on the train—and in short order we were in San Jose. We went back to the same hotel, a place that had really comfortable beds, free of mosquitoes. The room was perfectly air-conditioned—the experience very comfortable. We spent the next couple of days taking buses into the coffee country, walking through some of the little towns in these hills of coffee. We were trying to capture, freeze in time, these final days in Costa Rica, breathe in the air, feel the sunshine, drink the coffee. The next couple of nights, Glen and I hung out together, a sense of nostalgia settling in as our friendship and bond with this country deepened. We found little cantinas, some we had previously visited, and a few new ones—the liquid, fiery, electric guitar of Carlos Santana always decorating the background through the speakers on the little jukeboxes. I didn't look for my San Jose girlfriend—this time belonged to Glen and myself. I knew then—clearly realized it—that there would never be an experience quite like this again, and I vowed that I would one day tell my own sons about it. The edited version, of course. So Jonathan, boys, now you have it. Costa Rica—it changed my life. And you boys will remember this moment, this trip, in much the same way. It is your adventure. And it is just amazing, that I am here on this boat experiencing part of it with you. Let's jump in the water and swim to the shore. When do we have to get the boat back to Portofino, Roberto?" "In about an hour and a half," he answered. "So do we have time to swim to the shore and back?" "No problem," responded the captain who had become a good friend, practically a participant in my journey to Costa Rica.

"Boys, just another thing or two about Costa Rica, before we go for a swim. We got back to Golfito on time, but the boat had arrived before us and had already left. We were told that we could stick around a few more days, and catch another boat back to San Pedro. Or, they would refund our money so that we could buy an airplane ticket back home. Glen was ready to head back—and it was his opinion that it was probably just as well; how could we ever experience another boat ride like the one to Costa Rica? And, indeed, it was just as well. As I thought about it later, I realized that the return trip would have been about returning from the adventure, the emotions preparing for the "come down" of being back in Los Angeles. Better the memory be of journeying into the unknown, rather than heading back to the all too familiar. Costa Rica will always be about the journey into adventure, not the trip home. The return plane stopped in Mexico City for the night, the next day back to Los Angeles. The day after, arriving at my mom's house in the dry desert community north of Los Angeles, I sat in the front yard and started to sob. Everything was dry, where Costa Rica had been lush. There were Palm Trees all around Southern California, but they were brown. I had just been to Costa Rica; nothing would be the same again. My mom went into the front yard, as I sat there sobbing; she looked at me with deep compassion and tenderness. 'Brucie,' she said. 'It must have been so beautiful. It makes me sad to see you hurting like this.' She hugged me warmly and for a long time, and as she did, I continued to cry. 'Mom, I felt so alive there, so alive. I love you very much; I'm happy to see you. Maybe one day you'll get a chance to see Costa Rica, maybe one day you will.' 'Maybe I will Brucie; maybe one day I will. It must be so beautiful.' "

❐

We swam to the shore of one of the villages of cinque Terre. Walking up and down the beach, I tried to be nonchalant amidst these beautiful, bronzed, topless ladies. Woods looked over at me, offering a big grin—a smile fully across his face. "Good story Bruiser," he said. "Great Story." "Do well at Stanford; and enjoy the rest of this trip. And of course, look after Jonathan for me, will you?" "Will do Bruiser," he answered.

We swam back to the boat, Roberto starting the engine to take the boys back to their village. About 20 minutes later, we pulled into the little harbor, Roberto helping each lad onto the pier. I hugged each boy, from my soul, as they set out again on their own. "The highlight of the trip," offered Alex, as he made his way on to the pier. "Thanks Bruiser." "Great time, Great time," said Wyatt, that crazy hat back on his head. "Dad, I love you," said Jonathan. "Thanks for giving us such a good day." "Be safe, be careful, have a great time. Make sure I can reach you on the cell; keep it charged," I lectured. I looked into his brown eyes, his long, curly brown hair becoming increasingly golden in the sun. "I love this boy; I love him to the depths. And I will never forget this day," I said to myself. In its own way, it was a day that rivaled Costa Rica.

≈

July 11th, 2007

The plane is descending over the rather dry-looking hillsides and fields of Sonoma and Marin County. The announcement has just come on to get up and stretch and use the restroom now, because in about 10 minutes we will be required to be back in our seats, in preparation for landing at San Francisco International Airport. It is about 1:30 in the afternoon, and the blue San Francisco Bay is directly below us, not a cloud in the sky, the water dotted with dozens of sail boats and ferries, streaks of whitewater trailing behind. Now, the diamond that is San Francisco, a city that is a gateway to the east as it sits above its western bay is in full view, the elemental red—the color appearing to have come right out of the earth—of the Golden Gate Bridge directly below us. Directly over the city, I am sure that I am looking at the top of my apartment building as we fly above the north side, Pacific Heights. The tops of the financial district appear in full view, the highest tower, the Bank of America building as well as the impossible-to-mistake Transamerica Pyramid directly below. My office building is just down the street from the B of A building and, no doubt, my assistant, Mary, has had to field numerous questions from curious, concerned or nervous clients about this subprime situation and if it affects them. I can just imagine those questions have been coming in. I am preparing to answer these questions; and I am probably more up to speed on the issue than I would be if I had been in San Francisco these last couple of weeks. I have been reading the Financial Times, The New York Times, The Wall Street Journal, the International Herald Tribune to keep up on the economy. These pages have been filled with the growing number of financial institutions with exposure to this problem and the losses that keep being revised upwards. A few German and English banks appear to have more exposure than previously thought, and this is not to mention the potential for enormous losses amongst Wall Street's largest banks and securities companies. It seems that there has been greed everywhere.

Banks flush with cash due to the Federal Reserves strategy of significantly cutting interest rates a few years ago to avoid recession were aggressively making loans to unqualified borrowers without documentation. The loans were of variable rate, allowing for large increases if rates were to rise—which they have been doing over the last year and a half. Some of the loans were made with no equity on properties where the appraiser never stopped to even enter the house, the money just thrown at properties where the asking prices were higher than anything that had ever sold on the street. Speculators were jumping in and buying two, three properties at a time, thinking that there wasn't much downside—with no equity requirements they could rent them out, walking away if things ever got really bad.

And, apparently, things are getting bad—properties are falling well below the mortgages, and as interest rates rise, and the borrowing costs go up, many are walking away, putting these places into foreclosure. And this isn't only happening to speculators; it is happening to innocent homebuyers who were being offered big money by aggressive banks that had partnered with appraisers to get these people into the homes. Now, with mounting job losses and higher interest rates, these people who really couldn't afford to be in these homes are on the verge of losing them, banks taking the hit. Mortgage brokers, banks, home sellers, builders, appraisers were living the high life on these inflated, risky loans, but in a contagion that is undermining the U.S. economy and seems to be threatening the global economy, significant requirements for additional capital threatens to undermine the financial security of all sorts of financial institutions from banks to insurance companies. What further complicates the problem is that these subprime loans (loans given to under-qualified borrowers with little or no documentation) were used to increase returns on financial products known as CDOs (Collateralized Debt Obligations) that were purchased for their own portfolios by many, many financial institutions. I am reading about the potential for billions of dollars of losses for these institutions, possibly threatening their very survival. Hopefully, it will not get that bad, but from what I am reading it seems that it is going to get a lot worse, as the home prices fall, before it gets better. The bonds that are made up of these subprime loans do not have much of a track record in the financial markets, and it looks as though there is very little liquidity for the companies that hold them—in other words, traders are providing "very little quarter for those who need to sell."

This is the environment into which I will return to my office tomorrow. My clients do not own this product, which I will be pleased to tell them. But, no doubt, the trading of these instruments will have an effect on many financial instruments, even the conservative ones. The degree to which these subprime loans and the CDOs they are part of threatens the solvency of our large companies remains to be seen, but I have some fears that the problem is insidious, that we will find out that it is everywhere in the global economy.

❐

The "fasten seat belt" sign has just come on, and in a few minutes we will be landing in San Francisco, my home. There is an emptiness in my stomach as I consider that I will return to my apartment, just a few blocks from my wife, Susan, and the home in which we have raised our boys. I love her. I will always love her, and yet we are apart. When the boys return in a few weeks, I will be there more often to visit them. But for now, I'll come mainly to walk our beautiful Black Lab, Lucky. We are trying to adhere to the nature of our separation—we really are separated, and must act that way. But it hurts, and as I think about being so close yet remaining estranged physically, if not in my heart, I feel an emptiness in my stomach and a hardness in my throat. But what does one do; I just can't seem to change the state of affairs. There is something in me that wants it this way, I guess. Perhaps

I am expanding, evolving, penetrating some of the mysteries of life by allowing myself the freedom and giving up a comforting security. And honestly, there has been a yearning, a craving for something that has been there for me for a long while. This is my opportunity to find out what that is. The soul seeks, at a certain stage, the unpredictable, the unknown, uncertainty. And it seems that now my soul is calling the shots at this point in time. But there is no doubting a feeling of emptiness and sadness as we prepare to land. This feeling is a little mitigated by a pleasant thought that has crossed my mind—the healing that takes place when I visit the spiritual, calming environment of Dr. Gwen Jones, her gentle touches on my back in the practice of Network softening the edges of my day. She is calming, and I appreciate that she is there.

We are flying low now, the plane just above the bay as we approach the runway. This journey of the past couple of weeks has been profound—and I contemplate the self-discovery as our plane touches the ground. The landing was as smooth as butter; in a few moments I will be making my way through customs, into a taxi and back into the streets of San Francisco.

❒

It is now early August, 2007; both boys have resurfaced, and are back hanging out with friends at the family home, just a few blocks from where I sit on this foggy San Francisco morning, looking south from this green wooden bench at Alta Plaza Park, the city stretching out before me all the way to the Peninsula. The north side of this park, facing Jackson Street, is where I sat that day, sobbing, when the license plate "Alma Loves Ten" suddenly appeared. I sat on the wall that day waiting for my grade school boys to walk by, when that answer for a message appeared with such astonishing clarity. My sons are no longer boys; they are young men. Michael will be 21 in a couple of days, and Jonathan—Baby Jonathan, Michael used to call him—doesn't get much time at home before going off to college in New York as a freshman. The school requires that the entering students be there a few weeks for a seminar before the start of classes. So, in a couple of weeks, Sue and I will be taking Jonathan back east together, as a family.

I have been at the house more often now that the boys are home. I joke with the guys, get sarcastic and playful with their friends, as I always have, lecture, reprimand, encourage, joke, rough them up from time to time. I come by later in the evening reminding Michael to keep it under control, control the number of kids coming in and out, reminding him that the "neighbors will complain." Sue is usually asleep, upstairs, through all of the activity—I don't know how she is able to do that. When I am visiting the boys, I am in my home, and then I leave. I make way up the street to Broadway where I return to this apartment. And it hurts—sometimes like hell—every time I shut the door to the house and walk back to the apartment. But when I walk back into the apartment, the bay, the bridges, the lights of the city stretched out before me, boats and ferries sparkling in the darkness of the bay, I feel a calm, an inner peace amidst the deeply felt strain. And then I'll write. And when I do this, I realize that this is where I must be at this moment in time—that I need the quiet for reflection, that solitude is important at the moment, that space (mental and physical) is what the body seems to require. I question how long I'll be in this apartment, and whether a divorce is somewhere in the offing. I wonder if I will ever connect in a meaningful, committed way again, enjoying the intimacy and tenderness of love. I do go on dates from time to time, and now and then I'll feel a spark. But too much is unsettled, and I just cannot release of myself sufficiently at this moment to add enough kindling to develop a relationship. I don't want to be alone in this apartment for years or the rest of my life—living a solitary life—surrendering to the ease of being by myself, becoming set in ways that might make it difficult to ever be in a relationship again. I am a social person, and I meet people easily. And I can be easily tantalized with just the right hint of perfume as it blends with a smile and a look in the eyes. I have the freedom to pursue those suggestive glances if I choose, the smile that might lead to more—I don't live with Sue now—yet I remain so much a part of my family that I cannot seem to surrender to the fact that, perhaps, I am available. Am I available? I really do not know. How would I feel if Sue were to see me with someone? Probably similar to the way I would feel if I saw her holding hands with a man, or on a date. And yet I have to live. I don't want to hide. I live in this city. I don't want to live in such a way that I have to bury a social life, afraid that my boys might see me, or a friend who does not know that we have separated. It's confusing—I'm free, but between my ears, I am not. I am available, but I cannot offer a partner more than a glass of wine at a live music venue. And I look over my shoulder even then. So, it is difficult—it would be much easier if I did not love Sue, but I do. I just don't understand the way in which I love her. I strive to understand it. I struggle with it, as I sit here in this foggy park on an August morning, the wind blowing a chill through this sweatshirt. As I struggle with it, I seek to discard fantasies or illusions of what is possible. Is life destined, or is it an ongoing process of chance situations, random occurrences? We clearly have the ability, intelligence and will to make choices. But are many of the choices that we believe to be making with free will actually the consequences of a lifetime of actions responsible for where we are and what we do at this moment in time? It hurts like hell to acknowledge this separation, and the possibility of divorce. But for the life of me I cannot seem to be doing anything differently, to live my life in any other way.

❒

The breeze is picking up now and chilling me to the bone on this summer day. I often simultaneously love and dislike this city. There is a feminine energy about this place, an openness and freedom of spirit, a hypnotic seductiveness in the little neighborhoods where rows of ornate and delicate Victorians and Edwardians allow the mind to seek cozy refuge behind the dainty, delicate Ladies painted in purples, reds, greens, yellows—ornate designs, curved bay windows, rendering each one of these a masterpiece. These masterpieces cascade up and down hillsides more beautiful than Rome, the panorama as we look on the bay beyond compare in my travels. Yet, that bone-chilling cold on a summer's day can get to a person, even if you have lived here for 25 years. I wouldn't trade it, I wouldn't want to live anywhere else, but there are times on a cold August morning when I want to rip off my shirts, expose my bare skin to the wind and say, "San Francisco, you're a pain in the ass—hit me with it, give me all you have, I can take it, I can take all of it, you damn cold place." I'm hurting at the moment, and as I sit here, I do yell, "Damn it San Francisco, you are too beautiful for your own good! It hurts to be here; it damn hurts! And your are too damn, fuckin' cold. Do you hear me? You are too damn fuckin' cold!" And I do take off my shirts. There is no one around me at the moment, so I do not look like a crazy person to anyone—at least not to my knowledge. In a few minutes, I'll go and check on the boys, safely and comfortably tucked away within the interior of a Painted Lady, the one that I own. I love those boys with everything that I am, and may they always be safe, secure and cozy in a place that they love.

I get up from the green, wooden bench that sits atop this third and top tier of the three terraced levels that rise from Clay Street. This highest tier offers the most complete view of the city to the south. The distant parts of the Mission—clearly perceptible when the sun is brilliant—merge with a white background on this morning. I look down on the row of early Edwardian homes that look on this park from the street, thinking how cozy it would be to be in one just now, kicking back in a comfortable leather chair, reading and daydreaming. I would often do this on a morning like this in my house, but that doesn't happen anymore. I am not living in that calm and peaceful Victorian anymore—Sue and I used to talk about how the chi seemed right in the house, that there was a relaxing quiet that poured out from its walls. However, I experienced the greatest pain and sadness that I have ever know in that house.

❒

Several months after moving in, we learned of my mom's cancer. The calm energy within the house did provide some solace from the pain, and the attic in particular gave me a place where I could disappear from the world altogether with my tears. And, of course, the other half of the hard times within the house came in the aftermath of the revelations about "M." From that moment on, any day or night of the week would be unpredictable. Sue might go into anger or tears at any time—and there were so many late Friday nights, early Saturday mornings, Sunday breakfasts, the wee hours of Monday morning before having to get up to go to work that we lived in tortured despair—eventually hugging one another for comfort so that we could each get some rest. Drained from explanation, realization, rationalization, honesty and tears, we could find some comfort deep beneath the surface, in a refuge where the last comfort for each other was each other.

What was happening to us, we could not say. Or, perhaps I could not say. I think that Sue wanted to place all of our troubles on the fact that "M" entered our lives. And it was always implicit that everything would be all right if "M" had not entered our lives. And in these moments, this painful, troubled, tortured state of affairs possessed a layer of accusation, blame, suggestive of a guilt that I was supposed to feel. I didn't want to feel that guilt; I didn't want all of the blame to lay on my shoulders, and in the small hours of these mornings, I tried to talk of my yearnings, what seemed to be missing, struggling to recognize that I was a volcano erupting with feelings over which I had no control and that were changing our lives. I struggled to tell Sue that it wasn't all about me, that perhaps her pouring of herself into our children left me empty. But truth be told, I never went looking for something else; I was content that this is the way life is, that at a certain point, one just surrenders to the fact that we do not have romance in our lives, that there is no passion anymore. We were friends together, we would always be friends—what was there to dream about, what more was there to feel? Yet, there was a private yearning, and in my prayers I asked God to fulfill this yearning, to help me discover what would satisfy it. I was not interested in affairs; I was not interested in chasing women; I just wanted that sense of adventure again, a kind of Costa Rica of this time in life that I could share with the person that I love. But I slowly surrendered to the idea that there would never be a Costa Rica again, not in the real sense of an adventure, or a Costa Rica of the soul, where I would become more and more of the artistic, deeply feeling, compassionate, spiritual person that was my calling in this life. It was okay, though, I really didn't need more—just let me provide for all who depend on me and I'd be just fine. Little did I know, though, that my mine shaft was shallow, and just below the surface was a vein of soft yellow gold, a layer of thick black oil, a warm mineral well that needed the expression of consciousness. I suppose that I had buried it, but not as deeply as believed, after my mom died.

For a brief time, playing the soft Chopin Études, drinking wine, speaking softly with romance and passion for life, "M" tapped into a stream of emotion that so much wanted to be shared, and in sharing it, a spell was cast. And the spell lasted over many phone calls over many months, playing music for one another over the telephone lines, drinking wine all the while. And so we talked about "M," and we talked even more. I described how I couldn't shut myself down, that I didn't want to kill something that felt alive, and that for the life of me, there was not a thing that I could do, because the pain of Sue, "M," and myself was becoming too great. We talked of separating, then we cried about separating, and in the end we would just fall asleep, sometimes together after making love, other times apart.

I have walked only about 15 yards to the next green bench, these thoughts have taken the weight out of my legs, and I have had to sit again. That cold Siberian wind picks up again, and I start to wonder what is right and what is wrong. Perhaps looked at a certain way—as many in society will surely do—I never should have allowed myself to feel anything with "M." I might have acknowledged the feelings, but moved on as a married man. It would just be black and white, simple as that. All of the pain would have been avoided; I would still be in my chair, dozing off in the quiet of my home. But of course, I wouldn't be writing this, because there wouldn't be anything to write. I would be a provider with yearnings; but who doesn't have yearnings—that is just life. I wouldn't have been living this life that I never anticipated. But I can't go there; I simply cannot. I cannot succumb to this world of black and white, right and wrong. It is just not as easy as that, and I am not a stupid human being—something happened to me, and perhaps I'll be trying to understand it for the rest of my life.

A sense of direction; oh, God please give me a clear sense of direction. I say this in my prayers at night, and I repeat it as a mantra, sitting on this green bench, the view to the south now almost completely enshrouded in mist, the chill breeze that prompted the saying, often attributed to Mark Twain, that, "The coldest winter I ever spent was a summer in San Francisco" giving me no quarter. But I am not ready to get up; I don't want to go anywhere right now. I'm angry right now; I don't know why, I just feel angry. My feelings hurt; they hurt like that unrelenting sore throat that I seem to get about every other winter. The chill hurts; my feelings hurt; this cold breeze hurts; San Francisco hurts; my boys hurt; the death of my mom hurts; and there is no place to go.

❒

There have been so many fine moments in my life, and as we go through life, our experiences crystallize into serious memory. A little boy, perhaps four years old, big, clear, blue eyes walks in front of me on the path; he has light colored hair, and a disposition of pure sweetness and curiosity. I am startled at how reminiscent he is of my Michael at that age—my mom used to call Michael a

Gainsborough painting, so enthralled was she by his goodness and innocence—when the father, about 10 steps behind, offers, "Do you want some water?" "Yes, Dad, okay." comes the answer, as the dad catches up with him right in front of me and pours some water from a thermos into a cup, the boy drinking with great delight. "That's delicious, Dad," he says. "Its special water," answers the dad, the father and myself exchanging smiles, suggestive of the truth that "life really doesn't get much better than a son and dad sharing precious moments. It had to be yesterday, but goodness, it is suddenly 17 years ago that I walked in this park with Michael, along this very path, tossing him a ball, giving him a sip of water, putting him up on my shoulders. He is cozy in the house down the street now, most likely still in bed after being out too late. He will always be my baby; if I am around when he is 60, he'll be my baby for sure. Indeed, experiences crystallize into serious memory as we go through life, and it is wise to pay attention, because we really do not know going into the day which event, or snapshot, might alter our lives, and stay with us to our dying day. While there may be a heaven in some distant land that we might one day reach, the heaven that I can understand unfolds right in front of us—the dad who just walked by with his son, Michael, just walked softly across a stage in heaven.

I was present at the births of Michael and Jonathan; and while Sue, I'm sure, would not describe the experience of giving birth as being in heaven—she gave birth naturally, but she writhed in pain—the moment when Michael arrived, essentially impatient to be born, will be with me forever. A little more than six pounds, the eyes were searching for awareness, squinting from the light and shock of this foreign place. Indeed, he was impatient, perhaps scared, but unquestionably aware. I couldn't believe what I had just witnessed; it seemed mythological. How could it be real—this fully realized being coming from this place within a body? And I was a father. Heaven is in our memories, and that moment of his birth will always be heaven for me. Jonathan was calmer at birth, and isn't it interesting how he is just that way in relation to Michael now. His complexion and hair were a bit darker than Michael's, and he seemed quite relaxed at birth, not a sense of urgency in his body. Where Michael seemed to want to grasp everything right away, Jonathan appeared more relaxed, perhaps enjoying the experience. His lips were like a little rosebud, and that rosebud matured into a set of "kissing lips" that must produce envy in many girls. My thought after Michael was born was, "Well, I'd better stop here, because how will I ever experience this kind of feeling a second time?" And then the second time came, and the feeling for Jonathan, the sense of amazement of life, the immediate, overwhelming love for this boy of ours just overcame me—it was every bit as intense as the first time. The moment of his birth crystallizes in memory, and it is a piece of heaven.

❐

I recall an image of Sue that occurred during, of all times, the terrible period we were having after the revelation of "M." We had been going to couples therapy, and in this therapy we decided to get away by ourselves, so infrequently had we ever done this since the boys had been born. We went to Aspen for a long weekend in February and, on one of the evenings, we went to the outdoor ice rink in the center of town. The ice had been freshly watered, and there was no one on the ice except the two of us. There is nothing like skating on hard, cold, outdoor ice—I just love it. And on this outdoor ice, Sue and I skated, arm in arm. Getting tired—the altitude is about 8000 feet—Sue sat down and watched me display my hockey-skating style, my skates digging into the ice, making that fresh razor sound of blades cutting ice. She was impressed, as she had been when we first met, and I skated for her on the outdoor rink at Keystone in Colorado, the state of her birth. After my skating performance that day—I really wasn't performing for anyone, just having a fantastic time—a bunch of kids came up to me asking for my autograph. They were convinced that I had to be a professional hockey player. So I signed it for them—writing Bruce Farrell Rosen on their piece of paper. Sue had gotten such a kick out of that. After resting, she came back on the ice, her hands cozy in white gloves, and skated toward me, putting her hands around my waist. For a moment, everything to do with "M" didn't exist for her—we were kids again. Despite the torture of those days, and the estrangement that we both feel from each other—it seems that we hardly talk, and when we do, she doesn't want to talk about us, preferring to walk away—that moment will be forever crystallized in my memory as a piece of heaven.

And what about those great San Francisco 49er football days? Sue had moved to San Francisco the previous summer, and we were comfortably tucked away in a little studio with a gorgeous view of Coit Tower, North Beach, the financial district, the Bay Bridge. We had just bought a new TV for this occasion—the NFC Championship game between the 49ers led by the young, smooth as silk, ice water in his veins, Joe Montana and the Dallas Cowboys, the team that had buried the Niners' chances so many

Selected by lottery I purchased two tickets to Superbowl XIX against Miami; at Stanford Stadium, Joe Montana had a fantastic evening as the 49ers handled the Dan Marino-led Dophins 38 - 19.

times in the past. A couple of friends were over at the time, and we were all practically paralyzed as Montana—the team behind with time running out in the fourth quarter—rolled to his right, back tracked, nasty Cowboys virtually surrounding him, delivered a ball to the back of the end zone that had no business being caught. But Dwight Clark—a tall receiver to begin with—jumping and stretching to the absolute maximum permitted by his human frame, caught that ball with the very tips of all of his fingers. What were the odds of him catching that ball? It had to be less than 20 percent in my book. Replays of the "The Catch" as it will be forever called, showed how ridiculous such a catch was—it had no business occurring. There is a picture of The Catch on the wall in my office—and it will be there for as long as I work. It catapulted the 49ers into the Super Bowl against the Cincinnati Bengals, which we won. The Golden Age of the Niners had started, replete with many heroes over the '80s, and into the '90s. The names are now legendary in San Francisco: Joe Montana, Dwight Clark, Ronnie Lott, Roger Craig, Jerry Rice brought some of the greatest moments in San Francisco sports history, and along with them, some of the greatest times in our marriage. I acquired season tickets to the 49ers in those days, and together we enjoyed the Golden Years. There were so many memories going to those games, but that moment in our living room when Dwight Clark caught that ball, the hugging and ecstasy that occurred, will never be forgotten. The experience has crystallized into memory, and that memory is a slice of heaven.

There were many, many great 49er moments that Sue and I experienced together. Perhaps none more fun than that evening at Stanford Stadium, January, 1985, when the supercharged Miami Dolphins—they had rolled over every team in the AFC—met the Montana-led 49ers in the Super Bowl. We had been selected in the lottery for tickets, and Sue had taken a picture of me, huge smile on my face, being handed the tickets at Candlestick Park, home of the 49ers. The Niners dominated on that cold, foggy night, and Joe Montana was in a world unto himself. He walked on air that night;

he seemed to be playing in a special magical zone from which he could perform wizardry. He was brilliant—just picked apart the Dolphins. There were some people from my office that happened to be sitting a few rows in front of us, and there is a picture in the photo album, the album that we do not open anymore, of the joy in our faces together that evening. It is an experience that has crystallized into serious memory, and it is a memory that reveals a slice of heaven in our lives.

I get up from this green bench. The chill breeze has not subsided, and though my thoughts have kept me warm for a while, I am starting to get quite cold. I'll leave the park now, and head in the direction of my house. Perhaps I'll check on Michael and Jonathan.

August 4

I have just finished watching ESPN's highlights of an historic day in baseball. In the afternoon at Yankee stadium, Alex Rodriquez became the youngest player, at age 32, to hit 500 home runs. He hit it to left field, the ball staying to the fair side of the foul pole. The ball was hit against the Kansas City Royals, and as it cleared the fence, Rodriquez threw both hands into the air, the music of the movie, "the Natural," playing in the background. And, then, tonight at Petco Stadium in San Diego, Barry Bonds, after taking extra batting practice during the afternoon, also went to left field, tying Hank Aaron with his 755th home run.

With thousands of camera flashes going off through the stadium, Bonds hit a high and outside 2-1 fastball, tagging it off of a red advertising sign. Initially boos outnumbered the cheers, but in short order the majority of San Diego fans gave this accomplishment (however tarnished by accusations of steroid use it may be) its just celebration, applause and cheers eventually drowning out the boos. The replays show that quick, powerful Bonds swing, the "signature swing" that we have come to identify with, probably (steroids or not) the greatest hitter of all time. The extra batting practice must have helped; Bonds had gone 28 plate appearances without hitting a ball as far as the warning track. Sort of a surrealistic day, watching both players hit record home runs—seeing these home runs back-to-back in replay; perhaps time was providing a glimpse of irony, giving us a view of the present and future at once. The soon-to-be "home run champion" eventually overshadowed by the man who would one day break his record. Time will tell, but it certainly felt synchronistic to see these two sluggers achieve such amazing records on the same day of the calendar.

❒

This day, August 4, will be forever remembered by me for reasons other than baseball: It was on this day in 1967 that a man broke into our home in Montreal, Canada and attempted to rape my mother. I have described how we left for Canada on June 6, 1966—not the most auspicious sequence of numbers for making a drastic change in life—my father wanting to return to his roots. We had been pulled out of school a little more than a week before the end of the school year, the teachers wondering why my parents wouldn't just wait an extra week for there to be closure to the school year. But that is the way it happened, though to this day, I still feel like something incomplete had occurred. I think that in the deepest recesses of memory, I still look for closure to that school year, to have been able to say goodbye to my friends without a rush. And I have chronicled in earlier pages how rough a start it had been in Canada for all of us, but particularly for me, so desperately missing my friends in California, the feeling of California, playing baseball in the fields on the summer days, the vicious back of my father's hand to my lip, splattering blood against the wall. The psychological wound of that shot to the mouth must not have cleanly healed—there is painful scar tissue that makes me want to go into my darkened bedroom, close the blinds, pull the blankets over my head and sob.

❐

I recognize the very special work that my good friend Gwen Jones is performing with her Network Chiropractic—the light touching that she does two to three times a week to my back and legs is designed to release and free one from painful memory and trauma that becomes stored in our bodies, eventually working their way deep into our tissues, cells and bones. And over time these stored memories and emotions characterize our physical "bearing" as we carry ourselves in ways that defend one from experiencing hurt. Our posture takes on the form of armor as we guard against feelings, insulate ourselves from getting in touch with the self that wants to be known, and in being known wants to enjoy life and the freedom of being human. Sometimes my moments during our sessions are quite unsettling, emotions, feelings, thoughts, memories coming to the surface and dissipating. At other times, I gain a deep rest, my breathing slowing as I sometimes fall asleep on the table. And during some of the recent sessions, a deep inner pain becomes released, accompanied by the memory of seeing this man attempt to rape my mother.

❐

It was August 4, 1967, and my father had left Montreal to take a job in an electronics company in the outpost of a town called Campbellton, New Brunswick, Canada. New Brunswick is one of the Maritime Provinces of Canada, and Campbellton sits far to the northeast of Montreal, on the Gaspé Peninsula, at the mouth of the Bay of Chaleur, which feeds into the Gulf of St.

Lawrence. A job had been offered to my father in this place on a short-term basis, and if it were to work out and he liked it, we would all be pulled up to Campbellton. My father had at no time been easy to live with during that first year in Montreal, and this reprieve from his turbulence and anger had become a welcome relief during the month or so that he had been gone. None of us were really thinking that we'd end up in Campbellton; my mom saw it as a "get away" for him, and that he'd eventually be back in Montreal, at which time it would either work out for "us" in Montreal in short order, or we'd be making plans to return to California. And I never relented in reminding my mom how badly I wanted to return. I had just spent that day playing some baseball, in preparation for our upcoming playoff game. I had really entered a "groove" at this point in the baseball season, playing first base, being counted on to deliver clutch hits, batting third. The team had been doing really well of late, the same group of guys having an ordinary season the previous year, before I arrived to spray the ball around the outfield. We had just made the playoffs, and the honor of being captain of this baseball team eased some of the anguish of not being in California. I missed my friends, but had begun to make some nice new ones that summer of 1967 in Montreal, the summer of the World's Fair, and a full year after leaving California. That afternoon, the coach had just given us a "pep talk" for the playoffs. He said that he'd coached a lot of teams, but he'd never enjoyed coaching a team as much as this one. He was a tall, thin coach—early 20s—with pale skin, lots of freckles, flaming red hair. We had started slowly that season, and then picked up unstoppable momentum, winning the last several of our games to get into the playoffs. I can still remember his words during that pep talk on August 4, 1967. He spoke about how he had never won a championship, but had a good feeling about this team. Dismissing the team after practice, he walked over to me, put his arm around my shoulder, saying, "Bruce, I'm really counting on you to rise to the occasion; I really want to win this championship. Play your heart out, you California boy—I know you will." I was motivated when I went home that late afternoon. But in the evening, around bedtime I became frightened, as had been the case of late. I was 12 and my brother, Jeff, was 11. And since my dad had been gone, we would take turns sleeping in the same bed as my mom. It made us feel more secure. One evening a few weeks earlier, Jeff had been in the bed and got up to go to the restroom. As he was returning to the bed, he saw a man in the house walk past him down the hallway and head to the front door. Jeff described that as the man walked past him, he put a finger over his mouth, whispering to be quiet. He then left through the front door. My brother, white with fright, awakened my mom, scaring the "daylights" out of her. My mom filed a police report the next day, but the police were a bit skeptical at the time, offering a theory that my brother had been "sleepwalking." The window to the backyard had not appeared to have been tampered with, and the back door had remained locked, not violated. Jeff swore that he had seen this man, and I never doubted it for a moment. I knew my brother, and there was nothing illusory about his story.

We continued to trade off sleeping in my mom's bed—but Jeff became quite afraid, so being the oldest one, I took the preponderance of the nights. About a week after this "stranger intrusion," doctors discovered a pre-cancerous saliva gland in my mom's throat that they said should be removed as soon as possible. Surgery was scheduled for the following week, and the kids stayed with my aunt Vivian, just a few blocks away, the place where we had stayed on arriving in Montreal. My father remained in Campbellton—Jeff and myself growing up fast as we learned to travel around Montreal, taking the subway to visit my mom in the hospital, before and after the surgery.

My mom had been home just a few days on August 4, 1967, the bandage removed from her throat, but a scar clearly visible. She was tired and weak, but still interested in my excitement over the upcoming playoffs. I fell asleep in bed with my mom that night—the idea of that stranger intrusion back in my mind now that we were all back in the same house, and wanting to be next to her if she needed something during the night. She had fallen asleep before me; a "Gunsmoke" re-run had been on, and I was trying to stay awake to finish the episode. Then screams, and more screams from my mother—then I started to scream at the top of my lungs, screaming and screaming for survival. I looked up and clearly saw this man standing over my mother—his face quite visible in the white of the TV that had gone to static—a sick smile on his face. He had been leaning over her, trying to muffle her voice, and I saw him slap her across the face.

I continued to scream and scream, and then my brothers and sister started to scream. And then the man was gone. The front door had been left slightly ajar, and the window to the kitchen had been opened widely. My mom got up immediately and ran to check on the other kids to make sure that he hadn't done any harm to them. They were okay. My mom's face had fingerprints on it, just a few inches above the fresh scar. The police came, and along with them a fingerprinting detail. They lifted the fingerprints underneath the back window.

The street was filled with police officers, and cops were in and out of the house. It didn't take them long to identify the man—he lived just down the street. There had been a sexual assault on his record. He was a maitre d' at a well-known Montreal Chinese restaurant downtown. The police had already been called to the neighborhood before the break-in, because in his drunkenness to gain the courage to attempt to rape my mother, he had smashed a number of cars along the way, including his own car. The car had been left up the street. I see it in my mind as clearly as when it happened, the police waiting down the street for the man to surface. And about 5:00 in the morning, he did surface, trying to make his way into his house as he exited his garage. I was on the street when they grabbed him, twisting his arms behind his back, locking him in handcuffs. It was August 4, 1967, and I had played baseball that day.

It was a paralyzing fear that had overcome me that night as my mom struggled to keep this man away from her, her voice a muffled shriek, gasping to be heard after a surgery, his hands on her mouth and throat. The first reaction of my body was paralysis—I couldn't move, and I couldn't hear my voice as I tried to scream. In those first few seconds, I was aware that I could not move, and I had no voice. Then I could hear myself, though I never knew how loud it was. It seemed that the whole time that I was yelling, I was struggling for voice—but, apparently, my screaming became deafening, heard well into the streets behind and in front of the house. However, what has always stayed with me from that moment of horror is that initial sense of being unable to move or scream at all—an overwhelming sense of helplessness, fear, vulnerability.

I protected my mom, perhaps saved her life by being in the bed with her that night. But what I clearly remember of the immediate aftermath of this attack is that I was not able to physically stop this man from hurting my mom—I was only able to do it with screams. I was in a state of shock and disbelief, numb from what had happened a few hours earlier as I saw this man being taken in handcuffs into the police car, but amidst this overwhelming feeling of fear, was a sense of violation, rising to anger. I wished that I had been able to give that guy "a good beating," as he stood in that bedroom, and it was hard to accept that I was only 12 and unable to do so. That boy of 12 grew up quickly that night—he realized that he had to be a protector; that safety in this world cannot be taken for granted; that we live in a world where boundaries do not exist for some people intent on hurting others. I saw evil in that smile that night, and it is an awareness of such evil that makes it difficult for me to be a parent of young men today. I do let go; I won't stand in their way as my boys become men and pursue their lives, but I sometimes worry incessantly. I know that there is danger in life, and I so want to shelter them from all of it. I do pull back, I do let go, I do give them the space to go out and find out about life for themselves, but then when I can't reach one or the other, a cell phone goes unanswered, a text message is not returned, I sometimes go from zero to 100 miles per hour in a few seconds, moving from mild annoyance to full panic, not stopping anywhere in between. The boys are patient with me, knowing how I can be from time to time. And it is my struggle, challenge, to get over this sense of anxiety that can invade a quiet, calm state of mind, turning me upside down when only seconds earlier I might have been very much at peace.

A few days after the attack, my mom and myself were asked to come to the police station to pick this man out of a lineup. We went in separately, and I went in first. Initially, I could not identify the man, several of the men had dark hair and olive complexions, which was how I had remembered him. But then I had the police officer ask the men to smile, and when this happened, I identified the man instantly. The smile was unmistakable to me—it twisted into a wickedness that I will never forget. My mom followed, and she identified this man instantly.

In his confession the man admitted that he had gotten drunk to get the courage to go after her. He revealed that he had been watching her all summer, as she went to and from my Aunt Vivian's swimming pool at the apartment building across the street. And he did acknowledge that this was the second time that he had entered our home. He would be put in jail, we were told, but he would be offered bail.

To make sure that he would be put away for a long time, we would have to testify in court. The thought that this man would be out on bail and back on the street was ominous to me; I never wanted to see that face again. My father had been sending signals that this job in New Brunswick was working out, and that he wanted us to join him there. I simply wanted to return to California, and I was pleading with my mom to bring us back. But we were in no condition to return to California—that would take a lot of planning, and we didn't have the money. My mom had no more stomach for Montreal, and advised my father that, sight unseen, she would have all of our possessions boxed up and sent to Campbellton by the first of the next month. It would be up to him to find a place to live. There would be more of Canada to discover, but not before I played in that baseball tournament. We lost in the first round, 3-0. I got the only hit for our team, an opposite field double, against a flame-throwing French kid. This team went on to win the whole thing. But I wasn't myself in that game—the joy had left me. A few weeks previous, I had been preparing with excitement to play in a baseball championship—maybe even win it, but if not have a good time with my friends trying. Now, I was in a state of shock—a sense of joy, a feeling of fitting in had been replaced by sadness, shock, fear, vulnerability, a sense of just being out of place. It was thrilling and I felt "macho" getting our first and only hit off of that tough pitcher—in retrospect it was the only moment during the daze of that whole month that I felt like a kid, a 12 year old who hadn't been forced to grow up, a kid who loved playing baseball.

Campbellton, New Brunswick, Northern Canada

A few weeks after the baseball game, we had sleeping compartments on an overnight train from Montreal, through Quebec City, and on to the tiny, isolated, forested outpost of Campbellton, New Brunswick, on the Gulf of St. Lawrence in the far northeast of Canada. I shared a compartment with my two brothers, Jeff, 15 months younger than myself, and Elliot, seven years old. My mom was in the sleeping birth below us, with my little sister, Heidi, five years old. The train departed Montreal near midnight, and in short order everybody had fallen asleep. I felt safe on this train, moving out of Montreal, toward a destination where I would never again see this man who had attacked my mom. That man's face and the trauma of the night would penetrate that region of consciousness through which the mind travels en route to sleep. So I would do my best to think of happy thoughts, visions of returning to California, and playing baseball in the fields with my friends, or taking a hard "slap shot" beyond the reach of the goalie, my hands going straight up as I scored the winning goal in a hard-fought contest on the outdoor ice. My ice skating skills had developed considerably after that first year in Montreal, skating daily for hours into the night on the frozen outdoor ice, the temperatures often below zero. I had started to become respected by Montreal friends as a California kid who could play a bit of ice hockey. By the end of that winter, I had taken a large leap in ability and was now holding my own in some pretty competitive hockey games. So falling asleep was accomplished in the aftermath of this horror by visualizing exciting victories, remembering my friends out west, the fun times we had racing go-carts down a hill, or picking walnuts and oranges for money in the orchards of southern California. So much of southern California was orchards in those days, and we would all gather—my brother, Jeff, was amazing at this—in the orchards with the migrant workers, taking instructions on how to fill the buckets, where to put them. We would become excited about how much money we would receive for each one. My brother was an all-star at this; he certainly outdid me, and he was as good as any of the Mexican workers out there. These were the images that my mind produced as my body tried to heal from the shock of that night, my mind seeking the easiest route to sleep.

I slept deeply as we rolled toward Campbellton that night, lulled to a peaceful place as the wheels worked their magic on the tracks, the whistle sounding two short sounds, followed by a long third one as we rounded a turn in the darkness of this distant, unknown land. Indeed, though I wasn't going home to California, I was going to a place where I would never see that man again. And maybe there'd be a baseball team I could still join this summer—show these Canadians how the game is played. And, perhaps, I would become a really good hockey player after spending a couple of winters up here, no doubt skating every day of their long winters.

I had been asleep about four hours when, having to get up and go to the toilet, I gently climbed down the ladder from my top bunk. In the process my foot touched my mom as she slept below. She screamed with the fear of a woman under attack, waking up the entire car, the conductor urgently rushing to our compartment to make sure that all was safe. "I'm okay; I'll be all right now, I'm all right, my son just startled me when he went to the restroom," she assured the conductor. She fell back to sleep rather easily after that—she was desperately tired. But I wasn't able to sleep anymore that night. After some time trying to fall asleep, I again walked down the ladder, this time not touching my mom at all, and made my way to a lounge car with seats. I stared dreamily into the night, not sure where I was going, a 12-year-old boy trying to come to terms with a "kind of loss in his life"; a young boy who so much wanted his mother to be safe, his life to be happy, his family together. Now and then the lights of a tiny town, a couple of traffic lights visible in the darkness, would appear and quickly be forgotten, the train whistle announcing our presence, then retreating to the silent world, where its sound might one day trigger a memory, as it does now.

We came on Quebec City, where the train stopped, new passengers arriving, some departing. The blackness of night was giving way to the softening blue light of morning. The city looked old and intriguing—the architecture reminding me of the old section of Montreal, where my father would take me now and then after visiting his parents at 100 Villeneuve Street, just down from Mt. Royal. We would go sledding down Mt. Royal on cold, snowy, Montreal Saturday and Sunday afternoons. My brother Jeff would come with me, and we would meet my cousin, Melody, my Aunt Vivian's daughter. Those days sledding, caps covering our ears and heads, big mittens (they were supposed to be warmer than gloves we were told) keeping our hands totally warm, were among the finest of memories of our stay in Montreal.

Those memories brighten the darkness of the San Francisco Bay on this moonless night, the Golden Gate bridge unilluminated, except for a strand of orange teardrops of light that lines the outer rails, too low to prevent anyone from taking the plunge, as many have sadly done. The Romanesque-looking Palace of Fine Arts is dark tonight, and except for a few traffic lights switching periodically from orange to red to green, the only lights breaking the darkness are those veiled by curtains in the occasional apartments of Pacific Heights and the Marina down below. And atop Alcatraz, there is the intermittently shining searchlight, its beam brightening about every five seconds, and with each illumination that 12-year-old boy on the train now leaving Quebec City, sitting alone in the lounge car, is bathed in light.

We'd all had the opportunity to have breakfast in the dining car before the train pulled into the Campbellton train station shortly before noon. The screams of the night before were not brought up, buried under the surface, just as we all had tried to put in some far away place the horror of that August 4th, Montreal night. The train skirted the edge of a vast forest as it traveled alongside a cold and gray-looking gulf of water—the Atlas tells me that this was the Gulf of St. Lawrence—before turning inland through lightly forested expanses, broken up now and then by pastures and farmland, a pulp mill, the wind blowing smoke from its chimneys in a steady direction. In what seemed not much more than two hours after turning inland, the train's momentum slowed, eventually stopping on the edge of another gray and cold waterway. This was the Bay of Chaleur.

"This is your stop, Campbellton, New Brunswick," the conductor advised. "You'll need some help with these bags." He helped us offload the bags, and in short order, a guy in a little motorized vehicle brought the bags to a waiting area, where we would be met by my father.

He wasn't there, and was nowhere to be found.

We guessed that he had gotten mixed up over the time. The train station was near the water, and as we waited for my dad to show, I went outside for a short look around, my mom first telling me not to go anywhere, then letting me go, but telling me not to get lost and to be back in a few minutes. I walked outside the station to the shore of the cold, gray bay down a street. Looking across this bay, I felt that I might as well be on the moon, so far away from where I belonged.

❐

And where did I belong? I would have wanted to say California. But perhaps that was a dream that I would never realize again in my teenage years. All I knew was that my stomach felt empty, almost burning, as I looked across this waterway, the tiny train station behind me. Where did I belong? It certainly wasn't this place, that was for sure. A breeze picked up, and I took my first full breath of that acidic, sulfuric, scent of Campbellton, something like burning wood, with a tinge of pungent sweetness. We were in lumber-burning country, I realized, as this scent blended with a strong salty, fishy odor emanating from the bay. I continued along the shore of the bay for about five minutes, stopping in a place with a lot of little stones, picking them up and skipping them across the water. I fancied myself an Olympic champion at rock skipping—and indeed I was good. A few of the flat stones skipped seven, eight, nine, 10 times. I would become the rock-skipping champion of Campbellton, I fantasized. None of these kids would be able to match my success.

I looked around, the salty, sweet, sulfuric scent wafting through the air, filling me with a kind of mysterious sense of this place. There was an innate sense as I stood there, preparing to walk back to the station and find my dad, that I could depend on myself, take care of myself, that I would make the best of this place. And that maybe it might be fun? And I knew that I had a mom whom I would help out—I knew how much she loved me and that I would be strong for her. Next stop, Campbellton, I reasoned.

I was determined that nobody in this place was going to push me around, though I certainly wanted to be friendly. It was a vulnerability that I felt; after all, I would need to make friends in this foreign place, more than anyone here needed my friendship. But I was solid, I knew that, and I was determined to take care of myself.

Back at the station—I had been gone about 30 minutes—my father had still not arrived. We had come to meet him, and he wasn't even here. I wasn't too happy with my dad at this moment; he pulls us out here, and doesn't even show up to get us on time! Just like he never showed up after my mom was attacked. I was going to be strong—I knew that. But deep inside, I so much wanted my life to be normal again.

My father finally arrived, perhaps two hours after we did. Apparently, he had received information that our train would be late, the train actually arriving on time. In short order, we were driving through the main street of Campbellton, past Littwin's Drug Store, the only Jewish business in the town; the Woolworth Five and Dime; Maher's Funeral Home; toward the water where a couple of rooms had been reserved for a few nights at a little hotel on the outskirts, a small vacation spot where the locals would go for some summer sun. The beach along the shore of this large gulf of water was quite lovely, fine white sand, few rocks, lots of shells, and a sweet saltiness in the air, not quite as harsh as the seawater scent near the train station, where the sea blended with the sulfur from the pulp mill. My father, my mom, Jeff, Elliot, little Heidi, and I walked along the shore after checking into the hotel, Jeff and I continuing to walk along the shore, stopping to pick up shells, skipping stones (Jeff was amazed at my ability to skip them up to 10 times) after the others had stopped and turned back for lunch. We joined them a short time later for some fish and chips, the whole thing feeling like a little vacation.

❒

The following day, my father introduced us to the place that would be our home for who knew how long. My mom's face went pale when she saw the place, as though she had a stomach cramp. We weren't expecting luxury, but none of us was prepared for this place. It was on two levels, a family occupying the first level, the second floor only accessible in the back, up about 20 stairs that creaked and moved, practically crumbling beneath our feet as we made our way up. The outside obviously hadn't been painted in many years, the exposed wood of the place more prevalent than the green paint. We entered the place and it was pretty small. There were three bedrooms, one not much larger than a closet, one toilet with a shower and tub, floors that sloped sharply from left to right, a gradual incline in the hallway, giving the feeling that one was walking uphill on entering. The whole place was uneven, oddly shaped, very old, unsettling. "We'll be here for a few months, then see what happens," my father said after we looked around. My mom didn't challenge those words, but she definitely knew that we wouldn't "see what happens." It would have to do for the present, but there was no way, she told me that night when she saw the sadness in my face, that we would live like this for very long. She assured me of that.

My father didn't seem as disjointed about this place as the rest of us, and of course, he hadn't just come from Montreal where a few days after serious throat surgery a man had attacked his wife, threatened his family. He was in much better spirits than the rest of us. He told us that this house had been an army hospital, used by the Canadians as they sided with the British against the Americans in the War of 1812. People had been treated for serious injury, no doubt many died in these rooms that we now occupied. He was intrigued by living in a place with this kind of history; the rest of us, particularly my mom and myself, couldn't escape the pervasive sense of gloom that emanated from these walls, and coated the splintering floors.

❐

We hadn't been in this house for more than a week when playing in the little backyard, tossing a baseball as high in the air as I could, basket catching it Willie Mays style, my youngest brother, Elliot, seven years old, comes running to get me. "Bruce, come help Jeff," he yells, quite scared. "There is a guy out front, a lot bigger than him, and he is threatening to beat him up. Immediately, I throw down my ball and glove and run around the corner to the front patch of grass. He had my brother in a headlock, my brother's face very red. "Get your arms off of my brother!" I yelled, pulling the kid's arms off my brother, and pushing him. "You coward, you punk!" I said to him, "You like to pick on kids smaller than you? How about trying me?" "All right," he answered, raising his fists to do some battle with me. This was 1967, and I emulated Cassius Clay in those days. I followed all of his fights back in California, listening to the radio as Howard Cosell called the action, or watching them on TV whenever they were televised. I loved Clay from the time he beat Sonny Liston the first time, listening to that fight on the radio in our garage while my father worked on TV sets, his business in those days. He had the first television repair business in Simi Valley, California in those years, and he was getting contracts from many of the big department stores of the day. So, he would spend a lot of time in the garage, and I would often go out there and watch him, listening to various sporting events on the radio—Vin Scully calling Dodger games, Chick Hearn announcing Laker basketball games, and of course the moments listening to Cosell broadcast Cassius Clay championship fights. So, in emulating, imitating Clay, I tried to dance like him, move like him, spar like him, jab like him. My dad had purchased some boxing gloves, and I would spar with friends, my dad often refereeing to make sure that no one would get hurt. I was quite quick, very fast with my punches. I used to bounce on beds as a young kid, so it was a logical extension of that to enjoy jumping up and down as I practiced my boxing.

That kid in the front yard of the Campbellton house tried to immediately move in and hit me. I blocked his punch, spontaneously moving into my jumping, dancing style, à la Cassius Clay. I started to dance around him, left to right, right to left, throwing a few jabs and missing, but throwing a few more and connecting. Each time he tried to come in close and hit me, I either blocked it or danced away from him. He started flailing at me, clearly getting frustrated, and then I hit him, once, twice, three times, four times, bloodying his nose. My father had gotten word of this fight, and came around to the front to referee it—he didn't try to stop it, but wanted to referee it. By this time, there was a crowd of kids standing around out front, my brothers cheering for me, this kid's friends from the local hockey all-star team—it turns out that he was one of the better players from that team—rooting him on. The fight lasted, maybe, a few more minutes when, unable to beat me at boxing—blood dripping all over my shirt from his nose—he lunged at me, trying to wrestle me to the ground. It is at this point that my dad broke up the fight. The kid went back to his friends, congregating on the sidewalk in front, and they all took off. It was a moment that, essentially, set the stage for my life to come in Campbellton. Word had gotten out that, despite my size—I was not a big kid—I was a tough kid from California. A few weeks after that event, I had started to make a few friends. School had just begun, and there were a few kids who I liked and who liked me.

We went running around the neighborhoods one evening, playing hide and seek, running into backyards. I went hiding in one of these backyards, when a kid came out and told me to get lost, to "get out of here." He was wearing a black leather hockey jacket, an orange tiger insignia on the chest. In white, it had his hockey number on the arm. He had dark blond, sandy-colored hair, and came at me with authority. He was a little taller than me, but not a lot. "Okay, I'll leave," I said, "but you don't have to be such an asshole, punk," I said to him. "What did you call me?" he asked. "You're a punk," I said. "Wanna fight me right now?" I continued. He was startled. Apparently, nobody had ever spoken like that to him. He was the best hockey player in the town, captain of the team. Wayne Manley was his name. He pretty much had his way in the town. But this time, he backed away—not choosing to fight me. "Just get out of here," he answered. "Fine," I said, "I will, but you don't have to be an asshole about it." Leaving, the friends who I was with were shocked and dazzled about what had just happened. The two kids who I was with—David McDonald and David Barren—were not wimpy kids. It seemed that there weren't very many wimpy kids at all in this town, located on the edge of a forest, way up there in the Canadian outback. "Do you know who that was?" David Barren asked me. "No, who is he?" I replied. "That's Wayne Manley," they said in unison, David McDonald adding that he was captain and the toughest kid on the hockey team. "Okay, fine," I answered. "He sure seems like an asshole." As I walked away from his place, I started to think to myself that maybe I had "bitten off more than I could chew, challenged somebody a bit too tough." "But maybe I hadn't," I answered myself. I wasn't looking for trouble at all, but I certainly was going to defend myself in this new town—Wayne Manley or not. Wayne Manley didn't bother me again after that; perhaps he had heard about the fight in our front yard.

In this part of the world, summer quickly gives way to fall—summer best be treasured in these parts, because the snow thaws late into the spring, and by mid-September, the leaves are changing to shades of purple, red, gold, falling to the ground, the air refracting a thinning, dimming light as the sun sets earlier in the afternoon behind the forest.

Mid-September yields a kind of chill that reminds locals that it is time to announce tryouts for the new season's all-star, traveling hockey teams, banners put up on billboards at Woolworths, at the couple of candy stores on the main street, on the telephone pole outside the school, and over at the post office.

❒

The local ice-skating rink where all the Campbellton teams play their home games begins to attract large crowds of skaters on Friday and Saturday nights, lots of pretty girls nonchalantly making their way around the surface, dancing, moving their hips to the music playing on the loud speaker, lots of boys showing off for them as they build up speed, stopping suddenly and spraying the flaky ice. The best of the skaters, those most sure of themselves, wear black leather jackets, the orange tiger emblazoned on the front. It is a coveted jacket to have; it means that one has made it past the local recreational teams and on to the traveling all-star teams, representing Campbellton across New Brunswick. And one finds, on these Friday and Saturday skating outings at the local rink, a good number of boys wearing these jackets of honor. I admired how these kids skated; I wasn't as good as them, yet. And I envied the kind of non-verbal attractions and flirtations taking place between the local heroes and some of the prettiest of the skating girls; they obviously knew one another, they had grown up together as children, but the hormones were raging, which prevented them from becoming too familiar, sexual attraction putting in place a thick boundary between familiarity and desire.

I certainly had envy on these Friday and Saturday nights in late September, as I started to skate at this local rink. Some of the girls were so attractive—some of Irish, Scottish descent, others very French looking, still more a mixture of Irish, Scottish, English and French. And, of course, they were pure "North Woods Canadian." I didn't know any of these girls, and they didn't know—and at first didn't seem to care—anything about me. After a few skating sessions, I totally fell in love with this French girl, blond hair down to her shoulders, big green eyes, Denise Gadet. We got to know each other after a few skating sessions, she taking an interest in my stories of life in California, enjoying my accent. She had a low voice, emanating deep within her throat, not nasal, almost hoarse-sounding, that entranced me. Her blond hair was set against an almost Mediterranean complexion, her smile making me "light-headed." She had heard that I had stood up to the captain of the team, Wayne Manley, and that impressed her. She seemed to almost get close enough to let me ask her out, then she would disappear, rejoining her girlfriends, flirting with the guys in the leather jackets. It was so hard to take.

The music that played on the loudspeaker as we skated around on these Friday nights deepened everything that I felt. Herman's Hermits sang, "There's a kind of hush, all over the world, tonight, all over the world, you can hear the sounds of lovers in love." The song first came out when we were living in Montreal, that first winter, and I loved it. My mom loved the song as much as I did, and we would listen to it together in the car when it came on the radio. And we listened to it more often when I went out and bought the album. This song was a standard as I skated around the ice, my hands clasped behind my back, doing my best to show a bit of style. And the other song from that album, "Silhouettes," played through the speaker as well. "Took a walk and passed your house late last night. All the shades were pulled and drawn, way down tight.... Loved you like I'd never loved before.... Two silhouettes on the shade, two silhouettes on the shade." Not long after this song came, "She would never say, where she came from. Yesterday, don't matter if it's gone. While the sun is bright, and in the darkest night, no one knows, she comes and goes; Goodbye, Ruby Tuesday, who could hang a name on you? When you change with every new day, still I'm gonna miss you." I skated and skated, wanting to fit in, wanting to be popular, wanting to make friends, wanting to look every bit as good and respected as those kids in the leather jackets. And as I skated the music continued to play. "You say yes, I say no, you say why, and I say I don't know; oh no, you say Goodbye, and I say hello. Hello, hello; I don't know why you say goodbye, I say hello." That Beatles song evoked in me a mood that brought everything that I was feeling to the surface. The song seemed to mean nothing, and yet it meant everything. It had poignancy, silliness, melancholy, joy. My favorite treat at the snack bar on these skating nights was a Reese's Peanut Butter Cups—they were hard and cold at the ice rink. To this day, no treat tastes as good to me as a cold Reese's. "Hello Goodbye" of the Beatles went down with pure joy, when accompanied by the taste of that delicious chocolate-peanut butter.

Yet, if there was one song played on that ice-skating rink soundtrack—the person who put the music together really knew his stuff—that felt like Campbellton, evoked the mood of the place, it was Bobby Gentry's hit, "Ode to Billie Joe." The whole place felt alluring, foreign, slightly haunting as the song worked a kind of odd magic: "And Mama hollered out the back door, y'all remember to wipe your feet, and then she said she got some news this morning from Choctaw Ridge. 'Today Billie Joe McAllister jumped off the Tallahatchie Bridge.' " The song played over and over, and it was Campbellton.

Even though Campbellton, New Brunswick, was in the far Canadian north east, it was as country as the swamplands of Florida or Louisiana. The mood of the place, at its essence was a

"Choctaw Ridge." From the crumbling back porch of our home, we could see Sugarloaf Mountain. Up on Sugarloaf Mountain, was a large white cross, and the large initial of a woman who had jumped or fallen from the mountain and died. We saw it clearly from the porch. Sugarloaf Mountain was Campbellton's Tallahatchie Bridge. It will be forever inscribed in my memory like legend.

❒

The only Jewish family that anyone in Campbellton could name were the Littwins, owners of the pharmacy on the main street. News of the arrival of a Jewish family to this town had preceded us—apparently the job my father had been offered at this electronics company was a prestigious one, and news had spread that his Jewish family would be coming to join him. It became evident that we were expected when, thumbing through some 45 RPM records at the Litwin's store, Mrs. Littwin came over to ask me if she could help pick out something. She was very fair skinned, a full, thick head of gray hair obscuring most of the remaining black, a long, thin nose holding small-rimmed glasses that rested way down from the bridge of her nose, watery, pale blue eyes, peering out over the top. She looked at me with a mixture of curiosity, concern and compassion. "I haven't seen you in here before," she said. "Are you part of that new Jewish family that just moved here to join the electronics man from Montreal? You do look Jewish," she continued. I felt a bit embarrassed by her question, and curious as to her interest and apparent concern. It seemed that this lady knew so much about me, and I had never met her before. She was certainly nice enough, but her questions, directness, the fact that she had come right up to me, had me feeling shy. "Yeah, I'm Jewish, and my family did just move here from Montreal. But originally, I'm from California," I said softly. "How did you know who I am?" "Oh, the whole town knew that a Jewish family would be moving here," she answered. "The Littwins have been the only Jewish family in this area for a long time. There is some anti-Semitism in this area. Do you know what that means?" I nodded my head affirmatively. "We've had our windows broken a few times over the years. It hasn't happened to the other shopkeepers, only us." "Yes, I do know what anti-Semitism means," I answered. "I experienced it in Montreal." And as I said this, I was thinking back to a situation in Montreal, where I had to defend the fact that I was a Jew, or feel like a coward.

❒

In the mid-autumn after arriving in Montreal, a good couple of months before Montreal's bitter cold winter had arrived, I had gone to see a movie with a kid who was becoming a good friend, a Jewish boy named Marty Buxenbaum. He had dark hair, a dark complexion, a Jewish boy with Spanish blood. He was also a very calm, peaceful kid, and I enjoyed doing things with him. We would often take the bus from the suburb in which we lived, Ville St. Laurent, to the center of town, near St. Catherine Street. On this particular Saturday, we were waiting in line to get tickets to a movie when a couple of kids with long hair and army jackets tried to work their way ahead of us in line. They were speaking French with each other, and seemed to be having a great time, joking among themselves. I told one of the kids that it wasn't cool to be taking cuts, and to get behind us. He answered me in English, speaking with a French accent. "We were here first," he said. "You just got here; we've been waiting." That was so patently false, as to be a joke. "You're crazy," I said to the kid. "Get behind us, or I'm going to tell the ticket man that you're taking cuts, pushing ahead of everybody," I answered. He laughed at me, then walked behind me, further back in the line, to say something in French to a few friends. When he turned around, I saw for the first time, a Nazi swastika written in ink on the back of the army jacket. In a matter of a few seconds, he came back, placing himself, again, ahead of Marty and myself. The kid was about my size, and seemed quite hyper. Perhaps he was high on too much sugar and soda. His hair was greasy, scraggly, the longest part in the back covering the very top of the Nazi insignia. "It is not fair, and I'm not going to let you take cuts in front of me," I insisted. At this point, Marty was not feeling comfortable. "Bruce, just drop it," he whispered to me. "I know kids like this," he continued. "He has a big gang of friends and he is looking for trouble to impress them." "This kid is a punk, Marty," I answered quietly. "We can't let him do this." But, though I spoke quietly, it was not quiet enough for this kid's ears. "I'm a punk, am I?" he said. "Well you're a dirty Jew; you're a Jew, aren't you? You're a dirty Jew."

That was it for me; I had always had pride in who I was, and who I was, was a Jew. Despite all of the volatility, anger, emotional coldness that my father exhibited during my childhood, he, nonetheless, took seriously his role in teaching me how to defend myself—lots of boxing lessons—and sought to educate me as to the fact that I was a Jewish boy living in a world where there are a lot of bullies who would like to push Jewish kids around. My father is a small man—and I'm sure that when he was young he encountered these bullies. I suppose he had made up his mind that his own children would not be pushed around in such a way. He imbued within us a sense of pride in being Jewish, taking us to the synagogue for the "High Holidays," giving us a strong background of knowledge about the horrors of the Holocaust. This background, this sense of pride in who I was would not permit me to take this from the anti-Semitic kid. "I'm not going to take that," I said to the kid. "Not right now, but when this movie is over, we're going to fight," I said to him. "You're on" he answered me.

It was a movie I had really wanted to see, a John Wayne western. But there was no way that I could concentrate on the movie. I was nervous, antsy, anxious—this delay before we fought had me very apprehensive. "Perhaps I should have just fought him then and there," I said to Marty. "It is really difficult to enjoy this movie," I continued. And the event had spoiled the picture for

Marty, as well. He didn't know what was going to happen after the film, and he could see how nervous I was.

The kid was waiting for me when I left the theater. He pushed me; I pushed him back; he lunged at me, and I hit him squarely in the nose. And he did bleed profusely. He punched me a couple of times, one glancing off my arm, landing, but not squarely on my jaw. I was in my Cassius Clay dancing mode now, and I was hitting him, landing almost every punch. The kid was bleeding, and I had definitely beaten him. "That's enough," I said, and then I turned and walked away. After taking a few steps, the kid ran at me and jumped me, pulling me down. I successfully wrestled to get on top of him, and in so doing I punched him one more time. Then I left. "We're done," I said." "Let's go catch our bus," Marty said. "Let's catch it before this kid comes back with his gang." We walked to the corner, waited a few minutes, and then the bus came. But, boy, was Marty right; as we were getting on the bus, a whole gang of kids had gathered and were coming around the corner to find us. We had gotten on that bus in the nick of time. The doors had closed, the bus taking off, just as the kids had reached the bus stop—we had just sat in our seats, when we heard them banging on the rear of the bus, yelling at us. "That was close," I said to Marty. "I really beat that Nazi, Marty, did you see that?" "Yeah, Bruce," he said. "But it is nothing to brag about. Let's just drop it." "Okay, we'll drop it," I responded. Marty was a pacifist, and I never wanted any trouble with anyone. We were good friends my entire stay in Montreal, and, indeed, we never spoke of that fight again.

❒

"I'm Margaret Littwin," she answered. "And you are?" "I'm Bruce Rosen. Nice to meet you. I'm looking for a couple 45s. Do you have anything from the Beatles and Herman and the Hermits?" "Well there are two in here that you might like," she answered. "Here's one of the Hermits' early records, 'Mrs. Brown, You've Got a Lovely Daughter,' and here's a good one from the Beatles, 'No Reply.' " "I'll take both of them," I said. "I can't find my

'Beatles 65' album that has 'No Reply'; it is one of my favorites." I purchased the records and brought them back to my bedroom. I thrilled to the opening harmonies of "No Reply": "I tried to telephone, they said you were not home; that's a lie; cause I know where you been, when I saw you walk in your door." I had never heard more satisfying harmonies in my life—it was bliss. My mom came in when I put on "Mrs. Brown." She adored the song. "Mrs. Brown, you've got a lovely daughter; girls as sharp as her are something rare," intoned with the deepest, Manchester accent. We smiled as we listened to that song. In the middle of all of this unsettled dislocation, there are no finer memories of my youth than sitting in my room with my mother, the two of us putting on our strongest English accents, as we sang.

❐

The fact that I was Jewish had preceded me to the school that I would attend in Campbellton. The teacher was Mrs. Woodward, a heavy set, though not fat-looking woman, her weight appropriate for her large frame, whose gray hair had been made into a tight bun on the top of her head. Her face was round and full, the mouth permanently tilted into a smile, affording a kindly demeanor. She spoke clearly and in a measured manner, the outcome of many years of conservative educational training. They took their education seriously in these parts, the teaching showing an influence of the British system, where nonsense is not permitted. Mrs. Woodward smiled as she introduced herself to the class, and she might have been taken for an English "schoolmarm type," given those short, economic, stilted sentences, a kind of prudishness and moral authority underlying her words, except that she did seem genuinely nice. After introducing herself to the class—though, no doubt, all of the kids knew that she would be their teacher at the end of the previous year—she told us that we would have to be in our seats at 8:30 sharp every morning—and there had better be a good excuse if we were not—because she took reading the "Lord's Prayer" very seriously. "In a few moments," she said, "I am going to assign seats for this class, and it will be based on your academic record from last year. The highest score will sit in the first seat, first row, and the lowest score will sit in the last seat, last row. If you are near the bottom, there is an incentive to work you way up." As she was saying this, I was wondering, "Where in the heck is she going to put me? She doesn't know anything about me." And I was quite concerned that I would be put at the back of one of the last rows. "But before we begin this," she went on, "we will begin with the 'Lord's Prayer':

"Our Father, who art in heaven, hallowed be Thy name, Thy Kingdom come, thy will be done on earth as it is in heaven, Give us this day our daily bread, and forgive us our trespasses as we forgive those who trespass against us." I had never heard this prayer in its entirety before, but all the kids in the class knew it, since every voice was repeating it. I felt out of place as I looked up and down the rows of kids, sound coming out of each face, mine being the only one not saying anything. When the prayer was finished, Mrs. Woodward called attention to the fact that I hadn't been saying the prayer. "Mr. Rosen, young man, this is not to embarrass you, but it is my wish that you learn this prayer, so I will provide you with the words when we leave today. I know that you come from the Jewish faith, but the words are not disrespectful to your beliefs—we share the same God, though we pray to him differently." I could feel the color coming out of my face when she said this to me, though the words were not stated with any kind of meanness. All eyes were on me, the only Jewish kid in the class. I was so embarrassed, and felt like an outcast. "Yeah, its not my religion," I answered, struggling to find the words and to speak with some pride, trying not to allow the impression that I was meek or shy in any way. "But I will learn them," I went on. "That would be good of you, Mr. Rosen, and I'm sure you are a very bright young man, and that you'll learn them easily tonight." I nodded yes, all eyes on me, and then back on Mrs. Woodward, as she informed the kids that we would now be attending to the seat assignments. As she began to fill out the first row, before going to the first chair, second row, Mrs. Woodward announced that I would be sitting in the last seat of that first row. "You are a Jewish young man, and I'm sure very bright, so I will be seating you in the first row," she decreed. "I would like to see you stay in that row, perhaps working your way to that first seat, giving Nancy some competition for it."

Nancy was really cute, big, round, brown eyes, straight dark brown hair that was cut sharply at the bottom of her neck, a stylish cut where the evenly cut hair at the bottom of her neck curved upward toward the bottom of her jaw. She looked back at me when Mrs. Woodward said this, first a tinge of a smile, then a firm defiance, suggesting that she wasn't about to relinquish that first position. My immediate reaction to Nancy was that I would like to get to know her, much more than to try and unseat her as the smartest kid in the class. My new friends, David McDonald and David Barren, were in this class as well; Barren sitting at the front of the third row in a class of five rows, McDonald seated at the back of that third row. That first day had come to an end, and when I went to school the next day I was able to say the "Lord's Prayer" all the way through. As I said it, there was a smile on Mrs. Woodward's face—no words were spoken, just a smile of acknowledgement. By the end of that first month of school, I had hung onto my position in that first row. There had been a couple of tests, math and spelling, and I scored quite well, particularly the spelling. It was becoming clear that I was among the best students in the class, and perhaps the best speller.

But it was also the case that I had become increasingly friendly with both Davids, and as winter had blanketed the fields by the end of October, I had started to have a ton of fun—at the expense of homework—playing hockey from the end of school into the nighttime hours on the ice rinks that were being constructed all around town. Not only that, the boys had introduced me to snowmobiling, each one having a machine of their own. When we weren't playing hockey—and we were playing almost all the time—we would take off on the snowmobiles on trails deep into the woods. The two Davids knew the lay of the land, and by the end of November, I was experiencing some of the most fun I'd ever had in my life, bouncing on trails and through deep snow—wearing a big, black fur jacket with an eagle on the back, a ski mask sheltering my face, a lumberjack's fur hat with flaps over the ears—the temperature so damn cold that the lodges that we stumbled on in the woods were too cozy to leave. But when we did leave, the fun started all over again. And during this time, Nancy realized that I was not going to be a threat to her status—I had slipped into the second row due to my friendships—but, rather, an object of her affection. We started going out, first meeting at the local candy store for peanut butter cups on a cold afternoon, then to hockey games, where her brother was captain of one of the best hockey teams in New Brunswick.

Rick was 16, three years older than me. He played in the division just above Wayne Manley. He liked me, and he liked that his sister, Nancy, liked me. Sometimes, he came out on the ice with me, showing me a few tricks. They were moves that couldn't be learned right away, of course, but had to be practiced over a whole winter, but since I was skating, playing hockey every day, I had plenty of time to practice them. We used to work on taking a shot at the goalie, just as the puck was being dropped from the face-off circle. Not just winning the face-off, but getting a serious shot at the goal. He showed me his technique for backhanding the puck up over the goalie's shoulder, and so, aside from skating all the time, I worked on these techniques every chance I had. I worked on them on the local recreational hockey team—not the traveling team, of course; I wasn't nearly good enough for that—as well as during all the pick-up games that we played on the outdoor ice. And I was starting to get pretty good. My ability had grown in leaps and bounds since that previous winter in Montreal. I was starting to look like a hockey player. But, I'll never forget how good a player Rick was. He was able to implement what he preached. Nancy and I were watching him one game—he was playing against a team from Moncton, NB—and on two successive face-offs in the other team's zone, he scored right off the face-off. These were some of the best players in Canada—some of them, most likely, went on to the NHL—and he scored, not once but twice, right off the face-off. It was astounding to see then, and just as amazing to think about today. He was the best player on the ice, but I doubt that he went on to play in the NHL. He was Nancy's brother, which meant that he wasn't only a good hockey player, but a top student. I'm sure that he had a strong academic life in store for him. The day, though, is an indelible part of my memory: I'm with his sister, Nancy, it is so cold in the rink (even though it is indoors) that when you spit against the chain fencing behind the goal, it immediately turns to icicles, and he scores two goals right off the face-off, in a very competitive hockey game. And after he scored the second goal, he skates over and winks at me, not showing any ego at all, just a wink as if to say, "that's how its done lad; that's how its done." What a great day that was.

❒

The relationship between my mom and dad became very strained in the cramped quarters of this army hospital from the War of 1812, in which we lived. And the house had some heating problems. When the snows came in abundance and began to cover the bottom steps of the crumbling back stairs, the furnace and fireplace were ineffective protections from the draft that penetrated this place through the cracks in the window panes and the single-paned windows. The place was either excessively warm and stuffy as a result of turning up the thermostat sufficiently to compensate for the draft, or it was chilly to the point where one needed to be in sweaters to remain comfortable. And the temperature was not consistent; within the same room would be warm spots and chilly, drafty sections. And it was like this throughout the house. Just as the floors on which we walked sloped unevenly, the temperature was uneven and inconsistent. We all had numerous blankets piled on us at night, since the decision had been made that it would be better to be on the cold side than on the warm side when it came to bedtime. Lying in bed, sometimes unable to fall asleep easily during the cold nights of late November into December, I could hear coming from the front room of the house where my parents slept, voices rising in argument, followed by a, "Shush, you'll wake the kids," coming from my mom. These conversations turning into argument, becoming loud and contentious, followed by a sudden "shush," were becoming more and more frequent, and they were upsetting to me. The word "divorce" started occurring during these discussions; in the beginning I had to strain my hearing to decipher that word, but after a time it was clearly audible. I started to make sense of the nature of these arguments. There were rumors that my father was seeing another woman—and that he had started seeing her shortly after arriving in Campbellton, while we were living in Montreal. The rumors had come to my mom from various sources, and my father was vehemently denying them. And there were other things that she wanted my father to know. She told him that their son, Bruce (me), should be preparing for a Bar Mitzvah, but that there was no place to do so in this desolate town. I had started preparing for a Bar Mitzvah in Montreal, but those plans came to a sudden halt with the move to this outpost. She let him know that she saw no future for her family in a place like this, and that she didn't want to keep living in this "army hospital" any longer. Voices would rise, and rise some more, then become quieter—the "divorce" word inevitably occurring during every argument.

It was on a Saturday night in November—I had stayed home from school on the American Thanksgiving to watch the Dallas Cowboys play in the traditional football game; the nostalgia for Thanksgiving, the desire to be back home in California, was tugging at my heart, even though I was having fun with some friends in this birthplace of winter—when the building troubles between my parents reached a climax. I had been lying in my bed listening to the radio—there was a station that played all of my favorite stuff, and they did dedications to friends and lovers. I had called up about an hour earlier to dedicate a song to Nancy, and it had just played. Nancy liked to listen to the same station at night, and as I lay in bed, I wondered if she had just heard it.

During this contemplation, I could hear footsteps in the backyard (my bedroom faced the tiny backyard), followed by a person walking up the back stairs. I could hear some stumbling on the stairs, the person finally reaching the porch. At just this moment, my mom opened the back door. "Where have you been Larry?" she said. "You don't have to answer that—I know exactly where you were tonight!" she exclaimed with pure anger. "You smell of alcohol," she continued, "and I know why you're covered with all that snow," she followed. "I fell in the snow coming home," my father answered. "No you didn't," my mom said with disdain. "I was watching you cover yourself with the snow in the backyard. You did it to cover the scent of that woman. Everybody knows about that woman. You take me for an idiot? The whole town knows about her—and you think it is going to escape me? Do you take me for a fool? You bring us to this God-forsaken town, and this is what you do?" My mom's pain and anger were in full flight as she walked away sobbing, apparently impervious to the fact that her family might have been able to hear everything that was being said. She didn't care anymore—she didn't care if we heard every word. Perhaps she recognized that it would have to come to this, if anything were to change for us.

❐

The disconsolation that my mom felt on that frigid night in December when my father, covered with snow, drunkenly stumbled through the front door of this lopsided, nailed together, unimproved early-19th-century army hospital of a home in which we lived had deepened since that phone call from Toronto in late October from her sister, saying that her brother, Meyer Rush—waiting to stand trial on a $100 million stock fraud—had been blown up, killed in his bed as he slept in that city's Sutton Place

Hotel. Minutes after that phone call, my mom came to get us early from school—and the look on her face is forever etched in memory. She'd always had a sort of natural eye shadow encircling her large, round, deep brown eyes, but at this moment, that shadow had turned to black, as it contrasted with a face whose life blood seemed to have drained. I became scared when I came to the office where she had been waiting—even after her throat surgery she hadn't looked this ill. When my brother, Jeff, and myself were in the car, she explained that our uncle, Meyer, had been killed—blown up in his bed, and that she would have to suddenly go to Toronto. She had arranged for us to stay at a neighbor's place down the road—and that we were to put enough clothes together for about a week. She expected to be gone no longer than that. My younger brother, Elliot, and baby sister, Heidi, would be coming with her. My father might join her in Toronto, but he would be going to Montreal, first, to see his family. It seemed very difficult to get my mind around what had just happened. My Uncle Meyer had been blown up by a bomb in his bed? Why? I was shaken by this, just as I was starting to recover from the shock of the invasion of our home, and the attempted rape of my mother. There seemed to be no foundation to our lives, and as horrified as I was by the news, I was shaken to the core by the shock on my mother's face, the weakness overcoming her body as she broke down in tears in front of us. "Mom, it will be okay," I remember saying. "I love you, and I know that it will all be okay. Don't cry, Mom; let me come with you. Let me be there with you," I continued. "No," she said, firmly. "I can't take you boys out of school now. You need to be in school. I'll be all right, and I'll be back very soon." As she said this in the kitchen, the radio was on in the background. I can hear the words on that radio as clearly as I can say my own name: "In news of the world, Canadian stock promoter, Meyer Rush, awaiting to stand trial on his indictment for a $100 million stock fraud, died when a bomb detonated in his bed, as he slept at Toronto's Sutton Place Hotel. There were reports that he had initially survived the bombing, but died in the ambulance en route to hospital." This was my Uncle Meyer they were speaking about. I didn't know the meaning of the word, "surreal," but if the word has any meaning at all, it describes the way everything felt in the kitchen during the news report. My mom listened to the report almost stoically—no longer crying, she got up to continue putting her things together for the trip to Toronto. But about 15 minutes later, the phone rang, and I could hear my mom saying something to the effect of, "Yes, I just heard the news on the radio. What? He's not. Are you sure? I'm coming as soon as I can. I'll be there by tomorrow." "What's happening, Mom?" I asked. Who was that? What's happening?" "That was my sister, Sara," she said, nervous excitement taking over her voice, color returning to her face. "She says that Meyer is not dead. They say that he died twice en route to the hospital, but each time he was brought back to life by a young doctor in the ambulance. They massaged his heart; he is in the hospital, struggling to live, but she thinks he may make it. My God, oh my God," she continued.

About 30 minutes later, the news came on again: "Canadian stock promoter, Meyer Rush, preparing to stand trial in his indictment for a $100 million stock fraud, was bombed in his bed this morning at Toronto's Sutton Place Hotel. Initial reports were that he had died in the ambulance en route to hospital. There are new reports that Mr. Rush has survived the bombing, and is clinging to life. It appears that the stuffing from the bed absorbed much of the hemorrhaging. More details as they become available." This was my uncle they were talking about; he was this important to be talked about on the national news? This was my uncle—I hadn't known him that well, because he lived in Toronto, and I had grown up in California. But I did know him pretty well, recently. He'd come to visit us a few times in Montreal. He'd always have a bunch of candy bars whenever he'd come. My impression of Meyer was that he was about as tough a man as you'd ever want to meet—but with family, he was a teddy bear. He looked like he was made of iron, massive forearms, a thick muscular neck. He adored my mom, and my mom giggled, laughed, smiled when he was around. He told me that if anybody messes with me, I'd better let him know—and saying this, he'd give me a $20 bill to "go get yourself a nice Montreal smoked meat sandwich and a cream soda; and while you're at it get me one, too." I wish he'd been in the house when that man broke in that night. Surreal—again, if that word refers to anything, it refers to the way everything felt during those few hours when my mom picked us up at school, followed by the radio reports.

❐

My mom left that night; and by the following morning she was at Meyer's bedside. She phoned us at the neighbor's house the following evening to make sure we were doing all right. "He's in critical, critical condition," she told me, "but the doctors are hopeful that he might make it through. There are police outside his hospital room to make sure that nobody gets in, except immediate family. They want to make sure that those who tried to kill him can't finish the job while he is in here," speaking as though I had the full maturity to comprehend and grasp the significance of everything that was happening. She went on to tell me that the doctor in the ambulance saved his life two times; that she had spoken to him, and that the bed that he slept on was made by her sister's husband; her sister's husband's bed stuffing had been essential in absorbing the blood, giving him the time for the doctor to work his magic.

It had been a traumatic, nervous time waiting for the nightly phone call from my mom, but she did call every night to see how we were doing, and to let us know of Meyer's progress. The people with whom we were staying, initially nice and hospitable, became quite cold and unfriendly after our being there a few days. I could hear the couple in the front room—my brother, Jeff, was asleep, but I was having difficulty doing so—complaining about how much food we were eating, and that, "Wasn't it about time they came and pick up these kids already?" I felt a burn in my stomach as I heard this conversation, suggesting that we weren't wanted in their place. And later that evening—I was still awake, struggling to fall asleep—I heard the door to their bedroom squeak open; and as it did, the husband blurted out, "What do you guys want already? Go to bed!" I yelled back, "That's not us," and the wife responded with, "I'm sorry; go back to sleep." I finally fell asleep, but it had been a tough night. And though these people seemed pleasant the remaining few days of our stay, I couldn't relax with the sense that we were in a place where we were not wanted. I buried those feelings, knowing that my uncle would survive, my mom would be home soon, and that, someday, I'd be moving back to my California home. Initially I'd thought that these people might be comforting during a difficult time—I so wanted to be comforted by some nice people. But I hardened a bit when I realized that it certainly wasn't going to happen here.

❒

My mom returned home within a week's time, and it was a sure thing that Meyer would live. Those who had tried to kill him failed, but the government was still intent on prosecuting him. So, as soon as he was well enough to walk, eat, talk, they threw him into a prison cell—setting bail at a very high price. But bail was made, and within a few months time Meyer went to Panama, where he had land interests and connections that stretched to the highest place in the country. Protected by Panamanian bodyguards, Meyer was noticed by a journalist—perhaps he had gone there intentionally to get an interview with Meyer—from a national Canadian magazine. He asked for an interview, and Meyer granted it. The interview—the journalist gently nudging Meyer to suggest who might be behind the bombing and if there was a conspiracy involving organized crime and other forces—occurred in the presence of a top photographer. Within a few weeks, Meyer—photographed in a jeep on a hot Panamanian afternoon, skin grafts noticeable all across his neck—emblazoned the front page of this national Canadian magazine. Though he survived the bombing, Meyer's life would become increasingly difficult for years to come. He would continue to suffer tragedy, hardship, privation in his life. It is a story, biblical in scope, of a man's will to survive, struggle to live when hope seems lost; it is a tale of human will equal to the most powerful of oceanic currents, a determination of granite. Meyer gave me his story during several conversations in Toronto in the summer of 1980, before I flew to Denver to meet Sue for the first time, the woman with whom I would be given the gift of a precious family.

By mid-January the Bay of Chaleur was so thickly frozen that one might have been able to successfully drive a car across it to the Quebec side. The air was so frigid that it seemed a real possibility that my vapors of breath might turn to ice before they were out of my mouth. Working up some exertion on the outdoor ice rinks warmed the body in these below zero temperatures, but breathing air so cold burned those first few weeks of arctic blast. Just as one develops stamina through running distances, so one builds up some resistance to that burning feeling during exertion in these temperatures. After a few weeks, I didn't much feel the burning—though it never totally disappeared—but the toes, that was another story. Just as the body rejects exposure to cold water—swimming in the English Channel comes to mind—but as long as it isn't excessively cold to induce hypothermia eventually tolerates it by becoming numb, so was the feeling of my toes during the first several minutes after lacing up my ice skates. The toes would burn, become numb to the cold, then burn like hell as they thawed out after taking off the skates and burying them in boots thick with fur. The lungs burned, the toes burned, the face burned, but man, was it fun playing hockey on that frozen ice. You wanted your skates to be very sharp on this kind of ice—an ice so cold and thickly frozen that speed was the inevitable byproduct. I learned to skate really fast and shoot the puck hard, and in doing so, I would overcome for long stretches of time the unsettled nature of our home life. I was, after all, a kid, and kids have a knack for just being able to go out and play. But if I was a kid, I was also a mature son in whom my mom could confide.

❐

My mom confided in me on one of these cold January, 1968, afternoons, my toes burning since it had been just a few minutes earlier that I had taken off my skates. A letter had come asking that she testify against the man who had attempted to rape her—they were also asking that I come as well, since I was able to identify him. The prosecution wanted me to describe the kind of terror that I felt when I awakened to the sight of this person, to describe the sounds of my screaming. "I don't ever want to see this man again," she said to me. "And I don't want to have to bring you back to Montreal, take you out of school, and bring this all up for you again, Brucie," she continued. "Mom," I answered. "If we don't do it, he will get off without going to prison—and I want to know that man is in prison for a long time." "Brucie, I think that I'm going to let it go," she answered. "They say that if I don't testify, that he'll definitely spend at least a year in jail—but if I do, he might get the maximum sentence. But I've decided not to go back there—I went back to Toronto when Meyer was bombed, and I don't want to take this trip to Montreal. We will close this chapter and look ahead. I don't want to see his face, and I don't want you to leave what you are doing now—I can see you're having a little fun." "All right Mom," I answered. "But I hate to see this guy not go to jail for a long time." "He'll suffer the rest of his life for what he did, no doubt about that," she concluded. "But Brucie, there is some good news for you. We found a very nice house to move into, just up the hill from here. I am going to show it to you tomorrow. It is big, it is pretty new, it has a nice basement where you boys can invite friends over, play your games." "Sounds great, Mom," I answered. "That is really exciting."

The War of 1812 house was at the bottom of a hill, and across from a wide-open field where the large outdoor ice-skating rink was located. Directly across from our little back yard was where the kids sledding down the hill completed their ride. Very often kids would turn into our yard to slow themselves down, often ending up at the base of our crumbling steps. The new house had modern appliances, a brand-new working furnace, three nice-size bedrooms, and a large basement. It had been built just a few years earlier—it was part of an area of new homes, each built by individuals according to their own specifications. It wasn't an area of tract homes—definitely upscale by Campbellton standards. Within a few weeks we were in this house, and life had become much brighter. My bedroom looked out on the sledding hill—but instead of being at the bottom where tobogganers finished up, my room looked on the top of the snowy hill, at the top of the ride where kids lingered with nervous excitement. There was excitement, even a bit of fear, because one could really get a fast ride down that hill, if you knew how to steer correctly.

In no time at all the winter playground outside my back window was a paradise. My mom bought a sled for my brother Jeff and myself, and after a few cautious rides down the hill, we decided to go for it time and again. My brother was a hockey goalie, and a damn good one. He had just been asked to join the traveling team, and was given one of those coveted jackets—and boy, was I envious. But being a goalie, he was a bit crazy. You had to be to put your face in front of hockey pucks coming at you so fast that they're a blur. So he kept pushing me to see if we could get this going faster than any sled on the mountain. I would steer the thing, and he would be the brakeman, which meant that the brakes were never used. The thing would just hiss down the slope, now and then hitting an unexpected bump, sometimes quite icy, given that the hill was being used by kids all the time, propelling us into the air. At the end of the ride, we'd pull into the old backyard—within a few weeks, the fact that we lived there was becoming a distant memory. We'd then pick up the sled, one of us carrying the front, the other the back, and walk through the knee-deep snow of the back yard back toward the hill and back to the top. In no time at all we were confident that we'd be able to beat any sled down that hill. And Jeff would run around taunting every kid that he could find that we could beat the heck out of them in a race, even making little wagers. We called our sled "the bomb," and it truly has to be said that we were incredibly fast on that sled. So much so that I had fear every time we went down that hill. What had started out as fun turned into intense competition, and I truly do not believe that we ever lost a race, except for the one time that we tumbled and Jeff's nose was bloodied. But true to the world-class goalie that he was becoming, he got back on that sled right away, telling me that I had to steer better this time. My brother was crazy; and I sure envied him for making the all-star team and wearing that jacket.

Jackie and Janice

I'll never forget and have never forgotten Jackie A—but in recalling her, I remember Janice M with equal intensity. Jackie had been referred to my parents as a reliable, studious, high school girl of 17—an excellent student on the road to getting into a good college and a reliable babysitter. I was 12, almost 13; Jeff was 11; Elliot was seven; and Heidi was five. My mom started using Jackie in early December to make sure that the younger ones would be looked after—I was still going out with Nancy, though Janice Martin had entered the picture recently. Nancy didn't make out much, and the dates never seemed to get beyond the feeling that one was "square dancing at arm's length." I wanted to be more expressive in our relationship, and it just wasn't happening with Nancy. Janice was good friends with the sister of my friend David McDonald (of the two David boys), and she would often be at David's house when we were hanging out. She had long, dark hair, an olive tone to her complexion, a really pretty mouth (pretty in the sense that her lips were full and she always seemed to be smiling), and I could tell that she liked me. She'd often smile at me when I wasn't doing anything to make her smile. She didn't go to the same school as us, but went to a girls' Catholic school in town. So whenever I saw her, she was wearing the required uniform: a plaid skirt with blue tights to keep her legs warm, a white blouse and blue tunic. And while I had never had my hands on a girl's breasts before—and Nancy didn't seem to have much in that area—Janice was showing something there that really interested me. Eventually—within a few weeks from when we first met—David told me that Janice really liked me, that her parents were going to be gone for the evening, and she wanted to know if I would like to come to her party. Given that the two Davids would be attending, along with David McDonald's sister, I told him that I would go. And so I went.

The place was filled with kids on this cold, December night—all of us taking off our snow-covered boots, big fur coats, gloves, scarves, lumberjack hats and dropping them in the hall closet. She lived in a tract of homes across the wide-open field and down a hill from the outdoor ice rink that had been built beyond the backyard from the War of 1812 house; we were still living in that house when I went to her party, the two Davids coming to get me, as we trekked across that field on a moonless night, the snow deep to our knees. "Take the last train to Clarksville, and I'll meet you at the station. If you meet me by 4:30, you'll need no reservation, don't be slow," played loudly on the record player in the basement, as we entered the front door. Janice came to greet us from the back of the room, and this time she wasn't wearing a tunic, but a black sweater that got me quite excited. After a bit of talking and giggling—we seemed to be equally excited to see each other—Janice and I sat closely together on the couch, talking about our favorite music. "Hello, hello; I don't know why you say goodbye, I say hello," had just come on, and I told Janice how that song always made me happy. "I don't know what it is, but something about that song just puts me in the best mood," I said to her. The music stopped for a while, and then someone put a 45-RPM on the record player, instead of an album. "Cherish is the word I use to describe, all the feelings that I have for you inside," started to play, and as it did, Janice and I got up and started slow dancing. There was a scent about her—and it was natural, not perfumed—that aroused me in ways I had not known before. It wasn't sweet; it wasn't soapy; it wasn't perfumed; it had nothing to do with the way her clothes were washed; it was kind of musky in a way, but tinged with something like olives and cinnamon, and I don't think I have ever known a stronger aphrodisiac in my life. Our bodies pressed against one another as the words continued: "You don't know how many times I've wished that I had told you. You don't know how many times I've wished that I could hold you. You don't know how many times I've wished that I could mold you into someone who could cherish me as much as I cherish you." We kissed as that song ended—it was a short kiss, followed by a touch of embarrassment that we had moved so quickly. Yet, it was a kiss that meant that I had moved in another direction from the sweet, friendly, polite but hormone-empty relationship with Nancy.

When I returned from the party, my parents had not come home yet, and Jackie A was babysitting. It was the second time she had babysat, and we had all had a good experience with her the first time—she had brought candy, Reese's Peanut Butter Cups, made some popcorn, the whole crew having fun watching TV. Jackie was watching television alone when I walked in; all the kids, even my brother Jeff, had fallen asleep. Jeff had arrived earlier that evening from a day trip to Dalhousie, where his team had been impressive in victory. He had come very close to recording a shutout, the goal having been scored in the last minute of the game. He was totally conked out when I arrived. I sat down on the couch next to Jackie, just as the show that she was watching was concluding. She'd asked if I'd had a good time, and I answered that it was good fun, I'd met some new kids; they were playing some good music. Looking over at my albums, she noticed the record that I had just purchased earlier that day, but had not opened. "I've heard that new Beatles album," she said. "It is going to change everything in music—it is a very important record, and nothing will be the same again. It is the best thing anybody has ever done—but it goes beyond music, it expands your mind. Let's put it on." "Yeah, let's listen to it," I answered. The cover was real fun. "Beatles" was spelled in red flowers at the bottom; a large round drum above it, saying "Sgt. Pepper's Lonely Hearts Club Band"; above that were the Beatles in band uniforms, John Lennon, holding a French horn, wearing green; Ringo, holding a trumpet, wearing pink; Paul, in royal blue, holding a long woodwind instrument; and George, in orange, holding something that looked like a conductor's baton. To the side of the decorated Beatles was a picture of them in suits, as they first appeared in America on the "Ed Sullivan Show." And above them was a gallery of famous people: W.C Fields, Bob Dylan, Marilyn Monroe, many others. We spent some time looking at the album cover before opening the record. And when we put it on, Jackie went to sit on the floor, cross-legged in a yoga posture. "It was 20 years ago today, Sgt. Pepper taught the band to play...," a big band sound in the background, flowed effortless into, "I get by with a little help from my friends." Jackie rocked back and forth, closing her eyes, as entered the words, "Picture yourself on a boat on a river with tangerine trees and marmalade skies." "This is a vision of what happens in a psychedelic world," she said to me. "They were on a drug when they wrote this," she continued. "A drug?" I said. I had never thought much about drugs, and certainly hadn't thought of the Beatles taking them. Though this was 1967, I was not in San Francisco, but in Campbellton New Brunswick, Canada, a place a good distance back in time. But not for Jackie; she comprehended the essence of this album as we sat there alone that night. "Fixing a hole," played, and I was hypnotized by the sound. And I let my mind wander as they sang, "I'm painting a room in a colorful way, and when my mind is wandering, there I will go." The mood, the words, the other-worldly nature of the images brought me to an unusual place—a place that was enhanced by Jackie's hypnotic, seductive presence. She told me to listen carefully to the words of "She's Leaving Home"; that it was about the alienation kids are feeling today; that it was a sad song about a girl who had to leave because her parents refused to understand her. As it came on, I was entranced by the immediate, gorgeous harp giving way to a somber and moody cello; McCartney sounding ethereal, his voice filled with poignancy as he brings us to "Wednesday morning at 5:00 as the day begins." It continues with a sublime rawness as McCartney hits pure sweetness as he sings "she"; Lennon responds with stark, pure irony, his voice cutting the heart, "We gave her most of our lives"; McCartney continuing, "is leaving"; Lennon, again the voice of conscience, "sacrificed most of our lives"; McCartney following again, reaching the angels, "home." It tells the story from the girl's and parents' point of view—and it is a story simple and raw. We'd never heard anything like this in our music before. I immediately began to feel the sadness of the parents; it touched me, moved me in a deep way. Then that whole circus aspect of "Being For the Benefit of Mr. Kite" appeared, and it was spellbinding. I suddenly had this strong, strong desire to be in London, and to go to Bishopsgate. And then came the song "Within You, Without You." Jackie told me to listen, to let George Harrison's sitar penetrate me, move through me. She described how the Beatles had gone to India to meditate, and that this song reflected their journey to find wisdom. "We were talking about the space within us all, and the people who hide themselves behind a wall of illusion," the sitar weaving trance-like sounds within me and without me. I was drawn into this song, as I watched Jackie rock back and forth, eyes closed, serene and mature. My perception of music was being altered, subtle changes were occurring within me, I was in a deep and soft mood when piano chords were struck that seemed to reverberate right through me, the echoing voice of John Lennon taking me to places within myself and the universe that I had not previously visited: "I read the news today, oh boy, about a lucky man who made the grade. And though the news was rather sad, well I just had to laugh, I saw the photograph."

The album had taken me on a journey and there was no turning back. I had just awakened to something, and in my own way on that December, 1967, evening, though just on the cusp of 13, I had opened up to the life force that was changing culture in so many ways—change was everywhere, even in the living room of the War of 1812 house, where I, wide-eyed, listened to "Sgt. Pepper's Lonely Hearts Club Band" for the very first time, Jackie rocking back and forth in a meditative trance, her eyes closed, her thoughts deep within herself. What a night it had been; the places I had gone. From a gathering of kids my own age, my hormones coming alive to a cute, giggly girl whose developing breasts pushing through her sweater excited me— the Monkees' "I'm a Believer" playing in the background— to the deep introspection of Sgt Pepper's. Jackie intrigued me; there was a searching sense of wisdom about her that was seductive, a maturity that, in its own way, was spellbinding. As that final crescendo of "A Day in the Life" dissipated into far-away space, light years away, I had traveled a million miles in the frigid, December night of Campbellton, New Brunswick, Canada.

Jackie continued to babysit during those final wintry days of December, 1967, and whenever we saw one another, there was an unsaid kind of arousal that we shared. On the very next babysitting occasion—the other kids having fallen asleep—Jackie wanted us to listen to, specifically, two songs from the "Sgt Pepper's" album: the meditative, entrancing "Within You, Without You," the undulating sitar of Harrison seducing her as she returned to her yoga position on the floor, while I was stretched out on the couch behind her, and, "A Day in the Life." After moving the needle over to "a Day in the Life," Jackie did not return to her yoga position on the floor, but sat down on the couch, close enough that my feet extended over her thigh. As the song continued, she moved her thigh back and forth, my feet falling into a rhythm where they were, in effect, stroking the inner and outer part of this area. I had become aroused in a way that I had never known, blood obviously flowing more rapidly to my brain, a dizzy, light-headed feeling overcoming me. "I'd love to turn you on," Jackie sang, "I'd love to turn you on," she repeated in rhythm to the slow, hypnotic, dreamlike cadence of Lennon's intonation, and as she sang this, her thighs continued to move back and forth against my feet, absolutely turning me on. I had no means to express what I was feeling toward Jackie—just on the cusp of 13 years old; I had no sexual experience with a female, other than innocuous kissing, though the kind of kissing being done with Janice M the last few times were waking up the two of us to the potential for this sort of activity. I had become more bold in touching Janice's breasts during the last few times we kissed, but my feelings at this moment with Jackie had to be at least 10 times as intense. Jackie was tall, maybe five feet seven inches, maintained excellent posture from her practice of yoga, had boyish-looking, quite short brown hair at a time when virtually every girl wore it long, and was endowed with a very large chest, more pronounced because she was quite lean. She seemed to be always wearing—at least this is how I consistently remember her—a tight-fitting, long-sleeved green shirt, her breasts more like the peaks of mountain tops than rounded. When the song ended, Jackie lingered for a moment or two, my head on a couch pillow, and feet remaining on her lap, moving not quite as much as a few moments before, but continuing to slowly stroke her. Jackie's effects on my body had dizzied my mind, and while I had never had the experience of "making love" at this tender age, the rush of hormones moving through me, no doubt, had put me in an equivalent state. Perhaps Jackie didn't realize her effect on me that night—though given her sophistication and slow gentle approach, she most likely was totally aware— but she affected me in a way that was as profound as if we had actually made love. It was an unrequited kind of love that left each of us desiring something that just couldn't be completed.

Jackie continued to babysit as we moved into the new house atop the tobogganing hill. Through January and into February, after all the kids had gone to sleep, Jackie and I would watch TV as we lay next to each other on my parents' bed. She would rub her leg up and down my calf, eventually pushing off the sock on one foot, then the other. And I would do the same to her. This was always late at night, and on occasion, I had already been out with Janice M earlier the same evening. Janice had become a girlfriend—we weren't going steady in boyfriend/girlfriend way, but we clearly liked being together, and we were each others' dates at parties. With Janice, I was a 13-year-old boy (almost) with a 13-year-old girl. We were seventh-grade kids, doing things in a seventh-grade way. With Jackie, though, everything happening with us seemed dreamlike, chemical reactions creating new and unfamiliar sensations. She was deep into high school, and when we spent time together, I was on a voyage of discovery. Jackie A influenced my chemistry more profoundly, indelibly, than any drug, and while many people listened to that "Sgt. Pepper's" album under the influence of some narcotic agent, John Lennon's voice needed no greater compound than Jackie moving her thigh rhythmically beneath my feet. Janice M had become part of the routine of my life, along with playing hockey, racing down the mountain on "the bomb," and going to school. The scent of her skin when we kissed excited me every time. The world of Jackie A existed in the ether, the outer regions of space, within the quiet moments of stillness. There was only one occasion when I had to choose between the two. There was a late-night party on a Saturday night deep into January; the David boys came to get me at Janice's request. Jackie had been at the house babysitting—she had urged me to go off with my friends. I dissented, my friends a bit surprised. We rubbed our feet against each other later that night, in the couple hours or so before my parents were to come home, our socks falling to the floor, exposing the bare skin. "I wish you had motions," Jackie said to me that night; "I wish you had motions." "What do you mean by that?" I queried. "What do you mean by motions?" "Oh, I won't go into it now," she answered, "let's not worry about it." I put the thought away and didn't worry about it. It wasn't until later in my teens when, thinking back to the nights with Jackie, that I realized what she meant—it had become frustrating for her, she desired me sexually; she had become aware of the limitations. And as I have thought back on that night together, her comments, my limitations, I have wondered if I had made the right choice. Should I have gone off with my friends, spent the time with Janice?

As I look over this dark, dark bay, the Golden Gate Bridge unilluminated, except for the beads of light at the bottom along the road, my marriage in a place where the two of us have accepted that this change may be irrevocable, I also ponder how it all happened. Is it fate? Is it destiny? Is our place in life guided by the same forces that brought us together in the first place? Is the whole "darn shootin' match" just random? Did meeting "M" undo my marriage? And should I therefore have found a way to avoid the whole experience? It is clear to me that, no, it is not random, and that we do our best with the information that we have. I made the right decision in spending those moments with Jackie A—her effect on me was life-changing. And the experience of "M" was tantamount to being turned upside down in a hurricane—I had never submitted to anything like this in my life, but suddenly I was permitting myself to perceive possibilities, allowing boundaries to become blurred. Perhaps I had a choice in the matter, but it didn't feel that way—I just couldn't push the lever that said, "no, absolutely not." And so here I am, in a kind of limbo, an uncertain state somewhere between being "free" and desperately wanting to be grounded again. "M" still has no idea of this separation; there has been no communication. Her effect on me is irreversible, but

I move on into new territory. I continue this journey, though I hurt, sometimes deeply. Indeed, I have choice, but, perhaps, my inability to push myself back into the marriage, the inability to surrender this commodity of "freedom," is the difficult choice that I am making. Perhaps I am being decisive, more decisive than I realize, but that it all feels so complicated because of the pain that I feel. I love my family so deeply; these times are terribly difficult. The journey continues, comforted by the notion that we do have options; there are choices that can be made. We do not have as much control as we would wish, but we do have some, often more than we realize. We are shaped by our journey, by choices made and not made. The unmade choices are, indeed, choices made—if not by our own volition, then by the universe. All I can do is submit to this journey—submit with the realization that each step of the way, answers and ways of being unfold, as they always have. Let us be gentle with ourselves in difficult times—let us not engage in doubt or judgment. It will all unfold, as it must.

❐

The twin relationships of Janice and Jackie brought me joy and introspection; my senses of touch and scent were being altered; I was becoming more aware of my body and its capacity to respond to a female. With Janice, I was enthusiastic, happy to be my age with this girl my age; I traveled with Jackie, open to the possibilities of expansion, aware of the significant difference in age and maturity, but willing to have the experience, albeit with equal parts curiosity, excitement and caution. Jackie was quiet, secretive, seductive, mysterious, speaking with her body much more than her voice. I was amidst the unknown while in her presence, large spaces of mental quiet available for her imprint. The music enhanced my experience of both girls, and the entire experience of these months eased, tranquilized the trauma of Montreal, culminating in the horror of that night. I had moved way beyond that night—and as alien a place as Campbellton, New Brunswick, was, inevitably it was what God and the doctor ordered for this time in my life. And although it was a place to which I adapted well, I could not shake this inner necessity, this burning need to return to California. My mom recognized that this wasn't where she belonged either, but she was getting tired of the struggle. We had found a comfortable place to live, after the War of 1812 house. And though she truly wanted to move back to California, or even to Toronto to be with her family, she might have succumbed to the sense of settling down we were all starting to feel, if it had not been for me. It was as though I knew from the depths of my soul, I felt it in the soles of my feet, that California was where I belonged, and that I had to return. I sensed that whatever my life would be, whatever the future would have for me, my destiny lay in California, and it could not be ignored at any cost.

The feeling to return was continually being reinforced by the new National Hockey League team that just that winter had been located in Los Angeles. The Los Angeles Kings were one of the group of teams that included the St. Louis Blues, the Minnesota North Stars, the Philadelphia Flyers, and some others that had been part of the first NHL expansion from the original six-team league. Often on Hockey Night in Canada—a game broadcast all across Canada on Saturday night—the contest would feature one of the new teams. The L.A. Kings, with a big crown set against their jerseys of gold, excited me to the bone. I became incredibly nostalgic to go home whenever I saw them play on TV—and there were at least a few games that winter that were broadcast from Los Angeles. They had some really colorful players with great nicknames: Bill "Cowboy" Flett, Eddie "the Jet" Joyal. Flett was known for having an exceptionally hooked stick (much greater than they allow in today's game), and he was, apparently, well known in rodeo circles as a big star in that endeavor. He had longish hair, long black sideburns, and was known to have a wicked slap shot. I saw him score a few goals in the games I watched. Eddie "the Jet" Joyal was very quick, as the name implies. He was a bit of a "pretty boy," not liking to get his face in the corners. But he did go in the corners from time to time—you can't totally avoid it; this is the NHL after all—often coming out with the puck. He had black hair combed straight back—the hair flying backwards when he was in full flight. These were the day when players didn't wear helmets, so I can remember their faces quite well. Joyal scored a few more goals than Flett, but not many more. Flett was my favorite, though; I loved the way he played. He didn't look for trouble, but he seemed to be always willing to get into a mix-up, if one came his way. It was a thrill to watch the Kings, and by early March I knew I had to find a way back home to California.

I turned 13 years old on March 6, 1968. And though I had started to prepare for a Bar Mitzvah in Montreal, this moving to a town that did not have a Jewish place of worship, let alone the dislocation that we were all feeling, prevented this "coming of age" ritual from happening for me. Instead of a Bar Mitzvah, we had my birthday at Campbellton's only Chinese restaurant. We had Chinese food that night, and the only one of my family not present was my father.

I knew that my mom felt sad that she wasn't able to provide this "rite of passage" for me. "I'll be okay, if I can just get back to California," I thought to myself. It was a very clear thought in my mind, but I wasn't about to tell my mom about it anymore. I didn't want to put any more demands on her at this time—we were celebrating my birthday, and I wanted all of us to be happy. But I couldn't hold back when she told me to make a wish, and that whatever I wished she would make come true. "You mean it Mom?" I said. "Anything I want to come true, you'll make come true?" "Yes, as long as it is realistic, you know," she responded. "If it's within reason. You should be having a Bar Mitzvah tonight, and I want your dreams to come true," she continued, trickles of tears coming down her cheek. "Mom, is it realistic to bring me back to California, real soon? I want to go back so badly." "Brucie," she answered, "I am going to make this wish come true for you, I promise. Mark my words, by the end of this month, we will be on our way back to California. I promise." "How can that happen?" I answered. "Where are we going to get the money to do that? And I'm sure Dad won't want to go." "The pool table that we have is an antique; it is worth a lot of money. We'll sell it, as well as some other furniture, and that will definitely get us the money we need." "But Dad won't want to go—I'm sure he won't." "If he doesn't want to come, then we'll go without him, I promise." She said this with total determination, a kind of determination that comes from one place and one place only—the Rush genes and blood flowing through her veins. After all, she was the sister of Meyer Rush.

The next day my mom informed my father that by the end of March this family would be moving back to California. He fought her on it, and became enraged by her stubborn unwillingness to compromise. She told him in no uncertain terms that we would be leaving with or without him, and to do so we would be selling his cherished pool table. He was outraged, but he had no choice.

The Road to California

March, 1968

A slow thawing of the snow was underway when we left Campbellton; my brother's hockey season had finished just a week before, his team winning the division in which he played, but losing in the semi-finals to the team from Moncton. Wayne Manley had lit up the league during the season, and scored some important goals in the playoffs. A respect between us had occurred during the school year—he knew that I admired the way he played hockey, and respected me for standing up to him in his backyard that summer. While not ever becoming friends—I didn't travel in his circle—we became friendly acquaintances before and after the team's games, and when I rode the bus with my brother to the cities on the road. My brother, Jeff, wore his hockey jacket with pride—it had several emblems on it labeled "shut-out," marking the games when he had skunked the opposing team in goal—as we packed the car and drove off toward Maine, and all parts south and west toward California. My father had that angry, tense, tight, pale, thin look to his face as we left New Brunswick on the windy road through the forests, melting snow filling the fields, trees no longer bare, leaves beginning a life that would mature very quickly in this land of winter. The scenery was spectacular, and I tried to appreciate everything that I was seeing, knowing that my life as a northeastern Canadian—short in time (could it have only been seven months that we were in New Brunswick?), but indelible in its effect and imprint—would become something of my past, as I moved toward the place my heart craved. We stopped at small motels along the way, along a route that brought us through New England, across the mid-western states of Ohio, Missouri, Kansas, then south through Texas, New Mexico, Arizona, Nevada and into California.

❒

The trip west might have been, could have been, and as we departed I wished so much that it would be, an enjoyable adventure for the family—but my father just wouldn't let it be that way. I suppose that this return was difficult for him; he had left for Canada just two years earlier with grand hopes that he would be returning, perhaps permanently, to his home, his roots. Montreal did not work out for him, despite the fact that his mom and dad (my Bubby and Zeida) were there, and he very much wanted to be near them after many years apart in California. There was no permanence for his family in Campbellton, and he knew that, but he had grown to like the country life. It was not his choice, and it was against his will that we were on our way back west. He had no idea what kind of work he would find, and he made no effort to conceal his anger. To the contrary—when my brother, Jeff, and myself would argue too long for his liking, or if we were making too much noise when he wanted quiet, he'd swing his arm forcefully into the back seat, hoping to make contact. During a gas station stop in Columbus, Ohio, he had gotten so mad at my brother, Jeff, for answering him back that he drove off, leaving him at the station for a few minutes. Of course he wouldn't have kept on driving, even if my mom hadn't screamed with such anger at him, but the fact of its occurrence makes it quite clear the kind of ride we were having back to my homeland. Yet, it wasn't all this kind of craziness. During a long, dark stretch of road through New Mexico—my father wanted to just keep on driving through the night—I sat in the front seat with him when everyone else was asleep, and he actually asked me to tell him why I was so excited to be heading back. "I miss the long hot summers, playing ball in fields with my friends, going to baseball games at Dodger stadium, and now we'll get to watch the L.A. Kings play—I'll see 'Cowboy' Flett, and Eddie 'the Jet' Joyal in person. It's my home, and it's where I have longed to be since we left" "You know you won't get a chance to see Sandy Koufax pitch anymore," he said. "He's retired now." "I know, but Drysdale is still around. I can't wait to hear Vin Scully announce those games again; I just want to go to a ton of baseball games this summer." "We'll see," he said to me, "we'll see." That was his famous line; no matter how excited one of us would become about something, he'd always answer, "We'll see." But I knew that "we'll see" wasn't going to work for me; I had told myself that I'd figure out the bus route to the Dodger Stadium, if I had to. No doubt about it; I had made up my mind that I was going to get to know Dodger Stadium very well during the next several months.

There were a few more long nights of driving before we reached Las Vegas, a decision that my mom and dad agreed on. The days were warm, and my brother Jeff and I spent time in the swimming pool while my parents had fun, a babysitter at the hotel taking care of the little ones, Elliot and Heidi. Jeff had not been enjoying this cross-country drive very much—he didn't have the same urgency to return to California as I did—and my dad's temper was making him quite upset. He had really grown to like Campbellton, and was enjoying the high life of being the town's celebrated hockey goalie. But he did have one great moment, and it was the highlight of his trip. I had been watching TV in the room on one of the nights, when Jeff entered with huge excitement, my mom closing the door behind him with a big smile. "Tommy Smothers of the Smothers Brothers rode up in the elevator with us," said Jeff. "He made a whole bunch of funny faces at me, and told me he was going to put me in his show. He wanted to know if I was an acrobat. I told him no, but that I was a really good hockey goalie. He said he'd put me in his show as a hockey goalie, then. Mom says he means it, right, Mom?" My mom just laughed, smiled, "I think he really means it Jeff; I think he'll really do it." Jeff was convinced that this was going to happen for sure—that at any moment there would be a knock on the door, asking Jeff to join the Smothers Brothers show. Jeff was a little disappointed when we left Las Vegas and that knock never happened—but he got over it. We had stayed in Las Vegas three nights, and then it was the long drive into California. We entered California through the Mojave Desert, up through Palm Springs, then into Los Angeles, stopping at the Beverly Hilton hotel. Apparently my parents had won a little money in Vegas, and they had decided that they could afford a night at the Beverly Hilton Hotel. So that's where we stayed that first night in California. There were all kinds of movie stars and famous people coming in and out of the place, we were told, but I can't remember seeing any of them. There was only one person who I really wanted to see, and I looked for him everywhere: Sandy Koufax. I kept looking for him, and I thought I spotted him. It was embarrassing when I went up to the man and asked if he was Sandy Koufax. "No" he answered, "He's better looking than me, though I can pitch as well as him."

From the Beverly Hilton, it was on to a cheaper hotel in the San Fernando Valley, where we stayed about a week before finding a home in the San Fernando Valley.

We had been in the hotel not more than a day, our family occupying two rooms in this Motel Six-type place, when the television program was interrupted with reports that Dr. Martin Luther King had been assassinated. President Johnson appeared on the TV asking the country to "reject the blind violence" which had killed the "apostle of nonviolence." I remember seeing Vice President Hubert Humphrey's call for the nation to remain calm. And I'll never forget the words of Senator Bobby Kennedy, given as he was about to speak on a campaign stop in Indianapolis during his quest for the Democratic nomination for president. "Ladies and Gentlemen, I'm only going to talk to you for a minute or so this evening, because, I have some very sad news for all of you, and I think sad news for all of our fellow citizens, and people who love peace all over the world, and that is that Martin Luther King was shot and was killed tonight in Memphis, Tennessee. ... For those of you who are black—considering the evidence evidently is that there were white people who were responsible—you can be filled with bitterness, and with hatred, and a desire for revenge. We can move in that direction as a country, in greater polarization—black people amongst blacks, and white amongst whites, filled with hatred toward one another. Or we can make an effort, as Martin Luther King did, to understand and to comprehend, and replace that violence, that stain of bloodshed that has spread across our land, with an effort to understand, compassion and love. For those of you who are black and are tempted to be filled with hatred and mistrust of the injustice of such an act, against all white people, I would only say that I can also feel in my own heart the same kind of feeling. I had a member of my family killed, but he was killed by a white man." The words were spoken from the soul, and they were spoken softly, gracefully, they came easily, delivered with deep empathy and awareness of what this might do to America. I was 13 years old; I cried when I heard of Dr. King's assassination, and cried again when I heard Bobby Kennedy's comments and prayers for peace. I had been very much aware in my young life of Dr. King's struggle to emancipate blacks from a modern-day slavery. We had talked about his nonviolent approach and compared him to Gandhi during a civics lesson at school in Campbellton. I had recalled for the class the fear that I felt while living in Southern California during the Watts riots, and how I had respected Dr. King's approach, his appeal to his brothers to stop the violence. And even though I was only eight years old when he delivered his "I have a dream" speech, the soulful appeal, the phrasing of his words, touched me in an unusual way—I could see that this was a great man. I was perceptive at this age of eight—it was also when I was at this age that President Kennedy was assassinated. I loved his style; I was drawn to his magnetism when I saw him on television, and I was crushed, couldn't believe something like this could happen, when I was sent home from school the day of his assassination. I dreamt about Kennedy for years after the murder, my young psyche trying to make sense of such a thing. And so here was another murder of a great man, and at the age of 13 I felt its weight. During the remaining week, while my parents searched for a place to live, I often remained behind at the hotel, and my memory of significant transition for myself, my family and in the life of the nation, is filled with the scenes of rioting brought to the TV screen in the aftermath of the murder. While we were looking for a place to live in the land of my dreams, the country seemed to be coming apart at the seams.

Images of rioting across the nation contended for airtime with replays of some of Dr. King's great speeches, and these speeches made a strong impression on me. Taken together, they were telling a story of a tension in America much deeper than I had ever realized. There is an understanding in the Jewish faith that a boy begins to perceive the world in a more profound way on reaching the age of 13, thus the Bar Mitzvah coming-of-age ceremony. The young man begins to see the world in a more sensitive, reflective, philosophical way than at any previous time. As I sat in that hotel room during those few days, I apprehended, I think, a bit of the soul and the depth of the cause of Dr. Martin Luther King. The commentators were talking about how prophetic his speech had been in a Memphis church, the night before his death. That he was, perhaps, aware or had been informed that his life was in danger. Dr. King no doubt lived with the sense at all times that his life was in danger. But as I reread this speech tonight in the quiet of this apartment, it is astounding what this prophet had to say. He had had a vision of his own life and death, and of the glory for his people. Some of the words that were repeated over and again on the TV screen back in the first week of April, 1968:

"Like anybody, I would like to live a long life. Longevity has its place. But I'm not concerned about that now. I just want to do God's will. And he has allowed me to go up to the mountain. And I've looked over. And I've seen the Promised Land. I might not get there with you. But I want you to know tonight, that we, as a people, will get to the Promised Land."

❐

We eventually found a house in a middleclass neighborhood on Albers Street in Van Nuys. The guy who owned the house had been in years past "The Marlboro Man" in the cigarette commercials. There had been several Marlboro Men over the years, but this guy, so he told us, had been one of them. He was a tall, rugged-looking kind of guy, sandy-colored hair that was combed back, strands often coming unglued and dangling over his eyes. My mom and dad said they had recognized him from commercials a few years back, before leaving for Canada. Shortly after our moving in, he stopped by to see how we were settling. I was sitting in the backyard on an ornately designed metal love seat, its rod-iron back designed into hundreds of swirling flowers. "Enjoy sitting on that love seat," he said to me as he entered the backyard. "I decided that I'd leave it here for your family. But be sure to take good care of it, and tell that to your parents, all right? It's my favorite piece in this house." "Sure I'll tell them what you said," I answered, sitting quietly with a Coca-Cola and the baseball game next to me on a transistor radio. I was reveling in the sound of Vin Scully's voice, so I wasn't all that interested in a conversation. And to me, whatever I was sitting on was just a metal chair; I didn't see the magnificence of it. But I did make a mental note that this was something very important to its owner, and I made a mental commitment to not spill stuff on it and to be sure to dry it off if it got wet. During a commercial during the game I said to him that my parents had told me that he had been in Marlboro cigarette commercials, and that I had remembered the commercials very well, though not any of the actors. He had done the commercials in which he was riding horseback a few years ago, he said, and in doing them he met some really big names. He had become friendly with John Wayne and Clint Eastwood, he had told me. I wasn't all that familiar with Eastwood, but I loved, loved John Wayne. I asked him what John Wayne was like, and his answer was that he was "exactly as you see him in the movies, no different. He's a tough, strong, solid, honorable man, and a great actor." "Enjoy living here," the Marlboro man said to me as he got up to leave, noticing my interest in the next inning that had just started. "And be sure to remind your parents to take care of my love seat." "I will," I answered, "I'll tell them."

Van Nuys didn't exactly match my ideal of where I wanted to be in California, but I was all right with it. My parents had looked at parts of Orange County, a much prettier area, and places not far from the beach before settling on this spot for the time being. I'd had asthma as a kid, and the smog in this part of the city was giving me a wheeze. But I didn't let that stop me; we hadn't been living in this home for more than two weeks when I decided to take on a paper route. I was so good and efficient at working the route on my bicycle that the guy had given me another. When my mom saw how exhausted I was after doing both routes, she insisted that I give one of them up. "They're taking advantage of you," she said to me, "paying you peanuts for all of this hard work. And I don't want you riding your bike so late into the night, it's dangerous." I kept the easier of the two routes, which only took about an hour and a half after school. I liked having a job, and I enjoyed getting out and riding my bike.

I had been inserted into a seventh-grade class in the local junior high school. I didn't have any familiarity with the subject matter that they were studying, but I caught up very quickly. Whereas in Canada, we had been studying the roots of the French in Canadian society, here in California we were reading about the establishment of the missions and the state's inheritance from Spain. Notes on the War of 1812 were replaced with understanding the role of Father Serra in the establishment of missions up and down the State of California. I caught up very quickly and did well in school. The reading was less challenging than what we were doing in Canada, and the amount of homework was far less. I was way ahead of what they were doing in math, so I didn't have to study that at all. It all left more time to listen to Vin Scully at night. However, there was a definite culture shock that I experienced on entry to the new junior high. Generally, kids had much longer hair than the Canadian boys. And smoking seemed to be a big thing here in California. None of my friends in Campbellton smoked cigarettes, and while there were a number of kids who smoked, it was nothing like the kids that loitered before and after school, filling up the bathrooms with cigarette smoke. And it wasn't only cigarette smoke. I was being offered marijuana in the bathrooms—I had never encountered this stuff anywhere in Campbellton—and kids seemed to have an attitude when I turned them down. Acting as though I was "un-hip" and "square." And there was a real "rough" element that went to this school—lots of fights during and after school, many of them taking place between Hispanic kids and whites. This wasn't exactly Shangri-la. There was an independence that many of these kids had—some of them seemed to be able to do anything they wanted. Sitting in class one day, two kids across from me were discussing how they were going to hitchhike to see some rock shows in San Francisco. And the girl in front of them said that she'd like to hitchhike with them, since she was planning to hitchhike to Mill Valley to see a friend that very weekend. They made their plan to hitch together. Hearing this, I asked the long-haired blond kid across from me if his parents minded whether he hitchhiked so far away, and did they know he would be doing this. He looked at me derisively and said, "Sure, they're cool with it; what's the matter, your parents won't let you do that?" It seemed shocking to me that these 13-, perhaps 14-year-old kids would be allowed to do such a thing. Later that day, I saw the three of them—the two boys and the girl—smoking pot out on the track. This was a different life, no question about it.

Van Nuys Blvd. is about as ugly a street as one can find in Southern California. It is a long, loud artery through the San Fernando Valley, with great views of car dealerships, strip malls and fast food restaurants. The pavement is scorching hot on a summer's day and the air hovering over this street (in 1968, perhaps it is better today) is gray with smog. But the street became pure elegance, charisma and excitement one day in early June, 1968, the school year just one week from being over at the Junior High into which I had transitioned. I was standing on a street corner after school when a motorcade drove by, Bobby Kennedy smiling and waving en route to a speaking engagement a few days before the California primary, which he was hopeful of winning before the convention in Chicago later that summer. He had grown weary and tired of the Vietnam War. Recognizing that we were getting deeper and deeper into a conflict that was not winnable, he expressed the grief that America was feeling over the daily deaths of our young men that appeared nightly in our living rooms on the network news. The assassination of Martin Luther King had made him solemn, and he spoke in an intergenerational way of striving to breach the great divides that were deepening in America: the chasm between rich and poor, black and white, the young and the old. I was following him closely, and was starting to love everything about the man. There was a dynamism about him, an excitement whenever he appeared, and there was a love and compassion that flowed from him, an intoxicating energy. He had changed, matured, deepened in the years since losing his brother, John Kennedy. I so much wanted for him to be president, and given the crowds that were flocking to him wherever he went, it sure seemed that there was a really good chance of it happening. No doubt, though, I was partial to a Kennedy. When I was five years old in 1960, my mom used to ask me which way I wanted to part my hair: one way would be Nixon, the other Kennedy. I always selected Kennedy, and somehow, even at that baby-age, I rooted for Kennedy in the debates. I have a clear recollection of rooting for Jack Kennedy to win the election, waking up the next morning and asking my parents if he'd won. "Yes, we think so," my mom said at the time. "They're not sure yet." But he did win, and I was really happy. So I had a natural affection for Bobbie

Kennedy, but even still I was moved whenever I saw him on TV, campaigning, to see him in the motorcade that day was thrilling.

I was paying close attention to the results of the California primary on that evening of June 5, 1968. Kennedy had won and was giving his victory speech. He wore a magnificent, very happy grin, then finished his speech, giving a "V" sign (signifying victory and peace), accompanied by the words, "Now let's go on to Chicago, and let's win there." I was about to turn off the TV—it was already past midnight—when the cameras started to pick up expressions of anguish on the faces of celebrants in one of the large rooms where there had been revelry. There were a few seconds of quiet, followed by one of the commentators saying that he had just been told that Robert Kennedy had been shot. He would be getting further corroboration as quickly as possible, we were told. Within a few minutes celebrations had turned into mourning; commentators beginning to cry as they were starting to make sense of what had just happened. Robert Kennedy, apparently, had been shot twice in the back and behind his right ear in the kitchen pantry by a Palestinian man, Sirhan Sirhan, 24, who had apparently exclaimed, "Kennedy, you son of a bitch," before opening fire. There was talk that, perhaps, this man was angry at Kennedy's support for Israel in the Six-Day War. But what did it matter? This was too horrible to believe. I could barely sleep that night, not knowing if Bobbie Kennedy would make it—but I feared for the worst. The next evening it was announced that Robert Kennedy had died at the Good Samaritan Hospital, 25 and a half hours after he had been shot. I was grief stricken, and as I sit here reflecting on this time in my life and in the life of our country, the bay is a deeper black than I have, perhaps, ever seen. Or, perhaps, the bay is a canvas on which my mind reflects the darkness of that moment in time. I was so deeply sad. A few days after the assassination my friend's father showed me a $10 bill covered in blood that had been handed to him in the parking lot of the Ambassador Hotel, in the immediate aftermath of the shooting. The father had a job parking cars in the lot, and described to me how this bill had been given to him by a person in the security detail for Kennedy, as he left the lot. The father wasn't joking—there was nothing to joke about. I have never forgotten seeing that blood-stained bill a few days after the assassination.

By the end of June my parents had found another place to live, this time in a middle-class neighborhood in another part of the San Fernando Valley, Reseda. The place had a swimming pool, and I was excited about that. There would be furniture to buy, since the place in Van Nuys had come furnished. I had been sitting in the backyard one afternoon, listening to the Dodger game on my trusty transistor radio—Vin Scully's echoing, resonating voice keeping me satisfied, as it usually did—when the Marlboro man came by to inspect the premises. Looking around, he didn't see the "Love Seat." "What happened to the love seat?" he asked me. "I don't see it anywhere. Did your parents take it?" "Why is this guy asking me about his love seat again, when all I'm trying to do is listen to the ball game?" I said to myself. "I'm not the guardian of his love seat." "No, I'm sure they didn't," I answered. "I really don't know what happened to it." After a few minutes he walked away, leaving me alone, once and for all. Later that day when my parents picked me up to take me to the new house, I saw the love seat in the backyard. I didn't ask any questions; I didn't care about the darn love seat.

❐

I was true to my intention that summer of 1968—through figuring out the various bus connections (Los Angeles was not a public transportation–friendly city) I managed to make it to at least 10 baseball games at Dodger Stadium. The good friend that I had made in Van Nuys, Jimmy, the son of the man who showed me that blood-stained bill, came with me to several games. Then after we moved to Reseda, I pulled my brother, Jeff, with me to several more games, figuring out the bus schedule anew from our new home. All of the games that I went to were weekend day games, and it was surprising to me that my mom was so easy about letting me go on my own. But she saw that I couldn't convince my dad to take me—not even once—and surrendered to her faith and intuition that I would be all right. No doubt she was nervous about us going off by ourselves, and she was successful on a couple of occasions when she offered to pay for my friend's father's ticket if he would go with us, but she knew how much I loved and had missed the Dodgers. In Reseda, there were no new friends to go to games with. School was out and it took the better part of the summer to make some new friends, so she reluctantly allowed me to take my brother with me. It is amazing to me as I think back that my mom was able to surrender to a faith that allowing her 13- and 12-year-old boys to go off by themselves into the wilds of Los Angeles would not be a problem. It isn't that she didn't worry—she was a very accomplished worrier, but she didn't let that get in the way of allowing us to have our adventures; to grow up.

There is no way that I would have been able to permit my boys that kind of freedom at that age—I sometimes worry to the point of fatigue when I cannot locate my boys, and Michael turns 21 tomorrow, while Jonathan is 18. No doubt my mom was fully cognizant of all the things that could happen, but she didn't give those thoughts any energy. She trusted in the process of growing up—and I so wish I had her today to help me with the kind of faith it takes to raise two boys, to not get in their way.

Looking down on the grass field of Chavez Ravine, Dodger Stadium, brought joy to me every time. And the joy was only slightly diminished by the losing season that the Dodgers were having. The team still had some of the big stars from the World

Series years—Willie Davis, Don Drysdale, Ron Fairly, Claude Osteen, Jim Brewer, Wes Parker—but Sandy Koufax had retired. And with Sandy absent, the team was bereft of a kind of magic, charisma, charm, not to mention the 20-to-27 wins per season he would deliver. The team kept sinking toward last place, but Don Drysdale was having an incredible season. Before moving to Reseda, I listened on the radio to every one of his record-setting 58 scoreless innings—I'll never forget the moment when it looked as though the streak would come to an end somewhere in the 40s, when he actually hit Dick Dietz, forcing in a run. But the umpire ruled that the batter failed to try to get out of the way. Tom Haller—the former Giant in those bitter rivalry days of the early '60s, now with the Dodgers—was catching Drysdale that day, adamantly making the point that the batter did not attempt to get out of the way. I remember that moment so clearly, my homework having just been completed, the radio having been turned on just a few innings before. Several days later, Bobby Kennedy would be assassinated, and it was with a heart filled with enormous sadness that I listened to the game on June eighth, two days after the assassination, when the record reached 58 innings, before coming to an end.

August 7th, 2007

My family is gathered at Via Veneto restaurant on Fillmore Street to celebrate Michael's 21st birthday. Mossimo, the owner of the restaurant has blocked the entire back of the restaurant for the occasion, and created a special menu. My son, Jonathan, is here with his so-pretty girlfriend, Ana, and what a gift she has been during this period of dislocation within our family. She has been a reservoir of support for this sensitive, emotional boy, and has helped him to know how deeply loved he is by his parents—how his parents do, indeed, love each other—and that perfect families do not exist. It is a treasure to see the affection in their eyes for each other, the way they enjoy being together, the way they always seem to be celebrating whenever they are together. And isn't that truly what we want in a relationship with another—to enjoy one another, to celebrate in the other's presence, to do things together that bring happiness, essentially to share for however long the gift of this life? Not that relationships are 100 percent fun and games, or even 75 percent fun and games. We all know that. But if we can enjoy, delight, savor the other's company, if it is pleasurable to be together in ways that make us want to be with that person again, if we can partner with another through some, part, much, most, all of this adventure, then we are opening that present gift wrapped by God. Because after all, ultimately, God's gift to us, is our gift to one another. The gift that I have given to Michael this very special day, as he is surrounded by about 20 of his best friends—all of them home from colleges spread throughout the country—is three bottles of Beaulieu Vineyards, George Latour, Cabernet Sauvignon and Private Reserve, bottled in the year of his birth, 1986. Mossimo opens the bottles for us, pours glasses for those who can prove they are at least 21, and we all raise our glasses in toast to my son—so gifted on that Steinway, capable of writing stirring compositions, as he has at Oberlin, one of them recently performed at a concert in New York City—his deep turquoise eyes beaming with the joys of friendship, family, being in the city in which he grew up and to which he loves to return, and the satisfaction of finally being an age when he no longer will be "carded." When I bought this wine, the people at the winery assured me that it was at the perfect drinking stage; that we would be drinking a wine fully mature, but not overly so, and that we were in for a delicious experience with hints of cherry, chocolate, licorice, all coming together amidst an oak aroma that grounds the wine with body and soul. We taste the wine and Michael's first comment was, "Dad, this is incredible; I can't believe how amazing this tastes. What an awesome, awesome birthday gift, just to think that this was bottled and hasn't been opened since the year I was born." Sue tasted the wine, the corners of her mouth turning gently upward into a sublime sweetness—she has been beaming all evening, so nice to see compared to the pain that has been etched on her face so often lately—and she looks silky and stunning, her blondish hair pulled back into a braid resting partially down her back. She is wearing a purple dress with flowers, and I comment that the dress looks fantastic on her, that it sets off her eyes, and that I don't know whose eyes are the deepest blue tonight, hers or Michael's. She thanks me for the complement, and I tell her that she's welcome, and that this is just as much a celebration for us to see Michael come of age in a very nice way as it is for him to celebrate the birthday. "I just can't believe he's 21," she says. "I just can't believe it; it is mind-boggling. Where did the time go?" I tell her quickly of what a man once said to me when we were visiting Maui, and Michael was about a year and a half old. He had said that though he's only a baby now, you're not going to believe how quickly that time will go. You'll be celebrating his 18th, then 21st birthdays, and it will seem like a dream. At least that's the way it was for me," and he said it with a kind of realistic resignation," I told Sue. "I remember thinking," I continued, "that yeah, right, 18, 21 years, that's a very long time, and I'm sure that it will feel like forever when we get there. But here we are, and I am remembering that man's words very clearly. He was right—wow; how right he was! Yes it feels like a long time, we've done a lot in these years, but it also feels like a dream. Like it's gone by in an instant." And at this moment, Sue's smile turned into a wince of pain, a subtle melancholy altering her expression, and I felt that she was thinking back to that time and in many of the years that followed when we wouldn't have been able to imagine the present state of our marriage. As if aware of the thinning out of her lips as they started to tilt toward the beginnings of a frown, she brought the glass to her mouth for another sip, beginning to laugh at a funny expression of appreciation Michael had made after taking a large sip of the wine.

"Michael," I said, "I want to propose a toast to you. Everybody raise their glasses, even you guys that are just drinking water or whatever. This wine, this incredible wine that we are drinking tonight for your birthday is fully mature—another year or two and it will, probably, be overly mature, not as drinkable as today. And at 21 you have reached a milestone, a new level of maturity that permits you to go into bars and clubs, to do things that you've never been allowed to do before, legally. It's so hard to believe that this time has arrived. Mom and I were just talking about how quickly this time has flown by. We celebrate this moment in your life tonight, this rite of passage. And I am confident that you will appreciate the responsibility that comes with new choices." Michael starts to look at me as though I'm getting a bit too serious, but I go on, "So tonight we celebrate everything you are, and just how much you mean to Mom, myself, Jonathan." Jonathan gives me an embarrassed look, as Ana giggles slightly. "But also remember that unlike the wine, which is fully mature, there is much for you to learn in life, much to understand, just as there is for someone at any age. But even more so at 21. So, please, never fail to come to me or Mom to ask anything; just know that you have two parents who love you very much and are here to help and guide you, whenever the need arises. You have a long life ahead, kenahora, and may you always come to us as the fine wine that is Michael David Rosen continues to mature." "That was kind of serious, Dad," Michael says to me, "but thank you, and I always will." And with that, the table bursts into a low roar, Mossimo now coming by with the dinner's first course, of his amazing Minestrone soup, some of the best that I have ever had. As he delivers the soup, I pour Mossimo a glass of the vintage wine, telling him that it is from Michael's birth year, 1986. He takes a big sip from the glass—utters an expression of deep appreciation in Italian—then runs off, taking the glass with him, as he tends to other guests at the front of the restaurant. As we are finishing the soup, one of Michael's friends yells across the table, "Barry just hit number 756. My friend just texted me. He's sitting in the bleachers and this is what he says: 'I swear to God, the ball just hit my glove and bounced off. I was that close to catching the home run. I swear to God, it bounced right off my glove.' " The kid yelling across the table, Spencer, goes on to tell us that the kid who didn't catch the ball must be really mad at himself, because he is a good baseball player, that he played shortstop in high school. Indeed, number 756 had been hit on Michael's 21st birthday, August 7, 2007. Later that night I come back to my apartment, turn on the TV, and see the highlight of Barry Bonds circling the bases, the crowd going wild. He is lucky he hit it in San Francisco; with all of this steroids stuff I don't think it would have been a pretty moment if he'd had it on the road. Even so, it is an incredible accomplishment, achieved by probably the greatest hitter of all time, steroids or no steroids. And tonight is Michael's 21st birthday. The wine was incredible.

❐

It is late in the evening of August 21, the strand of jewels that are the lights below the towers of the Golden Gate Bridge glisten intermittently, red lights flickering synchronously atop the towers. The dome of the Palace of Fine Art is lit dimly in soft pinks and oranges—there is a soft opaqueness to its glow, similar to an antique Tiffany lamp—shaped like a finely chiseled diamond one might find in the Tower of London. Off in the blackness of the bay the light atop Alcatraz Island blinks about every five seconds, like a strobe, into all windows looking north on the bay. To my left, I see the lights on the hills of Sausalito, and to the right, way off in the distance I see the constantly flickering bulbs of the East Bay, Oakland and Berkeley. I look back again to the abandoned prison that is Alcatraz, and as I do I reflect on the joys of this past weekend, but also of the barriers and fences that prevent me from returning to the life that I once lived.

Sue and I returned from New York yesterday, where we had gone to take Jonathan to begin his freshman year at Bard College, an hour and a half out of New York City, along the Hudson. It was touching and poignant as Jonathan parted with Ana—Sue and myself watching from the taxi—as they embraced, kissed, parted, returned, kissed parted, returned. There was a bittersweet agony of sincere love speeding rapidly through time, but reaching the stoplight where parting was necessary and inevitable. There is a helplessness and desperation in that feeling, and their eyes were filled with that melancholy sorrow. Jonathan handed Ana the teddy bear that he had slept with since a small child, and our hearts were broken as Jonathan returned to the taxi, Ana clutching the ruffled bear as she walked away down the street, looking back several times until the taxi had disappeared. We stayed at the Essex House in New York City, Jonathan sleeping in Sue's room, while I had a room to myself. The three of us walked around the city the following day as a family, strolling through Central Park, stopping to spend time at Strawberry Fields, the memorial to John Lennon, across the street from the Dakota, where he lived and was killed. We continued walking through the day, eventually having some great Jewish food at the Carnegie Deli. We all gathered in Sue's room that night and watched a movie. It was a cozy night to a day filled with kinship and connection. The following morning we were on a train bound for Rhinebeck, just a few miles from the Bard campus, where a taxi had been waiting to bring us to Red Hook, where I had arranged to rent a car for the weekend. In due time we were at Bard College, located his dorm (a choice location in a stone building atop a small hill), and were off to purchase the bedding and supplies to make him feel at home. We found the softest sheets, the coziest comforter, the biggest, softest pillows that we could find—Jonathan wasn't hung up on this stuff, but we just had to make sure that the harsh edges of separation would be softened by a comfort where sleep would be easy. Sue was hard at work turning his dorm room into a makeshift home, Jonathan finding a chair in the corner, singing beautifully a song that he had written while in Mendocino the previous spring. My mother had come to him in his mind while visiting there during the final few weeks of his high school life, and he was singing a song about her, one of the lines being, "psychic blood in my veins." He went on to sing some more of his compositions, his voice and lyrics truly cut to the core, and I was already nostalgic about how quickly this was all passing. I didn't want to give him up, wanted to hang on with a tight embrace to this boy who stirs within me a boundless love, couldn't stand the thought that I'd be on a plane headed 3,000 miles away. But Jonathan seemed quite adjusted as Sue worked over his room. He was now playing Dylan's "Knockin' on Heaven's Door," followed by the Beatles' "This Boy," no doubt thinking about Ana. Just as he was starting to sing, "Here, There and Everywhere"—this is the song that I had the band play for Sue and myself, as we went up to give a wish for Jonathan at the party following his Bar Mitzvah—his new roommate walked in, holding a banjo. We knew instantly—the warmth of his expression—that Dave would be a kind young man with whom to share a room. There is a kindness and genuineness to this young man from Delaware, and of this we had no doubt. The time for us to leave Jonathan to his new life came abruptly—the barbecue for incoming freshman was about to start. We each embraced him with all of the life we had to give—and so the two of us left Jonathan to his new world, perhaps to see him for fall break if he wants a quick trip home, or maybe it wont be until Thanksgiving, such a long time away—and got into the car bound for our separate rooms in a little Motor Inn in Rhinebeck.

Together we walked the quaint streets of Rhinebeck in the early evening. The night had that August east-coast humidity, but not oppressively so. As we walked, stopping to enter a candy store with virtually every variety of candy cane imaginable—housed in a block of attached colonial-era homes converted to shops, this one of white wood, a large door the color of evergreen, carefully carved shutters framing the window, the same color as the door—a gentle breeze made a soft sound as it moved the maple leafs that fill the branches of many of the trees on the residential streets of the town. I bought a couple of root beer candy canes, Sue putting hers in her purse, while I immediately unwrapped mine, licked it a couple of times then becoming impatient and taking a big bite. We walked as old friends, perhaps even as a married couple that had raised two boys and delivered them to fine colleges, a calm nonverbal acceptance inherent in the language of our bodies, that we had reached a plateau at this moment in time, tension giving way to a feeling of satisfaction that we have produced two boys of gentle hearts and deep souls. We hadn't been seeing that much of each other in recent months, but we walked together with a familiarity and perhaps an appreciation for the other strengthened by the strife and passage of time. I knew at that moment, without a doubt, that whatever happened in our marriage, we would forever be friends. We truly are friends. "Jonathan seemed happy today, and his roommate is a great kid, I have no doubts," I said to Sue. "Jonathan is such a great kid," Sue responded. "We did something really right with our boys—we poured so much into them. They're such gifts. I feel so happy for Jonathan right now. He worked really hard, especially that senior year, and it was difficult for him, what was going on between us. We deserve to celebrate. You know I always loved you, even if you don't think that I always showed it. It's true; I wanted to be the best mother I could be. Just like you wanted to be the greatest dad for them. And whatever happens between us, I'll always love you," she continued. "I'll always love you, Sue, and I hope that you know that I always have. I really can't explain the changes going on inside me. I can't put my finger on it, or truly grasp everything. Perhaps there was a yearning in me to experience more of myself, the sense that I needed to expand, to allow the essence that is me to assert itself; maybe it has to do with knowing what it means to have choices. Whatever it is, I am going through a process from which I will emerge with direction and a feeling of completion. It is so difficult to be in this place; to always feel in-between and no longer settled as I had felt for so long in the family. It is a process, almost like a computer program that has to download and cannot be stopped prematurely. But it is so damn painful. This is not about other women; it isn't a rejection of you in any way. You are beautiful inside and out. Anyway, I don't want to get too heavy. Let's go get a glass of wine—better yet, let's go get dinner and have some wine." "Great idea," she answered. And so we found a veranda restaurant at a hotel in town. We each had the tasty veal dish, washed down with a bottle of California Sauvignon Blanc. By dinner's end, it had started to get chilly on the veranda.

We went back to the motor inn—the buzz from the wine not overwhelming but very pleasant—and changed into long sleeves. We met back at the front of the motor inn a few minutes later, thinking we might see if we were in time to catch a movie. But as we approached the movie theater, we heard some tasty-sounding rhythm and blues—a bluesy rock organ rising above some soulful vocals—from some club down the street. We were in time to see the movie, but the music exerted a gravitational pull. Our ears led us to a restaurant, with steps leading to an area down below. The little club had a bar to the left, a row of stools with tables for holding some drinks to the right, and a large area above the stools that was open to the outside, keeping the place well air-conditioned. The keyboardist was in the middle of a solo when we walked in; the drummer—a white man drenched in sweat—singing with the sweetest Detroit soul, "Ain't too proud to beg, and you know it; please don't leave me girl, don't let me go." The whole place was clapping, some sultry dancing already taking place, others getting up and joining. The song moved seamlessly into, "Just my imagination, slipping away, once again," and that in turn transitioned, without missing a beat, into that awesome Blood Sweat and Tears song, "You made me so very happy, I'm so glad you came into my life." "God, these guys are great," I said to Sue, and she added "Yeah, wow!" "Let's order another glass of wine," I continued, which we did. Two more glasses of California white. A few minutes later, the group took a break. And as the drummer walked by, I stopped him to say, "That's some great stuff you're playing. Do you play here a lot?" "This place is only open during the summer months," he answered. "During the winter we play in the city, as well as out in Woodstock. Where are you guys from?" he asked. "San Francisco," Sue and I said in tandem. "We just dropped our boy off at Bard; we'll be heading back to New York tomorrow, then back home," I added. "Love that town," the drummer said. "Used to make it out to San Francisco quite a bit a few years back—played at a few clubs out there. You know the Hotel Utah?" "Know it quite well," I answered. "South of Market—great open mike on Monday nights, and some excellent burgers." "You obviously know the place," he responded. "We had a few gigs there, as well a place in North Beach. We also played out in Mill Valley, in Marin County." "Let me guess," I answered. "Was it Sweetwater?" "That's the place," he answered. "A nice small club—and Mill Valley is a gorgeous little hamlet. It's a shame though," I added. "They're going to close the place down after all these years. They've seen some of the best since the '60s." "Yeah, I'd heard that; big shame," he answered. He went on to tell me how he'd played quite a bit with Levon Helm of the Band, that he is acquainted with Dylan." "Gotta get to the toilet, and when I get back, we'll do some folky stuff for you." "Sounds great," I said, Sue drinking her wine and enjoying the whole experience. When he came back, the group immediately went into "The Weight," by the Band. "I pulled into Nazareth, feeling about a half past dead; I just had to find a place where I could lay my head," and boy could he sing it, and the guitar player was no slouch, coaxing some sweet steel country sounds from that thing. From that song he moved right into "Stagefright," also by the Band. "See the man with the stage fright, standing up there with all his might; He got caught in the spotlight, and when he gets to the end, he's gonna start all over again." "I just love this stuff," I said to Sue. "This band is great" "Yeah, it reminds me of that bar in Evergreen that we went to, when you first visited me in Denver, remember the place in the hills? The music they were playing?"

We went to that club on my first visit to meet Sue, after we'd been talking on the phone for a few months. It was part of that trip that I had made to visit my Uncle Meyer in Toronto to talk to him about his life, then to meet Sue, after that astounding "wrong number." "I'll never forget that place, Sue," I said. "Isn't the place called 'The Bear,' or something like it?" "Little Bear," she answered. "Remember they were playing all that Dire Straits from their first album, 'The Sultans of Swing,' and 'Wild West End,' and some of their other stuff? Remember they were playing some Eric Clapton, like 'Layla'?" she responded. "Absolutely, I'll never forget that. I loved Dire Straits back then. Remember, I'd first heard them a few years earlier in London, before they had ever recorded an album. The guy who lived upstairs from me was a top hairstylist in London, and his brother was a producer. He had been given a new pressing of this group they had just signed, called Dire Straits. He pulled it out for me one evening when we were smoking hashish in his apartment. Said I had to hear it. The first song was 'Sultans of Swing.' I'd never heard anything like it before. Just flipped out over it. And the hash didn't hurt. The group had just started getting big when we went to the Little Bear, and it was so much fun to hear it in that little bar with you in Evergreen. I remember getting light headed from the altitude that night, hadn't been to Colorado before. And the tequila that we drank that night?" "Yeah, can't believe I drove home that night. I was pretty stupid to do that," she went on. "Naw you weren't stupid. You let yourself dry out a bit before driving home. You were young, having fun and falling in love. And so was I," I followed. "Yeah, this place feels a lot like that," I finished. And with that, I leaned over and kissed Sue. We made out for a minute, then hugged. "This is a celebration," I said. "I'm so happy for Jonathan." "Yeah, we've done some things very well," she answered. And then we were quiet, the drummer moving into some soulful, bluesy tune.

The following morning we changed our reservation for the train to New York City so that we'd be able to spend breakfast with Jonathan. We picked him up at Bard, and brought him into Rhinebeck for a great breakfast. Later that afternoon, we returned to New York. We went to see the "The Color Purple" that night in the city. The lead actress was amazing. And wow, what a voice. The following day we were on the plane back to San Francisco. We sat next to each other as friends, perhaps even as a married couple. But when we arrived back in San Francisco, the return was to our separate places of residence—the hard-core reality of our separation became the truth of our lives. The taxicab brought us to our house where Sue lives, and then on to this apartment, from where I reflect on the realities of my life. It seems that I can't overcome the barrier that separates me from my marriage, and as I look out on the bay, the light atop the prison of Alcatraz blinks about every five seconds.

High Holy Days

September 18th, 2007

This is a period of time on the Hebrew calendar known as the Days of Awe. Rosh Hashanah, the day of the New Year occurred a few days ago. I asked Sue if she would like to go to services with me, but she declined. She works as a pharmacist in a Jewish retirement and nursing home in the city; this home for the aged has its own rabbi and a quiet and peaceful little synagogue for worship. She is close with the rabbi who attends to the elderly in this facility, and it was her preference to attend the synagogue's worship service here. I understood Sue's reluctance to attend the New Year's service with me; though we are still married, we are not together as a married couple. It feels as though our souls are connected on a level that the travails of this world cannot tear asunder—there is a quiet, deep, and these days very-much-unsaid connection that beyond a doubt transcends our marital disconnection and will always be there. But we are not connected at all in the practice of our lives, and so while there is a cord that unites us, and I think has united us through many lives, we rarely speak to each other, our lives a void where there was once an intersection of our spirits. This void feels all the more empty to me given that "umbilical cord" that seems to never relinquish its gravitational pull, like the effect of the moon on the tides. There are no terms to our separation; nothing was put in writing that says we cannot attend a Hebrew service together. But, perhaps the consequences for Sue of our saying Hebrew prayers together—as we have at so many High Holiday services before, as we did at the Bar Mitzvahs of our two sons—are that it becomes just too difficult to carry on in a world where our "coming back together" is starting to seem improbable. She strives to shut down this part of her life that includes me—there is not one picture of me on the wall of the house. When I walk into the house to briefly visit, or take our beautiful black lab Lucky for a walk, it feels as though all color has been taken from my vision; the walls don't soften to my touch; there is a kind of blur in perception that would send one to turn the "contrast" button on the old TV sets. I feel it in my stomach; I feel the longing, the emptiness, the sweet oppression of our memories and dreams as a sensation—not intensely hot, but not comfortably warm—that covers all of my stomach. So I understand if Sue needs to shut down; she is certainly feeling her own sensations produced by our being together. I am trying my best, though, to not shut down, to remain open, to be with Sue and also not be with her. I suppose I can't have it both ways—perhaps we might one day enjoy the richness of our friendship, even if we are apart, but that day is not today.

I wanted to be with a friend on Rosh Hashanah, and so I asked Gwen Jones to come with me. She has become a soulful friend, a confidante when the days hurt and I have to talk, and the gentle touch of her Network Chiropractic is soothing. I am continuing to practice it a few times a week, and there are moments during these sessions when it feels as though I am moving through layers to a dimension where each breath, becoming slower and deeper, sends messages of gentleness from the bottom of my spine to my brain. I can best describe the experience as a "softness" in which I submerge below the choppy surface waters to a place where the current gently moves. And, indeed there is a current. The experience is one of movement—a slow, inexorable current.

Gwen had been to a few Hebrew services in her lifetime, and found special meaning in them. But she had never been to a Rosh Hashanah ceremony. The cantor's voice—prayers delivered in the desert by God in perfect form thousands of years ago—intoned these words in a voice low and textured, accented carefully so that each word was separated from the other and delivered unique meaning. He didn't own these words, but was a studied and magnificently trained vessel for their delivery. And as these prayers poured through him—as though they were organic, a form of life filled with heart and tears, carried within a wind ancient even to those who wrote their meaning in caves so long ago—tears welled within Gwen's eyes. She whispered to me that she had never heard anything so beautiful in her life. In his sermon the rabbi spoke of recognizing that "everything that we are exists in this moment—everything that we are, and all that we will be." This was a theme for much of what he wanted to say, and he said it in many metaphors. But it resonated deeply for me, and it felt so good to be in this synagogue, a place where I could surrender. The words of the sermon did something special for Gwen as well;

tears continued to well in her eyes as the rabbi spoke. In that moment, she no longer felt as a leaf on a limb—she felt connected to something much greater than herself. The words stimulated her in many ways she said, but particularly about her family, and her connection to it. I didn't question her further; it was comforting that she shared it with me that night, and that it was so meaningful for her. This was just a few days ago, and I contemplate at this moment the fast that I will take in a few days on Yom Kippur, the Day of Atonement when, "all that we are and can be in our moments" is known to God, as the gates that opened on Rosh Hashanah begin to close.

❐

It is September 20, and tomorrow night will be the Kol Nidre service, beginning the 24 hours of Yom Kippur. The ancient prayers that are sung and chanted on Kol Nidre enter the

On Television, the two Phils to my right, Sue to my left - taken at the Chicago Bears/49ers NFC Championship game, 1984. The 49ers defeated Chicago 23-0. The 49ers went on to beat Miami and win the Superbowl.

bloodstream and awaken the soul, the mind becoming a manifestation of spirit as it becomes possible to encounter through these sounds the connection to God. I have always become entranced by the sounds of this night, and as the words are delivered—and, again, they are repeated in a form that has been divinely given to the voice of the cantor trained in the art of hearing and repeating them—I have often become sure in a way that bypasses anything intellectual that God hears our prayers and offers us the ways to reach him. It is as though the prayers of Kol Nidre contain the DNA of man and God, and as we receive them, God's voice blends with the human in such a way that human words are also the words of God. And he responds to them, as they are being sung and heard. These prayers contain within them the deepest questions and sublime answers of what it means to be human—the conversation with God through these ancient words.

The music of this night embraces the human drama in its many dimensions—the existential dread of being alone, and the answer (the conversation) that we are not alone. In the prayers of this night God hears our sufferings and at once answers them. The words are sung with a voice aching to know God—and it is a voice that expresses the joys and sorrows of life at once—and is comforted by his presence. Tomorrow night is Kol Nidre.

❒

I heard some news today that was very sad for me. I called my friend, Phil Barbieri, to give him a bad time about missing the San Francisco 49ers first football game of the season. I hadn't spoken to him or seen him since the Yankees baseball game that we had gone to earlier in the summer. In an upbeat way as he could possibly sound—he was doing his best to sound tough and sure of himself—he told me that he missed the game because he had just started chemo therapy for the discovery of colon cancer. It had been diagnosed just a few weeks earlier. He hadn't looked very good, and couldn't eat when we went to the game that day. I had thought that his appearance reflected the grief of the recent passing of his mom, not long after the passing of his dad. And that grief was evident on his face, but now I understand it was much more than that, that he was sick with cancer. I haven't disclosed what I have been going through in my life to the male acquaintances in my life—but I did open up to Phil at the baseball game. I had never talked so personally with him before. It had always been about football, politics, and then football again. We loved to talk about the early Forty Niner teams—and the greatest games that he had seen. He started to go to the games in the early '60s with his dad, when the team was playing for the rough-and-tumble crowd at Kezar Stadium out in the avenues. He had some great stories of the games and the crowd. He had seen John Brody play about as much as he had later seen Joe Montana, and he talked with great respect about the talents of Brody. But he waxed religious when the conversation turned to Joe. It was during Montana's first season that I acquired my tickets, and together we witnessed one of the great eras in sports. It ranks way up there with the championship years of the Montreal Canadiens in hockey, and the New York Yankees. The Joe Montana–Bill Walsh era, and then the Steve Young period that followed, brought exuberance to the Bay Area, and it occurred during the youthful and innocent times of my marriage, before children and during the process of having and raising them. As they grew, each boy would alternate with Sue to go to a game, and all the while the two Phils—father and son—were steady fixtures in my life. So when Phil asked me how I was doing at that game, and how was Sue? I opened up to him. "We're not together now—we're living apart at the moment," I said. "I hate it when stuff like that happens," he answered me. "I don't know why this is happening, Phil," I answered. "I can't explain it—and I don't know what I can do about it at the moment. There is something going on inside me that I can't understand." "Don't be hard on yourself," he answered. "Its no one's fault," he answered. It was nice to hear this from another man—I needed to let it out, and I needed to hear it from him. It was just a few words of understanding, but it could have been a chapter in a book, it said so much. I am in shock that this has happened to him. The conversation was pretty short, and at the end, he said, "See if you have any clients who can use my two tickets this season. I'm not going to be able to go. I'm going to save my energy so that I can come back for a full season next year. "I would very much love to get closer with Phil; sadly it isn't going to happen this year.

❐

It is mid-afternoon on September 22, and I am deep into the Yom Kippur fast; during many of the fasts I do permit myself to drink water, but I have abstained on this one. I was in the synagogue all morning, and have come home to be alone for a while before returning to the closing services. My mind wanders—my body is somewhat emptied of the food and water that keeps our thinking grounded and practical—and I find myself listening to my voice as it goes someplace on its own, speaking fragments of memories, prayers, ideas about God. I am an observer as I start to doze off a bit, tired from the full day of serious prayer, my voice trailing off in the distance. But I am aware that God hears these feelings, and my mom seems everywhere around me. I am aware that this is an important Yom Kippur in my life; I am in pain, I feel it deeply, but I have never felt closer to God. I turn on my computer—not exactly Kosher in the strictest sense on Yom Kippur, when we should not be using anything mechanical—so that I will put these moments into the book that I am writing. It is important that I articulate these feelings, when I am so vulnerable and raw. Last year, Sue and myself were selected by the Synagogue elders on Yom Kippur to open the gates to the Torah. It happened during the time when we were deep into our "troubles" and my inability to let go of "M." It was as though God were giving us another chance to forge a spiritual bond that might keep us together. We opened the gates, surrendered to the prayers, and were washed in the "forgiveness" that is the essence of this day. God forgives on this day; as human beings, we need do no more than to surrender to this awesome energy with genuine heart. We opened those gates as a married couple on that day, but our spirits were plagued with strife. Sue did her best to hold back tears on that dais, and I felt in those seconds grief over the loss of our connection, the wish that we could be doing this as a couple whose spirits were unified and free of sadness before the Torah, a memory of all the times we came to the Synagogue with common purpose and slept peacefully together afterwards. But I did not cling to regret, and I do not do it now. There was no blame in our condition and there is not now; God brought us together in a miraculous way, and we were no less full before God as we opened those gates, than when we said prayers during those times of simplicity. God's forgiveness of us on Yom Kippur recognizes frailty and imperfection, and answers it with compassion. Sue and I were doing the best we could as we stood in front of the Torah, and I believe that, ultimately, God asks no more of us, and forgives us in all of those areas where we are not perfect. Forgiveness requires an honest heart, and we can demand no more of ourselves than that.

❒

My mind continues to drift to questions about our place in the universe, our importance. Are we so important that our lives are fated—that there is a divine plan to our days? Has God taken the time to imbue each of us with a divine purpose for our lives, or is all random? Is it random that we are here at all—that our lives are solely the product of the choices that we make, and that some choices work out, while others have untoward consequences? Are we so important in this universe that God sees each of us, or are we random events, in an impersonal universe? I deeply believe in God. And on this day, at this moment, I am filled with his presence. But I cannot avoid the part of me that wants to ask, as I sit here with a deep sense of longing for spiritual fullness and to not be alone, whether God knows my name, and whether my marriage can and should be saved. I'll try not to think so hard, and as I let my heart control my mind, I have no doubts that God knows the answers. And that even the notion of "random" has a place within a grander scheme of ultimate direction. There is even a place for random, though nothing is random. I miss Sue today; I miss her a lot. I cannot deny that there were large empty spaces in my heart when a couple, perhaps the ages of Sue and myself, walked arm in arm to take their places before the gates to the Torah. I miss my boys today, and wish that we might break the fast together. And the voice of my mother, Alma Lorraine Rush Rosen, echoes through my mind with a presence as clear as I have ever known. “Brucie,” she is saying, “Brucie.” Saying my name is her message; I am to know that she is here. In a few hours the gates will begin to close and the final shofar will sound; in a few minutes I’ll make my way into the busy streets of San Francisco, finding sanctuary in the synagogue where prayers given in perfect form by God thousands of years ago, contain His answers.

❒

It is the end of September, and I miss seeing Phil at the 49er games. The Niners started off well, winning their first two games by tight margins, but it looks like it could be a long season if they play like they have the last couple. I’ve been going to the games by myself—both boys tucked away in college—and it feels lonely doing so. There are some friends that I could call, but I haven’t wanted to discuss my situation in life at present. I must get over this; it is important that I reach out and connect with a few male friends. But I am cautious, not feeling that I can completely trust that details of my life won’t become little pieces of gossip. I’d rather be quiet at the moment; I’d rather keep my thoughts to myself, than hear my thinking played back to me by people who would judge, or question, or doubt, or be full of advice. Still, it would be nice to have a true, trusted friend who would care much for where I am, a male friend who could just listen with compassion and support. I don’t feel that I have that. If Phil were coming to the games we’d be talking about politics and the economy.

❐

The political rhetoric is really heating up as the Democratic and Republican candidates for the White House start looking to the Iowa Caucus and New Hampshire primary early next year. For most of this year Rudy Giuliani seemed the strongest of the Republicans for the nomination; he has been pounding away at the dangers that face us from terrorism and how he'll keep us safe. But this line of reasoning is predatory; it induces fear and preys on it by filling that vulnerability with the sense of security that only he can be strong enough and tough enough to keep the enemies at bay. Dick Cheney, in the Republican debates a few years back, used this approach when he stated that if the Democrats were to win the White House, the country would be attacked. I thought that this was shameless, and when we look back over the history of totalitarian regimes, we discover that leaders have been able to remain in power and have severely reduced freedoms by holding their "subjects" in a paralyzing fear of enemies from "without" and "within." Our economic troubles are building in this country as banks are starting to appear on the precipice of failing, due to their bad real estate loans on substantially overvalued properties across the country, as well as cut their horrible investments in bonds derived from speculative subprime loans (loans where money was loaned to buyers without the credit to qualify for conventional loans), and Giuliani seems to be impervious to it all, mechanically hammering this idea that he is here to save us from the terrorists. And the nation appears to be catching on to the poverty of his message, because he is slipping radically in the polls. Looking for alternative Republicans, voters are kicking the tires of other candidates, and Mitt Romney—the former Governor of Massachusetts, a Republican who successfully steered a Democratic state—is starting to appear attractive to many. Many of the experts, though, do not give him much of a chance because he is of the Mormon religion. To win the Republican nomination, it is argued, one has to appease the religious right—and that would be very difficult for a Mormon to accomplish. Let's judge a man by the efficacy of his ideas, his ability to manage affairs and think clearly, not according to the flavor of his religion, his form of prayer, or the color of his skin. I'm not saying that I am in favor of Romney, but I do believe he should be heard without preconceptions of "what he must be like, since he is Mormon." Television actor, Fred Thompson, has just entered the race and he is popular at the moment, but I can't see him lasting; he appears quite tired to me. John McCain, the senator from Arizona and hero of the Vietnam War for enduring torture and surviving as a prisoner for several years, is being quite overlooked at the moment, for his support of the war in Iraq. His support of the war has been die-hard, and this war is not popular at all—but one has to hand it to the man, he stands by his beliefs and keeps on going, even though he has almost no money left. Perhaps he'll start to see some support as Giuliani continues to fade, as I am sure that he will. McCain does appear quite old, and at times of less than peak health, and it is hard for me to see him getting the nomination. But perhaps he stands as good a chance as anyone; it is hard to see any of the Republicans getting the nod. On the Democratic side, Hillary Clinton is way in front, but the polls in New Hampshire and Iowa show her lead slipping a bit, with Barack Obama and John Edwards gaining a bit on her. Obama speaks from the heart, has the oratory style and dynamism of a religious leader, and certainly has a chance to catch on in the primaries. But Hillary, unlike Giuliani, has such a strong grip on the Democratic establishment, and her lead across the country is of such magnitude (in the 30-point range in many places) that it would be difficult to see anyone overtaking her. I'd like to see some candidates give her a run, though; there is a bit of an arrogance that I perceive, a sense that she is entitled to the presidency. Americans often like the "underdog," and I wouldn't be surprised to see someone give her a good run, but it is hard to know whom that might be. I'd like to think that America can overlook the color of Obama's skin and give him a fair hearing. We shall see.

The candidates are not saying nearly as much about the economic troubles as I would like to hear. And we are definitely at a "turning point," an economic crossroads in this country, and around the globe. For the last several decades, no country as had it quite so good as America. We have managed an enviable combination of steady growth and low inflation. The setbacks to our economy, particularly since the 1970s, in the form of recessions, have been remarkably shallow and of short duration. Coinciding with this period of prosperity has been a laxity in the available of credit, the old seasoned managers of money with firsthand experiences of "the lean years" giving way to younger decision-makers raised with the belief that the business cycle has been tamed and that prosperity can be "taken for granted." Real estate has been, essentially, in a bull market for the past few decades, and this has been fueled by the ever-increasing availability of money in large quantities to borrowers without track records. And as the availability of money with more lax requirements has continued to fuel the housing boom, permitting homes worth hundreds of thousands of dollars to be purchased with very small down-payments—homes becoming available to many borrowers who were banking on continued appreciation to "save their shirts" should their earnings capability be reduced—the process had continued to feed on itself. The double-digit appreciation in the housing market across the nation has permitted spending to routinely exceed income. And over time, this prosperity has spread across the globe, wealth growing enormously in the developed world as real estate values have surged, and there has been a creation of wealth of unprecedented proportions in the developing world as technology, cheaper labor and education have lifted millions into higher standards of living. But perceptions of risk are shifting, and America's economy, sheltered from any serious shocks for so long, has been growing meekly, brought down by a slump in home building, prices now starting to fall into the double digits in many places across the country. Many people are now saying that America's ability to "live beyond its means" has finally come to end.

Our ability to live beyond our means has been very much tied to this escalation in home prices. But, like all booms, the housing rush is dependent on ever-more risky borrowers to prop it up. Once credit conditions tighten, the marginal homebuyer becomes shut out of the market and, thus, the support to the housing market from the "ground up" is undermined, the pyramid beginning to collapse as home owners—many with speculative mortgages—are unable to continue to pay their mortgages or sell homes. Signs of this are occurring across the country, as banks are taking billions of dollars of losses from bad loans, and the speculative investments in bonds derived from the bad loans make credit far more restrictive. Thus, the Federal Reserve is forced to lower interest rates (as they did last week by one half of a percent, more than the expected quarter of a percent), despite the inflationary implications when commodity prices are rising and the dollar continues to fall to unprecedented lows against the Euro. The Fed is no doubt afraid that their actions might trigger uncontrollable inflation down the road—and certainly no one wants to see the drastic measures that must be taken when prices get out of control—but they are backed into a corner and must cut rates at this time. It is a strange environment in which we live at present, and I do fear that it will get worse before getting better. And it is not confined to the United States exclusively. The economic marketplace is very connected, and global banks are taking massive losses on their United States' asset holdings. Just last week in England, a major mortgage company was on the verge of collapse, receiving a massive bailout from the Bank of England. There appears to be a serious leadership vacuum in the U.S. at the moment; I hear nary a word about these troubles from the president or his cabinet. As the campaigns to decide our next president continue to "heat up," let us demand of our next leader the qualifications and ability to recognize and solve problems that corporate boards of the world's richest corporations require of their chairmen. America is at a crossroads now, and it is urgent that we acquire leadership worthy of the challenge.

Loma Prieta

There are times in life when the angels sprinkle stardust on our faces, and move us out of harm's way. It is the evening of October 17, the anniversary of the Loma Prieta earthquake. On this day in 1989 the Bay Area shook so violently that the foundations of homes on several streets in the Marina district collapsed to the ground, bringing fire and death. And it wasn't only in the Marina district—homes in other parts of the city suffered hundreds of thousands of dollars of damage. So violent was this quake that a piece of the road of the Bay Bridge, connecting San Francisco to the East Bay, cracked in half, there being a famous picture of a car dangling over the precipice. In the East Bay over a mile of Interstate 880 collapsed, killing 42 people and injuring many more.

The World Series had come to both sides of the bay for the first time ever, matching the powerful Oakland A's against the underdog San Francisco Giants. The quake struck just a few minutes before the first game was to start, its rumble shaking the concrete of Candlestick Park, spectators in absolute shock, then fear. I had been seriously excited about this World Series—how unlikely it was that these two teams would ever be playing each other in the World Series—and would have attended this first game at "the Stick," if it were not for being asked to be the best man at the wedding of Craig Jones, a special friend from college days at the University of California, Santa Barbara. The wedding was to be far from the Bay Area, down in Fresno, the home of his wife's family. Michael was barely three years old, and Jonathan six months. There was no question that I would attend the wedding as best man, but I wanted the family to come as well. And so did my mom. We hadn't been to Los Angeles in a good while—well before Jonathan had been born—and she encouraged us to all come down as a family, get a hotel on the ocean, enjoy a little rest, see the rest of the family, and take Michael to Disneyland for the first time. It was an easy sell; the trip to Craig's wedding would be extended to a longer trip afterward—and, for me, few things were as comforting as spending time with my mom. It had been a while since I'd had a tea-leaf reading, and I was going to "corner" her for one on the trip. There was some important stuff that I really wanted to know from her; our lives had been in disarray, and I needed some straightening out.

The disarray had begun a few months earlier when, now with two boys, I wanted to take the plunge and leave the city for the suburbs of Marin County. Sue and I had been looking at homes in Marin for some time since Michael had been born, never quite finding something in our price range that was relatively new and within walking distance of downtown Mill Valley. We had given up looking in the several months before Jonathan was born, and I had started to resign myself to the notion that I loved the city so much—arts, culture, views, coffee shops, movies, cultural diversity, walks, restaurants from every corner of the globe—that I wondered why I was even bothering with this idea of a move outside of the city. But after the birth of Jonathan I became antsy to look out there again. Jonathan was only a few months old, Sue still nursing him, when I called her one Sunday to come out and take a look at this house that I had discovered, up Blythedale Canyon, just several minutes walk from the center of town. It was late into spring, the sky was a pure blue, the scent of flowers everywhere in the air, berries growing along the road, Redwood trees towering high above the long street that led deep into the canyon, the part of the road closest to the town lined with an eclectic blend of cottages (they had been summer homes for residents of the city in earlier days); beautiful, turn-of-the-century brown-shingled Edwardians, and some homes that had been newly constructed on the lots of the older cottages that had been torn down. I had always been looking for a brown-shingled, turn-of-the-century home, but they were

Hiking with my boys on a gorgeous day in Marin County, California, 1991.

seldom available, and in this part of town were very expensive. In the "Open Homes" guide of the newspaper that Sunday, there had been something listed—in the outer regions of our price range—on that flat block of the canyon, and it sounded interesting. So I went to visit it on this pristine day, a large redwood tree in the front yard, the small back lot a veritable forest of redwoods, the scent of the bark being dried by the sun, sweet, earthy, rustic, triggering something almost primordial in me. Northern California has to be among the most gorgeous places on earth, and on this late spring day looking at this house as it sat amidst the redwoods on all sides, the red of the bark, the green of the leaves, the blue of the sky, somebody playing Grateful Dead music a few doors down—Garcia's sweet-as-candy vocals, "Shake it, Shake it Sugaree, I'll see you at the jubilee," the guitar notes as clean as a mountain stream, the taste not of wine but of chocolate—it was a can't-miss. Sue came out to meet me when I called her; about an hour later, she arrived with the three-year-old Michael in tow, while I put Jonathan against my chest in a "baby knapsack." She liked the place—though adoring the city, she always misses the earthiness of her native Colorado—and also became entranced by the beauty of the day. While I was caught up in the emotion of finding this place—the excitement and sensual pleasure of the location overwhelming reason in the moment—she was also under the influence of hormones, after all she was in the nesting, nursing stage of taking care of a baby. So we both overlooked the size of the place and the potential for dampness and darkness when we told the realtor that we wanted to put in an offer. The house did not have a family room, and the rooms were quite small and, perhaps, hastily constructed. It didn't have that feeling of "permanence" that one finds in the old homes. All of this was something that we didn't think about, until later.

We bought the place, and by the beginning of July, we moved in. But I could never let go of wanting to be in the city, though during the first several weeks, this didn't concern me that much. I wrote it off to a period of adjustment. But by late August, the sun was setting lower in the sky, and the brightness of morning and afternoon—taken for granted in early July—which reinforced a sense of well-being and confidence that everything that I was seeking in a home was on this front deck, gave way to impatience and moodiness as the air grew damper and the shadows longer. And the Redwood trees—their fragrance hypnotic and captivating in late spring/early summer—were becoming damper as the afternoons grew darker. The nights were very quiet on this Canyon

After Loma Prieta, Alma Lorraine Rush (my mom) brings joy to our home in Mill Valley.

road, and the feeling for me was becoming one of "electricity deprivation." I missed that electric feeling of the city in a way that I wouldn't have imagined; it felt as though a force of energy into which I daily tapped was no longer there to fill me, though I still worked there. On occasion, I would take a taxi over to the neighborhoods of Pacific Heights and Presidio Heights and just walk around, looking up at the flats filled with cozy chairs from which their occupants comfortably (not even knowing how lucky they were) gazed on the quaint street. Recognizing that I had made a mistake, I asked Sue if she would mind if we put the house back on the market. I had become almost "desperate" to return to the city; she went along with this, and by the beginning of September we had put a "For Sale" sign next to the big redwood tree in the front. And the house might have sold quickly to the man and his wife who sold it to us in the first place; they had missed the place greatly since moving out, and wanted to return to the same house. But, in my desire to gain some extra light in the back, I had trimmed and cut down several of the redwoods in the yard, though I'd left several standing. I loved the trees, but just had to clear away some of them to be able to get a decent glimpse of the sun in the dark months. When they saw what I had done to the back yard—though the gardener thought it was a significant improvement—they didn't want the place any longer. That overgrown back yard is one of the things that had drawn them back. So, the house languished on the market that month—homes just a few months earlier were going within a few days of being listed—and into the next month. The real estate recession of late 1989-1991 had hit at just about the time we had put the place back on the market; sadly we had paid top dollar for it at the height of the market. To sell it we'd probably have to slash the price, and this was a tough go for a young couple. So, we decided to rent it, and move back to the city. By late September, we had rented a place in the Marina district of San Francisco, with the intention of renting our Mill Valley home on our return from the trip to Craig's wedding and to see my mom.

❐

A few hours after the final Sunday open house that we held for the sale of our Mill Valley home before deciding to rent it I could see through the French doors facing the yard a little girl of maybe eight years approaching the front door. I got up from the dinner table and answered her knock. She possessed an angelic smile, a grin as broad and upwardly tilted as it could possibly be; it was radiant and formed a stunning impressionistic painting as it contrasted with a nose and cheeks full of freckles and long sandy-colored hair. There was a momentary surge of joy that I felt on seeing her face. "My mom wanted me to ask if the house is still available," she asked. "Is it still for sale?" "Where is your mom?" I answered. "Just over there on the other side of the gate with my little sister," she answered. "Yes, it is still for sale," I responded, "Does she want to see it? We're eating dinner, but I'll give her a little tour if she likes." "I don't know if she wants to see it, she just wanted me to ask if it is available," she answered softly, sweetly, suddenly appearing a bit shy. "Well you're welcome to go ask her and invite them in if you like; what is your name?" "My name is Angel," she answered, her tone a bit more assured as she pronounced her name. "My name is Angel," she repeated. "Well, feel free to invite your family in to see the house if you like, okay?" I continued. "Okay," she answered, again appearing a touch bashful, the voice the essence of the sweetness of a little girl—her parents must, no doubt, melt in her presence. She turned around and walked along the little walkway in our front yard, closed the gate behind her, and didn't return. So sudden, unexpected, magical was her visit; equally surprising was the fact that they did not return. Sue asked me about the visit when I returned to finish dinner, and I told her how odd it all seemed to me. I described how it felt timeless for a moment; it was as though the two of us went to a special little world during our few moments at the front door. "Her name is Angel, she told me, and you know what, Sue, I have the strangest feeling that we were just visited by an Angel."

Sue took in the full measure of what I was saying, reflecting for a moment, then going back to her work of feeding the kids and cleaning off the table. The house didn't sell after that Open House, and within a few weeks the movers returned to bring us to the Marina district.

The Marina flat was on the lower floor of a two-unit building. It was attached on one side to another flat, and we could hear virtually every word of the conversations that were taking place between the couple that lived there and their guests. The place had three bedrooms but felt quite cramped. It was about two-thirds the size of the Mill Valley house. It felt nice to be in the city, but I realized right away that this would only be temporary. Hopefully, we would be able to sell the Mill Valley house and buy something here. And if not, we'd stay here, maybe several months, and find a larger place up the hill in Pacific Heights; we were under my self-imposed time constraints to find a place. I didn't want to put us through an exhaustive search. And for whatever reason, I felt an urgency to return "home" to the city. But this place did not feel like home, and though I didn't want to be back in the dark, damp canyon I was feeling some emptiness in my stomach for our forfeiture of the quiet and independence the home afforded. We were in the flat just long enough to put things away before departing for the trip down south. But before leaving for the wedding I lay in bed one afternoon listening on the radio—the TV hadn't been hooked up yet—to one of the great baseball games in San Francisco Giants' history. Will "the thrill" Clark had had a fantastic season that year; he batted .333, with 111 RBI, losing the batting title to Tony Gwynn on the final day of the season. I lay in bed listening to the decisive game five of the playoff series between the Giants and the Chicago Cubs. It was the bottom of the eighth inning, the score tied 1-1, and Clark was taking his swings against one of the games "nastiest" relievers, Mitch "Wild Thing" Williams. After an epic turn at bat, with several two-strike foul balls keeping the duel alive for several minutes, Clark singled to center field to drive in two runs, breaking the tie, eventually sending the Giants to the World Series against the A's. It was an incredible moment, and out the window I could hear loud cheers and hollers, cars honking up and down the street. I went out for a walk, and beer was flowing in every Marina district saloon. Will Clark had become legend in that moment, and though I felt so unsettled with a place for sale in Mill Valley, now living in a cramped Marina flat with rent and a mortgage to pay, at this moment, it felt great to be in the city again, to feel part of it all.

The wedding was held in the backyard of Craig's bride's home in Fresno. It was a warm evening but they insisted that we at least start out wearing a tuxedo. The tuxedo fit, but the French-style shirt and cuffs were way too big. We were drinking wine, and I made a toast to Craig and his bride, but then I followed the toast with what I thought would be a funny comment about how Craig had finally settled down after his "checkered bachelor past, leaving a trail behind of broken hearts. You should have seen this guy in college—we became incredible friends there, but Craig took all the girls." Craig laughed nervously, but his wife didn't laugh at all. Nor did her parents, though his dad did smirk. Virtually nobody in the crowd chuckled, people's faces appearing quite tight. This was not a Jewish crowd, and the scene reminded me of that moment in "Annie Hall," when Woody Allen is having dinner with Annie's gentile family, feeling desperately out of place as he visualized how his Jewish New York family would be acting if he were in that setting. I made it through the toast, the evening, the send-off of my best friend and his bride; the following day we were off to the Ritz Carlton at Laguna Niguel, overlooking the sea, where my mom would be visiting us in a couple of days. I was looking forward to getting that tea leaf-reading. I so needed one.

The hotel is stunning as it sits on a bluff, the sound of the undulating surf below a rhythmic mantra of deep bass notes—thunder softened and fully contained—as the tide moves out to sea, inevitably overridden by the louder symphonic high notes as the waves cascade against the shore, the thunderclap of the cymbals unexpectedly punctuating this orchestra of the sea in the form of a swell sharply breaking. It was soothing to hear this music as I went to sleep that night, gaining some respite from my self-imposed melancholy of dislocation. I slept well that night, and I hadn't been sleeping more than three good hours a night for several weeks. The following morning we walked the immaculately terraced grounds, having breakfast with little Michael and "Baby Jonathan," as Michael loved to call his baby brother. The hotel—its resting places, lounges, restaurants, gardens—is opulent, the clientele often very wealthy and immaculately dressed. At 34 years old, two small children in tow, I felt too young to be staying in a place like this, and given the kind of lifestyle we had been living, not sure where we lived or were going to live, the two moves from the city to Mill Valley and back in a few months, I felt like a gypsy. Nonetheless, I wanted to be by the sea, wanted to find a place where my mom could gain some relief for a day from the constant readings (sometimes 10 people or more in a day) that enabled her to keep her head financially above water. After breakfast, I took the walkway down to the beach; strolling along the beach I fantasized, as I looked up at the balconies and magnificent windows to the sea of homes—new homes, some replicating the sprawling hacienda styles, others looking more Roman or Greek, with large posts and pillars—that occupied the bluffs just up the hill from the pathway. There were some homes just breaking ground and a number of new lots for sale. I had never had any desire whatsoever to live anywhere in Southern California, since moving to San Francisco as an adult. Everything about the place made me feel "sleepy" and "tranquilized." But not at this moment. "Yeah, I could live here," I thought to myself, the sweetness of the saltwater filling my senses, a deeper more pungent aroma of seaweed than anything on the north coast. "What's not to love? Waking up in the morning, taking a walk by the sea before going to work; returning to do the same after a stressful day of financial transactions. Sure, I could do this." I didn't have the financial wherewithal to live in a place like this, but one could still dream, couldn't we? I never really took that thought seriously; I knew that Southern California is not a place that agrees with my temperament, in the same sense that I couldn't live in a place like Hawaii. I require a bit of edge, and without that I would, no doubt, feel something missing. Nonetheless, perhaps I might one day be able to get a little cottage by the sea—have a little retreat where I might hear the crashing of the waves. There is no sound more soothing, comforting, quieting for me. Yes, indeed, living in San Francisco, but one day having a place by the sea to read, escape, write, walk and make love. This would be the fantasy that I would seek to make real for myself and family. At 34 years old, there is so much that I wanted to enjoy on this planet. I could barely stand still. I walked over to the sea, the cold sea water covering my feet above the ankles—my feet sinking into the sand as the current moved back out before the next wave moved in—and thanked God for being alive. I thanked him for this beautiful family; for the joys; the gifts, the blessings; for these two boys whose preciousness was beyond the measure of all the stars in the universe; for my lovely wife, Sue; and I asked him to please forgive me if I ever seemed to take anything for granted. This life is a gift, and I am grateful for every moment, every clear, clean breath that I take. Really, God, I desire nothing beyond being able to appreciate this gift of life. And I prayed for my mom; that her life wouldn't be so difficult. She had given every ounce of herself so that her family might make it through. The best parts of me I owe to my mom, so please, God, help her to have some fun, to enjoy. I so much want that for her. The difficulty of the previous few months was lifted in that instant, and I was so anxious for my mom to come and enjoy this place; when she arrived later in the afternoon, it was a sweet moment indeed.

My mom arrived at about 4:30 in the afternoon; she called our room after checking into the room that we had arranged for her. The first game of the World Series between the Giants and the Athletics was to begin in an hour and a half, so the plan was to order room service on the balcony of our room so that I would be able to watch the game. Michael was three years old and had become curious about baseball, showing a lot of interest whenever I watched a game. He had also started to become pretty darn competent at hitting the ball that I would toss to him in the little front yard of the Mill Valley house; he had become ecstatic—and, frankly, I was very impressed—when he hit the upper part of the house with a picture swing from the walkway near the front gate. I had put him on my shoulders and had run around the yard, pretending to touch all the bases as though he had hit a home run. His turquoise eyes shone pure, clear joy, and when we finished running the bases, I turned him around and showed him how to hold the bat from the other side of the plate, the left side. "Michael," I had said to him, "now that you can hit home runs from the right side of the plate, I'm going to make you a switch hitter." "Switch hitter? What's that, Dad? What is a switch hitter?" his voice the essence of innocence, curiosity, and the joy of his discovery that he was pretty good at this batting thing. "It's when you can hit from either side of the plate, Michael; the best baseball players can switch hit—and if you ever want to make it big in baseball, maybe make it to the big leagues some day, it's best we start learning how to switch hit." He was good at that from the "get go"; truly I was surprised at how quickly he picked up the changed stance and hand positions. Clearly, this little guy had nice coordination between hand and eye, and a pretty natural sense of physical coordination. He started hitting the ball from the left side with practiced dexterity—darn it, I was impressed. So shortly thereafter, I took him to a few Giants baseball games, and now he was really psyched to see this World Series.

Shortly before game time my mom arrived at our room. Now, it must be said that when she wanted to dress up my mom was a "knockout-looking woman"—after all, she had been a runner-up in the Miss Toronto beauty pageant when she was 18. And she did have the clothes—though there wasn't a lot of money to buy expensive things—to look great when she wanted to do so. But when she showed up at our room to greet us there was a disheveled, disordered look about her. There was a striped top that didn't fit her and was torn on one of the sleeves. The plaid skirt didn't match the top, it draped too long over her knees, and something had been spilled on it. The nail polish was coming off of her toenails, and she was wearing sandals that were on their last mile, smudged and on the verge of falling apart. She had run a brush through her black hair, but it still had an uncombed look. I gave her a huge hug when I saw her, and Sue did the same. And then I took a good look at her. "Mom, I thought I was a gypsy; you are quite a sight." "I read all day, had some real draining clients, so I just threw something on and came over. It is a good long drive here, and I didn't want to keep you waiting. Heidi came with me; she's down in the lobby talking to a very good-looking man—I think he's a chef or something—who is working in the hotel. Very Italian looking. This is some place that you picked out," her voice becoming a bit horse, whispery and out-of-breath sounding, as she took a drag on the cigarette. Every time I saw her, I invariably reminded her, chastised, lectured her on the perils of smoking. But she would never stop. Her answer had always been, and was the same at this moment when I sternly admonished her again: "I'm stopping very soon; you don't know it but I have already cut back a lot. Don't worry, boy (I loved it when she called me boy), I am definitely quitting, you'll see." "Mom, you say that all the time, and you never do. I don't believe that you ever will—you just don't get it. That stuff will kill you, and I want you to be around for a long, long time. I want you around to see your grandchildren grow into men. You're more out of breath now than when I saw you last time." "Enough about me, and what do you mean, I am quite a sight? You're quite a sight; you're looking pretty tired yourself," she countered. "Oh, God; I really need a reading. Maybe I can have one tonight? What do you think? And you are a sight, Mom—it's really funny. You look as though you dressed for a gypsy convention." My mom and Sue started laughing at that one. "See the way he talks to me, my son? This is how he talks to his mother. Lovely room the two of you got me, but it had just one king bed. So I changed it for another one with two single beds for Heidi." "I hope it has a view of the sea; I paid for a sea view room with a balcony for you." "Oh, it is lovely, and it does have a lovely view of the sea. Thank you very much; since you'll be watching the game tonight, we'll do a reading tomorrow. I know you need one. We'll sit out on the balcony and we'll do one." "Really looking forward to it, Mom," I said. And I gave her a huge hug. "So good to see you, Mom; so nice to see you." She sat down at the table in the room, as I turned on the TV to watch the game. It was a bunch of commercials at the moment. Michael sat at the table across from her; and Sue handed "Baby Jonathan" to her, and she put him down on her lap. "I see the strangest things," she said, the commercials blaring away in the background. I turned the sound down on the TV, so I could hear what she had to say. "Come a little closer, Michael," she said as Michael moved over to be next to her. "I see sparkles on the two boys; these children are protected. They will always be protected. There is a special sparkle on them—look at Jonathan, his forehead, his nose. Look at Michael, the little sparkles on his face. This comes from the angels. You are all protected." Sue listened intently to what my mom was saying.

"You know, Mom," I said; "I had the strangest experience the other day; I didn't tell you about it. There was a little girl who came to the door, saying that her mom wanted to find out if our house was still for sale. But the mom wasn't anywhere around. The girl said the mom was waiting on the sidewalk. I answered that, "Yes, it is still for sale," and that, though we were eating dinner—it was after an open house—I would be glad to show them around. She had the softest, sweetest voice, and an angelic smile—it was almost a beatific smile. She said that she would go tell her mom. Before she left, I asked her name. "Angel," she said; "My name is Angel." It was as though I had entered a mystical, unusual, magical place in that instant; a kind of happiness, a joy, a God-like sense came over me. It's hard to describe." "You don't have to describe it, I already know," my mom replied. "I know the feeling, the sense, and yes, an angel visited you. Sometimes angels show up unaware. Ever hear the saying, 'angels unaware'?" "Yes," I nodded. "You were visited by an angel on that day; I already know about it." "What do you mean, you already know?" I asked. "I won't go into it now, but I already know."

At just that moment the TV went to black. A few moments later, the announcer appeared to say that a major earthquake had just hit the San Francisco Bay Area—they were awaiting reports of damage. He described the shaking and rolling of this concrete stadium; how it first felt as though the crowd was making the place shake with their anticipation and excitement for the game, but that it became immediately clear that a major quake had occurred. The scene was now of crowds coming onto the field; the players had departed for some other place. There was a look of shock on the face of the announcer, and as the camera panned the stadium, looks of disbelief and shock covered the faces. Within a few more moments the announcement came that the game would be cancelled, and then there was a cut-away to the fires that were burning in the Marina district. We turned to CNN, and it appeared that the whole city was in flames. In reality that was not the case, though it did appear that way from the pictures. Then we saw the crack in the road on the Bay Bridge—a car dangling on the precipice. It was unbelievable. I was in total shock, as was Sue. My mom wore an expression of dismay, shock, but underlying that was an aura of a sublime understanding of it all. As she watched, she nodded a few times—no words, only a few forward nods of her head. Initial reports were that the Golden

Gate Bridge had collapsed, but then that was corrected. “This is unreal; this is surreal; I can’t believe this,” I offered to the room. Michael was trying to make sense of it all. “What happened to the game? Why are we seeing all these fires? What happened to the bridge?” He was all questions. “There was an earthquake in San Francisco, Michael. It looks like there is a lot of damage. The game was cancelled.” “They’re not playing the World Series? They’re not playing the World Series?” he wanted to know. “Not today, Michael; the game is cancelled. It is a really bad earthquake in San Francisco.” “Did it happen where we live?” he wanted to know. “Yes, Michael; it did. We’re very lucky we’re not there now.” And as I said that I hugged him, and then I went over to Jonathan and squeezed him against my chest.

All of the phone lines were down, so at first it wasn’t possible to get through to any friends in the city. But a short time later, I was able to reach the owner of the Marina flat in which we lived. The owner—a thickly accented Irish contractor who had remodeled this place himself—spoke with long pauses between his words. “We’ve just been to the flats” he said, clearly shock in his speech. “The place was knocked off the foundation. It didn’t collapse—no, no it didn’t collapse,” his words trailing off. “But it isn’t livable now; no, indeed not. You’re going to have to find another place to live—we’re terribly sorry, terribly sorry. You’re lucky you weren’t there, with the children and all. Very lucky you weren’t there.” He was in shock, no doubt about it. No doubt about it. I got off the phone and was speechless; just shook my head, put it down in my hand and was speechless. Telling the family that I was going to get some air, I walked outside, down the terraced, landscaped grounds to the sea. I sat down in the sand and lost conception of time and place. The sun was setting and I came back to the room. “We’re really hungry; let’s go to dinner,” Sue said. “The kids are hungry; your mom is hungry.” And, thus, we all went down to the very fancy, posh restaurant for dinner, my mom dressed as she had arrived. My sister met us there—she had been long engaged in her conversation with the chef (indeed he was the chef for this restaurant) and had just recently become aware of the quake. We dined as though we were on another planet. "Everything felt out of sorts today; I was picking it up when I left to come here. I threw these clothes on, not giving a shit," said my mom. "You are a sight, Mom; you definitely are a sight," and with that we all laughed, thankful to be together.

❒

Alma Lorraine Rush Rosen—Lorraine as she was known to her clients—gave me a tea-leaf reading as promised the following afternoon on the balcony of her room overlooking the sea. She had me turn the cup three times and make a wish. As I made my wish I said a silent prayer of gratitude to God for our being all together and safe. I prayed for the city to heal with God-speed from the horror of yesterday evening. And I made my wish—and the wish was for all of the people that I love in this world to be safe; to be able to live in the moment and be able to appreciate what was right in front of me to my utmost potential; for my heart and mind to continue to expand so that I might be ever more grateful for the little blessings that are in front of me every day, and to accept as necessary the parts of life that are difficult. And the wish included a special blessing for my mom—as it always did whenever she gave me a reading—that she be well and that we have much, much more time together, and that I appreciated fully the time we do spend together. The final sentiment of the wish didn't include a desire to find another place in San Francisco in which to live—so badly had I wanted to be back in the city—but to be at peace with whatever happens. We were so lucky, we had an undamaged home in a beautiful part of the world in which to live—we were not homeless—and I wished to be at peace with wherever we were supposed to be.

On looking into my cup my mom immediately began by saying that there are often angels put in our path to bless us, to bring messages, to simply make contact—and that often these people are "angels unaware." These people don't necessarily grow up thinking that they are angels, and they might not even believe in angels—but at a certain moment in time they'll be impelled to make contact and there will be a feeling of a "special lightness of being." And in "lightness of the moment" guidance is given, though neither person feels some sudden burst of wisdom. There is a magic in the moment, and life changes in a subtle way. Any of us can be "angels unaware," simple people living their lives that at a special moment in time have an extraordinary effect on another. "Are they born as angels, Mom—are they angels incarnate—or are they rather touched by angels during their lifetime and act accordingly?" I wanted to know. "There are angels, very special beings who are born that way, and they know themselves to be angels. Others are touched at certain moments in their lives by angels, and are called on to bring messages. I cannot say which one of these the little girl that visited you that day happened to be. But she came as an angel and touched your family in a special way; there was magic in the instant, and you were given information, though you knew it not. I knew that it had happened—but don't ask me how I knew, I cannot say.

"You were meant to move into that house in Mill Valley, because you were absolutely correct in thinking that it was time for the family to be out of the city. You were being pulled out of the city—it had been happening for some time—but there had been much the city still had to offer for you. So it didn't happen earlier. You found an area to which you were drawn, but after a little while you didn't love it. You didn't love it because you are a city boy at heart—you love the lights—and you will always be a city boy. And, indeed, had you found another kind of place in Mill Valley—something where it was sunny more of the time—you might not have moved back to the city, but the calling still would have remained. In truth, your path required you to move back to the city because there was a simple message for you, the message is that sometimes we cannot force things in life to be the way we want them to be. Everything has to come about in a natural way. You were a round peg forcing yourself into a square hole in that Marina apartment. It wasn't appropriate for you, and you knew that. In another month or two you would have moved again. But it wasn't meant to be. It is meant that you move back into the Mill Valley house. You'll stay in a hotel with the kids for a few days when you get back, then have different movers come this time to move you back—not the same movers. The City of San Francisco will go

After our move back to Mill Valley, following the Loma Prieta earthquake, my father comes to visit from Montreal. Sue, my father, and the boys, 1991.

through some suffering for a while; there will be gas leaks and chemicals in the air, and it is right that the family be back in that beautiful neighborhood, even if it's a bit damp. You'll be more grateful for it now. Don't even think of putting the house back on the market for at least a year and a half—when Michael is ready to go to Kindergarten—the economy will be better and it will sell then. But you may not want to leave at that point, though you'll have the chance to do so without having the burden of two places. You might move, I wont say for sure, but by then Mill Valley will have grown on you. Your business will continue to grow—you'll do very well—but the main thing for me to tell you is that you must return to Mill Valley, don't even look at new apartments." And with that, she put the cup upside down. She stood up and I moved over to give her a huge hug, so happy was I that she was here, so lucky was I that she was my mom.

A few days later we drove back up north to San Francisco, stopping to have lunch with my mom at her home in Santa Clarita, a gorgeous view of the mountains from her backyard. It was on that patio that she gave me the reading when she told me that I would meet a person named Sue; fully describing that she would find me at the appropriate time, that I wouldn't be able to locate her, and that her name would be Sue, not Suzanne or Suzette or any other derivation. She described her complexion, eye color, hair color and, as stated, it happened in exactly in the manner described. Astounding—it astounds me to this day. Late that evening we arrived at the St. Francis hotel on Union Square, where we would stay for the next five nights, organizing our affairs to return to Mill Valley.

That very night, at about one in the morning, the hotel shook with a pretty strong aftershock—apparently it had measured close to 5.00 on the Richter scale. My nerves were frayed, and I could only imagine what the residents were feeling, those who had suffered the full brunt of Loma Prieta. The next day, I went to work on the 21st floor—I had been suffering from vertigo before the earthquake, probably the result of not sleeping very well since the move to Mill Valley—and returning to this high floor created a great deal of tension for me. I didn't know how I would manage to do this, and hoped this condition would go away. I certainly didn't want to make another move to a different company at this time, one on a lower floor. But, man, this was difficult—the vertigo, the fear of another quake, and the excitability I was feeling just being in these quarters so high in a building. God forbid I get stuck in an elevator, as my assistant had.

Debra, my sales assistant, had been trapped in an elevator for about seven hours after the quake struck. The Regional Manager for the company had been visiting, and the two of them were in the elevator at just the wrong time—the elevator shook back and forth, then the lights went out as it stopped. Sirens could be heard

Bruce, after the Loma Prieta, at home and at peace after a day of work in San Francisco's Financial District.

everywhere in the city as the elevator remained stuck between the 17th and 18th floors. "My God, Debra," I said," that must have been unbearable, not knowing what was happening, clueless about when you would be able to get out," and I hesitated and kept quiet the idea that was forming about whether she had wondered if they would ever make it out. It was highly difficult to return to this building for me, but I had to do it. I had to come back to work! But every time the wind shook the building my nerves further frayed.

After work that night, I met Sue over at the Marina flat to survey the damage. The place was uninhabitable; the floors were lopsided, as they had been knocked off their foundation. Large cracks formed on the walls and on the ceiling, and there was a gaseous odor. Dishes had been thrown from the kitchen cabinet to the floor; virtually all the pictures had hit the ground, frames shattered, and the beautiful grandfather clock made of Cherry lay flat on its face, the time stuck on exactly the moment of the jolt. I turn my head away from this page, looking into my dining room, the dark bay again spread out before me, that very clock there as a living reminder of that moment. I had to have that clock, when I moved into this place. And one of these days I must get it fixed, so that it will chime again. But we haven't done so in all these years.

❒

Leaving the apartment, we walked all around the Marina district, parts of the area remaining very much untouched, but in other places essentially whole streets of homes knocked off their moorings, foundations exposed everywhere as these properties slant toward the sidewalks, wood exposed in much the way that the gums are exposed when the teeth decay or erode. We made arrangements for the movers to come on that Saturday, and as we waited for them, Sue and I—Jonathan in a knapsack against my chest as we held Michael's hand—walked up and down the streets filming the scene for posterity. There was a dust of debris, a gaseous and ash scent everywhere we walked, and I started to feel noxious from it. Sue had experienced enough. "Let's go," she said, and we walked away from the Marina, the camera back in its case. As we awaited the movers, I went over to the neighborhood sandwich shop—one of the best Italian delis in the world for sure—Lucca's, to order some sandwiches and potato salad. I must have been in a bit of a daze when they called my number—I'm sure that I wasn't the only one in that state—because the lady looked right at me and said my number three times before I responded. "Are you okay?" she asked. "Yeah, I'll be all right;

I'm fine," I answered. I wanted to remain in the city; I didn't want to leave, but there was no way that was going to happen. "It'll be okay," she answered. "It's all going to get better. We'll get through this," she continued. I nodded in agreement, paid her the money and left, a smile of compassion the memory I have of her as I walked back into Chestnut Street. We ate our sandwiches in the car, as the movers filled their truck with our belongings. By late that night, we had moved back into our Mill Valley Home.

We took the "For Sale" sign off the house, and didn't put it back on again until Michael was accepted at the school we wanted for him, the K-8 program of Town School For Boys, back in the city. But Mill Valley, as my mother had said would happen, had grown on us, and it was with bittersweet feelings, a real sense that this time we were really giving up something special, that we signed the contract to sell the house. Buyers swooped in very quickly this time, recognizing a good buy in a great neighborhood. We had put it back on the market rather philosophically, resigned to stay in the house and send Michael to a local school—after all, the public schools in the area were pretty good, and Sue and I had both gone to public schools—if it didn't sell quickly enough to send him to Town School the following September. But, again, it did sell and it sold fast, and to this day a lasting memory I have of Mill Valley in those days after we settled in following Loma Prieta is the joy of pushing both boys around in a double stroller on a warm late spring, early summer day—even the damper, darker days of autumn, when darkness covered our porch much too early in the afternoon for my taste, seems joyous—each boy wearing identical overalls with a cute dog face, a little red tongue of cloth protruding from the mouth. After the stroller ride, I'd bring them over to the Baskin Robbins in town, from which we would stroll over to sit on the soft green carpet of grass in front of the Fire Station. I recognized, as I had prayed that I would, that these were beautiful days and would not come again. I felt them to be priceless in the moment, and in retrospect I can only shake my head at the magic of it all.

Several months after returning to Mill Valley, the queasy feeling that I had on the top floor of the building continued to get worse, the vertigo and nervousness intensifying. I accepted a job at another company on a much lower floor; they gave me a tidy sum of money to come, but little did they know I was so desperate to find a company on a lower floor, I might have gone for free, or for certainly much less. And from that lower floor, I commuted back and forth to Mill Valley, enjoying that place, as I hadn't expected to do.

October 24th, 2007

Autumn is ablaze as I look out from this passenger train bound for New York City from Montreal, where I have been the past few days visiting my father, and my cousin Melody, who breathes through a mask as she waits for a double lung transplant to save her life. Her mother died in her early 60s from emphysema, and unless Melody—50 years old—undergoes this transplant in the not too distant future, her life will come to an end. She suffered from severe asthma as a child, and this was complicated by a cigarette habit that left her too breathless to ride in the wide-open fields the beautiful stallions that were her childhood fantasies that became realized in her early adult years. I wanted to see this gorgeous cousin Melody again—stunningly beautiful in her younger days, long black hair, brown eyes as round and bright as a full moon, complexion of silk—in these days before the expected transplant. She has been number one of the list for several weeks now, having moved from fourth to first in a very short span of time. I had known Melody from the early years of my life when her mother brought her to visit us in Simi Valley, where my family lived in the first years of our lives in California.

Simi Valley was just a few tracks of homes back then in the early 1960s, and there were wide-open fields filled with horned toads, lizards and the occasional rattlesnake. Melody and I would go into these fields and come back with a bag of horned toads, much harder to catch than the lizards. And, indeed, we managed to avoid a rattle snake on one of these adventures, slithering on its belly in the low grass as it made its way into the dirt about 10 yards from where we were cornering one of these toads. We told my mom of this near miss—a big mistake—and she refused to let us back into those fields again. But we did manage to sneak away a few times, undeterred. It is here in Simi Valley, where Melody came to visit us from sophisticated Montreal, that she first fell in love with horses. We lived very close to a movie location called Corriganville, where Westerns were filmed. Several episodes of Bonanza were filmed at this location, set amidst rugged mountainous terrain, huge rocks and boulders in varieties of odd, irregular shapes—a hillside that appeared to be not so much a mountain, but a series of massive boulders in shapes resembling hexagons and octagons, some looking like volcanic craters—forming the compelling scenery of the old west where, in the movies, the cowboys fought the Indians. Corriganville had horse stables, and on a day when we were not trapping horned toads in the fields, my mom took us to the stables to ride some tame horses within a little fenced in area, supervised by some cowboys. The horses had been used as "extras" in the movies, and while I was scared of falling off—I didn't quite acquire the flexibility to move in rhythm with the horses' movements, nor did I enjoy the jolting bouncing—Melody took to the animals as though she had been born on a saddle. We went back a few more times, Melody not able to get enough. And it was all she could talk or think about when she returned to Montreal; it had become a fantasy for her the rest of her childhood—to one day be able to own and ride at will, her own black horse. And this fantasy was realized in her early 20s, because by then Melody had become—her name exceptionally appropriate for the softness of her voice and ability to occupy and fill roundly every note on the register—a quite well-known songwriter and singer in Montreal, then throughout all of Canada. Many, many years had passed after our forays into the fields of Simi Valley and the riding at the stables of Corriganville (whose name had been changed shortly after she returned to Montreal, it was now called Hopetown, having been purchased by Bob Hope) before I would see Melody again. It wasn't until 1976 that we reconnected in person.

❐

I had come to visit my father that year after barely speaking with him for several years following his departure from California to Montreal, his violent temper in the aftermath of my return from hopping the freight trains culminating in the ultimatum to my mom, that either he would leave or I would have to leave, my mom answering in front of me, "That's easy Larry, it's time to pack your things." And it was a great time to visit, because Montreal was hosting the Olympics. Melody had just released an album sung exquisitely in French, with a few songs in English, and it was working its way up the charts. She had become an up-and-coming star in Montreal—and as a result had been asked to escort Mick Jagger to the closing ceremonies of the Olympic games, which she did. She had made enough money from the album in the next year or so, and also had done pretty well from a song that she co-wrote, which had gone on to win a Grammy for best Canadian film song, that she was able to find herself in fantasyland, riding her own horse, the dream that had started so many years ago.

And so as I leave Montreal on this train for New York, so many years after my 1976 visit, where I will attend in a few days Jonathan's parents weekend at Bard College—so looking forward to being with him and to see his school along the Hudson amidst the refracted light and burning colors of the autumn—I reflect intensely on the lunch at my hotel in Old Montreal with Melody, the oxygen tank next to her feet, the hissing of air pouring through her nose, as she bravely poured all of her energy into our conversation. I hadn't seen her since those 1976 games, and she had so many questions. I tried to explain—and I did so tearfully—the separation from my wife. We talked about the passing of my mom, and the death of her mother. And with the poignancy of adults who have suffered and lived—her grace; the courage to be so optimistic and cheerful amidst such a life-and-death situation that awaited her, inspiring within me the deepest admiration and respect—we reflected on the times in our life together, the days at Corriganville when she learned to ride, and those special winter moments when my family had returned to Montreal and we went sledding down Mt. Royal, just several blocks from where our Bubby made chicken soup at 100 Villeneuve street, then retreated to her parlor to read cards for her loyal followers, including the captain of Royal Canadian Mounted Police.

Zeida, blind, but perhaps not as blind as everyone believed, would find his way home from the tavern, beer on his breath. He would then turn on his radio and listen to Joe Pyne, a sort of reactionary radio commentator very popular at the time. I would sit at the corner of the bed with him—Melody sitting on the other side—and we would ask him for a little money as he tried to listen to his Joe Pyne. He'd give us the few bucks, and the three of us—my brother Jeff was there as well; he had always gone sledding with us—would walk down the street and pick up a cream soda at Rifka's. Rifka had some incredible hot dogs—I loved the way they were cut down the middle and put in the bun—and that soda washed them down to perfection. Then the soup was there for us, and of course the borscht.

One Hundred Villeneuve, I just had to see it again, and I would see it again, because following my lunch with Melody my father would be there to pick me up for the day. First on the list was 100 Villeneuve, then the gravesites of Bubby and Zeida.

And for dinner, it would have to be a Montreal smoked meat sandwich—no question about that. A smoked meat, accompanied by those red peppers—and the following evening the Montreal Canadiens were opening their home season against the Boston Bruins, and I had tickets against the glass on the blue line, to take my father.

The train moves around a bend at the moment, and in the offing is a forest of blazing reds, oranges, purples, the leafs scattered on the fields even more brilliant than those still on the trees. My chakras were open; I had come to Montreal at the right time in my life. I approached this city with the memories of a child, but also as a man who has endured 52 years of seasons. And I approached my father in precisely the same way.

I had flown non-stop on Air Canada from San Francisco to Montreal. And it is not all that difficult to confess that I am not sure whether—after a few sips of wine an hour before landing—the French Canadian flight attendant, gorgeous green eyes, black hair fully occupying the tops of her shoulders, silky long legs in black nylons, was encouraging me with her smile to be flirtatious with her, or if she smiles like that at every passenger. I concluded that there was a touch of "professional interest" on her part, kept strictly professional, a nice fantasy of interesting possibilities developing within my mind. This was not pursued as I exited the plane; I did not offer a card with my cell phone number on it or ask quickly where I might be able to reach her in the next couple of days, as she warmly greeted all passengers exiting at the front of the plane. Such a moment would have required total spontaneity, quickness, timing and absolutely compelling chemistry in a split second—nothing was revealed as I exited, save a warm, gracious smile, her eyes becoming even more fully round and inviting as I looked into them, pulling me in before she moved on to the passenger behind me and then the one behind him. I checked the fantasy at the door; gorgeous and elusive was this French

Canadian stunner, elusive in the same way of Denise Gadet, the beguiling French Canadian young lady with the green eyes and Mediterranean complexion who had stolen some of my breaths away in that ice rink in Campbellton New Brunswick, when I was 12. But that was a long, long time ago; I had arrived in Montreal as a 52-year-old man, about to see my father, who would be 78 in the next month. My bags arrived quickly—a "bon" omen, I had reasoned—and in a few minutes' time, I was in a taxi headed for Old Montreal

❒

It was a warm, sultry night; must have been about 70 degrees even though it was about 10:00 o'clock. This felt quite strange to me, given that we were on the cusp of November. The nights were bone-chilling cold at this time of year, 43 years ago when I endured that first Montreal winter as a 12-year-old boy. The air, this night, is much closer to that summer night, August 4, 1967, the evening that the man broke into our house and attempted to rape my mother as I lay beside her, leaving an indelible mark on my psyche. The traffic signs pointed in the direction of central Montreal, but one had an arrow identifying the direction of Ville St. Laurent, the area where we lived when this attack occurred. And for several long moments, I was deep in the throes of this moment in time, that 12-year-old boy feeling helpless; screaming for everything he had; searching for more oxygen so that the scream would be loud enough to overcome the paralyzing fear, awakening to the pure evil of this man's smile as he slowly backed away from my mom. Indeed, I had returned to Montreal, but I was much bigger and stronger and more powerful than this phantom of memory—it was a moment in time a thousand years ago, and it had no power over me now. Oh, but clearly the memory had not been fully defused; there was still electrical charge to it; it lay stored within cellular membranes of my brain, needing only a street sign marked Ville St. Laurent to revive it.

Bruce, L and Jeff R, in front of 100 Villeneuve St., Montreal. Approximately 1959.

The work of my good friend, Dr. Gwen Jones, is focused on releasing this type of memory from its location in our body—memory that affects the manner in which we carry ourselves, keeping us mired in defensive "fight or flight" postures, preventing one from opening up to new possibilities of thought and action. I momentarily reflect on our sessions together—the kindness in her eyes, her generosity to create about herself an open space, free of judgment, that permits for discussion of deeply held feelings. She seems to seek nothing in return, an outpouring of compassion that warms the spirit. I think of her as I emerge from this memory of Ville St. Laurent, and it is as though warm caramel flows through my veins and enters my heart. She has become a special friend.

I move on from the horror of that night, and I let dissipate into thin air the smoke of my memory of that terrible day when my father bloodied my face when I protested that he was late to take me to watch the football practice of the Montreal Alouettes, the Canadian Football League team that I was so excited to see. Though I was severely scarred by his violence that day, I am no longer under the influence of the electrical charge of the memory. But, again, I cannot minimize the emotional damage caused that day, and the effect is indelible. After that long flight and the surge of memory driving through the streets of Montreal, I slept exceptionally well in a cozy bed and room in old Montreal, a hotel so known for its charm that the Rolling Stones blocked out all the rooms for a few days during their last tour here. And as I awaited my father that next day, following my visit with Melody, I was relaxed, having slept better than I had in weeks.

Melody had just departed from the street in front of the Hotel St. James in old Montreal—we embraced about five times before she introduced me to her patiently waiting husband (apparently a pretty well-known radio personality in Montreal) as I carefully loaded into the back seat the oxygen tanks and other breathing equipment—when my father arrived in a blue Ford sedan, virtually occupying the very space that my cousin had exited just a few moments before. "Hi, Dad," I said, as I looked through his glasses into his green eyes, hoping to see a kind of acknowledgement, respect, compassion, a deep welcome for his son who had been going through such hard times in his life, and had come such a long distance to see him. However, these emotions were not readily discernable, as he met my eyes for a moment then turned away. But this didn't stop me from saying, "Dad, it's great to see you," as I broke through his possible discomfort with a strong, full hug. "It's great to see you, too," he replied a little nervously, pulling away to turn on the ignition and begin pulling out of this temporary stopping zone in front of the hotel. "How is Sue? Do you see her very often?" were his very first words. "I see her maybe once or twice a week, but some weeks, I don't see her at all." He took in my answer, absorbed it for a moment, responding, "I know this is a hard time for you right now, I had a very difficult time after I left your mother. We talked about my coming back for years, but it didn't happen, though I think it would have happened if she hadn't passed away when she did. You know, I never should have left California; I think I should have stayed nearby until we worked things out. I think we would have worked it all out." This was a strong statement for him to make, given that we hadn't seen each other in a few years. Clearly he had been thinking about his situation and my situation, and was looking at my experience in the light of his own.

And this forced me to confront some difficult feelings that I'd had about my father since my early 20s, several years after he had moved away. In order to protect himself from an enormous amount of blame, from an intense burden of guilt that could "eat a man alive," he'd had to go into a kind of denial that put blinders on his perception of our lives together. He had been so cold, distant, detached, but worst of all, violent, with his boys for so much of our lives. There were many times when my mom put herself in peril as she forced herself between him and myself or Jeff, as he was on the verge of losing control, rage pouring out of him over our disobedience. Those days before he finally left, when he made the threat that, "either Bruce goes or I go," were horrible. He had forbidden me from playing hockey anymore, because he couldn't accept the length of my hair; he'd forbidden me from surfing and threatened my mom that he would be gone within a week if she relented and bought me a surfboard, which she went ahead and did for me. My mom confided, crying on my shoulder one evening, that she couldn't take it anymore, and that when he "finally leaves," she'd support the family through her readings; that everything would be okay, and that she would hold it all together. And it was not long after that—my mom had bought me the surfboard just a few days before, and I had returned from a day at the beach—when he ran at me with both fists after I angrily responded to something he had said about stopping me from associating with my group of friends. This time, though, I stood my ground and did not back down, "Dad," I said to him with a calm anger, "this time I'm not running. You'd better stop, because if you come at me, I'm going to knock you down." I'm sure the look on my face revealed that for the first time in my life, I was prepared to stand up to his violence and temper, that as of that moment everything had changed in our relationship. In that instant, the dynamic between us would be different for all eternity; my father left for Montreal within a few weeks of that moment.

When I saw my father again at the age of 21—five years later during the Montreal Olympics—he talked openly about how my mom had chased him out; about how they agreed that he would leave for a little while and be welcomed back when he was ready, and how (even though he had his moments from time to time; got a bit strict, but that is the way fathers from his generation were taught to behave), he had been a good father to his boys, waking up at the crack of dawn on Saturday mornings to take us to our hockey practices and games. And, in truth, I thought to myself that he had at times acted like an interested father, but that anything he did do had to be repaid in total obedience, or else. Hearing this denial, I felt almost helpless, not sure what to do with these feelings of frustration and anger. It wasn't the kind of anger that I had felt when he left; I had come to terms with that over the past several years as I had matured and excelled in college. I was there to visit him because I could let go of those feelings, but I was troubled by the sense that he just wouldn't take any responsibility for his behavior, and in so doing essentially expected that our relationship would be a one-way street—that he had been a "good father," and that if there was anything that needed to occur for our relationship to succeed, it would require our coming to him. "I knew you boys would come back to me, one day; I'm your father, and I knew you'd want to come back," he had said at that time when I returned during the World's Fair. The statement left me empty, because it meant to me that we'd always have to come back; that no work would be required on his part. I wanted to say, "Dad, do you know how lucky you are that we are letting you into our lives—a lot of kids wouldn't speak to you again, forever." But I couldn't say that, of course. And in all of those years, leading right up to this visit as I sit next to him in the car and he asks about Sue—it has been thus. We basically never hear from him, unless we reach out and call. Oh, there are some exceptions, but this is usually the case. And it is so damn difficult for me to conceive of this behavior. I love my boys and reach out to them at every opportunity, perhaps too much. But I'll never stop giving of myself to them—it is at the core of the love that I feel for my boys. They mean everything to me, though I know that I must let them grow up and be men.

Driving away from the Hotel St. James, my father, thinking about my situation with Sue, shared some wisdom, and in it was compassion. He looked over at me, this time directly into my eyes, and said, "One day, you'll wake up and know what you have to do. It may be to go back; it maybe to leave, but you'll know; you'll just know." This was the compassion, the wisdom that I so craved.

"Thanks for that, Dad; I wish that time would come already. I so wish that I knew." "You will," he answered, "You will, for sure." "Let's drive to 100 Villeneuve—I so much want to see Bubby and Zeida's house. I miss having family around me; I so miss it." He didn't say anything to that—just looked ahead quietly, driving through the green light at the intersection en route to a special place in my past.

❒

My father lived at 100 Villeneuve street from 1940—when he was 11—until her met my mother in 1952. His parents—my Bubby and Zeida—continued to live there until their passing, about a year apart, between 1985-1986. The neighborhood had changed very little from that period of 1940-1952; it was where the Jews, after they had accumulated a bit of money in those hard-working years after the mass emigration from eastern Europe in the 1920s, lived and purchased some property. Rifka's grocery where Melody, myself and my brother Jeff would go—in that period when we moved to Montreal in 1966—and order those kosher hot dogs cut in half and smeared with mustard, washed down with a cream soda, had been there from the time my father moved there right up to that period when we returned, and then for several years after that.

Saul's Pharmacy—run by pharmacist Saul Shore and his brother, Harry, had also been there during the same period. But unlike Rifka's, which is still a grocery store, but has had legions of owners up to the current Puerto Rican ownership, Saul and Harry Shore still manage the pharmacy across the street from 100 Villeneuve. They no longer own it, having taken their money out of it several years back, but they are unmistakable—tall, sturdy, elderly men, bald across the top, full patches of white manes at the temples, faces lined with the wrinkles of generations, filled with the wisdom and knowledge of having been around to see children grow to become grandparents, grandparents for whom they issued prescription after prescription, grow old and pass on, their children becoming elderly as well. My father might be considered elderly, certainly quite senior of age at 78 years, though he works almost every day of his life at Radio Shack for mental and financial sustenance. The Shore brothers would be in their mid-80s, several years older than my father. After arriving at the corner home of my Bubby and Zeida—it sent chills up my spine as we parked in front, the number "100" in white against a blue background above the door as it appears in those pictures from early childhood in Montreal before we moved out west to California—I asked my father to take me over to the pharmacy. I had remembered the Shore brothers from the days when I was 12 in 1967; I'd go across the street with my mom from time to time to pick up a prescription, buy some Coffee Crisp candy bars. It was amazing candy; I had never known a flavor anything like it, the perfect combination of chocolate and coffee. It can still be purchased, but it doesn't taste as good today, and this is not because I am older, tastes jaded. It is way too sweet now; the company was sold to Nestlés from the original company Rowntree. I'll still eat the candy bar when I can find it; doesn't taste bad, is filled with memories, but it is not the same. Both Shore brothers were behind the counter filling prescriptions, and though it had been several years since seeing my father, they recognized him instantly and began the banter. "You're looking quite old there, Larry," Saul said to my father, you're totally white. Looking at Saul and his brother Harry, my father responded, "You guys haven't changed since I last saw yous several years ago; neither one of you looks a day over 90." The three of them laughed, and as they did, it seemed amazing to me that these three men were standing in the very same spaces that they'd occupied more than 65 years ago, so young at the time. In this world of such constant change, where obsolescence happens in months, this sort of meeting seemed to me to be impossible.

From this short little meeting, I so craved roots in my life; I desperately wanted to be around family, people who knew me from the beginning, craving a tethering pole in this dissonant, variable world. I started to think intensely that moment, as I listened to their banter and reminiscences, about how alienated I often feel these days. My mom is gone; my boys are off at college; I don't have any friends who I have known from the early years of my life, and though there are a few good friends (certainly Craig Jones, whose wedding I attended during the Loma Prieta quake) that go back with me more than 30 years, we have sort of lost touch. "I'm going to have to call Craig when I get back," I said to myself. "He's a great friend, and we've drifted over the past few years," I continued to think. Craig started a family much later than me, and he has been engrossed in the raising of his little ones. I have been in a very different place, giving all of my time to my boys as they were growing up. Instead of Craig going to games with me, it became my boys. And moments lead to moments, and before long four years have passed and we haven't spoken.

I supposed I haven't wanted to fill in my best friend on my life, the way it has been with Sue over the past few years; Craig remembers my marriage as having been something special. He saw Sue and myself as good friends, and indeed it was that way, nothing contrived. I just haven't wanted to go to that place of describing where I am today; perhaps there is a bit of pride in this, a fear that my friend might think less of me for where things are today, though I was there for him when his first marriage ended after two years. "I am going to call Craig when I get back," I affirmed to myself; "I must call him." The two brothers started to talk to my father—I looked on in total enjoyment of their camaraderie—about my cousin Melody, and the fact that her story had just recently been on the news, that she was first in line for a lung transplant. The story described her singing career—the notion that she could sing equally beautifully in English or French—and that she had been a star on the rise. "I was just with her," I chimed in. "Just spent a couple of hours with her. She had a big lung tank next to her, and was breathing though an inhaler attached to her nose. But she was in great spirits, and I have so much respect for this woman, my cousin, who faces the unknown every day, where another has to die for her to live. She came out to see me, struggling with these breathing tubes; I just love that girl. I told her, 'Melody, you watch, within two weeks of my visit, you will have your lungs, and the surgery will be a great success. You'll breath like a normal person again, and you'll be able to ride horses again. I'm sure of it.' " "I hope so," my father said. The Shore brothers remained quiet for a moment after I spoke, then Saul replied, "Sure hope it works out for the girl; I remember her mother, Vivian, the comedienne, so well—died of Emphysema, didn't she?" "Yes," my father answered, becoming serious and quiet as he thought of the passing of his sister.

My father and his sister hadn't been close for many, many years, but made amends in the months before she died. "I take care of her gravesite, as I do for my parents and my brother, Sollie, every week," my father said. "I always make sure that everything is taken care of, that there are flowers there, and that the grass does not grow over their stones," my father said, drifting off, his voice addressed to no one in particular. In the quiet of this moment, I asked Saul Shore if he remembered my mother very well. "Indeed, I do; Indeed, I sure do," he replied. "She was a beautiful woman; came from Toronto, didn't she, Larry?" "Yes," my dad replied. "She's gone now though, died of cancer a few years back. "Sorry to hear that," said Saul, and this was repeated by Harry. My father had stayed in a very quiet place, until I started with another question. "This area, it must have changed a lot in the years you've been here?" "Definitely has," answered Saul. "It used to be very Jewish; it had been Jewish middle class for many years. After that it became mostly Greek, then the Greeks left for the suburbs, and now it has a Puerto Rican, Indian, flavor to it—very ethnic, but quite colorful. Lots of mixes of people, a great variety of restaurants, even a few good Jewish ones still. And there are a lot of college students in this area—it is quite a young area now." With this my father said that we'd be going; the two Shore brothers shook my father's hand warmly from behind the counter. And then Saul, followed by Harry, reached over, each giving me a firm shake of the hand. "He's the eldest," my dad said, as we started to leave.

"His sister and two brothers are also out west." "Have fun with your dad while you're here; enjoy the moments," said Saul. "For sure I will; it's been a while, and I surely will," I answered.

We left the pharmacy and walked back across the street, standing in front of the black wrought-iron gate that came up to my waist; the same gate that was above my head in the picture from when I was three years old, with my brother, Jeff.

Walking across the street from Saul's Pharmacy my father and I stand in front of 100 Villeneuve.

I stand in front of this gate with my father, and in this instant I am that child again. In a few moments we'll go the gravesite of my Bubby and Zeida—I have never seen it. My father's brother, Saul, is there as well—he died sadly in 1979 from the smoke of a fire in a residence hotel, having fallen on hard times apparently beyond the scope of anyone to save him. I think back to Saul and his irrepressible laugh—there was so much good in him, and it was heartbreaking to receive that news, a few months after I had arrived in San Francisco to go to graduate school. This trip had started to feel very important to me, profoundly essential. A couple pushing a baby carriage walks past 100 Villeneuve, and as they do, I ask if they would please take a picture of me with my father in front of the black wrought-iron gate. As I write this at this moment, I think deeply about the passage of time. I glance at the picture of my brother and myself in front of this gate as small children, then over to the photo recently taken with my dad in front of that same gate, myself a middle aged man in his 50s, my father, now elderly. It is all so incredibly poignant. Life is precious, every instant is precious, and to the degree that we are able to open our hearts—freeing ourselves from anger and resentment—we are able to fully live the moments as time passes.

"How about Schwartz's?" My father said to me as we emerged from the gravesites of my grandparents and uncle. The day had seemed like three days already, and it didn't seem possible that the lunch with Melody had occurred in this same day. We had traversed decades during that lunch, my mind entering corners of memory from childhood that it had rarely explored in the past—Melody had been a large part of my life, but the experiences had been contained in a short span of time, and they had rarely been revisited. Thus, the recall of our times together, juxtaposed against her life and death struggle with the hissing of air pouring through her nostrils, created new trails in the snow, the mind like sharpened skis carving new tracks through memories not traversed before, or like the needle of a record player that cuts into an album for the first time, though they are songs from memory. And then the conversation with the Shore Brothers: they had remembered my mom—"What a beautiful woman," they had both agreed. They had ventured deep into lost time—each recovering in that moment something they hadn't realized that they had; vivid youthful memories, walking in the very footsteps they walked today. They brought 100 Villeneuve to the center of my universe in that moment, adding fresh pastels to the charcoal gray of memory contained in my picture of distant childhood. Oh, don't misunderstand, I adore, cherish, the charcoal gray of the memory, but life is not lived in black and white, and as the Shores discussed life with my father, the vision of a quite young, pasty-faced man, flaming, kinky red hair, entering his front door, suit soiled and wrinkled from driving a taxi all day followed by a night of revelry as he played clarinet in his band, dancing the night away in the speakeasies of late 1940s early 1950s Montreal, became emblazoned on my psyche.

I had seen in this moment my father—the passion to live, swing, be young and free—as a young man, and not a vessel filled with my feelings about him. He was 21 once; he knew these very guys, the Shore brothers, in those days of revelry and taxi driving, on this very turf where I stood. A few years later he would meet my mom, her mother taking her from Toronto to see Gertie, the noted card reader from Montreal. Stunning in her beauty, feminine in ways that stopped traffic, a chemistry occurred on the other side of that door, the very same door, beneath the sign, the very same sign, of 100 in white numbers against a blue background. My father awoke after one of those nights of revelry, still in his soiled clothes, just as my mom, Alma, always protected by her tough brothers and totalitarian Russian father, emerged from her card reading, entered the long hallway with that dark red rug that I had seen as a 12 year old, but that had been there since the 1940s, en route to the front door for a waiting taxi. My father intercepted her before she could enter that door. He held off the taxi, just long enough to obtain her number in Toronto, and then her pursued her for months until she finally relented, eloping within the year. The tough brothers of Meyer Rush, Davey Rush, Isaac Rush, encouraged by the tyrannical Abe Rush, her father, vowed to chase them down, destroy that Larry, if they could find him. The brothers said that they went to every hotel from Toronto to Montreal after they eloped, but there was no finding to be done.

He was brave, that father of mine, plucking Alma from deep within the Rush fortress. And he knew he was taking on the Rush family, not an enviable position, even for gangsters. But he knew what he wanted; he had to have her, and he was successful. How does one argue with fate: I write these words today, the product of his persistence and obsession. And it is all drawn with colorful pencils, the image before me of 100 Villeneuve Street. And then the graveyard, day three of this one day. “What is Schwartz’s?” I asked him. “It’s over on St. Lawrence Street, and it has the best smoked meat in Montreal. You ready for it? Hungry?” “Starving,” I said, “just starving.”

The place was packed, and after waiting in line for about a half an hour, they crammed us into a tiny table for two, barely large enough to hold the pickles in the jar—large, delectable, enticing ones, my mouth watering as I immediately pulled one out of the vinegar-flavored water—with us against the back wall and surrounded by dozens of other smoked meat eaters. The waiter didn’t waste any time: we had barely been seated, when he came to the table (now this is service!) to take the order. I took it for granted that people—usually all regulars—pretty much know what they’re going to order when they sit down. “What’s it going to be, dry or juicy?” he blurted out. And when I took a moment to think about it, he started speaking in Yiddish, then Hebrew to my father. I couldn’t quite grasp all that he was saying, but I made out a few things. The general gist of it was, “What’s the matter with this kid? Is he your son? He comes in here and he has to think about what he’s going to eat? Doesn’t he have a life?” This line of thinking was pretty much confirmed by my father when he told the guy, “He doesn’t really know from this stuff; he’s from San Francisco.” It was really quite cute; here I am, 52 years old, and I’m being treated like a 10-year-old kid, being taken out to dinner by his father. It felt great, actually—I was a kid with my father, only this time really enjoying the emotional embrace of my father, which I rarely experienced as a kid. After the Yiddish and Hebrew, the waiter slowed it down a bit for me: “Well, the dry is leaner, but the juicy is more delicious, but it has more fat.” “Can you give me the juicy, but take out the fat?” I answered. He shook his head from side to side, chuckled, mocked a derisive look at me, winked at my dad. "Sure thing kid, sure thing; you're getting the juicy." "Sounds awesome," I answered. "What is this awesome stuff?" he laughed, "Is that San Francisco language?" I just laughed. "I'll have a cream soda, as well," I offered, thinking back to those Montreal days at Rifka's. "I'll have the same," my father said, and bring me a cream soda too." Looking at me, my father said, "Do you like the large peppers or the small ones?" I looked at him a biz quizzically, like all of this was a foreign language to me. "You know; you remember—those big red peppers, or the smaller hotter ones?" I suddenly had a burst of memory—just in time, though, because I was starting to feel like a "smoked meat restaurant fool." "Oh, let's order the big ones—they're sweeter, aren't they? I remember them—God, it's been a long time, but I remember they were delicious."

In no time, just about the time I finished devouring the largest pickle in the jar, the peppers arrived, large, red sweet peppers from the "collective unconscious," archetypal peppers that would have made Carl Gustav Jung proud. And they were awesome. Just as the smoked meat sandwiches arrived, the table next to us—a family of six—got up to leave, the seats being immediately occupied by another group of six. There was a logjam, as the waiter pushed our table ever further against the wall. I was now totally pinned, unable to move; it was the least space I'd ever had in a restaurant, but the most enjoyable dining experience I'd had in recent memory. In short order, those sandwiches, except for the few extra moments of trying (almost to no avail) to cut off the fatty parts, were devoured. The moment is frozen in memory, and I salivate thinking about how badly I want another of those sandwiches. I want to have one with my dad again, and I wonder, indeed I hope, that we'll be able to do this again.

My good friend, Stuart, the owner of Mr. Ticket in San Francisco—man, he has put me in the front row for some of the great shows to come through San Francisco, the Rolling Stones, R.E.M., Neil Young, James Taylor, and as a kid I never had the wherewithal to see shows this close—had arranged for tickets up against the glass on the blue line for the Montreal Canadiens game against the Boston Bruins. I hadn't seen a hockey game with my dad since 1970, when I was playing hockey and he had seats for the Los Angeles Kings at the Forum. We would go to lots of games in those days, but a year later, the simmering, smoldering volcano that he had become erupted, and he returned to Montreal. He had managed a Radio Shack store in Montreal for a while, and was living comfortably enough to purchase season seats to see the Canadiens when they played at the old Montreal Forum on St. Catherine street. But that was many, many years ago; eventually he had to give up those seats, not quite able to sustain the profits and afford such a luxury in his advancing years. So this was the first game that he had attended—despite the fact that hockey is totally thrilling for him—in more than 20 years. He had met me at the Hotel St. James about an hour and a half before game time, and we each had a nice little shot of Scotch at the cozy, clubby bar downstairs, a warm fire burning just behind us, as we sat in oversized, super-comfortable leather chairs. I'd go back to that hotel in an instant, its living-room among the most comfortable places I have ever sat in my life. With dark-brown, fruitwood paneling, 19th-century, English-looking bookcases and desks, the place had an elegance but not a touch of stuffiness. It felt a bit like the Connaught Hotel in London before the major renovations—I still love that place but a touch of the charm has been lost with all the modernization—a kind of organic comfort where one might relax to the point of falling asleep and snoring, whether in faded jeans or finely tailored trousers.

The Scotch had gone down well, and the ride in the cab to the arena was quick. We had traveled a thousand miles in just a few minutes—the crackling of the fire and the clinking of the ice against the scotch glasses, the sound of Mozart from a piano not far away had given way to a loud organ, pouring excitement into the air, the referees in their black-and-white striped jerseys entering the ice (to a low chorus of boos), skating quickly to get loose, the sound of sharp razor on ice as they skated in front of us, fine little cuts into the ice trailing their blades. A few seconds later it was the vaunted Montreal Canadiens taking to the ice—they were wearing their white jerseys, trimmed in blue, the big "CH" (for Canadiens Hockey) on the front, as legendary a logo as one finds in all of sports, just dripping with hockey history, many a glass of champagne having been spilled on that insignia over the many years, poured in celebration from the Stanley Cup, time and time again as it was passed from man to man in the storied history of this franchise. There are a few logos that will bring chills to me, even if I do not worship the particular teams. The "NY" on the cap of the New York Yankees, not much more need be said; the "B" for the Boston Red Sox (has there ever been a cap more widely worn by a fanatical city than those worn for the Boston Red Sox?); the Maple leaf on the front of the Toronto jersey—nothing fills me with more desire to be in a cold place, playing or watching a hockey game than that blue leaf against the white background, "Toronto Maple Leafs" spelled on it; the "LA" on the Dodger cap, simply because my life cannot be truly understood without an appreciation for my early childhood love of the Dodgers, and my idolization of Sandy Koufax, the man on whom I projected my pride as a Jewish boy, and the virtues of all that was good; and the "CH" of the Montreal Canadiens. That jersey—it is the dream to wear it of virtually every wickedly fast, incredibly smooth, unbelievable skillful French or non-French kid in Quebec (and certainly those of less talent but no less the dreams)—is the symbol of championship hockey.

The Boston Bruins had just come on the ice, wearing the black and yellow, the "B" on the front of their jerseys also an icon of legendary performances. I had seen him play several times in the early '70s, and there has never been a player in my watching experience that could control, virtually take over a hockey game—making it bend to his command—like the greatest Bruin of them all, Bobby Orr. This "B" on the Boston jersey will always, for me, stand for Bobby Orr. The Bruins skated to their end of the ice—the other side from where we were sitting—and they did this to a loud chorus of boos. But not just the average boos; booing with a decidedly French intonation, accompanied by expressions of displeasure, sounding deliciously derisive in this language fully equipped for language of color. Wow! I was at a Montreal Canadiens game, watching it in Montreal! What a great decision to come here! How healing it was to be here with my dad. "You know, Brucie," my father said to me. "It is so great to be here with you. It's been 20 years, maybe more, since I've been to a game. And these seats; I've sat in some nice seats before but nothing like this." "My friend, Stuart, fixed me up with his guy in Montreal. Stuart is my ticket friend in San Francisco." "Wow; he found you some amazing seats. What did they charge you for these?" his naturally high-pitched voice becoming even higher with excitement. "Dad, I'm not going to tell you that. Let's just say I got a deal on them. I got a good deal." "Yeah, sure," he offered. He smiled at me, then turned away, shaking his head, as if to say, "That son of mine, he turned out all right."

I have known no sport that stimulates the zone of the brain associated with exhilaration and pleasure like ice hockey. There are many places in the United States where people have grown up without any exposure to the sport—kids playing ball hockey in the street before going home for dinner, then back outside again, this time to strap on the skates for a game on the outdoor ice under the lights is not a lifestyle in these parts—and prejudices about the sport have taken hold. In many places, ice hockey, because of the sometimes gratuitous violence that does tarnish its reputation, allowing for the impression that it is nothing more than brutal and barbaric when it is so often elegant and aristocratic in its display of precision, skill, finesse and grace at incredible speed, is barely above staged wrestling and roller derby. And so hockey is often looked on condescendingly in many parts of the country because its violence is often the only thing people read about or see on the quick sports highlights on TV. Thus, when a hockey-loving guy wants to take a girl out on a date in many places in the U.S., he

Bruce, captain of the Van Nuys Hawks hockey team, Bantam Division. Bruce upper left and his brother Jeff as the goalie—center front row—approximately 1970.

must do so with a lot of disclaimers attesting that he "really isn't a violent type at all, that he doesn't get excited by blood dripping from a players face, and that he really does have a sensitive, creative, poetic side to him." But such is not necessary, of course, in many parts of the land, where to love hockey is not to be seen as a member of a cult. And as the vibrant colors of autumn give way to the diffused light of winter where blue skies are shaded with white chalk, skates slash the ice, adrenalin pouring through us. On this particular night, Montreal was totally dominant. They conquered Boston in every facet of the game: speed, finesse, goaltending, hitting. And, goodness, was there some hitting. One might not gain the widest perspective of the game sitting where we were: up against the glass, inside the blue line. But what these seats lack in dimension, they make up for in visceral intensity. Players are as fast, if not faster than they have ever been, but on average they are considerably bigger and stronger than past generations. This combination leads to some astonishing contact—my father looking at me in amazement that a Boston player barely flinched, shaking off an enormous but clean hit by a Montreal defenseman, occurring directly in front of us. He smiled, laughed, shook his head; this was thrilling for him, immensely thrilling. Hockey is in my dad's blood and bones, and though he did his best to act as though he really didn't care who won—he'd given up pulling for Montreal years ago, he had said—it was pretty darn clear that he was surrendering to that childhood loyalty, a measure of satisfaction in his grin as the Canadiens dismantled the Bruins on this night.

During the intermission following the first period, my father's mind drifted to the players he'd seen as a young man at the old Montreal Forum, down on St. Catherine street. He told me of the jet-propulsion speed of the man known as the "Rocket," Maurice Richard. "Never has there been a player with more speed, more precision in his passing and shooting, more capable of faking a goalie out of his jock strap than the great 'Rocket,' " he said. "And I include Wayne Gretzky. The Rocket was even better than Gretzky." "Wow," I answered. "Better than Gretzky, you think? I've seen Gretzky play a few times, and I've never seen any player, including Bobby Orr, with an instinct with the puck like him. He seemed to know not only where the puck was at all times, but where it was going to be. He wasn't the fastest player ever, not the strongest, maybe not even the trickiest, but I don't know if there has ever been a player with the ability to be in the right position to score, or with the ability to put his teammates in the ideal situation to score like Gretzky. And the guy was a lot tougher than people give him credit for. I saw him take some pretty big hits, and bounce right back, even get in the face of somebody who was riding him too much." "You have to be tough to play in this league, I don't care who you are," my father went on. "Sure Gretzky was tough. No question that Gretzky is one of the all time greats. Maybe he was a better passer than the 'Rocket,' but for pure skill, there has never been anyone like Richard." "What did you think of 'Boom Boom' Geoffrion?" I asked my dad. "He played in the '50s and early '60s, didn't he?" "The women just loved Geoffrion. He was built like a tank, and could hit like a ton of bricks," he answered. "He'd hit somebody against the boards, practically knock him out, then look up and wink at a lady that he had spotted nearby. He was known for that wink to the ladies. He could shoot as hard as anybody I've ever seen—as hard as Bobby Hull, and that's saying something, because Hull could shoot. But also, don't forget Gordy Howe. I saw him play several times. He was a mean S.O.B. People learned to keep their distance from him, because he knew every trick in the book. You'd chase him in the corner for the puck, and come out with a broken rib, because he knew how to back you off when you got too close. Gordy would get you three, four goals a night, and also beat up the other teams' toughest player. They don't make them like Gordy anymore," my father concluded.

"The best hockey team that I've ever seen," I responded, "is after we moved back to Los Angeles in 1968. The next year you got season tickets to see the Los Angeles Kings, and we saw the Canadiens when they came to town. They had Guy Lafleur; Yvan Cournoyer; Serge Savard; Larry Robinson; JC Trembley; Jean Beliveau; Henri Richard, the younger brother of the 'Rocket.' Remember, they used to call him the 'Pocket Rocket,' because he was so shifty and quick?" "Oh sure, I remember the 'Pocket Rocket'—nothing like his brother, but he was great. That was a good team, Bruce," he followed, "A very good team." "I used to love watching Lafleur," I answered. "He was elegant on the ice; so fast and smooth, and when he found an opening, he'd thread the needle," I continued, totally excited to be seeing hockey in Montreal.

I had entered a zone, a hockey tent of the imagination that could not be invaded by the prickly needles of my thoughts, constantly reminding me that my life was out of sorts, a far-away location outside of that place where there is a steady stream of feelings letting me not forget that life is so solitary these days. I had found a location deep within the wilds of Montreal, occupied by my father, that was impervious, if even for a moment, to the reveries that always threatened to submerge me below the surface in a sea of emotion.

During the second intermission, my father began to talk to me about his memories of my hockey days. "You know, Bruce," he offered to me, "you were a fantastic hockey player when you were young. You were lightning fast; you were the captain of your team; you had a wicked shot, and boy could you hit. I really think you could have made pro, if you'd kept playing." Unsaid, of course, was the fact that because I wouldn't cut my hair, he forbade me to play anymore. The thought came and went like so many thoughts we are taught to release, images playing themselves out on the film screen of our minds, in the Transcendental Meditation that I started way back when I was 20. I still practice that exercise—have done it virtually every day since that time—and know that it has been very helpful in allowing me not to respond to insults or mechanisms that might trigger quick and unwanted responses. I think that it was very helpful in allowing the scene play itself out without my reacting, in much the same way that a baseball umpire reviews an image in his mind before calling a player out or safe at first base on a "bang-bang" play. I took the complement and continued to listen to what my dad had to say.

"You were a rough player, Bruce, but you were clean. Your hits were always clean. I took your mother to a game once, and she couldn't take it any more. She had to stop watching. She said that either you were going to hurt somebody, or you were going to get hurt. She said that she was going to stop you from playing hockey. 'That's enough,' she told me, 'He'll have to find something else to do.' I said, 'Come on, he's a boy, it's a rough sport, so what?' But she had to stop watching. After one of your games the parent of a player on the other team came up to me—I guess you had given him a good hard shot during the game—and said that you play the game too rough. I said, 'Come on, this is not a little boy's game; this is hockey.' He practically threatened me." he said. "You're kidding me," I answered. "I never knew some parent came up to you like that after a game; I don't remember there being such a reaction to the way I played." "You were a rough kid, Brucie. You played rough." "Dad," I answered. "I was pretty good, but not great. Maybe good enough to play college hockey—remember when I was offered a scholarship to Hodgkiss to play prep hockey back East?—but not good enough to play on this level. No way; perhaps if I'd started skating years earlier than I had. I progressed really fast—all that skating that I did when we moved to Campbellton. I was out there in 20 below zero, skating almost every night on those outdoor ice rinks. But the skill you'd need to play on this level—I'd never be able to play with these guys. But my brother, Jeff, now that's a different story. He could have played pro, no doubt about it." "He was one of the best goaltenders in Canada for his age," my father responded, "I sat next to the scouts when he was playing Junior Hockey out here for Dorval. He was being scouted by the New York Rangers. It is a shame he couldn't stay with it. But he had a temper, and he'd get mad and threaten to quit when the French coach would bench him, in favor of playing a French kid occasionally. He'd piss off the coach, so they'd bench him. The crowd was cheering for him to play, but the coach would hold him back, because Jeff wasn't willing to take his turn. But no doubt about it, Jeff could have made it."

My brother, Jeff, had just the right amount of thrill-seeking craziness to be a hockey goalie at the very highest level. And if not a hockey goalie, he might have made his way to the Ringling

Brothers, Barnum & Bailey tent, where he'd be shot out of a cannon and land on a high trapeze. He was a natural-born acrobat, and from the youngest age could move his body into all sorts of contortions. And though he might have been a genius at electrical engineering if he had pursued that course—he could fix absolutely anything, whereas I suffered big challenges plugging the right cord into the correct socket—Jeff was not intellectual. He rarely gave preliminary considerations to the consequences of his actions, seldom did he reflect over the possible outcomes of his behavior, including the dangers involved. Thus he became a hockey goalie, and excelled to such a degree that he was on the cusp of playing in the National Hockey League.

It all started that winter of 1966-1967, following our move the previous summer from Southern California to Montreal. While I was trying to figure out how to shoot a hockey puck while on ice skates—I had established myself as a street hockey player, but doing it on skates was a different thing entirely—Jeff had decided that he loved the acrobatics associated with goaltending. During one of our street hockey games against some very talented young Canadian hockey players, Jeff decided that he wanted to play goalie. He asked the kid who was in the net if he could have a try, hoping the kid might let him put on the mask, all the pads and play goal for awhile. "Sure," said the kid, "Let's see what you got." Jeff, the California boy who had just barely started ice skating, put on all the equipment, the big leg pads, the chest protector, the big facemask that looked like a massive catcher's mask, the glove for catching shots, and in a few minutes the game resumed. Jeff was astonishing—a huge smile comes to my face as I recall the moment with so much clarity that it might have been last week. On shots headed for the far corner, he did the splits, kicking them out, and he did this again, and again, and again. The ball came back to a kid who could really shoot the biscuit, and Jeff showed a glove hand that was wicked fast, dropping to a knee as he grabbed the shot headed for a score just under the cross bar. On another occasion, he was screened, as a missile hit him square in the facemask, startling him clearly, but only for a second until he started laughing from the sheer joy of it.

One of the kids told Jeff that he was going to introduce him to his coach. "You're amazing," the kid told Jeff, "I doubt that you can do this stuff on skates, since you haven't skated that much. But we've got to try you out for our team." The kid introduced Jeff to the coach at the next practice, and owing to serendipity, he was asked to start in goal the very next game, despite the fact that he was learning to skate, because the regular goalie had come down with a flu. I watched that game and really couldn't believe my eyes. Even though he wasn't much of a skater yet, Jeff had the balance and acrobatics to make several incredible saves, gloving a hard shot that was a sure goal. He was a natural, absolutely a natural, and he was mobbed by his new teammates, his victorious new mates, because Jeff's team had won the game, and in no small part due to his shocking play. The coach selected Jeff to start the next game, and he never relinquished the goal for the remainder of the season. During this time, he became better and better as his skating improved. The next season we were in Campbellton, New Brunswick, and in a place that lives hockey, breathes it like oxygen, Jeff played goal for the traveling team, wearing the prestigious jersey with the tiger on it.

When my father moved back to Montreal from California, after those torturous, brutal days when he refused to let me live my life with some peace, Jeff joined him to play hockey. The previous season I had played in a game against my brother. Jeff was a star, the top goalie in the league, receiving offers to play at any prep school of his choice. But Jeff didn't want anything to do with prep schools—he had no use for teachers and school. I was captain of my team—I still have the jersey of the Van Nuys Hawks, the big "C" for captain above the logo. The stands were filled to see the two teams play. I was among the league leaders in scoring; Jeff was impossible in the nets. It was an exhibition game, not part of the regular schedule. The two teams played in different divisions during the regular season. Going to the game in the car, Jeff assured me that I would not score on him. I answered by telling him that I'd get a hat trick, "three goals." The goalie for my team was overmatched. We were behind two to nothing after just one period. But during that period, I was flying down the wing. I barely took a rest before jumping back on. I was shooting the puck harder and more accurately than I ever had. Each of my shots was headed for the far corner—I'd shoot them on the fly, just above the face-off circle, as I skated down the right wing to Jeff's left. It was incredible, his goaltending that night. He did the splits on shot after shot, kicking out my low, hard shots that were bound for the far post. It wasn't until late in the second period that I broke through for a goal, not a clean goal, but a goal. I backhanded my own rebound, picking it up in front of the net. We tied the game later in that second period on another garbage goal, a forehand rebound of my own shot. I had two goals through two periods, and we had tied the game. I was within one goal of my predicted "hat trick." But he denied me time and again in that third period, his team going ahead to take a three to two lead. I continued to fly down the wing—it was the best hockey that I ever played in my life, and I can't imagine Jeff playing a better game on any level of competition. He robbed me, robbed me, and robbed me. Then, with maybe a minute left to play, we were still down three to two, I flew down the wing, this time faking the shot, centering to my assistant captain, the very quick Scottie Hamilton, who proceeded to deflect the hard pass straight into the air, headed above Jeff's head and clearly to a tying goal. Out of nowhere, his glove snared the puck behind his head, securing the win for his team. An incredible moment, and it is one that my dad is talking about, as he tells me that, "Jeff would have made it for sure." During those days when he went to stay with my dad, forgetting school to play hockey, Jeff impressed every coach he tried out for. But the coaches were French, and if they'd had their preferences, they'd prefer to play the French to the English. But Jeff was so good they had to put him on the team.

There were several coaches who showed no shame in trying to get their "hands on him." And so when he finally did decide the team that he'd play for—it was definitely Jeff's decision—he impressed immediately. But he didn't play as often as he would have liked—he wanted to play every single game—and made a total nuisance of himself, not respecting the coach's decision to alternate him. So he played less and less, and as this occurred, he lost his desire to remain in Quebec. The following summer he went to a hockey camp in Sweden, to learn from some of the best players in the world, including several from the National Hockey League. When Jeff stopped one of Sweden's all-time great players, Borje Salming, on a breakaway in a scrimmage, he was offered a position to play on one of Sweden's top teams the following season. He accepted the invitation, one of just a couple of North Americans permitted to play per team. He was spectacular, which is evident from the press clippings Jeff sent me to read. But he was lonely over there, and despite my insistence that he stay, "Give it a couple of seasons," I had told him," and you'll go straight into the NHL; you'll bypass all of the farm club stuff," he left after that season, returning to Montreal.

He didn't want to play in Montreal that following season, and so he decided to accept an offer to play in Newfoundland, Canada, for a very bad hockey team. He was the best thing that team had, but he couldn't single-handedly bring this team victories. He'd stop 40, 50, 60, shots a night, and I just marveled at this play when he sent me a copy of a radio broadcast, the broadcaster unable to come up with enough superlatives to describe Jeff's acrobatics. But the season wore him down, and it ended early for him when he suffered painful injuries to his knees, elbows and shoulders. That turned out to be the last season Jeff ever played hockey, and since then he has had something like 20 surgeries, some of them, I think, unnecessary (just lining the pockets of the surgeons). He can barely walk now, and in his side is a large, pillow-like device, a pain pump that constantly administers medicine for the nonstop pain. Jeff can't work; he lives on disability. And I have no resentment—I do so because I love my brother dearly—as I cover monthly rent on his house in Arizona.

Following the hockey game, my father was ready and willing to take the hour-and-a-half drive back to Northern Vermont, where he now lives, but I wouldn't have it. "Dad, you're going to be 78 years old; I don't want you driving back late at night on dark, narrow roads to Vermont. Let me get you a hotel room here. "You spent enough on the tickets; I'll drive; I'll be fine. The road is not that narrow," his voice trailing off. Clearly, he was tired. "And I do this all the time." "Well I just won't be able to sleep knowing that you're driving all the way back. I can't let this happen. "And furthermore, you daughter, my sister, Heidi, made me promise that you'd stay in Montreal tonight. And she has some of Mom's psychic ability, she can really be psychic." "I know Heidi can be psychic, I know," he answered, his voice becoming high-pitched, then trailing off. "I'm going to put Heidi on the phone, I'll call her in Los Angeles, and she'll tell you to stay, herself," I said as he started to show signs of defiance, first considering my offer then becoming resolved to go back and sleep in his own bed tonight. "Okay, okay," he said on my mobile phone, "I'll stay, I'll stay. Enough already, I'll stay," he answered the persistent Heidi—and she can be impossible to get off the phone when she wants to be heard—his voice beginning in the upper register, then falling several octaves, a Yiddish quality, a quite Jewish accent to his tone.

It's a shame my boys so rarely see him—they were relatively small children the last time they saw him in 1999, for the burial of my mom. His hair, once flaming red, has becoming totally gray, and with the Yiddish quality to his speech, he appears the prototypical Zeida. They could approach him clearly, cleanly, see him objectively perhaps, without all of the memories, cuts, scars, psychological machinations that attended my visit with him. And, of course all of this stuff cannot be forgotten, buried, removed of its influence—no doubt much of what happened between us during my childhood is stored in my bones, or the muscles surrounding my bones, or in my cells, perhaps the pores of my skin, the synapses within my brain—but as a man of 52 years I see him today as my father, simply human, full of mistakes and regrets, and love him deeply and totally. "So you'll stay," I responded. "That Heidi sure can talk," he answered. "I can't say no to her." "So you'll stay the night. I already checked—they have a few extra rooms. There is no problem." "Yes, I'll stay; I'll stay. You and your sister. You and your sister,…" his voice trailing off as the cab brought us to the entrance of the Hotel St. James, a welcoming porter greeting us as we entered the door to this place of comfort, coziness, rest.

The following morning we walked a few blocks down the street to a little breakfast place that specialized in waffles and pancakes, drenched in Canadian maple syrup; it was magnificent. But the breakfast was bittersweet, because within a few short minutes we would be saying goodbye for this trip. Hopefully, it would not be years before we see each other again. Though I do fear that as the distance of 3,000 miles reasserts itself, the intensity of these moments will fade to the point where the landscape is not so verdant, but in need of water. I am willing to keep it watered, but as he approaches 80, is he capable of doing so? "Brucie," he says to me, "It's been really great hanging out with you. I really wish that we could hang out more often." And as he says this, he begins to cry. The porter has just delivered his car to the front of the hotel. He sits in the drivers seat, and I slip into the passenger seat for a moment. "Please call me when you arrive in Vermont, Dad. Let me know that you got home, all right?" and I begin to cry. "I will," he answers, trying to get control of himself. "Take care of yourself," he follows, "and we'll talk soon. I love you dear," his voice trailing off. "I love you too," and I mean it, the words forcing themselves on my consciousness, struggling to be heard.

❐

The meditative clicking of the wheels against the tracks lulls me into a delicious half sleep as we move, the rails curved in a semicircle, half moon off in the distance, exposing a vast expanse of fields that are surprisingly green for this late in the autumn. Maple trees ablaze in red, gold, purple, dot the landscape sparsely, not a forest but solitary trees, each participating in the transition from birth to rebirth as its leaves reflect in color the maturation from the impatient urgency of spring, to the adulthood of summer, and on to the golden, wise period of the autumn, before falling to the ground, leaving tree limbs bare at the end of the cycle. The spring in full bloom is filled with possibilities; there is the emergence of hope and opportunity after the blanketing of the winter snows. The colors are irrepressibly green, the chlorophyll of youth, and the perfumes of nature permeate the air, knowing no moderation. There is naiveté, youthful folly within the abundant energies of spring—lessons to be learned, impulsive desire for experience, the indulgences and excesses of youth. It is a time of unbridled passions, some fulfilled, many not, as energies—some reaching their intended targets, others misguided, unfocused, not directed and never reaching fruition—fill up the universe in their excess. There is an instinctive aspect to spring; an almost uncontrollable, surge of being, the blood filled with oxygen after a winter of slow breathing. Spring can be too much: I often want to say, "Enough already; just relax a bit," to this season. I want to say, at times, "Let me rest, all right?"

Baseball season arrives just in time. Amid the thawing frosts, teams go south to cities throughout Florida and Arizona for the promise of a summer that is certain to come. Baseball is the passenger train that traverses the youthful innocence of spring—all teams, even the most undisciplined, inexperienced, careless, can have grand dreams of where they might end up in the fall, even though making it to the World Series requires more than big hopes and dreams, though the hoping and dreaming is necessary—through the summer, where experience is gained, and success depends on the application of understanding to skill and practice, and then on to the autumn, when energies are preserved, possibilities narrowed, experiences evaluated and lessons learned, wisdom gained and, sometimes, great dreams realized. A team will win the World Series by late fall, and its identity is the distillation of learning many, many things about itself from that period of innocence to the wisdom of age.

As the train moves rapidly but gently past the fields within my view—the gold, the brilliant red, flaming orange, deep purple leaves on the ground perhaps even more captivating than those on the trees about to join them, perhaps even more so because they represent surrender, their fate complete as they await the snows that will cover them—I contemplate the distillation of truths within myself. There is God and there is free will; have I surrendered enough to God? In the pursuit of free will, have I diffused my energies over ideas or possibilities that will not have any outcome in my life? The stark beauty of winter—white against black and the shades of gray; there is a beauty in winter unsurpassed in nature—is the manifestation of the surrender of all seasons into the quiet, still origins of life. All seasons move inevitably into the "empty" place of winter, from which all seasons are reborn. Do I understand inevitability? Do I struggle too hard against it? Is there an answer to my questions that I, somehow, do not hear clearly enough? Or, do I hear my truth clearly, but have difficulty being at peace with it? Am I taking the time to hear my mother's voice?—she vowed to talk to me from the other side. I consciously seek these truths, but I do know that the river of life will reveal them in the calm waters along the way. I cannot grasp; truth is revealed when, as John Lennon so beautifully said, "we are busy making other plans." I look on the colors of autumn and they speak to me: "This is the time for quiet now; let us not look to the future and all of its possibilities, which is the birthright of spring. Let us take a rest now; we have earned it." This is what I hear and see in the vibrant golden, blazing oranges and reds, the sublime purples of autumn.

≈

October 24th, 2007—Meeting Michael at Geisha

My son, Michael, is in New York for a few days—he is on a mini fall break from the Oberlin Conservatory—and we had arranged to meet here on my return from Montreal. Michael is enormously talented as a pianist and composer—he was given a music scholarship to the Conservatory as a composer, but could have qualified as a pianist—but in the past year has gravitated toward the Technology in Music program, adding this as a second major to composition. Sitting at a laptop computer for hours at a time, programming it to play an interstellar, intergalactic, assortment of sounds that cohere within a conceptual framework, a musical network of ideas that Michael's mind races to apprehend and put into form, is a great distance from the Shostakovich and Mendelssohn that he was playing at the San Francisco Conservatory of Music during his youth. His compositions are gaining recognition at Oberlin, and last winter, a month before my January separation from Sue, one of Michael's pieces was played at Symphony Space on the Upper West Side of New York City. His piece was played alongside one written by one of his professors at Oberlin, and when his piece was completed, the audience rose to their feet for a standing ovation, Michael nervously approaching the stage where he bowed—what a gentleman he looked, a young maestro in this special black suit—and shook the hands of the saxophone quartet that had just finished an extraordinarily polished (at least to my ears), rendition of this piece, which Michael had said was very difficult to play. The group is called Prism, a highly accomplished quartet of saxophonists whose music provides the backdrop for at least one major TV news program; they perform around the world, and their tastes range from the Baroque to the ultra-modern. It was an unusual arrangement of melody and cacophony, currents and crosscurrents of rhythm played in complicated time sequences, moments of gorgeous harmony in which time seemed to flow gracefully, followed by interruptions, sharp exclamations, pauses, and abrupt starts. It had taken Michael several months to write this piece—he had been commissioned to write it a few summers ago for winning the composition prize at the Walden Music Camp For Young Composers in New Hampshire—and what a moment it was to see him on that stage in front of a serious New York audience that had responded to this music and to him, as he bowed on the stage. I'll never forget how he tried his best to suppress the sense of accomplishment that, no doubt, was swelling within him—I could hardly contain my gratification in this moment, it being all the more joyful given the hard days Sue and I had been experiencing—as he saw his name on the poster at the entrance to Symphony Space, announcing his piece to be performed. "Nice job, Michael," I had said. "How does it feel to have your name in lights on Broadway?" "Oh Dad," he answered, "you're making too big a deal out of this; it isn't that big a thing," he said tightly, nervously (he was very nervous about this debut), his tight lips then breaking into a full laugh as I tickled him, saying, "Yes it is, Michael, it is a big thing; your piece is being played in New York City. You are just a little kid"—I said this as I continued to tickle him—"and you have this serious piece being played in New York." He gained control and became serious again; and as he does I tell him how his grandmother "Tudy", my mom, Alma Lorraine Rush, would have cherished this moment. "I think about her all the time," he tells me in this moment that has suddenly returned to seriousness and anxiety for him. "She is always with you Michael, always. She loved with you with all of her heart. Remember, she said—I know that you remember this—that she will always be with you during the important times in your life. Remember, we were on vacation in Copenhagen when you were little and you had a dream that alarmed you. We called her back in Los Angeles, and she said that during moments in your life when you need guidance or her presence, she'll always be there; you'll always be able to find her. Your grandmother Tudy is with you now, Michael. Enjoy the moment."

I gave him a big hug, and then he went inside to spend time with his professors and invited guests. Now, as I am a few hours outside of New York City, he calls me every 20 minutes to find out if my train is making up some lost time, or whether we are being further delayed. He wants to meet at his favorite restaurant in New York—Geisha, where they have the best sushi I have ever tasted—and he is starving and wants me to be there already. "I can't make this train go any faster, Michael," I say with a touch of perturbation after his fifth call in the last hour. "You know what, go there with your friends, start a tab, order food, and I'll be sure to get there before they close. Go ahead, don't wait, just start without me." "Okay, Dad, but come straight here to the restaurant. Don't stop at the hotel first." "Michael, I have this enormous suitcase"—we always called it "the monstrosity"—and I'm not about to wheel it into this narrow little restaurant. "You brought the monstrosity? Why did you bring the monstrosity?" Michael says impatiently, the energy of New York working its way through his metabolism. "Michael, I'll see you soon; I'm looking forward to seeing you. And be careful with the drinks, that place can cost enough for a down payment on a house." "Okay, Dad; but hurry up."

Within an hour and a half, I was wheeling "the monstrosity" through the narrow aisle of Geisha, the well-heeled crowd pushing their feet in, backing up as much as possible—I am trying my hardest not to run over sexy shoes attached to gorgeous ankles, long legs fitted into black fishnet stockings grabbing my attention—as I work my way to the back of the restaurant, where Michael waits for me. "I feel like one of the Beverly Hillbillies with this monstrosity," I say to Michael, as he gives me a huge hug, as do his friends who have come with him from Oberlin. They are all a bit buzzed, and I can only imagine how much this tab will already cost. I sit down to a nice glass of crisp white wine, as I savor the hamachi, blanketed by a spicy avocado cover. Sometimes life is great; sometimes it is absolutely great.

It is close to midnight when I wheel out "the monstrosity," and it is a good bit easier to do so now, the crowd having thinned out quite a bit. Michael has plans to stay at his friend's house—Orin, an Oberlin friend 20 years old whose family lives in Hell's Kitchen—and I see him into a cab before grabbing one myself to take me to the Essex House on Central Park South. Michael and his friends are a bit too tipsy for my liking by the end of the evening, and I admonish him, telling him that it is absolutely no fun to drink so much that you spend the evening throwing up. "Dad I'm fine, I'm perfectly okay; I'm in New York, I'm on a break, you tell me this all the time," he answers. And I suppose that is correct, I am concerned about the drinking that goes on at these campuses—when it comes to my boys I worry, worry, worry. I inherited that "worry" gene from my mom, but as I have said, she found a way to not let it control her life, and I am struggling to find that "happy medium" between concern and acceptance, between having some control over their lives and being able to "let go" and let myself relax. I suppose living alone makes it much harder—I keep these concerns, anxieties within myself, finding it difficult to release them in the middle of the night when I wonder what the boys are doing far away in their college environments. But while I do trust that all will be okay, that these guys were raised to be intelligent and conscious, my concerns are justified. I have visited the campuses of both of my boys, as well as a number of other campuses over the past few years when we were exploring college choices, and I was overwhelmed by the amount of drinking—the abundance and sheer pervasiveness of it—on these campuses. It is difficult for kids to get into these liberal arts schools; the baby boom of the baby boomers, coupled with the discretionary capital to pay for these schools puts intense pressure on kids from early in grade school. Their high schools are places of serious competition, the amount of quality study required to succeed and be competitive equivalent to the toughest work one will do in college—the requirements and work load, including the demand that kids be actively involved in programs outside the classroom as well, far more intense than anything I ever encountered in high school in the early '70s—and it is no surprise at all that college becomes a place, finally, of being able to let go and party. After all, they have made it; they are "in." But the drinking goes beyond acceptable limits from what I have seen on occasion. This is not an indictment of Michael (Jonathan doesn't enjoy alcohol very much)—an unscientific survey would reveal that he drinks no more in quantity or frequency than the average college kid. It is just that the drinking is on such a wide scale, the amounts being consumed seemingly well beyond anything I remember in my day. Perhaps there was less overall drinking when I was in college because marijuana played a much larger role than it does today—but I'm sure there are people who could put up a strong argument that marijuana is as prevalent as it was in the '70s, and that kids are smoking as much as we did, and drinking more. I don't know, but I can say that the drinking makes me quite nervous, as I lie awake in my apartment on a Friday or Saturday night, knowing that the kids are out "letting go." The schools seem to do nothing to curb this abundance of drinking, even among kids under drinking age. Perhaps these institutions are concerned that they will acquire "negative reputations" as places where it is difficult to party, thus discouraging applications and causing their acceptance rates to decrease, which then might have an effect on their status and fees. They might not seem as prestigious in the annual college report of school rankings that is released in the "U.S. News and World Report." But I find it outrageous that the schools across the country seem to take such passive attitudes to the drinking of the kids—I do not want campus cops barging into my boys dorm rooms, but I do want to know that these colleges are playing some kind of role in making sure that our kids are going to school in environments where there is supervision and education with regard to the dangers of drinking. Something, I'm not sure what, but something does need to be done on campuses across this country!

I arrive at the Essex house, and I have struck it rich again. This bed is absolutely delicious; it is incredibly comfortable. Perhaps as comfortable as the one at the Hotel St. James in Montreal, though this hotel in New York is much more corporate in its size, not the boutique of the St. James. After calling Michael on his cell to make sure he arrived at his friends house all right —he didn't answer the first call, but did the next one a couple of minutes later, putting me at ease—I turned on ESPN, where highlights were being shown of the first World Series game between the Colorado Rockies and the Boston Red Sox. The Sox had cruised to a game-one victory 13-1, behind the superior pitching of Josh Beckett, who struck out the first four batters that he faced in the game. There shouldn't be any doubt that Boston will win this series, but baseball can drive odds-makers crazy. The Rockies have been perennial doormats in the national league, sad-sack losers for years. Whenever we would visit Denver—Sue's birthplace and where she grew to adulthood—it would be easy to get tickets to games, even for the best seats. This is not to say that the city didn't support the team; the games seemed well attended, but it wasn't difficult to obtain tickets to a game at a fair price. After all, they'd finished either in last place or close to it since their inception. And they started this season as an average, middle-of-the-pack team until late in the season. And then something happened. There was a kind of team magic that can happen in no other sport the way it happens in baseball. Late in the season they could do no wrong, and the city of Denver became more and more feverish as thoughts of a pennant became a serious possibility. The city had never before know pennant fever, and by mid-September, it was under the spell of an 103-degree, certified pennant flu. The Rockies entered the series having won an astounding 21 of their previous 22 games, going back to the end of the regular season, including sweeps of the Philadelphia Phillies in the National League Divisional Series, and the Arizona Diamond Backs in the National League Championship Series. They also had to beat the San Diego Padres in a tiebreaker to get into the playoffs in the first place. This was miracle baseball. The team had started the season with grand hopes of making it to the World Series, as all teams do. They had acquired through great draft picks, plus a few nice acquisitions, a nice little club, one that might seriously compete in a few years time. However, along that train ride from spring into autumn, the ingredients and chemical reactions that produce a baseball champion—often taking several seasons of percolation before they coalesce into the fall magic of a championship team—occurred as though a magic wand had cast a spell and the "will to believe" transformed into unstoppable action. Yes, they lost 13 to one tonight, but as I lay in bed waiting for my room service order of toast and warm milk—I had acquired this need for toast before going to bed years ago from Sue, and will, probably, never shake it, so accustomed is my stomach to it—I reflect on the notion that this Rockies team made it to this series against enormous odds. In baseball, as in life, there is much that defies prediction and programming. I surrender to the fact that, sometimes, chemistry and magic must have its way.

I am back in San Francisco, having returned a few days ago. Indian summer is history for 2007, and a chilly wind was biting my skin, penetrating my bones earlier this evening when I went to dinner at Via Veneto, the Italian place owned by Mossimo, the proprietor who has become a sympathetic acquaintance over these past years as I visit his restaurant for something wholesome after work. I visit his place about three times a week, and the Japanese place across the street, perhaps, another two days a week for Sushi. I usually visit these places alone, eating alone, because I don't want to be embarrassed if Sue walks in and I am having dinner with a woman. I do not date as often as a single/separated person might—but I am not a hermit, I am not reclusive and certainly allow myself the company of a woman on occasion. But it is so difficult to have a date that one knows from the beginning must have limitations, that there are intimacy boundaries that cannot be breached as long as my marriage is in limbo. And it is in a deep, icy state of limbo. It is fun to hear music, go to the theater, go to a movie, have dinner in my apartment, take a walk down by the bay with a woman, but though there are many opportunities to do so, I avail myself of very few occasions. There are those who would say, who do say to me, "Bruce, you are free now, at least for the time being, enjoy yourself, take advantage of dating, go out and have more fun, loosen up a bit, you are in your 50s, life is short, whatever is going to happen will happen, but in the meantime have a bit of fun." And, indeed, this makes sense. But there is a price to be paid for this freedom, and this price has much to do with this feeling that I have every day—I feel it in the depths of my stomach when I am at work—that I am not tethered in my life; that I am missing the "safe harbor" that I can call home. The price of the freedom that I now have has stiffened my neck to the point that I have tension headaches that I have never known quite like this before; my shoulders tighten to the point that they often feel like plates of steel.

The economy continues to unravel from this subprime mortgage crisis, the banking system seeming to become increasingly fragile (domestically and globally) as companies are finding it hard to figure out just what their overall loss exposure is to these mortgages and overvalued real estate. Fortunately, the nature of my investment business is the sales and analysis of tax-exempt municipal bonds—and this is an area of investment insulated to a high degree from the substantial declines in asset values associated with mortgages and real estate. But it is not entirely immune, as bonds become downgraded due to the insurers of the issues losing their AAA ratings as a result of exposure to these mortgages. So, indeed, my tension is not strictly a result of the uncertainty in my life, though it is heightened because I cannot share my thoughts, concerns, the need to be understood, nurtured—to be able to give love and nurture to a person who can receive it. In good relationships and marriages—and our marriage often had this magic through the years—a kind of third world emerges, a world where something new and unique occurs from the coming together of two separate but unified selves. It is made up of the two souls, but is something entirely separate, a dimension of experience that can continue to evolve through the growth of two expanding selves, evolving but expanding together. This third place, this world where a thriving marriage resides, requires an equal contribution from both parts, with several tablespoons of chemistry thrown in for all the ingredients to combine. It is sad when the chemistry is there, but the selves have lost their separate identities—thus taking one another for granted—in the union. Eventually one side or the other, possibly both at the same time, emerge from this loss of separate identity—waking up to the fact that the marriage or relationship is not only not growing, but stifling the growth of the vital souls involved—and a differentiation occurs, the result being a redefinition of the relationship. Is it no longer working? What can we do to make it work? Is it worth saving? Or are the demands for individuality now so great by one party or the other, possibly both at the same time, that the structure of the marriage can no longer hold together the pieces, however much love there might be, however great the chemistry, however strong the sense is that these people are soulmates?

I have a difficult time dating other women because our marriage is in limbo. And then limbo exists because neither of us deep within our hearts wants to let go of the other. This is true. But we do nothing to go forward, and our sense of love for one another is based on the sense that we have always had—and will always know—that we are special friends, that our souls are connected, and not only because we have a lifetime of memories and shared experiences. Not only because we have raised a family of two beautiful boys—boys who were meant to be in this world, and so our connection was inevitable and right, as my mom had seen in her reading that afternoon—but because there is true love between us, but our relationship had stopped evolving—we had become roommates, and neither of us had added anything new to each other in the form of closeness, romance, an interest in the depth of the other person beyond talking about the affairs of the day—and that third world (that definitely had some special moments through the years) became dormant, and then more than that, empty. There were special ingredients that brought Sue and myself together, and for much of our lives contributed to that third world that allowed our marriage to thrive. But eventually, neither of us was depositing enough in the "bank account" to make it work. Was it inevitable that our situation would go in this direction? I ask myself this so often. Perhaps it was? Perhaps a spiritual marriage contract exists, a priori, before experience. Possibly this is the time that the marriage is supposed to conclude. I think about free will and determinism so often. We have choices; we can act differently. We can move our affairs in a direction. But the universe does exert limitations on our choices, our freedom does not exist in a vacuum. To make one choice eliminates the possibility of the other choice. Ultimately, well-meaning people are doing the best they can. We are human; we must be gentle with ourselves. We are not perfect, and we must forgive ourselves our humanity. We can make ourselves ill with worry and regret. Let the troubles fall away from us—let us move on when we must, move on with the sense that we are trying the best we can to make our lives right for ourselves and the ones we love. Sometimes this involves staying together in a marriage; at other times the individuality has become too strong on the part of one or the other or both, so that change must occur for each of the selves to evolve. Let us repair what we can repair, and not force ourselves to repair what cannot be repaired. God, please grant me the ability to change what I can for the best, to understand where I cannot effect change, and the wisdom to know the difference.

❐

It is very dark and late as I write these thoughts about life. A mist enshrouds the Golden Gate Bridge and hides the bay and the lights below me. It was an amazing trip to Montreal and New York. After spending time with Michael, I went up to Annandale-on-Hudson to visit Jonathan at Bard College. I stayed in Rhinebeck in a little bed and breakfast, from which I attended a few seminars at his school for what was parents' week. The school was leafy with golds and browns, purples and reds, the sky a diffused blue of fall. It was a great stay, and I was quite sad when I had to leave. Jonathan will be back for Thanksgiving, and so will Michael. We'll get together at the family house for Thanksgiving, and though it cannot be the same, it will be what we have. And we will give thanks.

I arrived back in New York to see the final game of the World Series. Boston's overwhelming strength was too much for the will power and magic of the Rockies. Though the Colorado team fought hard to come back, making it close at the end, Red Sox took the series in four straight games, winning the last one four to three, the game ending as my warm milk and English muffins were being delivered to my room at the Essex House, somewhere just past midnight. Though I had the freedom to do so—I was alone in New York on my return visit from Bard—I did not look up" M," or give any thought to calling her, though I certainly was aware, and felt her energy, her place of work being just a block or two away at the Steinway store across from Carnegie Hall. Her impact on me was enormous, nothing more need be said. Her smile was similar to my mom's; her velvety voice had the quality of my mom's; she had a zest for life that got deep into me. But meeting her and experiencing its effect on my marriage was, next to my mom's passing, was the most painful time in my life.

Just a little while ago, before starting to write tonight—filled with moodiness and inspired by this dark and misty night—I put on the "Led Zeppelin 3" album. I hadn't heard this album in a couple of years and there are some songs on it that have always affected me in a substantial way—it came out at a time when I was getting in touch with my deepest feelings, the marriage of my parents coming to an end, my mother going through grief because of the loss of her mother, my father moving on like a hurricane finally letting go after causing destruction.

One of the greatest rock concert memories that I have—maybe the greatest—is seeing Zeppelin after the release of this album. I had just finished smoking a pretty strong joint of Colombian weed when the lights at the Los Angeles Forum go totally dark, except for the fire coming from people's lighters throughout the area. Then one had the sense that something was happening on the stage, shadowy figures moving into their spaces. All of a sudden the insistent, repetitive chords of Jimmy Page transport you to some place in the future or, maybe, way back in time to the era of the "cave man." Without any light on the stage, the chords to the "Immigrant Song" get louder and louder, then all of a sudden the stage is bathed in light, the pounding drums of John Bonham intensely illuminated, a spotlight on Robert Plant, tight pants and long flowing golden locks that have girls lunging for the stage. Then the howling opening verse, preceded by that haunting loud chant, the entrancing sound that brings one to a world where you may not want to live full time, but what a visit it surely is. Later in the concert, after the hypnosis they have worked on the crowd, Plant says that they want to slow it dow, two chairs are assembled for Page and John Paul Jones to play acoustic guitar, Plant standing between them. The gorgeous, sweet, melodic melancholy acoustics begin to play, Plant's vocals softening to become a masterpiece of irony in the song "Tangerine." The song describes loving and being loved deeply, and there is the regret of lost love. The voice evokes powerful youthful yearnings and it fills my bloodstream, the oxygen of the possessing mystery and irony of Plant's voice transporting me to the moment I saw it performed, the intensity of the idealism of that time almost heartbreaking right now. I so deeply wanted and believed in true love, and that 17-year-old boy felt that once discovered, a marriage would last forever. It would last forever because true love would be its essence.

The album and the song gave me the recognition that true love might continue while the marriage might not is shattering. I am proud of the man I am today, but it is so hard to give up the boy of such pure dreams.

Thanksgiving

The boys came home for Thanksgiving yesterday and I wrapped my arms around both of them at the same time, squeezing them against me in the biggest bear hug they have had since, perhaps, early grade school. Thanksgiving is my favorite holiday of the year; it has always been the moment in the year when my internal clock slows down, seemingly much more time between the seconds, the hours unwinding slowly, opening up broad spaces into which my love for my family, the sense of the preciousness of time together, expands. There is something inherent in a Thanksgiving Day—that train about which we earlier spoke, that starts in the spring with youthful, impassioned enthusiasm and continues into the fall where unbridled energy transforms into a quieter, reflective thinking, a slowing down that includes the opportunity for wisdom—that doesn't occur at any other time of the year. This slowing of the clock and the opportunities for deeper intimacy, an intimacy of thanks between friends and those that we love, however far away, exists in a peculiar way on this day—as though it is a special energy handed down to our culture from someplace "on high."

Sue invited me to Thanksgiving dinner in a formal way—she called to tell me that I was invited to have Thanksgiving with the family, that it would be just our family. I was welcome to come, but if I had other plans it was okay. "Of course, I don't have other plans; there is no place that I'd rather be than having Thanksgiving with my family," I answered. I went on to say that despite the differences between us, even though we were doing our best to honor our separateness and the reality that we are apart, nothing would ever be more precious for me than the special moments with my family. "This part of me will never change, Sue," I told her. "If the two of us are never back together again as a couple, the moments when we are all together will be sacred. And you know how I feel about Thanksgiving—it is such a special time to finally unwind, reflect, let go a bit, get out of my mind and to settle into my body." "I do know," she answered; "of course I know. You know that it is the same for me." "Yeah Sue, I know how you feel about this time of year as well. I'll definitely come." Her voice then became low and very quiet—on occasion Sue's voice can become almost a whisper—and with a distinct trace of sadness she concluded, "Well, come about 1:30, so you can do some of the carving. Michael is going to make his famous mashed potatoes." And perhaps just as sadly, though not quite as quietly, I answered that I would see her then..

At the dinner table, our black lab, Lucky—my God how I miss spending more time with him—is at his annual Thanksgiving Day place just beyond reach of the turkey. His head is cocked a little to the right, the longest tongue in the world dangling practically to the floor, eyes in a kind of pitiful longing, a low moan becoming more high pitched and turning into an occasional bark, before Jonathan sneaks a piece of turkey from the plate at the center of the table and drops it into Lucky's salivating mouth. And then I say a prayer; the boys take in every word, not the usual goofing off that they do when I would get serious for a moment and talk about the preciousness of these moments, and how lucky we all are. My college boys recognize that these are important times—that our moments together are short and fragmented, compounded by the dislocation within our family—and when I am speaking, they have also gone to a place of consideration and thought. But just for a moment or two; after that they dive in and enjoy the turkey. It was delicious, and for the first time in quite a while I linger in the front room of our charming Victorian with the high ceilings, late 19th-century crown moldings. Michael plays the Steinway, and after about 20 minutes, Jonathan throws the football at me, and we go down the street—to Alta Plaza Park, across from Town School For Boys where they went to grade school—and throw the ball until my arm falls off. Jonathan is impressed that I "still have it." He makes some gorgeous catches of my tight spirals, and if I do say so myself, I was pretty good. After football Jonathan and I went to see a movie—Sue wanted to stay at home and watch one on the movie channel—and we enjoyed ourselves in the simplest and deepest of ways. The music in the movie was great—can't go wrong with Bob Dylan—but the movie itself wasn't phenomenal, an experiment that didn't quite work about showing the different faces of Bob Dylan. We went back to the house afterwards, Sue asleep or resting in the upstairs bedroom, and Jonathan played some gorgeous Dylan tunes.

Several years ago I had a very strong sense that Jonathan should take guitar lessons, to complement this voice that struck me as having tinges of Paul Simon, a splash of McCartney, Dylan when melodic, and elements of Ricky Nelson from the "Lonesome Town" era. He had been writing some poignant, touching lyrics, but just didn't have an instrument to back them up. He started taking lessons, and within six months was surprising his teacher with his ability to put chords seamlessly together in harmony with the lyrics that he was writing. After a while, he started to play some of these compositions around town at open mics, eventually being asked to come back and play whole sets of music at some of these venues. About a month and a half ago, taking a short break from Bard College during an autumn recess, he played a set at the Hotel Utah in San Francisco to a standing ovation. He was invited to come back and play "anytime he wanted." Sitting on his bed, I'm lying down in a beanbag on the floor against the wall across from him, he begins to strum some chords that massage the pleasure center of my brain, no doubt a big joyous smile on my face. Then, invoking the soul of Dylan, the verses come flowing:

My love she speaks like silence,
Without ideals or violence,
She doesn't have to say she's faithful,
Yet, she's true like ice, like fire.
People carry roses,
Make promises by the hours,
My love she laughs like the flowers,
Valentines can't buy her.

"Love Minus Zero/No Limit" is, maybe, my favorite Dylan song. Jonathan knows this, and as a Thanksgiving gift to me, he brought tears to my eyes in the singing of it.

Listening to Dylan always puts me in the mood to write, and so, on this late Thanksgiving eve, these thoughts from the day pour through me. There is a picture just off to my right—it sits next to the picture of Joe Montana, the number 16 boldly displayed on his chest, his trademark hands held high in the air after throwing a touchdown—that was taken before Jonathan was born. Michael was about two years old, and had a paper Native American headdress on his head. I am holding him in my arms, his arms wrapped around my neck. The caption below—taken from the

Torah—reads, "The pleasures we get from children are far more precious than gold." That about says it all. It just says it all.

I am back at work now; and as November winds toward its conclusion, the financial news is not sweet and melodic, but dismal and discordant. Banking losses in this country and in Europe are deepening, as they continue to write down losses on their mortgage portfolios due to the steady decline in American home values. The values of these mortgages are continuing to fall, requiring these banks to put aside more and more capital to meet the financial requirements that call for healthy reserves of cash to offset losses. And though this situation is not a crisis, it is starting to feel like a flu that wont go away, a contagion that appears to be spreading instead of being contained. The mortgage-backed bonds that were packaged to institutional investors—large banks, insurance companies, financial institutions—paid substantially higher than average returns because they contained these low-grade, subprime mortgages that were offered to buyers with little or no credit ability to receive them. Home values are falling, defaults are increasing, and there is, virtually, no market for these mortgages. If they continue to plunge in value due to their limited liquidity, the global banking sector will have severe problems. Nobody really knows how pervasive the problem is or how severe it will be. Perhaps it is just a couple of banks that will have trouble—perhaps it might be worse. I am concerned about it. And so is the stock market. Over the last month and a half, the market has recorded its first 10 percent correction in five years. There is a credit crunch—a tightness of lending—that has corporate borrowers facing the most restrictive borrowing terms that they have seen in several years. This, in turn, has triggered recession fears, both domestically and globally.

The Bank of England just announced that it needs at least two rate cuts to stem a serious slowdown. The music today is Mahler at his heaviest, not "Abbey Road" at its sweetest. "I read the news today oh, boy," Lennon had sung on the "Sgt. Pepper's" album, the echoing, resonating piano chords and voice underscoring a poignancy of the moment and sense of irony. How powerful these words still are today as we apply them to the news. The war in Iraq rages on, Bush's popularity continuing to plummet, car bombs, roadside bombs, ambushes killing or maiming our young boys. Candidate Barack Obama—he seems to be gaining a lot of steam and is raising enormous sums of money, though the safe money is on Hillary—argues in campaign stop after campaign stop that he is opposed to the war, will get the troops home under a "time table," and reminds us that unlike his opponents, he advised against the war when it was unpopular to do so. John McCain—his campaign close to being finished as he seems old and tired on the stump—stands by his conviction that this is a "just war;" that we need more troops, and that had he been president the "strategic mission" would have been much better thought out. Billions of dollars are going into Iraq, as the U.S. infrastructure begins to crumble, and health care is a privilege for those who are employed or have money. We will have to wait for history to be the final verdict on whether this adventure in Iraq was worth the enormous sacrifices that it has cost. If we are there to promote democracy in this country then we must be prepared to accept the democratic choices of these people: it is certainly possible that democracy might lead them to a Muslim extremist government that looks to Iran for inspiration. The safeguard that this does not happen is a constant presence in Iraq: indeed, McCain has said on the campaign trail that we might have to be there for 100 years. God willing, Iran does not occupy Iraq eventually, finally winning the war that they lost to Saddam.

We are in a quagmire. To defend the west from Iran will require a constant presence in Iraq. It is unlikely that the government will become strong enough to defend itself from the numerous enemies that seek to destroy any government that makes friends with the west. And yet what do we do? Leave? Leaving would result in a civil war of mass destruction and bloodshed.

Much of it will be directed at those who sympathized with the Americans. We invaded this country—taking on the full cost of it ourselves—when we could have had cooperation from the rest of the world in controlling Saddam. This cooperation might have led to forcing him from power, eventually, without the price tag of war. History will judge; I believe that it will not be kind to President Bush, as our dollar continues to tumble in value, the cost rising exponentially. I read the news today, oh boy.

The Abu Dhabi Government is providing a $7.5 billion infusion to beleaguered Citigroup to keep it afloat, as its survival is threatened due to the enormity of its losses in the mortgage market. Stocks continued their tumble on the news—the fear is that if this is happening to Citi, then how many other institutions might require similar assistance, and will it be there if they need it? The tentacles of fear are spreading through our economy and around the globe. The U.S. dollar is tumbling; the prices of Gold and Treasury bonds are soaring as investors seek safe havens and inflation protection. The headline on my news summary as I sat at my desk this morning is that, according to the U.S. Conference of Mayors, the value of U.S. homes in the United States will fall by $1.2 trillion, and at least 1.4 million homeowners will lose their homes to foreclosure in 2008. So, if this is true—and my God, I hope it isn't—what will be the fate of the country's banks if they are holding the paper on all of these foreclosures? Maybe these dire predictions are wrong, and the doomsayers are having their day. We have certainly seen that before.

Predictions of economic collapse are made, so that those making the predictions can reap some benefit from the government to fund this project or that. There have been newsletters prophesying all kinds of doom and gloom for decades—this attracts attention and sells subscriptions. There have been many economists that I have read over the years who, amidst the very best of times, were predicting that the very worst of times was just around the corner. For some of these people every economic slowdown or recession was the beginning of the end of all good times for the American economy. And each prediction in short order was rendered wrong, pessimistic, flatly incorrect as the resilient capitalism of America pushed through stagnation on its way to acceleration and innovation. Maybe these prognostications will be substantially exaggerated, based on trends, but not nearly as bad as stated. Maybe. But I have a feeling in the depths of my stomach that, this time, due to so much excess and greed, things might become as bad, even worse than what is being said. Perhaps, it is just my mood at the moment, and I am being completely subjective in my thinking. But I don't think so, though my mood reflects some sadness, born of melancholy—a loneliness and frustration that I cannot seem to get through the barriers in my mind that prevent me from reconnecting to Sue, and yet I so deeply want connection and intimacy.

I miss the tightness of my family before the boys went off to college in the years before meeting "M." Perhaps I fantasize; the truth is that I craved a closer intimacy with Sue than either of us was able to offer. We poured ourselves into our boys, then retreated back into ourselves. The separation from Sue was inevitable, part and parcel of the Costa Rican adventurer within me who just had to take a chance. So here I am. Free. But not free. Desiring freedom, perhaps the opportunity for a profound experience with a woman other than Sue, but still tethered to the institution of our marriage, struggling to re-enter the cocoon of its comforts, but thoroughly unable to point myself in that direction, let alone take the steps. Indeed, my mood colors my feelings about the economy and where it is headed, my intuition tells me that this time those economic doomsayers might have their once-in-a-lifetime chance of being right.

I stop to answer the phone. My cousin Melody had asked her husband to call me and let me know that she is resting comfortably following a successful lung transplant. It happened quickly, unexpectedly, no time to tell anyone, and it is a perfect fit. The prognosis, while guarded, is excellent. "Melody wanted you, Bruce, to be among the first that know," he tells me. "She wants you to know that you were right, you brought her luck." I take a deep breath, a bit stunned by the news, so deeply happy for her, but obviously concerned that she will recover well. "Tell her that I love her, and that I want to see her as soon as she is up and running, and I'm sure, knowing Melody, that this will be in no time at all. Tell her that I love her, and that her mom and my mom were there in that operating room" "I will buddy, I will," he says with fatigue but elation.

Life and death put everything into perspective. Melody entered that life-or-death surgery with wit, a disarming sense of humor, belief in God and the arrogance—her famous arrogance—that there was no way that she wouldn't make it. No doubt, the morning of the surgery she looked at the people she loves, inhaled the sky, the trees, whatever air could make it into her lungs, and so desperately wanted to have the opportunity—given to us by God—to be able to continue cherishing her days of life, to sift slowly through the diamonds, the rubies, the emeralds, the sapphires, the pearls that are the treasure chest of the days of our miraculous lives. It is so great to be alive! May I never, never take it for granted!

❒

It is early December and the politics are heating up as we move into the final month before the primary season. Early next month begins the Iowa Caucuses, and from there it will be a fast and furious season of primary after primary—the huge prize of Super Tuesday in early February when there will be 23 contests that some say should decide the nominees for the two parties—en route to an election that will replace in my judgment the most arrogant, least reflective, stubborn, perhaps worst president of all time.

Economic difficulties are appearing as wildfires dotting the landscape all across the country, and if we are not careful, if we do not react quickly and decisively by establishing the firebreaks that would contain these fires, they might become uncontainable as they threaten, metaphorically, villages all across the nation. The potential for thousands on thousands of loan defaults is clearly evident. And this would be horrible for the banks that underwrote by the truckload mortgages for homebuyers with poor credit, requiring little or nothing down in equity. But, it isn't bad enough that banks loaned money, and accepted appraisals for properties that were appreciating to the moon, they took their own money and invested in the debt obligations (collateralized debt obligations) that were backed by the these insanely speculative mortgages. What happens when the banks try to sell into the open market these bonds, which are backed by problem loans they are forced to foreclose on (what a dreadful situation, to own in your own portfolio the bonds whose collateral one must foreclose on)? Given that these investment vehicles are relatively new and not well-understood—and that there is not a highly competitive and efficient market for the trading thereof—the losses on this stuff might be enormous. And so I come back to President Bush. It is clearly evident to people in the investment community that these problems might become very serious, but the President refuses to take off his deregulation hat and get involved in tackling the problem. President Bush steadfastly refuses any government involvement—though if he could he'd have the government interfere in the abortion choice of what a woman does with her body, or seek to write into the constitution a ban on gay marriage—in the free market system. Well, the free market system needs some oversight, right about now!

The President needs to understand that the Citigroup situation—where they had to go to a Middle Eastern government to obtain the cash necessary for survival—is unlikely to be an isolated event.

Given the interrelatedness of our banking system, it is probable that many other institutions have made the same mistakes that occurred at Citi, and if such is the case, America is on the verge of giving away ownership of prized businesses, or risk seeing them fail. The President has steadfastly stood by his commitment to deregulation, even at a time when, in the early part of the decade, major utilities were on the verge of bankruptcy, because their cost of power had considerably exceeded the rates they could charge. Pacific Gas and Electric in California went bankrupt for that reason, and the State of California had to step in and purchase power under duress, agreeing to long-term contracts that we now know were enormously too expensive. They were too expensive because, as we now know, one of Mr. Bush's largest and wealthiest contributors—Enron—was illegally manipulating and controlling the market, the administration all the while adamant that they would not intervene in the free-market system and control the price of energy so that California and its largest utility might remain solvent.

Is it possible that this philosophy of deregulation as it pertained to the bankrupting cost of energy was influenced if not dictated by Enron, a company that used this deregulation to corner the market? It is more than possible. Is it possible that Mr. Bush and his closest advisors knew of the illegal practices of Enron, but turned away? It is very possible, I would argue. The unfolding mess in this country derives from the stubbornness, arrogance, shortsightedness, murky thinking of our leadership.

Although we do not live in a society based on the Confucian principles of filial piety, this Confucian notion that when the leader of a government—as is the case with the head of a family—loses his moral authority, the political structure breaks apart, remains accurate in understanding leadership. The President has squandered moral authority, and the result is mistrust of his policies domestically and internationally, a loss of confidence in the ability of the United States to act in accordance with its lofty principles. The dollar is in a freefall, but what would one expect when we are, virtually unilaterally, spending hundreds of billions of dollars on a war, while at the same time cutting taxes? The lack of confidence of the world in the leadership of the United States contributes to the further erosion of our currency, continuing to make the war more and more expensive in depreciating dollars. And as the value of our currency falls, we fall deeper and deeper into debt, depending on foreign governments, particularly China, to fund our dysfunctional form of capitalism. Isn't it ironic that the most socialist of socialist countries, China—and this is no criticism of China particularly—is now depended on to fund our debt so that we can continue to run this dysfunctional form of capitalism?

Everything is interconnected and interrelated. The declining value of our dollar is connected to the arrogance of our "go-it-alone" philosophy in Iraq—we cannot afford this war and the value of our currency reflects this. It seems that the priority of our leadership is to protect and increase the wealth of the wealthy and of its largest donors. How abhorrent is it that as our soldiers were waiting for orders to fight a war, our government was signing contracts with its largest donors to rebuild the country after the war? Meanwhile the infrastructure crumbles, and there is no healthcare insurance for those who are not employed or covered by a private plan; this tears at the fabric of fairness. The economic condition continues to decline because, in the absence of oversight to mitigate greed, anarchy prevailed. Amidst this leadership vacuum at home, the rest of the world loses confidence in our ability to manage our affairs competently, further eroding our global influence.

Next November cannot come soon enough from an economic point of view; we desperately need a change of leadership. Barack Obama, on the Democratic side, continues to gain popularity in the polls, and is a magnet for raising money. He is campaigning hard in Iowa, but the safe money remains on Hillary to win the nomination after Super Tuesday in February. There is, though, a hint that Obama—due to his strong field organization—could win in Iowa, which would be a huge setback for Clinton. Edwards also seems to have a chance in Iowa. But, again, Hillary's machine might be too formidable to conquer on a national level. I saw the Democratic debate a couple of days ago, and she is becoming shrill-sounding, as the Obama candidacy seems to be becoming something of a movement, his support no doubt stronger than she had expected. Her line, which she seems to be repeating frequently these days, is: "So you decide which makes more sense: entrust our country to someone who is ready on day one, or put America in the hands of someone with little national or international experience, who started running for president the day he arrived in the U.S. Senate." Fun stuff. On the Republican side, the former governor of Arkansas, Mike Huckabee, seems to be gaining a lot of popularity among the Christian right, with his anti-choice position, "down-home" folksiness, and Bible-Belt preacher style. Giuliani is slipping like a rock in the polls, while Mitt Romney remains within striking distance with his presidential style. John McCain is starting to be looked at all of a sudden, as Republicans kick the tires but are having a hard time finding a candidate who can speak to the whole nation, including independents.

It has been dry since last spring—virtually no rain, until this very minute. Low clouds obscure the view from my picture window, and rain is splashing across this window, as I look out over the top of my personal computer. I need the moisture to add some Yin to my parched Yang. I have been moody—Pisces, the water sign is said to be moody—but the moods have been dry, in need of moisture. Perhaps the tears might flow a little easier now. I welcome this rain, and could use a good solid few days of it. My throat hurts a bit, so I'll go have a cup of tea. Perhaps I'll splash a bit of Scotch into it. I haven't been sleeping very well; but I think that I will tonight.

❐

The space next to the Pets Unlimited, over on Fillmore street, a block from our family home, is having its annual Christmas tree sale. It is Saturday, and I walk amidst the trees, comforted with what the Bittersweet chocolate shop calls their "Classic," a euphoric, deeply rich cup of hot chocolate containing just the right amount of thick cream to mellow the decadence of the chocolate. I am evidence that a cup of chocolate can bring happiness, and I drink it in the kind of weather that I love during this time of year. There is a time and a place for bright, clear, blue skies; warm days when short sleeves are comfortable. I don't want that in late December, and it is amusing to me when, in giving his weather report this time of year, the weathercaster begins by saying that the weather news isn't so good: "It will be getting colder, the rain will be with us for a while, so everybody better have that umbrella ready to go." And at the end of the weather report, the newscasters in a jocular banter ask the weatherman to bring some better weather, so "we can get out those golf clubs." How foolish it all sounds to me. This is mid-December—get a life, will you? Enjoy it! Mid-Decembers only come around once a year, and it doesn't get any more beautiful than walking amidst the fantasy Victorian homes on a day when I am dressed for the chill, the coolness bringing life to my face, the drops of rain deflected by my plaid umbrella of green, white, black and brown, the sound a softness that brings an inner calm. It is that kind of day this afternoon, as I hold the hot chocolate in one hand, the umbrella in the other. The Christmas tree lot is full—just a week before Christmas, and trees are going fast. The taste of the chocolate meshes with the scent of pine as a boy of about seven says, "It's that one Daddy; that's the one I want; it is that one." The dad answers that, "This is the most beautiful tree I've ever seen; Santa will have a good time putting some presents under that one." This brings a glow to the boy's face, an enormous smile as he grabs the hand of his dad. It was only a few years ago that we'd walk with the boys to this lot, picking out a tree. We never picked out the biggest or most ostentatious tree, because it wasn't supposed to be a Christmas tree, but a Hanukah bush. But we couldn't let the season pass without the smell of pine in our front room, and some gifts under the bush. The boys will be home from college for winter break in a few days, and I miss them deeply today. From the tree lot, I continue up Washington Street and enter Alta Plaza park.

The rain continues to fall as I walk up the steps to the first level of the park, then along a path to the next level of steps, which leads me to a bench overlooking the city of San Francisco to the south.

The rain lightens, almost to the point of a mist, but still hard enough to keep the umbrella open as I move from the bench to some steps above Clay Street. I lean my back against the wall next to the steps, taking in the picturesque row of Victorians—handsome homes, a palette of colors, some ornately painted in a variety of colors, others less intricately colorful, but no less aesthetic in design. This city at its best is captivating; the homes built as works of art, first, places to live second. And, on a day like today, as I look above the variegated facades of the homes below me, the city stretching out in the mist, San Francisco is a fantasy, a place that lies behind a "hidden door" that a "lucky few" are able to discover. As I sit on these steps, my back against the wall, the rain remaining steady but gentle, a woman—maybe late 50s, a few years older than myself—walks past me as she brings her dog out of the park. "Wouldn't you rather be inside by a fire?" she asks. "It's miserable out here." Slowly, calmly, I shake my head, "No; enjoying the beautiful day." "Gonna go home and get out of this soup," she answers. "Don't catch yourself a cold," and on she goes. Then a few minutes later, as I remain on these steps, enjoying the winter light and mist, the colors of the day, a rather good-looking man with jet black hair, a scarf wrapped around his neck slows down as he walks up the stairs into the park, saying, "Beautiful day, isn't it? A lot of people wouldn't call this beautiful, but it's absolutely gorgeous; don't you agree?" "You're so right," I respond. "Actually, it doesn't get much more beautiful than this." He nods his approval, stops on the steps for a moment, takes in the view above the rooftops toward the city below, brings in a deep breath, then continues on. "Enjoy it," he utters; "You do the same," I respond.

After a few minutes, I get up and begin walking toward our family home, just a few blocks away, down Washington Street. I am missing the companionship of our black lab, Lucky. Seeing people with their dogs, I decide that I'll go take him for a walk. Lucky resides with Sue, but of course I get my visitation rights. I call Sue to tell her that I'm coming over to take him for a walk, but there is no answer. Hopefully, when I ring the doorbell, there will be that bark. And indeed that is the case. I ring the doorbell several times, but no answer. And then I call Sue again—no answer again. I unlock the door—I am careful to observe Sue's privacy, but clearly she isn't home—and I am greeted by Lucky, jumping all over me. His collar and leash are next to the door. "Want to go for a walk?" I say, as he continues to jump all over me. "Walkies? Walkies?" I utter, in my highest dog voice. "Want to go get a treat?" He continues to jump all over me. He's ready to go now, and as I turn to open the door, I see above the mantle of the fireplace in the front room, three stockings. One is for Michael, another for Jonathan, the third for Sue. It hits me like a ton of bricks, like a dagger in the heart. There is no stocking here for me; I don't live here anymore. For Sue to put a stocking up for me would be too painful a reminder for her that I am not in this house. She does not omit the stocking to cause me grief—what is she supposed to do? She must move on, attempt to come to terms with our situation the best way that she can. I understand this. Indeed I do. But all the understanding in the world—and there is no blame here; I try my hardest to understand the gap that separates us, but to comprehend a rational reason that we go through this does not prevent the overwhelming sense of being alone at this moment. I am outside walking on the wet sidewalk—Lucky looking not too pleased that he has to be taken for a walk in the rain, spoiled guy that he is—feeling homeless, as I pass the Christmas tree lot. The boys will be here in a few days; indeed, I'll see them soon.

❐

It is January 1, 2008, the first evening of the new year, and so much of life feels very far away from me. My boys—home for their winter break—are staying at our house a few blocks away, and they feel so far, far away. We have been spending precious time together during these holidays, and have shared some sublimely sweet moments, inherent in them a recognition of the depths of our bond, our closeness and affections. But at this moment of this first night of '08, as I sit overlooking a very dark San Francisco Bay, their lives seem so very far away from me. I desire in the "living room of my thoughts" a couple of "big overstuffed chairs" to be occupied by the presence of Michael and Jonathan, but there are no such chairs in this place of thought and reverie, a place that feels spartan and deficient at the moment. The boys are moving, inexorably, into their adult lives; we love each other deeply, but they feel so far away, beyond my reach, in an orbit where the gravitational pull has lessened, their orbit becoming further away. This is an inevitable process of separation and individuation—it is evidence that we have raised them well. They separate and pursue their journey with love in their hearts, compassion for others, an understanding that they are deeply loved and possessing the capability to love deeply. I understand that, even if I were living at home, these feelings of their orbit becoming "further and further away" would produce a sense of sadness and loss, leaving empty spaces in our lives that our marriage would have to expand to fill. But our marriage has not expanded, it has become further and further away. Instead of one empty nest that a married couple might fill with the precious straw of their past, and the soft cotton of their new intimacy, we have two empty nests that we must furnish individually—alone and apart—with the trinkets or soft pieces of cloth from our time alone. I furnish my "empty nest" with the writing of this book, and I know that Sue does the best she can to find peace in a world that is foreign and unexpected. Indeed, I know it would all hurt, even if Sue and I were together; but we are not together, and the fact that their orbit is becoming further and further away—that they are not sitting in those "overstuffed chairs" in the living room of my mind—hurts deeply as I sit here tonight.

I reflect on those moments sweet, precious, and vulnerable when—it might be Jonathan sitting me down and telling me that he just has to play this song for me; or Michael, reluctant as he is to ever give a big bear hug, punching me on the arm, the big blue eyes laughing and mocking me with love, then the derisive thin-lipped smile, followed by, "How are you Bruiser, I've missed you?"— their Dad means "everything in the world" to them. I cannot think of a better feeling than the recognition of their love, and, though they may not know it, I drink in this feeling whenever it occurs. They are not, though, emotionally dependent young men, and I am so appreciative of this. I seek to observe a boundary that allows them to live their lives, without their feeling a need to attend to whatever empty spaces might exist in my life. I am grateful that they are young men with passion for the adventures yet to come, eager to pursue their artistic dreams, to quest for their own sense of legend. I'll let these spaces occur as they must; there will surely be other times of contentment. But, for now, there is a pervasive sense that "everything feels so very far away." I am thankful that I am not numb; I am sad at the moment, but I have never been more alive.

Tomorrow, January 2, would be my mom's 74th birthday. And I feel the void of her absence acutely. She feels very far away from me tonight, as far away as the darkened bay and unilluminated bridge off in the distance. Tomorrow, I go to my office with zero commissions for the year. It all starts again at zero. This will be my

25th year of starting at zero, and the whole notion of another year of financial undertakings, while I am quite skilled and productive, seems heavy, and far, far away from me tonight. I just finished listening to John Lennon's first album post-Beatles—the one where he and Yoko are lying in a field together. It is raw with emotion, highly personal, but charged with such honesty, sadness, anger, loneliness, disillusionment, and soul-searching intensity that it shocks one into being awake. In the song "God" he sings that: "God is a concept by which we measure our pain." And he goes on to deny belief in anything but himself. From the depths of his aching soul he chants, implores, repudiates:

I don't believe in magic;
I don't believe in I-Ching;
I don't believe in Bible;
I don't believe in Tarot;
I don't believe in Hitler;
I don't believe in Jesus;
I don't believe in Kennedy;
I don't believe in Buddha;
I don't believe in Mantra;
I don't believe in Gita;
I don't believe in Yoga;
I don't believe in Kings;
I don't believe in Elvis;
I don't believe in Zimmerman;
I don't believe in Beatles;
I just believe in me.

He is in search, ultimately, of quiet, as he struggles to tear away from his identity all brands, labels, false images, oppressive ideologies. It is not the words, particularly, or the sense of nihilism implied that touches me so deeply tonight as I listen to this song. It is the raw honesty, the quest to be alive and feel, the inherent sadness that affects and touches my soul in a hypnotic way. And then in another song, "Look at Me," he sounds beatific as he sings,

Look at me;
Who am I supposed to be;
Who am I supposed to be;
Look at me;
What am I supposed to be;
What am I supposed to be?

And then on to the song, "Hold on John," his voice penetrating deeply beneath the surface as he seeks a calm:

Hold on John, John hold on
It's gonna be alright
You're gonna win the fight;
Hold on world, world hold on
It's gonna be alright,
You're gonna see the light.

And then, of course, the song, "Love":

Love is real, real is love,
Love is feeling, feeling love,
Love is wanting, to be loved.
Love is touch, touch is love,
Love is reaching, reaching love,
Love is asking, to be loved
Love is you,
You and me,
Love is knowing,
We can be.
Love is free, free is love,
Love is living, living love,
Love is needing to be loved.

The texture with which he sings this song is heartbreaking; and his voice is sheer bliss, even more so because of such vulnerability. As he sings this song the piano chords reverberate to his touch, layers of emotion aching to be expressed. And as I wind down to prepare for the first day of the new year, I ache to love and be loved. I am sad, though, because at the moment it all feels so far away.

It is the evening of January 3, 2008 and the journey to elect the next president of the United States has begun in earnest. I have just finished watching the final returns of today's Iowa Caucus, listening as a visibly tired, slightly hoarse, fluidly eloquent Barack Obama describes his victory as a "defining moment in history." A few months ago it had seemed a foregone conclusion that the "Big Clinton Machine" would glide through the primary season en route to Hillary's "coronation" next summer as the first woman nominee of a major party for the presidency. She had a significant number of "super delegates" already pledged to her, and there seemed a sense of inevitability about her. However, in the past month or so, but particularly in the most recent couple of weeks, it has become evident that there is a movement in place, a beautifully formed Hawaiian wave that Obama appears to be gracefully surfing. The wave is clearly a rejection of what has happened in this country during the past seven years, but there is an aspect to it that feels much deeper than solely a rejection of the status quo. There is a "power," a kind of "soul force," an empowered urgency that every person who desperately wants change in this country has the ability to act and bring about that change.

There is a charisma, charm, eloquent magnetism to Barack Obama—he is the gifted surfer apparently capable of riding this wave. The movement at the moment, the public mood behind this emerging "volcanic activity" that is propelling Obama, is a willingness to embrace an "authentic agent of change" over the known quantity of experience. Clearly, there is a sense that this country has been led astray, has been told lies—and there is a sense of developing trepidation as people look to their futures and those of their children. The Obama factor, his clarity, freshness, lack of Washington experience, the color of his skin—represents a definite departure from our political past. It remains to be seen, though, whether this wave continues to form and roll all the way to the shore—continuing to be shaped with energy from the depths below the surface—or if it will break sharply, expunging its energy, the selection process moving back toward the industrial power of Mrs. Clinton. And it remains to be seen to what degree Mr. Obama is skilled enough to ride this wave all the way to the shore.

Barack Obama's winning of his party's nomination—and, no doubt about it, it would mark a defining moment in history—will require a social movement that comes along, perhaps, once in at least a generation, maybe longer. And it will also require the ability of a master—an ability that also may occur only once in a generation or longer—to draw in the energy from its source, all the while harnessing it like the conductor of a great symphony or surfing it all the way to the shore. I was impressed as I heard him give his short victory speech tonight. Speaking with an intonation reminiscent in moments of Bobby Kennedy or Dr. King, Obama declared this the moment when we tore down barriers that have divided us for too long. When we rallied people of all parties and ages to a common cause. When we finally gave Americans who've never participated in politics a reason to stand up and do something."

This gifted orator, words calming and more inspiring than anything that I have heard since the great, assassinated men of the '60s, went on to offer a vision of hope. Speaking as though he were a lightening rod for change, Obama looked to convert America: "For many months, we've been teased, even derided for talking about hope. Hope is that thing inside us that insists, despite all evidence to the contrary, that something better awaits us if we have the courage to reach for it, and to work for it, and to fight for it."

The Republican side of the Iowa caucus was won by the former Governor of Arkansas, Mike Huckabee. Languishing in the single digits in the polls until very recently, Huckabee began to play very well in Iowa, his folksy, friendly, country style of social conservatism striking a harmonious tone. The Conservative Mitt Romney, former governor of Massachusetts, placed second. John McCain spent very little time in Iowa, and is banking on a strong showing in New Hampshire in a few days to keep his campaign alive. Down and out just a few months ago—virtually deplete of campaign money to continue—McCain has been seeing a surge of money come into his coffers to compete in New Hampshire. Polls show him likely to finish second in that state, Romney the probable winner. I cannot see Huckabee having a message inclusive enough to win the nomination, though he'll play well, no doubt, in parts of the mid-west and the southern Bible Belt, putting a lot of pressure on the other candidates to raise money. Giuliani—there always appears a meanness to his demeanor—drew virtually no support in Iowa, banking that he'll do well on Super Tuesday in early February. A one-time likely nominee of his party, he is languishing at the bottom of the pack. Huckabee's win in Iowa was impressive, though. He was vastly outspent by his opponents, and came away the winner. Grinning widely on his victory he told his supporters, "People really are more important than the purse, and what a great lesson for America to learn." The times they definitely "are a changing"; it is going to be interesting to see how it all unfolds.

It is the evening of January 9, and last night went the way Hillary Clinton and John McCain hoped that it would. Obama had gone in to the New Hampshire primary riding high from his Iowa win—some polls had shown him to have a four- or five-point lead—but was defeated in a come-from-behind victory for Mrs. Clinton. Buoyed by the support of women—who apparently had not come sufficiently to her side in Iowa—Clinton received an injection of energy into her campaign, and no doubt money will continue to flow. The Democratic race is evolving into a contest for the ages: a battle between the first would-be female nominee of a major party for the White House, and the first person of African American descent. The drama is captivating. From a raucous, celebratory New Hampshire campaign headquarters, Mrs. Clinton told her supporters that she came to them "with a very full heart." "Over the last week," she said, "I listened to you, and in the process, I found my own voice. Now, let's give America the kind of comeback that New Hampshire has given me." A little while after Mrs. Clinton's speech, Obama emerged to congratulate her, and his message was upbeat: "I am still fired up and ready to go," Obama said, adding: "A few weeks ago, no one could have imagined what we would do tonight in New Hampshire." He went on to say that he was ready to take the country in a fundamentally new direction, his comments interrupted by the chanting of his supporters of, "We want change, We want change."

It had been a record turnout in New Hampshire, and the night revived the hopes of Republican John McCain, seven months after he was on the verge of putting his "straight-talk express" bus in the garage, barely enough gas to ignite the spark plugs. Tapping into the independent spirit of New Hampshire, McCain bested Mitt Romney (who has spent millions of dollars of his own money in hopes of getting a fast start and winning Iowa and New Hampshire, second-place finishes in each) by about five points, Huckabee finishing a distant third. "Tonight, we sure showed them what a comeback looks like," a grinning McCain told supporters as they chanted, "Mac is back! Mac is back!"

As we come to the end of this month of January, the political battles build in intensity, amidst a backdrop of fear over the economy. Mrs. Clinton won a caucus in Nevada, then campaigned and won in Florida and Michigan, states uncontested by Obama and other candidates because their delegates had been disqualified, due to the states violating Democratic party rules preventing them from moving up their primaries to January. Obama won the primary in South Carolina, and in so doing was dismissed by the very partisan Bill Clinton, who compared his victory to Jesse Jackson's victory in that state. The comment was not well received by the general electorate—at least that is what the polls say—because it was interpreted as being "mean-spirited," condescending, and to some, having "racist undertones." I can't see racism in the remark; but in his fierce loyalty to his wife, he may be doing more harm than good at the moment. Politics will be very interesting next week, when something like 22 states hold their Democratic primaries. Several months ago, one would have thought that this would be the week when the "Clinton Machine" waltzed to victory, virtually securing the nomination for the presidency. Clearly, that is unlikely to happen for her at this stage of the campaign, and to the contrary, it could push Obama into a commanding lead. The way I see it, this battle will go down to the bitter end in June, perhaps continuing all the way to the convention. We shall see. The month has been a pretty good one for McCain, who went on to win the South Carolina primary, a contest that many thought would go to Huckabee. Romney finally won a primary in his home state of Michigan; but there is starting to appear a kind of inevitability or invincibility to McCain's candidacy. Again, we shall see.

All of this, though, is occurring against a troubled electorate. The economy is taking center stage on the campaign trail, polls showing for the first time that it is becoming even more important than the war in Iraq. A lot of talk has been about recession. Are we in a recession? Are we going to enter a recession? We may or may not be technically in a recession, but to investors watching the stock market plummet, homeowners witnessing a dramatic loss of value in their homes, consumers heavy in debt and afraid of losing their jobs, the technical definition does not matter very much: it sure feels like a recession. Further evidence of this is that the Federal Reserve just cut the Federal Funds rate by 75 basis points (three-quarters of one percent) in one fell swoop, as large a one-time cut as I can ever remember. There is a lot of fear out there, as consumer confidence numbers continue to plummet for current conditions and future expectations. Amidst this fear, investors are selling some very sound stocks, stocks that have no relation at all to the housing troubles. The money is going into short-term treasury bonds, pushing those interest rates down significantly. And the losses are continuing to mount at financial institutions. The other day I learned that my own company, Wachovia, had to take a write-down of $1 billion for some commercial loans gone bad. Commercial loans? These are supposed to on the safer side of lending. If it is this bad on the commercial side ($1 billion is an enormous sum of money), what will my company's books look like if the subprime fiasco continues to get out of hand?

This stuff is starting to get to me tonight—and it doesn't help that Sue and I must come to some understanding of the state of our marriage, where it is going, what must be done. I must move beyond this limbo where I cannot go forward toward intimacy or backward to an ideal place in our past that exists only in memory. We communicate little, but I do love her to my soul. What to do about that? Again, I do not know. Or, perhaps I do know, but am so afraid to lose our connection. If we cannot remain in marriage, I so much want to be the best of friends. I love my family deeply. And yet, the barrier to returning to my marriage remains almost impenetrable. I need to lighten up a bit; I'm turning off this machine and will put on some Larry David, "Curb Your Enthusiasm" re-runs.

❒

As the country prepares for the big political extravaganza of Super Tuesday in a couple of days, the biggest football game of the season—the Super Bowl game matching one of the great teams of all time, the 18-0 New England Patriots against the New York Giants, a team that entered this game as a wild card into the playoffs, not winning its division—took center stage. This game was a rematch of the final game of the regular season. In that contest, the Patriots won 38-35 to complete the first perfect regular season since the 1972 Miami Dolphins. Going into this game, the Patriots were favored by 12 points. As I write this, on Sunday night, February 3, I ponder that I may have witnessed today the best football game I have ever seen.

In saying this I take into full account the game I attended in Miami in 1989 with my good friend Craig Jones. Sue was pregnant with Jonathan at that time; so when I was selected, as a 49er season ticket holder, in the lottery to go to the Super Bowl in Miami that year, she good-naturedly suggested that I take my best friend. Craig was overwhelmed with excitement when I offered the ticket to him, and in a week or so we were off on a charter entitled the "Tail Gate in the Sky"—for 49er fans to attend the game in Miami. I still have that T-shirt, given to us when we landed in Miami, that says, "I survived the Tail Gate in the Sky." I tried the shirt on a few days ago when I happened on it—once again throwing clothes to the floor as I frustratingly search for a coveted shirt that I was hoping to wear but was not able to find, and this happens all the time, not being able to find clothes that I know I have but cannot locate, the drawers a complete mess (my goodness this gets me upset)—and it was a bit snug. I made a mental note that I would give it to Michael or Jonathan, telling them the great story behind it, the party we had in the air en route to one of the great football games of all time.

In this game, Joe Montana and Jerry Rice were absolutely "otherworldly." The Niners were being slightly outplayed through most of the game—the Bengals on the verge of winning a Super Bowl against the favored 49ers, avenging the loss they took against the Niners in Detroit in 1982, from which the Bill Walsh–coached team would go on to be considered the "Team of the '80s." A gentle mist of rain had been falling through much of the game, but by the late Fourth Quarter, when the oh-so-cool Joe Montana joined the huddle after the TV time out, the team losing 17-13 and buried deep in its own territory on about the eight yard line with less than two minutes to play, the sky had cleared, the heavens afforded an unobstructed view of a magician quarterback and a master wide receiver at work. Football aficionados have heard the story: With less than two minutes to play and about 92 yards to go, needing a major comeback on a stage watched by much of the sporting world—the Bengals on the verge of winning their first Super Bowl—Montana observes funny man, John Candy, in one of the nearby seats. As "cool as a cucumber" he announces this sighting to the huddle—"Hey, there's John Candy"—and suddenly a "lightness of spirit," an easing of the tension, moved through the offensive unit. The drive is now legendary. Precision pass after precision pass to Jerry Rice—several fingertip sideline catches to go out of bounds and stop the clock, which were simply astounding—punctuated by some clutch, high-stepping running by Roger Craig, brought the Niners to inside the Bengals' 50-yard line, with just under a minute left to play. The vibration in the stadium was pure electricity—I looked over at Craig and his jaws were tight, and mine must have looked exactly the same, so much did we not want to fly home losers of this game—and I was spellbound by the cool, precise, unflappable way that Montana was running this offense. I was getting dizzy from the tension—putting my finger on the pulse in my neck to make sure my heart was beating properly—and Montana (indeed the whole offensive unit) were ice cool. With my binoculars I looked across the field at the Cincinnati sideline, where head coach Sam Wyche (he had coached

Joe Montana while with the 49ers and knew first hand what this guy was capable of doing) was a wound-up ball of nerves, his face twitching. No doubt he felt a sense of foreboding—after all, this was Joe Montana in a clutch moment that he was up against. The 49ers have moved deeper into Bengals territory now, just a handful of seconds left. Montana drops back to pass—we were seated close to the action, our seats behind the mayor of San Francisco, Art Agnos—Montana has time, the offensive linemen picking up their assignments effectively, and finds the so-talented, ever-consistent John Taylor cutting into the end zone. Touchdown 49ers! Touchdown 49ers! Touchdown 49ers! It was a night that Craig and I will never forget; and we will be forever bound by that experience.

Indeed, I must say the game tonight rivaled that one, and perhaps even exceeded it, if such is possible. I can only imagine what it must have been like to have seen it live. The first three quarters of the game were a pitched defensive battle; usually a defensive battle is not filled with thrills and excitement, but this one had a kind of "defensive tension" that for me was every bit as exciting as an open offensive game. The teams combined for only 10 points during these first three quarters, the Patriots leading 7-3 entering the final quarter. New York finally scored their first touchdown to take a 10-7 lead. New England eventually responded with a touchdown of their own, to take a 14-10 lead, with about two-and-a-half minutes left to play. Then, perhaps the greatest highlight in Super Bowl history occurred.

Faced with third down and five yards to go from their own 44 yard line, a little over a minute left to play, Giants quarterback Eli Manning somehow stays on his feet to avoid what appeared to be a certain sack, completing a 32-yard pass to wide receiver David Tyree, who made a leaping catch, pinning the ball on his helmet. I'll never know how he made that catch, clutching the ball with one hand against his helmet while being pummeled. And the get-away by Manning at the beginning of the play was equally impossible. When that happened I knew it was the Giants' game, and that we would see one of the great Super Bowl upsets. Sometimes it just seems—in football as in life—that fate takes over. Four plays later, New York wide receiver Plaxico Burress caught the winning touchdown, just 35 seconds remaining.

This had been a football game for the ages. And afterwards, about an hour ago, I called my good friend Phil Barbieri—so many games we had watched together out at Candlestick before his cancer diagnosis—to get his comments about the game. It has been a while since we have spoken, and he promised to keep me informed with regard to his progress in this battle. Last time we spoke, he was optimistic about winning this fight—the chemo appeared to be shrinking the tumor and he was feeling strong enough to keep on fighting. His answering service came on, and I left a message. "Please call me, Phil," I offered, "What did you think of that game?"

❐

The Super Tuesday primaries have occurred and there is a sense of inevitability with regard to the candidacy of Senator John McCain. Facing long odds just a few months ago—the intelligent betting money would have been placed on someone else, Romney or Giuliani—McCain followed up on his big wins in New Hampshire and South Carolina by taking more than half the states that voted on this day, including big prizes, California, New York, and New Jersey. Huckabee—his anti-abortion stance and intention to teach creationism as a theory equal to Darwinism well received in the Bible Belt—took all of the southern states that voted on this day. He was successful in Georgia, Arkansas, Alabama, Louisiana and Kansas. Romney, his fortunes beginning to fade, won just enough states to stay in the race, perhaps, but it was a showing far less than he was hoping to achieve. But, again, the big prizes and momentum belonged to McCain. Like a football team down 17-0 in the third quarter, he has put together an efficient message and a strong offense, pulling well ahead, perhaps something like 27-17. The drama of his comeback is captivating. But even more captivating to me is the Democratic race. Going into Super Tuesday, Obama won the coveted support of Senator Ted Kennedy, by far the most important endorsement of the campaign.

His support had been seriously sought by both candidates, and it was with the kind of eloquence that only Ted Kennedy can deliver that he described Obama as a once-in-a-generation politician, comparing his charisma and vision to that of his slain brothers. Super Tuesday, though, did not decide the Democratic battle in any way—the drama intensifying as the candidates prepare to battle all the way to the convention. One must, I think, give Obama the edge for this reason: There was a sense of entitlement that Mrs. Clinton had carried with her prior to the primaries, and along with this came a feeling of virtual certainty and inevitability that she would become the first female candidate for the presidency from a major party. There is not inevitability about her candidacy now, and her machine that had been thought to be invincible has, like the British proudly marching in their colorful uniforms through the center of America's colonial towns, been vulnerable to sabotage by the extremely well-organized revolutionary resistance. She may yet win, and she certainly has shown her self to be very tough, like a prize fighter, absorbing stinging jabs, only to bounce off the ropes and land some telling shots. But she does appear to be up against a movement that seems to be larger than the Obama candidacy—she seems to be struggling not only against Obama, but against a force for change that keeps moving him forward, like a tidal current or a wind at his back.

This race for the presidency has become increasingly dramatic, historical, epic. I talk to Michael and Jonathan as often as I can about the times in which we live and the incredible political race that is unfolding. I tell them to be aware that they are living through a period that historians will write about and debate, much as we do now of the '60s. My words are not lost on them; they are very involved, interested, engaged in the unfolding.

Valentine's Day

February 14th, 2008

It is the evening of Valentine's Day, and I struggled emotionally today. I had a sense that it would be difficult, but it was even more than I had imagined. Sue had called me at work to say that she had a card for me, and I was welcome to come over and pick it up. And I wished her a "happy Valentine's Day," telling her that I had something for her as well. I brought her a heart-shaped box of Godiva truffles, a little note attached that she will "always embody the sweetness that is at the heart of Valentine's Day." I also delivered a note to my friend, Gwen Jones, thanking her for her "unconditional kindness, and being so willing to hear me in my moodiness and sadness." I also wanted to let her know that she, sometimes, seems wise beyond her years, and that it is often comforting to be in her quiet presence during tumultuous times for me.

After dropping off the card to Gwen, I went to the house to bring the gift and card to Sue, receiving hers, which had a simple but heartfelt message: "I wish you a happy Valentine's Day." We hugged platonically, our arms around each other's back, but our bodies several inches from touching. I delivered the box of truffles, which she opened, taking one and offering another to me. We enjoyed the chocolate surge of pleasure for a brief moment, and then I was out the door, down the steps, a chill wind blowing into my face as I walk down Broadway Street to the corner of Buchanan, and then up to my apartment where I put my head down on my desk—my forehead touching the top of the personal computer with which I now write—and began to cry. I love Sue, but as I have said many times through the journey of these pages, we each seem to be unwilling, unable, to overcome an invisible, yet 50-foot-high barrier to our marriage. In the moment of these tears I feel so powerless to change the circumstances of my life, frustratingly feeling that I cannot move forward, but the past receding in the rearview mirror. And I remind myself of that wise prayer: "God, please grant me the serenity to accept what I cannot change, the courage to change what I can, and the wisdom to know the difference." I am powerless, and amidst these tears I surrender to this sense of powerless and to God's will.

The tears clear for a moment, but return again when I open the Valentine's Day card that Sue and I used to pass back to each other every Valentine's Day. I had given her this huge, bright orange card—perhaps a foot and a half in length—the Valentine's Day before the summer that we were married, back in 1982. On the front of the card was written, "You've got what it takes to be my Valentine." and then one opens it up to read "and you know how damn fussy I am!" The following Valentine's Day—February 1983—the first of our marriage, Sue wrote these words, surrounding a big heart: "Bruce, this is a recycled Valentine! You gave it to me first and now I'm giving it to you. Maybe we can pass it back and forth each year, and as our love continues to grow so will the writing on this card. All my love, Sue."

Indeed, we did pass this card back and forth throughout the course of our marriage. The card is an historical record—a priceless, organic, living, breathing chronicle of our souls—of the love we shared and will always possess in our DNA.

Reading through the card is difficult, but I do it. On February 14, 1987, Sue wrote to me:

To my husband, I thank God for all he has given me, a wonderful husband and a beautiful, healthy baby. Michael and you are the most important people in my life. We are a real family now and I love you both so much that I can feel my heart burst with joy.

The following Valentine's Day, 1988, I wrote to Sue:

To the finest wifely this planet has ever known. Each year you outdo yourself with kindness, patience, love and generosity. The gentle touch with which you are helping to raise our gifted little boy has an influence only matched by the beauty of our child. Perhaps next year, at this time we will be ready to receive Michael's mate, but from now through eternity my love is yours. Love, Hubbs

Then in 1989, a few months before Jonathan was born—a stomach that little Michael called a "bumpy," she wrote to me:

What better place to be for Valentine's Day than this beautiful island of Maui, with my handsome husband, my little boy Michael and my "bumpy." The other night as we sat on the beach looking at the stars and thinking about God, I could feel God all around us. I know that I am really blessed to have such a wonderful husband as you. Love, Sue

And then the following year, February 14, 1990, the Valentine's Day following the Loma Prieta earthquake, the trying, difficult period in which we moved to Mill Valley, back to San Francisco, then back to Mill Valley again, all within a couple of months, Jonathan just several months old, I wrote:

> *In turbulent times and quiet times, through periods of color and times of change, you remain the same; your peaceful, loving, charming and heavenly kindness are the best gift God can give to a man and his children. Love you for all eternity, Hubbs*

And the Valentine's Day after that, 1991, Sue wrote to me:

> *Bruce, this has been a year that has been difficult, but I feel as though much emotional growth has come out of it all. We are growing as a couple and a family. I know I don't say this enough, but I just want you to know that I could never think of spending my life with anyone but you. I love you as my husband, friend, lover, and a father of my boys. I love the philosopher in you, and the writer, and yes even the broker. Love, Sue*

It is so hard, but I read on. Life takes its twists and turns, sometimes robbing innocence and our best intentions like a thief in the night. Does God guide us? To what extent does our free will interfere with God's will? Is the whole damn universe a place where we suffer alone? I feel so alone as I read these words from February 14, 1993:

Dear Husband, with the demands and responsibilities of our children and our parents, it is easy to feel like "the sandwiched generation." Just remember that my love for you is always a constant, and it is a love crested from the heart. Next month my parents will be celebrating their 50th anniversary, and in 40 years, I know we will. Love, Sue

After we moved into a new home in 1998, I wrote to Sue:

I'm looking out the window at this beautiful view of the bay, the grey clouds thick and low above the earthy bridge, and I'm thinking about the incredible gift God has given me in a woman of such radiant inner beauty, strong, compassionate and kind; so pure in her morality, such a mentor for her children, such a loving wife. The gift of this family fulfills the dreams of all past lives, and I pray that we will all be together for eternity. I'll miss you very much the next week when you are in Colorado. Happy Valentine's Day. Love, Babbs, Hubbs, Bruce

February 14, 2000 was the first Valentine's Day following the passing of my mom. I wrote to Sue:

This is the first Valentine's Day of the new millennium. It has been the most painful year of my life, since the last Valentine's Day. I would never have thought that a year later my mom would be gone. It has been excruciating painful for you to hold this family together, but you do an amazing job. While there isn't much romance in our lives right now, and I feel more in pain than romantic, I still love you from the depths of my being. We will be in love together for all of this life and, God willing, for all of eternity. May we next Valentine's Day look back on a year of goodness, love and simple pleasures. All of my love, Bruce

The year before The Troubles, February 14, 2004, I struggle to come to terms with the romance that was missing, but love Sue nonetheless:

Dear Sue,

Thank you for the love that you give me. And even though times are not all that romantic these days, my sleep hang-ups, the teenagers, your early bedtime, my grouchiness, as I approach 50, please know that you are my soulmate—and I love you very much and forever.

And then the final entry on this card; it was written February 14, 2006 during the torturous time following my meeting of "M":

Dear Susan,

This Valentine's Day is not light; it is not filled with the aroma of roses and chocolates; there is not the sweet fragrance of floral perfume. Rather, it is made of the heaviness of two hearts weighed by pain and anguish, struggling to hold on to one another, trying to survive as one—despite unforeseen, unexpected, and incomprehensible obstacles. But please know, my dear Susan that the love that I feel for you at the moment is greater than the sum of all these greetings. I'm sorry for the pain that you have felt, sorry for the sadness that I didn't mean to cause, sorry for all the tears, mine and yours. Please, please know, though, that I do love you. I do love you. All my love, Bruce

New York City

February 19th, 2008

It is Tuesday evening and I am in the cozy hotel room of the place that I like to stay in New York City—the Essex House, where the beds provide sumptuous sanctuary from the difficult emotional moments that often alter the comfort of sleep for me—having come here to meet Jonathan and take advantage of a rare opportunity to see my beloved hockey team, the San Jose Sharks, play the New York Rangers in Madison Square Garden. Jonathan is almost as big a Sharks fan as myself—I introduced my boys to hockey at young ages, and they devoured the sport, not just loving hockey but becoming hooked on the teal-clad boys from San Jose, the menacing Sharks logo perhaps permanently in their bloodstream—and he hasn't had an opportunity to see the Sharks this year at all, the price one pays for going to a far-off New York College. It is a rare event for the Sharks to play in New York City—the schedule is structured such that they only play there every few years—and for the contest to fall on Presidents' Weekend was a gift from above for a Father and Son weekend in one of the world's great cities.

The game was played Sunday afternoon, so I met Jonathan late Saturday afternoon at Penn Station, from which we jumped into a cab and made our way to the Stage Deli, filling up on chicken matzo ball soup—I simply cannot find, for the life of me, a good Matzo ball soup in San Francisco—pastrami sandwiches, washed down by a New York–style cream soda. Jonathan hasn't been eating well at college—he doesn't like the food very much, so he doesn't eat as much as he should, and he is looking a bit thin—but he had no trouble putting down everything in front of him. My spirit mellowed, a soft warmth working its way from my stomach and easing the palpitations of the heart, as we sat there together eating at the deli, eventually ordering—but not finishing—a piece of cream pie that was gigantic but delicious.

We went back to the hotel and watched movies together—Jonathan in my midst for a whole couple of days, my not having to worry about where he was at the moment—the wounds of Valentine's Day easing as I started to doze off on my bed, my son telling me to hush as I apparently started to snore. "You never stay awake for a movie, I don't think I've ever seen you stay awake for a movie," he admonished, as I quickly returned to full consciousness, trying to catch up with the "jewel heist" that had just taken place on the screen. I did catch up with the plot, and by the movie's end I was right there at the finish line—thinking that I'd seen the whole film, save for a moment's lapse—only to be informed by my son that I'd have to see the film again, that I'd missed way too much. I assured him that I had only dozed off for a second. "No way Dad!" he answered. "You were snoring off and on for more than a half an hour." "No way," I answered. "I caught up with the plot instantly. I probably dozed for not more than a moment." "Believe what you will, Dad," he offered. "You missed at least a third of the movie." "You're a tough movie policeman, a tough movie cop," I responded, jumping over onto his bed, holding his arms down. I went on to take a long bath, and when I came out, he had fallen asleep with a schoolbook on his chest. Goodness, it was nice to be here with him.

There is nothing like seeing a hockey game on a chilly day in February on the east coast. The temperature in San Jose is mild—seldom is it bone-chillingly cold as one walks to the arena from the car—almost all the time. The weather for Sunday's game didn't disappoint. There was no snow on the ground, though the weather report foretold that some was definitely on its way, but the temperature was in the upper 20s as we made our way into the Garden. We had stopped at a little café and ordered a cup of hot chocolate before entering the arena, and were on a combination chocolate high, hockey high, New York in winter high, as we made our way to our seats. And what seats they were. Stuart, my ticket friend in San Francisco, had arranged with a company in New York to hook me up with some excellent seats near center ice for this game, but little did I know that we would be just a handful of rows above the Sharks bench. I'd never seen the Sharks play on foreign, enemy ice, and I felt a chill go through me as the boys entered the ice to the boos of the New York fans—enormous excitement and pride for his team spreading across Jonathan's face—eventually taking their place on the players' bench a few rows below us.

Initially, the Sharks got off to a quick start, Jonathan Cheechoo scoring the first goal of the game to put our team ahead 1-0, but though they were the better team on paper and in the standings, they eventually fell flat, losing the game by a few goals. They had just arrived in town for a long eastern trip, and no doubt they were jet-lagged. It would have been sweet had they won the game, they have been playing incredible hockey this season, and are one of the elite teams in the league, but I'll never forget the thrill of seeing it with Jonathan. Hockey in Madison Square Garden in midwinter—it would have been thrilling to see any game there, but it was incredible to be there with my son, seeing our team.

Jonathan spent the night at the hotel with me again on Sunday, and then left yesterday morning to go back to Bard. The emptiness was palpable when I dropped him off at the train, staying to the final second as he boarded. When I went back to the hotel, I pulled out my ice skates—I had never skated in the Central Park rink before—and walked across the street from the hotel to Wolman Rink, where I skated for hours. Halfway through the skate, my phone beeped with a text from Jonathan, saying he had made it back to school. The sensation of missing him poured through my veins, as I put on my hockey face, slicing the outdoor ice with precision. I can still skate, no doubt about it. I'm sure I look quite competent on my blades, even to easterners on this outdoor ice. The thrill was intense as I skated as fast as I could for several laps, my breath creating clouds, the city of New York, soaring above and beyond.

❒

I am still in the hotel tonight, though I was scheduled to leave today. The flight, scheduled to leave late morning, had been delayed to early evening. They offered me another flight for tomorrow if I wanted it, and I took it. So, here I am, Tuesday night, reflecting on a long weekend that was more than I ever could have imagined.

When I arrived Friday night, I had a quick dinner at the hotel, then rushed over to the Carlyle Hotel on the Upper East Side to see if I could buy a standing-room ticket to see Judy Collins. She would be playing there several nights a week for the month of February, but the tickets had been sold out well in advance. Before flying to New York I had been advised to "try my luck" and come on down, that maybe I'd get lucky and get one of those tickets at the last minute. The odds would not be great for a Friday night, but now and then, they try to fit in another body, I had been told. So, finishing dinner, I grabbed a cab, entered the small lounge at the hotel where—to my amazement—there was an empty seat at the bar, just as Judy was entering the stage. Excited and enthused, I asked the usher if that seat was available, "Please tell me it is!" I implored. "You're in luck my dear boy," he said, a friendliness so full and warm that I was taken aback: one doesn't expect to happen on an empty seat at a bar for a venue such as this, and to be greeted by such warmth at the same time in New York City. I ordered a thick, red, California Cabernet Sauvignon from Beaulieu Vineyards, relaxed from the long flight as I sat in my cherished seat, and took in the charm of her banter, the poignancy of her lyrics, the soaring grace, clarity, enchanting tones of her voice.

I thought of Sue as Judy sang; I thought of how much Sue loves Judy Collins, and how she would be in her bliss if she could hear her in such a small venue in New York City. And then Judy began to sing, "There is a young boy that I know, he's only 21; he comes from Southern Colorado. Someday soon, going with him, someday soon." The vocals filled every ounce of oxygen in the room, resonating with ethereal clarity. The poignancy of the moment soothed my soul, but with a bittersweet longing for something no longer available to me: Sue is from Colorado, and it is where our relationship started. "Sue," she had said her name. "Sue from Denver," she announced that day when she had called me by "divine accident," intending to call her friend Jamie. There was a young girl that I knew, and she came from Colorado. I won't be going back to her someday soon; I know that, but it aches to realize it. "Someday soon, going with him, someday soon," Judy continued to sing. It was beautiful and sad; it was all that I could handle in that moment.

When I left the Carlyle Lounge after the show the usher—what a cool, gracious guy, made sure that both of my glasses of wine were promptly brought to me, and was generally full of good cheer all night—told me to "try my luck on Monday night," because that's when Woody Allen plays the club with his Dixieland style jazz band. He told me that he'd be working that night and, though the seats were sold out well in advance, he'd try to fit me in for standing room. "Thanks, thanks a lot; I'd love to see Woody in person; I've heard that he plays in New York City with his group from time to time, but I didn't know it was here, and that he'd be playing Monday." "Plays every Monday night during the fall and winter, at least when he's not working on a movie," he told me. "Come on by, and we'll try to fit you in." "Thanks for the tip, super nice of you," I responded, reaching into my wallet and handing him a 20 for treating me so well.

I returned last night about a half hour before starting time and the lounge was totally packed—definitely no seats available at the bar this time. I didn't see a lot of standing room availability when I walked in, but it turned out not to be an issue: my usher friend had just finished seating a group at one of the reserved tables when he spotted me, brought me over to the cashier, telling the guy, "Take his money for a standing room." "That's the last one," the cashier said. "Can't let any one else in tonight," he added. The usher, about my height, five nine, a relatively good-looking guy of about 40, Mediterranean complexion, though a bit oily, black hair that was parted from left to right, dropping down over his right eyebrow, partially obscuring his eye, smiled, winked, elbowed me in the ribs as he walked by, saying, "Got you in, right? Enjoy it," and continued with his very busy job of seating people, taking drink orders, clearing people out of the aisle to make room for walking, carrying on a variety of conversations and activities.

All of the tables in the lounge were taken except one, and just as I was finishing the thick, mellowing Beaulieu Vineyard Cabernet that I had drunk the night of Judy Collins, Mr. Allen walks from a door at the back of the lounge, brushes against me as he makes his way over to the vacant table. He is carrying a black instrument box, and as he sits—a lot of whistles and applause as the room discovers him—he looks straight down at the clarinet that he is assembling. He looks neither to the right, nor the left, nor straight ahead. There is not an acknowledgement of the crowd, his head bent straight down, a serious expression (which I interpret to be shyness rather than an unfriendliness). Clarinet assembled, Woody gets up and walks to the stage to join his mates waiting for him. He walks to the stage, head down, looking neither to the left, the right, nor straight ahead, a serious expression—shyness? Almost a frown—until he takes his seat at the center of the group, smiling economically in the company of his band mates. The mates are jovial, almost festive—laughing and smiling heartily—as Woody nods to his left, then to his right and the band breaks into their Dixie Swing.

And Woody is damn good on that clarinet, enjoying himself immensely, though reluctant (shy) to make eye contact with the audience. The band goes seamlessly from one song to the next, barely taking a break between pieces, Woody taking his solo after the others had taken theirs. Woody sits quietly, head down and avoiding the crowd, as he listens to his mates taking their turns at a solo. This is in sharp contrast to the movement, smiles, "rocking out" of his mates as they take their turns listening to the others solos.

As the band works up a full head of steam—the music happy and infectious in contrast to Woody's demeanor—a silky, stunning, curvy, blonde woman, a few inches shorter than me, is dancing in front of me, rubbing her backside generously against my front side. And as she does this, she speaks Swedish to a girlfriend next to her. The blonde friend is almost as gorgeous as the blonde in front of me, but not quite. And both are full of joy and smiles, dancing continuously. Well into my second glass of red, I am enjoying the moment immensely. Eventually she stops dancing, orders a Vodka drink in English with that Swedish accent, looks back at me and smiles. I just can't let the moment pass, so I ask her where she is from, and if she is enjoying Woody. "Woody is a legend," she answers. "And he is a really good musician," she continues, perfect teeth, big blue eyes, nice cleavage. "But he never smiles," she continues. "Yes," her friend nods, "he doesn't seem very happy," she continues, also an enticing Swedish accent, the voice a bit deeper from the chest than the woman dancing in front of me. "I just think that he's a bit shy," I respond, "He knows everybody is here to see him, so he has a hard time dealing with it. But, I am impressed by how well he can play that clarinet."

"What is your name?" I ask the woman whose backside has already been introduced to my front side. "Greta," she answers. "And you must be from Scandinavia, I would guess Sweden," I respond. "Good guess," she follows, and the two friends giggle and smile at each other. It is clear that both ladies—I would guess early 30s—are a bit buzzed from the Vodka that they have been drinking all night. And they are, indeed, having an outstanding time. "I'm coming to Europe this summer, or at least I plan to," I tell Greta. "I'm thinking of going to Greece, but maybe I'll change my mind and come to Sweden." She smiles, opens her eyes widely, saying, "That would be nice. Do come." With this she opens her wallet, and hands me her card. She works at a medical clinic in Stockholm. "What type of work do you do?" I ask. "I'm a medical student, and I work in this clinic on my card," the music going into full swing as she begins to dance full throttle again. She continues to dance directly in front of me, brushing against my front, but not quite as closely as before.

After about an-hour-and-a-half of non-stop, full-Dixie swing—Woody Allen style—the music comes to an end. Woody's big, full bellied, jovial cohort—he'd been laughing, grinning, generally carrying on all evening—thanks the crowd for coming out. As he says this, Woody ever so slightly and quickly looks up at the crowd, musters a bit of a thin lipped smile (shy) and proceeds to walk back the same path used to walk out. He walks past me, and as he does (a couple of glasses of wine have me feeling quite nice at the moment) I say, "Great job, Woody, great playing, thanks for the fun!" to which I hear some kind of mumble, the words to which I could not make out. My Swedish friend is making her way to the restroom, and I catch up with her, not appearing to be in pursuit, since I also have to use one as well. As I catch up to her, I tell her that I'll definitely call her if I come to Sweden, and in my slightly buzzed state I tell her that it is pretty likely that I will come. She smiles, giggles—wow! She is a knockout; before I ever settle down in my life, I must go to Stockholm at least once I resolve—and joins arms with her friend. I exit the restroom and the girls are gone. I walk back through the lounge and cannot find them anywhere. "Well, maybe I'll catch up with her in Stockholm," I offer myself, entering the cold night air, easily catching a taxi back to the hotel in Midtown..

❒

The angst builds, as this Tuesday night—the room service waiter has just delivered a pot of hot milk and English Muffins—becomes Wednesday morning in this hotel room. It is my hope that the hot milk will coat my synapses, decrease and soften the electrical charge that my brain is releasing into my bloodstream, manifesting as tension, worry, anxiety. I text-messaged Jonathan about a half hour ago, hoping that I'd receive a quick response that he was safe, secure and cozy in his bed—Michael had already responded to my message to him at Oberlin, and he responded that he was in bed reading and ready to go to sleep—but I haven't heard back from Jonathan yet. I shake with nervousness at the moment, a tightness that moves up my right forearm, into the shoulder on the same side, up into the neck and temples. I am overtaken with the need to "control" the world around me; to be sure that all is okay with my boys; to find certainty and a sense of security that everything in my world is safe, will be safe, that God is there to protect. I know, rationally, that Jonathan is safe, and it is illogical, almost insane to assume that because I cannot reach him—as though his telephone must be an appendix to his body—that something is not all right. But I simply cannot relax until I gain that assurance, and the more I strive for that assurance—the more phone calls I make and text messages that I send—the less certain I become. So, the synapse activity increases in frequency and intensity, and I worry, essentially a victim to the chemical changes that pour through my bloodstream. The uncertainty yields more uncertainty, the anxiety leading to greater anxiety, worry feeding itself—and the trigger point, an ostensibly innocuous inclination to "check in," leads to an emotional experience that speeds the heartbeat, the respiration, ravaging any sense of calm or equanimity that might have existed previously—until I begin to walk around nervously, more and more desperate for security.

Once the worry or need for assurance kicks in, its like a car going from zero to 100 miles an hour, never stopping at the lower speed limits to gain composure, apply common sense. But I don't allow myself the use of an antianxiety medication—Valium or Ativan—when these moods occur, preferring to allow my system to return to normal on its own, perhaps eventually exhaust itself, from which, in a tired state, a sense of calm, common sense might return. I will fly home tomorrow, but the plane doesn't leave until the mid-afternoon: I'll be able to sleep in, so I write into the night, hopefully assuaging this anxiety until Jonathan calls or texts me. If I do not hear from him tonight, tomorrow is another day—I'll be okay when the sun shines again. Eventually the synapses will become more "mellow," as I become more tired. The release of these thoughts will help, aided by the warm milk that—a little honey added to it—soothes the nervousness of the stomach.

This need for security, this struggle for the certainty or emotional calm that all is all right in my world, is a manifestation of a deeper struggle that I must be having with my perception of God and sense of faith. I have always felt protected in my life. There has continued throughout my life a sense that my world is safe. My mother imbued within me—from earliest memory—a deep sense that God is available to me, and that all one need to do to hear his voice is to envision within our minds a candlelight burning brightly. This candlelight is the light of our soul, an eternal light, and that deep within the halls of man—all of mankind—there lies this eternal light, this everlasting light. The failure to perceive of this light is the failure, she taught, to see oneself—for in seeing oneself, one truly finds and hears the words of God. "Envision a candle," she would say, "and in envisioning the candlelight in a moment of quiet, ask God what you need to know. He'll answer you. You'll hear him clearly." And I do believe that in my moments of deep need—as I am feeling at the moment—I have been able to hear God. And if it didn't happen right away, the moment I was hoping to hear the words, it did eventually happen in a quiet moment when I could slow down sufficiently to envision the light, and hear the words. I do know that even if my mother had not told me of the nature of God in our lives, I would have believed innately. From earliest memory, I had the urge to kneel at my bedside before going to sleep, to pray for well-being of those that I loved, to thank God for allowing me to have him in my life.

I have always believed in God, have always had a profound sense of a Holy Spirit that is the essence of what it is to be human, an essence that is inseparable from all of the physical form that is the composition of this universe. But then my mother passed away, and I saw her suffer painfully—though mercifully not for too long a period—from lung cancer that had spread to other parts of her body. I tried to rationalize that God had taken her for a reason—that she had another calling, perhaps as a special emissary to do very special works—and that her time had been fulfilled on this planet. She did do incredibly wonderful things for people—she helped so many people set their lives back on the right track; her gift allowed her to heal with her words and sometimes with her touch; she was blessed to see ahead the winding path that is our lives, and the detours one must take on occasion, and she would often "read" for free for the poor people who needed her help, as well as accepting the "little extra" from the wealthy and famous who could afford it. She died at the age of 65, and I wasn't ready for her to die. She helped to plan Michael's Bar Mitzvah, and came within a month of seeing it. It had been her dream to see the Bar Mitzvah of the grandson she called a Gainsborough—"Gainsborough could come the closest to painting the innocence and blue eyes of this precious boy," she had said—but didn't reach it. The pain of her passing was so deep that I wanted to rip off my clothes. The gap that was left will never be filled; perhaps I would have been able to accept her passing some day, but not when it happened. There was just too much of a role for her in our lives, and in the future of my boys, her grandchildren.

My mom was taken, and, no doubt, there lingered within me a sense of doubt. Perhaps not a doubt about the existence of God, but about his compassion. I think of the holocaust, and I think of the horrible injustice, and I think of the horror that affects the innocent. And in a profound intellectual sense, I question the safety of my own world. "What is there so special about me, that I should be protected?" I begin to ask. And then I feel a sense of guilt that I ask that question. "I know better than that," I tell myself. "This is not a question that I need ask," I continue. But the worry builds, and Jonathan still has not responded to my text message. "I'll give him a break; I won't bother him tonight. I'll write until I am so tired that I have nothing left tonight. And then I'll sleep," I tell myself. I think about my marriage. It was a gift from God. How astounding it was in the way we came together—and my mother saw it in the cup just as it happened. These boys—Michael and Jonathan—were meant to be, just as the sun is assured of coming up tomorrow. But the marriage seems to be ending. And it is profoundly sad for me. How do I reconcile this with my sense that this union was a gift from God? It is not—in any way that I can see—an act of pride or stubborn will that now keeps us apart. I strive to know God, to never take for granted his gifts, but a sense of doubt, watered by fear, permeates in ways that are unwelcome. I strive to find the quiet, envision the flame, hear the voice, and in so doing, I see my mother, hear her voice, perceive her flame. "Within the halls of man," she said to me, "There lies an eternal light, an everlasting light.".

❒

There is a gravity in my soul as I sit here in this New York City hotel room. There is a gravitational pull of the soul to family, the familiarity and comfort of Sue. I swim against it, but it hurts, and it feels as though I am fighting a strong current. Though I have had a few alluring dates in the year plus since our separation—and a few, quite attractive women have used above-average charms to entice me to pursue them further—I remain quite alone in my world at the moment. I haven't let anyone become too close to me, because I simply cannot make promises or imply commitment—though it is quite difficult for me to date without there being an excitement over the possibilities, the potential for discovery, the fantasy of deep and lasting connection. As I begin to release myself from the obstruction to enjoying a woman fully in the moment—allowing myself the freedom to not think of boundaries, limitations, suppressing (with a glass of wine) the notion that the enjoyment of this connection in the moment cannot possibly perpetuate in any lasting form because I am way too much in limbo—that gravitational pull will too often reassert itself, pulling me back into a psychic commitment to Sue, which feels hollow. We are not doing anything, either of us, to fill that form with the ingredients for emotional reconnection: We do not show the laughter that comes from sharing a thought or sentiment that nobody quite understands in the way that we do together; we do not permit the smile to occur and linger between us, that smile that comforts the stomach with a sense of well-being; we do not express a sense that "this is all foolishness," and that we shouldn't be wasting any more of our precious time being apart. Perhaps underlying our daily approaches to life is the sense that "this is all foolishness and we really shouldn't be where we are." But, on the other side of the coin, maybe it is my wish that this sentiment were shared equally by each of us, when it really is not. Perhaps the barrier that I feel is the same barrier that Sue feels as well. We love one another for sure, but maybe it is just not the case that either of us thinks that, "This is all a bunch of foolishness, and that we are wasting the precious time of life not realizing it." Perhaps what I do not want to acknowledge as real, is very real. Our journeys have diverged, and maybe it is a sacrifice of precious time to not acknowledge this. The gravitational pull makes it difficult to come to terms with our being apart: but the pull is, simply, not bringing us back together.

Though I am alone, I have found quiet, intimate moments in the comfort of my friendship with Gwen Jones. Her hands have the power to lift the heavy energy from the spine; there is a healing quality when she touches my shoulder and neck. I sometimes feel as though I am making my way through a vat of soft, delicious, thick caramel when I am around her. She is 16 years younger than I am, and we do not have many of the historical reference points that I am passionate about—she was born after the breakup of the Beatles; does not know much about Jack, Bobby or Martin; no recollection of Vietnam; no sense of Watergate; she can only observe as I enter a melancholic, holy nostalgia on watching the black-and-white print of McCartney and Harrison singing into the same mike, Lennon bent over and rocking back and forth on "Hard Day's Night," as they sing, "If I fell for you, oh please, don't run and hide"; doesn't get the chills to Jagger singing, "She comes in colors everywhere, she combs her hair, she's like a rainbow"—but there is something so soothing about being in her midst. I'll take a break from the stresses of the financial marketplace day to have a cup of tea with Gwen, and it becomes a quiet, comfortable release and escape. That gravitational pull often lifts when I am with Gwen, only to return and then lift again. I observe all of this carefully—sometimes as though I am a third person—and I often wonder if there can be much more to us. She does have a window into my soul; she truly sees me. She perceives the aching of the soul, quietly permitting a space of calm that surrounds her like an aura. Often when I leave her presence, I so much want that intimacy to be permanent, and then the gravitational pull occurs, and I know that in this moment I can belong to no one. There is a message in this gravity, and I must understand it before I can fully succumb to the adventure.

I continue to think of Gwen. Using the metaphor of playing a piano, she wouldn't have command of all the chords or be able to use all of the notes up and down the keyboard to play complicated pieces. Her playing though—using the chords and keys she knows well—would sooth the soul, quiet the mind, bring in stardust, lull to sleep. Gwen cannot share the experience of growing up in my era—she wasn't there, and cannot go there with me in the way that I sometimes crave—but she brings an awareness, sensitivity, understanding of life that is unique, possessing a kind of gravitational pull of its own.

Gwen can calm me with her velvet touch when I am troubled, worried over the whereabouts of my boys. I can honestly, without judgment, open up to my fears—and she occupies that space with me, even seems to love me in that space. The currents of life move within me and without me: the gravitational pull of the life that has been mine; the inclination to expand and be free; the vat of caramel that consist of the moments with Gwen, and her gravitational pull. It is now four A.M., and I have said—while not as completely as I would like—much of what was in my soul. This has really been a substantial trip—and then my mind returns to Jonathan, and the text message that I anxiously want returned. I turn on the power to my phone—I must have turned it off by accident, I didn't realize that it was turned off—and the red light is on, indicating a message. And it is from Jonathan: "I'm in bed, Dad; stop worrying. Have a nice flight. It was a lot of fun. Love you." If I could only feel this way all the time.

❒

I was cramped into a middle seat on the ride back, and I read the entire flight. By the time we arrived it felt as though a metal rod had been inserted up the entire right side of my neck. My back ached, and I was feeling the tightness that has been becoming more chronic in my right arm lately, almost an arthritic kind of feeling, where there is an aching in my hand that extends all the up my arm into my shoulders. The process of writing is quite physical, and I don't give myself much of a break by day, navigating the little "mouse" on my work station for eight or nine hours daily, striving to make my daily living as I move across the pages and pages of investment inventory, intermittently switching to clients' pages as I do my best to respond to every call that comes in. And, most likely, I hold my body in a tense fashion anyway, the stress of my personal life inevitably transferring to my hands, jaws, arms, shoulders. Yoga; I vow to find a yoga class—but not just find one, actually take the time to practice it. I know that this will help, and I have been telling myself for months that I absolutely must do this—but so far, I haven't followed my best advice.

I was looking forward to a hot bath—Gwen had told me about some sea salts that detoxify to drop in the bath water, and I had been using them and feeling transformed after each bath—on getting home, and also cleansing myself from the negativity that had filled the papers during this return flight. I should have read some funny stuff on the flight—Augusten Burroughs' book, "Magical Thinking" is hilarious—but forced myself to get caught up on as much financial information as I could stuff into my head. And I read this stuff until my head hurt. The articles discussed Federal Reserve Chairman Ben Bernanke's honest assessment of the economy, and it was one of great concern. According to the chairman, the U.S. economic system—and indeed that of the world—was worsening daily, the deterioration happening so quickly that the traditional levers of cutting interest rates and loosening money supply might not be enough in the face of this erupting volcano of financial deterioration. He talked of the government needing to be prepared, to become involved in the bailout of the financial system, particularly if banks and insurance companies began to fail.

Banks were placing larger and larger subprime loan losses on their balance sheets, and if this continued it might undermine the survivability of some of the nation's largest banks, such as Citigroup, Washington Mutual, even the company for which I work, Wachovia. Traditional Wall Street investment firms, Lehman Brothers and Bear Stearns, were reported to have made significant commitments to mortgage-backed bonds, and were losing billions and billions of dollars. There was an in-depth article about how the municipal bond market—my area of expertise and specialization—was on the verge of taking a massive nose dive in values, if the municipal-bond insurers cannot survive, or have their AAA ratings cut to much-lower credit quality. Triple A ratings on insured municipal bonds is something the investment community—the municipalities that buy the insurance; the financial advisors who sell the bonds; the individual investors who buy the bonds—has always taken for granted. The fact that these major insurance companies—Ambac, MBIA, FGIC and others—might fail or become so severely downgraded as to not be able to honor their guarantees to investors is astonishing to me, seemingly never in the realm of possibility. This is a harsh awakening, a cold dose of stark reality.

Another article discussed how the trillion-dollar market for mortgage- and debt-backed securities could collapse if the insurers continue to suffer crippling losses. Another article talked about how the economy has clearly entered a recession, there being the first contraction—and one of significant proportions—in five years. Another article talked about the fear of the debt-plagued consumer, and that consumer confidence had plunged in the recent survey to levels not seen in many years. And yet another piece predicted that within a year the economy might see the unemployment rate come close to eight percent. And I kept reading and reading, through calm air and turbulence, just drinking in this enjoyable financial news..

❒

The political arena, though, was entertaining. The New York Times had published a front-page exposé that had John McCain fuming and counterattacking. The article detailed questionable ties between McCain and a Washington lobbyist. It stated that during his 2000 run for the White House, McCain wrote letters to government regulators on behalf of the clients of the lobbyist, a rather sultry looking woman. At the time, McCain was Chairman of the Senate Commerce Committee. The article made the accusation—rather bold and inflammatory it had seemed to me, because there did not appear to be much evidence to back up such a claim—that McCain was having an affair with this woman. It brought up that campaign aides at the time believed that this was a fact. McCain, according to the article, had admitted back in 2000 that he had acted inappropriately, and had vowed to "keep his distance." McCain had lashed back that this article was basically a bunch of garbage, and that it was a "hit piece" on him. And I might agree. Why bring up such circumstantial stuff dating back to 2000? It does appear to be shoddy journalism, and one can certainly question the motivations. But, for McCain, it might be good that this sort of stuff gets brought up now; better to deal and dispense with it during the primary season, than to have to respond during the general election.

On the Democratic side, Hillary and Obama continue to go hard at each other. On the verge of their debate in Texas, Mrs. Clinton is belittling Obama as being "all talk and no substance," an "inexperienced choice for Commander-In-Chief in a dangerous world." Hillary, though, seems to be fighting an uphill battle, doing her best to swim against a rapidly rushing Obama current: fundraising for January shows that Obama raised $36 million, three times the amount for Hillary. This is certainly a "contest for the ages," and no doubt, fundraising records for a presidential campaign will be set on the Democratic side, a rather incongruous notion when the economy is hemorrhaging..

❒

I walk into my apartment—it is mid-evening, and a foggy mist envelops the bay, lights vaguely appearing through apartment windows, as though obscured by window shades, a hazy light illuminating the elemental rust red of the Golden Gate Bridge off in the distance—and I turn on the water for the bath. It is the very first thing that I do, after putting down my bags and looking out my window. As the water runs, I dial my landline phone to see if there are any messages. And there is one. It is the voice of a woman that I hear—a high voice that I recognize only when she tells me that it is Charisse, the girlfriend of my football buddy, Phil Barbieri. She is responding to the message that I had left a few weeks ago when I had called to ask Phil how he is doing, if he needed anything, if he was handling the chemo okay. Did he see that incredible Super Bowl game?

"Phil died," she said. "He never had a chance to see the game. I know that you two were good football buddies, and I wanted you to know. I would have told you earlier, but I only got your phone number when you left it for Phil. Good-bye."

The words shocked and shook me to the core. Phil was my age, 52. All of the good times at those games with him and his dad. The Joe Montana, Steve Young, Bill Walsh eras; the George Seifert, Jeff Garcia era. Then the losing seasons—losing seasons but with the hope of a comeback. Talking the ins and outs of the 49ers every home Sunday for the past 25 years. And now he's gone. And we were starting to talk about life outside of football recently, just before he had been diagnosed with cancer. We had vowed to get together a bit during the off-season. I saw the potential for Phil to be a really deep friend, with whom I could share my feelings—and I have so much wanted that lately. Now he's dead. Just doesn't seem possible. First his dad, Phil, a couple of years ago, and now, Phil, the son. Don't know how I'm going to be able to go out to those games in the future, when the two seats to my right—12 rows above the field and just off to the side of the 49er bench—are empty. The two Phils—his dad would put his arm around me and tell me that I needed some sun on that office complexion, and I'd turn to his son, asking him if he'd ever seen a tougher cornerback than Ronnie Lott—will never return to those seats. Football will never be the same for me again. I soak in the hot bath, as I remember and miss Phil Barbieri.

I get out of the bath, put on my reading glasses and go directly to the stand that holds my catalogue of music CDs. In the days when my life seemed more orderly, these things were in alphabetical order. But not these days; when I moved into this apartment, it was all that I could do to put these couple of hundred or so pieces of music in some sort of order—so I prioritized them in order of preference. The music that I was likely to listen to the most, was placed on the upper shelves; the less likely to be played often relegated to the lower areas, where I'd have to bend over and get on my knees to find them. And it is a hardwood floor, so getting on my knees is painful and requires finding a pillow to put under them. Pink Floyd's "Wish You Were Here" album is at eye level, and it fit neatly into my hands, virtually falling into them, essentially asking to be played. As I select it, I in no way disturb any of the other cases—sometimes when I pick one out, three others come falling down—everything just flowing smoothly for the listening of the music. And then comes on the song for which I selected this album, "Wish You Were Here." The song opens with background static, mumbling of voices—as though we are overhearing a bit of a conversation—and then moves into some of the most deeply, emotionally satisfying acoustic guitar I've ever heard. Each note cascades into the next, building in pitch, rhythm, ecstasy, penetrating the emotions and the soul as it reaches poignancy.

Phillip Rusty Siegler

I'm in my rocking chair now, an old Stickley chair from the early 1900s, rocking back and forth as "Wish You Were Here" intoxicates, filling me with reverie; wanting to live fully; missing my mom desperately; the early days of innocence with Sue; the days when my boys were young and in those overalls with a dogface on the front, big red dog tongue of felt sticking out; wishing for the football days with Phil and his dad; and missing another old friend, the best friend that I ever had, also named Phil. This friend from my youth, Phillip Rusty Siegler, knew of no other way to be, except loyal. We did so much together as kids, came of age together in the late '60s and early '70s, and then I went off to college, and he fell on hard times, desperately hard times. I miss him a lot right now. I'm looking at a picture of myself with my brothers, Jeff and Elliot, and best friend, Phil. There is so much chemistry and connection in this picture—we fit like a building held together by gravity and not cement or nails. There is joy, intensity and attitude in this picture. Elliot, my youngest brother, is about 16, good looking, with brown, wavy hair that is growing toward his shoulders. He wears a full smile—he's enjoying the company of his brothers and their best friend. Jeff, the stud hockey goalie, has a mini-afro hairstyle, a beer in his hand as he looks off in the distance. I must have been influenced by the new disco craze, my shirt collar open, revealing a gold chain; a blue, unbuttoned vest; hair nicely styled into a long, round, natural; a mustache; and my carefully honed hockey glare. Phil is sitting on the arm of the sofa, leaning over on me to get into the picture, the haircut like John Fogerty, the plaid shirt right out of Creedence Clearwater's "Cosmo's Factory" album. It's interesting; Phil's look in the eyes is very much like mine, in contrast to my two brothers, who appear in a lighter frame of mind. As I look at this picture, the words fill me—Phil and I heard them so many times together—"We're just two lost souls, swimming in a fish bowl, year after year, running over the same old ground, what have you found? The same old fears. Wish you were here." "Wish you were here," I sing to myself, but loud enough to fill the whole apartment. "Wish you were here," and tears start rolling down my cheek. When the song finishes, I play it again, because once is not enough. "Wish you were here!" I sing loudly; "Wish you were here."

The song finishes and I go over to pull out a stunning, gorgeous vinyl that I bought at Bleeker Street records in the Village, across from John's Pizza. I had first heard about John's Pizza from "M," and I went there with Jonathan on this last visit. After having the most delicious pizza that I'd ever tasted—sweet, ripe tomato sauce, with the perfect thin crust, baked in the brick oven; it even surpasses Tommaso's of San Francisco's North Beach—washed down with a couple of glasses of hearty red wine, we made our way over to the record store. It wasn't cheap, but high up on the wall—far enough out of reach to require someone with a ladder to go up and get it, no doubt to discourage touching by window shoppers—was a first pressing of "Rubber Soul," recorded in the original mono. I would have wanted this album at any time of day, but in this slightly buzzed condition—the wine had nicely washed down the pizza—I had to own it. And so I paid the couple of hundred dollars for the album. I put it on now for the first time.

Is there a song any more true of life, of reverie, of missing people, of trying to make the most of every minute, of accepting all of life, the good, the bad, the joyful, the painful, than Lennon singing thus:

> *There are places I remember*
> *all my life, though some have changed*
> *some forever, not for better, some have gone and some remain*
> *all these places had their moments, with lovers and friends, I still can recall*
> *some are dead and some are living*
> *In my life, I've loved them all."*

The tone, the irony, the vocals from deep within the chest, emanating from the heart; the absolute beauty of feeling encapsulates the world for me at the moment. I play it again as I sing softly to myself, "Some are dead, and some are living; in my life I've loved them all."

My mind drifts to summer of 1968. My family had moved on from Van Nuys, where we had landed after departing Campbellton, New Brunswick, Canada—the nation still in shock and mourning following the assassinations of Martin Luther King and Bobby Kennedy—and had settled on Calvert Street in Reseda, deep in the bowels of the smog-filled San Fernando Valley. Calvert Street was like so many of the rows on rows of cheaply built residential housing tracts that made up "the Valley," but we were among the lucky ones, because the house we had purchased had a swimming pool. My brother Jeff and I had become relatively popular on this street just weeks after moving in—and, of course, one of the chief reasons for this popularity had to do with our willingness to invite kids over to go swimming during those summer months, when eggs literally fry on the sidewalk.

Having been in Canada the past couple of years, it was surprising to me just how insanely hot this turned out to be. I marveled at how many of the neighborhood kids were able to walk down these incinerator sidewalks barefoot; their feet so calloused from absorbing the sidewalk coals that there would be very little to gain from sandals. It was crazy to me to see this—it was as though kids had several layers of extra skin on their feet. Given the competitive kid that I had been, it was paramount that I catch up to the barefoot abilities of the neighborhood establishment. But it didn't happen easily. The first day I handled the hot stones for about 10 seconds; the second day, maybe 20 seconds; and by the end of the month I painfully walked about a couple of hundred yards on hot coals to hang out with some kids. And it was on one of these scorching one-hundred-degree-plus days that I met and admired Phillip Rusty Siegler. His middle name was "Rusty" for a reason: his hair was short, cropped along the ears and against the neck, but glistened copper as it grew longer on top. It was too brown to be blond, and too red to be brown. "Rusty" would be the only way to describe it. We were both 13 years old, and about the same height, maybe five foot six. But Phil was stockier than me, broader, and with more girth. If I was built like a wide receiver, he was a linebacker. If I were a centerman in hockey, he'd be the defenseman. His blue eyes were deeply set—a lot of eye bone surrounding them, and he had a squarish jaw, the chin dimpled. Freckles scattered across his nose and onto both cheeks.

Phil didn't live in this tract of homes, but rather several blocks away on one of the streets that ran perpendicular to the train tracks. He had been visiting one of his buddies, Mark, hair dark at the roots, then moving progressively from red, to blond to white, starting out straight, then becoming exceptionally bushy, frizzing out at a 90-degree angle very reminiscent of Bozo the Clown.

Mark and Phil had been throwing a football around when I arrived. And then I joined in, trying to impress the new guys with my spirals. And, indeed, good at sports, I was pretty darn impressive that day with the straightness and tight spirals of my passes. Phil and Mark had been passing the ball barefoot on the sidewalk when I arrived, but it was all I could do to make it there barefoot, so I quickly made it to the cool, comforting grass from which I participated in the throw around. Eventually Mark went into his house, leaving Phil and me alone to throw the ball. And this was where I became extremely impressed with Phil. The pavement was absolutely scorching, and he ran pattern after pattern down sidewalks, into the harsh pavement of the street, diving for balls across sidewalks into peoples lawns, jumping on the hoods of cars to catch a pass, running into chain-link fences, eventually ripping open some skin on the top of one of the fences. I kept throwing those passes from the sanctuary of the cool green pasture on which my feet rested. After about 45 minutes, Phil came back to where I was standing and suggested that I run some of the patterns into the street. "If I had some shoes, maybe," I said," but I can't run on that stuff barefoot," I continued. "You ain't got feet like mine, ha," Phil answered, the words bathed in a drawl that was country, but not deep, deep country. "I like the way you throw the ball, you play Pop Warner growin' up?" he started. "I did, as a kid in Simi Valley, but I wasn't a quarterback; I was a halfback," I answered. "But ice hockey is my main game now," I continued. "Been living in Canada the past two years, and really started to get into it. We've been back a few months, and I've started playing for a team out here. Do you know how to ice skate?" "Naw, though I sure like watchin' it," Phil answered, stretching the words out in a mellow, slow way. "I sure like watchin' it, but I'm from Arkansas, only been here a couple of years, and we ain't got any ice skating in Arkansas. But I really like the sport; be fun to go to a Kings game one of these days." "Yeah, maybe we'll go to one together sometime," I answered. "How would you like to come out and watch some of our hockey games when the season starts in a few months? I'll introduce you to my brother, Jeff, he's an incredible goalie; he was on the All-Star team in Canada." "That would be real cool," Phil answered. "Be real, real cool." "Hey how about coming over to go swimming now? I'll introduce you to my brother, Jeff." "Man, that would be real cool, let's do it." "Let's do it, let's go," I followed.

Mark had apparently disappeared somewhere, so Phil and I made it over to the backyard pool, where Jeff was already in the water. As we walked through the fence into the backyard, Jeff gets out of the water and onto the diving board. "Hey Bruce, watch this," as he proceeds to do a one-and-a-half flip. "When did you learn to do that?" I ask him. "Just a few minutes ago," he answered. "That's pretty good," responds Phil, as he gets up a full run and jumps far into the pool. After getting out, Phil makes his way over to the diving board, brings his toes to the edge, and does a sweet back flip. "Hey, pretty good," Jeff yells out. "What's your name?" "Rusty," answers Phil. "Hey, nice to meet you, Rusty," the bonds formed from the very first day.

❐

There is a period during the development of a friendship when mutual respect is established. Sometimes this respect is earned through proving to the other guy that you are just as tough as he is, and that you are willing to "take his best punch" if need be, but he better be prepared to take yours as well—this certainly was the case on the playgrounds of Sequoia Jr. High School in Reseda, California, an area at the very core of the sprawling lower-middle- to middle-class, tract-home wilderness of the San Fernando Valley. It is late November 1969, the early days of the Nixon administration—will never forget the horrible images of the war in Vietnam pouring into our living room each night, Nixon saying he had a plan to end the conflict with dignity—and Phil and I stayed after school to play football on the school field. A bunch of kids began to join us as we were throwing the ball around, and given the size of the gathering, it was inevitable that we would choose up sides for some tackle. Since Phil and I had been there the earliest—and it wouldn't have been fair to have us both on the same team—we made ourselves captains and picked our teams. Our kicker kicked the ball deep to their team, Phil taking the kick for the runback. Phil wasn't real fast, but very thick, and just as he fought off one of our tacklers I came in and made solid contact with him, my shoulder hitting his chest, my arms wrapped around his waist as I struggled to bring him down. I do bring him down, but as he gets up, he throws the ball at me, wiping blood from his lip onto his forearm. "Rosen, you tackle me like that again, I'll pop you one," he says with that slight Arkansas drawl, then walks head down, not even giving me a second glance, back to the huddle.

On the next play, I'm lining up wide to defend the receiver; Phil stands to the left of the quarterback and goes in motion to the right side, my side of the field. The quarterback pitches out to Phil and he turns the corner—not running straight up like a graceful track runner, but bent over like Rocky Bleier, a cannonball gaining density and speed—as I come up, adrenalin pouring through my veins, to take him on for the tackle, which I do successfully, but not before he buries his head in my stomach, hurting the shit out of me, driving me hard on my back. He gets up, smiles, "You okay Rosen?" After seeing blackness and a few stars for a split second, I get up and laugh at him. "I'm okay, Siegler," I respond, "but at least I can catch you. Wait till we have the ball; I'm putting you in my dust." "Oh really, Mr. fast guy, hockey player," he says to me, "We'll see; we'll just see." "Yeah, we will see," I answer. They had scored a touchdown on their first possession, and I am the deep guy for our team on the kickoff, taking the kick and running straight in the direction of Phil. He starts taking an angle toward me as I am running away from everyone down the sidelines; I see this and start slanting back toward the center of the field, at which point I'm caught and tackled from behind by Pat, a surfer kid, tanned, with long, sun-bleached blond hair, a good friend of Phil's. Pat was a very nice kid—good athlete, quite non-aggressive—and I had recently started to get along nicely with him. "What happened to the speed burner?" Phil says to me, head down as he walks back to his defensive huddle. "Phil, what is it with you?" I say. "You're acting like a punk!" I yell. "And you're a pussy," he answers. "Fuck You," I say, at which point the other kids on the field begin to take notice. "Say it to my face," answers Phil. And I walk up to him and say, "Fuck You," about six inches from his face. He answers by pushing me, and I follow by pushing him. He pushes back, and I follow with another push. These pushes are getting harder and harder, beginning to take the form of miniature punches. After about six or seven of these back and forth shoves—it had become crystal clear to both of us that we didn't want to fight each other—Pat comes between us and breaks it up. "What are you guys doing?" he says. "I thought you guys were really good friends. This is stupid." At this point Phil and I look at each other and acknowledge that there is no real reason for this; there is not any good future in it for either of us. "Alright Pat, we'll drop it," I say. "Yeah, okay," says Phil, "but one day we should spar in my backyard with some boxing gloves," he follows. "I'm for that," I answer. At this point we decide to end the football game, a relatively short time after it had started. And so Phil offers me a ride home on his motorcycle. Even though Phil was only 14 years old—not old enough to legally ride one—he had taken his brother's motorbike to school that day, parking down the block.

I get on the back, thinking that bygones had been bygones. But, apparently, that isn't what Phil was thinking. He starts up the bike and begins to warm up the engine loudly, bringing it to full throttle a couple of times. "Ready?" he says. "Ready," I answer. At which point he quickly accelerates, bringing the front wheel up off the ground several times, speeding quickly down the street. "God damn it," I say, "What the fuck are you doing?" I yell. "I'm getting off this thing." "Got you scared, ha?" he answers. At which point he calmly, smoothly drives me through the streets of scenic Reseda, oil leaks staining virtually every driveway—there always seemed to be someone working on a broken-down Mustang or Chevrolet—back to my house on Calvert Street. "See you at school tomorrow," he says as he revs up the engine to go home. "Thanks for the ride home," I answer, the Arkansas smirk tightening that square jaw of his as he rides off.

Phillip Rusty Siegler was a master at carefully rolling up a towel in such a way that from top to about three quarters down was a firm solid stalk, the remaining quarter a tail of cloth that he would snap with precision. After being stung a few times by his whip towel, my brother Jeff and myself learned his art and started using it back on him. He didn't particularly enjoy being stung by the whip towel, and we learned early on that the key to deterrence with Phil was to come right back at him with your own trick, prank or sabotage. To this day, I consider myself a master at rolling up a lethal towel that I only use when I am trying to knock a fly out of the air. My boys used to lecture me about knocking innocent flies out of the air, but I persisted in doing so in homage to my memories of Phil.

The first time that I saw Phil's whip towel in use was in the shower room after gym class, perhaps a few weeks after our confrontation on the football field. Eighth grade at Sequoia Jr. High was the first time that I ever had my own gym locker for class, and it was also the first time that I had been in a gym class where I had to take showers with a class full of guys. One realizes at this point of human development that all kids do not mature in the same way as others, and that the Good Lord has provided early endowment for some, while withholding the fruits of maturity until later for others. It is certainly startling at first to be thrown into this jungle of male nudity, just as the body is going through major changes. Some boys are shy, holding onto their genitalia so that others cannot fully catch a look, but all the while trying not to look obvious in doing so. Others may not have much to be proud of yet, but they're not inhibited at all, just letting it out without any embarrassment whatsoever. And once in a while there is a kid who appears much too manly for this age group, hair growing on his chest, well endowed, furry genitalia. And in this class there was such a man-kid. He was a Mexican kid, and he used to parade around the shower like he owned the place. He was, I think, in the next grade above Phil and myself, ninth grade. Phil' s locker was at the opposite end of the bench from myself, and the Mexican kid had a locker right behind mine. The guy was always friendly toward me, joking with me from time to time as he dressed and put on that Brut aftershave. That Brut aftershave; I can smell it to this day. He'd pour a heavy splash onto his hands and rub it on his chest, neck and face. "Makes the girls go crazy," he joked to me once. And as he put it on, he'd sing, typically, one of three songs, a really good, deep voice, tinged with a touch of a Latin accent. His words ring clear as a bell to me at the moment.

With the strong scent of Brut as a backdrop, he'd sing the great Otis Redding: "Oh she may be weary, them young girls they do get wearied; wearing that same old miniskirt dress, but when she gets weary, you try a little tenderness." On another occasion, he'd sing a song or two from Three Dog Night:

"How can people be so heartless; how can people be so cruel; easy to be hard, easy to be cold; how can people have no feelings; how can they ignore their friends; easy to be proud, easy to say no." When he sang one Three Dog Night song, he'd usually follow it with another: "One is the loneliest number that you'll ever do; Two can be as bad as one; It's the loneliest number since the number one." He could really sing. On one of these occasions, just as my Mexican friend is wrapping up with "but when she gets weary, you try a little tenderness"—he's not fully dressed at this point, well-endowed genitalia proudly dangling—Phil comes up from behind and snaps his whip towel squarely on the guy's ass. I absolutely was stunned, couldn't believe my eyes. He snaps the guy squarely on the ass to the sound of stinging skin. The Mexican guy had a choice at this point, and in his eyes I could see the decision being made. He could have gone after Phil, grabbed his towel and destroyed him with it, or he could laugh it off. He did the latter, but vowed to my good buddy that he'd get even, and that Phil should never feel safe again when he was in that locker room. Perhaps Phil secretly knew that the "Latin lover" would take it as a joke and not retaliate, but he certainly couldn't have known it for sure. It was pretty damn ballsy of him to snap that guy; from that time on I waited—probably more concerned that it would come than Phil was—but the retaliation never came.

As we moved into 1970, Phil was in the front row for virtually every hockey game in which my brother, Jeff, and I played. Just as our winter weekends were consumed by playing hockey, Phil's weekends were spent eating slices of pizza and burritos, always downed with a large Coke, pumping a fist at me as I laid out a solid, glass-shaking body check, or yelling an opposing player's number at me for revenge when I was on the receiving end of a hammering. And at Jeff's games, Phil would sit directly behind the net encouraging the league's top goalie—indeed, Jeff was an

Phillip Rusty Siegler, myself, my brother Jeff, and my brother Elliot. We looked like a rock band. Approximately 1975.

incredible goalie, lightening-fast reflexes, courageous almost to the point where he was stupid—to stay focused. At the end of a period, my brother might swing his stick against the glass in acknowledgement of Phil's presence, and Phil would respond by yelling at Jeff that he couldn't let in more than two goals because he had a serious bet on the game. Jeff would turn around, take his mask off, and make a kind of ape face at Phil. Those two had great banter with each other, and just as Phil and I had become completely tight as buddies, Jeff and Phil had the bond of brothers.

By the time we were deep into 1970 the enjoyment of music had become a huge part of my friendship with Phil. His older brothers, Johnny and Nick—they loved Jeff, and I was always pleased that they took a liking to me as well, because they might be very scary if one found themselves in their disfavor, arms as large as tree trunks, driving a low-rider car, barely inches off the ground—had passed down to Phil the love of the Motown sound. We'd come home from school, each grabbing a corner of my bed, and Phil would pull out his cassette tape of the The Four Tops. It was with Phil that I heard these words for the first time, and I was totally blown away:

Now if you feel that you can't go on (can't go on)
Because all of your hope is gone (all your hope is gone)
And your life is filled with much confusion (much confusion)
Until happiness is just an illusion (happiness is just an illusion)
And your world around is crumbling down, darling
Reach out for me
I'll be there with a love that will shelter you
I'll be there with a love that will see you through

The song begins with the high, delicious, strawberry-candy notes of the organ, the snare drum sounding almost as though someone is keeping a perfect beat on a garbage can—raw, primitive, rousing—then the lyrics burning a slow ember of soul, the texture of deep, dark chocolate sauce; unforgettable. "Now if you feel that you can't go on, because all of your hope is gone, and your life is filled with much confusion," the chorus chanting the refrain like honey, a few octaves above the burning embers of the vocals; the song hypnotized me (and as I listen to it now in the middle of writing these words, it has the flavor of a rare scotch, a smoky, tobacco flavor that lingers on one's breath, a scotch from one of the islands off the Scotland mainland, such as Islay).

And from this song we started bouncing up and down on the bed as these words took over:

> *Standing in the shadows of love*
> *Waiting for the heartaches to come*
> *Can't you see me standing in the shadows of love?*
> *I get ready for the heartaches to come*
> *I'd run, but there's no where to go*
> *Cause heartaches will follow me I know*
> *Without your love, the love I need*
> *It's the beginning of the end for me.*

And then on to, of course, could there be anything better, Phil dancing and snapping his fingers, lip-syncing to an imaginary mike:

> *Ooooooooooooooh, Sugar pie, honey bunch,*
> *You know that I love you,*
> *I can't help myself,*
> *I love you and nobody else*

When I think of my soul-buddy Phil, I go no further than the Four Tops.

Phil's love of motown influenced me irrevocably, but I had an equal effect on him. He had never really sat down to listen to a Rolling Stones album until one afternoon after school when I put on "Big Hits (High Tide And Green Grass)." Even at 15 years, Phil was not a big talker—though he definitely was a prankster—but he always had a serious, thoughtful answer when asked a question. When listening to music, there was a side to him that enjoyed relaxing quietly, laying back, head down and grooving to it. Given his R&B- and soul-influenced tastes, he immediately took to this album. I'll never forget the sheer bliss that came on his face—really truly hearing this song for the first time, though no doubt he'd heard it on the radio before—when this one came on, Jagger intoning his reverie and bluesy philosophy, Richards bathing it in a warm, sensuous pool:

Time is on my side, yes it is
Time is on my side, yes it is
Now you always say that you want to be free
But you'll come running back
(said you would baby)
You'll come running back
(I said so many times before)
You'll come running back to me

After this there followed—Jagger measuring his words clearly and slowly, the Englishness dripping from his London accent, invoking an almost Southern United States R&B at the same time, the texture of the vocals coming from a warm place deep within his core—the base notes and the words:

There've been so many
Girls that I've known
I've made so many cry
And still I wonder why
Here comes the little girl
I see her walking down the street
She's all by herself
I try and knock her off her feet
You'll never break, never break, never break
This heart of Stone.

"That's fuckin great," Phil had said. "It's my favorite by the Stones," I had answered. We listened to that song again and again for years. Several years ago the Stones came to the Bay Area for three shows. I went to one of them and got lucky. About halfway through the concert, Jagger—thanks to my ticket guy Stu at Mr. Ticket, I was really close—says that "we're gonna dig way back into the past and do one that we rarely do in concert," and then I'm drenched in those opening English, southern-blues licks followed by "There've been so many, girls that I've known." It was ecstasy, and I was back in that moment when Phil and I were sitting on my bed, laying back against the wall and listening to it for the first time.

❒

It is early in 1971, and I had just tried marijuana for the first time. A couple of friends, Chad and Glen, had been smoking it for a few months and had been trying to get me to try it, but I had steadfastly refused. Walking home from school through a little alley that I always used as a shortcut, I happened on the two boys just as they had lit up a thin, but tightly rolled joint. Actually, I smelled the stuff—an alluring scent, sweet and earthy, something like a combination of burning flowers and rope, with a hint of mint—as I turned the corner to go into the alley before actually finding my friends. "Brucie boy, sit down and smoke this joint with us," Glen said. "Yeah, nothing to be afraid of my dear boy," followed Chad, his eyes closing as he takes a deep, long hit, then exhaling very little of what he brought in.

Both these guys had very short hair, as short as mine, up until just a few months before, but at this point—the culture of marijuana taking over their brains—their hair was becoming quite long. Chad's hair was dark brown and totally, perfectly straight—I had always envied guys with hair so straight, mine always an unruly ball of curls and frizz—and was approaching the top of his shoulders. He wore a green headband inlaid with native American designs, and was doing his best to grow a beard, which at this point amounted to a crop of red fuzz from one ear, continuing along the jaw line to the other ear. Glen's hair was blond, very thin, also perfectly straight. It was crossing the boundary from short to long. He played on my hockey team, and was a good skater, though not really fast. But he had good puck-control skills, and just a few months earlier had given me a beautiful pass as I was breaking toward the center of the ice, hitting me in full stride as I got past the two green-clad defenseman of the Burbank team, assisting on my third goal of the game, as I whipped a shot low and to the stick-side of the goalie. I had so badly wanted to score a hat trick (three goals in a game) and it had evaded me all season. But on this day I scored one against one of the best teams in the league, though I wouldn't get another one the rest of the season. Yes, Glen's hair was getting quite long—though not as long as Chad's at this point—and he was starting to receive a lot of flack for it from our French coach, Guy Fournier. Guy kept threatening to bench Glen, if he didn't cut his hair, but up to this point Glen had been playing well enough to avoid being benched, managing to retain his locks. So, just several weeks earlier, he had assisted on my hat trick, and now he was trying to assist in "turning me on."

Chad passes the joint to Glen, who takes a deep hit, but doesn't hold it in as long as Chad does, releasing more smoke than Chad had done—releasing it into my face, the alluring scent of those burning flowers mixed with dirt, rope and mint. "If you're ever going to try it, this is the stuff to try," Chad says to me. "It's Panama Red; no shit, it is the real thing, Panama Red, I assure you of that." "Try it," Glen follows, "We just started; you can finish it with us." I sit down next to them and receive the cigarette from Glen. And then I take a shallow hit, holding it all in as I feel the warm smoke infiltrate my throat, mouth and lungs. I exhale virtually no smoke at all. "Good hit!" exclaims Chad; "Nice hit," follows Glen. I pass it to Chad, who takes another of his long, slow inhales, holding it in as long as he can, closing his eyes, a beatific look on his face—Chad is in ecstasy, totally absorbed in the enjoyment of the moment. He passes it to Glen, again taking a deep hit, but letting out a fair amount of smoke; and then back to me, as I bring in a shallow, but full hit, again releasing very little smoke as I exhale. We finish the joint, and at first I'm not sure that I am experiencing anything different, though I do definitely notice that the ground on which I am sitting has a unique texture, softer than pavement, my hands and ass feeling as though they are melting into the ground. And as my hands and ass begin to become one with the asphalt, my entire body begins to heat up. I feel as though I am getting warmer and warmer, beginning at the core of my stomach, extending to my legs (as we stand up), through the arms to the fingertips, continuing into my chest, heart, into my ears. Suddenly my ears are burning, and though I am not scared, I am a bit alarmed. "Are your bodies hot, do you guys feel this in your ears, are your ears hot?" "You are stoned!" Chad says, "This guy is really stoned." "Want to play some hockey?" Glen says to me, pretending to take a slap-shot at an imaginary goalie. "No really, my whole body feels hot," I continue. "Are you guys hot?" "No, I'm not hot," Chad answers, "but I'm buzzing, that's for sure," he continues. "I'm really ripped," Glen follows, "Let's go up to my house to listen to some music." And we all walk across Tarzana Avenue, turn onto a street that brings us up a hill (it felt as though we were climbing Mt. Everest, never had this hill seemed so steep), and then up another hill to Glen's place. Glen had a gorgeous house, built on different levels up a hillside.

The middle level had a pool, though this being early winter, the pool was drained. His parents—the father was really cool, Jack was his name, he had long hair, entertained a lot of people from the counterculture, famous people, though Glen would never tell me their names, and was, clearly, very wealthy, giving us a ride from time to time in his blue Corvette—lived in the upper house, above the pool, while Glen had the lower house, below the pool, to himself. Glen's bedroom was exceptionally comfortable, with a few cushiony beanbags on the floor. I blissfully land in one of these bags, Chad crashing in another one, as Glen puts on an album he had bought just a few days ago. The needle crisply cuts through the vinyl like freshly sharpened ice skates slicing through outdoor ice on a cold winter's day, the speakers conducting the sound with such precision that there was no separation of the music from my ear.

Four times Jimmy Page strikes the opening chords—two chords each time of pure fire power, raw, electric, filled with heat and gravity—followed by John Bonham introducing himself for the very first time, keeping time in the background as he breaks into his pounding, muscular, rhythmic beat. And then I hear Robert Plant for the very first time, as he sings with raw energy about the confusion of a boy reaching manhood. The song is "Good Times, Bad Times."

That was it for me. There was no turning back. Led Zeppelin's marketing had its desired effect: I was hypnotized. I remain hypnotized to this day. Led Zeppelin's first album—this was their debut album, incredible, it was the realization of a platonic musical form, if one might apply it to rock music—entered my bloodstream, a bloodstream warmed to receive it by an agent they call Panama Red. It just kept getting better. The gorgeous, acoustic, slow, bluesy, rainbow of notes played by Page, as Plant begins to sing the opening lines of "Babe, I'm Gonna Leave You."

And then, eventually, the slow, deep, descending bass notes, leading into the stratospheric, piercing high notes of Page, the mournful wail of Plant taking over, in "Dazed and Confused."

And this followed by the pure fire of Page's guitar.

"Phil has to hear this music in this way," I thought to myself. And while I had a real sense that smoking this stuff was taboo—and I knew that Phil would absolutely think so—it was something I wanted to try and experience with my best friend.

A couple of days later I told Phil that I had tried marijuana with Glen and Chad, and that I had heard this Led Zeppelin album that was "just unbelievable;" that it brought you to "another place," and that I'd never heard anything "sound as incredible as that." Phil looked me directly in the eyes, shook his head with a touch of derision, and tilting his head to one side said, "I can't believe you did that. If your mom ever finds out, she's gonna be really, really pissed, and you'll be in big trouble. And you know what will happen if your dad finds out."

This occurred in the months before I hopped the freight trains, during that period when my father's anger, his desire to control every aspect of my life, his threats to "smash my head" had become intolerable. This was the period when I had decided that I wouldn't back down from him again, if he came after me violently; and it was during this period that his threats to my mom that he would "leave if I didn't leave" (my mom answering, "That's easy Larry, just leave") had become constant. "He's a total asshole, Phil, a total asshole, and he'd better not come after me, because I'll knock him down next time," I said. "Naw, that's your father, you won't knock him down. He ain't all that bad; he takes you to hockey games," Phil answered. "You don't know half of it, you don't know half of it," I answered. And then Phil addressed my request that he try smoking this stuff with me, and that we then go hear music afterwards. "You don't need to smoke that shit, like Glen and Chad; you don't want to be like those guys. Just drink beer; what's wrong with drinking beer? I ain't gonna smoke that stuff; if my dad ever found out, he'd absolutely destroy me." And so I dropped it. But in dropping it, I didn't stop smoking, though I would only do it on weekends, after my hockey games were finished.

≈

Phillip Rusty Siegler, I love you like a brother, and how nice it would be to have a friend who cares about me as you did, a friend who gave and received friendship like you; who wanted nothing more than to be a friend. I miss you buddy; I really miss you, I think, as I look out on this very dark February night in San Francisco, pellets of cold rain splashing against my window. The foreground is dark, the ever-present beam of light from Alcatraz breaking through the darkness in rhythmic, timed sequence; the Golden Gate Bridge visible only by the lights that distinguish it. I am that boy, late in his 15th year, my hair getting longer now—I hadn't cut it in a few months, and my father was raging about that—lying down in the bedroom of a friend of Chad's, headphones on as I'm listening to Jimmy Hendrix for the very first time.

❒

A group of us had just smoked a couple of joints—didn't have the burning sensation this time, but rather a feeling of drifting on a magic carpet—and I had plugged in some headphones to the cartridge player. I press play and am taken over by the music of rocket ships transporting me to a place far into the ethereal night. After that opening intro known as, "And the Gods Made Love," the musical currents flow seamlessly into the sound of an instrument—I had never heard a guitar make music like this, virtually the essence of a sound, but more like a vibration of gently, flowing waves, flowing for miles. And then the voice, rich, soft, layers of depth below the surface, the texture of silk that caresses. He sings or rather glides, "Have you ever been to Electric Ladyland?"

During this song I had visions to which I succumbed. I saw the vision of a rabbi, full beard, yarmulke on the head, and he was saying words to me in Hebrew. I remembered the words briefly, but cannot remember them any longer. And he kept saying them. He was at peace. Was he a guardian spirit? Was he an ancestor? A universal archetype of a rabbi? I don't know, but the experience was profound. He came to me with a message, and I succumbed to it, inherited it, allowed it in, though I knew not what it meant in words. But I did have a knowledge on another level, and I feel that I carry that knowledge with me today.

The music poured through me; and it was a journey into the recesses of my mind that I had never explored. Mr. Hendrix's magic wand had had its effect, and to this day I remember the journey of experiencing "Electric Ladyland" for the very first time. The spell was partially broken, though, when I came walking toward my front lawn late that Sunday afternoon, Phil playing ball with Jeff. Thinking that I'm being nonchalant, I walk up to Phil and say hi, my intention being to go directly into the house and to my room. Phil takes one look at me and says, "You are totally stoned. You should see your eyes. They're completely red. Better get some Visine or something. If your mother sees you like that, she's gonna know instantly that you're stoned. I wouldn't go in there if I were you. Come over here, Jeff; look at how high your brother is." I start to smile it off, saying, "No way, I'm not high." "You can't fool me," Phil answers; followed by my brother saying, "Bruce, you really look stoned." I take Phil's advice and walk down to the corner store and have a Coke, and did that ever taste delicious. By the time—an hour and a half later—I returned to the house, I was much more presentable, according to Phil.

During the next couple of months, I continued to smoke the occasional joint, but not pushing Phil at all to join me. He wasn't interested, and I certainly didn't want to be the kid his parents would call a "bad influence." And, clearly, there was a touch of guilt that I felt in smoking, because if I couldn't share it with my best friend, and if I was afraid of my mom finding out, then it was hard to fully embrace. But the music was so delicious and electrifying, mind-changing after smoking, that I continued to partake and enjoy. One afternoon after school I met up with Phil and he offered to give me a ride home—he was now a legal rider, having recently turned 16—on his yellow motorcycle. We pulled into the local liquor store, located just across the railroad tracks that abutted the alley I would take to walk home—the same alley where I had met Chad and Glen that Panama Red afternoon—to get a Coke. We get on the motorcycle—each holding our Coke in one hand—and Phil crosses the tracks, diverting from the main street, and pulls into the alley for the shortcut to my place. Pulling into the alley we come on the nice, slightly secluded open space where I had smoked that first time. "Phil, pull over, right in here," I say to him. "Why?" Phil answers. "Just pull over for a second, I want to show you something," I answer. So he does, and as he gets off the bike, the wool is not pulled over Phil's eyes. "You're gonna try to get me to smoke with you, aren't ya?" he says. "You're a bad influence, Rosen," he says to me. "Phil, I haven't asked you in a few months, ever since that first time when I tried it, but yeah, you're right, I have a joint on me. It's really, really good—and you won't believe what music sounds like on this stuff." "Okay Rosen, all right, I'll try it. But if I get busted for this, you're in big, big trouble."

I pull out the tightly wound cigarette, and it is aromatic, sweet, another version of the combination of mint, dirt, flowers, dry grass, warmly but not hotly filling the lungs. Phil smokes it like it is second nature to him. He inhales, holds it in, slowly exhales. We smoke the whole thing, and I'm very, very buzzed. Getting back on the motorcycle Phil says, "I don't feel a thing.

Maybe this stuff won't affect me. I've heard that it doesn't affect some people." It is just a few blocks to my house, and when we get there, Phil pulls down the kick stand, looks at me, smiles; I laugh at him, he laughs back at me, and then we are laughing together, and it is getting louder and crazier, completely euphoric. "You are high, Phil," I say to him. "I know," he answers, "I have no idea how I ever got my bike here. It's like it drove itself." My dad was gone, my mom was at work—she had recently taken a job (her first job in many years, outside of reading teacups) at a Country and Western record label in Hollywood, working with Buck Owens, Dusty Rhodes and other country names—so we went into my bedroom to listen to music. I had recently graduated from the "Led Zeppelin 1" album to "Led Zeppelin 2," and I put it on for Phil, just as our high was reaching its crescendo. Jimmy Page's opening chords to the first song are raw, elemental, combustible, and for a 16-year-old guy, really buzzed on some good stuff for the first time (Colombian, I had been told), life changing. And then Plant begins to sing the "crawling on the floor and wanting to fuck" opening lines of "Whole Lotta Love."

And this occurs against the pounding, throbbing (centurions could be marching to the sound of it), powerful, muscular, testosterone-filled drumming of John Bonham, in my mind the greatest rock (maybe of any genre) drummer of all time. From here, Jimmy Page soars, the language of his guitar not so much audible as penetrating the entire circulatory system, Bonham again taking over as he trades solos with the magician on guitar. And then again, Mr. Robert Plant.

The look on Phil's face—absolutely shocked, astounded, intoxicated, cerebral, ecstatic, intense, happy, very very happy. "See what I mean, Phil?" I say. "These guys are fuckin' amazing—this music is incredible; incredible." "Yeah, I see what you mean, Rosen, Mr. Hockey Player," he answers; the Arkansas drawl more prominent in his very stoned marijuana state. And we start laughing uncontrollably as the words "I want a Whole Lotta Love" are repeated again, and again, and again.

❐

About a month and a half after our voyage with Led Zeppelin I went on my own brief, but very intense journey of self-discovery when I hopped freight trains across the country with my friend of Native American descent, Steve Pencille. That trip, as I have described, will be with me, has become part of the chemistry of my blood, forever. I reflect on it now, and there are very few weeks of my life when some of those moments do not present themselves to me.

I am thinking of the time that the train stopped for a complete day in the red clay desert of Texas—Steve and myself eating the peanut butter and jelly sandwiches that we made from that revolutionary jar, where the peanut butter and jelly were mixed together; I marvel at the significant risk I took that night when I took leave of the train stopped in the Tucson yard—searchlights beaming all around the train yard, where I read a sign that said that, "Stowaways will be prosecuted to the fullest extent of the law"—darting across the tracks to buy the few groceries (including the peanut and butter and jelly in the jar), barely making it back to the accelerating train as I jump on it (trying to stay below the search lights) several cars down from our home car; I remember the phone call I made from the El Paso train station to my tormented mom, the phone ringing and ringing to no answer; I'll never forget the horrible breathlessness I felt from an asthma attack that stormy night in the Midwest, as I tried to sleep in the boxcar; and the words play in my head, just as they did the day that I heard them, the words telling me that if I wanted to go home, it wouldn't happen unless I took the action to turn myself around—the music of Bob Dylan's, "Like a Rolling Stone," the sound track to my thoughts. "How does it feel, to be on your own, no direction home, a complete unknown, like a rolling stone?" were much more than the lyrics of a song to me; they cut to the core of this adventure/crisis as I considered that I had gone far enough, and that I would need to split apart from Steve and return home. I did, of course, make it back home, and about a month and a half after that, my father left the family for good. That he left was a good thing at the time, because I don't think that I would have ever been able to expand in my youth, actually live out the "call of the wild" for which my soul ached, been free enough to travel the roads of Costa Rica and the trains of Europe, so overwhelmingly repressive and violent had he become. Not long after he left, Phil, my brother Jeff and I hitchhiked to the Colorado River in Arizona, where Phil's family had a trailer just yards from the river.

The banks of the Colorado River in Arizona had been an extremely popular place for high school and college kids to come with their sleeping bags during Easter break or spring recess. It was festive, with kids forming circles around a few guitarists; lots of Dylan, the Beatles, Cat Stevens, Arlo Guthrie songs filling the air, the hashish peace pipe being passed around, lights of matches and lighters flickering up and down the shore, billowing clouds of sweet, rope-smelling smoke forming wherever the circles of kids had congregated. I didn't actually experience the river during spring break until I went with Phil during my first year of college, 1974, my father well into establishing a new life for himself in Montreal. We'd hang out at water's edge into the evening, partying, singing songs—I have vivid memories of us all singing, "Coming into Los Angeleees, bringing in a couple of keys, don't touch my bags if you please, Mr. Customs man," by Arlo Guthrie—then the two of us would go back to spend the night at the trailer, which his family kept at the river year-round. But the first time I ever went to the River was in the last weeks of June 1971, just weeks after my father left, and a couple of months after hopping the freights. Indeed, we had hitchhiked there, but chills run up my spine when I think back to the fact that two 16-year-old boys—granted I was seasoned from the train tracks and felt mature, and Phil was certainly a reliable foxhole partner—and a 15 year old (my brother, Jeff) were hitchhiking across the desert. We had told my mom we were getting a ride there, but the truth is we hitchhiked. Yes, it was much more common than it is today—as a father of two college-aged young men, I am horrified at the thought of it—but, Lord knows, there were huge risks. But I was not averse to taking risks, as was the case in the late morning of our second day at the river.

It starts to become very hot at the Colorado River in late June, so you don't find many people sunbathing on the banks. Those who come here at this time of the year to play usually do so in their motor boats, enjoying the miles on miles of this snaking river—the current passive in some places, quick and accelerating in others—fishing poles sometimes extended, the sun strong on their backs, the dry air soothing the bones and comforting to the spirit. Near to where Phil's trailer was situated was a bridge that is not much wider than the train tracks for which it was used to bring freight across the river and on into the desert to its destination. The bridge stood maybe 50 feet above the river, and if one jumped from the bridge, there was a little island in the river, about 100 yards from the landing place. And that is exactly what we did that hot, hot morning—jump from the bridge into the water, the destination being the island. It had been Phil's idea to do so; Jeff was enthusiastic, and I not that much so. It wasn't something I was excited to do, and I had a hard time convincing myself that I would enjoy it. Their minds had been made up, so I followed along with them as they walked up the road to the entrance of the bridge.

The sun had become oppressive at this point, its hot rays feeling like prickly needles on my scalp and back, an itchiness up and down my back that I wanted to scratch but wasn't able to do. "No problem, it will be nice to cool down in that water," I had thought to myself. First Phil jumped, barely looking down at all, just going up to the edge of the bridge beyond the tracks, looking down for a second and jumping. Then he began his swim to the island, and he was swimming smoothly and easily. Then

Jeff jumped; he looked down for several seconds, doing his best to bury his fear, and followed Phil into the water, laughing with exhilaration when he came up, splashing his way without too much difficulty to the island. When I approached the edge of the bridge, Phil was just making his way onto the island, Jeff about 50 yards away. I stood there, essentially paralyzed with fear, unable to jump. It looked very far down, though their jumps lasted just a couple of seconds. "Jump, it's easy, it feels great when you get in," Phil yelled from the island. I continued to stand there, totally psyched out by my perception of the distance, my thought process interrupting the action of jumping. And the more I thought, the more I started imagining the things that might go wrong. What if I landed the wrong way; what if I couldn't make it to the island? A few minutes pass, Jeff and Phil relaxing on the island, veterans of the jump. "Is it a hard swim, any kind of current?" I yell at them. "It's really easy," answers Phil. "It'll be a piece of cake for you," follows my brother. "Go on and just jump," continues Phil. "Don't think about it, Bruce, just do it," follows my brother.

So I jump. I was petrified as I did so, hyperventilating when I came to the surface. And now the swim. Gasping for air as I started the swim, I was at a huge disadvantage. I swam earnestly, but felt short on oxygen. I was using way too many strokes for the distance I was moving. And then I started to get tired. I continued swimming with all the energy that I had, but it didn't feel to me that I was getting very far. And I continued to become more and more out of breath. I had barely reached half way to the island when I realized that it was too far to go. I decided to turn back. "Come on Bruce, keep swimming; you're halfway here," yelled Phil. "You can make it Bruce, it's not much further," echoed Jeff. But I proceeded to swim back toward land. And as I did, I found myself being caught in a current. There was no current against which I was pushing as I was making my way toward the island, but now that I was heading back toward land, I was up against one. "Guys, I'm in a current, and it's pushing me. It's hard to make it to land; it's pushing me down the river," I had the strength to yell. There was a moment of deliberation—just a split second of pause—and then Phil yells to Jeff, "We better go after him." I'm in this current, unable to swim against it to get to the land that didn't seem very far away at all, and Phil and my brother are ripping through the water like Olympians, their strokes quick, efficient, life saving. I'm keeping my head above water, but as I'm so doing, I find myself nearing exhaustion. And I'm afraid. And I was particularly afraid of some motorboat ripping by, not being able to see me. In the current, I was right in the path of these motorboats.

Phil is on me, Jeff just behind him. As he approaches me, Phil yells, "Keep your head up; don't let it go under. Keep it up." Phil reaches me. "Grab my arm," he says calmly, "Just grab my arm, and I'll get us to shore. "Push him," Phil yells to Jeff. "Push him, as I'm pulling him." And then what do I do? I jump on Phil's back. "Get off my back!" he yells. "Just grab my arm." My brother, Jeff, all the while pushing me forward. Phil then has the presence of mind to make a joke, "They always tell you to make sure they don't jump on your back, if you're saving somebody. Now I know what they're talking about," and then he starts laughing. As he laughs, my momentum now going forward, cutting through the current, I start to become relaxed, gaining my wind, taking it the remaining 30 or so yards to the shore myself. When I reach the hot, scorching sand, I go into a prayer position, kneeling, hands outstretched on the earth, "Thank you God," I say. And then I kiss the ground. Phil and Jeff laugh as I do this. I get up and hug Phil with everything that I have, and then I hug my brother. They didn't say that they had saved my life, but it was understood. They saved my life. And I carry Phil and my brother Jeff with me forever.

Daurie and Cheryl

In the early winter of 1972, I had become charmed by the lightness, joy, carefree nature, infectious laugh of a girl named Daurie. She was 17 like myself, had gorgeous, clear, olive-hued skin, brown hair with blondish highlights that was styled in such a way that it accentuated her angular features—the high Cherokee-looking cheekbones, the thin, athletic, elegant neck, the chiseled jaw—as it cascaded in layers along her face and fell aesthetically upon her shoulders. Daurie was a beautiful girl, all the more so because of her inner love of life, acceptance and trust in the goodness of people, the total lack of judgment one felt in her presence. One cannot think of Daurie without remembering those penetrating, emerald green eyes, eyes that saw right into your soul. They became known as "Daurie eyes," and anyone who came into her presence was captivated by them. I have never seen a green like them in all the years since meeting her; and though they were large and round, they were framed by lids that provided them an almost Asian quality, forming the shape of an almond. What fun one saw in those eyes, but not just fun, a knowingness and wisdom way beyond her years. Daurie and I would often walk home from school together, find a grassy spot in the park, and smoke a bit of weed, then go over to my house or her house and listen to music. Her favorite song was "Surfer Girl," by the Beach Boys; and under the influence of my friend Chad's weed—he would turn me on to just amazing stuff—Daurie and I would groove to the sweet, euphoric vibration of Brian Wilson as he sang:

Little surfer little one,
Made my heart come all undone;
Do you love me, do you surfer girl?
I have watched you on the shore,
Standing by the ocean's roar;
Do you love me, do you surfer girl?
Surfer girl, surfer girl,

But Daurie also loved the Rolling Stones, and herein lay my influence on her. She hadn't been into the Stones until she met me. But when she heard the relatively recently released "Honky-Tonk Woman," she was hooked. After Surfer Girl, she'd get up and dance, shaking her hips in a very sexy way as Jagger put her in the mood:

> *I met a gin-soaked bar-room queen in Memphis*
> *She tried to take me upstairs for a ride*
> *She had to heave me right across her shoulder*
> *'Cos I just can't seem to drink you off my mind*
> *It's the honky-tonk, honky-tonk woman*
> *Gimme, gimme, gimme the honky-tonk blues.*

We had a ton of fun in brief moments together; and it was a friendship that we had—sort of like a girl buddy—neither of us letting it become romantic or sexual. We enjoyed each other's company a lot, and so there was a sort of unwritten, unsaid rule about it that we wouldn't want anything to threaten the fun that we were having. By the spring of 1972, Daurie had become a best friend.

❒

I had known Cheryl for a couple of years, meeting her not long after we moved to Calvert Street in Reseda. In those early days of knowing her, she was very shy and bashful. She had a "little girl" quality about her, maturing physically a little later than many girls in their mid-teens. We went to the same junior high school, and she sat directly in front of me in homeroom my first year there. Her long, wavy, brown hair fell on my desk, and I would tie strands of it together, Cheryl turning around, blushing, pretending to slap me. A friend once told me that she had a crush on me, but I couldn't take it seriously, since she seemed much more like a little sister than a peer. She was quite a pretty little girl in those days, an olive complexion (one of her parents was Hispanic), with freckles covering much of her nose. She had thin lips, and a sweet, melt-a-daddy's heart kind of smile. She had to be in quite early on Friday and Saturday evenings, so she was never part of the crowd of kids that would hang out in the park on many weekend evenings. She was very smart and proper—always seemed to have the right answers when she raised her hand in class, thanking the teacher when being complimented for having done her homework. While I was into the Beatles, Rolling Stones and Herman's Hermits in those days—these were the pre-Led Zeppelin days—she still loved the Monkees and the Jackson Five. She loved chewing bubble gum, and "bubble gum" would be an apt description for her taste in music.

By late 1971, when Phil, my brother Jeff and I had really gotten into the musical journeys, stimulated by the quality hemp that always seemed to be available, Cheryl had still not changed very much physically. She was tall, thin, remained very proper, still having all the right answers in class, her musical tastes in a totally different world from the stuff that I was listening to with Phil, Chad, Glen and my brother Jeff. Cheryl seemed to be in a time warp, much closer physically and in terms of personality to my little sister, Heidi, than any of the girls our age. But by spring, 1972, wow, something had changed. I hadn't seen her for awhile and she showed up one evening at my place with Daurie—they had become good friends of late—sitting cross-legged on the floor, partaking of the joint that was being passed around by several of us guys.

Over the past few weeks, Daurie and Phil had become sexual, and were now, for all intents and purposes, boyfriend and girlfriend. I sat there listening to Steve Miller, a good friend of mine, strumming his guitar. He was playing several Steve Miller (of the famous Steve Miller Band, no relation to my friend) tunes. I was overwhelmed by how beautiful Cheryl had become. She was showing cleavage with a V-neck top, arms and feet tanned, hair thick and wavy as it draped her arms, sitting as she was in the yoga-style, cross-legged position. She was stunning, so much so that she seemed untouchable, amazing. But this was Cheryl I was looking at—and I must have really been staring at her, because she turned to me as she took that first hit, her eyes saying, "Okay already, don't flip out, I'm hot; I've grown into a young woman." The joint makes its way over to me, I take a deep, long hit—my friend, Steve Miller, eyes looking intense behind those thick-rimmed glasses, having switched from singing Steve Miller songs to "Lay, Lady Lay" by Dylan—and pass it over to Phil, who tells me not to "Bogart that joint, my friend," and then leans over and kisses Daurie, blowing the smoke from his hit into her mouth, continuing to make out for a considerable period of time afterwards. We must have been in that garage for about an hour after Daurie arrived with Cheryl, and I must have had my eyes on that beautiful, enchanting woman virtually the whole time, the softness of her whole being, the long, wavy, brown hair flowing over her arms mesmerizing me.

During that spring, 1971, I had discovered one late night, while listening to the Los Angeles underground FM radio station KMET, quite buzzed on some Afghanistan black hashish, an electric guitar solo that had to be Jimmy Hendrix. But Hendrix's pieces eventually led to those sublimely mellow vocals, and this song was a strict instrumental. It wasn't until the end of the song, when a voice comes on and says, "Oh, 'Maggot Brain,' " that I realized it was not Hendrix, but from the same distant galaxy. Its searing, scorching, ozone-piercing, shrieking guitar penetrated the outer layer of the atmosphere and brought me in touch with interplanetary objects. The brilliant flashes of comets and meteors, the blackness of the filament occasionally penetrated by the blue-hot distant suns, my mind soared through space at somewhere near the speed of light, undeterred by gravity, contained in its own vessel of mental energy, my headphones the fuel for the journey. It was an incredible discovery that night on the radio. There had been a couple of pieces of music before that, but the only thing that I can remember was that incredible pulsating guitar. In a deep midnight voice that was a conduit for dreams, the announcer provided the titles and artists of what had been played in the set, concluding by saying that, "The final song in the set was "Maggot Brain" by Funkadellic. You're listening to KMET, 94.7, Los Angeles."

Funkadellic, I had never heard of them; but my God, what an insane, absolutely incredible guitar piece I had just heard. In the next couple of days, I requested the song be played again on the radio; and one night we were all obliged—Phil, Chad, Mark Webber, my brother, Jeff, Daurie, Cheryl and a few other kids. We had smoked some more of that same Black Afghan hashish, and the disc jockey came through for us. And to a person, each of my friends was hypnotized by it—none of us had heard anything like it. This was a total revelation, and it sounded just as amazing that night with my friends as it did on the journey in my bedroom with headphones.

A couple of days later, the music was replaced by intense, bewildering, panic and dread. My mom had told Daurie and Cheryl to never hitchhike. I can hear her words loud as a bell, as I look out over the black bay, no illumination of moon, just the consistent, rhythmic beam of the light on Alcatraz rock. She had pulled Daurie and Cheryl aside, in front of me one afternoon. "I want to tell you girls something," she had said. "I don't want you girls to hitchhike. I don't have good feelings about it." The girls smiled, then nodded with seriousness. "Okay, Mrs. Rosen," they had agreed. "We won't hitchhike."

Not long after that conversation, Daurie and Cheryl were missing. They hadn't come home one night. Each had told their parents that they were going to the mall for lunch and shopping. The next night led to the next day. And the next day became the next night, and they still had not come home. Panic and dread; panic and dread; panic and dread, as their parents searched everywhere, day and night for them.

I asked my mom what she thought, and she wouldn't answer. But the look on her face, the aura surrounding her said everything. It had become clear to me as I looked at my mom that we must be prepared for the worst. We prayed, we hoped; we prayed, we hoped; we prayed, we hoped, but a few more days went by and Daurie and Cheryl still hadn't come back.

The police, having been told that my mom was very psychic, asked her what she felt, could she steer them in some direction. Her face was ashen, cheeks sunken, as she shook her head, perhaps not wanting to say anything that would cause anybody to give up hope. She prayed and hoped against what she deeply knew. All of Daurie's and Cheryl's friends—all of us—were interviewed by the police detectives on the case to see if we could shed some light. None of us could. I remember a detective showing me a picture of a camp site, a sign in the background saying, "Party Place." He wanted to know if I had ever seen this place before. I didn't recognize it; couldn't identify it. Seeing it, I asked him if they believed Daurie and Cheryl had been taken to this place. He became quiet and said that he couldn't answer that question.

A day or two later, and the details were all over the news. Daurie and Cheryl had gone hitchhiking. They were picked up in a pickup truck by a group of boys and girls. They had been taken to some kind of campsite, where they had been murdered. I have blocked out the details of what had been done to them. It was gruesome. Arrests had been made. We saw the faces of those who had done it. The horror.

A week or so after the discovery, our group of friends gathered together one night. We called KMET and requested to hear the song "Maggot Brain." I had told them that we were remembering our friends, and what had happened to them. The announcer knew the story very well. A few minutes later, the piece was played. And then it was followed by the deeply affecting song, "The Wind Cries Mary," by Jimmy Hendrix

There is nothing more that I can say tonight. I walk over and put on that beautiful first pressing of "Rubber Soul" that I had bought on Bleeker street. I have to hear John Lennon at the moment; and he sings to me:

There are places I remember,
All my life, though some have changed.
Some forever, not for better,
Some have gone and some remain.
All these places had their moments,
With lovers and friends
I still can recall.
Some are dead and some are living,
In my life
I've loved them all.

I am reliving that time intensely at the moment; reliving it, viscerally, emotionally, in a way that I have not since those days. It seems that I have carried these girls with me through my whole life. I'll see a girl with tanned arms, gorgeous bare feet, flowing wavy hair hanging down past her waist, a smile that is gentle, pure, captivating, and I think of Cheryl. I often think of Cheryl. And those eyes of Daurie's are the stuff of legend. They were feline, bewildering, seductive, friendly, hypnotic, spiritual and carefree. If you'd known Daurie, you'd know what I mean about those eyes—maybe there is one, but I can't think of any artist that could have painted them.

❐

My mind echoes with memories of Phil. I can truly say that I have known the loyalty of a true friend in my life. I reflect on that time in the Fall of 1973, my first year of college, when I had come home to find Phil with a clean-shaven head, those beautiful, golden, thick flowing locks fully shorn. His head was bald, and it was hideous to me. At that time in my life, hair represented freedom, the expression of my soul, feeling it blow wildly in the wind represented liberation from the years of physical and mental abuse of my father's punishments. The longer, the better; the wilder it was, the further removed I was from the world where he would threaten me with beatings, stopping my hockey playing, of chasing away of friends that he didn't like. And the girls liked my wild hair.

I was a college kid studying philosophy—quite adept at recounting the thinking of Nietzsche, Freud, Marx, Sartre—and was enjoying the intellectual and sensual freedoms really for the first time in my life. I didn't bring up these philosophers and their ideas just so I would appear intellectual and bring girls to bed—girls just loved the intellectual types with the long hair—but my hair and conceptual understanding of these thinkers certainly combined for some fun times. The deeper into philosophy I delved, the longer my hair grew. And the longer my hair grew, the easier it seemed to get girls. Now, Phil never went to college. He worked tough construction jobs—he seemed to get a serious injury to an arm, a hand, a leg virtually every month—and most of the time after work would come over and hang out with my brother Jeff. Jeff had taken a break as a hockey goalie during that fall—early that winter he would move to Montreal where he was wanted as a goalie for a junior team in Montreal—and was hanging out with Phil quite a bit. "Phil, what in the fuck did you do to your head?" I asked him that afternoon, arriving at the house after a day at college. I was going to California State University, Northridge, this first year of college, and was living at home. "I decided to join the army. When you get out, the benefits will be really great. They'll basically give you the money to buy a house." "Phil, are you serious? There is a war going on in Vietnam right now. Do you want to go to Vietnam? You're crazy. You've got a great life. You really want to run off and do this?" "I'm going to do it. And guess what?" "What?" I replied. "Your brother is going to come in with me, too. We' re going to do it under the buddy system. They promised that if we join together, we can go in together, go to training together, and be together through the whole time." "And they'll send both of you to Vietnam as well? The fuckin' buddy system?" I continued. At this moment, my brother Jeff walks in, still with a full head of hair. "What is this shit I'm hearing," I say to my brother. "You and Phil are going to join the army? What about hockey? Have you decided to quit playing hockey? You might even make it to the NHL. Do you know that you might even end up going to Vietnam? This is fuckin' stupid you guys. Do you guys think that you'll be able to just kick back, smoke a joint, listen to Zeppelin, Tull, Hendrix any time you feel like it? Do you think you'll be able to go over to the field and play ball like we do any time you like? Do you think that you'll be able to go to all of these rock shows that we've been going to anytime you like? Or to go to a Dodger game? Or a Rams game? Or a Kings hockey game whenever you want? Don't do this; this is crazy. And, Jeff," I went on, "How come Phil shaved his head, but you didn't?" "I am doing it tomorrow," he answered. "Does Mom know about your plans?" "I just told her a little while ago," he answered. "What did she say?" "She said that she didn't like it, and that your brother will try to stop you, but if this is what you kids think you have to do, then I won't stand in your way." "Well I'm fucking standing in your way," I followed. "This is stupid. Have you already committed to it? Do you now have to go?"

"They gave us a couple of days to change our minds," answered Phil. "Well, change your fuckin' minds," I answered. "You know what, let's smoke a joint and talk about this. If you still want to do it tomorrow after we smoke a joint tonight, then do what you want."

And so we sat in a circle together a little while later, smoked a really good cigarette that I laced with just a touch of hashish, and got royally high. Once high, I said, "Okay guys, let's hold hands so that we can feel each others energy. Let's really feel how connected we are." After a few minutes, I go to the eight-track player and put on some early Rolling Stones: "Time is on my side, yes it is; Time is on my side, yes it is; You always say that you want to be free; but you'll come running back, you'll come running back, you'll come running back to me," intones Jagger. Phil, my brother Jeff, and I are just rocking back and forth, back and forth, digging, grooving to the sound. And then I say, "Do you guys really want to join the fucking army? Seriously, is this not stupid?" And they agree that it is stupid; and they decide to revoke their application the following day.

"And grow your fucking hair back, will you Phil?" He laughs, says its only hair, but that it will grow back soon enough. And, indeed, it grew back, longer, more flowing and beautiful than it had looked before.

❐

I think of the loyalty of Phil, and my mind drifts back to that Fleetwood Mac concert in mid-'70s, somewhere around 1977. I was about a year away from graduation, and Phil was deep into working construction. My brother, Jeff, had just completed a year of playing hockey in Newfoundland, where they recruited him for a team based on his success as a top goaltender in a Swedish league. He had been scouted by the New York Rangers of the NHL that year in Newfoundland, but when the season ended he decided that he wouldn't play hockey anymore. The team had been terrible, and Jeff had been forced to make 50, 60, sometimes 70 saves a night. His body took a terrible toll, so he decided to quit. He should have stayed and played in Sweden—I tried desperately to convince him to do so—but he couldn't be convinced. He might have gone from Sweden to the NHL; he was making a big name for himself there. But it didn't happen. And so he returned.

The three of us go to this concert at the Los Angeles Forum, and it was fantastic. You can say all that you like about Stevie Nicks, but Christine McVie is the heart and soul of that band. She isn't with them anymore; Stevie Nicks is the star attraction in their proposed comeback tour. But this concert in the late '70s belonged to Christine McVie. I can still hear the pure melodic texture of her euphoria-inducing vocals as she repeats the verse at the end of the song, "Songbird": "I love you, I love you, I love you, like never before." Lilting, elegiac, her voice resonated throughout the hall that night.

I had enjoyed the show immensely, and was feeling a mellow sense of joy as I left to go home with Phil and my brother. My brother had darted off ahead of Phil and me, and as we approached the walkway leading to the exit from the arena, we suddenly see my brother in some sort of Kung-Fu stance, his body hunched and low to the ground, threatening to attack some security guard who, apparently, had given him a hard time as he was trying to go to the bathroom. As we get closer to him we hear sounds that I had never heard a human being make. From that low Kung-Fu stance there is a high-pitched scream/shriek/wail, sounding something akin to how I'd imagine a cat would sound if it were going through a sex-change operation. Jeff had been watching a lot of Bruce Lee movies, and now he was putting it all into practice. As he made these horrifying screeching sounds—his right arm fully extended with the index finger and middle finger becoming a dagger, the left arm bent as the fingers were curled into a claw about to strike—he would turn quickly, aggressively at angles, eventually covering 360 degrees. As we hear this, Phil and I start to laugh, Phil saying, "I ain't never heard anything like that before." All of a sudden there were about three security guards encircling my brother. Phil and I look at each other, and make our way to the scene, whereupon I walk up to one of the guards to make the case that he is no threat to anybody and that I'll "calm him down" and bring him home.

"He's a hockey goalie, and he's had a few too many pucks hit him in the head, I think," I began to tell the guy. Just as I'm doing this, a security person grabs me from behind, carrying me to the exit with an arm lock around my neck. Another guard does the same to my brother Jeff. Phil, seeing that I am choking, runs over and absolutely "cold cocks" the guard with his arm around my neck—hits him with a vicious shot to the guys jaw and knocks him down, freeing me. I then run over and grab the arms of the guard who has my brother around the neck, causing him to release my brother, who is struggling for air. Phil then starts walking over toward me, when the security person that he has hit comes over and knocks him down with a return punch to the face. This has, of course, gotten very, very ugly. The situation is diffused when Phil and Jeff leave the Forum, the police nowhere in sight. But I wasn't finished. Adrenalin is pouring through my veins, and as Phil and my brother exit the place, I walk back toward the guy who had grabbed me around the throat. I ask him for his name, his I.D. number, and tell him that he could have suffocated me. I tell him that I'm going to pursue this brutality in a legal way, and that, he's lucky I'm gonna take this route, "because what I really want to do is "kick your fuckin' ass fair and square." He was a bit taller than me, but I summed him up as not being as strong (I was a very-well-built young man). He told me that if I wanted I could wait for him outside of the Forum till he was off and "we could take care of business." And I assented to this. So (and I'm not saying I wasn't nervous as hell; of course I was) I wait about 30 minutes for the guy to come out, and he eventually does. We go up to each other—chest against chest, eyes inches away from the others—and we stare for a good couple of minutes. At this point the security people come out and break it up, Phil and Jeff each taking one of my arms to pull me away. Needless to say, I wasn't as mellow as I had felt in those first few minutes after the show. I'll never forget the Fleetwood Mac show that night, and I'll always remember the loyalty, the fierce protectiveness of my friend, Phil. They don't make very many of that kind in any era.

❐

In the years following my graduation from U.C. Santa Barbara in 1978 and my moves to London, Boston and eventually San Francisco in late 1979, where I attended graduate school and eventually stayed and began my adult life, I saw very little of Phillip Rusty Siegler. My brother, Jeff, moved to Arizona where, with my mom's help, he purchased a fabricated home looking down on the Colorado River. Phil moved with Jeff to the river for quite a while, and then returned to his roots in Arkansas, where his parents had moved to retire. For many years, Phil would continue to visit Jeff at his place near the river, and Jeff would venture off to Arkansas to stay with Phil for weeks at a time.

My sister, Heidi, ventured out to try to start a life as an actress and model, getting some small parts on game shows and appearing in the background of some films. My brother Elliot remained at home deep into adulthood, and during this period developed some traumatic psychological problems—a bipolar disorder and a form of schizophrenia where he would hear voices directing him in his affairs, leading to intense instability and paranoia. He lived at the house with my mom, and she lived her life deeply troubled and worried about him. He would often disappear and not come back for a few days, and on more than one occasion, she received phone calls from police stations, telling her that he had been picked up because he had been wandering aimlessly, sometimes not quite sure who he was, where he was going or had been. The situation into the early '80s had become so severe that my mom—my sister Heidi at her side—had to call a Pet Team (Psychiatric Emergency Team) to come to the home, subdue him in his agitated state, and bring him to a mental hospital. It became extremely difficult for my mom to read the tea leaves that she had to read to survive, worrying so desperately about Elliot as she did. But she did read, and the groups became larger and larger, actors and actresses flying in from all over the world to see her, sharing space in our small living room with the poorest of the poor from Watts, for whom she would read for a couple of dollars. She found it difficult to draw boundaries around herself, as the calls came in morning, noon and night. She often answered these calls at midnight—and I would get very angry at her for so doing—feeling that she just had to be there for a desperate soul. "Mom, damn it, you've got to take care of yourself, you have to give yourself some rest, some peace; you have to learn to turn it off and rest, shut this phone off late at night!" I yelled more than once. But over time, as the Pet teams had to come several more times to take Elliot back to the mental hospitals for evaluation and hospitalization, her blood pressure continued to get out of hand, she put on large amounts of weight, she developed diabetes, and she continued to smoke. Her gift, though, continued to develop: people looking for lost relatives hearing of her; police detectives coming to her to solve crimes; doctors looking for answers; criminals trying to stay out of jail; lost souls trying to find themselves; the sick looking to be healed; lovers, whose love had grown cold, coming to her to discover if the marriage was worth saving, might the love become rekindled?

During these years, the dark circles that encompassed her eyes became deeper and darker; I would beg her to stop smoking, plead with her to come up here to San Francisco to live, where I would help her get situated. She kept planning on doing that; she just loved visiting us, spending time with her grandsons, Michael and Jonathan. She loved opening the window at night and breathing in the cool San Francisco air. She would fall asleep on the couch in the living room watching a movie, the open window allowing delicious breezes to bathe her. She would sleep through the night. Often, by the time she went home in a few days time, the dark circles would begin to diminish, a happiness beginning to come over her. And she would promise yet again that she would begin the process of moving up here to San Francisco.

For several years she talked about it, but couldn't follow through. "I have to get Elliot situated before I can do anything," she would often say to me. And we decided that she would sell the house in Canyon Country—where she had given me that reading that dry gorgeous day, the sky deep blue, the mountains perfect in the background, "Her name is Sue," she had said, "Don't try to find her, she'll find you; you wont be able to find her" (and indeed, she did find me so soon afterwards)—and move to a little condo in the city with Elliot. "Elliot would love it up here," she would say. "And he is doing so well now that they have found the right medicine for him. He is such a sweet boy; so smart, actually brilliant, and the medicine is working. And he promises me that he'll always take it—that he will take it the rest of his life." Indeed, Elliot is brilliant. He has a photographic memory for statistics. And he is even more intense about sports than I am. The disease made him even more brilliant in a certain way, the manic phase of it. But that phase always leads to the intense paranoia, then the terrible "let down." The medicine, I had observed, had made him quite tired, he was sleeping for great periods of time, whenever I went down to visit. He was putting on weight, as he lived in a bedroom, not getting out very much from the back room of my mom's house. "Yes, Mom," I would answer. "Elliot would love it here. I'll take him to hockey games, football games, baseball games. We'll get him out of the house, maybe even find him a job." It all sounded so right; but she just couldn't seem to put it all together. The readings continued to demand more and more of her time, draining her. I would always worry when summer arrived to the desert area where she lived. It would become so hot, days upon days well above 100 degrees, without a breeze. And the smog would often settle in on what eventually became known as the Santa Clarita Valley, where she lived. And so I worried about a stroke; I worried about her lungs, as she continued to smoke. Then she would visit, and over the years she looked more and more tired; her eyes grew darker and darker. Then the cool breezes would come as she lay on the couch watching TV, Michael and Jonathan at the foot of the couch, then the foot of the bed. And again, she would promise that she would come, give up this kind of life, move here and read just enough people to get by. "You'll be able to read as many or as few people as you want when you move here," I would tell her.

"Once you start reading, your name will spread like wildfire. And, of course, your loyal clients will certainly fly up here for a day for readings. You'll have it much easier," I would always encourage. And she promised, she promised, she promised.

During these years, I continued to keep in touch with Phil, but very infrequently. We'd talk on Thanksgiving every year, very often when he was with Jeff at the River, or Jeff was with him in Arkansas. But, though we rarely spoke, I always felt very connected to Phil. And this connection led to dreams that I would have about him every several months. The dreams were always ominous. And the dreams kept coming time and again. The dreams were always similar, though different, manifestations of a sense of foreboding and danger. For years I would dream of Phil running from the law, being chased by a posse with guns drawn, unable to find him as he hid in the corner of some barn, covered with straw and blankets. I would have dreams where he was being chased by the law, he staying just ahead of them as he scaled barbed wire, slicing his hands, arms and feet. Each dream had this ominous sense of danger around him, and I dreamt them for years. Another dream had him sliding on his belly, again running from something, in a field next to a barbed wire fence. And still another dream had him finally caught by the law, Phil backed into a corner of an alley, the posse surrounding him with guns drawn. I didn't see Phil during these years, but these dreams were keeping me very close to him.

I did hear from my brother Jeff that Phil and his wife had ended a very bad marriage, and that the wife would become very violent with Phil, suspecting him of cheating on her everywhere he went. They would drink large amounts of hard liquor many nights a week, and that Phil had become an alcoholic. But he had kicked the habit, met a healthy woman in the nursing profession, married and had a child with her. But the hard drinking had done some serious damage to his liver, and he had also contracted a dose of hepatitis C, further damaging the liver. The disease would emerge and submerge at various times, and, apparently, it was active during much of the time he was drinking the hard stuff so heavily. And, so, he had been on a medication for it. And he was doing well. But then the phone call came on a July night in 1995, as I lay awake in my bed watching a San Francisco Giants baseball game. The phone was near my bed, and I thought not to answer it, so engrossed was I in this good, close game. It is my brother, Jeff; tears are in his words, abject pain coating his voice. "Bruce, I have terrible news," Jeff cries. "Phil is dead. He had woken up from a sleep to go take out the garbage back in Arkansas, and he passed out on the floor. His wife called the ambulance, but he was dead when they arrived. They say he died of a heart attack." I went into total denial; it just couldn't be. I wouldn't let it be. And as I sit at this desk on this dark night, the cool San Francisco breeze pouring into my apartment from a little crack in the window, I think of my football buddy, Phil Barbieri, and his dad, Phil. I think of the best friend a guy could ever know—a loyal friendship that is so rare in life—Phillip Rusty Siegler, whom I so deeply miss.

❐

Flashes of memory come back to me as the words of Pink Floyd once again echo through my living room. Phil, my brother, Jeff, and I went back to visit my father in the summer of 1976, and to see the Montreal Olympic Games. It was the first time that I had seen my father since he left the house on Calvert Street, Reseda, in the weeks following my freight-train hopping to the outskirts of Chicago in 1971. And I could probably count the number of times on one hand that I had spoken to him during those five years. But here the three of us were in Montreal, and my dad was being a very welcoming host. He took us to a few of his favorite jazz clubs in old Montreal, and showed us where we could obtain tickets to the games. We three boys were really attracted to the boxing, and were able to procure tickets to a few of the fights. I remember how tough the Thai and Korean fighters were during those games. And there were some devastating Cuban fighters. We saw several fights, but the best of the best was watching Sugar Ray Leonard do his thing. Sugar would go on to become the champion of the world in a couple of weight classes, eventually fighting classic fights against "Hit Man" Hearns, "Marvelous Marvin" Hagler, and Roberto "Hands of Stone" Duran. But here we were, way before those epic matches, watching Sugar Ray demolish an opponent on his way to winning the Olympic Gold Medal. And during the fight, we had the great fortune to say hello to Howard Cosell as he walked past us on his way to the press box.

When the Olympic games had ended, the three of us decided to drive northeast for a few days to that place of deep and lasting memory for me, Campbellton New Brunswick, the home of Jackie and Janice. It had been nine years since our family had moved from Campbellton to California, but memories of Janice and Jackie were very strong for me. It was summertime and the scenery promised to be amazing. And amazing it was. Once past Quebec City, the country road into New Brunswick wove through hundreds of acres of stunning forest, deer now and again darting across the road. We were three long-haired boys—we looked like a rock group—heading into the backwoods of Eastern Canada. On one particular stretch of road, Phil lights up a joint and the three of us pass it around until it is fully smoked. The windows are open and the scent of the forest is alive in our senses. The smoke of a distant pulp mill is visible, and along with it, the scent of its somewhat contradictory odor, woodsy, sweet, but slightly acrid. The last time I smelled something like that was on a trip to visit some clients in Humboldt County, on the road from Fortuna to Arcata in California. The woods are enveloping us—and minutes before lighting up, a deer had darted in front of the car, my goalie brother showing lightening reflexes—and we are all singing and rocking our heads to the words. And I sing along to these words right now in memory of my true friend:

So, so you think you can tell Heaven from Hell
Blue skies from pain.
Can you tell a green field from a cold steel rail?
A smile from a veil?
Do you think you can tell?
And did they get you to trade your heroes for ghosts?
Hot ashes for trees?
Hot air for a cool breeze?
Cold comfort for change?
And did you exchange a walk-on part in the war for a lead role in a cage?
How I wish, how I wish you were here.
We're just two lost souls swimming in a fish bowl, year after year,
Running over the same old ground.
What have you found? The same old fears.
Wish you were here.

And I'm thinking of Phil at this moment, and how much I wish he were here.

The stay in Campbellton was short but memorable for me. I couldn't find Janice in the phone book. But I did manage to locate Jackie's number. Jackie had moved on to Ontario and had gotten married. Her second sister, Margaret, had also moved away. But the baby of the family—I can't remember her name, but she had just completed her freshman year in college to my junior year—answered the phone and remembered my name when I reminded her that I was one of the kids that Jackie used to babysit before we moved back to California. She really wanted to see me, and so we arranged for that to happen later in the evening. Jeff and Phil drove me to her place, with a prearranged time to pick me up, somewhere around midnight. It turned out that she was a lot of fun, and as we drank wine, she put on all the music that I loved.

We made love (well, had sex) on her couch that night. And the following morning—after Jeff, Phil and I had had breakfast at the cheap roadside motel—I met her to go for a walk by the bay. We took a long, enjoyable walk along the water—the sweet but acrid scent of a distant pulp mill wafting from off in the distance—and we enjoyed one another's company very much. I really liked her, and it felt mutual. We vowed to stay in touch, but the distance was too great for this chance encounter to develop into something deeper. A letter and long distance phone call were exchanged, but it ended there. Phil and my brother knew of my story of Jackie, the babysitter, and they just couldn't believe that I wound up connecting in this way with her baby sister. Clearly, I had an unusual connection with the girls in this family.

I put the song on again, as the memories of Phil pour through me. I recollect again the split decision that he made to rescue me in the waters of the Colorado River, and the way he started to laugh in a crisis moment as I jumped on his back to save myself. And those early days when we played tackle football hard against each other: "Rosen, you hit me like that again, and I'll pop you one," he had said with that Arkansas, country drawl. And the "whip towel"; that moment in the locker room in junior high school when he snaps the "Latin Man Child" sharply on the ass, as he is in the middle of singing one of his locker room songs. I think back to the time when the two of us were in the back of a pickup truck on the way to the beach, Phil singing the words of his favorite singer and song at the time. I hear Phil's voice singing Cat Stevens as clear as a bell:

> *Oh, I'm bein' followed by a moonshadow, moonshadow, moonshadow*
> *Leapin' and hoppin' on a moonshadow, moonshadow, moonshadow*

And I'll never forget one of Phil's all-time great moments, though the joke was on me. It belongs in his greatest hits. Phil knew that I was kind of a flower child; that I would like on occasion to stop and smell the flowers in a garden. The two of us were in the back seat on our way to a Los Angeles Kings hockey game. He leans over and quietly says to me, "Bruce, before we got in the car, I smelled this amazing flower. It was one of the most beautiful flowers that I have ever smelled." "Really?" I had answered. "Do you want to smell it?" he asks. "Yeah, for sure," I answer. I lean over to smell whatever is in his hand, as he places a couple of fingers at the very opening of my nostrils. I take a deep inhale, and practically throw up. "What the fuck! That smells like shit!" I yell at him.

And he laughs uncontrollably. And so does the rest of the car when he says that he had just put his finger up his ass. Phil, I gotta tell you, I Wish You Were Here.

It is February 24, Sue's birthday. It is a Sunday, and all week long the weather people have been predicting a big storm. We had some drizzle toward the end of the week, and the winds have been pretty steady. As I look out my window this early morning, the city is waking up, dark gloomy clouds hovering above the elemental rust-red Golden Gate Bridge, the bay dark and choppy, white caps clearly visible off in the distance across the Marina District. I want to wish Sue a happy birthday, but though I know that she must be awake—she is an early riser—I'll wait a little. Earlier this week I called her at work, spoke to her briefly, wishing her a happy birthday in advance. Her voice sounded thin and tense. "Thanks," she said, but there was some hospital pharmaceutical business in the background, so I told her that I would let her go for the moment, since it seemed so busy and that it appeared that she couldn't talk. "Just wanted to wish you a happy birthday in advance," I repeated. "Thanks," she said again; "I'll call you later in the week," she followed. But the call later in the week never came. Days like her birthday, especially, but also Mother's Day, Valentine's Day, Christmas Day, New Year's Day, the first day of Passover, the first couple of nights of Hanukah are so very damn difficult since our separation. I want to tell her how much I love her, even if we are not together. I want to tell her that I care so deeply for her, and want everything wonderful for her, but despite these feelings, I cannot bring myself to return to our marriage nest—and she doesn't ask me to come back, though I know she loves me very much. I put my head down on my desk, just below the keyboard, dozing off for a good while. I must have fallen asleep for at least an hour in this position. My neck is stiff as I get up to call Sue. The fear in calling her is that she doesn't answer—so often when I call her (though I do not call frequently), that is the response, no answer—and this is what happens this time as well. I leave a voice message: "Sue, I want to wish you a happy birthday. A very happy birthday. Hopefully, you'll do something really fun for your birthday. If you're going to be around, I'd like to say hi, and take Lucky for a walk." A few hours go by and there is no answer. So I text her the same message, referencing that I had left a phone message. An hour goes by and there is no answer. Then another hour and no return phone call, no answer to my text. I check in with the boys to see if they had spoken to their mother on her birthday. But no response from either of them. I can't get Jonathan on the phone or get a return text, same for Michael. I call Sue a second time, but this will be the last for the day. "I've tried to wish her a happy birthday; I can't do more," I verbally, audibly, say to myself. But, of course, I start to get worried. When I do not get a response from my boys or from Sue, my worry genes kick in—and they go from zero to 60 in about five seconds. I walk to the house to check in on her. The car is gone; the dog doesn't bark when I ring the bell. Did she fly somewhere? Did she drive somewhere? Hopefully she got there safely. And so I continue to worry. And now I'm worrying about everybody, as my stress and worry genes metabolize throughout my body. I text the boys again, no answer. I call the boys again, no answer. It is early afternoon, as I head down to the bay to go for a walk. I'm heading along the walking path toward Fort Point, just below the Golden Gate Bridge, when I get a text from Sue: "I'm in Monterey; wanted to get away. Went to the Aquarium."

The Monterey Bay Aquarium is where we would take the boys when they were young. It has an incredibly interesting array of undersea habitat and marine life. I was totally amazed at the variety and texture of the jellyfish. I really love that aquarium, but haven't been in a few years. And the boys, Jonathan particularly, were hypnotized by the place. Michael's mind would dart from one form of marine life to another; Jonathan would stay transfixed on one aquarium for a long time, lost in the strange, fascinating world. We had several captivating family days when the boys were young at this aquarium. The wind is blowing and I continue my walk along the bay, a bit of drizzle splashing against my face. As I approach the bridge I receive one, then another, texts from the boys. Indeed, they had spoken to their mother today on her birthday. I continue to walk toward the bridge, and I feel very sad as I do. It is Sue's birthday, and I want the best for her. I want joy for her; I don't want her to know sadness. But I seem helpless to do anything about it. Why? I just can't answer that question. I simply cannot change the state of affairs. There is a barrier I cannot go through, and I cannot climb over it. I am sad today; and as I walk back toward the city, the wind rendering my umbrella useless, there is a feeling of emptiness and loss that overcomes me. I am so very sad today.

❒

It is March 5, the day before my 53rd birthday. The political landscape has become decisive on the Republican side, but on the Democratic side, Hillary is fighting back intensely, lashing out like a cornered cat, cutting and stinging her opponent, Barack Obama. Mrs. Clinton got her campaign back on track with wins in Texas, Ohio and Rhode Island last night. Delegate-rich Texas and Ohio were considered must-wins for her campaign. Obama, who claimed victory in Rhode Island, had won 12 straight contests since Super Tuesday on February 5. "You know what they say," said Mrs. Clinton. "As Ohio goes, so goes the nation. Well, this nation's coming back and so is this campaign." But Obama had his rejoinder. "We know this: No matter what happens tonight, we have nearly the same delegate lead as we had this morning, and we are on our way to winning this nomination," Obama told his supporters in Texas. In February, former President Bill Clinton said that if his wife won Ohio and Texas, she'd go on to win the nomination.

As the democrats struggle for supremacy, potentially taking this fight to the floor of the convention in Denver this summer, the race is decided on the Republican side. The last obstacle to the nomination for McCain, Mike Huckabee, conceded the nomination to him after McCain swept all four Republican contests to become his party's presumptive nominee. McCain won the primaries in Texas, Ohio, Vermont and Rhode Island, giving him more than the 1,191 delegates needed to clinch the GOP nomination. "I am very, very grateful and pleased to note that tonight, my friends, we have won enough delegates to claim with confidence, humility, and a great sense of responsibility, that I will be the Republican nominee for president of the United States," McCain told his supporters. It will be a tough road for McCain, because whoever wins the Democratic nomination McCain will be tied to the failed programs, unpopularity, misery, of the Bush Administration. That cannot be made any more clearly than seeing McCain on TV today visiting the White House and asking the President for his help, most likely in fundraising. It is a very big risk for McCain to even be seen with such an unpopular president. He needs Bush's help with the party's conservative base, but any ties to Bush could alienate moderate Republicans and independent voters who are a key to a possible McCain win in November. But John McCain appears to be very much his own man, and no doubt will do as he sees fit, despite the criticism from parts of his party.

Faced with the unpopularity of his presidency, Bush said today that, "They're not going to be voting for me; I've had my time in the Oval office." What a sad and lonely feeling it must be for the President, as his own party debates the issue of whether their nominee should even be seen with him. Perhaps the President—his arrogance and swagger often repulsive to me—deserves his unpopularity. He is an isolated man, and the country has told him that his thinking, ideas, priorities, have not only been out of step with this country's needs but have also been destructive. History will, of course, judge his time, and the prediction is that it will judge it to be among the greatest failures in American history. Nonetheless, I feel sad for the man and his failures as I see him on TV tonight—a man the nation so eagerly, desperately wants to see out of its collective life.

❒

It's my birthday, March 6, and Sue called this morning to wish me a happy birthday, before leaving for the pharmacy. I fall asleep very late these days, and it just gets later and later every week. It is often the case that I don't fall asleep before three A.M., as I lay in bed listening to a sound machine of ocean waves that Gwen had loaned to me—she obviously cares about me deeply, this machine is a treasure that she inherited from her very beloved grandmother. I crave the ocean, wish I could go to sleep to the sound of it every night—I never sleep so sweetly, soundly, blissfully as I do when I can hear the sea at night—but this machine is very soothing. Anxiety creeps into my thoughts the later it becomes at night, and so there is a sort of vicious circle at work in my sleeping pattern. The later it gets, the more anxiety I start to feel, wondering if the boys are okay, vacillating between surrender to a "Higher Power" that deep within my being I know is real, but then trying to wrest control of my life from that surrender. And as I try to seize control of my life, to tell myself rationally that all is well and will be well,

I start to ask the deep, unanswerable questions like, "How do I know God will take care of me, when so many believers see so many unhappy circumstances? Why should I be different?" But then I answer these issues by allowing myself to surrender, if just for a moment. The energy from the thought, worry, manifests into an anxiety whose presence cannot find release from this body as I lie in bed, the night advancing inexorably toward morning. And the later it gets, the more tense I become, the symptoms occurring in a tightness in my temples which starts as an ache in the neck, upper back and shoulders. And so I tell myself that I will sleep as late as I need to sleep, and that I'll go to work tomorrow when I am ready. If I come in later, then I'll stay later. After more than 25 years of handling clients' money, keeping it as safe as I can, spending years of "cold calling" from early morning to early evening in the early stages of this career to build a business, I'll give myself the earned respite that I need.

❒

I have been among the "top producers" in my field for more than a couple of decades, but I do not torture myself to be successful. The success has arrived as a result of trying to understand the world the best that I can, trying to listen to what my clients are saying, endeavoring to return every call the same day that it arrives, following a "bluish-collar" work ethic that directs me to work as hard each day as I might if I were a janitor spending long days cleaning buildings, or a typist required to type documents for multiple of hours every day, their shoulders and arms "on fire" from the amount of work. Prior to entering this business, fresh out of graduate school, I typed hundreds and hundreds of telexes a day for a bank, my neck, shoulders, arms "on fire" from the enormous load. And as a student in college, I worked as a janitor for close to seven hours a day after class—often from four P.M. to 11 P.M.—at a private school for kids in grades K-8. I was there to lock up night after night, after sweeping room after room in dark, eerie silence. When the school principal caught the other janitor cheating and lying about the hours he worked, they asked if I wanted his hours. And so, to take pressure off of my mom—I wanted her to not have to give me any money, so she could take care of the rest of the family—I accepted the extra hours. And it was quite scary on occasion when I left that dark school so late.

I approached this job with full determination from the beginning, working as hard as I could, because I didn't know how to do it any other way. I am lucky to make phone calls for a living, and for many years tried to reach as many people as I could in a day. I've made fewer phone calls to prospects these past several years, focusing on caring for the clients whom I have. Indeed, I never forget how lucky I am to speak to clients on the telephone to make a satisfying living, how fortunate I am to be trusted, and how I strive so hard to return that trust. The markets have been in chaos lately, particularly the last few months. Given their exposure to subprime debt, the municipal bond insurers' ratings are starting to be downgraded to levels well below the AAA that clients and financial advisors had taken for granted as being a constant. And with the downgrades and enormous need for liquidity that we are seeing in the municipal bond marketplace—the result of banks not lending enough, hoarding capital for survival—the values of municipal bonds are tumbling, client statements showing substantial declines. In the end, though, the bonds pay the interest rate for which people acquired them, and unlike stocks they will mature or be redeemed at 100 cents on the dollar (assuming they don't default, which I take for granted is extremely unlikely, given the quality of the bonds that I sell), however low the price might be today. More and more clients are calling with panic in their voices, as a result of the declines in values on their statements. I am spending a significantly greater percentage of my time answering these questions than being able to "go forward" with sales of new offerings. And, given what has happened to the market recently, there are some of the best buys that I've seen on municipal bonds in many years. However, I do all that I can to explain the situation, to let clients know the reasons for these substantial declines in value, to assure them that it has more to do with the lack of liquidity in the economy—that we are seeing an incredible amount of selling of bonds due to the need to raise cash—and less to do with impending defaults of quality bonds. The days are difficult, and I come home to a world that is, essentially, just me at this moment.

My life is in limbo, and though I crave the balance and stability of a steady relationship, I just can't get there at the moment. And, so, at the end of the day, I often fall asleep in my cozy, leather reclining chair, eventually making it into my bed. At three A.M., the sound machine works hard at helping me reach a subliminal consciousness, and often the fog horns issue a peaceful reminder—the cool sea air bathing my face through the slightly open window—that I live near the sea, not the desert. Eventually I fall asleep. Often it is interrupted, but at other times it is deep. And I allow myself to sleep in, because I have no other choice. And I arrive to work later than I ever have, but it all seems to work out.

"Happy Birthday," Sue said to me. "I wanted to be the first to wish you a happy birthday this morning." "Thanks," I say, "thanks very much." "Well, enjoy your day," she follows. "I'll try; I will," I reassure. And then she hangs up. And then I go back to sleep, and I sleep a few more hours.

As the day wears on, I strive to be able to leave early. I haven't made plans to do anything with anyone tonight. There are some movies playing at the Embarcadero Cinema at about four o'clock in the afternoon, and I would love to break away early to go see one, just by myself. I am looking forward to a chocolate bar and a cup of tea in a peaceful theater on my birthday. But the calls keep coming in. It is early in the month, and clients are receiving their statements—statements showing declines in values from the previous month. I am trying to answer the calls—hopefully make a sale or two as well—and go to see this movie. I finish the last phone call at about 10 minutes to four, just as the phone rings again, resulting in a red message light. "I'm not answering this one, that's for fuckin' sure," I tell myself. "They've taken enough of my kidney and liver for one day." I rush to the movie, buy the ticket for a showing of Oscar-nominated shorts, buy the chocolate bar and tea. I kick back in the chair, see a few of the shorts, then fall asleep for a few more, coming to full consciousness for the last one. I walk back to my office, and as I do, I turn my phone on, listening to a message from Gwen. She wants to come over and cook me dinner—we had talked about this yesterday, but I wasn't totally committal about it. "I insist," she says, "and I won't take a no answer." I get back to her and we arrange for her to come over around seven thirty to cook my favorite meal, lasagna. She shows up at about 8:15, and by nine o'clock we are enjoying a delicious lasagna. I was prepared to be alone on my birthday, perhaps would have preferred it. Gwen would not let that happen, and I try not to take for granted the sweetness of her friendship.

❒

It is late in the evening, about 11:30, of Thursday, March 20th. I am bewildered, astounded, dazed, in shock, over what has been transpiring in the United States economy over the past couple of weeks. On Monday, March 10th, the fifth largest brokerage firm in the United States, and one of the oldest, stated to the financial community that they had the liquidity to survive the meltdown in the mortgage markets and the collapse of its two hedge funds several months ago. Bear Stearns confidently assured the markets that they had over $18 billion in cash. But by the end of the week, the stock, which a year ago had been trading as high as $170 a share, had crumbled into the low single digits. By the time the sun illuminated Wall Street the following Monday morning, the Federal Reserve—concerned about the severe loss of capital of other financial institutions that do business with Bear Stearns as a result of their insolvency, as well as the undoing of many financial money-market instruments tied to repayment contracts required of Bear Stearns—had provided JPMorgan Chase with a $30 billion line of credit to enable them to take over the once-vaunted trading powerhouse for $2 a share, little more than the cost of a subway ride across Manhattan. Earlier in the week, the Federal Reserve—concerned about the failure of the financial system—announced the most massive commitment it has ever made to the private sector by agreeing to lend money to struggling investment banks. The Central Bank said its new lending program would make money available to the 20 large investment banks that serve as "primary dealers" and trade Treasury securities directly with the Federal Reserve. In what amounts to, essentially, a bailout of the financial infrastructure, $200 billion had been committed to enable financial institutions to borrow Treasury securities, posting illiquid mortgage-backed securities as collateral. In essence, the Federal Reserve printed fresh capital, putting in its inventory, and saddling taxpayers with billions of dollars of assets that are basically little more than worthless. There was, however, little choice for the Central Bank. Fearing a financial collapse as a result of the lightning-fast demise of Bear, the Fed had to do something to provide confidence and promote liquidity, lest the arteries of the financial system totally freeze, causing a collapse of financial commitments and agreements throughout the world.

The acquisition of Bear for $2 a share by Chase is an incredible opportunity for the acquiring bank. But the direct involvement by the Fed to make this happen is very alarming—we haven't seen this sort of involvement by the Federal Government in the banking sector since the Great Depression. What is next? Where will it stop? Many fear that Lehman Brothers—with enormous leverage and considerable exposure to the bonds backed by subprime debt—might be the next to fail. Lehman, though, is assuring the market that they have the capital to weather the storm. We shall see.

What was it that brought Bear Stearns down so quickly, when their stock price reflected relative liquidity just a few days earlier? Savvy market analysts and conspiracy thinkers alike are seeing this as product of "short sellers" going wild. Many are saying that a general nervousness in the market prompted clients and lenders to rapidly get cash out of the firm—and that this run on the firm was prompted by rumor fed by the short sellers that the firm was "going under." These people are saying that without the shorting of the stock, the company—with its cash position—would have survived. The rumors became a self-fulfilling prophecy. Certainly a lot of money was made on the part of those who dumped the stock, buying it back as it tumbled in a free fall. And, perhaps, there was this conspiracy of rumor, greed and fear; maybe one day we will know. But one thing, though, seems clear: if Bear Stearns had been allowed to collapse, it could have put the whole financial system at risk. The Fed had no other choice. The rescue of Bear Stearns might be just the beginning, not the end, of the troubles in the financial markets. That is now the concern of the entire financial world. It is likely the case that the worst of the financial crisis is not behind us.

During these past couple of weeks the state of the U.S. economy has continued a free fall, the U.S. dollar falling to a record low against the Euro. And there is no telling how much lower it might go, given the continued fears over the state of the banking sector, amid worsening credit conditions. And against this backdrop, the price of gold reached a record, trading at $1,000 an ounce for the first time, pushed up by the failing U.S. dollar. On top of all of this—but not unexpected—housing data released this week shows that U.S. home prices fell almost 13 percent in February, compared to a year ago—and how much lower will this go? During my tenure in the financial business—I've been doing this about 25 years now—I have tried to understand the fears of the reluctant, fearful older investor, the person almost too paralyzed to put their money any place but in a Certificate of Deposit. Many of these people had first-hand experiences of the Great Depression, or were very close to relatives who had. "Never would I ever want to experience that again, never, never, never!" is the refrain that I would often hear. And I would try to assure people that such an event would be extremely unlikely, and that we were living in a different world of Federal guarantees of banking deposits, and insurance companies that could be depended on for their guarantees. I would argue that certainly we will continue to see booms and declines in the economy, stronger and weaker periods of growth in the business cycle. But a depression again? Not in our lifetimes. But now I'm not so sure. Has our economy killed the "goose that laid the golden egg"? Has all of this excess, leverage, creation of financial instruments tied to speculative collateral, overzealous lenders, appraisers, greedy buyers of homes taking the bait and moving in with virtually nothing down in equity, backfired? No doubt it has, and my fear is that given that nearly two thirds of the gross domestic product of our country is tied in some way to real estate spending, that this will go much deeper. Will it produce a depression? There has been "blood on the streets" the past few weeks, and nobody can say for certain where all of this is headed. Perhaps I'll sleep well tonight, but I bet I won't.

❒

Amidst the economic chaos of the past couple of weeks the front-runner for the Democratic nomination for the presidency, Barack Obama, has come under severe political pressure to disassociate himself, essentially to disavow his relationship with, the pastor of his church, the Reverend Jeremiah Wright. Senator Obama has listened to Reverend Wright's sermons at his Chicago pulpit for more than 20 years, and credits the religious leader with introducing him to his Christian faith. But Reverend Wright has become the epicenter of a political firestorm that threatens to undermine the candidacy of Senator Obama. During the past few weeks, the reverend has spewed flames of anger—showing no sensitivity to the political aspirations of his famous parishioner—directly at America. Perhaps using his popularity as the Pastor for a potential president, Wright has used language that reflects the anger that can be heard on Sunday mornings in an America that many white people do not know, though it is hard to believe that this thinking speaks for anything more than a very small percentage of African Americans. There is hatred in these words, a kind of hatred clearly borne of generations of racial segregation and racism in America. And in these words, Wright clearly cannot forgive:

"The government gives them drugs, builds bigger prisons, passes a three-strike law and then wants us to sing 'God Bless America'. No, no, no, God damn America, that's in the Bible for killing innocent people. God damn America for treating our citizens as less than human. God damn America for as long as she acts like she is God and she is supreme.

"We bombed Hiroshima, we bombed Nagasaki, and we nuked far more than the thousands in New York and the Pentagon [on 9/11], and we never batted an eye. We have supported state terrorism against the Palestinians and black South Africans, and now we are indignant because the stuff we have done overseas is now brought right back to our own front yards. America's chickens are coming home to roost."

In addition to blaming American policy in the Middle East for bringing the 9/11 World Trade Center destruction on itself, he has accused White America of creating the AIDS virus to destroy people of color.

Clearly the image of Senator Obama has become tarnished over the past couple of weeks, as it became evident that the Reverend Wright had been a spiritual advisor and mentor to Obama for 20 years or more. How could he sit in the Reverend's church and not hear this rhetoric, journalists were asking. And if he did hear this rhetoric over such a long period of time how could he go on and associate himself with such a person? How much of this ideology does he share deep within his private thoughts? As both candidates campaigned for the Pennsylvania primary, Mrs. Clinton, trying to find a balance between staying out of the fray and watching the destruction absorb Senator Obama, and using the moment to her political advantage, offered the subtle dagger that, "It would be safe to say that Reverend Wright would never have been" her pastor.

Until this maelstrom, Obama had tried to mold himself as a transcendent American political figure, not viewed uniquely as an African American running for president, but rather a candidate who is African American, uniting the country behind him. And as long as he was able to assume such a role, he effectively stayed clear of the very divisive issue of race in America, an issue rife with numerous landmines for an African American politician striving to be a unifying figure. But, now, he is in the middle of a controversy that threatens to undermine him, as the story is discussed over and over again on news programs and talk shows around the country. And on these shows the viewer is inundated with images of the Reverend and his language. Against this backdrop Senator Obama had no choice but to delve fully into the issue of race in America, and with honesty, compassion and stinging criticism, he described his relationship with the Reverend Wright. Delivering the speech before a small audience of local supporters, elected officials and clergy members at the National Constitution Center in Philadelphia, the Senator's comments were broadcast live on cable. Condemning the more incendiary remarks of the pastor, Obama nonetheless tried to explain to white voters the anger and frustration behind Mr. Wright's words, and to urge blacks to strive to understand the sources of the racial fears felt by whites. With a deep, profound and soothing voice, Obama sought a tone of reconciliation that would deliver a thoughtful message from a man born to an African father and white mother, and raised by a single parent; he sought to link this theme to the issues at stake in the election during a deepening economic gloom:

"The remarks that caused this firestorm weren't simply controversial. They weren't simply a religious leader's effort to speak out against perceived injustice. Instead, they expressed a profoundly distorted view of this country—a view that sees white racism as endemic, and that elevates what is wrong with America above all that we know is right with America; a view that sees the conflicts in the Middle East as rooted primarily in the actions of stalwart allies like Israel, instead of emanating from the perverse and hateful ideologies of radical Islam. As such, Reverend Wright's comments were not only wrong, but divisive; divisive at a time when we need unity; racially charged a time when we need to come together to solve a set of monumental problems—two wars, a terrorist threat, a falling economy, a chronic healthcare crisis, and potentially devastating climate change; problems that are neither black or white or Latino or Asian, but rather problems that confront us all. Given my background, my politics, and my professed values and ideals, there will no doubt be those for whom my statements of condemnation are not enough. Why associate myself with Reverend Wright in the first place, they may ask. Why not join another church? And I confess that if all I knew of Reverend Wright were the snippets of those sermons that have run in an endless loop on the TV and YouTube, or if the Trinity United Church of Christ conformed to the caricatures being peddled by some commentators, there is no doubt that I would react in much the same way. But the truth is that isn't all I know of the man. The man I met more than 20 years ago is a man who helped introduce me to the Christian faith, a man who spoke to me about our obligations to love one another. I can no more disown him than I can disown the black community. I can no more disown him than I can disown my white grandmother—a woman who helped raise me, a woman who sacrificed again and again for me, a woman who loves me as much as she loves anything in the world, but a woman who once confessed her fear of black men who passed her by on the street, and who on more than one occasion has uttered racial or ethnic stereotypes that made me cringe."

In another section, Obama talks about the anger that underlies Wright's remarks:

"For the men and women of Reverend Wright's generation, the memories of humiliation and doubt and fear have not gone away; nor has the anger and the bitterness of those years. That anger may not get expressed in public, in front of white co-workers or white friends. But it does find voice in the barbershop or around the kitchen table. At times, that anger is exploited by politicians to gin up votes along racial lines, or to make up for a politicians' own failings. And occasionally, it finds voice in the church on Sunday morning."

In another section he shows empathy with the white experience:

"In fact a similar anger exists within segments of the white community. Most working- and middle-class Americans don't feel that they have been particularly privileged by their race. Their experience is the immigrant experience—as far as they're concerned, no one's handed them anything; they've built it from scratch. They've worked hard all their lives, many times only to see their jobs shipped overseas or their pension dumped after a lifetime of labor. They are anxious about their futures, and feel their dreams slipping away; in an era of stagnant wages and global competition, opportunity comes to be seen as a zero-sum game, in which your dreams come at my expense. So when they are told to bus their children to a school across town; when they hear that an African American is getting an advantage in landing a good job or a spot in a good college because of an injustice that they themselves never committed; when they're told that their fears about crime in urban neighborhoods are somehow prejudiced, resentment builds over time."

And in another section he ties it all into the issues that confront us today and that are vital in the election:

"And if we walk away now, if we simply retreat into our respective corners, we will never be able to come together and solve challenges like healthcare, or education, or the need to find good jobs for every American."

The reviews of the speech—even among begrudging Conservative commentators—were essentially stupendous. There is a moment during an election when a candidate and an era are defined. I think back to the Ronald Reagan-Jimmy Carter debate when Mr. Reagan admonished—the head tilting just slightly to the side, the body language becoming just slightly condescending, the smile turning ever so wry—" Now there you again." From that moment the election was decided, in my mind. That expression defined the man and the era. The speech by Barack Obama a week or so ago revealed the character, charisma and depth of the man, and defined the era in which we live. It had elements of Martin Luther King and the Kennedys, but it was uniquely Barack Obama. Will it put to rest the maelstrom? We shall see. But, clearly, the man rose to the occasion and even transcended it, delivering a speech that will, likely, stand the test of time. It was also a very political speech, designed to unite the working class of all colors behind him, and as such it had subtle elements of class conflict. There were layers to the speech, at once strategic and political, yet designed to take a risk and honestly confront race and our higher calling at the same time. This will likely be talked about well into the future. These are interesting times.

Hawaii, Spring Break

It is Mid-April, and I returned about a week ago from an unexpected, spontaneous trip to Kauai with my son, Michael. A few days before his spring break at the end of March, Michael called, saying, "Dad, can we go to Hawaii for spring break? It has been so cold, snowy and windy for months, and I am in these music rooms, doing all of this abstract, conceptual music so that I barely ever see the sun. I have a craving to go to some place lush and tropical. But I don't want to go to a commercial place with a lot of hotels, I just need to get to some place with a tropical breeze and lush green all around." "Yes, Michael," I had answered. It felt so affirming, gratifying, I felt so privileged that my 21-year-old college son—he certainly might have asked if I would help him go somewhere warm for spring break with a friend—had asked to go with me to Hawaii. It isn't just the warmth and green that he craved; clearly, he wanted to also spend time in this place with his Dad. "Michael, absolutely, we'll go." "But break begins in just a couple of days, Dad; do you really think we can do it? I'm sure it will be really expensive last minute like this. Can you really get away last minute?" "We're going Michael; we'll definitely go." And I told him that I'd get back to him in a day or so to tell him of the plans.

I really wanted to find a house on the water in Hanalei, but no doubt—this is spring break—those places would have been booked months, even years in advance. I started calling all the real estate companies on Kauai—leaving dozens of voice messages—to see if in the next few days there might be a last minute opening for a house on that gorgeous crescent of a beach. Everything had been spoken for—there were condo spaces much further up toward the middle of the island—but no way would there be anything in Hanalei, even if I had called a few months ago. But then a phone call came in—it was a very nice woman with whom I had spoken the previous day, by the name of Christine, there was a sultriness to her voice, and I could hear the ocean waves in her Hawaiian accent—and she said that "your timing is amazing. We just had a cancellation. And even though we have a waiting list, you sounded so nice, and it is so sweet how you want to spend some time alone with your son, who is off at a cold, wintry college. It is a house right on the beach, and it had been booked by the same family every year for several years. You can have it, but you have to tell me today." "I will tell you today, I will tell you right now that we'll take it." And with that, I provided my credit card, paid a pretty high price for some last-minute air tickets, called Michael and made him very happy. I had been thinking that I'd like to get back to Hawaii sometime in the not distant future, but I didn't think that it would happen anytime soon, until that phone call from Michael. But it did happen just a couple of weeks ago, and it was fantastic to be there with Michael.

"Puff the Magic Dragon lived by the sea, and frolicked in the autumn mist in a land called Hanalee," is the opening verse to "Puff the Magic Dragon." And when one arrives at the sublime white sands of the crescent half-moon beach, the bath waters a pristine turquoise and aqua, lush green hillsides in the offing, it becomes obvious that what the islanders tell you is correct: the Hanalee of song represents Hanalei, and if you sit back on the sands and begin to surrender (which in a short span of time begins to occur naturally, though decompression from a frenetic world rarely happens in one sitting), dragons of magic or any kind of peaceful dream of fantasy become the stuff of reality. The Aloha spirit is often talked about in sales literature to encourage travel to Hawaii, and it can easily be dismissed as a slick marketing program. But there truly is something to it in Hawaii. The cooling breezes of the afternoon trades are infused with soul; suddenly the faces of the ancestors and gods of legend are images in the sand, travel amidst the trees, become the design of the lush hillsides, are etched into the canyons and mountainsides. And as the breezes move gently amidst the life of the islands, connecting souls of the past with the living, moving as the maestro George Harrison sang on the album "Sgt. Pepper's," "Within You and Without You," one succumbs to this spirit of friendship, welcome, an amnesia-inducing life force that calms our thoughts, softens our memories, pushes aside our recriminations for a moment or two or many more. This Aloha spirit I have felt in all of the islands—it is a true spirit, a soul of the ocean, volcano, the heavens, the gods—but I have never been more aware of it than on the island of Kauai.

I experienced it in this way when Sue and I first traveled here for our honeymoon, and I feel it on the island with Michael. I feel it, and begin to enjoy its movement through me from the moment I get off the plane and step on the tarmac, and even if the weather is stormy, the spirit of tranquility resides in the winds. It is blissful to be here, this place of Heaven or "Heavenly Earth," and it is so right that Michael and I spend this precious time at Hanalei, rather "Hanalee." We will be forever richer for it.

I hadn't been surfing since those days shortly before my father left, when my mom defied my father and bought me the surfboard as a compromise for quitting ice hockey. But on this trip, Michael

"I'm on vacation, Mrs. Blum, your bonds are fine. I'll get back to you when I return."

and I took a full day of surfing lessons together, and my son would surely admit that his 53-year-old dad was quite surprising to the teacher and the young students—they were pretty impressed that I was able to paddle (it came back to me) through the oncoming waves, keeping ahead of everybody. And I got up on the board the first wave; my form wasn't great, but I stayed on it all the way to the white water. It was awesome fun, and in short order Michael was up on a few waves as well. What a healthy change for him from the music rooms where he resided most hours of every day, amidst the serious cold and wind of this Oberlin winter. The day of paddling through the oncoming waves, pushing us a little bit harder to find the next series of swells, the excitement of doing something in the sea so exhilarating, eventuated in a serious afternoon hunger. And to satisfy this we followed the directions of the surf instructor to go the taco stand near the pier and order some fresh fish tacos with salsa, followed by a tropical juice or beer. Kicking back against a palm tree, we downed more than one of those tacos, and finished it with a cold, cold cerveza. I hadn't felt this kind of relaxation and satisfaction in such a while, peace overcoming both of us, our energy spent, the tacos working their way through our stomach and into our souls.

The next day we hiked an ancient Hawaiian trail for about five miles. The trail begins at the very north tip of the island, beyond Princeville where the movie South Pacific was filmed. The trail is made of small, uneven stones, and winds through lush tropical flora. It is relatively steep for the first three or so miles, continuing up more often than leveling off. But when it does level off, one is overwhelmed by the panoramas of the sea splashing below against rocks, filling little inlets and bays, the color a desperately gorgeous blue. And then we continued, the sun beginning to take a toll on our energy; this is where we showed our age, Michael not quite as affected as his dad. But maybe I was a bit more tired than Michael at the outset because I was holding the pack on my back for most of the first section. Realizing that maybe I was pushing too hard, I gave the pack to Michael for the next few miles down to the beach, teasing him that as soon as he takes the pack, the trail moves downhill. And so, to prove to me he could handle the load, Michael insisted—and I didn't argue—that he carry it on the way back. We ate lunch on the secluded beach—water and a turkey sandwich, followed by a Lara bar for energy (highly recommended by Gwen) had never tasted quite like this, Michael and I dining together as we lay on the sand—and after about an hour of rest and fantasy, we made the trek back. About a mile from the end of the trail on the way back, Michael takes a picture of my red face as I pour half the bottle of water on my head, weary was I but so incredibly happy.

And as I write this, looking on the bay, the wind whistling a baritone as it pours through my slightly opened window, I am looking at this picture. Michael is back at college now, and I called him tonight. I wanted to hug him, but could only do it with my voice.

On another day we took an expedition, in two-seat kayaks, up an inland river to an ancient Hawaiian burial ground and campsite. It was an organized tour; but paddling together for miles up the river and back gave us sublime father-and-son moments. I kept chiding him to row faster, the competitive instinct coming out in me, because I wanted to stay ahead of all the other rowers. And we did. And we did again on the way back. We ate lunch that afternoon under a freezing-cold, roaring water fall; after lunch we jumped into the waters fed by the falls, but Michael survived it much longer than I could. Goodness, that was cold. And goodness, that lunch tasted good, resting after rowing in the hot sun, the breeze from the falls bathing our bodies.

The cottage we had been given was on the sea as promised. It was described as being cozy; but it was even cozier than I would have imagined. Very clean, the beds comfortable, about 50 yards of well-tended green lawn that eventually reaches the white sand by the sea; there was a big barbeque that Michael—he loves to cook—took full advantage of several times. At night, there was the sound of the sea—the sound I had been hoping would be loud and soothing—filling my senses and bloodstream as I easily fell to sleep. The cottage had a name, the Paniolo. Paniolo is a word derived from Spanish, and it was given to the Hawaiian cowboys, who were taught to ride and manage the wild herds, by the Spanish cowboys who were brought to Hawaii by King Kamehameha III in 1838. The name eventually came to be associated with the uniquely Hawaiian arts, music and dress. Symbolizing its name, there was a wooden carving of a horse on the mantle in the living room. And next to the horse was a miniature model of a bridge, looking something like the span of the Golden Gate Bridge. From my first look at this horse and bridge, I started to think that maybe there might be an omen here for me, a message important to the meaning of my life at this time. I thought back to what happened that first weekend that I met Sue in Denver, on the return trip from Toronto, where I had gone to interview my Uncle Meyer, about his life for the book that I would write about him. Sue was wearing a cowboy hat—a big, tall one—when I met her. We became instant friends; there was a friendship from the beginning that is hard to describe, one in which all the formalities of getting to know a person seemed unnecessary. This was a friendship from the soul; one that probably spanned many eras and many lifetimes, I had thought at the time. There was a friendship that seemed a priori, not dependent on romance or sparks to be ignited. It seemed to have always been there. We had gone to Aspen on that trip, and I was looking at some pictures recently of how I looked light-headed running up a hill—I wasn't a mountain boy, had rarely ever been to a high altitude—after drinking a couple of beers. And on the way back from Aspen, we stopped in a convenience store to buy some souvenirs and refreshments.

By accident I bumped into a wooden horse and it fell to the ground and cracked. It was my fault, so I paid for the horse, put the pieces in a bag and gave it to Sue. I didn't think much more of the horse on that trip, until at the airport Sue took it out of a bag for me to bring back to San Francisco. She had glued the pieces back together, and had done a very good job in the operating room. One could barely tell that it had been fractured. During the years of our marriage I had often reflected on the meaning of that horse, its breaking and being put back together. I came to believe that it represented that there would be a time in our marriage when things might get difficult, when the marriage was beginning to show cracks, and that it would be held together by glue. Perhaps the very nature of our marriage had implicit within it a crack; and maybe if that horse had not broken—we certainly would not have bought it—there wouldn't have been a marriage at all. And so, to be married to Sue meant that the marriage would at some point be fractured and put back together. Is that where the future resides with Sue? I begged God for the answer to this question one night late, the sky moonless, as I walked the length of the lawn down to the sand and sea. I prayed and asked for the answer. Will the crack in our marriage be glued back seamlessly, though the crack will always remain? Does the crack mean that we will no longer remain married but stay in some sense as one, always spiritually connected, certainly connected through the boys? I search for those answers then as now. There was only one horse on that mantle, and there was a bridge next to it. Does this symbol of the Paniolo represent a message to me, a message that, maybe, I will ride this horse alone as I live in the city by the bridge? I ask many questions, looking for answers in the omens. But only God knows; truly only God knows.

It is the first night of May, the clock on the verge of becoming the wee hours of morning on the second, the incessant beam from Alcatraz rhythmically penetrates the darkness about every five seconds, entering my living room, darkened except for the big lamp on my 19th-century, mahogany, English pedestal desk.

I bought this antique desk—I have loved 19th-century English furniture since first seeing it at the Victoria and Albert Museum the first time I visited England, the trip that gift from my mom when I graduated high school in 1973—maybe 20 years ago, after a particularly good month selling municipal bonds. There is a peaceful energy from the desk, perhaps the merging of my energies with the vibrations of those who have used it for their thoughts during the hundred plus years before it became mine. The desk resonates with me, it is alive, a friend to my thoughts. The writing that I do is usually quite late into the evening, and I tend to measure how late it is in the night by whether I can see the light of a TV in a rather high floor of the condominium building in the offing to my right. Very often I'll stop writing before the lights of the TV are put out, and at such moments I do not feel alone. But often, when the lights are put out while I am deep in thought, the feeling can be quite empty.

It is an unusual connection that I have with the person who lives in that space, a man who appears very cozy and comfortable each night, kicking back in a lounge chair, sometimes visited by a female friend. I see slightly more than the outlines of these figures; they are close enough so that I can partially make out their images. Usually, though, it is a solitary male figure who is up into the wee hours watching the TV that creates the bluish light, and I sometimes wonder if he is aware of this solitary figure who sits at his desk, writing deep into the night. It is, of course, not essential that this person be aware of me, and, perhaps, I would prefer that he not be. It is, though, interesting that the signs of life in that condominium space are comforting when present, and that I feel rather empty when they're missing. The light just went out, perhaps a bit early this evening. And, indeed, a touch of loneliness has come on me. I observe and reflect.

I am writing with my right foot on a bag of frozen chickens. My instep hurts, and the foot has started to swell as a result of some violence that I did to my telephone. A couple of hours ago I threw the phone and receiver to the floor, and started stomping on it with my stockinged right foot, unprotected by a shoe. "Fuck! Fuck! Fuck! Fuck! Fuck! Fuck! Fuck!" I had repeated again and again, first out of anger then out of pain. I had been talking to my sister Heidi and my phone kept disconnecting me (I have been having trouble with the receiver lately), and every time I called back, it continued to disconnect me. This was particularly annoying because I had been waiting for a few weeks to set up a psychic reading with my sister, who has always had a sizable percentage of psychic ability inherited from my mom, but who has recently been startlingly accurate with people.

Just a month ago she had given an old friend—a man for whom my mom once read—a reading over the phone, telling him that he must get a physical and treadmill test done right away, that there was something serious that had to be corrected. He took her advice, went to the doctor, and was told that there was something that needed to be looked at in more detail, and that a stress test would be necessary. The man delayed going to the doctor, and then delayed some more. Unaware that he had been delaying getting this test performed, my sister called him to find out if he had followed up with the test. On hearing that he had not, she told him that she felt that it was urgent that he go back to the doctor and have the follow-up tests performed. He listened to her this time, and a few days later he was in the hospital for emergency heart surgery. The doctors told him that if he had not returned and had the diagnostic test performed, he most likely would have died. There was serious blockage in the arteries revealed by the tests; Heidi's reading saved his life. And the whole family was eternally grateful to her. And there have been other messages that she has passed on to people. Heidi, indeed, has become very good, as she matures. I love my sister, and was looking forward to talking with her tonight; I deeply wanted to talk with her about my life in a focused way. And then that damn telephone started acting up again! And again, and again, and again! So I started stomping on it, cursing it, cursing everything! After all, what is a man to do? How much can a man take? This fuckin' economy! The incessant assuaging of people's fear! The limbo in which I find myself, a sense of helplessness to change anything in the moment! All I wanted was a bit of time for myself; I was prepared to really hear my sister. I wanted to hear her thoughts, though ultimately I will always make my own decisions. And that fuckin' phone! I totally destroyed it with my stocking foot, and so here I sit, the light in the condominium across the way out now, no TV set on, my foot on this icy bag of chickens, feeling like shit. After the damage and cursing, my sister called me back on my cell phone to see what had happened. "I heard cursing and destruction," she said to me. She went into hysterics when I told her what had happened. She offered to give me the reading on the cell phone, but I declined. I get a strange feeling—a dull feeling in my brain—when I hold a cell phone to my ear for very long. I told her that tomorrow I'd go to Radio Shack to buy a new phone. We rescheduled for a few days hence. "What about the portable phone?" she asked. "We can use that; I know you have one with your land line." "I destroyed that too," I answered, and she went into hysterics again. "Once a hockey player, always a hockey player," she answered. And as I sit here looking out over the darkened night, my foot throbs on this bag of frozen chicken.

❐

The last week and a half or so certainly has been interesting in the political arena. While John McCain glides toward the Republican nomination later in the summer—the big question being who will he pick as his running mate, and some of the serious money is on Mitt Romney because of his attractiveness, conservative credentials to provide balance and money—Hillary

Clinton is staying alive for the nomination on the Democratic side. Making Pennsylvania her home state for the past month, she defeated Obama by 10 percentage points there, a blow to him given that he is looking for the "knock-out punch," and is striving to market himself as the presumptive nominee, a candidate who can win in any region of the country and among all colors of people. After winning Pennsylvania—she succeeded by winning the white vote by a margin of 60-40—Hillary had the following comment: "I won the double-digit victory that everybody on TV said I had to win, and the voters of Pennsylvania clearly made their views known—that they think I would be the best president and the better candidate to go against Senator McCain. She went on to say that the "tide was turning." In recent weeks Hillary has fended off calls to drop out of the race—raising less than half of what Obama was raising in funds, she has ignored calls from many within her party that extending this bruising fight, this constant battle of charge and counter-charge so deep into the season would only weaken the Democrats' chances in the general election. But no doubt, emboldened by this Pennsylvania victory, she moves on, hoping to convince the working-class voters of Indiana, West Virginia, North Carolina, that she has the mettle to come from behind and claim the nomination; that she has the stuff to beat McCain. Most pundits say the math is against her, and that she would essentially need to sweep those three primaries, and also take Oregon later in the month (Obama is seriously ahead in that state) to even have a chance. Her hope is that she can do that, that the money will begin to pour in from the Pennsylvania victory, and that by drawing to a virtual "dead heat" with Obama, she'll gain the support of the super delegates at the convention. Clearly the fallout from the Reverend Wright controversy has hurt Obama, and has forced him to tackle the racial issue in a way that he had hoped to avoid. He never wanted to be seen as the African American candidate, but as the candidate representing the best hope for change in a country desperate for it, that he would be the agent of change for all colors, and that there was much more that united his constituents than separated them by color. And, so, in defending himself against the claims that he shares the sentiments (or perhaps agrees with them in his deepest private thoughts) of Reverend Wright, Obama severed ties last week with the reverend. It was something that he absolutely had to do, given the rambling tirade of hatred and anger that the reverend delivered at his National Press Club appearance a few days ago. At the question and answer session following his prepared talk, the reverend quoted the bible and suggested that the U. S. Government deserved to be attacked on September 11, and that the government had genocide in mind when it created the HIV virus to eradicate people of color. He emulated the Nation of Islam leader, Louis Farrakhan, and went on to ridicule the accents of JFK and LBJ. I watched it again tonight on YouTube and thought it was hilarious in its madness and insanity. Ultimately, though, it was just sick. After seeing this and suffering the fallout, Obama offered that, "Whatever relationship I had with Reverend Wright has changed. He doesn't show much regard for me, or, more importantly, for what we are trying to do for the American people." He went on to say that, "I have spent my entire adult life trying to bridge the gap between different kinds of people. That's in my DNA—trying to promote mutual understanding, to insist that we all share common hopes and common dreams as Americans and human beings." It now remains to be seen whether Obama will gain the support of the white industrial workers in Indiana and North Carolina, where victory would effectively knock Hillary out of the race.

❐

It is late in the evening on a Wednesday night, May 7. Usually when I write, the room is illuminated on opposite walls by the softened lights that sit deep within casings that look much like large oyster shells. The owner of this building has done a very good job maintaining it, they provide nice security with cameras and a doorman up front, and there are tasteful touches that one wouldn't expect to find in a rental apartment. The bathrooms, for instance, are tiled with lotus plants, a rather unusual touch, but quite artsy. In any event, the lights that are usually on when I write are off at the moment, the bay is dark, no boats on it, the incessant, rhythmic beam of the light tower on Alcatraz island continues, the Golden Gate Bridge not illuminated, except for the strand of pearls of lights that spans the couple of miles of expanse across the bay. The only light that I have on at this moment is the green lamp, a gorgeous green glass from the early 1930s in the shape of a Turkish turret, which I purchased from Chuck, my favorite antique dealer, whose store is on Sacramento Street, over in Presidio Heights. It is this lamp—and it is such that a genie might appear from its narrow opening at any moment—and the light from the computer that provide the illumination in this front room. I reflect, meditate, let my mind wander, as I focus on this hypnotic green lamp, and I answer the "three wishes" that my mind tells me that are mine to have. "I want my boys to be safe in all they do," I tell the genie. "I want them to be safe, to have fulfilling lives, to reach some if not all of their dreams, to do what they love, to be healthy until old age, to be safe. And, of course, this only counts as one wish, okay?" And the genie agrees. The second wish that I have is for Sue to accept her life, to accept our relationship, in whatever form it takes, to not suffer, to never know want, to be content, to live healthy and with some joy. "This is, again, only one wish," I remind the genie. And he agrees, the apparition smiling on me, as it colorfully emerges from the narrow opening of turret-style green glass. And for the third wish, I wish for my own good health, long life, to know joy, to understand my relationship with Sue, to accept it in whatever form it continues, to love easily without regret, to find balance in my life, to know serenity, to feel the presence of my mom and God. "But, please, Genie, this is only one wish," and he agrees. As I look across the darkened city, I am heartened by the light that is on in the condominium at eye level off in the distance. The man is lying back in his chair, watching the big TV set. I am not alone on this lonely night

❐

Earlier in the week I had so much excitement over my beloved hockey team, the San Jose Sharks. The Stanley Cup playoffs were in full swing, the team was expected to go deep into the tournament, perhaps even make it to the finals for the Cup. So many years, now, I have been disappointed by the Sharks' performance in the playoffs, but this year they are so good. I have been "living and dying" with each game of the playoffs. In the first round of the playoffs, they were fiercely tested by a tough, physical, punishing, mean-spirited Calgary Flames team, which took the Sharks to a decisive seventh game. It was a bruising, demanding series, and the Flames are not the team that I would have wanted to see the Sharks play in that first round. The Stanley Cup playoffs are a painful test of endurance. A team must win four series—has to be the victor in 16 games—of fast, grueling, torturous hockey to claim the cup. And it helps if the team can escape the first round in five or six games, without having to endure too much punishment. I knew the Flames would be a difficult match, and that they would exact pounds of flesh, win or lose. The Sharks beat them in that seventh game, but, clearly, they had spent the better parts of themselves doing it. This was evident in the way they opened the series against the Dallas Stars in the second round of the playoffs. The Sharks were playing at half speed, it seemed, not able to get into that desperation mode that is required to win games in this kind of competition. They lost the first game in overtime, 2-1. And then it got worse. Losing, like winning, can become habit-forming. And they followed that first loss with a pathetic performance, losing 5-2. They were now down two games to none, in the best of seven series. They became desperate in game three, played back in Dallas, after the first two games had been played in San Jose. They outplayed Dallas in every way, on Dallas ice. But they lost again, 2-1 in overtime, sending the Sharks into a do-or-die mode for the rest of this series.

They had been expected to beat Dallas; the Sharks were definitely the better team on paper. But Calgary had pulverized them, though the Sharks had emerged from that series with the victory. Desperation, the "will to live" had taken over for the Sharks, and they won that fourth game in Dallas, 2-1. Then they came home to play game six, and the Sharks won that game in a gut-wrenching contest, taking the contest in overtime, 2-1. We were now within a game of tying this best of seven series, 3-3. The teams flew back to Dallas for that sixth game, the decisive seventh looming on San Jose ice, if only we could get that far. This game six turned out to be "one for the ages." One might have expected the Sharks, living a "do or die existence" for the past two games, to have shown fatigue, emotional exhaustion at this point. But they did not. And the two teams battled as though no hockey would ever be played again. Dallas didn't want to see this series tied, after holding a 3-0 lead, and, certainly, they didn't want to face the Sharks on San Jose ice for game seven, having blown a three-game advantage. Early in the second period, Dallas scored to take a 1-0 lead. And the score stayed that way until my favorite player, Ryane Clowe—he isn't the most skilled player on the team, that goes to Marleau or Thornton, but he has an incredible tenacity, focus, toughness and will to win—scored early in the third period to tie the game. I was going out of my mind wanting to see the Sharks pull this out! I texted my boys, Michael at Oberlin, Jonathan at Bard, to keep them up on every new development, every bit of tension. Michael was not able to get the game at all, but Jonathan, finally, after waiting through various TV programs watched by other students, was able to get the third period in the recreation room at Bard. Sue called me and said she had to stop watching it, the tension was too much for her. She asked that I let her know the result, when it happens. And that result did not come for a very long time. It became the eighth-longest game in NHL history, going deep into the fourth overtime. The score at the end of regulation had remained one to one. The goaltending was just unbelievable through four periods of overtime—they had played more than two games of hockey on this night in Dallas, and not just regular hockey but gut-wrenching, vomit-inducing, do-or-die playoff hockey. After several major chances for San Jose throughout the overtime (they had, by far, the better and more frequent chances) Dallas wins the game on a power play, deep into the night. I texted Michael the result and he was heartbroken; Jonathan had just seen it on TV, and he could barely talk. Sue had fallen asleep, I awakened her to tell her, and she sadly went back to sleep. It was one of the most excruciating sports losses I have ever experienced. And, on this night, I am barely getting over it.

And, so, it is now back to baseball, and though I love baseball—it will inevitably bring me back to myself, I feel my soul unwind at beautiful ATT park in San Francisco—it will take a while to adjust to its pace, after hockey. The Giants are off to a very poor start, though the pitcher whom I had mentioned as a rookie about a year ago, Tim Lincecum, is a revelation, pitching "lights out." What an exciting find for this team, which is searching for a "star" and identity in the aftermath of the Barry Bonds era.

❐

It was a tough day at the office today; many clients were calling, not to discuss their portfolios, but whether they were safe at Wachovia Securities, the firm for which I work. The demise of Wachovia seems far fetched. But the calls kept coming in. After the failure of Bear Stearns, and now with Lehman Brothers showing signs of serious weakness, clients are losing confidence in Wall Street firms. The questions about Wachovia were precipitated by the fact that Wachovia has been in the news virtually every week because they are taking heavy losses in their mortgage portfolios. The acquisition of World Savings is proving to be a financial quagmire, if not disaster. They had reported today that their previously announced loss for the first quarter had nearly doubled to $708 million. And the articles are suggesting that there are more major losses to come in future quarters. But I soldier on, doing the best that I can for my clients, during this very difficult and volatile time. The economy has continued to deteriorate, and Fed Chairman, Ben Bernanke, slashed the Federal Funds rate to two percent this past week, in an effort to hold off a serious recession. The rate was at 5.25 percent, just last September.

And if the economic situation isn't bad enough, with the potential failure of financial institutions and the deep recession that seems to be looming, crude oil hit $120 last week, stoking serious worries of a systemic inflation that could haunt the global economy for years.

❒

The politicians are staying away from the quagmire of how they would fix this economy, instead blaming it all on the policies and ineptitude of the Bush administration. And as the election gets closer and closer—just six months away—it is becoming seemingly inevitable, now, that the Democratic party will have its first candidate of African descent for the presidency. After winning yesterday's North Carolina primary, Obama exuberantly declared to supporters that, "We find ourselves less than 200 delegates from the nomination." Hillary won the Indiana primary, but it was much closer than many had thought it would be, and considerably closer than the polls had predicted a week ago. It seems that Obama has successfully put the Reverend Wright fiasco behind him. It was a good night for Obama, winning North Carolina by 14 points, while Clinton squeaked by in Indiana by just two points. Clinton vows to continue campaigning, but given the fact that she is loaning her campaign millions of dollars, while Obama has millions of public money pouring into his coffers, it is all but over. Even though many of the young do not find it incredible that an African American stands so close to the presidency, and is on the verge of his party's nomination—a testament to the degree to which multiculturalism has eradicated racial barriers—it is astounding for me to watch. Even though I was in my early teens, I so remember the speeches of Dr. King and his dream of a "Promised Land," which in my mind would not likely occur in this lifetime.

≈

June 9th, 2008

I spent my afternoon walking around the streets of San Francisco, trying to view the city with fresh, uncensored eyes, striving to not be disturbed by the incessant sirens that seem to always be a soundtrack to a walk anywhere in the city, from the Marina, through Pacific and Presidio Heights, over to Nob Hill and Russian Hill, into the Financial District, up the stairs of Telegraph Hill, and then across town to the Haight. And I can add testimony to that notion as I sit at my desk on the second floor of the Merchants Exchange building on California Street in the Financial District. The main office is in the Bank of America building across the street, and Wachovia Securities occupies a very high floor, with a sweeping view of the city. But I never go up to the main office, very content and satisfied to be able to walk up the elegant marble staircase to my office that looks on California Street from the second floor.

It is an older building, owned by Clint Reilly, the quite well-known political consultant. He purchased this building many years ago, and it is a gem. The building has been around since the very early 1900s, and it exudes the essence of San Francisco; I feel the ancestral soul, the spirit of this intoxicating, eccentric, gorgeous city pour into my pores as I practice my trade in this building.

I am in this building because when I decided to join Prudential Securities about 10 years ago—they later were acquired by Wachovia—the condition was that I would not work on such a high floor. My claustrophobia in elevators and vertigo in high places had already become well known amongst managers of brokerage companies in the Financial District. I was, though, quite sought after and Prudential agreed to find a small space for me to do business, one that would be near the main office. After shopping for space one day, I suggested we look at space in the Merchants Exchange building. I had always loved the building and its lobby, and was aware of the staircase that would make it easy to avoid the elevators. An office was available on the second floor; and though it was in serious disrepair as a result of some aging and sloppy lawyers who had just vacated it, the manager and I could see the potential of the space. So, I have been there for nearly 10 years, and in this location my business has thrived. Not without a lot of daily stress of course, and chief among the stresses of a financial market's day—particularly during these troubled times—is the incessant, piercing, assaulting sounds of, perhaps, the loudest sirens in America.

I walk across the city, harsh sirens moving past me on Fillmore Street, turning left on Jackson and headed in the direction of Presidio Heights. I go over to Alta Plaza park, enjoy a very good turkey sandwich from Mayflower Market—I bumped into Clint Reilly there a few weeks ago and he said he thought they made the best sandwiches in the city—and sit on the bench looking down to the South, as San Francisco stretches out to the Mission District and beyond. The fog had lifted about an hour before and there was no wind. It was a beautiful Sunday afternoon in a city—taken only on appearances— that would have to be considered in the top five of the world's most alluring, along with Paris, Rome, New York and Hong Kong. The incessant demanding sirens that I had heard over on Fillmore Street minutes before had abated, but there is still a droning off in the distance of sirens—an undercurrent that San Franciscans block from their consciousness in much the same way that one no longer pays attention to that persistent but barely perceptible ringing in the ear. After finishing the sandwich, I walk toward Chinatown, walking up and down Sacramento Street—I'm thinking to myself that I have never been to Alcatraz, and how cool it would be to take a tour of that place, and how much I have always wanted to do that, dating all the way back to when my parents brought me here and when I fell in love with the city in early childhood—eventually standing on the corner of Sacramento and Grant in the heart of Chinatown.

When I was a child visiting with my parents, Chinatown was the most exotic place on earth to me. The color of the place, greens, reds, golds, the dragons breathing fire as they sat on posts, the lanterns that were light fixtures written in calligraphy, the wafting scents from Chinese kitchens, captivated me. About once a year for a few years we'd come to San Francisco to visit from where we were living in the Simi Valley of Southern California. And every time we visited, I pleaded with my mom to convince my dad to bring us here to live. It called me, and it refuses to ever let me leave.

❐

I was a big Los Angeles Dodgers fan in those days, Sandy Koufax being the ultimate idol and father figure rolled into one for me. He is Jewish, didn't pitch on the Jewish holidays, and was so devastatingly good. I looked up to him, was charmed by his quiet dignity, hypnotized by his pitching brilliance. Thinking about him, I remind myself what Mickey Mantle said to the Dodgers catcher, Johnny Roseboro after striking out to Koufax during the 1963 World Series: "How are you supposed to hit that shit?" Mantle apparently had spoken to the catcher, dejectedly dropping his bat and walking back to the dugout. Or the words from Willie Stargell: "Trying to hit Koufax is like trying to sip soup through a fork." I just loved the guy, and came to San Francisco wearing my Dodgers cap. But the rivalry was intense up here—the Dodgers were not loved. I'll never forget how ardent Giants fans would tell me politely that I must remove that cap and replace it with a Giants cap—this was the land of Willie Mays. I smiled a big kid's smile and politely answered that, "No, I'll keep my Dodgers cap on, but Willie Mays is incredible." And I followed with, "But you know, he has a hard time hitting Sandy Koufax's fastball." The city had affected my imagination with a fantastic magic that felt like fantasy. It was a circus, a carnival, a parade, replete with all the music. As I stand here looking up and then down Grant avenue, I realize how lucky I am to live in this city, and I remind myself to never forget that living here is a dream come true.

It is interesting to note that I see an abundance of Obama banners as I walk up Grant avenue into the center of Chinatown. Perhaps there are four or more Obama banners for every Clinton one. And so, today, the politicos of Chinatown must be pretty happy with their presumptive nominee. Last night Hillary Clinton gave an impassioned, enthusiastic, inspirational speech conceding the nomination to Obama, urging support of him, and in so doing reminding America what they were not getting. And what they didn't elect is a very intelligent, charismatic woman with clear leadership capabilities. She looked quite attractive as well, I must say—I have a client in his 80s who had been telling me that he wants Hillary to become president, thinks she is very sexy, and hopes that he is alive long enough to watch her occupy the White House the next four years. She sure did come on strong against Obama at the end; perhaps if she had not been so confident in the early going, had hired people that took nothing for granted, showed her human side a bit more during the whole campaign, she would be the nominee. We'll never know. But, no doubt, Obama was able to ride the beautifully formed Hawaiian wave—extremely skillful in surfing it, correcting mistakes and confronting issues as they arose, the incredible speech on race—all the way to the shore. He certainly has to be a favorite to reach the Promised Land against McCain. But, again, we shall see.

Chinatown

As I walk up Grant avenue, memories come flooding through me of my first days living in San Francisco in 1979. I am walking by the green building that houses the tiny offices on the upstairs, the printing presses on the first level for Asian Week newspaper, as well as some other publications that they own. This is the first place I worked when I moved to San Francisco to become a graduate student. Trying to find a job in the city to supplement the dollars my mom had planned to send me—at this point I didn't want her to have to support me, I knew how hard it was to keep up these tea-leaf readings, day after day—and also wanting to be a writer, I found on the bulletin board at San Francisco State University an advertisement for a reporter for the Asian Week newspaper. It had said that previous journalism experience was preferred but not necessary, and if one felt that they had strong writing skills to go ahead and apply for the job. And so, that very day I called to set up an interview for the following day. The person with whom I had spoken on the telephone that afternoon was an elderly sounding Chinese man, but he spoke very clear English. "Just ask for me, John Fang," he had told me. I was excited about the opportunity, to say the least. I arrived at the old, wooden green building on Sacramento Street, just up the hill from Grant Avenue, and was greeted by a quite attractive Chinese woman with long black hair. She introduced herself as Florence Fang, and brought me upstairs to see Mr. Fang. Mrs. Fang had been involved with the printing machines when I walked in, and she was doing this work with two teenage Chinese boys. I remember the very clear complexions of the two boys—they might have been a couple of years apart in age—the straight black hair clipped above their ears, the diligence with which they worked, and the rather good-natured way that they went about their jobs, smiles on each of their faces. The whole place smelled like ink mixed with something herbal. Mrs. Fang brought me upstairs to meet the Mr., who stood up from a metal desk strewn with an abundance of papers, and came over to meet me, slightly hunched over and squinting above his glasses as he did so. He shook my hand, while Mrs. Fang smiled and left the office. On his desk was a book with very tiny Chinese calligraphy, and it had been opened to somewhere near the middle. Mr. Fang seemed to have been poring over the words on these pages when I walked in, squinting over the top of his glasses as he read it.

The room looked down on Sacramento street, and smelled of herbs, the tea that he had been drinking, the ink from the room below, and tobacco. Mr. Fang asked me—again squinting above his glasses as he looked at me, his teeth were clean and straight, his hair completely gray—if I had ever written for a newspaper before. I answered that I had done some journalism in college and high school—that I'd actually had my own column in a high school newspaper—but that I had never worked as a reporter for a newspaper before. I tried to impress him—and I was very enthusiastic—that I was not unfamiliar to writing, being a graduate in philosophy from the University of California, Santa Barbara. And that I was in San Francisco to attend graduate school in International Relations, and what a great experience it would be to be able to cover issues of concern to English-speaking Chinese while studying for my master's in International Relations. I wanted to impress him that as a philosophy major, I had a very strong interest in East/West philosophy, with a particular interest in Chinese philosophy, particularly Lao Tzu and the Tao. We discussed a bit about Taoism and Confucianism, and he was pleased that I had familiarity with the ideas and practice. I described how I had meditated a bit at a Taoist temple as a student in Santa Barbara, and that I was very attracted to Chinese culture, philosophy, thought. Mr. Fang was nice to me, but I could tell that he wasn't sure that I had the stuff that he was looking for, particularly because I had no experience as a journalist. "You are not a journalist, and I really want a young journalist, someone who knows San Francisco," he had said at the end of the interview. I responded that I knew that I could do the job well, that I was a very strong writer, and that his ad did not demand journalism experience. "I'll take you to my editor," he said, "and I'll let him make the decision. I will leave it up to him." I politely thanked him for the chance to move on to the next interview; at which point he brought me into the next room, introduced me to a man in his early 30s, rather good looking—an experienced, somewhat jaded, editorial look about him—with sleeves rolled up to the elbows. "This is Mr. Rosen, see what you think; I leave it up to you," Mr. Fang said to his editor. Then he turned to leave the room, walked toward me to shake my hand, peered into my eyes above his glasses, offered me just the slightest smile and "good luck," then walked back down the stairs to the printing press room, and then out the door to Sacramento Street. As our interview started, I could see out of the corner of the window, Mr. Fang walking slowly, a bit of a limp, slightly hunched over, crossing the street and disappearing into the wilds of Chinatown.

The slightly jaded, not incredibly enthusiastic editor with rolled-up sleeves was not overwhelmingly impressed that I came to him without any journalism experience. However, he did give me an assignment, which he said would be rather difficult. "We'll see how you do with this," he said, "and if you do a good job, I'll consider you for the position. But, again, it is not an easy assignment." He wanted me to go out into the streets of Chinatown and describe what I saw. To write everything that I saw. "You can do it tomorrow if you like; you don't have to do it now. And when you finish, just bring it back to me." I was excited, enthused, and wanted to do it that very minute. I informed him that I would go out and do it immediately. This is what I wrote:

"Red and its various hues of orange, magenta, and maroon pervade the eye amidst the decorations of Chinese characters, the dwellings that are pagodas, the scents that only Chinese chefs can create and the feeling that one is for a moment in a fantasy.

"On the corner of Grant and California streets, one gains a revealing look at Chinatown. To the right, down the 600 block of Grant, one might feel that he is in a Pearl S. Buck novel. The words, "Chinatown Wax Museum" appear against a brilliant red background, typical of Chinatown. The building is made of yellowish brick. In the upper center and left corner of this exciting structure, on its fourth level, is recorded a most elegant trademark. Long-tailed dragons, suggestive of mythical conflict, face each other and breathe fire as they circle an eight-sectioned mandala, framed in the green of life. Against its red background, denoting luck, are written the eight Chinese characters of the legend. The center of the mandala recalls the study of Chinese philosophy with a circle divided into North, South, East and West, and a curved line of Yin and Yang, the two elements of Chinese cosmology, reveal themselves in the center of this beautiful trademark.

"My mind drifts across California Street, still on Grant, and I might think myself in Asia if it were not for the signs written in English. I look across California, and find another four-floored yellowish-colored brick building. This graceful dwelling is topped by a three-tiered Pagoda that is crowned in red and silver. It recalls the Emperor.

"Continuing my gaze across California, and the other way down this one-way street of Grant, the beautiful Asian background is framed by two elegant Chinese lanterns posted either side of the street. They are miniature Pagodas, supported on either side by aqua-green posts and golden dragons. Bells hang from the roof of these pagoda lanterns, and I can just imagine the fantasy they must cause on a night when the streets are wet with rain and reflect the lights of these lanterns as they frame both sides of Grant across California.

"I walk down Grant and I come to the intersection of Sacramento. The color red and its various hues provide the background for Chinese characters, which satisfy my yearning for far-away places. Just above me, I look up and see the sign 'Bank of America' written in Chinese. Looking for the entrance to this bank, I discover the most spectacular Bank of America that I have ever seen! The entrance is in another of Chinatown's beautiful Pagoda buildings, and its hearth is marked by two stunning pillars with ornate golden and fierce dragons facing one another from either pillar. The clash of this violent gold against the red calls to mind that if I were to take a picture and send it to a friend, he would probably think that it was a picture of the bank's Asian branch.

"One is also reminded that Chinatown is bordered by a bustling business community. A glance down Sacramento, and I have a view of the Bay Bridge, as it provides a backdrop for the many modern executive buildings. At first glance, these buildings oppress the Asia in which I now stand, but from another point of view it is an interesting example of East meeting West.

"It's lunchtime now, and I contemplate the pungent scents of Oriental kitchens. I relax for a moment in the quiet space of a park that is filled with red benches. Chinese people speak Chinese behind me and I view the modern executive buildings. This park links the East with the West.

"English-language signs, such as 'City of Shanghai,' 'Buddha Fine Arts,' 'The Far East Café,' remind me that I am still in America, but they also tell me that I am in Asia. Yes, this is San Francisco! And as it sits like a diamond on its Western Bay, it is a Gateway to the East!"

I went home to type the piece and made myself a peanut butter and jelly sandwich. Then I got back to the paper as quickly as I could, one of the Fang brothers opening the door for me. It was before five o'clock, and the editor was still there preparing the articles for the next issue—he had been drinking some coffee, his hair pushed back even more than it had been when I left for my assignment. “Let me see what you’ve got,” he said, then proceeded to focus intently on what I had written. “This is very good stuff, very colorful, descriptive, well written,” he said. “It’s very good; it’s good enough that I’ll give you the job on a trial basis.” “Thanks!” I responded. “That’s just great, really great!” In the following edition he printed my piece:

A Chinatown Fantasy
For a Newcomer, Area Has Special Meaning
By Bruce Rosen

I called my mom instantly to tell her of the job, and when the article came out, I sent her several copies. She was overjoyed with excitement and pride. And as I walk past the green wooden building on Sacramento Street today, I am proud of myself; I feel a part of this city and I miss my mom. I dearly miss my mom.

The very first assignment handed to me at Asian Week by the disheveled, coffee-drinking (he seemed to always be drinking coffee) rugged, but good-looking editor, with the combed back sandy-colored hair (though a few strands were always falling down and dangling over the eyebrows), and rolled-up sleeves, was a plum question and answer session. He wanted me to interview the attorney, Arlo Smith, who was challenging the incumbent District Attorney of San Francisco, Joseph Freitas. A once highly popular DA, Freitas had become controversial, the object of anger and frustration among many San Franciscans, for the light sentence handed to Supervisor Dan White in the slayings of Supervisor Harvey Milk and Mayor George Moscone. Using his now notoriously famous “Twinkie Defense”—his attorneys arguing that Dan White was under the influence of the high sugar content found in Hostess Twinkies, thereby causing him to act irrationally—Dan White was not found guilty of murder but rather involuntary manslaughter. The decision shocked the nation, and left the gay community—but not just the gay community, of course—in abject outrage. The decision led to the White night riots of May 21, 1979, the gay community organizing in the Castro and marching on City Hall. Freitas would come under attack for the light sentence, and for not directly prosecuting Dan White. So, the first question that I asked the challenger—he arrived with a small staff about 20 minutes late to a little hole-in-the-wall Chinese restaurant off the beaten path in Chinatown, I had just finished a cup of hot and sour soup and some jasmine tea—was his take on the prosecution of Dan White. The strong, forceful, bald-headed Arlo Smith wasted no time in going after Freitas: It was "outrageous, absolutely outrageous" he told me, that the DA didn't directly prosecute White. He then glibly added something to the effect that, "Perhaps he thought it was such an open-and-shut case that he had nothing to win politically by taking it on directly."

"Do you think he was playing politics with this case?" I remember asking him. "Do you think that he was afraid of alienating the constituency that supported Supervisor White, with an election on the horizon?" I continued. Arlo Smith said something to the effect that, "A murder had been committed, possibly a premeditated murder," and that the sentence was outrageous. We moved on to other areas, with me asking some questions on crime in the city, drugs, guns, prostitution, that the editor had wanted answered. The interview lasted about 30 minutes, at which point Smith said that he had a full schedule and had to leave. He thanked me for conducting the interview professionally, we shook hands, and then he was outside the door of the small Chinese kitchen, into the narrow side street of Chinatown, turned the corner onto Grant Avenue, where a car had been waiting for him and his small group. I was impressed with Arlo Smith, his leadership capability, power and energy. He looked like a formidable challenger. I would have wanted to interview

Joseph Freitas, but that interview had already occurred a few weeks before I started writing for the paper.

A couple of minutes later I walked over to the upstairs offices of the little green building that houses Asian Week, and wrote up the interview. By the end of the day, the article was on the desk of Mr. Rolled-Up Sleeves, and in a few days it made the front page of the newspaper, virtually intact. I was enjoying this.

During the next few months, I would come to the paper part time, often on the days when I wasn't taking classes in my graduate program at S.F. State, and edit a few articles for the paper from columns to which the paper subscribed. And I would often get an assignment. I did a story on a Chinese artist who did stunning landscapes in a very tiny upstairs room of a Chinatown boarding house, the smell of fish being cleaned in the bathroom down the hall permeating the air. In another article, I interviewed a Chinese chef on the benefits of tofu in the diet; there was a piece on acupuncture, and another on the economic conditions. But, then, about three months after landing the job—and, it seemed doing quite well, there had been letters to the editor commenting about some of my articles—my editor was fired (or maybe he resigned, was never quite sure) and I was also asked to leave by John Fang. "We're going in a another direction," he had told me. "I think I'm doing a good job, and I'm enjoying it," I responded, and then I described some of the articles that I had written. "You were fine," he said, peering over the heavy glasses. "We are going to do something else." And that was it. Disappointed, I left my job at Asian Week in Chinatown..

While writing for Asian Week I was, of course, aware of that newspaper's competitor in Chinatown, the other English language weekly aimed at the Chinese audience, East/West. Trying to be a good journalist, I would read the East/West each week of its publication, trying to gain background and knowledge of the Chinatown community. While the philosophy of Asian Week was to cover stories of interest to the broader Asian Community of the Bay Area—particularly reaching out to the Japanese and Filipino readership in addition to the Chinese—East/West appeared to be much more focused on the social, economic, political stories affecting the Chinese of San Francisco. It emphasized the personalities of Chinatown more so than Asian Week, and they had a very talented film critic—he could have been writing for any major publication in the country—Richard Springer. During the several months that I worked at Asian Week and read East/West I had started to arrive at the perception that Asian Week had a philosophical/political bias in favor of Taiwan, while East/West tilted somewhat toward mainland China. I didn't have any inside information or hard facts supporting this, just a general sense that there was a strong competition and political rivalry between these two papers. And so, armed with a stack of articles that I had written for Asian Week, I made my way up the tiny, narrow elevator—I didn't like elevators in those days, and I do everything I can to stay away from them—to keep the appointment that I had made with Gordon Lew, the publisher of East/West.

Mr. Lew had a large round face, was about five foot, six inches when he stood to greet me, and had the belly of a Buddha when he sat back down. He was dressed nicely in a suit, white shirt and tie, hair black and oily as it sparsely covered a rapidly balding crown. I wouldn't say that he smiled on meeting me, but neither was it a frown. The look was impassive, not particularly happy that I was there, but in no way dismissive—after all, he did consent to this interview. "What can I do for you?" Mr. Lew had said to me with a distinctly professorial tone, the words not flowing together, but expressed in a clipped fashion, a pause before each word: "What-can-I-do-for-you?" And though Mr. Lew's lips and jaw seemed tight as he greeted me—almost stoic in their lack of expression—I could see depth and kindness in his eyes, an initial suspicion about my reason for being there, then an appreciation for the kid in me who wanted a chance to be a journalist. "Mr. Lew," I started, "here are all of the articles that I wrote in the several months that I wrote for Asian Week. I think that I am a very good writer, can be a really good journalist for you. I'd like a chance to write for East/West. For whatever reason, Mr. Fang at Asian/Week wanted to do something else. He let the editor go—the guy was an excellent writer and editor—and he asked me to leave. But I don't feel that I'm ready to leave the Chinese community—I am starting to become familiar with it, and enjoy meeting the people, writing the stories—and would very much appreciate writing for you. I am quite familiar with the paper. And I want to say that I think Richard Springer is outstanding in his movie reviews. He is excellent." "Mr. Rosen," Mr. Lew began—I surmised that he was from Hong Kong, given the hint of British English in the Chinese accent in which he spoke his words in that abrupt clipped fashion—"I am very familiar with your writing. We really do not need another writer here, and can't afford anybody full time. But if you would like to come a few days a week after your studies—I understand that you are a graduate student, is that correct?" "Yes," I responded, "studying international relations with an emphasis on China at S.F. State." "If you would like to come a few days a week to do some odd jobs around here, a bit of editing, writing some articles, we would pay you $60 a week. I don't expect that you can afford to do that. But that's all that I can pay." "I would be willing to do that for now," I answered. "The experience is what I'm looking for right now." "Well then," the words spoken with that tinge of English pronunciation covering the Chinese accent, "come on Monday at five o'clock and we'll get you started.

"Come hungry, because at about 6:30 the office goes to dinner, and you will be invited to join us." "I very much appreciate the opportunity. I'm glad that I'll be able to continue to work in Chinatown." "We shall see you Monday, then." And with that, I put my articles back in their large envelope, made my way over to the tiny, narrow elevator, and got into it when it arrived. I hated that elevator, but the enthusiasm of the opportunity to continue working in Chinatown helped to put that claustrophobia to the back of my mind.

I was now in the employ of the East/West, weekly, English-language Chinese newspaper, and I would visit the office between two-to-three times a week. The job involved riding that narrow, claustrophobic, tight-fitting elevator up four floors. The thing really shouldn't hold more than about four people, but (and this is no prejudice; it is simply the case) the Chinese do not necessarily

Bruce Rosen, the journalist, writing an article for the East/West newspaper. He is also Bruce Wong, the ad salesman.

observe personal space requirements—very often it was filled with 10 or so, many of the riders making their way to dinner at the top of the building, the quality Mandarin restaurant, the Empress of China. Whenever I entered that elevator, I prayed that it would open at my destination and not get stuck. And when it filled with so many people, I would often get out and wait for the next one. But quite often it would fill up several times in a row, so fairly often I would just get in, "bite the bullet" and hope that I wouldn't start hyperventilating from the claustrophobia. But it always opened at my destination, never once stopping between floors and getting stuck. However, it did become quite difficult for me to ride elevators after than period in my life; I had always had—since childhood—an anxiety over being in elevators, but from that time forward the line had been crossed into a new territory of anxiety.

It was usually on Monday nights that the office would meet for dinner at the Empress of China restaurant, and it was here that Gordon Lew taught me the art of using chopsticks: one stick resting effortlessly on the bottom two fingers, the other held in between the other two and pivoting. And in short order I had become professional with the technique. After a month or so—while not understanding a word of Chinese (though I did start a class while in grad school, but had to drop it because it would have taken about eight hours a day for me to get anywhere with it)—I had become proficient, virtually fluent in the language of chopsticks. And during these dinners I really got to know Gordon Lew, not as a stoic competitor in the Chinatown newspaper business, but as a dignified man with a kind, loving spirit, a learned educator with a foundation in the teachings of Confucius and Lao-Tzu. And from time to time at the dinner table up at the Empress Restaurant, while many in the group would be talking about the news of the day, we'd get into discussions on wu wei, the Taoist notion of "action that is actionless"; the idea that we "achieve by not striving to achieve"; the concept of water being the most powerful force on earth, simply because it is the lowest and most humble; the idea that we walk behind and therefore we walk in front. And in the Confucian school of thought we discussed the idea that "order on earth and in the universe" derives from order in the microcosm of the family— that all things derive from the proper order within the family, and this order is based on filial piety and respect. I had studied these concepts as a philosophy major in college, and in the presence of Mr. Gordon Lew I listened to a man of deep Chinese understanding describe their use in daily life.

During the next several months I had begun to make a name for myself at the publication and within the Chinese community as a writer capable of revealing the truth within a story, cutting through the superfluous stuff to get to the inherent meaning of the event. Suddenly, there were "Letters to the Editor," referencing a piece that I had written, discussing it or elaborating. I continued to work for $60 a week, yet I was really loving what I was doing, enjoyed the recognition within the community, and truth be told would have done it for nearly free, so satisfying was it to be a member of this paper and a writer.

A few months after starting at the newspaper, the date was January 30, 1980, to be exact, the East/West published a controversial piece of mine that created a serious stir within the Chinese communities of San Francisco and Oakland. The story was even picked up by TV news in San Francisco. Gordon Lew had given me some names to call about the prospective cancellation of the Oakland Chinese New Year's parade. These names revealed a lot more than anyone intended, and the story cut into a bitter feud between supporters of mainland China and Taiwan. Under the byline Bruce Rosen, the article appeared on the Editorial page, with the title: Oakland Parade is a Political Casualty. Most people had thought—and basically the article that I was asked to write started out as just a basic corroboration of the fact—that the cancellation of the parade occurred because an Imperial Drum Corps had been disbanded. But in interviewing and probing several people—and I was astounded at what and how much they were telling me—I learned that the reason for the cancellation was due to the fact that the financial sponsors wanted no mainland Chinese representation, including no communist Chinese flag. When this couldn't be accomplished, according to these sources, the Taiwanese donors withdrew all funding.

This was a major firecracker in the Chinese communities; the Chinese New Year's parade—something ostensibly free of politics and representing all Chinese—was a cherished institution in Oakland, as it was in San Francisco. The fact that reliable people had said—and their stories had been corroborated by others—that it had been cancelled for political reasons was a major insult to this community. As East/West prepared to publish my piece, the newspaper was—according to what I had heard—contacted by interested parties asking that they not do so. But Mr. Lew did publish it, and next to it, he wrote a scathing editorial about the cancellation, titled, "Free From Politics." For a few days there was tension in the air, and it was exciting to be in the middle of it.

I had only lived in San Francisco for six months when I was a news reporter for East/West in January 1980, so I wasn't much aware of the various television news reporters and personalities of the Bay Area media. Thus, when I sat down at a table one afternoon at the San Francisco Culinary Academy to write a piece about the delicious lunch that was being prepared by world-renowned Chinese chefs, I had no clue that I was seated next to the team of Channel 7 reporters that had just returned from a groundbreaking visit to China—a momentous journey on an inaugural Pan Am 747 charter flight from San Francisco to Shanghai—that revealed "behind the scenes" views of Chinese life previously not allowed by the mainland government. During the first half hour or so of the luncheon, I very much enjoyed sharing pleasantries and discussing the delectable deliciousness of the food with a Chinese man next to me. Eventually he asked what I did, and I told him that I was a graduate student in International Relations at S.F. State, with an emphasis on China, but also had a part-time job as Bruce F. Rosen, the reporter for East/West weekly newspaper. He had seen some of my articles, was very aware of the political controversy that had been depicted in my recent story about the cancellation of the Oakland New Year's parade, and wanted me to tell the publisher that he appreciated his willingness to run the story. "I'm David Louie," he said to me, "and you just might be the right person to write our story of the China trip. We are going to run a daily report on the trip next week on Channel 7 News, followed by a documentary within the next month or so. Would you be interested in writing the story?" "I would love to do the story, sure, absolutely; it would be a lot of fun and very interesting," I answered. Mr. Louie then proceeded to introduce me to the rest of the Channel 7 team, the producer who had gone to China and another reporter who had also participated. He told them that, "This is Bruce Rosen, a very talented writer for East/West—he broke the story on the controversy over the cancellation of the Oakland New Year's parade—and I'm going to recommend to his publisher that he write about the China trip in advance of the broadcast next week." I received smiles and handshakes from the very attractive Chinese woman who was the producer, as well as from the rest of the television team seated and enjoying the delicious delicacies. David and I talked for about another 30 minutes about the China trip, and about my studies in International Relations. When his team eventually stood to leave, David gave me a big, warm handshake, saying, "You'll be hearing from us." And, indeed, it didn't take very long to hear from him.

I left shortly after they did, taking an hour walk to burn off the lunch, so that I would be clear headed enough to write the story about the luncheon. When I made my way back up that tightly fitting elevator to the newspaper office, Gordon Lew greeted me immediately with the news that he had just been contacted by

David Louie from Channel 7, and that he was quite impressed with me, and had requested that I write the piece on the China trip. There were several more senior writers for the paper who, no doubt, would have loved this "choice" assignment, and I did have the feeling that if Gordon were to have his way—Confucian as he was in respecting seniority within the paper—he would have preferred to give one of these people the piece. "Do you feel confident writing this story?" he asked me. "Definitely," I answered. "I think it would be a lot of fun." "Well he asked specifically for you," he responded, "so I really don't have much choice but to let you take it. Here is Mr. Louie's phone number; he would like to do the interview tomorrow so we can make it in this week's edition, in advance of their reports next week." "That's great," I answered; I'll go call him and set it up now." David sounded very pleased that I would be doing the piece, and I must admit the thought did occur to me, "He really doesn't know that I haven't been a journalist very long; I really am an amateur at this," but I swallowed that feeling, knowing that I really would do a good job on it. That night, I turned on Channel 7 News to see a segment being reported by the person with whom I'd had lunch that afternoon. I was in San Francisco, and it felt like the Golden Gate was opening for me!

❒

My focus as a graduate student in International Relations had been China, particularly on the emergence of modern China following the long march by Mao, through the Cultural Revolution and the Gang of Four, into the development of capitalism with a communist face. During these studies I delved as deeply as I could into the collected writings of Mao, and so it was fascinating to me to speak to Mr. Louie and gain insight into the modern China, the degree to which it was still Maoist and to what extent it was bursting through the yoke of Maoist repression. The piece that I wrote complemented my graduate studies and was informed by them. I spoke with David Louie for about two hours, before going home to my typewriter to write the piece. He was an ebullient man with whom to speak—charming, bubbling with enthusiasm about his work, thrilled with the revelations of the groundbreaking news trip to China. He had been quite satisfied that the objective of the trip, to gain a "free hand to penetrate the uncensored life of China," had been to a great extent fulfilled.

He described his visits to the Gifted Children's Palaces, the places where youth beginning at about the age of five are taken to coordinate both sides of the brain in the complementary studies of music and tai chi. He described a very impressive scene of watching these young people—film crews rarely if ever had been granted such full access to these studies—brilliantly playing music and moving gracefully, artistically through the martial art. In contrast to the Children's Palaces, Mr. Louie described the spartan and unhealthful conditions that existed for the Chinese factory worker. He described the freezing conditions within the factories, where coal was inadequately employed to keep workers warm, causing lung problems for those who had to breath the dust daily. I probed him on current attitudes toward Mao and the Cultural Revolution, and whether the Chinese had repudiated and vilified the founder of Chinese communism. He answered by telling me the story of an educator, Xue Sheng, who was a principal at a school before the Cultural Revolution. Because of her recalcitrant nature, her resistance to so radically change her teaching style in conformity with Mao's requirements, both of her legs had been broken, and she had been forced to become a janitor, working very long and difficult hours. But the woman had equanimity—which many of the Chinese he interviewed appeared to have toward their painful past—feeling that her experiences were part of China's growing pains, difficulties that are necessary toward the greatness that China will eventually enjoy.

At the time of my interview with David Louie, China had been imposing fines of 10 percent of a family's income for producing more than two children, while adding an additional 10 percent income to people with one or no children. He had wanted to study old-age homes, but officials were vague about their existence, and he also had hoped to see the inside of prisons. They had been given free access to many places, but the prisons were totally off limits. Talking about the distribution of resources on an equitable basis, Mr. Louie came to the conclusion that, "You can't help but leave with the impression that they have found something that works for them." He was fascinated to no end by his experience in China, and the sense that the clock had been turned back about 50 years.

I still see David Louie on the television news, always enjoying his charisma and infectious charm. And I tell myself that one of these days I will give him a call to reminisce about our interview and the radical changes that have taken place in the world and in China in the almost 30 years that have passed. I simply cannot believe it—I conducted that interview, virtually 30 years ago, and I still think of myself as a kid. I really mean it; I think that I am a kid. God willing, I'll always think of myself that way, all the way to the last breath when, hopefully, I will have gratitude for having been alive a long time and having lived a full life, cherishing as many special moments—taking mental snapshots of them—as God permits. But getting back to China, it is ironic that the country he described in that piece back in 1980, a country barely out of the Communist revolution and horrible repression (China's version of McCarthyism), is leading the world out of the gloomiest recession since the Great Depression. They are growing at about 10 percent a year, and while the world is mired in debt that threatens to collapse the foundations of capitalism, China is flush with liquidity and little debt. The country is a paradox, and it would be fascinating to explore it.

Apparently my story on the television news crew's trip to China enhanced the ratings. This is what David Louie so appreciatively told me in the thank you note that he had sent after the publication. He wanted me to know that it was a great pleasure working with me and reading the story. "You have" he said, "created the images of the story" that he was hoping to reveal. At that moment I so wanted to be a writer, and I felt that the path was opening for me. I was privileged to work with such nice people in Chinatown, and, indeed, it felt like I was living out a fantasy. I had been entranced by San Francisco when brought here by my parents as a child; I was hypnotized by the place and pleaded with them to bring me back soon, practically begging my dad (my mom was very interested in doing so) to move us here. No place that I had ever visited exerted a gravitational pull on me like San Francisco. I had to be here. But Chinatown, in particular, had me spellbound. Situated somewhere atop one of the city's "magical mystery hills," it felt like an exotic jewel; and whenever I would think of San Francisco from boring Simi Valley where we lived, the image of Chinatown— all of the lights and the streets dampened by the rain reflecting the colors, pungent delicious scents wafting through the air, the little trinkets in the foreign shops, the cable car scaling the heights and stopping just beyond the welcoming lanterns—beckoned my return. Indeed, it felt as though San Francisco and its Golden Gate—the bridge the color of red rust, elemental and earthy—were opening to me a world of possibilities, the opportunity to pursue and live my dreams.

Bruce Wong

After several months of working upstairs in the cozy writing and editorial quarters of East/West, I became aware of a man who would visit the office at the end of the day, delivering a stack of papers to Gordon Lew, parting with a few words in the street-smart, New York–sounding toughness of a Damon Runyon character. This tough-looking, tough-sounding Irish guy seemed very out of place in this Chinese newspaper space. He stood about six feet tall, slightly hunched shoulders, a full combed-back mane of grayish-turning, reddish hair, a nose that looked like it had been broken a few times, and a well-packed pipe (tobacco spilling over from the sides) dangling from a mouth whose front teeth were missing. He would deliver his package of papers, sometimes picking up an envelope from Mr. Lew, and take a glance around the room, with a tough sounding, "See ya tomorrow," or a, "See ya Monday," or a, "See ya next Wednesday." Gordon would nod graciously, in his dignified way, acknowledging that he would be there to see the guy on the appointed days. The tough-sounding guy would turn around, often taking a glance around the room, drop his head and leave, having put the envelope in his brown leather case. This toothless guy did not dress particularly well—there was a soiled blue sport coat clearly in need of a dry cleaning, very often a blue and white striped shirt that needed ironing, gray trousers. But the brown case was clearly expensive, and so were the brown leather shoes. So his appearance had the element of contradiction. And, again, at first he seemed clearly out of place in this space. And over the next couple of months his visits to the office became more frequent, his deliveries to Mr. Lew much more often, the exchange of papers for an envelope now more commonplace.

On one of these occasions the guy stopped at my desk to ask me my name. "Bruce," I said, "Bruce Rosen. I write for the paper." "Yeah, I've seen the articles," he answered. He didn't say whether he liked them or not, just, "Yeah, I've seen the articles," delivered with a slightly derogatory attitude, or maybe it was just his street-tough tone, suggestive of a sense that, "This is all a bunch of bullshit," or, "Who do you all think you are up here, feeling so smug and self important; you're a far cry from the New York Times." "Gordon Lew told me that you're from Toronto," he said, "and that you're a good writer, but not making much money writing." "Why would he tell him that?" was my first thought.

"No, I don't make a lot of money," I answered, "but for the time being it is okay; I'm a graduate student, working on a master's degree in International Relations out at San Francisco State, and I'm enjoying what I'm doing. I'm not worried about the money right now." I continued, "Yeah, I was born in Toronto, but I haven't lived there since I was a small child. We moved to California when I was young." "Well, I'm from Toronto originally," the guy said, the pipe dangling from the corner of his mouth. I found it amazing that he was able to speak so well with that pipe dangling from his mouth, not tied down by any hands. "But I lived in New York for quite a while before coming here." "When did you live in Toronto?" I asked him. "Were you there in the '60s?" "Yeah, I moved there in my 20s. I was born in England, actually, flew a Spitfire in the Battle of Britain, then moved to Toronto after the war." "Are both your parents from Toronto?" he asked. "No, my father is from Montreal, but my mom was born and raised in Toronto. And (now this is not something I would necessarily tell somebody, but since the guy had such a toughness about him, I decided to let it rip), if you lived in Toronto in the late '60s, you've probably heard the name, Rush." "Rush, as in Meyer Rush and Dave Rush?" he replied. "Yes, as in Meyer Rush and Dave Rush; they are my uncles, my mom's brothers." He stood up straight, clearly very impressed, and went on: "Dave was one of the richest men in Toronto for a time, and nobody would fuck with him. He was known to be very tough, very, very tough. He was behind the first heavyweight fight ever fought in Canada" "Yep, that's the guy," I answered. "I worked for him in his glass factory in London, when I graduated college a year ago. He's an intense uncle, but I love him." "And Meyer," he responded, "Everybody in Toronto knows Meyer Rush. The guy is a legend. Used to go in and pay cash for Cadillacs. Would buy two at a time as gifts sometimes. He survived the bombing; they thought they killed him. How in the fuck did he survive that?" "Yes, that is my Uncle Meyer," I answered. "I saw him about a year ago when I was in London working for Dave." "Well, I'll be Goddamned," the toothless guy said. “I’m Owen Duffey, and I’d like to train you to advertise with me. You’ll make 20 times what you’re making here writing articles. You’re a Rush; what are you doing this for fuck sake?” “I’m not really interested in doing anything else right now,” I answered. “I’m into the writing.” “Well the boss thinks you should work with me,” he replied. And this, of course, was new to me. “Well, he hasn’t said anything to me about it.” “He will,” Owen Duffey replied. “You’re going to advertise with me, and you’ll make some money. None of this $60 a week.” And as he says this, Gordon Lew walks by, entering the room from somewhere else. He smiles an embarrassed smile as he walks to his desk, nodding, with a “Hello” to Owen Duffey.

“I overheard what Mr. Duffey said, and I’m sorry that he spoke with you before I had a chance to do so; he shouldn’t have done that,” Gordon said, after calling me over to sit at his desk. “But he is correct, he can train you to make some good money selling advertising, and I feel bad that we cannot pay you properly for the work that you are doing. He had asked about you a few weeks ago, his partner has just moved on, and he was very excited to hear you were born in Toronto. He’s read your articles, thinks you are obviously very smart, and I told him you are a very intelligent young man. I can’t force you to work with him, and if you do advertise with him, you’ll still be able to write some articles. But I cannot pay you more; and I cannot keep you for so little money.” “I’ll talk to the guy, Gordon, but I want to write. If I can’t do it here, I’ll look for some other paper. The guy is pretty gruff looking and sounding.” “I think you should go to his office where he advertises, see what he does, let him show you his method, and give it a try. It might work out very well for you and the paper. I cannot force you to do it, obviously, but I won’t be able to keep you on here if you do not do this. We’ll still go to our dinners and I will continue to give you some articles to write, just not as many.” “I’ll have to think about this Gordon and I’ll let you know if I want to do this in a few days. I'm not sure that I want to be around this guy." Gordon nodded, smiled that reserved and dignified smile, stood up, patted me on the shoulder, and said that I should think about it. And that he would like me to do it.

A couple of days later, I called Gordon to tell him that I would at least go and listen. I had spoken to my mom about it and her advice was to "follow the signs as they appear. Go look and listen; the path often leads to places you do not expect. It might be nice to make a bit of money, and these guys from Toronto sure know how to do that." She was impressed that Duffey knew her brothers. "You'll not go in any direction that is not right for you. Follow the signs; you'll be able to tell if this is something that you are comfortable doing. Maybe just give it a try for a couple of weeks." And, as I usually did, I followed my mom's advice. My mom's advice was always "as good as gold," and without a second thought I called Gordon to arrange to spend some time with Owen Duffey.

The following week I walked into Owen's space on the first floor of a two-story building over on Kearney Street. He had a cubicle whose walls were covered with various advertisements culled from many papers, particularly the San Francisco Chronicle, the Examiner, and the Wall Street Journal. Most of the ads were small classified, particularly for help wanted. There were, though, some large advertisements placed by the city and the state, public service types of stuff. The room smelled heavily of pipe tobacco, and the radio was on, the popular and opinionated Jim Eason pontificating about "the total mess" Jimmy Carter had made of our country. Owen had just finished a conversation when I walked into the office. He observed no formalities. "Sit down over there Brucie, and I'll show you what we do here, how to sell ads, how to make some money." "Brucie" had an endearing ring to it for me. Few people called me "Brucie," but the ones who did were very close to me. My uncles Dave and Meyer called me "Brucie," and of course my mom did quite often. It was odd to be called Brucie by someone who didn't know me at all, but it did loosen me up toward this guy. It just had that effect.

"I go by the name Ching Lee" in here, said Owen, "and if you do this, you'll have to have a Chinese name. Keep your first name but think of a good last one. It's got to be a very common name, the equivalent of Smith or Jones. "How about Wong?" I answered. "Nice ring to it," answered Duffey, "Bruce Wong; that will be your name. Now, let me show you how this is done," he continued, "We take copy out of newspapers—it's all camera-ready stuff—and call the phone number on it, asking for the guy who is responsible for running the ad. Very often, it is not the person listed in the ad. It may be his boss; it may be somebody else; it may be she or he stated in the ad, and sometimes they'll refer you to an advertising agency. You tell them where you saw the ad, and then tell them that you represent East/West, an English-language Chinese weekly that reaches approximately 150,000 readers, mainly American-born, college-educated, and affluent. You tell them that these are the people who most publications haven't tapped, and we reach them directly. Brucie, you let them know that these are the people who can afford cars, who are educated and qualify for jobs; they have a lot of money in the bank, and can buy homes during this recession. I haven't had time to solicit some of the real estate ads, particularly the big display ones, but I would like you to take a shot at those."

And then he went about showing me how it is done. He pulls an ad out of the Wall Street journal, an ad selling farmland in the Central Valley of California. He asks to speak to the real estate agent responsible for placing the ad, and discovers that he has the right person on the phone. He tells the guy that he is Ching Lee (and I am deeply chuckling inside, trying to be careful not to break down in outright hysterics, because this guy is a tough-talking New York Irishman, and he makes no attempt to sound Chinese), and represents East/West, an English language weekly in San Francisco, reaching approximately 150,000 readers, primarily American-born, affluent, educated, English-speaking Chinese. He continues that these are the people that like to own farms; that they come from a farming background; that farming is in their bones. The guy on the other end wants to know the rates, and Ching breaks it down for him, recommending four runs to achieve the biggest discount and maximum exposure. The guy on the other end commits to the ad, saying he likes the concept and will recommend the idea to his colleagues. He wants Ching Lee's phone number. Ching Lee gives it to him, he covers the phone, winks over at me, and says, "See how easy it is Brucie? I got him, Brucie, I got him."

When he gets off the phone, he tells me that we should start on the real estate ads, first the small ones, then we'll graduate to the larger ones. I ask him if this paper really reaches 150,000 subscribers. "Not subscribers, Brucie, readers; there are about four readers per subscription. The paper actually has a subscription of about 40,000. Remember, you won't get into any trouble if you call them readers, there is no way they can quantify that." He cut out several ads from that day's real estate section of the Journal, handed them to me and listened as I went to work.

The first ad that I ever called on was culled from the section of the Wall Street Journal advertising "Acreage For Sale," and promoted dozens of acres of fertile land for farming. "Hello, I'd like to speak to the person advertising land for sale in the Wall Street Journal." "You've got him," a hoarse, gruff-sounding guy immediately responded on the other end. "Can I help you? You lookin' for choice row-crop land?" "I'm not a buyer, but rather I'm interested in telling you about a great place to advertise for this." "I'm not lookin' for any more advertisements," his voice becoming louder and annoyed. "We've been runnin' this for weeks in the fuckin Wall Street Journal, and haven't had a bite. You reckon you're better than them?" "Well, I'm Bruce Wong with the East/West newspaper in San Francisco. We're an English language weekly reaching about 150,000 mostly educated, upper-middle-class, English-speaking Chinese, primarily in the Bay Area, and these are the people currently buying property, investing money, and they are big buyers of farms and ranches." "I've never ever sold anything to any Chinese out here, and you don't sound Chinese," he answered me. "I'm American-born, American-educated Chinese, I assure you of that. Farming and ranching is in our blood, and if you've never tried reaching this readership you should. You are targeting a market that can afford what you are selling, and more than that, the Chinese tell each other about opportunities and they very often like to invest together." "Kid, not a bad pitch," he responded effetely, practically surrendering to the likelihood that during this horrible recession—interest rates in the high double digits—he would never sell this acreage or anything else for that matter. "But I don't believe it. Where are your Chinese from, Taiwan or China? If they're from China, then they don't have any fuckin' money. And if they are from Taiwan, then they're sending all of it back to their families in Taiwan. I've hardly ever seen a Chinese out here, let alone sell him some big acreage. Not interested buddy, but good try. I'd try to sound a bit more Chinese, though." And with that he hung up the phone on me.

Mr. Duffey went about critiquing me, and critiquing me hard. "He didn't think I sounded Chinese," I started to tell him. "Buddy," he answered "why the fuck would he think you're Chinese when you sound like a jackass? You sound like you're trying to impress him that you are out of Stanford Business School for Christ's sake. You sound too fuckin' proper. 'I'm American-born, American-educated Chinese, I assure you of that,' you answer him. What a bunch of tedious, proper bullshit! If you're gonna work with me and make some money, more money than any of your grad student friends, then you listen carefully to what I tell you. 'Hello,' you tell him. 'I'm Bruce Wong with East/West newspaper in San Francisco.' Slow it down a bit. Sound natural. 'We reach about 150,000 readers, mainly American-born, English-speaking, educated Chinese. These people have money pouring out of their safe deposit boxes and mattresses. If you've never reached this market you should give it a try. These are the people buying these days. We've had excellent results running ads. But you should try an ad about four times, so you get full penetration. They see the ad, then show it to friends and family. We've found that most sales come around the fourth run or so,' something like that Brucie. And if they question your Chinese heritage. Just laugh it off. Just tell them if they ever saw you they'd have no doubts about your being Chinese. Laugh it off; take it lightly. And slow the fuck down, for heaven sakes. No doubt, they've never heard of this rag, so you'll have to send out dozens of papers in the beginning. But you do what I say and you'll do very well. You have the smarts for it—it doesn't even take any smarts—let me rephrase that, you have the glibness and charm for it. And you've got something going for you, a very nice telephone voice. When I heard you talking to Lew upstairs, I knew instantly you'd be good on the phone. And you're a Rush for fuck sakes; you should be able to sell anything."

By the end of that first day I had made two sales, and much as how a fishing guide teaches you how to bait and hook, then clean the fish afterwards, Owen Duffey taught me the mechanics of being Bruce Wong, then how to deal with the paperwork afterwards. "Not a bad fuckin' day, after a rough start," Duffey said as he turned off Jim Eason, locked up the office, the pipe dangling from the corner of his toothless mouth. As he locked up, I looked over his shoulder at the place where I had just spent the last three hours, my cubicle now having a few dozen ads that he had cut out for me to call on in the next week or so, the walls above his cubicle filled with numerous advertisements, many a faded yellow from decay or his pipe. "We'll see you tomorrow, Brucie," he said as I bounded down the stairs ahead of him, then onto Kearney street. "We'll see you tomorrow."

I did come back to the Owen Duffey boot camp the next day, and for the successive three days, right after my grad school classes in the morning. He'd hammer me when I didn't show enough interest, or spoke too quickly, compliment me when I delivered a smooth Bruce Wong presentation. I sold something like 12 ads or so that week, making somewhere in the vicinity of about $300. "It would take you about a month and a half to make at East/West what you made this week Brucie, and you're just a trainee," he said to me. "And not even that good a trainee, but you'll get better; you have the potential for it."

After working with Owen for about three weeks, I'd almost had enough of him and the whole damn Bruce Wong thing. I was getting deep into my graduate school studies, and I had not been given one writing assignment, not even one. He was, no doubt, very pleased with the way my advertising sales were taking off, and all the new ads coming into the paper. By the end of the third week, after a particularly tough boot camp, I'd had enough of this guy hammering me. "Fuck you," I said to him. "Fuck you, I've had enough of your bullshit. Take your fuckin' Ching Lee and Bruce Wong and stick it up your ass," I told him. "What am I doing in this God damn place?" "You think you're too damn good, ha?" he responded, coming at me with a pocketknife. My immediate instinct was to wrap my arms with my jacket to protect myself as he came at me, but then "flight" reaction to "flight or fight" took over and I ran out the door, Duffey coming after me, but stopping at the doorway before the hall. No doubt he didn't want any of the other tenants of this office building seeing him chase after me with a pocketknife. And what I sight he was: pipe dangling from the toothless mouth, reddish-grayish mane falling into his face, wide and broken-looking nose, cheeks getting redder by the instant, the anger of a madman all over his face.

I didn't return that day or the next day. But the following Monday, I did return. When I walked back into the office, my clippings were neatly organized. "Ready to go to work, Brucie?" he said to me. "Ready to go to work," I answered. And for the next couple of years I was Bruce Wong, working right alongside Ching Lee, and Jim Eason, on the radio, pontificated and blathered on about this or that, the soundtrack to our times. During these times, the hostages remained in Tehran, and Ted Koppel's "Nightline" show becoming the immensely popular chronicle of each day of their captivity; during these days, Jimmy Carter debated and lost the presidency to Ronald Reagan; during these times, the USA Olympic Team defeated the Russians and went on to win the impossible gold medal at Lake Placid, in what will be forever remembered as the Miracle on Ice; and during these times, Reagan was shot by John Hinckley, Jim Brady becoming paralyzed; and during these times, John Lennon was shot and killed outside the Dakota in New York City, my hearing about it from Howard Cosell on Monday Night Football; and during these times, the phone call came in from Sue—the wrong number that was the right number—and I made enough money to fly to Denver every month, and to fly her to San Francisco every other month.

Owen Duffey was an intense drill sergeant but he knew when to let up, to leave me alone, when I needed to be left alone. Eventually, the ads were pouring into that newspaper.

❐

During the first few months of working alongside Owen Duffey I tried to remain a part of the East/West journalism establishment, going to the dinners now and then, pestering Mr. Lew for a writing assignment. But before long, the success of Bruce Wong the advertising guy made it so that the newspaper didn't want me to do anything but sell, sell, sell. This is not to say that I wasn't writing—I was deeply immersed in the theoretical language of my MA thesis on International Political Violence: The Problem of Revolution in a Nuclear Age, a paper that I eventually sent to Ted Kennedy, receiving a very nice handwritten letter from him, thanking me for the consideration and the ideas. He had been attempting to unseat Jimmy Carter at the time, and I wished him well; I really felt that there were some foreign policy ideas that he would find useful, and I had the chance to tell him this on the telephone (to my amazement) when I called his office on a whim one day. He said to send the thesis and he would read it, and in his letter he addressed a few of the ideas articulated, the letter on my office wall to this day. But be that as it may, during this nearly two-year period as Bruce Wong, the newspaper's advertising revenue had grown exponentially, so much so that they were printing more pages to accommodate the ads. Whereas in the past, articles and news would occupy the preponderance of the page, now with all of these ads, many pages were almost entirely advertising. I no longer had the byline—and I really did miss that; I still defined myself as a writer, but my influence on that paper had become quite significant indeed. I really did miss going on assignments and meeting some of the people who were movers and shakers in Chinatown—being appreciated for a piece I had just written—but it certainly didn't hurt to be able to pull out some bills from the pocket rather than small change. And the small change turned to bills primarily for this reason: We had stumbled on an advertising gold mine. Owen Ching Lee wanted me to go after the "big game" of the large, full-page ads that homebuilders were placing in the San Francisco Chronicle and Examiner. These ads had rarely if ever appeared in any of the Chinese publications, Chinese or English language.

Making dozens and dozens of phone calls, following like a bloodhound the trail from decision maker to decision maker over a period of a few months, we were eventually led to advertising agencies, whose clients directed them to try several runs in our paper, and when one homebuilder saw the ad placements, the others wanted to follow. I'm not sure that anybody ever received any decent response from the paper's readers—I don't think any client ever came back to tell me that they were continuing the ads because of increased sales—but the ads kept flowing. And they kept flowing, and flowing, and flowing during this severe economic downturn of the early 1980s.

I really never felt like I was an actor playing the role of Bruce Wong. I was Bruce Rosen—very much myself—selling newspaper ads in a publication that seemed to me should really draw in some buyers. I really did believe in this demographic, and the advertisers no doubt picked up on my enthusiasm about their chances. And sales is always a "shootin' match" anyway, certainly no guarantees. But the possibility of success in this paper made sense to me, and I tried to convey that to the buyers of space. And the buyers of the space—smart people—made the kind of commitment that should be made to determine whether something works: you give it ample opportunity to work by trying it for an extended period of time. During the halcyon days, the Irish cheer was flowing from Owen (Ching Lee) Duffey, and while working on my thesis a bank account was building for me.

Perhaps it might have been easier in my social and business lives if I had just been Bruce F. Rosen. I wasn't able to go meet prospective advertisers in person, because there was no way I could suddenly become an English-speaking, American-born Chinese. Certainly, I might have sent somebody in my stead for these special occasions—there were a few well-spoken, English-speaking photographers and journalists at the paper who would have qualified—but that would have been totally crazy, and I wouldn't submit to that. Owen did think it to be a good idea on one occasion when a man said he would only advertise—and he was promising big-time advertising, several months worth of a large display ad—if he could meet me in person. I never followed through on it, content to let the money slip away rather than represent myself as Chinese and show up as Jewish, with curly hair and large round eyes. I wrote it off to being an occupational hazard—though Owen was not pleased I wouldn't submit to having someone impersonate me—and reasoned that I probably gained more business than I had lost as a result of having that Chinese surname.

There were also some highly charged flirtatious moments during the approximately two years of my tenure as Bruce Wong that had to be abandoned as conversation, never able to reach fruition. Several advertising women over this period had expressed that they had been quite attracted to my voice and that we should at least meet for business. I wasn't married—and for much of this time hadn't met Sue—and as a man in my mid-20s, had the interest to follow-up, if even for business (though no doubt these opportunities might have compromised the lucrative sales if I had been the Jewish Bruce F. Rosen).

These flirtatious moments would occur on occasion with different advertisers, but there was one woman in particular (her name was Pamela) to whom I was very attracted on the telephone, and that interest was clearly mutual. She had a soft, melodic voice, whose tenor accentuated the lower chords of the scale, and she spoke not from her nose or throat but from within her lungs. It wasn't a husky voice, not in any way thick, but had a sexy breathiness to it that was in no way self-aware; and her personality was filled with charm. Pam was very professional, and she looked at several issues of the paper—apparently calling a number of other advertisers—before making the appeal to her clients that they use our paper as a component in their media purchases. She advertised at East/West during the duration of my stay, and in this period of time we had developed a kind of telephone relationship, there being a strong underlying current of attraction. Pam was Chinese, well educated, from an Ivy League college, about my age, and single. She loved to ski, and was a frequent visitor to Tahoe. I had expressed to her my love of skiing, my interest in all winter sports, particularly hockey, and that I had been born in Canada. She had expressed on a few occasions that we get together for a drink, and implied that if we "hit it off," we might go skiing together. I ached to meet her; desperately wanted to let her know that I was Bruce F. Rosen the journalist in Chinatown, the graduate student in international relations at S.F. State. Owen talked me out of it more than once: "Don't be fuckin' crazy; look at all the business you're doing with the broad. You want to go fuck that up? And if you meet her, you will fuck it up. Just for a fuck? And there is no way you two are going to get married or anything like it, Brucie. So don't fuck it up; stop thinking with your prick." So, I stopped thinking with my prick, and the business relationship remained the most lucrative one that I had over that tenure at East/West. I had never, ever seen a photograph of Pamela; but several years after my leaving the newspaper—it was at some point in the later 1980s—her name was in the business page of the S.F. Chronicle, a picture beside it. She had been promoted to head of advertising for her company, in charge of the whole show. And in the photo, she appeared virtually as I had envisioned her: full lips, hair fashionably cut around her face as it rested on her shoulders. It was a business photo, but she was stunning. I was deeply married to Sue at the time, Michael was about two or so, and Jonathan had not been born yet. I was in the municipal bond business and rarely saw Ching Lee, but on occasion would pay him a visit in that room still smelling of sweet tobacco, the walls covered with yellowing and fading newspaper clippings. I brought in a copy of Pamela after I saw it that day. We had a chuckle together. "You never let me meet her, Owen," I playfully chided. "You didn't need to fuck her, Brucie; it never would have worked out. Though she is a good-lookin' broad." We laughed a bit and I rarely saw him much after that. As I think about him tonight at the typewriter, I really do miss this guy—this guy who went after me with a pocketknife, and was so impressed with my Toronto birthplace and the uncles of my history.

Angels come in many disguises, and for me an angel took control over my life when I was about 25 years old. That angel, with a pipe always dangling from a mouth devoid of front teeth; a nose that had to have been broken a few times; a full head of mussed-up hair, once red, now almost completely gray; a ruddy complexion suggestive that there was still a lot of fire and vinegar remaining in the belly; saw that I needed to make money, that I had the potential to be successful for him and in life, and that I needed to move away from the $60-per-week job as a newspaper reporter, toward my destiny. I'm not sure if Owen was truly thinking more about my ultimate destiny than about how much money I might make for him when he insisted that I sell ads with him, but he did respect me, valued the person that I was, and told me that I would be very successful in sales one day, if I just listened to him. That angel did love me, and I do love him back.

❒

I often marvel at the effect human beings can have on the lives of others, and how chance meetings or simple recommendations from one person to another can affect one's destiny and possibly spawn generations. Chance encounters, and the ways in which they have changed lives, fortunes, destinies, I particularly find fascinating; the simple stories of how couples met, lived their lives together, raised families. These are the miracles of life, and they happen in the most simple and ordinary ways. The greatest choices are the simple ones, the encounters we take for granted, the life that unfolds as "we are busy making other plans," in the words of the noble John Lennon. Tonight I think back easily to two such encounters in my life that changed my destiny, as though a hand were placed on my back to turn me in a certain direction. And both of these involve a friend, Jeff.

Jeff and I moved to San Francisco together in 1979. I came up first—I had been living in Boston after living in London following my graduation from college in Santa Barbara in 1978—to find a place for us to share. Jeff had been accepted to attend the master's program at the S. F. Conservatory of Music, and after turning down a graduate program at Boston College in Philosophy, I moved to San Francisco, where I had been accepted to attend graduate school at S.F. State. Jeff and I shared a place for six months in

Pacific Heights, but given how costly it was and the little amount of space available, we moved to a larger flat in the Haight-Ashbury district with some of Jeff's music school friends. Here, we had our own rooms, no longer sharing a tiny bedroom with twin beds. In Pacific Heights, we had shared one phone number. We kept that phone number initially on moving into the Haight apartment, but after several months, Jeff (his music teaching business starting to take off) set up a second phone for me, keeping the number of the first one. It was just about a week after the change in phones and phone numbers that Sue called me by accident—the wrong number that was so much the right number—asking for her friend Jamie. "This sounds like long distance," I had said to her. She lingered on the call, saying that it was long distance, that she was trying to find her friend, Jamie, who had moved to San Francisco from Denver, and that this was the last phone number that she had for her. I told her that I loved her voice, and we talked at length. I had been preparing to go down to Haight Street to get some dinner, but lingered, talking to Jeff for awhile, not saying anything, when that phone rang. When Sue's picture arrived, I looked at it, knowing that I would one day marry her, and that we would have children together. I absolutely knew it; I could see it as clearly as a beautiful blue-sky day. I simply knew it, and this had nothing to do with the reading that my mom had given me; when I asked her to give me the name of the woman I would meet and one day marry, she answered not Suzanne, or Susan, but Sue. "Sue from Denver," my future wife-to-be had told me; "Sue from Denver." Had I not moved to San Francisco with Jeff, and had Jeff not changed the phones at precisely the time he did, and perhaps if I had not lingered just long enough to hear the phone ring in my bedroom, I wouldn't have met Sue; Michael and Jonathan would not be who they are, and my life would be something else.

Jeff also played another vital role as an agent in the life that I would live. He had been struggling in music, not making any money, barely having enough come in to pay his rent. We had gotten together for a couple of hearty pints one night when I told him that I was going to get out of the Bruce Wong role; that I had had enough, was ready to do something else. I told him that I was going to tell Owen sometime in the next week; and that if he was interested, I'd ask Owen if he'd like to train Jeff for the job. Jeff was interested and very excited about the possibility. I told him that there were some accounts already established, and that, perhaps, Owen might let him make some money working them, though no doubt most of the money he would make would come from new ads that he'd learn to sell. A few days later, I introduced Owen to Jeff; and a few days after that they started working together, when I accepted a job working for an international bank.

Owen was a drill sergeant with Jeff, but in time, Jeff started to make some money selling ads, though Owen kept all the commissions on the real-estate display ads that had been our "gold mine." I had become very frustrated with the banking job—I couldn't stand the regimentation and bureaucracy—after about six months. One afternoon I had made plans to have lunch with Jeff, whose office with Owen was just several blocks away. We had met at a burger place at the time owned by Francis Ford Coppola (it is that very interestingly shaped, ornate green building in the heart of North Beach) when Jeff pulled out a newspaper ad that Owen had given him to give to me. It was in the S.F. Chronicle Sports section, and it was from a municipal bond sales company that had just expanded to Marin County from Los Angeles. "Owen wanted you to see this; he thinks you'd be good at it, and that you should definitely give them a call," Jeff had relayed from Owen Ching Lee Duffy. "Tell him thanks, and I will call, for sure," I answered. The name of the firm sounded familiar, California Municipal Investors. I was racking my brain to remember where I had heard the name before, when it came to me: Neal, my roommate in college at Santa

Barbara, had started working for them about a year earlier—I was virtually positive it was the same name firm. That night I called Neal, and I was correct, it was the same firm. I asked Neal to let the principals of the firm know that I would be calling for an interview; I wanted to qualify on my own merit, but it would be nice for there to be an introduction, and Neal unquestionably made the contact for me. He called me the next morning with the name of the person to call. I made that call, visited Marin, won the job, and continued to work at the bank while I pored over the voluminous study literature for the Series 7 exam that qualifies one to be a broker. I passed the exam, cold-called 10 hours a day for years, and have become successful in this field. I excelled in this field not only because I worked exceptionally hard on the phone for years, but because I read everything I could find on economics. The language of bonds—unlike stocks—felt intuitive to me, and I grasped the relationships between interest rates and prices, the elements of security and risk, the language of bonds, quite readily. I started out thinking that I'd try it for a little while, and it became my career to this day. And, though these are challenging times economically, I value the knowledge that I have gained from the years of watching bonds trade; appreciate the trust afforded to me by my clients; do not take for granted the freedom that I have to follow my own ideas; give thanks to God that I have been able to afford to educate my boys and enjoy what I had always dreamed of doing, traveling the world. That little newspaper ad in the sports section culled by Owen, given to Jeff, who, strategically, was working with Owen, had changed my life, the hand on the back guiding me in a direction. I marvel at the simplicity, the simplest ways in which our lives can be forever changed, and the angels, unaware, that play a part.

I have been writing for many hours in this chair tonight, and my back and neck ache. The darkness over the bay is of the "deep in the night" variety, and it was relatively early evening when I started. The rustic red of the bridge had been illuminated earlier in the evening, but is now totally dark, save for the pearls of little lights that span it. I lived the fullness of my life in memory today—and I allowed Chinatown to enter into me, and the way I had once lived. My life in San Francisco begins in Chinatown; its people, flavors, the characters I have met there, will forever remain inseparable from the Bruce Farrell Rosen who I am. And again, I must say to Owen, thanks for the love, though perhaps you did not know it as love or experience it that way. But, then again, perhaps you did. And when I think back to the "unseen" hand on my back shaping my destiny in those days—though I certainly had free will; I could have left and never returned when Owen came at me with that knife, but I chose to return; I might not have lingered, telling Sue that I liked her voice and it sounded like long distance, but I stayed on that phone, drawn in by the moment—I realize that my path was laid out for me to follow, and that though other choices existed, they did so only in theory.

All of this makes it hard to explain the situation in my life today, where it seems that there is no hand shaping my destiny, gently moving me in a direction. I love Sue, and yet no matter what I try to do in my mind, I cannot cross that threshold back to our marriage. In this case I have a choice, but cannot make it. And I ask myself why, a thousand times. And, perhaps, Sue feels the same; she loves me, but for the life of her cannot seem to bring us back together. But the choice is right there in front of us—and we just can't seem to make it happen.

The issue at present seems quite different from the past, when I followed a path that unfolded, not questioning the choices. Today, I dwell on the past, question the choices I make in the present, and hope that it continues to unfold in the way it was meant to be. I just don't have that kind of certainty today

How I would so deeply love a tea-leaf reading from my mom. What would she tell me today?

She would tell me that the present is unfolding as it should, to continue to follow the signs, and not to force my life into being any specific way, but to let it happen naturally and with simplicity. I suppose that is what I am doing, though to hear her words in my ear would be a gift from heaven.

❒

The newspaper headlines over the past week reveal an economy that is paying the price for years and years and mountains and mountains of debt. An economy can only grow so long when earnings are based on the bad faith (or the amnesia) that greater and greater leverage will continue to boost profits and that this debt can be overlooked into perpetuity. A certain amount of debt might be considered necessary to drive an economy, to provide the liquidity that makes its way back into spending and not savings accounts. But there is a tipping point, and, clearly, we have gone beyond that tipping point—it happens imperceptibly, the money flowing like champagne in a World Series locker room, spewing every which way like an oil rig gusher—into a place where the economic "house of cards" begins to collapse on itself. We are at that point. And it is my deepest hope that the mess will end in something short of total collapse—that fear and ensuing chaos (the selling of assets to survive) will not push the U.S. economy (and the global economy) into a free fall that drives equity and asset values to levels that threaten the survivability of the financial institutions that provide the capital that feeds corporations, the purchases and sales of homes, the household liquidity that allows people to fund their daily needs, including buying food, enjoying leisure, paying for their children's education, and planning retirement.

No doubt, we will see a period of serious and substantial de-leveraging in this economy, whereby companies will sell assets (given the erosion of consumer confidence in their own net worth and ability to hang on to jobs, homes) to eliminate their debt whose interest costs threaten survival. This will push down asset values as the supply of assets of all kinds floods the marketplaces. Fear can make matters much worse than necessary, and I do hope that in the next several months the values will not fall to levels way below what might be considered their true worth. It will be a great shame if companies fail or have to be bailed out with more debt, the debt levels of these companies overwhelming their worth like a tidal wave submerging everything in its wake.

The newspaper headlines, indeed, are troubling and foreboding. A couple of days ago, the board of Wachovia Corporation—the company at which I am employed—ousted their CEO, Ken Thompson, amidst an avalanche of bad financial news. As a sign of how quickly deterioration seems to be occurring, Mr. Thompson had recently enjoyed strong support by the bank's governing body. On the same Wall Street Journal front page as the article about Wachovia is the story about massive losses occurring at Lehman Brothers Corp. Apparently, Lehman has greater exposure—relative to its size—to securities tied to residential and commercial mortgages than any other financial institution. It has just taken its first-ever quarterly loss since going public, and must raise about $4 billion of new capital, in addition to the roughly $6 billion it has already raised in the past year—pretty darn scary when the assets securing this capital are collapsing in free fall. The headlines of the Journal for the weekend edition, June 7-8, talk about the recession into which our economy has sunk (clearly we have been unofficially there for months), and how the price of oil notched its largest jump ever—nearly $11 to the incredible price of $138 a barrel. Unemployment is rising sharply—up to 5.5 percent from 5 percent the previous month—and payrolls are continuing to shrink, five months in a row now. Amidst this "great news," the Dow industrials fell nearly 400 points in a single day. The "triple whammy" of huge spikes in oil, precipitous drops in stock values, substantially rising unemployment, occurs against the backdrop of unbelievable debt levels in the economy, particularly in real estate–

backed securities. And we have very little knowledge of how much of this stuff is owned by whom. We must hang onto our seatbelts here, and cherish those we love.

❒

It is late in the evening of June 28, and baseball always brings me back to myself. When I wrote and recorded the series of "slice of life" pieces for the BBC program, "Up All Night," I did a piece on baseball. It began just that way: "Baseball always brings me back to myself." I have deeply etched memories of that golden, echoing, resonating voice of the magnificent Dodger's announcer Vin Scully—that voice belongs in the Smithsonian—dating back to about six or seven years old as a kid growing up in Simi Valley, newly arrived from Toronto, Canada. I cannot separate my love of the Dodgers from my childhood, and Scully's voice is the soundtrack to those memories. I listened to that voice call the 1963 World Series—my Jewish idol, Sandy Koufax, winning two games as the Dodgers beat the highly favored Yankees four games to zero—and clearly remember the assassination of JFK just a couple of months after that, watching as a stunned child the funeral procession, the salute of John John, and then the perplexing, confusing sequence of events when a man wearing a hat lunges in front of the television camera to murder the alleged assassin, Lee Harvey Oswald. I listened to Scully call the final game of the 1965 World Series from Minnesota—I was the student council representative from my class and was allowed to listen to the game on radio during class, dutifully putting the score of each inning on the blackboard as the game progressed—with my idol, Koufax, pitching on two days' rest, throwing smoke and winning the game and the World Series for the Dodgers. Koufax, I clearly remember, did not have his curve ball that day, was a bit wild, but threw pure, almost unhittable smoke, to conquer the Twins. When we returned to California from our two-year stay in Canada, I listened to Vin every night if I could—and he continued to quiet my mind during those dark days when my father left and I had stumbled upon drugs. In my 20s, after moving to San Francisco, I searched the tiny little corners of my radio to hear him call Dodger games, eventually buying a shortwave radio to pick him up. Indeed, baseball always brings me back to myself, and the voice of Vin Scully will always be the catalyst for an immediate return to my youth.

I have been back just an hour or so from a baseball game played over in Oakland between the very poor San Francisco Giants and the slightly better Oakland A's. I would not normally venture across the bay to see a game, but tonight, Tim Lincecum is pitching, and I went with my son, Michael, now ensconced at home after his academic year at Oberlin. Earlier in this memoir I talked about the phenomenal ability of this young man—the incredible talent and potential he has—and that he might become a superstar. Indeed, this has happened. Only 24 years old, perhaps about five foot, nine inches, not more than 175 pounds (I would guess), this kid is probably the most charismatic pitcher in baseball today. He throws the ball about 98 miles an hour, with pinpoint control. And he can paint the corners with that blazing fastball. But, like Koufax, he has this curve ball that breaks "off the table," thrown with the arm motion of the fastball but arriving 15 miles per hour slower. It is, at its best, almost un-hittable when following the wicked fastball.

Tonight Tim Lincecum beat the A's, striking out 11 batters in seven innings. If he keeps this stuff up, this kid might win the Cy Young award; I can't think of a better pitcher in all of baseball right now. My hope is that he'll be more than a one-or-two-season wonder and that there is longevity here. But, man, at this moment he is the real deal. And it was so great to watch this masterpiece with Michael, who loves baseball as much as I do. After a long year at Oberlin, it is bliss being at a baseball game with him.

As the price of petroleum goes well above $100 a barrel, and the mortgage crisis continues to threaten the survival of banks and insurance companies, and this economic crisis expands and threatens the well-being of so many people, it is nice to put it out of my mind for a night, enjoying the company of my son and this young pitcher—they call him the Freak—whose pitching prowess shows Hall of Fame potential, but looks not a day over 16. What a delicious night, indeed.

❒

It is the evening of July 22, and the economic gloom of the world, as well as the uncertainty in my own life—a painful sense of not being anchored, that cohesiveness of being in the home, all of us under one roof, a mom and a dad together as a unit no longer the story of my life—have pervaded my dreams on an almost-daily basis lately. It feels as though roots have been pulled up, my equilibrium off balance, my branches too vulnerable to the wind. But that is how I feel; it is not necessarily the way other people perceive me. My business remains strong; my advice to clients clear and accurate. I advise them not to panic, to hold steady, to not feel off-course, rudderless, vulnerable. And I mean it. As bad as things are economically—and they are getting worse—I have no doubt that we will avoid the doomsday scenario. I sell State of California General Obligation municipal bonds to California residents. My phone rings several times a day with worries, the need for reassurance from me that the state will continue to pay the interest, not fall into the ocean, not go bankrupt. And I explain, many times a day, dozens of times a week, hundreds of times a month, that a state cannot declare bankruptcy, that as the seventh-largest economy in the world, California has the cash flow, the legal, financial and moral obligation to meet its interest payments, and that it will surely do so. "The state may have to make draconian cuts," I tell my clients, and "the cuts might get progressively more draconian over the next several months, but, no doubt, the state must continue to exist, and to exist means that it must make good on its debt." And yes—despite what I hear every day from worried investors fresh from reading the papers—the state does have the money to pay their bonds; but given the deficit and the amount of interest costs that must be met, the piece of the pie available for the social services that had been given with large promises by politicians drunk on surplus revenues when times were good, is substantially less than expected. Indeed, though, "The state will pay its bond interest, because if it did not, there would be no credibility to borrow money from the taxpayers again, not to mention the legal ramifications that would tie up the assets and cash flow of the state until the interest was paid." And, of course, I continue to repeat, "Not paying interest to bond buyers, that were promised this interest by the good faith and taxing authority of the state, would be something akin to a financial nuclear bomb (or at the very least serious carpet bombing) being dropped on the state, and this is not going to happen."

The days are difficult and they require clear thinking, accurate logic, the confidence to seize on opportunity (and to seize on opportunity requires confidence that these conditions will improve). And so I carry on, strive to be positive, though not necessarily sanguine, while the news headlines tell the public that we are seeing beginnings of financial collapse, and that they have everything to fear.

"We must live amidst uncertainty, we must live, love, thrive amidst uncertainty," I tell my clients and myself. And this uncertainty becomes deeper and more pervasive virtually every day. Not only do I receive numerous daily calls about the viability of the State of California and the bonds they have issued, but I receive an equal, perhaps greater, number of enquires about the fate of my own financial firm, Wachovia. The news has been terrible about this company, and it keeps getting worse.

In the past week the economic news has become gloomier and more troubling. My company, Wachovia, the fourth largest U.S. bank, plunged to an $8.9 billion loss in its second quarter, cut its dividend for the second time in three months, and said it would cut more than 6,000 jobs. A few days before this news was released, a relatively major bank—Pasadena-based Indy Mac—became undercapitalized because of deepening mortgage losses, and was seized by the FDIC. It is estimated that the failure of Indy Mac will cost the FDIC between $4-8 billion, the costliest failure in history. Depositors are becoming increasingly concerned—given the Wachovia news, the Indy news, the troubles at Lehman Brothers, the failure of Bear Stearns, the deepening problems in the insurance industry, municipal bond insurers being severely downgraded and the world's largest company, AIG, showing serious cracks—that they have nowhere to hide. And all of this does not take into consideration that the Treasury and the Fed have had to pledge aid to keep solvent the two mortgage giants, Fanny Mae and Freddy Mac. The Treasury has said it will seek authority to buy "equity" in either company if needed, so that they have sufficient capital to continue their mission of providing a steady flow of money into home mortgages. This is just unbelievable—Fanny and Freddy are on the verge of "blowing up" without (and probably with) government aid.

❐

All of this has affected my outer life and inner life. A couple of days ago—July 16—marked our 26th wedding anniversary. We are still married, but we're not married. I live alone, but the ties are there; the gravitational pull continues to connect us: I am free but not free. I make payments on our home but I really can't go there without making an appointment. When the boys are there, it is "like my home"; but it isn't my home, and when I come over I feel like a visitor. The boys do not perceive me that way, I am sure; the facts of our lives, the circumstances that have entered in no way diminish the love, care, bond, profound sense of identity with family that we all share apart and together. But I am not under that roof, I am free to date; so is Sue, and it all feels like it is in an unsettled place of confusion. We need to straighten this out, Sue and I; if we are not getting together, perhaps we need to put our

Victorian on the market, find a cozy, smaller place for Sue to live when it sells, and then situate myself in something more permanent when she is settled. This limbo pains me so deeply. Divorce? I guess we will have to do that. But, damn, it is hard to think about, let alone do.

On the day of our anniversary I went to a movie alone. I have become closer with Gwen; she is a true friend. She is there to hear me when I hurt, but at this point, I cannot say the direction our relationship will go, though it is difficult to not see her in my life. I believe she will always be there in some way, though I do not know the manifestation. I must admit though, I don't want her to be gone. But, on the anniversary, I went to a movie alone. And the choice of movie was probably not the best for my mood. I went to see the amazing "Dark Knight." In this film, the recently passed Heath Ledger is insanely brilliant as the Joker, an anarchist mastermind unleashing chaos, pushing Batman to the absolute limit. Heath Ledger, in my mind—how could he not—is sure to win a posthumous Academy Award for Best Actor. He is startling, riveting. But it probably wasn't the film to see alone in a movie theater on my anniversary.

❒

I have been looking for truth, and it is showing up in my inner life, my dream life. The other night I had a very profound and strange dream. I was meeting various high-ranking leaders of the Christian faith, priests, perhaps even the Pope or his representatives, and they were in the process of canceling my marriage in Christianity. They were ending our marriage—going through rituals that brought it to an end, as far as the religion was concerned. It wasn't an excommunication or assignment of blame for anything—there wasn't a sense of guilt in the process—but it definitely took matters into their control and brought closure through the rituals. I started to feel quite sad as I realized what exactly was occurring. This was unusual, given that our marriage never occurred in a church—it has no Christian element to it all, except that Sue did convert from Catholicism to Judaism. In the dream, the marriage was not ending in the Jewish faith, just in the Christian. During the ceremonies, I met various high-ranking religious leaders, and they were gracious as they conducted their rituals. There was never a sense of blame or guilt. And in the end, I met a frail Nelson Mandela, as he shook my hand. He was shaky, but charismatic—no doubt very wise. He is among the greatest political/spiritual figures the world has known—and I was moved by the opportunity to meet him—though after shaking his hand, I didn't quite know what to say. Perhaps I am looking for guidance from great leaders and teachers—and as far as the marriage being annulled in the Christian faith, I very probably suffer guilt over the separation and my freedom. I have become free to choose, and this likely is producing guilt for me.

There seems to be an inner sense that I cannot conform to a strict marriage—the Catholic church in the dream—if I have to sacrifice a longing for freedom. Maybe I cannot do this with Sue anymore, though it is so hard to accept, and the church (my conscience) is telling me that it is over.

❒

It is late in the evening, Monday, August 18. Sue and I had a conversation over the weekend about putting our Victorian on the market in the fall, when the boys go back to college. She lives alone in that big house most of the year, the boys off at college, and we agreed that the equity in the place could be put to better use by finding a smaller, more cozy home for Sue and, eventually, a condo for me, instead of paying all of this rent that offers no tax benefit. I don't want to pay rent for more years, when the money could be invested in a property that I would own and go to the boys one day. This apartment is cozy, I have settled into it, the view to the bay and bridge offers serene moments for reflection, contemplation, writing. But, it feels like an interim place for me, and this feeling of limbo never goes away. We have to address our marriage—how can we stay married for months, years to come, without marital relations, companionship, intimacy, connection, living together—and decide how we go about making our separation official, which means divorce. I pay attention to my reaction to that word, "divorce," and experience an electrical charge running through my body that I would describe as an intersection of grief with sadness. It is terribly difficult to allow that word to become action for me; it is laden with a sense of failure, guilt, "deviation from the path," "letting down my family and highest self," and "walking away from love." It is extremely painful to allow this word to eventually become action, and then to become part of my "identity." But we have to do something. I want to go forward; I want intimacy again, perhaps on a deeper level with Gwen. Or to allow for the possibility of that happening. It just seems to get complicated; I want to go forward, but I do not want to surrender the past. Sue was a deep, trusted friend of my mom; I was close with her parents, and was there for her when her father died of complications from Alzheimer's, then her mother from a fall when she was on her way to dialysis. It is hard to go forward into a life without Sue being my partner, she is a trusted friend; but we just can't seem to make it back together. So, in this tough economic environment we had a sincere talk of putting the place on the market; we'll be realistic with the price and, hopefully, take advantage of a buying opportunity when we do sell. I'm thinking that in a few months we'll find a place for Sue to buy—using a large percentage of our savings—and then put the place on the market a month or so later. I would take a large risk in doing this, having two mortgages and a rent for heaven's sake, but I think the house will sell if we are realistic in price. And, as a last resort, we can rent it to cover our mortgage. I just want to give Sue a stable foundation if we are not together; I want her to have the stability of a home that would be hers. It would be difficult to remain in the place, people parading through during open houses; and to give ourselves the best chance of selling, it would be best to have it staged, a designer making it as inviting as possible. We'll paint it as well, just make it gorgeous, though it already has the charm, the high ceilings, original moldings the elegance of the San Francisco homes built before 1900. I'm thinking that we'll take the chance, find Sue something really nice, smaller and cozy, and then put the place on the market. But it would be a big chance, because every single day the economy continues to unwind, consumers becoming more and more frightened, the entire globe now, officially, in recession.

Certainly it does not boost one's sense that good times are around the corner when the front page of the San Francisco Chronicle today reads, "Another Day; Another Deadlock." They are referring to the sea of "red debt" that envelops the State of California as it goes into the 48th day of a budget stalemate. Something must be done about the requirement that a two-thirds majority be reached to pass a budget—a simple majority is necessary to get anything accomplished. There are too many politicians who view public service as a career—taking enormous sums of money from interests to whom they make the promises that get them elected. It is absolute political warfare, a zero-sum game where compromise is too often considered defeat. But as the stalemate continues, the costs keep going up, the confidence falling (clients calling me everyday asking if the state can go bankrupt and not pay their bonds), a sense of gloom grows deeper. It is against this backdrop that I consider taking the bold step of buying, then trying to sell, but we must go forward, Sue and I, as well as the economy, and gloom becomes a self-fulfilling prophecy when people become too paralyzed to act.

❒

In two weeks, the political parties will anoint their presumptive nominees for president. There has been much speculation about the vice presidential running mates. Many people think that Evan Bayh of Indiana would be a good pick for Obama; others believe that Hillary in the end will be offered the nomination, creating the strongest possible Democratic ticket; I feel that Joe Biden would be a good choice, a guy long on foreign policy knowledge, a tough guy and good debater who adds some establishment gravitas to Obama's campaign. The Republicans are hampered by the strong "pro-life" wing of the party, and that makes it difficult for McCain to offer the job to his good friend, Joe Lieberman. Many think that Mitt Romney would be a strong, attractive choice. He certainly has the pro-life conservative credentials, but he really slammed McCain during the campaign and, no doubt, political ad after political ad would exploit that. I have no idea who McCain might pick. But one thing seems certain, McCain seems quite eager for the race to begin. He has been hammering Obama for being weak on defense, being flat out-wrong for not supporting the surge of troops that was successful in driving the enemy out of key strategic sections of Iraq, for denying "funds to soldiers who have done a brilliant and brave job in Iraq."

Obama counters that he didn't deny funds for the troops, but voted against a flawed bill that set absolutely no timetable for withdrawing from Iraq. He admonishes that while Bush was destroying our global standing, invading Iraq, cutting taxes and spending billions of dollars that we couldn't afford, the Taliban continued to organize in Afghanistan and al-Qaeda went unpunished. He ties McCain to George W. Bush—one of the most unpopular presidents of all time—every chance he gets, pointing out that John McCain voted with Bush more than 90 percent of the time. And he pounds away at the economic "elitism" of McCain, again tying him to Bush. A couple of days ago, in San Francisco, where Obama raised $7.8 million on one visit, the Democratic contender made his attack clear: He told his supporters that, "We have an economy that, frankly, for the last eight years, has been focused on the very few, and we have not seen economic growth from the bottom up." Therein lies the Obama philosophy: The government must have a larger role in creating jobs for the working man—an appeal for union support—and that if taxes are to be cut, they must be done so for the middle- and lower-economic class, to be paid for by the wealthy in the form of higher taxes. It is class warfare to a degree, but in this economy it offers to be very effective. The irresponsible, greedy, wealthy are a great scapegoat right now—and anytime a country is unified against a scapegoat, dangerous, totalitarian temptations lie beneath the surface. Obama's candidacy is fascinating, particularly in the "cult of personality," the mystique that surrounds him. I am, though, concerned about cultism of any kind, and particularly during these tough economic times when there seems to be developing a national inclination to find blame in a "narrow elite"—Jews were such an elite in Germany.

❐

It is late August, the late evening of the 23rd to be exact. I have not taken an extended vacation this summer, rather a Friday at the beginning of a weekend or a Monday at the end. Three-day weekends can feel like mini-vacations, refreshing and recharging, when the preceding four days have been so intense. So, I have done this a few times this summer, three days of wandering around the city—possibly taking a bus to walk amidst the Redwood trees and quaint village of Mill Valley, where we lived during those days just before and after the Loma Prieta earthquake when the boys were so small—in lieu of a longer vacation that would require the transition of leaving and returning. I have given a chunk of the money that I would have used on a vacation to my friend Stuart, at Mr. Ticket, who has sold me his best seats directly behind the plate at Pac Bell Park, where the Giants play. I have gone to about 14 games this summer—sitting in these incredible seats, hearing the sizzle of the fast ball, watching the curve ball snap to the left or right, close enough to see the seams and spin of the ball—and a day at the Park is a journey out of time and place to a land faraway but incredibly close, where the Brucie who grew up loving the voice of Vin Scully and idolized Sandy Koufax merges with the self that daily strives to soothe the frayed nerves of his financial clients and understand the dislocation in his life. "Baseball always brings me back to myself," I wrote for that BBC program, and that is so very true. And it is true every single summer, despite whether the home team is four games in front or 14 behind. So between the three-day weekends now and then, the days at the Park, I am having the equivalent (perhaps better suited to me at the moment) of a very fine vacation.

❐

During the past several months music has been less a part of my life than I would like. Music stirs me, allows me to release feelings that need to come out, inspires me, gives me hope, fills in the concepts with color, fragrances, brings joy, stimulates the memories that define my past, enriching the present. However, amidst the toil and burdens of the days I often come home to my apartment, recline in my chair, put a blanket over my head, and do not turn on any music. It is as though there is a part of me that doesn't want to permit the other part to feel, because feeling hurts too much. I am very "on" during the day, my analysis of the financial situation and where clients stand is pretty accurate—clients need not dump good bonds at a loss. I need the music to balance the stress, but I either haven't wanted it, or just do not permit myself to listen to it. I do listen a bit, but I really need so much more of it. Yesterday, I put on the Beach Boys' "Pet Sounds"—the album that inspired the Beatles to do "Sgt. Pepper's"—and it brought moments of sheer bliss.

Is there anything sweeter than the opening lines of the very first song on the album, "Wouldn't It Be Nice?"

Wouldn't it be nice if we were older
Then we wouldn't have to wait so long,
And wouldn't it be nice to live together,
In the kind of world where we belong;
You know it's gonna make it that much better,
When we can say goodnight and stay together."

No, it just doesn't get any sweeter than those Beach Boys harmonies. Brian Wilson really was incredible. So, I listened to this last night and it snapped me out of a gloom, cleared some of the energy that settles in from the day. Tonight when I came home, I leafed through the CDs and put on one of my all-time favorite sax players: Stan Getz. He was once a client of my mom's—he came to her for many years—and she saw him during the last days of his life when he was suffering from cancer. The album is entitled "Anniversary," and on the cover there is an inscription from 1979: "To Bruce and Sue with sincere affection, Stan Getz." He met us just a couple of times, but it was as though he had been a lifelong soul connection. He exuded a warmth and familiarity that made one feel as though he had been a long, loyal friend. My mom really enjoyed his visits, and he found her readings extremely valuable to his life. So, I put that CD on tonight, followed by a shot of single malt that tasted like distilled dirt—but it went down well. The album was recorded 12 years before he signed it for us, back in 1987; it is a live recording from Copenhagen. The playing pulls out the tears and fills in the empty spaces with love and joy—truly love and joy is what I experienced in listening to that tonight after sipping the tasty, distilled dirt. So, I must return to music; I need it. It is the moisture to my dryness, oxygen to the blood.

❒

The Democratic National Convention is next week, and the Republicans follow the week after that. Today Obama announced his vice presidential nominee as Joseph Biden. It is a good choice in my opinion. Biden is Chairman of the Senate Foreign Relations Committee, and he brings decades of experience that will help counter Republican attacks on Obama's lack of experience in foreign policy. On the shared stage in Springfield Illinois, where Obama first announced his candidacy for president, Biden came out swinging at McCain.

"John McCain served our country with extreme courage, and I know he wants to do right by America," he said of his Senate colleague and the presumptive Republican nominee. "But the harsh truth is loud and clear: You can't change America when you supported George Bush's policies 95 percent of the time." Biden will be formidable, no doubt about it. And it will be interesting to see whom the Republicans will put up against him. We now enter the final stages of the long campaign; in the meantime, there seems to be not a voice anywhere that provides confidence to this declining economy. I won't take it so seriously though, I've got my music.

❒

During the nearly two years that I have been taking a journey at this keyboard as I have traced my own journey in life—the inception of this work occurring just a few months after my jolting, almost surreal-feeling separation from Sue—I have observed the tiny seeds of our economic decline, where we were just beginning to hear of the exposure of banks to this new "subprime mortgage problem," blossom into a multi-headed monster, the full nastiness of which we most likely have not fully experienced yet. And during this unfolding of time—again, a personal odyssey where I have strived to be pure in my recollection of the emotional, spiritual, philosophical, musical, experimental, confrontational, passionate, sad, painful, and wonderful moments that comprise the organic historical being who is Bruce Farrell Rosen. It has been astounding to watch the political fairytale that has brought Barack Obama to this day, Wednesday, August 27, 2008, when the delegates officially provided him with the Democratic nomination.

How uncanny it was to observe an interview that was played on television news a few weeks ago, when Bobby Kennedy said sometime in 1968 that he could envision an African American being elected president in about 40 years. Racial tensions in this country were as severe as the schism, the personality conflict, this country experienced in Vietnam. The likelihood of a black president in my lifetime seemed possible in fiction, not reality. "I might not get there with you, but I've seen the Promised Land";

Dr. Martin Luther King's words chill the spine. He anticipated his death, but saw the future in a moment of divine prescience, illumination. The young people of today—not raised during the "March on Washington" or the incredible brutality in Alabama and Mississippi—do not find it so startling that a man of color could become his party's nominee for president, there being a very strong chance that he will win. But to me, and those of my age or older, this is astounding. Not because I am prejudiced—I would like to think that I am absolutely not—but because we just couldn't perceive America as a place where this would happen. He defeated the leader who had the prestige, base and money; Hillary Clinton was the presumptive, practically anointed nominee of the party—until she wasn't. They fought bitterly; many thought the convention would not be decided on the first ballot, and that there would be a bitterly divisive fight. But it didn't happen. Tonight these were Hillary's words: "With eyes fixed firmly on the future, in the spirit of unity, with the goal of victory, with faith in our party and our country, let us declare together in one voice, right here, right now, that Barack Obama is our candidate and that he will be our president." Following these words, a loud celebration took over the hall. And I love the words this night—tears pouring down his face—of representative John Lewis of Georgia, the icon of the civil rights struggles of the 1960s: "I'm more than happy to see the large number of young people who are not African-American—they are white—saying to their grandfathers, to their grandmothers, "You must vote for Barack Obama. Barack Obama is not an African-American nominee. He is the Democratic nominee for President of the United States. That's what this struggle is all about—to create one America, one house, and that is what Barack Obama represents."

It is now Thursday, the 29th, and Barack Obama has given his acceptance speech, tears pouring down the faces of so many in the audience. I am not a big Jesse Jackson fan, but it was touching to see his eyes filled with tears—whatever his belligerence, he has fought hard for racial equality. His face added poignancy to an already strikingly profound moment. The speech flowed like the beautifully formed Hawaiian waves from which he emerged.

The charisma was spellbinding; the words turning into rainbows. The speech was hypnotic—I couldn't pull myself away for a moment—perhaps more so because of the sense of history unfolding. But it wasn't all poetry. He hit the notes for the fall campaign. Announcing that healthcare is fundamental he said: "This country is more decent than one where a woman in Ohio, on the brink of retirement, finds herself one illness away from disaster after a lifetime of hard work." Striking the populist position of preventing jobs from going overseas, he stated: "This country is more generous than one where a man in Indiana has to pack up the equipment he's worked on for 20 years and watch it shipped off to China, and then chokes up as he explains he felt like a failure when he went home to tell his family the news." And while showing respect for the service of John McCain, he went after him hard: "John McCain has worn the uniform of our country with bravery and distinction, and for that we owe him our gratitude and respect. But the record's clear: John McCain has voted with George Bush 90 percent of the time. But really, what does that say about your judgment when you think George Bush has been right more than 90 percent of the time?"

Next week the Republicans will have their turn, and I am enjoying the theater.

❒

The verdict is in, and I have no clue who she is; I must confess I've never heard of Sarah Palin. It is very late at night on Saturday, August 30th, the strobe of Alcatraz focused directly on me; it is a light that always demands answers, searching for the truth, not quite as harsh as a "third degree," but insistent as it beams into my living room about every five seconds. We have gotten to know each other quite well over the period I have been sitting down to write—it probes me for answers, encourages my poetic side, urges me to supplement these writings with the music that I love. I have asked it to be kind, not so insistent and harsh, to soften its light. And there is no question the light has taken on a softer glow recently, has become more patient in its search. Someone is watching the closing moments of Saturday Night Live on the television in the building off to my right—I know because curiosity got the best of me and I pulled out my binoculars to see what they were watching—and I am comforted again by this particular watcher or couple of watchers that I am not by myself. No doubt they have seen me at my desk, as they gaze out their window to the top of Pacific Heights behind them. In any event, I reflect on this vice presidential pick. It is either the smartest pick in presidential campaign history, or the dumbest and most desperate. I have never heard of her, and no doubt huge swaths of the country have never heard of her. Her résumé shows that she has been governor of one of our least populated states, Alaska, for about two years, before which she was mayor of a tiny town, Wasilla, where, apparently, she was quite successful in reducing taxes. She has absolutely zero foreign-policy or international-relations background and, if elected, she becomes a heartbeat away from the presidency of what would be the oldest elected president in history.

She is a strong "right-to-life" advocate, and this clearly plays well with the base of the Republican Party that strongly objected to "right-to-choose" candidates like Joseph Lieberman (the likely preferred choice of John McCain). But if they wanted a "right-to-life candidate," there were some well-known people from which to choose: Romney and Huckabee put up good battles for the nomination. Most likely the McCain handlers have decided that the paradigm needs to be broken: that McCain's age and following in George Bush's footsteps can only lead to a landslide loss unless people are given something brand new to think about.

The hope would be that she would attract enough of the female votes—women who are disaffected by the fact that Hillary is not on the ticket—to make this a competitive race. But if he wanted a woman with conservative credentials, what about someone like Kay Bailey Hutchinson of Texas, someone who's has been exposed to the big issues? Clearly, the party wants to shake things up in a big way, and they must have confidence that Palin is charismatic, passionate, exciting enough to energize the Party, reach out to women, and make McCain appear presidential.

My initial reaction, though, is that it makes him appear to be less presidential, prepared to put a person, for strategic political considerations, a "heartbeat from the presidency" who doesn't belong there in the slightest. Using a corporate analogy, it is like taking an application from someone interviewing for a management job and deciding that you want to make them vice-chairman or CEO. The whole thing seems crazy to me. She is quite cute, though, in a kind of country sort of way; I found myself reacting to her sex appeal when she was being introduced alongside McCain. She does have a "star quality" about her, very photogenic, and McCain (30 years her senior) looks quite elderly in her presence. My initial impression is that he'll have a hard time keeping up with her. And—a big hockey fan—I do like her comments on being introduced: "I was just your average hockey mom in Alaska before getting into politics. When I found corruption there, I fought it hard and brought the offenders to account." Showing that it is a choice that, hopefully, would excite all women, she energized the crowd and received a strong, positive response when she offered, "Hillary left 18 million cracks in the highest, hardest glass ceiling in America. But it turns out the women of America aren't finished yet, and we can shatter that glass ceiling once and for all." So, indeed, they knew that she would be charismatic and she is, but it is tough for me to buy into this one. A heartbeat away from the presidency? A person America will only get to know for about two months, when there are so many people more qualified and who have undergone a vetting process for a few years? Apparently John McCain only met her once, maybe twice, before asking her to join the ticket. This is sheer desperation, the way I see it—not putting the country first.

It is the fifth of September; the Republicans have had their turn to excite the nation, their convention now complete. No doubt about it, Sarah can excite a crowd, and she showed that she can be an attack dog, clearly not intimidated by the Obama wave and mystique. "In politics, there are some candidates who use change to promote their careers, and then there are those, like John McCain, who use their careers to promote change," she offered, deriding the whole "change" mantra that has propelled the Obama campaign. In another barb, she traced her career as mayor of Wasilla, Alaska, to governor of her state, adding: "I guess a small-town mayor is sort of like a 'community organizer,' except that you have actual responsibilities." As a young man, Obama did a stint as a community organizer. She smiled, sardonically, after the statement, the crowd standing with enthusiasm.

For his part, McCain tried to reclaim the mantle of maverick and outsider, even though he has served in congress for more than 25 years. He suggested that his choice of Sarah Palin as his running mate gave him the license to run as an outsider: "Let me just offer an advance warning to the old, big-spending, do-nothing, me-first-country-second crowd: Change is coming." Patriotism played a large role in his speech, and in a very moving moment, he brought to the screen his struggles as a prisoner of war in Vietnam. But, for my money, there was something "out of step" in his speech. In almost every sentence, he talked about the "fight," continuing the "fight," forever "fighting." Fighting about what, I do not know. It was a bit "over the top," in my opinion. The economy is collapsing, nary a word mentioned about it, but we get a steady diet of "fight, fight, fight." "Stand up, stand up, stand up and fight," is the way he concluded the speech. Perhaps we've had a bit too much of that attitude from the outgoing administration. I was not impressed.

❐

It is an ordeal going to San Francisco Forty Niner football games. The food isn't so great at the park—not like those kosher dogs, the barbeque beef sandwiches, the combination taco plate that you can get at Giants baseball games—so I always wait in line at about 12 o'clock at the Mayfair grocery store on Jackson and Fillmore, before walking down to California and Van Ness Streets to catch the Forty Niner express bus to Candlestick Park. It's been called a series of names, Monster Park, 3Com Park, and some others since it was first named Candlestick, but I've never called it anything else. It is an ordeal because there are far more fights in the stands than there used to be in the glory days of Joe Montana, Jerry Rice, Steve Young, and tickets are much easier to get these days. So, far too many of these tickets now fall into the hands of Neanderthals, whose primary focus is getting drunk, cursing loudly enough to bother people who just want to have a good day watching football, alienating parents who don't want their kids to be exposed to goons, their language and behavior. And these people—practically daring anyone to say anything to them about such behavior—provide a somewhat-depressing backdrop to the enjoyment.

And the Niners are just not that good anymore, and haven't been for a while—certainly not since the glory days of the Eddie DeBartolo regime; Eddie, who, sadly, lost his ownership rights and had to turn over the team to his sister's family, the Yorks, because he was banned from football ownership for life due to a scandal he was involved in down in Mississippi. What a shame! Because the ownership is inept, hiring a series of coaches who are poor, not putting the proper people in place to make good personnel decisions, squandering money on bad players, not hanging on to or properly paying the good ones. It's just not that much fun to come out here anymore, but I do come to at least four or five games these days—instead of the complete eight game schedule that I would never miss in the good ol' days. And, of course, they were the good ol' days because Sue and I would always go to the games together; or when she didn't, I'd go with my friend Craig, whose best man I was on the weekend that Loma Prieta hit—the wedding pulling my young family out of the city's Marina District, to which we had moved when I was desperate to escape back to the city, after moving to Mill Valley earlier that summer. And when the boys started to become old enough—I'll never forget that Forty Niner game that Sunday, it must have been at least 100 degrees out there, when pieces of dark ash were wafting through the air, a smoky haze in the background, Michael's eyes burning so much that we had to go find seats much farther behind us in the shade of the overhang, he was about three at the time of that devastating Oakland Hills fire—I would alternate between them, Sue and Craig.

The point is that I was never alone at those games. Because even on the days when I couldn't get anyone in the mood to come with me, or they were all doing other things, I still sat next to my father-and-son best friends, the two Phils, the Barbieri boys, father and son. It is just insane that they are both dead, and for the past couple of seasons—since the boys have been off in college and Sue and I are no longer together—I come to these games most of the time by myself. On my empty seat to my left I put my lunch, and to my right are people I never know, the Barbieri estate sending the seats back to the team or a ticket agency. There are always different people occupying those seats, and I become lonely just sitting there. But, I do love football, and I continue to come, even though I experience sadness often at the games. And sadness is not something I ever felt in all the years I came out here, until recently.

The 49ers lost the game today, 23-13 to the Arizona Cardinals. We made it close for awhile, but by the middle of the third quarter, we were out of it. It was, however, a gorgeous day out there, perhaps 70 degrees, the day starting with just a touch of overcast that burned off by about the time I bought that sandwich and made my way up Fillmore Street, down to California, and on to Van Ness. I am now tired from the day; sad for sure that my good friends were not there, but lay in graves.

Today is September 7, 2008, nine years to the day that my mother passed away. And she lies in a grave at the Home of Peace Cemetery down in Colma, just a few miles from where I watched the game today at Candlestick Park. God I miss her, and I expect her to come back, like the tingling feeling of a missing limb, even after all these years. I do believe she is with me, but sometimes I just surrender to the truth that she is dead. And there is the aura of the two Phils at the game—their energy in the form of memory will never disappear from those two seats—but as I look out on this very black night (there are lights out there, but I don't see them), I admit that I will never sit next to them again. I'm tired from this day; I didn't enjoy the football game today.

If You Ever Need Me, I Won't Be Far Away

My mom had planned to come up to San Francisco to visit us for Jonathan's 10th birthday, April 17, 1999. That was just one of the plans we had for the spring through fall. In June she would come to Hawaii with us, enjoy the boys—take a needed break from the daily tea-leaf readings (how draining it is to be psychic for a living almost every day of your life)—and revel in a grandmother's joy. We would plan Michael's Bar Mitzvah, which would be in late October, basking in the soft tropical breeze, listening to the calming, peaceful surf. For months, Sue and she would talk about that Bar Mitzvah—my mom would arrange for the invitations, print the messages in gold leaf, make it into the party of her lifetime, she was so excited and proud of her grandchild.

Gainesborough, she called him; he reminded her of the innocence in the works of children by Gainsborough.

We had agreed to fly up some of her favorite people for the Bar Mitzvah, mostly the poor, but a few of the stars would make this "A" list as well.

At the last minute, several days before Jonathan's 10th birthday, my mom called to say that she was quite sick. Now, I was used to her being sick; she suffered from diabetes, high blood pressure and emphysema. She would come down with a bout of flu or a cold, and shake it off after a few days. I was always nervous when she was "under the weather," but was used to her getting over things, at least enough for it to not deter her from plans, but this phone call had a different "feel" to me, a tone to her voice that troubled me, her voice nearly a whisper as she struggled for extra air to continue the conversation. "We'll monitor it, Mom," I said, "but I'm sure you'll be well enough to come in a week. I know you'll get over it by then, and we'll celebrate Jonathan's 10th birthday, and have a lot of fun. Remember when you made that birthday cake for my 10th?" I reminded her. "Yes, I do," she whispered, the sound of her breath more audible than the tone of her voice, "I do—it was the 'Bozo the Clown' birthday cake. You loved Bozo the Clown, and the whole chocolate cake was his face." "It was one of my favorite birthdays," I answered, "I remember that one better than any other birthday growing up. So we'll make Jonathan's special as well. You'll come; you'll be here, I'm sure." "I'm sure too," she said, "I know that I'll make it."

I spoke to her each day leading up to that birthday, and though she didn't seem to be getting worse, she also was not getting better. The day before the birthday, she had to withdraw from coming. "I can barely get out of bed," she said. "When I go to take a bath, I hardly have the energy or breath to get out of the tub. You know how I get dizzy from time to time, from the high blood pressure? Its probably more in my head than anything else—I'm just nervous these days." "Mom, have you been to a doctor for this flu that doesn't seem to be going away?" "You know what I think of going to doctors," she answered. "But I did call in for a prescription of Ativan—that seems to be helping. It is relaxing me. It's probably just a bad flu that is triggering this emphysema, and making me nervous. I'm sure that it will get better." "I'm sure that it will as well, Mom, but you really have to get some X-rays. This has to be looked at. Maybe you need to be on some heavy antibiotic for this? You have to go." "I'll go," she insisted, "I'll go." But my mom could be very stubborn, especially where going to doctors was concerned. Frankly, I don't know if there was anything that I could get her to do that I really wanted her to do. Whenever she would come over, she'd pour a ton of salt on her food, even before tasting it. "Mom, you have high blood pressure!" But she'd pour a little more. Then she'd go for a cigarette. I'd say again, "Mom, you continue to smoke! I just can't believe you. High blood pressure, diabetes, emphysema, and you continue to smoke!" "Leave me alone already. I'm not really smoking that much anymore at all, and I'm quitting soon." "Mom," I'd reply, "you are one of the great psychics and healers this world has ever known; you have an amazing gift. But not for yourself. You should know you can't continue to do this stuff. I want you around for a very long time." "I'll live as long as I'm supposed to live," she'd answer. "And I'm sure it will be long enough." "Mom, I want you to be here for both grandchildren's Bar Mitzvahs; I want you to watch them go through their teens, go to college, hopefully get married. I think you can do it if you take better care of yourself, stop the smoking, pouring all this salt, and I'm doing pretty well now in this business;

I'd like you to sell the place in L.A., with all that smog, move up here where the air is clear; we'll get you a nice little condo, and you can read just enough for your expenses." "That sounds lovely Brucie," she'd say to me. "And that is my plan. I will come up there in the next year or so, and my life will get much easier. That will be the plan." It was the plan for five years or so, until she couldn't make it to Jonathan's 10th birthday.

From mid-April to early June, she didn't improve, but didn't appear to be getting a lot worse. She would read tea leaves a few times a day, then retire to her bed for hours, waking to take that bath that was so difficult to take, returning breathless to bed again. As far as I knew she hadn't gone to the doctor for an X-ray, but apparently, in mid-May, 1999, she did go. She was too ill to come to Hawaii with us, but she promised that nothing would get in the way of attending Michael's Bar Mitzvah. While in Hawaii, I'd call her every day, but rarely had the chance to speak with her. She was either reading cups or asleep. Perhaps she just couldn't handle telling me what I found out the minute I arrived home from the airport: "Heidi, is Mom up? How is she feeling today? I could barely reach her in Hawaii. Has she gone to the doctor yet? We need to get her to the doctor." "Bruce," my sister said, "Mom went to the doctor last week and the tests came back. She has lung cancer. The doctors say it is inoperable, a massive tumor."

A strange calm came over me when she said this—no doubt a defensive mechanism given to human beings to make them numb during times they can't handle emotionally. I had been anaesthetized by a chemical in the body, but when I looked in the mirror, my Hawaiian tan was gone. I was pale.

"Heidi, what does this mean? How long does she have?" "I don't know," she said, "but it isn't long." "Does Mom know it is cancer? Does she know what kind? Does she know the prognosis?" "She knows it's cancer, but she doesn't know how bad. We're all hoping that miraculously she can overcome this the way she has overcome everything else in her life. She is thinking that she can do this, too." "Well I'm not giving up hope; maybe she can. She'll overcome this. I will fly down next weekend," I replied. "That would be good Bruce. Mom would love to have you here." "Heidi, I'll come down next Friday night."

I listened to the airplane music with headphones on that Friday night flight. As we reached mid-air the powerful song of R.E.M., the simultaneously soaring, haunting, chanting hymn of Michael Stype poured through my bloodstream:

I've watched the stars fall silent from your eyes,
All the sights that I have seen.
I can't believe that I believed I wished,
That you could see.
There's a new planet in the solar system
There's nothing up my sleeve.

I'm pushing an elephant up the stairs,
I'm tossing up punch lines that were never there.
Over my shoulder a piano falls,
Crashing to the ground.

And all this talk of time,
Talk is fine.
And I don't want to stay around,
Why can't we pantomime, just close our eyes,
And sleep sweet dreams.
Me and you with wings on our feet.

I'm breaking though,
I'm bending spoons,
I'm keeping flowers in full bloom.
I'm looking for answers from the great beyond.

I want the hummingbirds, the dancing bears,
Sweetest dreams of you.
I'm looking to the stars,
I'm looking to the moon.

Hearing this music, I knew that nothing would remind me more of this time than this haunting, gripping, soothing, sad, mournful, elegiac sound. At 35,000 feet—en route to Burbank Airport, and then from there up Highway 5 to the dry mountainous landscape of Canyon Country, California, where my mother, whose compassion for others was a fountain of limitless depth, struggled for breath—I was deeply looking for "answers from the great beyond."

Late in the evening of the first night that I was there, we had to drive my mother to emergency at Cedars Sinai, about 50 miles away. The oxygen machine was not providing enough air; the house was very hot (this is the high desert in mid-June, and the air conditioning was suddenly not working properly) and my mother became very scared. We arrived at about 11:00 P.M.; she was rushed immediately to the intensive care, where they filled her with oxygen until the blood oxygen reached an acceptable level. When she arrived, it was at a level where life would not be long sustained. We left at about 4:00 A.M, arriving back to the hot house at about 5:00, where she fell asleep. I retired to the bedroom that I had had as a high school kid, worrying as I went to sleep that she might not be alive when I woke up. She did make it through that night, and the following day, the oxygen-supply place provided another oxygen machine that delivered a greater burst of air, making her more comfortable and, apparently, better saturating the blood. The next afternoon we had her favorite Thai food delivered, and she was in good spirits. It was usually the case that my mom would visit us up in San Francisco; I hadn't been down to Los Angeles to visit very often. Now, I found myself wishing that I had come down more often to share with my mom this delicious Thai food in her home. After dinner, my mom went to her bed and asked that I sit next to her. "There is a quiet around you that I feel, Bruce; you will be okay. You have an inner peace. Life is all very simple, really," she went on. "We all make it so complicated, but it is all so simple." She went on to say that she felt bad for the way black people are treated in our society. "It isn't right; it isn't right at all the way these people are treated, what they have to go through." I nodded, listened intently, our hearts intertwined. "It's just so simple, really so simple," she continued as she drifted off to sleep. "It is nice that I don't have to read so much now; now I can take a break, get some rest." She fell asleep, and I went off to a take long walk around this neighborhood that I'd known in high school.

I walked up the hill and sat next to the water storage shed—day becoming twilight, how nice it was to sit in a T-shirt, a warm breeze on my face; it had been a good while since escaping that San Francisco chill—impervious to the memory that I'd once come dangerously close to a coiled rattlesnake on this very spot. I had been gone a few hours, and when I returned, my mom was sitting hunched on the blue velvet sectional couch (very '60s looking) in the darkened living room. She stayed there until quite late; I wanted to stay up with her all night, but she wouldn't let me. She insisted that I go and get some sleep, and when I refused she started to get testy with me. "I just want to be alone, and you need your sleep. Don't worry about me; I'll be fine tonight." So I gave her the space, went back to the warm back bedroom—goodness, how many times had I smoked weed back in this room with Phil, my brother, Jeff, the whole gang—and tried to absorb the idea that I'll be in this room maybe a couple of more times in my life, and that my mom—sitting hunched on that blue sectional—may not make it through many more nights in her home. I wanted to sob so desperately that night, as I went to sleep wondering if she would be alive the following morning. But I could not sob; I could only be present with the deep pain. Eventually I fell asleep, and my first destination on waking was to enter my mom's room, to see if she was breathing. She had survived another night.

I flew down a couple of weeks later, and again we had to go to emergency at Mt. Sinai. This time we arrived in the afternoon and stayed until late evening. The oxygen saturation level had weakened seriously. She sat in the bed, an airtight oxygen mask on her face, the nurse telling me that I was not to allow her any water, not to open the mask. She was desperate for water, so I would go over to the sink, repeatedly filling a tablespoon with water, carefully fitting it under the mask. She gave me a conspiratorial wink—we were a team violating these stupid rules. Later that day I had gone to the Jewish Deli down the way and bought a Pastrami sandwich. For dessert I had some chocolate Halvah. It was her favorite dessert, and so I snuck some under the mask for her. Momentary joy spread across her face as she tasted that Halvah. When we left that night, the doctors advised to be ready, to have all affairs in place, because the end was near. I listened. And when I flew back the next day, the song sounded more mournful than it ever had, but it spoke to my soul, my mind, my pain:

I've watched the stars fall silent from your eyes,
All the sights that I have seen.

I'm breaking through,
I'm bending spoons,
I'm keeping flowers in full bloom.
I'm looking for answers from the great beyond.

❐

We spent August 7, Michael's birthday, at my mom's house. Sue, the boys and I drove down to see her. Michael turned 13 that day, and he read to her the Torah portion that he would read for his Bar Mitzvah. We stayed at a motor lodge out in Valencia. It was so hot outside that I had the sensation of prickly needles poking me up and down my back. I liked the sensation after all these years in San Francisco. My mom—her mind drifting quite often now—had suggested during a moment of clarity that I take the family to Universal Studios. We did that, and we enjoyed it immensely. While there and on the way back to my mom's house, I wished with everything I had inside me that she would make it to Michael's Bar Mitzvah, and I wished that we had come down here more often to take the boys to Universal Studios and Disneyland. The next day we traveled back up Highway 5 to San Francisco. The boys would never see their grandmother again. She is a legend to them now.

I saw her one more time while she was conscious. In late August I flew down. It had become torturous for me at this point, because every night I lay in bed wondering if she would be alive the next morning. My doctor had recommended that I take an anxiety medication for these times. Resistant as I was to taking anything, I started taking it every second night. It helped immensely. At least I could let go and fall asleep. On this late August visit, my mom had some remarkably clear moments. She actually seemed clearer for longer periods of time than she had during our visit with the boys. Heidi, my mom and I went out to a barbeque place that she just loved. The lung machine by her side, she would carefully remove the mask and put down some pieces of spare rib. She loved it and was able to eat. That night, the evening warm, gorgeous, a soft desert breeze reminding me again of how nice Southern California can be, I wheeled her in her chair up the road to the water storage shed.

She talked about it not being a mistake to live here, and that her father had done her a very big favor in helping her to buy this place when she had absolutely no money in the period after my father left. She so desperately—as did we all—want to escape that home in Reseda that had been so hellish during the rough years with my father. She told me that she would still love to move to San Francisco, that she just loved the cool breezes, but that this place had not been a mistake. "It was meant to be," she said as I wheeled her back down the hill. "I love you, Mom," I said. "I love you too, Brucie, very much," she answered. "I will always be with you and all of my children," she followed. "And if you ever need me, I won't be far away, just on the other side." "I know that, Mom; I know that," and the pain was hard to bear.

The next day, I flew back home. When I left for the airport, my mom seemed disoriented. She wanted to know if I was going to the store. And if it could only be that way, I thought to myself. I just wish I were only going to the store. "I'm going home to San Francisco, Mom," I answered. "But I'll be back here soon. I promise." At this point, she wore a sort of sly expression, giving me a little wink. "Don't give up on me. I'm not done yet." I ran over to hug her. "I'll never give up on you, Mom. And I know you're not done. I'll be back in just a few days."

And on the flight home the music played,

I'm breaking through,
I'm bending spoons,
I'm keeping flowers in full bloom.
I'm looking for answers from the great beyond.

While at work on September 7, I received a phone call from my sister that Mom had almost stopped breathing, and that she and a friend were driving her to Cedars Sinai. And that I'd better come down right away. They practically crashed the car into the glass entryway at Cedars Emergency. Just before arriving, my mom had stopped breathing, but they were able to revive her. When I arrived, she lay in a coma. After several hours we decided that we would mercifully let her go.

≈

In a small anteroom just down the hall from where my mother had passed, I sat with brothers, Jeff and Elliot, sister Heidi. Elliot had been living at home with my mom, and her greatest concern was that he continue to take the medication that had normalized him from the devastating effects of a bipolar condition. Jeff had been living in a fabricated home in Arizona, just above the Colorado river. But he could barely get around from the dozens of surgeries he had had over the past many years, the result of being a daring, brilliant, acrobatic, partly crazy hockey goalie. The summers out there in Arizona—where the days would routinely get to above 120 degrees—were too much for him. And he would have to leave. He was very isolated, and would sometimes become a bit delirious from the heat, suffering dehydration and becoming confused, sometimes forgetting to take his medication, then overcompensating by taking too much.

Heidi was struggling financially, taking odd job after odd job, none of them seeming to last. During the last few years of my mother's life, a period when my career had substantially blossomed, I would send her as much money a month as I could spare. I know that a substantial percentage of this went for the shelter of my disabled brothers and financially challenged sister. As we sat in this room—the pain of losing such a cherished person is so intense that it is God's grace to make us numb, a feeling of unreality protecting one from the painful feelings of loss that will continue to unfold during a lifetime—I promised my brothers that I would purchase a place for them to live together. But Jeff would have to make me a promise that he would look after Elliot, and I demanded a promise from Elliot that he would take the medicine everyday (he would often miss some days, manic symptoms returning, because it made him a bit sleepy from time to time) as my mom so desperately wanted him to do. They made these promises to me. I assured Heidi that I would always be there to help—financially, and in any way I could. These were going to be very difficult times to get through, "but we'll make it because of the deep love that we all have for each other, and because Mom will be there with us all along, to pull us through."

I hugged my brothers and sister with all of my soul, called the hotel where I had spent the night, and purchased rooms for them. Heidi walked into her room, dark circles under her deeply set, stunning green eyes, her face pale and filled with sorrow; Elliot and Jeff were bewildered, dazed, as they went into their room. "I'm there for you, I told them both; you'll never have to worry about having a place to live or food to eat." My own personal numbness had started to wear off, like the anaesthetizing effects of whatever the dentist uses these days, and my personal grief must have been all over my face as I tried to "sell" my brothers on what I would do for them. "I love you boy," I said to Elliot, following Jeff into the hotel room. "Don't call me boy," he snapped back, "Only Mom can call me boy." "Okay," I answered, nodded my head in understanding, hugged him, walked down the hall into my own room, looking forward to returning to my home in San Francisco. I fell asleep quickly, but was awakened incessantly through the night with dreams that didn't make sense in this foreign place.

Rabbi Alan Lew of Congregation Beth Shalom in San Francisco had been working closely with Michael in preparation for his Bar Mitzvah. The last period of Michael's Torah study coincided with the last few months of my mother's life. And so during this time I had gotten to know Rabbi Lew as Michael's Bar Mitzvah mentor and guide through the Torah, and as a grief counselor. He asked that I call him anytime when the feelings of pain seemed hard to handle, anytime day or night. I told him that I would try to respect his privacy, but would call him during times of need. And indeed, I did call him three or four times.

Rabbi Lew had been a devout, deeply insightful Buddhist before he heard the calling to become a Rabbi. He had a mental clarity developed through years of meditation and spiritual practice, and his words were spoken directly from the depths of heart. Several years before the Bar Mitzvah preparation, a family friend had urged us to listen to his sermon at a Saturday service. We did, and never returned to the synagogue we had been previously attending. Sue and I were so moved by his authenticity, the "earthy, in-the-moment wisdom," that we had to join his congregation. He was a marvelous writer, deeply intuitive and willing to acknowledge that there is a dimension to this world wherein we are in touch with those who have left this earth. He didn't dwell on messages from the "other world," but was sensitive, aware of the energies around him. He had just completed a book, "One God Clapping," during this time of my grief and Michael's Bar Mitzvah preparation, and this time in my life will be remembered by that period in his life, when Rabbi Lew would read portions of this book at various book signings. There was a particularly moving passage in the book that I underlined at the time, it was a statement about "going easy on oneself," allowing one's "Divine Name" to present itself:

> "Each of us has a divine name. Mindfulness is the key to understanding its secret. The term in the Talmud for mindfulness is kavanat halev, 'the directing of the heart.' Real mindfulness comes about not by an act of violence against our consciousness, not by force, not by trying to control our consciousness, but rather, by a kind of directed compassion, a softening of our awareness, a loving embrace of our lives, a soft letting be."

In the days of my mom's passing these words provided a message of "letting go" and embracing my life, accepting the pain and loss as part of my divine name, my own calling. Allowing myself to not run but to be present in my world, to experience this moment in all of the intensity as I did the joyous ones. And, again, it is a special message for today, 2008, when I so deeply strive to understand the "whys and wherefores" of my life: "We must not commit violence against our consciousness to arrive at an understanding, but rather a kind of directed compassion, a softening of our awareness, a loving embrace of ourselves." Very special words, indeed.

I did not find Rabbi Lew to be excessively warm most of the time—he could feel distant at times—but he was deeply mindful and present. And when it really mattered, when one's soul called out for help, he would be compassionate to the core. And he had that compassion for me during the final months of my mom's life. Just before I took the taxi to the airport on the final day of my mother's life I called Rabbi Lew to explain that my mother now lay in a coma in the hospital:

"This is your life," he said, "I love you, and now it is your time to attend to your mother. Be courageous, but do not be a hero. Do what you feel is appropriate. It is your time now, Bruce. Go with my thoughts and I will be here when you return." "This is the moment that I have dreaded my whole life," I answered. "Bruce, this is your life and it is your turn." There was really no more that he could say to me, but, again, I put on the airplane headphones and the music played:

I'm breaking through,
I'm bending spoons,
I'm keeping flowers in full bloom.
I'm looking for answers from the great beyond.

My mother passed just a couple of days before Rosh Hashanah; I returned home in the evening, and the following morning I summoned the strength to go with Sue to the memorial chapel, where I purchased her coffin. The coffin salesman was well intentioned—he wanted to make sure that I had all of the burial options—but he just didn't seem to know when to stop talking. He had to make sure that I had all of the information to make an educated decision. I started to become a bit agitated at the incessantly talking voice, each word creating further tightening of my back and neck, stiffness in my jaws, overwhelming emotion being barely stifled by a thin veneer of mortuary etiquette.

Sue could see that I was hurting, hurting badly, and she offered that we should purchase the simple box with the Star of David inscription. "Yes, that is the one that we will take, for sure. Please prepare that one." I wrote the man a check, and we were on our way to the Home of Peace Cemetery, where I would purchase her resting place. Again, the man that ran the burial site was full of words, nonstop words—he seemed even more impervious to my deep grief than the man selling the casket. He kept going on about the various financial plans and payment schedules, and that there were other sites adjacent to the one for my mother that we could include in the agreement. Words, a cascade of words. I paid cash for the site—forget the damn payment schedule—and I told him to hold two more sites for Sue and myself. He told me that he could place a one-week hold on them at most—there was a lot of interest in this quiet resting place under an olive tree—and we would need to get back to him within a week's time for sure, if we wanted to hang onto the sites. "You know what, we'll take them," I said to this businessman who seemed not to have an ounce of mercy. "I'll give you a deposit with my credit card." And so I did. I was so happy to leave that office, though I was pleased with the resting place for my mom and eventual resting place for Sue and myself.

Sue had picked out the location when I was in Los Angeles the previous day, and I thanked her for taking control and making a nice choice. "I really didn't like that guy," I said to Sue as we drove away. I continued that, "Obviously, he has done this thousands of times, and he was so totally cold. I don't know how you do this day in and day out. I guess you develop an inability to feel, otherwise you couldn't do the job. It must take a certain kind of person for this work. Certainly, he is the right guy for the job," and with that I broke into a deep sobbing, the pain of loss overwhelming me. Back in the city, Sue ran into a supermarket—

we hadn't had lunch yet—while I waited in the car for her to return. When she returned what I felt was uncontrollable—I was heaving with grief, tears pouring. "It's good that this is coming out now; it's good," she said.

We returned home—there was now a break in this storm—and we had the Sushi. I had to find a place to be by myself, and went up to the attic of our Victorian. The attic had many of Jonathan's paintings, a train set that he enjoyed watching, some incredible Lego constructions—that young man would spend hours up here playing by himself—and way off in the corner, a little chair in front of a small window that looked down three stories to the street. I sat in this seat, and it felt peaceful for the moment to be out of that hospital to which I had rushed to find my mother in a coma, her body becoming cold; to not be in an airplane; no longer in the chapel where I had to look at coffins; away from the businessman selling me gravesites; to be at peace with my grief. I closed my eyes, and I didn't feel like sobbing anymore. And for a few moments, I found peace. But grief is a sickness, and like a severe flu where vomiting can come on at any time, I began to sob again uncontrollably. It came on like a rainstorm, starting slowly, then becoming more intense, the wind picking up and the rain lashing against the window, coming from virtually every direction. The rainstorm has a rhythm, and the tears were rhythmic, pouring, then abating somewhat, then pouring again—my breathing, like the wind driving the storm, becoming shallow or deeper with the intensity of the tears. The most ferocious storm of tears that I would experience occurred in that attic on that day, and while I would cry deeply, off and on for days and weeks, the eye of the hurricane of my grief had passed through me that day.

The following morning I fulfilled my appointment to select the stone that would mark the place of my mother's body at the Home of Peace. The location was just down the boulevard from the entrance to the cemetery, and it was clear as we approached it that we were at the correct place. Out front was a wide variety of the different kinds of grave stones: from the ornately decorated, sleek stone to pieces of rock that appeared to come right from a quarry; from the large mausoleum, Romanesque style, to the simple, unadorned polished stone of the fireplace mantle. We parked and walked past the rock toward the small office—large German Shepherd dogs barking ferociously behind a chain-link fence, there obviously to scare away intruders after hours—entering a small cottage, where there were books on a desk illustrating the kinds of stones available.

It was a small man, slight of build, late 60s in age, perhaps, his face tanned and exposing freckles, hair (the color oddly black, as though it had been dyed) receding well back from a brown forehead, a warm greeting of a smile welcoming us. This man clearly was not a talker or a salesman. He gave us the space to sit down and settle in, then he offered coffee or tea. I asked for some herbal tea, which he had the office lady prepare. "This is not easy, I know," he said. "It doesn't get much harder than preparing a stone for your mother." I nodded, trying to put together a piece of a smile through what must have been tight lips. "Those are some German Shepherds," I responded; "I don't know how you do any business, they must scare everyone away." "We have them behind the fence, not to worry; you wouldn't believe how many people try to break in at night and steal stones." "It's not something I've ever thought about," I answered, "but I guess it must be a problem." He looked at me for a second, then changed the subject to the mission at hand: selecting a stone. Sue and I quickly settled on a dark gray, simply carved, but elegant stone. At the top was a rose, my mother's favorite flower. "This is the one," I said quietly; this fits my mother, quiet, simple, the look of antiquity, elegant." "A very nice choice, indeed," he added, and we then worked out the details of the size. He then gave me a piece of paper and asked that I compose the inscription. I wrote the following:

Alma Rush Rosen
January 2, 1934–September 7, 1999
A seer of truth
A teacher of wisdom
Whose compassion overflows
A mother, Biblical in nature
She will be deeply missed
By those fortunate enough
To partake of her grace

Later that day we met with Rabbi Lew in his study to tell the story of my mother; from this he would prepare his remarks for the service at the gravesite early the next afternoon. The following evening would be the first night of Rosh Hashanah, and the cemetery was going to hold the grounds open past the closing time for the Holy Day, so that we could lay my mom to rest. I couldn't hold back the tears as I told the Rabbi how my mother grew up with a very violent father, a tyrant from the Russian old country who had settled in Toronto, Canada. Her mother had been a delicate woman from Austria, but her father, Abraham, had been given to serious rage. Her brothers were very successful and notorious in Canada. I told him about her brother Dave Rush, who at the age of 29 owned 29 department stores in Canada. And how he had promoted the first heavyweight championship fight to ever come into Canada, between Archie Moore and James J. Parker. And I told him about Meyer and the bombing that he survived. And how Meyer—a story I always loved—picked a man out of a police line-up—he was one of the men that had broken into Meyer's home one night and beat him with a baseball bat to try to stop him from testifying—and instead of identifying him to the policeman, knocked him out cold. "Is this the man?" Meyer had been asked. "I don't tell no tales," Meyer had answered, as he walked away. This was all part of my mom's life, and it had to be told, so the rabbi would understand from where she came. I described the elderly English women in Toronto that had befriended my mom when she was maybe five or six, discovered in her a very special psychic gift, and taught her how to read tea leaves, and how, when she started using this gift at a very young age, she began to scare people so much that her mother had said, "Alma, for now you'd better keep this to yourself; people are becoming frightened of you; they are saying you are a child witch."

I described the moment when she went out with her father to collect rent one evening—her father reluctantly letting her come in the car with him—and told him as they approached a dark alley not to open the door because "a man was there and would try to kill him." "Nonsense," her father said as he started to open the door; just then a man with a crowbar appeared from behind something, my mother screaming, her father slamming the car door in the nick of time to save his life. I continued with the story of how my mom had to escape this tyrannical father, and did so at the age of 18 by eloping with my father, a 22-year-old taxi driver from Montreal. She had gone with her mother to visit Gertie Rosen, a famous card reader, fortune teller, whose notoriety was big in certain circles of Toronto. My father woke up from a nap after being out all night—clothes soiled from sleeping in them—and discovered the most beautiful woman he had ever seen. And indeed my mom was beautiful—she had been the runner-up in the Miss Toronto Beauty Pageant, her brothers almost going after the judges because they believed they must have been bribed to not have chosen her. The bottom line, though, was Larry Rosen had to have her, couldn't imagine not having her, and eventually did have her. They eloped, and the Rush brothers—as Meyer once told me—took the next three days to try to find them, checking out every hotel they could find between Montreal and Toronto.

I told Rabbi Lew this story. And I told him about the horrible moment when my father—having taken a job up in New Brunswick, Canada—had left his beautiful wife and family in Montreal. On August 4th of the summer of 1967, a man had broken into our home—he had drunkenly smashed cars all the way to our kitchen window—and had attempted to rape my mother as she slept—myself lying next to her—she just recovering from throat surgery. I described the fear that had been so intense that I wasn't sure sounds were coming from my throat as I tried to scream. But apparently I had screamed loudly, waking up my brothers and sister, also screaming, as the man exited through the front door. The horror of that night as the police came, lifted his fingerprints from below the open kitchen window, located him and caught him in the wee hours of the morning. I told Rabbi Lew that I didn't think I'd ever been able to overcome the horror of that night, my constant need to be safe no doubt stemming from the break-in and watching a man try to rape my mom.

I told him everything I could in as quick a time as I could, and I started sobbing, not the uncontrollable convulsive tears of the day before, but a steady rain shower without the thunder. Rabbi Lew, with eyes that see right into one's soul, a man focused like a laser, listened to me; and as he did, it occurred to me that he hears many, many stories—and that he always listens for the authenticity—but he was hearing me from the depths of my soul, from the depths of my mother's soul, as it emptied through myself. He continued to listen intently—darkly handsome, as he sat upright in his chair, the Zen discipline very evident—as I described the reading that she had given me when I asked, "Mom, when will I meet a woman that I will marry?" "It will happen very soon," she had answered. "Very soon, maybe within the next few months. But she will find you; you won't be able to find her. She will definitely find you; so don't even try to look for her. She will be of fair complexion, maybe blonde. She will be very intelligent, as intelligent as you, but in a different way. And her father will be quite quiet; quiet but very intelligent. And he will like you very much." "What is her name?" I had asked.

"What is her name?" I just had to know. I told him how she thought for a moment, then said, "Sue. Her name is Sue. But don't look for her, she will find you." And then put the cup upside down, signifying the reading was over. He listened deeply, intently, as I told him how the "wrong number that was the right number" came in; and it was, indeed, Sue, looking for a friend, Jamie, who had changed her phone number within the last few weeks, the old one becoming mine. He shook his head from one side to the other, smiled, and continued to focus beyond my words, looking into my eyes at my soul. I told him that I really hadn't thought that this "Sue from Denver" as she had said it, would be the one that I would marry. But described how I did know when I saw the picture. "When I saw that picture," I told him, "I just knew that she was the girl that I would marry. I absolutely knew it." I went on to tell him of the hardship after my father had left to go back to Canada, and how she had read teacups day and night to feed us, and put me through college. I described how I had told her about the high school class going to Europe the upcoming summer—I was just telling her, not ever expecting that we would have any money to go, not even thinking about going—and she had said, "You'll go." "How will I go, Mom?" I had said. "We can never afford this." And she just said, "I don't want you asking that question. You'll go. It will happen; so make your plans." She knew how I had to see the world; how I needed to expand my soul; and through her readings, she made it happen for me. And, indeed, that trip provided the inspiration for me to go out in this world and succeed, to keep learning, to grow. The trip was "everything to me," I explained to Rabbi Lew. At the end of my story I said to Rabbi Lew that I hoped at some point soon I would be able to stop crying, that it kept coming uncontrollably. He said that my soul was telling the story of its grief in my tears, and that if it were to still be "happening months from now or a year from now," it would be something to look at. "But I don't think that will be the case," he had said. "You will be okay; you will be okay, Bruce."

And with that we had come to the end. We hugged and prepared to meet for the service the following early afternoon. And he had a full-nights' work ahead of him, because now it was time to write the Rosh Hashanah sermon. "I'm sure it will flow; I'm sure the words will come," I said to him. "The words will be beautiful."

Late that night, perhaps around 11 o'clock, and before the following day's burial service on the day of Rosh Hashanah, Sue picked up the telephone and told me that Rabbi Lew wanted to speak with me. I had called him a few times during this period of my grief and Michael's Bar Mitzvah preparation, but I had never received one from him. "Bruce, there is a rather extraordinary reason for my call," he said, speaking slowly, the slight Brooklyn accent underlying his deep, warm tones, a satisfying voice with a touch of Yiddish quality, and no doubt he had spoken many wise and funny Yiddish phrases growing up. He followed that with the obligatory courtesy, "I hope I am not waking anyone or calling too late." "No, Rabbi Lew," I answered. "It's very nice to hear from you." "I'm calling at this hour, because I have to ask your permission for something. I think your mother hijacked my Rosh Hashanah sermon. I think she wrote it for me. I started out with other ideas, but I felt her message coming through me and I went with it. Did your mother know of or quote John Muir?" he asked. "I don't think so; but I am familiar with the simplicity of his words. And my mom's great wisdom was in the simple, homespun truths. She spoke layers of truths in the simplest words." "Well, I would like to deliver this sermon tomorrow night, and I would like to know if I could have your permission to do that. It will be called 'Alma's Sermon.' " "My goodness, Rabbi Lew. What a privilege and honor that would be. And no doubt my mom will be there to hear it; I have no doubt that her presence will be very strong and uplifting." "I will point your family out to the congregation; I hope this will not be embarrassing for you or your family?" "It will be a blessing for us all; please follow your feelings." "Thank You," he answered, "My Rosh Hashanah sermon is written. It will be Alma's sermon. Please get some sleep now, and I will also. I'll see you tomorrow," he concluded.

When I finished the telephone conversation, I told Sue what Rabbi Lew had said. She listened, grasping the essence of what had occurred. She didn't say much, quietly accepting that my mother had spoken to the rabbi, as she knew Alma could.

The service at the gravesite was very hard. It was the most painful thing I'd ever known, to see my mother's coffin—the simple one that we had selected, the beautiful Star of David engraved at the top—placed in full view. Sue sat to one side of me, Michael to the other. My brothers, Jeff and Elliot, sister Heidi a little further down, my father to the outside of Heidi. Jonathan sat on my lap; I wanted him there. He had a way of calming me, nurturing me when I needed it. I treasured having him on my lap at that moment. The rabbi had said some magnificent words, and had read some poems and letters written about her—about how she had healed, inspired, provided insight, purpose to the lives of those who had written, and there were many letters from which he could select—and then asked if anyone wanted to add anything. I wanted to, but I couldn't; normally a person of words, it was enough for me to be quiet. I had no words. And so we moved on to the Hebrew tradition of shoveling dirt on the lowered casket.

It is the physical act of burying my mother—putting her body back into the ground and covering her with the earth, which is the clay from which our bodies are formed. It is an ancient and wise tradition because it is the physical act of knowing ultimate humility. We are reduced to love and humility, despite the pain, in the face of putting the people we have loved and cherished to their humble conclusion. Her eldest son, I was the first to shovel, and I shoveled with strength to work through the grief. Next, my brother, Jeff, in a lot of emotional pain, and the physical pain of his hockey injuries and surgeries. Then Elliot—he had promised my mom to stay on the medication to keep him balanced amidst this debilitating bipolar disease—and he shoveled with anguish. Then Heidi, shoveling and crying. Then my father—he had cried mightily that morning, cried because he would always love her, said that there could never be another one like her, mourned the misery of his mistakes—shoveled with not a lot of strength. Then Sue, shoveling amidst tears; Jonathan, shoveling shyly and sadly.

Then Michael, shoveling with strength, bravely, because he was missing her so much. Then some of my friends that had asked to come, and then some of her clients who flew up from Los Angeles. And then Rabbi Lew shoveled as well.

As we were about to leave, Rabbi Lew took me aside to tell me that, "I think some of the people up there shoveling were getting help." I thought for a moment, then understood his message. He was very much aware of a spirit helping those who were grieving, and he felt very much in touch with the spirit of my mom.

That evening, on Erev Rosh Hashanah 5760, Rabbi Alan Lew delivered Alma's Sermon. And it began thus:

"You never know what's going to happen in this life. Just this past week we had a death in the congregation. Bruce Rosen's mother died in Southern California. Now everyone—every human being who ever came to live on this planet is unique, special—a snow flake—irreproducible and irreplaceable. But Bruce Rosen's mother, Alma Rosen, was a little more special than most. Bruce Rosen's mother was a psychic—a professional psychic. People came from all over the world to consult her and they always came out of these consultations shaking their heads in amazement: How did she know that? How did she manage to say exactly what I needed to hear?" The Rabbi then went on to recount how Alma had saved her father's life the day that she had gone out with him to collect the rent and had the vision of the man with the crowbar. He continued to tell how my mother described that my future wife would find me, and that I couldn't find her. He told how she could see her complexion, the details of her personality and family, and that her name would be "Sue." He described how Bruce had been dating a girl of darker complexion at the time, whose name was Suzanne. "That's not the one" Alma had said. "She is blondish and her name is not Suzanne, but Sue. You haven't met her yet."

He continued to tell about the English women who had discovered in the very young Alma a very special gift, and had taught her to read teacups. He then went on to tell some very profound stories of John Muir, and one in particular went like this:

"John Muir was up at the timberline in the High Sierras, and he noticed a very strange pine forest there. It was a forest of Tuberculata Pine, and there were two things about this forest that were strange. First of all, none of the trees ever let go of their pine cones. The cones sat stuck very high up on the trees, and they never fell off. There wasn't a single pine cone on the entire forest floor. Secondly, all the trees in this forest were exactly the same age—the same height, with the same number of rings in their trunks. If the trees never let go of their pine cones, how did they reproduce? And whoever heard of a forest where all the trees were exactly the same age—the same height, with the same number of rings in their trunks? It was just as absurd as a human civilization where every single person was the same age—just as unlikely, just as impossible.

"And John Muir was up there contemplating all this from a ridge just across from the forest, when suddenly a big summer storm came up, thunder and lightening, which filled the entire horizon. And just at that moment, a bolt of lightening struck one of the Tuberculata pines and the pine caught fire, and pretty soon the whole forest was ablaze, and then, in an instant, John Muir had the answer to his two-fold mystery. As if by the signal of an unforeseen hand, every tree in the forest suddenly dropped its pine cones at exactly the same instant. This was how the Tuberculata pine had learned to survive in the unforgiving climate of the timberline. It had learned to hold onto its pine cones until a fire came and burned it down. And this was why every tree in the forest was the same age, as well.

"Muir was thunderstruck. He sat on the ridge trembling with awe in the face of the Divine Intelligence he had just seen revealed in all this." The inspiration was pouring through the rabbi, and

Alma had given him new insight into the Divine Wisdom, seeing it a new way, of the great naturalist.

Rabbi Lew continued to tell other stories of John Muir, apprehending the man's wisdom in ways he had never quite before known. And then he concluded with the messages from Alma:

"So now I know what it is that Alma, having so recently passed from this world, wants to say to us on this Rosh Hashanah evening, and Alma, you know, means soul, and at this very moment, Alma is all soul, flowing out of the tip of my Mont Blanc pen.

"Sh'ma Minah tarti—Alma wants to tell us three things.

"Alma wants to tell us that we have been given far more than we realize. We think we are up against a sheer rock wall, when we think there's no hope, we think we can't go on any more, but then suddenly some wonderful new strength announces itself, some aspect of being human we never dreamt of, some vision, some reserve of strength, some capacity, some power we never knew we had. And it seems to take being up against a rock face, being absolutely desperate before we come to this new strength; but don't worry, because we all come to that rock face, that absolutely desperate place sooner or later—I wrote this from such a place—so it's important to know this. We are equal to our lives, absolutely equal to it. We are never given more than we can handle, and just when we think we have nothing left, something new comes, something we didn't know about, something wonderful.

"Please remember this the next time you're up against a sheer rock wall. And Alma wants you to know—you will be some day.

"And the second thing Alma wants you to know this Rosh Hashanah is that there is a Divine Intelligence in the world. Einstein was right. The universe is not playing craps. When the forest burns, the pine cones drop. It took an eternity to work that out—an eternity and an eternal consciousness—and that consciousness permeates everything, and when your forest burns, your pine cones will drop. The world is hardwired that way. Here it is Rosh Hashanah, the time of Teshuvah—and the thing you need to make Teshuvah about keeps bumping into you and making you uncomfortable, and it will continue to do so until you get it right. This is the way the world is wired. This is the way it works."

"We read the Torah on Thursday morning while all that lightening was still falling on San Francisco and the thunder was still booming. Parshat Ha'azinu. Ha'azinu Hashamaim vadaberah, tishmah haeretz imreifi.ya'arof camatar lichachi. Give witness heavens, and I will speak, listen earth, to the words of my mouth. My doctrine falls like the dew. My will, my consciousness, is expressed by everything that happens, every drop of dew, every pain on every heart, every dysfunction that calls you to Teshuvah—to wakefulness, every heartbreak which breaks you open until you are new and fresh and alive again. That's the way the world works. Divine Consciousness permeates everything. Ya'arof camatar likachi. My doctrine falls like the dew. The pine cone drops when the forest burns, and not one instant before.

"And Alma wants you to know this, too. Alma wants you to know that the pain you are carrying in your hearts is purposeful pain, and Alma wants you to remember that when your forest starts burning, and Alma wants you to know that your forest will certainly burn some day.

"And this is the last thing Alma wants you to know. You may be amazed that Alma can still talk to you even though she died some time last week, but that's not what you should be amazed at. You should be amazed by the way your body works, by the love in your heart, by the fact that you can hear my voice right now and understand it, derive meaning and feeling from it.

"You should be amazed by the light in this room and the light around the bodies in this room and the light in your mind and the light in your soul.

"Parlor tricks shouldn't amaze you so much. This life you've been given should amaze you more. Miracles are just distractions.

"Thus speaks the miracle Alma:

"Shuvi nafshi limnuchaichi—return my soul to your rest.

"Ki adonai gamal aleichi—because God, the great flow of being, has given gratuitously to me.

"Ki chilatzta nafshi mimavet—because God saves my soul from death every second.

"et eini mi dimah—my eyes from dissolving in tears.

"et ragli mi dechi—my feet from stumbling.

"Please stand up, and pay very careful attention when you do. How did you do that? You don't know how to do that.

"Now please sit down and pay close attention again. You don't know how to do that either.

"Why do we take these miracles for granted? Why do we waste our lives searching for miracles?

"Alma says come off the ledge.

"Let go of your pine cone.

"You've been given everything you need

"And every moment of your life is suffused with the sacred.

"Shannah Tovah Tiketevu."

❐

I look into the approaching midnight, as September 30 is about to bring us to the month of October. I have been saving the newspapers during this past month, putting in a pile the San Francisco Chronicles and Wall Street Journals that I read daily, because the history lesson that is unfolding this month cannot rely on memory. I save the proof that I will pass on to my boys, a conversation that I will have, perhaps, a few years in the future, when they are out of college and begin to understand the commitment that it will take to build financial lives for themselves. They understand money abstractly at this point, I have paid their school bills since childhood, they have known nice vacations with the family over the years. But the wherewithal for all of this did not come easily to me; it required thousands of hours of cold calls in my 20s to acquire clients, the cultivation of almost obsessive attention to detail to retain these clients and attract others, considerable focus on the economic factors so that I could understand and grasp for myself the fundamentals, inform these principles with daily practice, then over time offer the acquired knowledge to my clients.

What I take from the more than 25 years of navigating financial waters is that patience is a remedy for volatility. Our nervous systems need not vibrate with the thunder and lightning; we do not have to become seasick in choppy seas, and like pilots, we can navigate to calmer air above the storm. It is my experience that reason, informed by caution and patience, leads to longevity in the financial world and in our personal lives: longevity of wealth requires a stability of mind that relies on reason to curb the impulse to overreact to fear or the euphoria of irrational exuberance. Many inherited fortunes are lost because the beneficiaries do not understand the mental side of what they own, and wealth is often acquired, even during very difficult times, when people understand that money is a commodity that can multiply, but that obsessing about this multiplication can lead to greed that undermines its very creation.

I want my boys to appreciate that money isn't the only fruit of our labor (they are artists and it is my prayer for them to know the joy of creation throughout their lives), but that it is a measurable one, and that it is necessary for the comforts (home, food, clothing, enjoyment of culture, travel, the arts, bringing a family into this world) of this world. And they will work hard for this, no doubt, and in working hard they will understand the value of money. But I save for them the newspaper articles of September, 2008, so that they will acquire a memory of what collapse looks like on paper, and how dangerous it can be out there if reason is overridden by greed, impulse, stupidity.

I divert my eyes from the blackness of the bay to focus for about the 20th time today on the surrealistic photograph of our Congress at work, on the front page of the San Francisco

Chronicle. The big, black, bold headline reads "Now What?" and above it are the faces of congressional leaders facing the camera after a day and night session, following days of agonizing negotiations to try to arrive at compromise to print enough money to halt the slide into financial collapse and a potential depression. Ben Bernanke, the Chairman of the Federal Reserve and Henry Paulson, Secretary of the Treasury, have been pleading for quick action to provide the liquidity needed to prevent the continued collapse of our major financial institutions, to make available enough money for the most solvent companies to rescue and acquire their competitors, lest the lack of liquidity undermine even the ready cash of money-market instruments, whose short-term maturities are invested in corporate guarantees heretofore considered inviolable.

But we have seen from the events of this month that the sanctity of these money-market funds can no longer be taken for granted; that the notion of "In God We Trust" no longer applies to the abilities of our Federal Reserve and Treasury to prevent financial catastrophe. The grave, sullen, tight, disbelieving (indeed, their expressions surreal) faces of the congressional leaders appearing before the cameras in a long red corridor, say everything that needs to be said: They could not arrive at agreement for a rescue plan, providing the requested $700 billion of freshly printed money that the Fed and Treasury were begging for, to secure financial instruments; they cannot prevent further collapse of financial products as a result of collapsing banks and insurance companies; they cannot forestall the drying up of credit, perhaps the primary reason we had the Great Depression.

The picture has House Speaker Nancy Pelosi on the left, a heavy necklace weighing like an anchor on her neck, cheekbones protruding above a severe grimace; an incredulous Majority Whip James Clyburn, D-SC in the center; and to the right the Majority Leader, Steny Hoyer, D-Md., shoulders practically up to his ears, mouth agape, bags under his tired, watery, disbelieving eyes. And as a result of this failure to act (and there had been optimism that congress could not possibly fail us now), the stock market hit the panic button, declining nearly 800 points today (seven percent), the worst point drop in history. Investors had seized on the bailout package (while it did not address the long-term solutions to revive this crumbling economy) as a signal that the loan problems paralyzing the financial system were finally being addressed. With the failure of this rescue package, the country is left, momentarily, with no roadmap to exit this crisis that has dried up credit amidst raging financial forest fires. The future is now. The unwinding of an economy built on a pyramid of debt—a financial house of cards reaching the rarefied air of senselessness, culminating in financial products backed by mortgages on mortgages on insolvent mortgages—has hit home. It has happened; it is here.

❒

September 30 culminates a month of disbelief. On September 8, the two pillars of the mortgage market, Fannie Mae and Freddy Mac, had to be rescued by the Federal Government. Ousting the CEOs of Fannie Mae and Freddy Mac, the government promised $200 billion of capital to keep afloat these quasi-government agencies that provide up to 75 percent of the funding for new home mortgages. With this move, the U.S. mortgage crisis entered new and unchartered territory, potentially saddling American taxpayers with billions of dollars in losses from home loans made by the private sector. Bush administration officials argued that the cost of doing nothing would be far greater because of the toll on the economy of falling home prices and defaults in the $11 trillion mortgage market. On the same day that the government took over the mortgage giants, one of the nation's largest lending institutions, Washington Mutual, forced out its CEO. The institution's shares have fallen nearly 85 percent in the past year, and its financial position is among the worst of any major U.S. financial institution.

Well do you, don't you want me to make you?
I'm coming down fast but don't let me break you.
Tell me Tell me Tell me the answer.
You may be a lover but you ain't no dancer.
Look out Helter Skelter,
Helter Skelter.
Look out Helter Skelter,
Helter Skelter.
Look out Helter Skelter,
She's coming down fast,
Yes she is!

I don't think there could be better background noise to what was happening to our economic structure than this cacophonous song from the Beatles' "White Album," which depicts a world coming unglued, torn from its moorings, shattered apart, knocked off its axis. "Helter Skelter, Helter Skelter," as the events of mid-September unfolded. The bold headlines of the Wall Street Journal say everything:

"September 15—Crisis on Wall Street as Lehman Totters, Merrill Is Sold, AIG Seeks to Raise Cash."

"September 16—AIG, Lehman Shock Hits World Markets; Focus Moves to Fate of Giant Insurer After U.S. Allows Investment Bank to Fail."

"September 17—U.S. to Take Over AIG in $85 Billion Bailout; Central Banks Inject Cash as Credit Dries Up."

"September 18—Mounting Fears Shake World Markets As Banking Giants Rush to Raise Capital; Morgan Stanley in Talks With Wachovia, Others."

"September 22—Goldman, Morgan Scrap Wall Street Model, Become Banks in Bid to Ride Out Crisis; End of Traditional Investment Banking, as Storied Firms Face Closer Supervision and Stringent New Capital Requirements."

"Helter Skelter, Helter Skelter, Helter Skelter"

I watched this collapse, if not in disbelief, then with astonishment, 150 miles-per-hour hurricane-force winds, a 7.0 economic earthquake, a perfect storm, a massive tidal wave all hitting at once. Where to go? What to do? What is safe? Is it the end of the world as we know it? Into what do we place our faith? Has our government failed, and is too late for a rescue? $700 billion had evaporated from retirement plans, government pension funds, and other investment portfolios. Lehman Bros, an investment bank that predates the Civil War and had weathered the Depression, filed the largest bankruptcy in American history. The fallout from that collapse will be felt severely across the economic landscape, as there were billions of dollars invested in Lehman money-market funds.

No doubt investors will pull money out of Lehman-backed funds, undermining the security of cash deposits all around the world. In response to this, banks agreed to create an emergency fund of $100 billion to protect themselves from the fallout. The Federal Government has also decided to add multiples of billions more, to provide liquidity against falling asset prices and prevent further failure. The sense of gloom deepens as it is clear that the United States has entered a deep, dark recession; and the financial crisis that started over a year ago with the falling of housing prices and the crash in value of mortgage-backed securities has, now, reordered the financial system. Bank of America's deal to buy the teetering Merrill Lynch and its "thundering herd" of 17,000 advisors means that three of the top (Bear Sterns, Merrill, Lehman Brothers) five U.S. investment banks have fallen prey to the subprime crisis within six months.

While the government allowed Lehman to fail, it certainly could not do the same for the massive AIG insurance company. Fearing a financial crisis that might tip the world into irrevocable Depression, the Federal Reserve agreed to an $85-billion bailout of the company, a move that gives the government control of the desperate insurance giant. This move, only two weeks after the Treasury took over Fannie Mae and Freddy Mac, is the most radical intervention in private business in the Central Bank's history. What frightened Fed and Treasury officials was not simply the prospect of a massive corporate bankruptcy, but the chain reaction from its inability to back its insurance guarantees.

AIG is an enormous provider of financial insurance contracts to investors that bought complex debt securities. These required AIG to cover losses suffered by the buyers in the event (now very probable) the securities defaulted. AIG is potentially on the hook for billions of dollars worth of risky securities that were once considered safe. If AIG collapses—and is unable to pay its insurance claims—institutional investors all around the world will be instantly required to mark down the value of those securities, substantially reducing their own capital, indeed the capital and net worth of the entire financial system. This, of course, in much the same way as with Lehman Brothers, would mean that small investors, and anyone who owned money-market funds holding AIG investments, would be hurt—there would simply be no guarantees for the massive losses in these funds (companies just not having the capital to do so). The spillover from a collapse of AIG might be absolutely devastating.

"Helter Skelter, Helter Skelter, Helter Skelter"; it's not music that my mind wants to play, but I just cannot turn off the soundtrack playing in my head. "Helter Skelter, Helter Skelter, Helter Skelter."

During this economic melt down banks and brokerage firms have been desperate to reduce their leverage, but this has been very difficult in an environment where buyers of distressed assets are nowhere to be found, and would-be buyers are holding tight to whatever cash they have, hunkered down in the bomb shelter. And so the desperation to unload assets only increases, further reducing the values of everything in the marketplace, except the safe haven of U.S. Government bonds. Corporations are in trouble, so the prices of even high-grade corporate bonds like General Electric are plummeting.

The Hedge Funds had loaded up on municipal bonds—because they were paying considerably more than government bonds in the last year (very strange since tax-free bonds in normal times should be paying considerably less than taxable securities, the tax benefit going to the investors, the lower interest rate going to the issuers)—but have had to unload them in droves to raise cash to unwind their leverage in the real estate and mortgage markets. Thus, municipal bond prices are plummeting, yields rising, even though overall interest rates are dropping like an anchor.

The weakness in the municipal market is further accelerated by the collapse of the bond insurers, companies that had insured municipal bonds, but had become greedy and put their capital behind the insurance of derivative products secured by ugly, subprime debt. Mutual funds that by prospectus had to hold only AAA-rated, insured bonds have had to dump bonds into the marketplace, because the insurance companies have been downgraded well below AAA ratings, adding tons of new supply to the supply created by the liquidation of the aforementioned hedge funds. And, of course, mortgage-backed securities of all kinds have seen their values drop by 50 percent or more, almost overnight.

And none of this takes into account the daily erosion of the stock market, the latest a 449-point sell-off that brought the Dow to its lowest point in three years, and 23 percent lower than mid-September of last year. And so, against this backdrop, the Federal Reserve, in an attempt to prevent the crisis on Wall Street from bringing down its two premier institutions, took the extraordinary measure of agreeing to convert investment banks Goldman Sachs and Morgan Stanley into traditional bank-holding companies, thus preventing a Lehman-ization (potential bankruptcy) of these two pillars. This move puts the finishing touches to the radical transformation of a Wall Street that was once a coterie of independent brokerage firms that bought and sold securities, advised clients, and were considerably less regulated than traditional banks. Now the two most prestigious institutions on the Street will come under the close supervision of national bank regulators, subjecting them to considerably more oversight and less profitability than they have ever known.

The move will buy Morgan Stanley considerably more time to remain independent, its position rumored to be very fragile, as it sought suitors of equals, apparently the most recent negotiations taking place with my company, Wachovia, which struggles to stay alive. I don't think anyone in the country can fully gauge the severity of this crisis, and the ground beneath our feet feels a long way down.

❒

But life must go on, we must live our lives, and for Sue and me, it means trying to find a way out of this limbo, this torturous place of no gravity, wherein we realize that we love each other more deeply than phrases can utter, but the likelihood of our living together again has diminished to deeply unlikely—it might seem that McCain has a better chance of defeating Obama (and that is becoming very remote as the economic crisis is being tied to Bush-McCain policies, by a clever Obama campaign) than Sue and I of moving back in together.

Sue is in the big house by herself; a large percentage of equity is tied into the place; I can never just go there, unless the kids are in town, and even then it doesn't feel like mine anymore; and it hurts like hell to be in this estranged place. It all feels so complicated, my neck aches, and I'm in pain all the way to the base of my spine, my shoulders tightly pinching the neck, my body always tight. My face hurts, the psyche aches, and how did it all get so complicated? I crave simplicity, and I do my best to shield what is going on in the economy from the quiet I seek in my personal life. And I acquire that quiet often enough, enough to survive—but the pain of the limbo returns and returns. So we must get ourselves out of it, despite the economy. We must make choices; go forward. And we decided to purchase a house for Sue;

we'll look together in the next few weeks, try to take advantage of this paralyzed market. We have enough savings to do this, and then, in this horrible economy, we will put the big Victorian on the market, prepare to get out of there after the inauguration and the Super Bowl. It's a beautiful house; it will sell; there are not a lot of gems around like this. And if we have to take a bit less we'll be okay, because we'll buy for less. I don't know what else to do; life has to take shape; we must go forward again. And when we do sell the house, then I will think of myself, search for my own place, make the move from this apartment where I cannot grow roots. This is the plan; and it remains the plan even though it is now clear as I write this during the first couple of days of October that my company, Wachovia Securities, will not survive.

Wells Fargo appears to have emerged the victor over Citigroup. How bizarre it all is, because, just a few weeks ago it seemed Wachovia—less leveraged than many of the other institutions—had the capital to remain independent. So, it appears, I will be part of Wells Fargo, and Wachovia will be no more. The nice thing about having a clientele that one has built over the years is that I can always move somewhere else if a takeover doesn't work out; I have moved before, and clients have almost unanimously followed. But given what is happening in the economy, is there any safe place to go? Wells is a good name; and it would be my hope that this acquisition will finally put an end to all the rumors surrounding my firm, the paranoid calls from some, very few, but still some, removing their money—clients asking if my company is going to survive.

Yes, against this backdrop, Sue and I will go forward with our lives. There is no roadmap, and in this storm, I can only see several feet ahead, even with headlights set to their brightest. I pray that all will be well.

❒

The first of the three presidential debates occurred a couple of days ago, amidst an economy in collapse, a stock market in free fall wiping out billions in net worth and retirement savings, and a government seemingly incapable of acting for the greater good beyond partisan bickering over special interests. I was put off by McCain's snarl, his unwillingness to show Obama the respect of an equal as evidenced by his tendency to refuse to look at him, and when he did, to frown derisively. The body language of McCain suggested to me that he felt his opponent was not sufficiently qualified, significantly inferior to himself, a man who had served his country as a hero in war, and a political leader in government for most of his life. The picture on the front page of the San Francisco Chronicle captures the handshake moment at the end of the debate very well: Obama turning to McCain, pressing hand against forearm, McCain's face turned away, a tight, unfriendly grin above a clenched jaw. The debate, itself, though was disappointing to me: It was a highly programmed affair, heavily rehearsed by the combatants, taking place in a world far removed from the crisis. It was a stage play divorced from the enormous urgency on the ground, and there was no sense of the electrical charge that underlies these tumultuous days. It was a debate originally scheduled to be on foreign policy, but because of the state of affairs there was a focus on the economy. But how disconcerting it was to listen to the candidates' answers for these troubled times. McCain's response to the question about whether he planned to vote for a rescue plan taking place in congress was, "I hope so"; no further elaboration. Obama's answer to the same question was a cool, aloof, "I do think there is constructive work being done." McCain hammered away at how he would control "earmarks," saying, "I've got a pen, and I'm going to veto every single spending bill that comes across my desk containing earmarks."

Obama shot painful darts, tying McCain to the failed policies of the Bush administration, noting that McCain voted with the President 90 percent of the time. "To stand here after eight years and say that you're going to lead an administration offering change and reform, I think is kind of hard to swallow." Both men talked of the greed of Wall Street, an easy scapegoat during these harsh times, and hammered home the idea—each blaming the Bush administration—that lack of regulation and failure of oversight was responsible for the troubles. But again, if we're going to have a discussion on the economy, let us listen to an intelligent exchange on the importance of the bailout that is stalled in congress, the liquidity essential to oxygenate the blood of an economy gasping for air. The longer the delay, the further the damage. Let us hear constructive questions and answers about where this money goes—pro and con—and steps that might be taken down the road to allow us to exit the enormous piling up of debt.

Each candidate tried to defend his positions on Iraq, McCain pounding away that his support of the surge of forces in Iraq was a successful strategy, one opposed by Obama, suggesting that Obama was ignorant of the difference between a "tactic and a strategy." Obama countered that, "Over the last eight years, this administration and Senator McCain have been solely focused on Iraq. In the meantime we have weakened our capacity to project power around the world." The play was well rehearsed, and provided some profound moments of drama and story; but, again, it was so, virtually, separate from the frantic moments of the day as to be essentially meaningless. In the end the press reported that polls showed Obama to be the victor by a wide margin, and I would concur. People say the race is close, but it sure doesn't feel that way to me.

❒

It is October 9, the birthday of my brother, Elliot. Perhaps my mother knows from the place where her soul lives that her wish that Elliot be stable—that he remain on the medicine that shields him from the mania, wherein voices would haunt his thoughts, lead him to the brilliant but insane scribbles on the walls of bedrooms, and the severe lows of the crash, causing sadness, anger, depression—is continuing to be realized. Those horrible occasions when the Pet teams would have to enter the house, my agonizing mother who so loves her children watching powerlessly, and remove my brother, bringing him to hospital confinement until he might be stabilized, have not occurred in the years that she has been gone. I continue to pay the rent for both brothers, Jeff and Elliot, as they live together in the desert of Kingman, Arizona. Jeff remains close to the hospitals that can monitor his pain, his body almost crippled from the dozens of surgeries—perhaps needed, maybe not—after his years of being a hockey goalie. And on Elliot's birthday today, I contacted the manager of the supermarket in town, gave him my credit card number, as he agreed to allow the boys to come to the store and purchase as much food as their refrigerator can hold. Jeff cooked a big steak dinner, and baked a cake. It was a good birthday for Elliot today.

It is also the birthday of John Lennon, and had he lived he'd be 68 today. The nature of these days has made it difficult for me to sleep well—goodness, I haven't had more than one or two decent night's sleep in weeks. And, so, in honor of John's birthday I woke up this morning from another fitful sleep and put on one of my favorites. It is a rumination on the joys of being groggy from a good nights sleep, and as he sings it in that plaintive way, I can envision his body rocking forward and back in rhythm, the intonation deep and Liverpudlian, the tone wry and ironic:

When I wake up early in the morning,
Lift my head, I'm still yawning.
When I'm in the middle of a dream,
Stay in bed, float upstream.

Please don't wake
me, no,
Don't shake me,
Leave me where I am,
I'm only sleeping.

Happy Birthday Elliot, and Happy Birthday John Lennon.

❐

What can one say? The economy continues to unravel, and there will be a bottom at some point. Yesterday the stock market fell 679 points. Over the past seven days the market has fallen more than 20 percent, and that is a crash. Everything has the feeling of happening in slow motion to me, though it is occurring at breakneck speed. All of this is happening despite the fact that congress finally passed a few days ago a $700-billion rescue package. The markets domestic and global are demonstrating a massive show of no confidence that this rescue will succeed as implemented, European stocks showing over the past few days their most substantial drop in more than 20 years. The relentless sell-off is based on fears that this is just not enough money to prevent more massive banking failures, and that even double that amount of money wouldn't be sufficient. Nobody really knows which major banks might fail—and the economy appears so perilous that fear is the "new rationality."

In my own backyard, the takeover of Wachovia is now fully decided. Wells Fargo and Co. is the victor, agreeing to pay about $15 billion for the combined bank and brokerage arm—a fraction of what the company had been worth barely more than a year ago and hardly more than Wachovia had paid for the mortgage lender, World Savings, a couple of years ago. Hopefully, now, I will stop hearing from clients thinking about pulling their money out of my company—fortunately almost all of my clients have hung in there, but the going has been treacherous. The name Wells Fargo is synonymous with stability, and I'm pleased that this is the suitor that prevailed. The government and stockholders should be as well. The government would have to absorb billions of dollars of losses to merge the bank with Citigroup, and the transaction would have wiped out the stockholders. The Wells transaction is for $7 a share, and very little in the way of government dollars or guarantees. I am glad this acquisition talk is over and that I know the company for which I will be working.

❒

Last night was the second debate for the presidency. McCain was much more civil this time around, and appeared less stiff. He walked around the stage as he took questions, perhaps allowing him to feel more folksy and release some of that pent up energy. If he were a boxer, it would be the move-around-the-ring-and-jab style, every once in a while stopping to throw a hard shot. Obama remained contained, confident, a fully defended boxer holding his ground, deflecting shots. Since the last debate, Obama has gained up to 10 percentage points in the polls, taking a commanding lead. He is leading now in all of the swing states of Ohio, Florida, Illinois, Indiana and Pennsylvania, even moving ahead in conservative Virginia. McCain needed, if not a knockout in this debate, then a clean victory, and one was not achieved. He unveiled an interesting plan of providing an additional $300 billion to help out individual mortgage holders to stabilize the real estate markets in the country. I found the plan interesting for sure; Obama sought to share the initiative, arguing that the $700 billion bailout included this provision, and that he had recommended similar funds for distressed homebuyers a month ago. McCain hammered that Obama would raise taxes at the worst possible time, and Obama continued to tie the failure of this economy to the lack of regulation during the Bush-McCain era.

It is quite humorous how it has become the Bush-McCain era, and, frankly, I just can't see a Republican winning in this shadow. The more the economy remains the major story, and it becomes bigger and bigger every day, the harder it will be for McCain to dwell on foreign policy. Hitting him on his strength, Obama landed a heavy blow to McCain's body during the debate: "It's true," he said, "there are some things I don't understand. I don't understand how we ended up invading a country that had nothing to do with 9/11, while failing to capture Osama Bin Laden" The debate was good theater, as these debates always are, and the contrast between the two men was amusing. But, again, it seemed a charade, light years removed from the real world. How many homes might have been spared from the hundreds of millions of dollars spent on this "cotton candy"?

Its very late and I have to go to work tomorrow. I'd like to sleep in; I'd love a good night's sleep. I put the Beatles song back on, sung by Lennon. I have a craving for it and have to hear it one more time; maybe John will sing me to sleep:

Please don't spoil my day,
I'm miles away.
And after all,
I'm only sleeping.

❐

Although John McCain's poll numbers are sinking substantially—some polls giving Obama a double-digit lead among likely voters—his ratings are rising on the Comedy programs. The statistics show that through mid-October the Republicans were the target of 475 jokes by Letterman and Leno alone, while the Democratic team was the victim only 69 times. That is nearly a 7-1 ratio. And according to Robert Lichter, a George Mason University professor and head of the Center for Media and Public Affairs, in no other campaign over the past 20 years has one party's ticket been jabbed more than the other by even a two-to-one ratio. A sampling of the comedy:

Letterman: "John McCain said he's going to win the third presidential debate. Of course, he also told Custer the surge was working." Extremely funny stuff. And equally funny is this from Leno:

"According to a recent poll, 61 percent of people surveyed said they'd rather see Sarah Palin in a bikini than Pamela Anderson. Although 99 percent said they'd rather see Pamela Anderson as vice president."

The jokes about the Obama campaign are far fewer than those about the McCain camp, and also much more tame. Perhaps because Obama is black, comedians tend to veer away from anything that can be taken as racist. Such is the case with this Craig Ferguson joke:

"In an interview, Barack Obama forgot which wedding anniversary he celebrates this year. Michelle Obama just changed their slogan to, 'Yes you can; sleep on the couch.' "

But contrast this to the biting quip from the same comedian about McCain:

"At this point, it's a race to see what drops faster—the stock market or John McCain's poll numbers." Is the humor about John McCain increasing due to his falling poll numbers? Or are his poll numbers sinking because of the humor? Clearly, the body language of McCain doesn't help his cause—its seems hard for him to remove that scowl, and his posture is such that he seems ready to fight, fight, fight—as compared to Obama's self-contained elegance. And Palin's attack-dog style is clearly backfiring; she offers few answers during these harsh times, but instead focuses on the scare tactic of "Obama palling around with terrorists." No doubt people in these troubled times are getting very "turned off" to these Dick Cheney–style tactics. And it certainly doesn't help her with the comics when she lists her foreign policy experience as including that, in Alaska she "can see Russia" from her backyard. The truth as I see it is that the McCain-Palin combo makes for a very comedy-friendly tandem. And though Palin is charismatic and attractive—hey, I've had a few fantasies about her, I must admit—she just isn't ready to take over for a would-be President McCain, who seems to be aging before our eyes on the campaign trail. She has a folksy quality to her, and she does say some things that conservatives want to hear about abortion, guns, and so on, but to me, there is a cartoonish quality to her—and I'm just amazed that she is on a ticket for president, given some of the names that were available. This is not to say, though, that Joe Biden is immune from great comedy—I've never seen a prime-time candidate put his foot in his mouth as often as he does—and it's surprising there isn't far more comedy about him. But the man—despite his propensity to embarrass Obama from time to time—has some public policy gravitas, which just doesn't apply to Sarah. In any event, in just a few short weeks, the decision will be rendered; and I hope we still have an economy by then.

The Panic of 2008—historians will be writing of this time for decades to come—continues to burn out of control, thick clouds of black smoke blocking the sun. The fires, which started in the United States in the form of manufactured investment products backed by insanely overvalued real estate, often owned by borrowers with credit so poor that they shouldn't have been able to qualify for credit cards—let alone being able to purchase homes with virtually nothing in down payment—has spread all over the world. Much of the world's banking system bought into Wall Street's investment creations with "blind faith," but it now gasps for air as the toxic smoke from these fires renders breathing difficult. These complex, higher-yielding investment delicacies contained the seeds of a virus that now spreads as a virulent economic disease.

It is a beautiful, blue-sky, Indian summer San Francisco day as I write this on Saturday, October 11. The bay looks Mediterranean, calm, barely a ripple, as I look out from this window seat at my desk. We wait all year for this weather in San Francisco, and it is here at last. The red of the Golden Gate Bridge looks elemental, like metal mined from the earth, as it rises above this bay, a passenger ship (my binoculars bring into clear focus the travelers on the decks, enjoying this fantastic sight of the glistening city of hills, colorful architecture hugging the hillsides) moving peacefully inland, almost as gently as the sail boats in its midst. I drift in the calm of this moment, thinking that I should be on a ferry over to Sausalito or Tiburon about now; that I should be out there on the water. It is not often that I write during the day, but I do so today, for whatever reason. There is an urgency that I feel, and there is an urge to express; but it is not so urgent that I do not realize in the moment that I live in the "greatest city on earth."

❒

Yesterday, it was announced by Treasury Secretary Paulson that for the first time since the Great Depression the United States will invest directly in banks to prevent a total collapse of the global banking system. This move will be done in concert with the G-7 ministers, because no amount of direct investment would be sufficient if the panic caused global banks to withdraw substantial sums from the United States. "The current situation calls for urgent and exceptional action," said the G-7 ministers, which include Japan, Germany, Britain, France, Italy and Canada. This direct investment has become necessary because it is now clear that the $700 billion bailout passed by congress last week is insufficient to unclog the arteries of credit that threaten to strangle the economy. It has become so bad that even the biggest banks will not loan to one another overnight, given the possibilities of failure. This direct investment in the banks of the developed world would insure all deposits and use all "available tools to support systemically important financial institutions and prevent their failure," according to the communiqué. It is one of the great ironies of this crisis that the developing world—Brazil, China, India, and other countries once considered non-industrial or second tier—might be asked to organize a "bailout fund," given that they are flush with cash, and have far less debt than the mature economies.

These times are strange—unusual, unpredictable and strange. But on the promenade along the bay there is no such thing as a collapsing economy, just the sweet, salt of the air, the sunshine as it glistens against the water on this pristine day; and that is where I am going when I turn this computer off in 30 seconds.

❐

I watched the third and final debate tonight, then went out with Sue to take a drive by the very cute, charming, two-story yellow house, a sweet, large, white porch reminiscent of the homes in the Deep South, that we have agreed to try to purchase. She had been looking at homes for about the last month, but just this past Sunday saw this very special one. I went to see it with her, and right away I understood that there was a simpatico between her peaceful calm and the quiet, delicate, welcoming energy of this home. It is located in the inner avenues of the Richmond district. It is a short walk to two synagogues, and Clement, the street that truly represents the diversity of San Francisco: cozy cafes and bookstores, delicious Italian food, the best Chinese, Vietnamese, Thai, Burmese restaurants in the city. People don't realize what this section of Clement street has to offer; I had always liked this area, but I never fully appreciated its diversity until walking up and down the street a few times before we decided to put in the offer for Sue. I loved it; it doesn't have the pretense of Pacific Heights, though I settle in Pacific Heights because I am often hypnotized by the fantasy of the Victorian masterpieces and the views that captivate me on my walks. It is certainly not cheap to buy a home in the inner Richmond District—homes that go for well over $1million cannot easily be defined as working-class residences—but the area has a feeling of ordinary folk, a melting pot of students, an increasing Russian population, a significant number of Chinese walking the neighborhood streets, from the teens to the elderly, and a lot of middle-class white families, the driveways showing more in the way of average American cars than the status quo Mercedes in the Heights. I try not to generalize, but it is certainly the case that this area in which Sue will live feels a lot more friendly and eclectic than the Pacific Heights street from which she will be moving.

The home would have been about 15 percent higher in price if it had come on the market a year ago; but still it is very difficult to figure out its worth in an economy like this, when the stock market plunges almost daily. Perhaps it helped the seller's motivation a bit that the stock market fell 733 points on the day they accepted our offer. Again, though, I am concerned that the real estate market will continue to fall, perhaps less precipitously in San Francisco than the rest of the state. The purchase though, is an action based on faith: faith that Sue must be settled and grow roots in a place that is right for her, a home that she loves. The sale of our home after the purchase of this one for Sue, will give me liquidity to eventually find something for myself. But that is a good bit off; we must begin the process of selling our home, polishing it within and without so that it glistens like the Victorian emerald that it is. Homes like this do not come on the market very often, certainly not in this neighborhood, and I have faith that it will sell, and that there will be a buyer whose fate it is to own this home. It is the time to move on with our lives, and we'll put it on the market after the inauguration, perhaps after the Super Bowl. But, oh my goodness, how bad it is out there! And I can't stop myself from asking, "What the heck are you doing, buying a home in this economy, without first selling yours? For such a prudent person you are acting absolutely crazy!" But what are we to do? Wait years? Live with paralysis? Forward we must go, and I do this with faith. The state of limbo overwhelms me. As much as I love Sue—

and I do ever so deeply—the barrier remains. Why this barrier? I've asked the question dozens of times, reflected on it repeatedly in these pages. I just do not know. I just do not know.

❒

The home for Sue is lovely. It has a similar layout to the one that we will sell. The moldings lend a grace, and the flow of energy (chi, the Chinese call it) seems soft and uninterrupted. The back yard is deep, beautiful green grass, landscaped with blossoming flowers everywhere. There is a serenity to it, a graciousness that is conducive to quiet and meditation. I loved the place for Sue; it is she; it is for her. How could we not go for it? And so what does this mean? I don't see myself living there; it is for Sue. I suppose this is the step that truly separates us, and sends us off to live separate lives. We must always be friends, the warmth of our friendship is so evident in the way we looked at this home together, cooperated on the purchase, enjoyed the moment of its purchase. It is very strange though, to be buying a house with Sue, loving the place, but loving it for her! I would love to sit in that zen-like backyard anytime I like, but that won't happen. I'll visit the backyard when I'm invited. It is for Sue, and this feels so odd. We get close in the moment of this special event, but then I go back to my apartment, knowing that the separation is inevitably permanent. The moment contains joy and sadness—and I can't seem to shake the sadness. No doubt, the move will not be easy for Sue, all of that stuff to get rid of, all of that furniture to move! And the pain of going through the dozens of photo albums, pictures of our lives together. How will she handle the salt of those memories on the open wounds of this move? It will not be easy. But at the end, she will have her peace; the home is smaller, cozier than the other one, and she will make it hers. The plan is to be in by mid-November, and the boys will be home for Thanksgiving. We'll have Thanksgiving in Sue's new home. I look forward to that.

We had a glass of wine tonight on Clement street, after driving by the house. Relieved that we had come to terms on the new house, we talked about the third debate. McCain needed a knockout—he is way down in the polls—but could only deliver glancing blows. McCain launched a renewed call for Obama to detail his relationships with former '60s radical Bill Ayers, and the controversial ACORN voter registration drives, saying that, "Americans need to know the extent of those links." But Obama calmly deflected McCain's jabs, offering, "The fact that this has become such an important part of your campaign, Senator McCain, says more about your campaign that it says about me. Both candidates aimed to seize the mantle of change—Obama continuing to link McCain to the legacy of Bush, and McCain painting Obama as an out-of-step liberal, not knowledgeable about foreign policy, and one who would increase taxes and spending. "Senator Obama, I am not President Bush," McCain snapped, "if you wanted to run against President Bush, you should have run four years ago." Obama's response: "If I've occasionally mistaken your policies for George Bush's policies, it's because on the core economic issues that matter to the American people—on tax policy, on energy policy, on spending priorities, you have been a vigorous supporter of President Bush."

It was the best debate of the three; McCain appeared sharper than in the past, and very much on the attack. However, Obama also was at his best, deflecting the blows, gracefully jabbing and moving like Ali, and in the end he wasn't touched. The reviews of the debate show Obama widening his lead, now into double digits.

❒

Indian summer in San Francisco follows the clock almost to perfection. About a week before September, usually around the 24th or 25th of August, the thick layer of morning and evening fog peels off, pulls back, and the city becomes awash in sunshine, the temperatures often reaching the 90s for several days at a time all the way into late October. But somewhere around the 27th or 28th of October every single year (there are exceptions of course to the beginning and ending dates, but it is almost without exception that these are the dates in my 30 years of living in the city) autumn kicks in, and the days become chilly. It isn't the foggy chill of summer, but more of a bone-chilling feeling—especially at night—as the light becomes refracted and the days grow shorter. Very often Halloween night is quite cold, when just a week or two earlier the evening might have been considerably warmer.

It is Tuesday, November 4, and the phone rings at about 8:30 in the morning. I wake up, groggy, run to get it as it reaches the last ring before it goes to voicemail—it takes seven rings to get to voice mail, and I pick up the phone just at the onset of number 7—and it Sue on the other end, her voice tinged with emotion. I hear her voice as I look out at the overcast that has settled in over the grayish, autumn bay. "I just voted," she says, her voice quivering with emotion, the voice signaling eyes of tears. "I was just overcome with such a powerful, strong feeling that this is such an historical time, that we are voting at a time of great change. I just started crying and couldn't stop when I saw Barack Obama's name on the ballot," she continued. "I don't know what's wrong with me, but I couldn't hold back the emotion," she went on. "Yes, this is an astounding time, a monumental time in the history of this nation," I answered. "It's been a long eight years, but Bush will finally go away," I continued. "I think of the words of Martin Luther King, before he was killed, those prophetic words that, 'I've been to the mountaintop and I've seen the Promised Land.' Remember how he said, 'I might not get there with you, but I've seen the Promised Land'? A lot of kids growing up today do not see 'color,' and don't quite appreciate how amazing it is that a man of color will likely win the presidency; but, God, it is astounding to me that this is happening. It is beautiful, and if he wins, it will show the world that America is a place where democracy is truly possible, a place where real change can occur, and that we are capable of taking back control of our government, our fate as a nation, and casting it in a different direction, that we are capable of breaking through and trying something different. That we are not just the nation of George Bush, Dick Cheney, Iraq, unmitigated power, and that the world doesn't matter as long as we get what we want. It is amazing Sue." I had been groggy a second before, but her voice triggered emotion and adrenalin in me. I was now wide awake. "I've spoken to Michael and Jonathan this morning," she followed, "and this is the first election in their lifetimes that really matter to them—they are so excited, their campuses are really into the election. Both of them have voted already. Well, I've got to get going to work, and I had to share this feeling that I have. When are you going to vote?" "I'll vote on the way to work this morning. I'm going in late. Trying to get a little extra sleep; I just haven't been sleeping too well." "Well, take care of yourself," she offered. "I will; I'll check in with you this evening, especially if Obama wins." "I may not be home," she answered, "I'll be at the home of some friends, watching the election results. I'll probably be home pretty late; we're hoping it will be a party." "I'm just gonna stay home and watch the returns come in, but if it goes well I'm sure we'll have a chance to share the moment." "Yeah, I'm sure we will; I've got to get off to work now, so take care," she answered. "Okay," I responded, "I've got to get going now, as well."

Hanging up, I felt that painful void in my stomach and chest; I often feel this way after speaking with Sue, because we were kids when we met, we've shared so much in our lives together; life goes on, but not together. And it would be nice to experience this historical time with family, not alone. I would invite Gwen over, our friendship continues to deepen; but she is so anti-Obama that I don't think it would be fun. She's a Libertarian, and lost interest in the election when her darling, Ron Paul, was no longer involved. I try to impart to her the great historical import of this time, but she isn't moved. And so, I will enjoy it more by myself tonight. God, it would be great to have the boys here tonight—their colleges feel so damn far away today!

I have pizza delivered from my favorite place in the city—Tommasso's, and I've asked for extra tomato sauce—and it arrives at about the time Barack Obama is being projected as the next president of the United States! Sue calls with a lot of party noise in the background; she was so excited, and couldn't contain herself. She was exuberant, her voice clearly revealing tears of joy. Then Michael calls from Oberlin. He doesn't have a lot of time to talk, but just wants to let me know his school is going crazy, parties are breaking out everywhere. "Dad, I love you; let's talk all about this soon!" "We will, Michael; this is such an amazing time in history, there is so much to say" Then Jonathan calls from Bard College in New York, and he wants to spend a little bit of time on the phone talking about the significance of the election. "Dad, do you think he will be a great president? Do you think he'll get us out of Iraq? Do you think he can get everyone healthcare; will your sister, Heidi, finally be able to get healthcare one day soon?" Jonathan is a film major, and he tells me that he is filming the joy that is breaking out everywhere on his campus; he understands how special this moment is, he is overwhelmed by feelings of hope, and is proud of America tonight, proud that it would take a chance on a new direction with a black man. He is proud of his generation for getting so involved and making a difference.

"Yes, Jonathan, there is great potential for Obama to be a great president. Great presidents are born of great challenges. I can't think of another president-elect who has faced so many difficulties. The country will be looking for success quickly, and given the problems in this country, success will not come quickly. And if we do not get a turnaround within a year or so, he'll start to be blamed for the problems. That is how politics works. You get a bit of a honeymoon, then you have to deliver. Right now people see Barack Obama as having an answer to their problems, or they are at least extremely hopeful that he will change the direction, offer leadership the world will respect, set in motion new events that will get this country on the right track. There is a huge void in the lives of millions of people right now, and there is the tendency to see a person as a savior. But he cannot be a savior, and it will be dangerous if he tries to be one. He should enjoy this great victory, but discourage cult worship. Because, just as people may see you as the "savior" or "answer," they can turn on you just as quickly if you do not deliver. Yes, I do think he'll get us out of Iraq, but then we have Afghanistan. Will we get involved there? I do think, given his enormous popularity, he'll be successful getting healthcare for everyone, and God willing, someone like Heidi—who tries so hard to find work and has these constant health issues—will finally be protected by a safety net." "Dad, I really have to go now—there's a lot going on here, and I'm going to join some of the parties. But thanks for sharing your ideas and let's talk a lot more soon. I love you." "I love you too, Jonathan; have some real fun tonight."

And with that I went back to the pizza, opened up a Coke, and listened intently to the solemn words of John McCain's concession speech. Though the loss had been expected in the final couple of weeks, there is always the campaign hope that the final poll of the voters themselves would prove differently, and that the country would in the end turn away from the untested political novice and elect the war hero, the sturdy political warhorse, John McCain. It was not to be, and there was sadness on all of the faces. Some started to shout over the gracious McCain as he sought to give credit and due respect to the man who had defeated him to become president. McCain, gently admonishing the hecklers, spoke from the heart:

"Thank you. Thank you, my friends. Thank you for coming here on this beautiful Arizona evening.

"My friends, we have—we have come to the end of a long journey. The American people have spoken, and they have spoken clearly. A little while ago, I had the honor of calling Senator Barack Obama to congratulate him, to congratulate him on being elected the next president of the country that we both love.

"In a contest as long and difficult as this campaign has been, his success alone commands my respect for his ability and perseverance. But that he managed to do so by inspiring the hopes of so many millions of Americans who had once wrongly believed that they had little at stake or little influence in the election of an American president is something I deeply admire and commend him for achieving.

"This is an historic election, and I recognize the special significance it has for African Americans and for the special pride that must be theirs tonight.

"A century ago, President Theodore Roosevelt's invitation of Booker T. Washington to visit—to dine at the White House—was taken as an outrage in many quarters. America today is a world away from the cruel and prideful bigotry of that time. There is no better evidence of this than the election of an African American to the presidency of the United States.

"Senator Obama has achieved a great thing for himself and for his country. I applaud him for it, and offer him my sincere sympathy that his beloved grandmother did not live to see this day, though our faith assures us she is at rest in the presence of her Creator and so very proud of the good man she helped raise.

"I am so deeply grateful to all of you for the great honor of your support and for all you have done for me. I wish the outcome had been different, my friends. The road was a difficult one from the outset. But your support and friendship never wavered. I cannot adequately express how deeply indebted I am to you."

In this concession I saw a greatness in the man, a momentary appreciation of a heroic, graceful American hero and fighter. I had certainly not seen anything of this sort in the angry body language of the debates or the nasty insinuations during the campaign—but in the moment I felt the greatness of the man and this country. My eyes were filled with water as Mr. McCain concluded his words. A few moments later, the water turned to tears as President-elect Obama addressed a massive crowd filled with incredible joy in Chicago's Grant Park.

There was a glow, a radiance, elegance, to the man as he appeared on the platform before the crowd, the nation, the world. The aura had elements of a victorious Muhammad Ali, though there was not the puffiness of a physical battle; the expression of joy seemed to emanate from a source deep within and conveyed the kind of charisma, charm and magnetism of the great champion. His face had the exuberance of a Michael Jordan pulling off an incredible acrobatic basket to win a championship. The oratory, it was spellbinding; I don't think I've heard a political leader speak in such an effecting way since the days of JFK and RFK.

His voice had the solemnity of Martin Luther King, sober and incredibly soulful and hopeful. The memory of watching Dr. King deliver his speeches and interviews—though he was a free man, he would never feel free as long as his people were enslaved—and now a black man ascending the throne of president of the United States was startling, dreamlike, surreal, fantastical in its reality.

Dr. King, often facing enormous hostility, forever walked assuredly, proudly, with dignity, never hunched by oppression. I thought of this as I watch the president-elect deliver his words proudly, assuredly, his gait purposeful and elegant, the inheritance of Dr. King. His expression revealed a sense that really this had to feel absolutely amazing to him—a reality but a dream. The look in his eyes told the story that such things are only possible in this great, great country of ours. Indeed, the tears rolled down my cheeks—perhaps out of recognition of the irony and enormity of the moment, the feeling of history unfolding, a feeling of hope and optimism that infused the oxygen—as the man began to speak:

"If there is anyone out there who still doubts that America is a place where all things are possible; who still wonders if the dream of our founders is alive in our time; who still questions the power of our democracy, tonight is your answer.

"It's the answer told by lines that stretched around schools and churches in numbers this nation has never seen; by people who waited three hours and four hours, many for the very first time in their lives, because they believed that this time must be different; that their voice could be that difference.

"It's the answer spoken by young and old, rich and poor, Democrat and Republican, black, white, Latino, Asian, Native American, gay, straight, disabled and not disabled—Americans who sent a message to the world that we have never been a collection of red states and blue states; we are, and always will be, the United States of America. It's the answer that led those—who have been told for so long by so many to be cynical, and fearful, and doubtful of what we can achieve—to put their hands on the arc of history and bend it once more toward the hope of a better day.

"It's been a long time coming, but tonight, because of what we did on this day, in this election, at this defining moment, change has come to America.

"The road ahead will be long. Our climb will be steep. We may not get there in one year, or even one term, but, America—I have never been more hopeful than I am tonight that we will get there. I promise you: We as a people will get there.

"America, we have come so far. We have seen so much. But there is so much more to do. So tonight, let us ask ourselves: If our children should live to see the next century; if my daughters should be so lucky to live as long as Ann Nixon Cooper, what change will they see? What progress will we have made?

"This is our chance to answer that call. This is our moment. This is our time—to put our people back to work and open doors of opportunity for our kids. To restore prosperity and promote the cause of peace; to reclaim the American Dream and reaffirm that fundamental truth that out of many, we are one; that while we breathe, we hope, and where we are met with cynicism, and doubt, and those who tell us that we can't, we will respond with that timeless creed that sums up the spirit of a people: 'Yes we can.' "

It takes 270 electoral votes to win the presidency. It appears that Obama will win 365 votes. It seems clear that he will win 51 percent of the popular vote, the first time since President Johnson in 1964 that a Democratic has won the majority of votes cast. Bolstered by a tidal wave of young, African American and independent voters, Obama has been declared the victor in virtually all of the battleground states. He wins in Florida and Ohio, highly contested states that went to Bush in 2004. He wins in Iowa, Colorado, New Mexico and Nevada. And he wins in Virginia, which hasn't backed a Democratic presidential candidate since 1964. The only battleground states won by McCain were Georgia and Arizona, his home state, which suddenly became "in play" in the last couple of weeks of the campaign. The victory is overwhelming and decisive. But is it a mandate for new liberal leadership, in much the same way that the Reagan revolution swept away Jimmy Carter and ushered in an era of conservative thinking and leadership? I suppose the answer to that will be discovered as the new president endeavors to provide universal health coverage; pull us out of Iraq; makes decisions about whether we become and how deeply we get embroiled in Afghanistan; figures out how to prevent the collapse of, and eventually stimulates, the economy; deals with the ongoing threat of terrorism; decides whether we can possibly raise taxes during an economic collapse, and so much more. Will he be remembered as the president who oversaw a depression, or prevented one? While the country recognizes that the president-elect inherits problems beyond belief, he will eventually be blamed for not fixing the problems if he is not successful. Charm, magnetism, cult of personality, mantras of "hope" and "yes we can" will only go so far if he cannot obtain the cooperation he needs to implement the change he seeks. And, are we looking at change for the "sake of change" or the kind of change that history will judge to be absolutely necessary for our time? We will come to learn all of this in good time. We will discover soon enough whether this decisive election result represents a national tilt toward liberalism or a strong vote against one of the most unpopular presidents of all time, George W. Bush. After speaking with Sue this morning, I went out to vote, and on my way down Broadway Street to the polling station, I read on the frame of a license plate the words, "New Era." It wasn't an advertisement for anything in particular; perhaps it was the name of the dealership where the car was purchased. I do not know. But the words struck me in the moment as a message of our time. Indeed, it is a new era, and as I write this late in the evening of Obama's election night, I am deeply moved by the moment, the new era into which we journey, and the prospects for the tangible effects of hope: for the nation and in my own life.

The Journey to Tibet

When we remember who we were, we become more fully who we are. And in the moment of our memory, we hear our voice as it has traveled through time, affected by the places of the journey, and the echoes of those we have loved, perhaps feared, run toward, run away from, have cherished, forgiven, or have tried to forget. In the tone and timbre of my voice there is the 10-year-old boy enraptured by baseball, worshipping Sandy Koufax, desperately wanting my dad to take me to see him pitch, and he never would. My voice of today reflects the voice in the letter that I sent to Sandy Koufax, which was never answered. In the letter I said how much the man meant to me, that he could be so great and Jewish touched me deeply, and that he seemed humble and not boastful (and I valued this as deeply as a 10 year old, as I do today), thoughtful and heroic. I told him that I wished that I could have a dad like him, because my own dad never seemed to want to love me. And I didn't say this because I didn't love my own dad (I so desperately wanted to love him and be loved back) but because my dad seemed forever angry, unwilling or unable to take me in his arms and let me know that all was good, that I was his boy. And, indeed, the tone and timbre of my voice today includes the disappointment that my dad finally promised to take me to see Sandy pitch, but when the moment arrived he had a friend do it. I suppose, also, that the disappointment never quite went away that Sandy never answered my letter, though maturity convinces me that he received thousands of letters and that mine was a "needle in a haystack."

In the tone and timbre of my voice there no doubt resides the stunned anguish and pain of the 11-year-old boy—just after arriving at our new home in Montreal from California—who had been promised by my dad that he would be home in time to take me to see Montreal's professional team, the Allouettes, practice. He came home very late, the practice over, and when I approached him with some anger and disappointment, he smashed my mouth with the back of his hand, blood dripping on my clothes, splattering against the walls. My mom said at that moment that she would never forgive him for that, and that in her mind she was finished with him. Her words are part of the tone and timbre of my voice today, how could they not be? I have long ago forgiven this, but I will never forget. And because I can never forget (the memory is part of my cellular structure, as my good friend Gwen Jones would say), it is the raw material of the tone and timbre of my voice.

I try to quiet the pure horror, the speechless horror, that I felt when, at the age of 12, I lay next to my mom in bed when pure evil stared down in the form of the man attacking her. Just a couple of weeks earlier she'd had a pre-cancerous gland removed from her throat, the scar fresh and raw. My father had taken that job in Campbellton, New Brunswick, and we had remained in Montreal for the time being. The evil in the attacker's eyes, the wickedness of his face, the sound of his palm hitting her across the cheek as she screamed—and as I screamed, fighting through the speechlessness of pure fright—will never be forgotten. The memory is cellular, it is deep in my bones as well, and it is in the tone and timbre of my voice.

The 53-year-old man of today is also the boy of 12, all those years ago, when my father moved the family to Campbellton, New Brunswick, following this attempted rape of my mother. My mother had been aware that my father had been having an affair, and that it had started while we were in Montreal, I guess about the time that the man tried to rape her. In Campbellton my father had come home late on a snowy night; as I lay awake in my bed about 2:00 A.M., my mother went out to meet him on the back porch, and started yelling that she knew what he was up to, and that she saw him rubbing snow on his jacket to, as she said, "cover the scent of the woman." He said, "You're crazy," and she started to scream that this was the "unhappiest" she had been in her life, and that with him or without him she would begin the process of bringing us all back to California, which was something I desperately wanted. I am that boy within these 53 years, and in my voice is the voice of that boy.

Yet, in the tone and timbre of my voice today is the exuberance of playing hockey on those outdoor rinks in Montreal and Campbellton. I had become pretty darn good at the sport by the time I returned to California. In California I continued playing, eventually becoming captain of my team and a big goal scorer. The exuberance of those days is clear and evident in the tone and timbre of my voice today—particularly when I'm at a San Jose Sharks game, recalling my own heroics to all who will listen.

I carry within me the voices of Daurie and Cheryl, two of the sweetest girls on earth, two of my closest friends at the age of 16. They went out hitchhiking and never returned. The murderers were found. The darkness of those days is part of my fears today, and I hear their voices often and will never forget their faces. Their voices form the tone and timbre of the voice with which I speak today.

I am that boy of 16—the loss of Daurie and Cheryl still very raw—who departed home, hopping freight trains across the land. There were no telephone answering machines in those days, so my mom was not aware that I had tried to call her from El Paso, a few days after leaving. I knew she must have been worried, but had no idea of the severity until I reached her from that phone booth just outside Moline, Illinois. My hair was filthy, and below my headband the reflection from the metal front of the telephone revealed black train grease smeared across my forehead and cheeks as I heard my mom's voice for the first time since beginning the journey. "Brucie, are you okay? I'm so glad you're all right; I've been worried sick; I prayed and prayed that you'd be okay. Did you have an asthma attack? Don't move from that spot! Give me the phone number where you are in case we get cut off! Go get the phone number from the nearest store and I will arrange to get you back!" "Mom, I want to come back the way I arrived, by hopping freights. It's the easy way out if I fly home." She brought me home, as I've described. It is an experience that is deeply ingrained in the person who I am, and the sound of my mom's voice, her fear, her relief, forms the tone and timbre of the voice with which I speak.

As I excavate the layers of myself it isn't hard to discover the boy of 20 who went on an adventure of a lifetime aboard a Merchant Marine ship to the jungles of Costa Rica.

To this day I haven't seen a place so exquisitely lush and intoxicating. I saw the loneliness of the sailor at sea, far away and many days from family, but the enormous camaraderie that they had with each other. I'll never forget the arrival in that port, the way they lathered us up, then brought us upstairs to meet the ladies. After that, Glen and I were on our way across Costa Rica, the music of Santana playing on those cantina jukeboxes in tiny jungle towns, hot, sultry, humid, the ladies dancing inches from our faces. Costa Rica, one of the most treasured, hard-bound, finely illustrated books in the library of my experience; the people, places, my traveling partner, Glen, inform my imagination and are located in the tone and timbre of my voice.

I will forever hear the voice of my departed friend, Phil (Rusty) Siegler. You'll no doubt remember the incident of when he snapped the towel (he folded a wicked, rat's tail towel) on the golden-voiced, Mexican man-child, as the guy was singing a song in the locker room. He forever won my respect when he did that—I couldn't believe he had the balls to do it. And then he and my brother saved my life in the Colorado River. The tone and timbre of my voice today includes the country accent of Phil, and now and then I break into an accent that sounds just like him. Phil, I love you, man. I've never had a friend as loyal as you.

And it is hard for me to go to a San Francisco 49ers football game anymore, because the two Phils, father and son, have passed away. The son had incredible football knowledge, he had the answer to any football question I would ask, and his dad would put his fatherly arm around me as Joe Montana or Steve Young (he finally gave in to the charms of Young, but it took a while, loyal as he was to Montana) went about their work. He could see the work stress in my face and tell me how nice it is to be able to come out here and get rid of that "office pallor," as he called it. He had been a butcher at Safeway throughout his career; and he would often give me a half of his finely cut roast beef sandwich. The two Phils are part of who I am, and in the tenor and timbre of my voice resides their voices.

I help my brothers, Jeff and Elliot, and sister, Heidi, and I love them with everything I am. And in their voices I hear my mother's voice, and in her voice I hear my own. Though she isn't here physically, her voice is as clear as when she could talk without the cancer. She had the voice of mellow Costa Rican coffee, with a touch of caramel. Her voice was a shamrock, a magical charm, and it moves within me and without me; every time I hear my own voice, I hear the voice of my mom.

"What's her name, Mom; please give me a name. This girl that you say I'll meet; what's her name?" I implored. "You won't be able to find her; she'll find you. Her name is Sue. You will meet a girl named Sue, but remember, you won't find her; she'll find you."

And so it was. "Sue, my name is Sue," she had said on the wrong number phone call that was really the right number. It was a voice of absolute, unadulterated, pure goodness and sweetness. And it could not be ignored. She was shy, but not too much, and the cute giggle devastated me on the spot. I had to get to know this wrong number, and, apparently, she really had to know me. I sent her a picture taken in one of those department store camera booths, and the note that said, "I'm sure I look nervous." She sent me a photo, and I knew it for sure—I swear to God—I knew that this was the girl who I would marry. It isn't because my mom said it—I was dating a few girls at the time—but I just knew it when I saw the picture. And she happened to be "Sue."

Sue's voice is part of every word I say; I love her deeply, and she is in every syllable of every word that I say. How does one get divorced, when one loves a person? The stigma is that divorce means that you don't love the person anymore; but I do, and will forever. I have tried to dissect it, understand it, grasp it, and I accept that the logic about our situation will not lead to understanding. We are not together anymore, and I suppose divorce will lead us from this limbo. But Sue, you are in my soul, and I know I am in yours. And, as we go through life, I know it will always be that way.

Recently, my son, Jonathan, spoke to me about how a beautiful dress on a hanger in a closet is nowhere near as beautiful as it is on the right woman. The insight struck me deeply. On the hanger a dress is pretty, but it is only material. The power of the soul transforms that dress into something beyond the elegance, refinement, beauty of the design; it is the power of the soul, not just appearances, which makes that dress on the hanger a living thing. Sue loves Laura Ashley dresses, and when in London together we would go to a store where she would try one on. It is as though these dresses were designed for her soul and hers only; these dresses come to life, they become spiritual when she wears them. And on her, it is clear what the designer had intended these dresses to become, a refined adornment for the most refined of souls.

In my voice I hear my mom, an awareness that she is always there, just a fraction away on the other side. And I hear her voice in the voices of my boys, with them as they travel their own journeys of discovery. Thank You, Mom.

We inherit and embody all of the voices of our lives. And our lives reflect the choices we have made. Every choice informs every other choice as the wheels of our lives are set in motion. The creator has given us free will, and very often, human beings do not choose wisely. The Buddhist notion of karma sees this as inevitable, and that over a period of, perhaps, many lives, humans might learn enough to break through suffering and karma, eventually reaching enlightenment. In the Hebrew tradition, sin is defined as "missing the mark," and that over time, with the forgiveness of God, guided by the Torah, we will make better choices. There is a recognition that we are human, fallible, flowers that blossom and disappear from the earth forever; God's love, goodness, kindness, renews our strength with the desire to make better choices, live more complete lives. I wrestle frequently with the question of whether the choices we make are truly free, or if there is often just the appearance of freedom. Perhaps there is, often, a hidden hand in the choices we make; if we're lucky there is a God or guardian angel watching out for us to prevent us from going in the wrong direction, pushing us in the right direction toward a better destiny. And just maybe, we are given this benefit after several lifetimes of learning, and by having the right intentions in a human, fallible, mortal world. I don't know the answer to the issue of free will versus determinism, but I suspect that there is a God who has a hand in our lives, especially if we get out of the way and allow God to help. I think back over my own life to the moment that I met "M." If I had known what kind of emotional turbulence and pain that I would go through by going to the play that night, would I have gone ahead and done it? I think the answer would be no. But I did not have the luxury of knowing that at the time. I struggled mightily within my heart and soul to withdraw from the temptation to communicate with "M," but to no avail. Though I had a choice, it certainly didn't feel that way at all. It is, perhaps, an experience that was unavoidable. Or was it? The reality is that it happened, and my life has been turned upside down. To this day, she does not know that I am separated.

So, clearly, my separation was not solely about her. Maybe she was a catalyst for something that needed to be released from deep within. I believe that is true. Without that event, I would not have written this memoir, and the journey of its writing has brought me to the depths of my feelings of love, adventure, loss, forgiveness. And, certainly, in the process, there has been deep despair and alienation. Yet, I have never felt more deeply about the power of goodness and love than I do today. So, perhaps, it has all been meant to happen to me. Where is my life going? The adventure continues; and life is a journey.

Over the past few months I have been reading the wise quotations from the Dalai Lama. There is a path to tranquility if one can truly live these words. The theme of love appears over and over again; it is within our human power to practice and it is our real salvation:

"If there is love, there is hope to have real families, real brotherhood, real equanimity, real peace. If the love within your mind is lost, if you continue to see other beings as enemies, then no matter how much material progress is made, only suffering and confusion will ensue.

"Human beings will continue to deceive and overpower one another. Basically, everyone exists in the very nature of suffering, so to abuse or mistreat each other is futile. This foundation of all spiritual practice is love. That you practice this well is my only request."

I would love to go to Tibet, but though I've never been there, I know that my soul has traveled that far.

Afterword

During the course of this writing, the San Francisco Jewish community, indeed the community and world at large, lost a profound teacher, Rabbi Alan Lew. The story of how this Buddhist monk had become a rabbi is told—how he discovered and answered his inner calling—profoundly and with gentle humor in his book "One God Clapping." Before flying to my mother's bedside while she lay in a coma before passing over, Rabbi Lew counseled me to be brave, not heroic, but brave, and to be aware that "this is my life," to be present and conscious as it unfolds. He guided my boys through Bar Mitzvah studies and was available to me anytime I needed him to discuss the depths of my emotions and conflict after meeting "M." I so much wanted him to be able to read this book; and I have thought of him often during its writing. I have the sense that these words have reached his ear on the "other side."

I also want to say that my eye for baseball talent was absolutely correct. However, no doubt most of the San Francisco Giants baseball fans had the same sense that Tim Lincecum would become an amazing pitcher upon seeing just a few outings. Early in this book I described how good this rookie is, and that he might be a great one some day. During the course of this writing, Mr. Lincecum won two back-to-back Cy Young Awards. He was essential in the Giants winning their first ever World Series in San Francisco. Maybe in about 15 years or so we'll see him in the Hall of Fame.

Lyrics Credits

A DAY IN THE LIFE; © 1967 Sony/ATV Music Publishing LLC. All rights administered by Sony/ATV Music Publishing LLC., B Music Square West, Nashville, TN 37203. All rights reserved. Used by permission.

AIN'T TOO PROUD TO BEG; Words and Music by Edward Holland and Norman Whitfield. © 1966 (Renewed 1994) Jobete Music Co., Inc. All Rights Controlled and Administered by EMI Blackwood Music, Inc., on behalf of Stone Agate Music (A Division of Jobete Music Co., Inc.). All Rights Reserved International Copyright Secured. Used by Permission. Reprinted by permission of Hal Leonard Corporation.

CHERISH; Words and Music by Ronald Bell, James Taylor, Charles Smith, Robert Bell, George Brown, Curtis Williams and James Bonnefond. © 1984 Warner-Tamerlane Publishing Corp. All Rights Reserved. Used by Permission.

COMING INTO LOS ANGELES; Written by Arlo Guthrie; © Howard Beach Music (ASCAP); administered by Kohaw Music (ASCAP), under license from The Bicycle Music Company. All Rights Reserved. Used by Permission.

EASY TO BE HARD (from "HAIR"); Music by Galt MacDermot. Words by James Rado and Gerome Ragni. © 1966, 1967, 1968, 1970 (Copyrights Renewed) James Rado, Gerome Ragni, Galt MacDermot, Nat Shapiro and EMI U Catalog, Inc. All Rights Administered by EMI U Catalog, Inc. (Publishing) and Alfred Publishing Co., Inc. (Print). All Rights Reserved. Used by Permission.

REACH OUT, I'LL BE THERE; Words and Music by Brian Holland, Lamont Dozier and Edward Holland. © 1966 (Renewed 1994) Jobete Music Co., Inc. All Rights Controlled and Administered by EMI Blackwood Music, Inc., on behalf of Stone Agate Music (A Division of Jobete Music Co., Inc.). All Rights Reserved. International Copyright Secured. Used by Permission. Reprinted by permission of Hal Leonard Corporation.

RUBY TUESDAY; Words and Music by Mick Jagger and Keith Richards. Copyright © 1967 (Renewed) Abkco Music, Inc., 85 Fifth Avenue, New York, NY 10003. All Rights Reserved. Used by Permission.

SGT. PEPPER'S LONELY HEARTS CLUB BAND; © 1967 Sony/ATV Music Publishing LLC.. All rights administered by Sony/ATV Music Publishing LLC., 8 Music Square West, Nashville, TN 37203. All rights reserved. Used by permission.

SHE'S LEAVING HOME; © 1967 Sony/ATV Music Publishing LLC.. All rights administered by Sony/ATV Music Publishing LLC., 8 Music Square West, Nashville, TN 37203. All rights reserved. Used by permission.

SILHOUETTES; Words and Music by Frank C. Slay Jr. and Bob Crewe. © 1957 (Renewed) by Regent Music Corporation (BMI). International Copyright Secured. All Rights Reserved. Used by Permission. Reprinted by permission of Hal Leonard Corporation. SOMEDAY SOON; Words and Music by Ian Tyson. © 1991 Four Strong Winds, Ltd. All Rights Administered by WB Music Corp. All Rights Reserved. Used by Permission.

STAGE FRIGHT; by Robbie Robertson. © 1970 (Renewed) WB Music Corp. and Music, Inc. All Rights Administered by WB Music Corp. All Rights Reserved. Used by Permission.

SURFER GIRL; Written by Brian Wilson. © 1962 (Renewed 1990). Guild Music Company (BMI)/Administered by Bug Music. All Rights Reserved. Used by Permission. Reprinted by permission of Hal Leonard Corporation.

THERE'S A KIND OF A HUSH; by Les Reed and Geoff Stephens. © 1966,1967 by Tic Toe Music Ltd. Copyright Renewed. Administered by Songs of Peer, Ltd. in the United States. Used by Permission. All Rights Reserved.

THERE'S A KIND OF A HUSH (ALL OVER THE WORLD); Words and Music by Les Reed and Geoff Stephens. © 1966, 1967 (Renewed 1994, 1995) Donna Music, Ltd., and Tic Toc Music, Ltd. All Rights for Donna Music, Ltd., in the U.S. and Canada. Controlled and Administered by Glenwood Music Corp. All Rights for Tic Toc Music, Ltd.. in the U.S. and Canada Controlled and Administered by Songs of Peer, Ltd. All Rights Reserved. International Copyright Secured. Used by Permission. Reprinted by permission of Hal Leonard Corporation.

TRY A LITTLE TENDERNESS; Words and Music by Harry Woods, Jimmy Campbell and Reg Connelly. © 1932 (Renewed) Campbell, Connelly & Co., Ltd. All Rights in the U.S. and Canada Administered by EMI Robbins Catalog, Inc. (Publishing) and Alfred Publishing Co., Inc. (Print). All Rights Reserved. Used by Permission.

WILD HORSES; Words and Music by Mick Jagger and Keith Richards. © 1970 (Renewed) Abkco Music, Inc., 85 Fifth Avenue, New York, NY 10003. All Rights Reserved. Used by Permission.

WISH YOU WERE HERE; Words and Music by Roger Waters and David Gilmour. Copyright © 1975 (Renewed) Roger Waters Overseas, Ltd. and Pink Floyd Music Publishers, Inc. All Rights on Behalf of Roger Waters Overseas, Ltd. in the U.S. and Canada. Administered by Warner-Tamerlane Publishing Corp. All Rights Reserved. Used by Permission

WITH A LITTLE HELP FROM MY FRIENDS; © 1967 Sony/ATV Music Publishing LLC.. All rights administered by Sony/ATV Music Publishing LLC, 8 Music Square West, Nashville, TN 37203. All rights reserved. Used by permission.

WITHIN YOU WITHOUT YOU; © 1967 Sony/ATV Music Publishing LLC. All rights administered by Sony/ATV Music Publishing LLC., 8 Music Square West, Nashville, TN 37203. All rights reserved. Used by permission.

WOULDN'T IT BE NICE; Words and Music by Brian Wilson, Tony Asher and Mike Love. © 1966 Irving Music, Inc. Copyright Renewed. All Rights Reserved. Used by Permission. Reprinted by permission of Hal Leonard Corporation.

YOU'VE MADE ME SO VERY HAPPY; Words and Music by Berry Gordy, Frank E. Wilson, Brenda Holloway and Patrice Holloway. © 1967 (Renewed 1995) Jobete Music Co., Inc. All Rights Controlled and Administered by EMI April Music, Inc., and EMI Blackwood Music, Inc., on behalf of Jobete Music Co., Inc. and Stone Agate Music (A Division of Jobete Music Co., Inc.). All Rights Reserved. International Copyright Secured. Used by Permission. Reprinted by permission of Hal Leonard Corporation.

A few weeks before the publication of this book the woman referred to as "M" passed away after a year and a half battle with cancer. She fought gallantly until the end, because she felt life was so very precious. I've never known a woman so passionate about living life to its absolute fullest. She had a smile that could melt ice caps, and a voice in harmony with the sublime notes she played on those Steinway pianos. She will always be in my heart.